1,001 THINGS
THEY WON'T
TELL YOU

An Insider's Guide to Spending, Saving, and Living Wisely

BY JONATHAN DAHL

and the editors of SMARTMONEY,
The Wall Street Journal Magazine

WORKMAN PUBLISHING • NEW YORK

ISBN 978-0-7611-5137-1

Cover design by Janet Vicario
Interior design by Francesca Messina
Illustrations by Lidija Tomas

WORKMAN PUBLISHING COMPANY, INC.
225 Varick Street
New York, NY 10014-4381

Printed in the United States of America

Contents

INTRODUCTION
One Thing Personal Finance Magazines Won't Tell You

There's one core concept that every personal-finance magazine worth its salt quietly embraces but never says outright. Behind all those feature stories on asset allocation and today's hottest investing sectors, between the lines of every housing survey and retirement worksheet, lies the hidden truth of the matter: It's what you *aren't* told by the experts that is almost as important as what they do say.

The folks at *SmartMoney* have always understood this, especially when there is money involved. Toward that end, the magazine's popular monthly feature "10 Things" offers a peek behind the veil of the various industries, institutions, and professions that have become a part of our daily lives. The goal is simple enough: to provide an insider's view of how these worlds operate—often to the detriment of ordinary consumers—and to arm you with the tools to protect yourself.

From the very start, the feature has been a huge hit. Indeed, back in April 1992, the editors at *SmartMoney* knew they were on to a good thing when they published "10 Things Your Real Estate Broker Won't Tell You" in the front-of-the-book "Street Smart" section. After all, who doesn't love a list? By the second issue, "10 Things" was already beginning to play a more prominent role in the magazine, this time reaching beyond the scope of simple nuts-and-bolts investing information while sticking fast to its reader-advocacy roots. In this second appearance, "10 Things Your Lawyer Won't Tell You" explained the various ways consumers can often lose ground when they don't have the same information as the guy working the other side of the desk. Before we knew it, an institution was born.

Since then, more than 150 issues later, "10 Things" has become one of the most popular—and sometimes controversial—features of the magazine, covering a range of topics from the conventional to the outrageous. In "10 Things Your Tax Preparer Won't Tell You" (March 2008), staff writer Janet Paskin exposed the latest gambits in the tax-preparation game, including No. 6: "You hired me, but your return is being done by some guy in Peoria." As Janet discovered, tax pros have begun outsourcing returns—sometimes transmitting your sensitive data electronically, "in one bright, shiny package," as Beth Givens, director of the Privacy Rights Clearinghouse, calls it. "That's a great gift to the identity thief."

At the other end of the spectrum, writer and film critic Ian Grey deciphered the language of movie-ad hyperbole in "10 Things Your Movie Critic Won't Tell You" (March 2006). In No. 2—"Beware of blurbs"—Ian offers, among other tips, what he calls "the law of three": Don't trust any film ad that doesn't "boast full sentences from at least three media sources you've heard of." Hardly conventional personal-finance journalism, but advice you can take to the bank? You bet. Just ask anybody who's gone to the movies lately—shelling out up to $12 a ticket, on average, and facing concession markups of up to 80 percent—only to sit through the latest overhyped flop. And

that doesn't even include the cost of gas and a babysitter.

So when the folks at Workman Publishing wanted to bring together 100 of *SmartMoney*'s "10 Things," we thought it was a great idea. After all, we regularly get mail from our readers suggesting "10 Things" topics that have already been written about—why not make the lot of them available in a single volume?

That's when we assembled our team, led by assistant managing editor Kim Bernstein and staff reporter Renée DeFranco, to begin the monumental task of culling the best of the best of "10 Things" across every topic imaginable. With the aid of a group of skilled and relentless fact-checkers, we set about updating the originals. First we weeded out old statistics and filled in fresh data where it was warranted, then we added some helpful sidebars containing to-do lists and advice, fun facts, and insights from experts in the field.

The results—well, you can see for yourself. The next time you need to rent a car or hire an exterminator or get your taxes done or even buy flowers for your sweetheart on Valentine's Day, you'll go in better informed, knowing a thing or two—or 10—this time that you didn't know before. And what better way to wield your wallet wisely?

—*Jonathan Dahl*
Editor in Chief

Your Family

■ Families are very important. They are also very expensive. From the day you get the first pediatrician bill to the time you are picking out colleges, you are reminded that taking care of loved ones is something of a balancing act. Indeed, just when you think you have one family issue mastered, along comes another period in your life.

With that in mind, we've culled the information to help you through the various stages of family life, from putting together a wedding to taking care of your aging parents and everything in between. In "10 Things Your Child Care Provider Won't Tell You," for example, we help you secure the best and safest supervision for your young kids, while in "10 Things Your Veterinarian Won't Tell You," we walk you through the care and keep of your beloved family pets. (After all, who says family doesn't include our four-legged friends?)

10 Things Your
Wedding Planner
Won't Tell You

1 *"SOMETHING OLD, SOMETHING NEW—AND EVERYTHING OVER THE TOP."*

In recent decades, a rise in what couples expect to spend on their wedding has boosted the wedding biz to a $120 billion industry, according to David Wood, president of the Association of Bridal Consultants. Today's nuptials, costing $27,000 on average, tend to be " grander," Wood says. And the grander the affair, the more a couple needs help putting it together. Enter the wedding planner, a profession that emerged in the 1950s. Once catering to the wealthy elite, wedding planners have gone mainstream in recent decades, doubling their numbers over the past three years to 20,000. Some 270,000 couples hired planners in 2006, up from 200,000 in 2003. Today, according to industry estimates, roughly 20 to 30 percent of weddings involve the use of a wedding planner.

What accounts for the boom? For one thing, people are waiting longer to marry and are often too busy pursuing careers to plan their big day, says Shane McMurray, founder of research firm The Wedding Report. For another, more couples expect to re-create the lavish affairs seen in movies and tabloids, says Kathleen Murray, deputy editor of the bridal site The Knot.

2 *"YOU SAY YOU NEED A REFERENCE? WELL, YOU'RE LOOKING AT HER."*

When Keisha Barnes and Christopher Johnson, of Cerritos, Calif., first met with a wedding planner, they say she showed up an hour late, then took them to see churches much too far away. After the next appointment, when she recommended Lutheran churches (the couple are nondenominational Christian), they began researching venues on their own. "I felt like I was the wedding planner and that I was servicing her," Barnes says. "She clearly had no idea what she was doing."

Since wedding planning requires no formal training, anyone can hang out a shingle, and a growing number of former brides are doing just that. "Many enjoyed the planning process themselves and have made it their living," says Claudia Hanlin, founder of consulting boutique The Wedding Library. So how to tell a pro from a novice? The Association of Bridal Consultants (*www.bridalassn.com*), June Wedding (*www.junewedding.com*), and the International Special Events Society (*www.ises.com*) all recommend certified planners nationwide. Or ask a recent bride for a referral. Either way, contact former clients, and ask to see photos of the event if possible.

3 "I'LL DO WHATEVER IT TAKES TO KEEP YOU CALM, COOL, AND OBLIVIOUS."

Just 15 minutes before setup, wedding planner Sasha Souza of Napa, Calif., found out that the deejay she'd booked had been arrested. In a panic, she called up a sub, who lived three hours away, and told him to get there ASAP. What did she tell the bride? Nothing. Instead, she went to the groom, explaining that the deejay had been in a minor car accident and that a replacement was on his way but would be a little late. Playing the sympathy card worked beautifully: "I'm so worried about him," the groom responded. "Please tell him we're sorry." Says Souza: "I felt bad lying, but it was really for the best. The last thing you want is for the client to freak out on their wedding day."

Indeed, the best planners are those willing to take matters into their own hands when necessary. "There's no such thing as a perfect day," says Souza, who has planned weddings for boxer Fernando Vargas and for *Extra* host Dana Devon. Celebrity wedding planner Colin Cowie concurs: "If someone comes to me and says, 'I want the perfect wedding,' I'll tell her she's come to the wrong man. Things are always going to go wrong—but that's why you need a professional."

4 "I WON'T NECESSARILY BE THERE ON YOUR BIG DAY."

As the industry continues to grow, wedding consulting has gotten more specialized—and confusing. Planners now offer tiers of service, from full (meaning they manage the entire process from start to finish and charge about 10 to 15 percent of the total wedding budget) to partial (they select the photographer, caterer, and other vendors for an hourly rate of, say, $25) to day-of (they oversee the event as it happens, usually for a flat fee—though there can be a hefty hourly rate tacked on if the wedding runs over time).

In addition, many venues now offer complimentary "wedding planning" as part of their package. Unlike the independents, these venue-employed coordinators operate interchangeably, like a help desk; sometimes the bride and groom have never met the person who shows up on their wedding day. The problem is, couples often mistake this type of help for a full-service planner, says Robbi Ernst, founder of consulting firm June Wedding.

Fortunately, couples often have more leverage in this situation than they presume: A simple request for the same coordinator to help out on the day of the wedding can be worked into most contracts, Ernst says. Be more specific in communicating your wishes, then "get it in writing."

5 "CONGRATULATIONS, GLORIA AND BILL . . . UM, I MEAN MARCIA AND TOM!"

Tracy and Taj Haynes had timed their Jamaica wedding to begin at 6 P.M., just as the sun set over the Rose Hall Resort in Montego Bay. But they say that by the time the staff finished removing decorations from a previous wedding and redoing the venue, it was after seven and already dark. Where was their planner? Running between the resort's three locations, where various weddings were taking place. Adding insult to injury, the seating chart for the reception was botched and champagne not provided to the guests. The venue "simply had too many weddings to deal with on that one day," Tracy Haynes says. (Rose Hall wedding planner Charlene Henry counters, "It is highly unlikely that somebody's wedding would be pushed back.")

A good planner knows how to handle high volume while making each couple feel like their wedding is the only one. Start by asking prospective planners how many events they work at once and how they cope with the overlap. "A consultant shouldn't have more than two weddings in a month, certainly not more than three," Ernst says. If they exceed that, "they don't stay in business very long."

6 "MIXED MARRIAGE? KA-CHING!"

With an increase in multicultural and interfaith weddings, consultants are cashing in on the opportunity to incorporate more than one tradition into a single event. Planner Heather Rohrer of the Wedding Lounge in Annville, Pa., says she recently suggested custom yarmulkes for guests as a way to honor a groom's Jewish heritage, a gesture that runs from $2 to $5 a head. "In our initial consultation, I'll ask if there's anything unique about a client's wedding, and that will open the door," she says. Just how much are these twofer ceremonies costing couples? They add roughly $10,000 to the total amount, after factoring in additional dresses, tents,

and extra cocktail hours, Rohrer says. And that's just for one-day affairs, never mind those that run two days or longer.

To minimize the tab on your own blended ceremony, it helps to have a clear vision of what you want and to communicate that in the earliest stages, says planner Charles Banfield, of Charles Banfield Productions in Los Angeles. Also, if you're having more than one ceremony or event to accommodate separate traditions, consider working with the same vendors. "Many times, they'll come up with a special package," Rohrer says.

7 "THE EARLY BRIDE GETS THE WORM."

Good wedding planners live by the calendar. So when you're getting ready to hire one, it's helpful to take a page out of her book: Start your search well in advance—we're talking 10 to 15 months ahead of time, minimum. Not only will the planner you hire have more time to realize your vision but she'll be more willing to cut you a good deal. That's because she'll be able to save money by locking in vendors, such as photographers and reception halls, so far ahead—and before these vendors effect their annual rate increases, generally every January.

8 "GETTING MARRIED IN HAWAII? I'LL BRING THE SUNTAN LOTION!"

More than 250,000 couples held destination weddings last year, according to The Wedding Report, and most of them

4

paid a pretty penny for the experience. While there's no getting around the extra fees and added cost of travel accommodations that make excursion weddings an expensive proposition, one place you may be able to score some savings is on your planner. Why? Destination weddings tend to attract a higher class of consultants, who are often more willing to underbid one another to get an enticing gig. "The more appealing the wedding is, the more I'll try to win a client over," says Claudia Hanlin, co-owner of The Wedding Library in New York City. "The Four Seasons in Nevis? We could tack on a vacation before and after!"

And that doesn't apply only to destination weddings—local celebrations with a unique appeal can likewise land couples a better rate. For example, Hanlin says she might offer a price break when a particular wedding would make a nice addition to her portfolio because of its pleasing aesthetics or it's held at a venue with which she wants to forge a relationship—say a five-star resort. Seattle-based wedding expert Martie Duncan adds that planners may also offer discounts for weddings that could give them entrée into a specific demographic, such as the close-knit Greek community, where weddings tend to be large and expensive affairs. To finesse such a deal, "it couldn't hurt" to play up anything that is significant or unique about your event to prospective planners, Duncan says.

9 "CUSTOM SILK WEDDING FANS, ANYONE?"

Nowhere is there more room for trimming the budget than in the realm of wedding frills being foisted upon eager couples hungry to make their day unique. From gourmet chocolate wedding-bell truffles to custom sparklers that guests light when newlyweds depart for their honeymoon, the favors at today's nuptials are plentiful, and pushed hard by the industry. "The wedding becomes an outlet to make a statement about your life," Wood explains. Needless to say, wedding planners have a big stake in this trend. Roughly three quarters of full-service planners are now charging clients a percentage of the wedding's total budget rather than setting a flat fee. And since a wedding consultant's commission grows in tandem with her clients' budget, she has a powerful incentive to encourage couples to pull out all the stops on their big day—and virtually none to negotiate with vendors for the best deal.

Fortunately, you can nip this kind of budget inflation in the bud. "This issue begins and ends with the contract," Kathleen Murray says. It's important to request a blueprint up front, everything from a statement of the budget to what the planner will do to meet it and how many hours of service will be given, she recommends.

10 "YOU DON'T REALLY NEED ME."

When the industry started, wedding planners "mostly addressed invitations, rolled rice [in tulle swatches for guests to throw after the ceremony], and showed up on the wedding day and created havoc," Ernst says. Since then, the magnitude of their responsibilities, as well as their reputability, has improved by leaps and bounds: "Now wedding planners are like Broadway producers for a one-day show," he says. But just as not every play is made for Broadway, not every wedding needs a professional planner. Given the amount of information readily available today—including bridal magazines, how-to handbooks, and the vast array of wedding-related websites—couples can easily put on their own show if they choose to. "It sure isn't rocket science," Ernst says.

How to get started? Ask newlyweds and even big venues, like a prospective reception hall, for referrals for a deejay, photographer, or other services, Ernst says. Chances things will go smoothly increase when you hire vendors that have worked together before. Then, once you've selected vendors and collected contracts, devise an event-day schedule and send it out to all your vendors two to three weeks prior to the wedding. The rest is icing on the cake, so to speak. Still daunted? Recruit your maid of honor or most reliable friend to help out. "Everyone wants to give a memorable wedding gift," Ernst says. "So ask for a gift of administrative help on your wedding day." Now that's priceless.

THINGS TO DO

- **Find a certified wedding planner** at sites like *www.bridalassn.com*, *www.june wedding.com*, and *www.ises.com*, then check references. Don't be shy about asking former clients to give you the full story.

- **Ask prospective planners** how many weddings they're willing to juggle in a given month; if the answer's more than two, run away, bride!

- **Request a contract up front,** spelling out your budget, how your planner intends to meet it, and how many hours she'll devote to the gig.

- **Another way to save** is to get married during the "off season"—typically December, January, and February—when wedding planners may offer reduced rates.

10 Things Your
Adoption Agency
Won't Tell You

1 *"JUST BECAUSE WE PLACE CHILDREN DOESN'T MEAN WE'RE GOOD PEOPLE."*

Adoption may seem like an altruistic endeavor, but it's also big business— and a loosely regulated one at that. "Nobody's watching for cheaters," says Adam Pertman, executive director of the Evan B. Donaldson Adoption Institute and author of *Adoption Nation*.

Adoption has always been a local, not federal, issue, and statutes governing it vary from state to state. And few states, Pertman says, go far enough in monitoring and enforcing standards that would prevent adoption agencies from tactics like pressuring pregnant women or lying to adoptive parents.

So how can prospective adoptive parents start the process with confidence? First, avoid searching the Web blindly; the Internet is replete with agencies that lack a physical location—a major red flag. Instead, check out the National Foster Care & Adoption Directory (*www.childwelfare.gov/nfcad*), a database funded by the Department of Health and Human Services that lists licensed agencies by state. You can also research an agency's history of complaints by contacting the licensing specialist—also listed on the site—in the state where

your adoption will take place. Finally, the directory can point you to support groups that offer independent references for an agency.

2 *"WE HAVE NO IDEA HOW LONG THIS WHOLE THING WILL TAKE."*

When prospective parents ask how long an adoption will take, agencies often quote an average of one to two years. But the process can take even longer. First, a social worker must conduct a home study to gauge your ability to become an adoptive parent; this can involve multiple home visits and FBI clearance. When agencies estimate time frames, they typically don't include the duration of a home study in their estimates, so be sure to factor in the four months it often takes.

Next, you must wait for a child or birth mother to be identified, then go through the legal steps—mostly paperwork—to finalize the adoption. International adoptions, in which the children often come from orphanages, can get slowed down by the country of origin's political problems or red tape. In domestic infant adoptions, the adoption agency compiles a profile describing each family and the environment it can provide a child. The birth mother chooses adoptive parents based on these profiles, and she can be swayed by a seemingly unimportant detail, such as the prospective parents' native state or even a pet's name. So to avoid disappointment, prospective parents should ask what the average wait time is for people who have yet to be picked by a birth mother.

3 "SURE, WE PROMISED YOU THE CHILD—BUT THAT WAS BEFORE WE SPOKE TO THE FATHER."

Although domestic adoptions are very rarely contested in court, experts estimate that about half of birth moms decide to keep the child at some point between the initial verbal commitment to adoption and the official termination of legal rights after the birth. Given that statistic, if an agency promises brisker-than-average results, take it as a signal that it may not be adequately investigating who else in the birth mother's family is involved.

To avoid being misled, ask the agency if it has ruled out the possibility of any biological relatives trying to claim the child. Maureen Flatley Hogan, a Boston-based adoption lobbyist, cites recent cases in which the child's paternal grandparents challenged an adoption. You'll also want to ask what steps were taken to include the father in the process. Beware if the agency tells you the birth mom doesn't know who the father is—it could leave the door open for a potential father to make a claim later.

Sometimes a birth mother contacts an agency within days of her delivery. In such cases, relinquishment shouldn't happen until she's out of the hospital and has received 8 to 12 hours of counseling with a social worker from an agency with extensive adoption experience. In such a case, confirm with the agency that this procedure has been followed—and get it in writing if you can.

4 "YOU MAKE A LOT OF MONEY? WELL, OUR FEE JUST WENT UP."

Using an agency for an adoption costs as much as $20,000 to $35,000, according to Adam Pertman. Your out-of-pocket costs can include the home study, the process of identifying a child, placement fees, and postplacement visits by a social worker. For international adoptions, they may also include the price of visas, document translation, and a financial contribution to the orphanage. The precise fee you'll pay for each service varies from one agency to the next, so it's important to comparison shop. Ask prospective agencies for an itemized list of charges, and consider dropping any firm that won't cooperate.

Also, be wary of any agency that asks for your financial information before providing an itemized list of charges. A home study, required for all adoptions, usually runs between $1,000 and $3,000, but lobbyist Hogan once came across an agency that was charging consumers 10 percent of their annual income. Other agencies have been known to inflate charges when consumers are eligible for the adoption tax credit. (If your 2007 income was below $210,820, you could claim all or a portion of the $11,390 credit on that year's return; check with your tax preparer for updated amounts.) "If the agency knows a family will be eligible [for the adoption tax credit], they may increase the cost of the adoption because, after all, the family will get it back in their taxes," Hogan says.

5 "OUR QUOTED PRICE IS ONLY A FRACTION OF WHAT YOU'LL END UP SPENDING."

Besides checking the breakdown of an agency's fees, you'll need to ask about extra charges that often aren't listed at all. In an international adoption, for example, many parents find that once they arrive in the country where their child was born, they are asked to fork over money for bribes in order to grease the wheels with government officials. In domestic infant adoptions, on the other hand, agencies may not tell you about your responsibility for the birth mother's living and medical expenses—which can run several thousand dollars— until later in the game. "It's especially disturbing when a mom's fees are charged 'retroactively' for periods of time when the couple didn't even know she existed," Hogan says.

If you're paying a birth mother's living expenses, ask to write the check directly to the provider of services, such as the birth mother's electric company, instead of having the agency give her your money. You'll also want to see proof of the birth mother's medical expenses; to preserve her privacy, the agency should be able to delete any identifying information. According to Adam Pertman, some agencies have gone as far as charging adoptive parents for the full price of the birth mother's health care even though she was already covered through Medicaid or a state-subsidized program.

6 "WE'LL PRESSURE YOU MORE THAN A USED-CAR SALESMAN."

Preadoptive parents are understandably hesitant to question the kinds of activities that would in other circumstances send them running for the hills. Every adoption agency understands this insecurity; the worst firms exploit it with pressure tactics more commonly seen in an automobile dealership. There's even the adoption world's version of the bait and switch—you arrive in a foreign country only to find a child who is much older than the one you thought you were adopting or who has serious medical problems.

Another tactic in international adoptions: ratcheting up the pressure after the parents have received the medical history and a photo of the child and must decide if they want to adopt him. Some agencies will call the couple on a Friday and give them the weekend to make their decision. Or they're told that other families or agencies are considering the child, and whoever decides first gets him, which may or may not be true.

Of course, it would be irresponsible to allow a child to languish in an orphanage while a couple takes six months deciding whether to take him. The best agencies balance the interests of both sides by giving the prospective parents about a week to turn down the referral or to make a tentative verbal commitment with the caveat that they can ask for additional information.

7 *"THE PEOPLE WE WORK WITH OVERSEAS HAVE NO BUSINESS DEALING WITH ADOPTIONS."*

When evaluating a U.S. agency that does international adoptions, ask about the people the agency works with overseas. Often called "agents" or "facilitators," they act as liaisons between the agency and the foreign orphanages. Most adoption agencies have every intention of working with reputable facilitators, but in too many cases, the go-betweens have sketchy qualifications at best—as a Michigan family learned after adopting a child from Russia. In the course of a wrongful-adoption suit alleging that the agency failed to disclose the child's multiple congenital anomalies, the parents discovered that the facilitator had no social-work training; he was a furniture refinisher and didn't even speak Russian.

To avoid such problems, ask agencies about their overseas liaisons before committing to anything. Are these people trained child-welfare professionals? To what degree does the agency assume responsibility for the acts of employees and facilitators abroad? And how are facilitators paid? Some receive salaries, which is a good sign, while others are paid for each successful find, which encourages unethical players who just want fast cash. Finally, make sure your agency is insured. Most are; they have to be to get accreditation. If it isn't, you'll have little recourse in a potential lawsuit.

8 *"THIS CHILD MAY HAVE MAJOR DEVELOPMENTAL PROBLEMS."*

Some agencies would have you believe that children adopted overseas are mostly healthy kids in need of nothing more than your love and care. But many children adopted from other countries arrive in the U.S. with serious emotional and physical problems—as great or greater than those faced by children in domestic foster care.

Frequently, children adopted overseas have spent time in institutions. As a result, there is a strong possibility of medical and developmental issues that adoptive parents should explore before bringing a child home. For example, fetal alcohol syndrome is common among children adopted from Eastern Europe. And research has repeatedly indicated that children who were institutionalized as infants can have difficulty forming close relationships as they develop.

The good news is that even the most severe problems can be tackled with early intervention. Some of the best adoption agencies offer classes to prospective parents that cover these issues. To learn more on your own, check out *www.adoptionlearningpartners.org*, which provides a comprehensive online education program entitled "With Eyes Wide Open: A Preparation Guide to International Adoption" for about $45. In addition, the list of adoption experts at *library.adoption.com* includes relevant articles and studies.

9 *"OUR INFORMATION PIPELINE IS SERIOUSLY FLAWED."*

Once you know the potential for health problems, you'll face another hurdle: getting specific medical information about your prospective child from the birth country. Record keeping there might have been slipshod, or the child may have been abandoned. Even in such cases, however, some helpful information is usually available—if your agency bothers to secure it. According to a survey conducted by the Adoption Institute, 15 percent of the 1,600 responding families adopting overseas reported that their agency withheld details or gave them inaccurate information about their child.

The best adoption agencies continue to help out parents after the child has been placed in the home.

At a minimum, the agency should have material on what the child looked like the day he was brought in—how much he weighed, whether he was responsive—and his current physical and mental health. Typically, the agency will provide you with a photo or video of the child and will hire a translator to provide a summary of his medical report. As soon as you receive the information, ask a pediatrician who specializes in international adoptees to review it—the American Academy of Pediatrics' website, at *www.aap.org/sections/adoption,* offers a list of such pediatricians in various states. You can also ask your agency or state medical society for a referral.

You should request the original documentation so that your pediatrician can compare it with the translation, checking for missing pages. Ann Arbor,

Mich., pediatrician Jerri Jenista once saw two different medical reports from two different agencies about the same child. One agency had failed to translate a critical sentence: "The mother was an alcoholic and murdered the child's sibling."

10 *"ONCE YOU'VE GOT YOUR CHILD, YOU'RE ON YOUR OWN."*

The best adoption agencies continue to help out parents after the child has been placed in the home. Some offer postadoption services that guide parents through a range of problems, from how to explain adoption to the child to dealing with "postadoption depression," a surprisingly common phenomenon among these parents.

If a child develops a medical condition, parents should be able to call the agency to ask whether it runs in the birth parents' families. One top adoption agency even arranges to have social workers meet with the child's teachers to help them understand any problems. And many parents return to their agency when the child is old enough to consider getting in touch with the birth mother.

But not all agencies are so diligent— many end their services the day you bring your child home. To weed out the lesser agencies, ask for the names and phone numbers of three clients whose adoptions were completed at least three years ago. Contact those adoptive parents and inquire about how the agency handled both postadoption services and the adoption process itself.

THINGS TO DO

● **Check with your state's Office of the Attorney General,** child-welfare state licensing specialist, or Better Business Bureau to see if the agency you're working with has a history of legal action or complaints.

● **When dealing with international adoptions,** you may want to hire an adoption doctor to do pre- and postmedical screenings. Find one at *www.theadoptionguide.com.*

● **The National Adoption Foundation** offers $500 to $2,500 grants to families, as long as you sign up for a home study or have one in progress.

● **International adoptees aren't eligible** for financial assistance in every state. Contact the North American Council on Adoptable Children at *www.nacac.org* to see if your state will help with nonrecurring adoption expenses.

● **If your agency abandons you** after the adoption and you still need some help, you can locate adoptive-family support groups in your state at *www.childwelfare .gov/nfcad.*

10 Things Your
Child Care
Provider
Won't Tell You

1 *"WHEN YOUR KID TAKES A NAP, SO DO WE."*

Leslie Thurman was at work when she got a call no parent could prepare for: Garrison, her eight-week-old son, had stopped breathing at his day care center. Although paramedics got Garrison's heart beating again, he died the next day. An autopsy later determined the cause of death as apnea, which occurred when the baby was placed on his stomach for a nap. The Thurmans sued Applebrook Country Day School in Ringgold, Ga., and were awarded $1 million by a Catoosa County Superior Court jury in a controversial wrongful death lawsuit in September 2002. "The mother assumed that they would place the child correctly," says Renzo S. Wiggins, the Thurmans' attorney. "Unfortunately, that was an incorrect assumption." The day care center appealed, and the decision was overruled. (The appeals judge deemed the original testimony of a child care expert characterizing Applebrook's actions a breach of standard care was "not helpful to the jury" in the context of a wrongful death suit.)

Despite the legal outcome, this case helped spur Georgia to add a regulation requiring that infants be placed on their backs at group and family day care centers. But it's still important for parents to check that a prospective day care facility follows that regulation, since there are still some that may not: A 2000 study by Rachel Moon, a pediatrician at Children's National Medical Center in Washington, D.C., found that 25 percent of licensed child care centers in the Washington metro area were unaware of the American Academy of Pediatrics' 1992 recommendation that infants be placed in the nonprone position (i.e., on their back) while sleeping; a 2003 study conducted by Moon showed that 20 percent of nighttime child care centers still positioned infants prone at least some of the time. "You'd think it would be common knowledge by now, [but] we're bumping up against a lot of tradition," Moon says.

2 *"WE SPREAD GERMS LIKE CRAZY..."*

Day care centers are supposed to give working parents a chance to do just that—work. Pat Murphy wishes it were that simple. The Oradell, N.J., mother missed so much office time—a full week out of the month sometimes—caring for her two sons who were sickened by germs picked up at day care centers, that her absences started to raise her boss's eyebrows. Both boys, Liam and Conor, contracted their first ear infections before they were three months old, and both needed tubes put in their ears by nine months. The family's doctor classified the infections as day care-related. "They were sick constantly," says Murphy, who finally pulled her sons out of the centers and hired a nanny.

There's no getting around it: Put a large group of kids together, and you can expect a marked increase in colds, ear infections, and upper respiratory infections. Says pediatrician Cathryn Tobin, author of *The Parent's Problem Solver*, "I see some day care kids twice as much as other children not in day care." Toy-sharing is a big factor. Nicole Queen, assistant director of Parents of Preschoolers Inc. child care in Bethesda, Md., says that some centers require caregivers to clean toys with bleach and air-dry them every two weeks, but that "only a couple of centers I worked at did that." How can you keep your kid healthy while in day care? Be scrupulous about sanitation. Pay attention to how caregivers handle toys and bottles, change diapers, and clean the facility.

How can you keep your kid healthy while in day care? Be scrupulous about sanitation.

3 "...ESPECIALLY WHEN NOT ALL OF OUR KIDS HAVE BEEN VACCINATED."

Spring means chicken pox time, and day care centers can help pass the virus along faster than you can say tic-tac-toe. A 2001 chicken pox outbreak that infected 21 kids in a Philadelphia preschool was attributed to a single child whose parents had chosen not to vaccinate. While immunization rates are generally rising, "it's an increasing concern that some parents are choosing not to have their kids vaccinated," says Karl Heath, a registered nurse with the Philadelphia Department of Public Health.

For day care providers, it's not a simple issue. Day care owner Gale Walker, who oversees more than 300 kids at her Children of the Rainbow centers in San Diego, says that the center will occasionally admit a child who isn't fully immunized due to religious reasons. Still, Walker says, she is hesitant to allow very many vaccine-exempted children in her care because "some childhood diseases can be very detrimental, not just to children but to everybody."

4 "RECALLED TOYS AREN'T THE ONLY SAFETY HAZARD YOUR CHILD COULD FACE."

Day care centers may be fun for kids—but they can be dangerous, too. The hazards range from the simple, such as recalled toys or unsafe playground surfacing, to the flagrant. Don Keenan, an Atlanta lawyer who specializes in negligence involving children, says he's seen cases dealing with day care injuries more than double in the past decade.

Keenan is most troubled by the "alarming increase in intentional injuries," he says. "That is, sexual predators or child abuse."

Case in point: In March 2002, a Nevada district court sentenced Gary Hanneman, a former day care worker at the Children City Learning Center in Reno, to multiple prison terms for molesting nine children at the center. Videotapes of his acts were included as evidence. Several of the victims' families filed civil suits against Hanneman as well as Children City Learning Center. "[Hanneman] had access to more than 200 children," says Sherry Bowers, an attorney for several of the families. "There were many red flags that should have put [the center] on notice that it had a problem." (The victims' families reached an undisclosed settlement with Children City Learning Center in June 2002.)

5 *"OUR EMPLOYEES DON'T TEND TO STICK AROUND VERY LONG ..."*

Ann Douglas, author of *The Unofficial Guide to Childcare*, puts the turnover rate for day care centers at "a mind-boggling 30 percent per year." You can blame low salaries for part of the problem. The U.S. Bureau of Labor Statistics tags the average hourly wage for child care workers at about $7.00 an hour, or just over $15,000 a year.

Even when quite young, kids can be affected by high turnover in early caregivers. According to a study combining the efforts of researchers at the University of North Carolina at Chapel Hill, the University of Colorado at Denver, UCLA, and Yale, children who developed closer relationships with their early child care teachers demonstrated better classroom behavior and exhibited stronger social skills through early elementary school. That's one very good reason Douglas urges parents to seek out day care providers who manage to retain their top employees, since such an environment is more conducive to the type of relationship that will enhance your child's development and better prepare them for their K–12 years.

Children who developed closer relationships with their early child care teachers demonstrated better classroom behavior and exhibited stronger social skills through early elementary school.

---

6 *"... AND THOSE WHO STAY MAY DO MORE HARM THAN GOOD."*

The average cost for a four-year-old in a child care center runs anywhere from $3,000 to $9,600 a year, depending on a variety of factors including location and the range and type of services provided. But is cost necessarily the best indicator of quality care for your kid? Studies have shown that the education level of caregivers is a major predictor of quality child care, yet 20 states, including Michigan and Texas, still allow their licensed day care centers to hire teachers with no prior training, according to data compiled by the Wheelock College Institute for Leadership and Career Initiatives. Even worse: In Maryland an individual can work with children as an aide at age 16 and with no training. (Maryland licensing officials stress that all aides are closely supervised.)

"There could be safety and self-esteem issues" for kids who are placed in the hands of untrained staff, says Sherry Workman, CEO and executive director of the National Association of Child Care Professionals, based in Austin, Tex. "People who have not had training interact with people the same way they were interacted with as a child, which may or may not be positive." For a state-by-state list of child care regulations, check out Daycare.com.

7 "YOUR CRAZY WORK HOURS ARE NOT MY PROBLEM."

How many times has your 9-to-5 routine turned into a 12-hour marathon? Or has your boss called an emergency meeting—for 5:45 P.M.? If you're like a lot of people, too often to count. And if you have a kid in day care, such delays can be tough to manage, not to mention costly: Many providers charge late fees—up to $1 a minute—for parents who miss their scheduled pickup time. What's more, a 2002 YMCA survey on child care in the U.S. revealed that more than two out of three parents lacked programs in their community offering extended-hour child care—a situation that can be extremely hard on parents whose work hours include evenings and weekends. According to Workman, the problem still holds true today. "There aren't enough child care programs offering extended hours to meet the demands of parents," she says. "This can definitely be improved."

Just ask Wendy Walls. A former room coordinator for Medical City Dallas Hospital, Walls worked two 16-hour shifts on weekends so she could be off during the week to care for her son. But for six years she was unable to find a local center that covered her work schedule and was forced to shuttle her son among friends and family. "Having to rely on other people was very stressful," she says. Walls finally found professional care at Children's Choice Learning Centers, a company specializing in 24-hour care. Unfortunately, the 24-hour model is hardly the norm; indeed, says Workman, there's a very real need for more round-the-clock child care facilities.

8 "THE ONLY LICENSE WE HAVE AROUND HERE IS A DRIVER'S LICENSE."

Restaurants need a license. Barbershops need a license. But don't be surprised if your day care center lacks any state certification. Many centers, such as some faith-based programs and health-club nurseries, legally operate without licenses. Yet even if your child's day care provider is licensed, it doesn't ensure that the facility offers a high-quality program. "All [that does] is establish a minimum floor below which a facility should not go," says Faith Wohl, former president of Child Care Action Campaign.

State licensing agencies set minimum standards designed to reduce the risk of harm to children from injury, unsafe buildings, and the spread of disease. But because states decide on their own what those standards are, requirements for things such as group size, the child-to-staff ratio, and maintenance of environments vary widely—for example, in New York the child-to-staff ratio for four-year-olds is 8-to-1; in Texas it's 18-to-1. A better indicator of a center's quality is voluntary accreditation by either the National Association for the Education of Young Children (*www.naeyc.org*) or the National Association for Family Child Care (*www.nafcc.org*). Both organizations set requirements, from age to training, that a center's employees must meet; you can search their websites for accredited child care facilities.

9 *"GOOD REFERENCES MEAN LITTLE IF YOU DON'T DO SOME DIGGING."*

You might think that going the nanny route and bypassing day care centers altogether will ensure consistent help. You just need to vet your prospective help via a few references and your worries are averted, right? Not necessarily—references aren't always foolproof. Many reference providers "do not know what the qualities of good care are and may be too invested in the situation" to be objective, says Julie Shields, author of *How to Avoid the Mommy Trap.*

What to do? Go beyond simply verifying obvious information, such as dates of employment, when checking references. Instead, ask such questions

Go beyond simply verifying obvious information, such as dates of employment, when checking references.

as "What is the aspect of this person or arrangement that you liked least?" and then listen for negative clues. "If a reference is very negative, that is probably more accurate than a very good one," Shields says. As an extra precaution, consider conducting a criminal background check, as Valencia, Calif., mom Dawn Walker did. Walker made her top nanny candidates give her their Social Security and driver's license numbers, then hired a company through the Internet to investigate her first choice. "It came back clean," she says, and "definitely gave me peace of mind." The cost? Less than $75.

10 *"LOOKING FOR CHILD CARE ON VACATION? GOOD LUCK."*

Be prepared for some angst if you want to sneak away on your summer vacation for a day trip or romantic dinner sans Junior. Securing child care in a hotel can be dicey. While on vacation in London, Fran Falkin and her husband arranged for a babysitter through their hotel to care for their son after they scored theater tickets. But the sitter never showed. The hotel management "finally scrounged around and found a maid who was free," Falkin says. "When we came home, [our son] was still awake, they were watching a movie we wouldn't have allowed him to watch, and the room reeked of smoke."

And that's when you can get a sitter at all. The fact is, just 14 percent of hotels that responded to an American Hotel & Lodging Association survey in 2006 said they provided child care for guests. And among the minority of hotels that do offer it, services are less than ideal. Very few babysitters provided by hotels, for example, "are trained in water safety and lifeguard techniques, and are actually permitted to take a child to a pool," says Kyle McCarthy, editor of Family Travel Forum's website.

THINGS TO DO

● **To locate an accredited child care provider** near you, start with *www.naccrra.org*, where you'll find a list of Child Care Resource & Referral (CCR&R) centers. Through your local CCR&R, you can also learn about complaints and licensing violations in your community.

● **Your CCR&R center should also** be able to steer you toward any local financial assistance. In addition, check to see if your employer has a program to pitch in on child care costs.

● **Always visit and interview** potential child care providers before signing on, and be sure to ask about a center's child-to-staff ratio, its age-specific education plan, and the people supervising your child and their backgrounds. Call parents as references.

● **Also, inquire about a center's** safety measures: Are caregivers trained to handle medication? Are they CPR-certified? Do all children enrolled have the required immunizations?

● **Once you choose a provider,** build a relationship with its employees. Check in regularly about your child's progress, and participate in events to show you're involved and committed to your child and the center.

10 Things Your
Summer Camp
Won't Tell You

1 *"ACCREDITATION? WE DON'T BOTHER."*

According to the American Camp Association (ACA), there are currently about 7,000 overnight "sleepaway" programs to choose from in the U.S. And the number of day camps, where kids return home each evening, has increased 90 percent since the 1980s, to roughly 5,000 today—in large part because they're now offering extended day sessions to meet parents' needs and are accepting younger children. But picking the right camp for your kid can be daunting: Of the 12,000 or so options, only about 2,400 have ACA accreditation, a voluntary process in which the camp meets more than 300 different standards. (Visit the organization's website, *www .acacamps.org*, for its "Find a Camp" database of accredited programs.)

While other, nonaccredited camps may be perfectly legitimate options, you'll need to do a little more homework to be sure. First, check out the Web directory KidsCamps.com, where you can search a database of camps based on geography and interests. To get a better feel for how a camp operates, call its director and ask about staff screening procedures—whether the camp does background checks—and its staff return rates (anything over 50 percent is good). Then ask about the staff-to-camper ratio: Look for 1-to-4 for very young kids and 1-to-8 for older campers. And make sure the camp has a state permit or license that requires it to meet minimum safety requirements. Most important, get references from a prospective camp. "Ask for people in your hometown," advises Christopher Thurber, a New Hampshire psychologist and coauthor of *The Summer Camp Handbook*. "That means they can't handpick the people you talk to."

2 *"WE PAY FOR REFERRALS."*

Camp advisory services, which advertise online or in the yellow pages, can help streamline the process of choosing a camp by doing the legwork for you. They tend to be long-standing mom-and-pop operations, and they're free. Jill Tipograph, founder and director of Everything Summer, says she keeps records on more than 2,000 camps and teen programs around the world. "Parents don't know if these programs are safe or what their reputation is," Tipograph says. "They prefer to work with programs we have been sending children to."

These companies have to make money somehow, however, and guess who pays? The camps. That's not to imply that all advisers recommend only camps that pay them. Tipograph, for one, says she has referred parents to nonclient programs. You should ask advisers how they charge: If they're paid a set fee, regardless of how many referrals a camp gets, that's good. If they're paid based on how many kids they refer, that's less reassuring. When you contact a camp, ask about its relationship with the adviser who sent you, just to double-check.

3 "WE MIGHT NOT BE THE RIGHT CAMP FOR YOUR KID."

In an effort to attract business, some camps can be notorious about flip-flopping on their supposed "philosophies," says one East Coast camp official. "I've called up camp X and said, 'My kid is Jewish. How religious are you? [Because] my kid hates services.' And they say, 'Oh, he'll be perfect here.' And then we call again and say, 'How religious is the camp? My kid is very religious,' and they say the same thing."

Specialty camps, a fast-growing area, can be big culprits. Naoko Halloran realized she'd made a mistake in choosing the art day camp her then nearly five-year-old son went to in Maui. "He was the youngest one there and found the day too long," she says. While her son came home with some "amazing" oil paintings, Halloran says he felt lost "hanging out with 10-year-olds."

To avoid such misunderstandings, be honest in evaluating your child's personality, and be sure to check the referrals a camp provides. Ask, "How would you describe the typical kid at this camp?" According to Stacy DeBroff, author of *Sign Me Up! The Parents' Complete Guide to Sports, Activities, Music Lessons, Dance Classes, and Other Extracurriculars,* "Matching the culture of the camp to the personality of your child is the formula for success, period."

4 "AND YOU THOUGHT GETTING YOUR KID INTO HARVARD WOULD BE TOUGH."

Camp registration rates have been growing steadily for years: In 2005 a record 10 million children attended day or resident camp, according to the American Camp Association. As a result, it's become increasingly difficult to get your kid into his camp of choice. "The entire period of time for signing up has shifted dramatically," says Laurel Barrie, who owns camp advisory company the Camp Connection. Some camps fill up as early as August of the previous summer.

Philip Margolis, of Glastonbury, Conn., found that out the hard way a few years ago, when he and his wife decided to send their then eight-year-old son, Jacob, to an overnight camp affiliated with their temple. They registered one or two weeks before the camp's March 1 deadline, but their son's age-group was already full. "Jacob's enthusiasm after hearing the camp's presentation [less than two months earlier] made our first decision easy," he says. "When he didn't get in, we had to go back to the drawing board."

Still, if you get stuck registering close to a deadline, don't panic. "There are plenty of camps available," says

Nancy LaPook Diamond, president of KidsCamps.com, "but act quickly." For best results, start researching camps by January 1 and make appointments to visit camps in early April, advises Barrie, before the more common deadline of late May. But what to do if your first-choice camp is already full? Ask that camp's director what other programs he or she recommends; then, if need be, get on wait lists at your preferred camps. Registered kids often change their minds about attending.

5 "WE'LL PUT YOUR LITTLE LEAGUER THROUGH THE GRINDER."

The most popular alternatives to traditional camps these days are sports specialty camps. But for kids who don't have NBA or Olympic dreams—and abilities to match—many may be too hard-core. Several summers ago Dayna Bergman, a stay-at-home mom in Bucks County, Pa., was a chaperone at the cheerleading camp her then 11-year-old daughter's school squad attended. It turned out that the camp, chosen by the school coaches, was geared toward high school girls who were serious athletes. "They were getting up at 7 A.M. and working out until they couldn't walk," Bergman says. "The kids weren't very happy."

Before registering your child at a sports camp, ask the director to describe a typical day and the level of competition. "Say, 'If my child is tired at 4 o'clock because he's been playing lacrosse for five hours, can he sit down?'" suggests Rick Echlov, former summer

programs director for Babson College in Wellesley, Mass., which runs 17 camp sessions of one to three weeks for soccer, basketball, baseball, and other sports. "The answer might be, 'No, he'll be in the middle of a game.'" Also, ask who's going to be coaching your kids. Many sports camps feature a former college or pro athlete or a big-name coach. Stars attract a huge enrollment, which means your kid may get little face time with a featured athlete. Make sure that whoever works with your kid most of the time is more than an enthusiastic counselor and is a coach with solid experience and training.

Before registering your child at a sports camp, ask the director to describe a typical day and the level of competition.

---

6 "OUR ADD-ONS REALLY ADD UP."

The basic cost of camp can range from reasonable to resortlike. Tuition at an accredited day camp ranges from $100 to $300 per week, according to the ACA, and overnight camps run about $597 per week. The median rate for overnight camps in New England is the highest, costing $780 per week.

But more often than not, costs don't end at tuition. Stacy DeBroff thought the $6,000 she paid to send her then nine-year-old son to a seven-week overnight camp would include everything, so she was shocked, to say the least, when she received a catalog of required clothing—including camp-logo T-shirts, sweatshirts, mesh shorts, and sports jerseys. "The required uniform included 17 things!" she says. "It added about $300." Another unexpected extra: a $30 fee to have the camp print out the e-mails she sent her son.

KidsCamps.com's Diamond advises parents to ask about extra fees before booking. Activities and extras often not included under tuition, she says, are swimming lessons, horseback riding, transportation, uniforms, and even food.

7 "OUR PRICES ARE NEGOTIABLE."

Struggling to afford camp for your kids this summer? Try asking for a discount. In a recent survey by the ACA, 49 percent of accredited camps reported offering campers some level of financial assistance. Called "camperships" in the industry, discounts often depend on income; some camps provide partial camperships because of a family medical crisis or if a parent is in the military. Ask about these as soon as you begin contacting camps.

Even if you don't qualify for aid, many camps offer discounts of 5 to 10 percent for early registration, full-season enrollment, or enrollment of multiple family members. Marci Rose, an artist and mother of three in Churchville, Pa., saved $300 off a $6,800 tab by signing her daughter up for camp on visiting day during the previous summer. Because her other daughter was attending, too, Rose got an additional $400 "sibling" discount.

8 "YOUR KID COULD GET SICK HERE—REALLY SICK."

Poison ivy rashes, head lice, and sore throats are staples of camp infirmaries. Make sure your kid's camp is equipped to handle such basics. The American Academy of Pediatrics recommends that overnight camps with more than 50 kids have an onsite registered nurse with access to a supervising M.D.

But whenever groups of kids get together, more serious ailments can become an issue. When Nancy Springer sent her then 14-year-old son, Nick, to an overnight camp in Massachusetts, he contracted meningococcal meningitis after sharing a water bottle with campmates, including one who was an uninfected carrier. "We sent a healthy child away to summer camp," Springer says. "Two weeks later he was on life support." In a move that probably saved the boy's life, the camp's doctor recognized the purple rash, started Nick on an IV of the right antibiotic, and called an ambulance. Other campers haven't been so fortunate: In 2002, a 12-year-old Oklahoma girl who was diagnosed with bacterial meningitis after attending a Girl Scout camp in Joplin, Mo., died.

While cases of meningitis are rare, the conditions at camps—sharing close living quarters as well as food, water bottles, utensils, and even lip balm—put kids at greater risk for the disease. What can parents do? Tell your child not to share such personal items, and consider having him vaccinated. Menactra, manufactured by Sanofi Pasteur, protects against four of the most common strains of meningitis. For more information, visit the National Meningitis Association's website at *www.nmaus.org*.

9 *"OUR VALUES AREN'T THE SAME AS YOURS."*

When one New York mom received a phone call from her daughter's camp director saying they had a serious disciplinary problem, she was shocked—until she heard what the problem was. "She got in trouble for writing her name in toothpaste on the bathroom mirror, which I didn't think was such a terrible thing to do," the mom says. The camp disagreed, considering it harming public property. "She was really demonized by the authority figures," the mom continues. "She was docked from evening activities and had it marked on her camp records. She was in tears."

Rule breakers—no matter how silly the infractions may seem to parents—are often sent home, so make sure you know the rules ahead of time and that you feel comfortable with the repercussions. What happens, for instance, if your kid raids the girls' cabin or gets caught using a cell phone? If the offense is bad enough for him to be sent home—hazing and drinking are two obvious ousters—parents can get punished too, at least financially. "If you bring certain things to our camp," like fireworks, says David Phillips, president of Maryland's Capital Camps & Retreat Center, "you're going home, and you're not getting your money back."

10 *"YOUR KID'S HOMESICK? HE LOOKS OKAY TO US."*

A whopping 95 percent of kids who go to overnight camp feel some degree of homesickness, says New Hampshire psychologist Christopher Thurber. But chances are you won't hear about that from directors. "Camps want to help kids adjust," he says, "but they're hesitant to bring [homesickness] up, because that doesn't sell slots."

Thurber recommends that families prepare for separation by having the child practice spending time away—at a sleepover, say—and honing coping skills. But also ask your prospective camps about parent-child communication policies before booking. Most resident camps allow few or no phone calls, "and that's a good thing," Thurber says. In case it's needed, make sure the camp provides counseling you approve of should your kid end up with more than just a day or so of the blues. "Some camps provide [staffers with] specialized training in homesickness and adjustment, but others don't," Thurber says. Specifically, counselors should be able to recognize signs of distress and be trained in talking to kids about homesickness. Just don't expect them to offer any consoling hugs. Fearing accusations of inappropriate behavior, Thurber says, "many camps are training their staff not to hug kids. Some think the only acceptable touch is a pat on the shoulder or a high five."

THINGS TO DO

● **The majority of summer camps** are unregulated. You can find accredited camps listed at *www.acacamps.org*.

● **Some sport camps** can be too hard-core for the average child. Talk to as many former campers as you can to figure out if a camp is going to be the right one for your child.

● **Advisory services,** like *www.summer camp.org*, can be helpful in picking the right summer camp. Avoid biased advice by sticking to services that are paid a flat fee by camps, not those that get paid by the referral.

● **Don't be put off** by the brochure price—almost half of accredited camps offer some form of financial aid. Also, be sure to ask what discounts are available. You can search camps by price at *www.campparents.org*.

10 Things Your
Veterinarian
Won't Tell You

1 *"GOOD THING YOU LOVE SPARKY LIKE A SON. HIS CARE COULD COST AS MUCH."*

After a New York City taxi struck Jessica Malionek's dog, Mojo, flinging him 30 feet in the air, she spent $4,000 for veterinarians to perform emergency treatment and then lifesaving surgeries on her beloved companion. "It was like they were treating a person," Malionek says.

These days veterinary medicine can be every bit as sophisticated as human health care—and the costs reflect it. The amount of money that pet owners spend on vets is expected to have reached $10.8 billion in 2008, according to the American Pet Products Manufacturers Association. And per-visit costs are skyrocketing: From 2002 to 2006, the average cost of a veterinary visit for a dog rose from $172 to $219; for cats, from $133 to $172.

Why the steep price hikes? Chris Green, an attorney and member of the American Veterinary Medical Law Association, says vets are happily obliging owners who want to keep their pets alive at all costs. That means paying for the latest high-tech procedures, such as feline kidney transplants, cancer surgery for rabbits, CAT scans, and even MRIs. There

are also more aged pets today, which require more care.

2 *"VACCINATING YOUR PET MAY DO MORE HARM THAN GOOD."*

For years the primary reason for seeing a veterinarian was to get your pet vaccinated against a host of diseases ranging from distemper to rabies, either with individual vaccinations or "combo wombo" shots that could cover seven separate conditions. Indeed, annual vaccinations have been an economic bulwark for many vet practices. However, some veterinarians say they're not only unnecessary but can actually be harmful in some cases. Marty Goldstein, a veterinarian in South Salem, N.Y., says he sees a range of vaccination-related reactions in animals, everything from cancerous sarcomas to epilepsy. Another reason to think twice about certain vaccines: The immunity provided by some of them can last well beyond a year and even as long as the pet's lifetime, Goldstein says, negating the need for some annual shots.

Both the American Veterinary Medical Association (AVMA) and the American Animal Hospital Association now say vaccinations should be assessed yearly and tailored to an animal's age, health, and lifestyle. For example, an indoor cat with limited exposure to some diseases may not ever need certain common vaccinations, says W. Jean Dodds, an immunologist and veterinarian with Hemopet in Garden Grove, Calif. Only a veterinarian who has access to your pet's complete medical history can determine which vaccinations should be administered and how they'll be most effective. Also, talk with your vet if you're considering traveling with your pet.

3 "I HAVE MORE COMPLAINTS FILED AGAINST ME THAN A USED-CAR LOT—NOT THAT YOU'LL EVER KNOW ABOUT IT."

When she picked up her kitten, Pumpkin, from the veterinarian after a routine spaying, Mount Pleasant, S.C., resident Marcia Rosenberg was stunned to find the cat nearly comatose. Soon Pumpkin's body was wracked with seizures, and her stomach swelled. Rosenberg rushed Pumpkin to another vet, who saved the cat, but the distraught owner called her state's veterinary board to complain. Told that the board had no procedure for alerting consumers about disciplinary actions taken against incompetent vets, Rosenberg mounted a successful campaign to have such actions posted on the South Carolina veterinary board's website.

Tracking complaints against vets often requires a bit of detective work. Some state veterinary boards list disciplinary actions against vets, while others do not. And complaints typically aren't disclosed until a board investigation and judicial ruling have determined a case of

wrongdoing. On her own, Rosenberg says she was able to find that the veterinarian had previously had his license suspended in Ohio and since then had more than a dozen complaints against him in South Carolina.

4 "REAL DENTISTS ARE FOR PEOPLE."

When John James, an academic adviser in Los Angeles, took his geriatric cockapoo, Amber, to his veterinarian for a chipped tooth, the vet told him his dog needed a root canal and that he could take care of it. Amber died during the procedure. James's lawyer later learned that the veterinarian's canine dentistry training came from a weekend course. What's more, elderly Amber should never have been a candidate for the intensive procedure.

How do you know whether your pet is in the hands of a skilled specialist? The AVMA lists 37 specialties for veterinarians, ranging from anesthesiology to dermatology. Legitimate specialists have done graduate work in their specialty and have been certified by an industry medical board. Some vets may claim a "special interest" in an area, meaning they've taken some continuing education, but they aren't necessarily certified specialists, says Peter Weinstein, former president of the California Veterinary Medical Association. If your pet needs a specialist, ask the vet about his educational background and certification. Also, inquire about how many specialized procedures he performs annually; having a "special interest" may be fine if the vet has had enough experience.

5 "SURGERY'S A CINCH. IT'S THE OVERNIGHT STAY YOU SHOULD BE WORRIED ABOUT."

We'd all like to think a beloved pet will be tenderly nurtured through the night after surgery at a veterinary office or hospital. But many vets don't staff their offices overnight—it's important to ask about what happens in the wee hours.

Laura Ireland Moore, an animal law attorney in Portland, Ore., says she represented a client who took her dog to the vet after stitches from a routine spaying came undone. The veterinarian repaired the stitches with metal sutures but neglected to put a cone over the dog's head to protect the wound during an overnight stay. The office was unattended through the night, and by morning the animal had chewed through the sutures— as well as 15 feet of its own intestines. The agonized dog had to be put down. The moral of this unpleasant story: "You should definitely check if anyone will be on the premises overnight," Moore says.

If the facility doesn't have a night attendant or if you don't trust his credentials—a late-shift babysitter may or may not be a veterinarian or even a vet technician—you should ideally find a facility where a licensed vet stays over, Moore advises.

6 "PERSONALLY, I THINK DECLAWING IS INHUMANE. BUT, HEY, IT'S YOUR DIME."

Animal activists have long held that cosmetic and so-called convenience surgeries, such as declawing a cat or clipping the ears of a Doberman, are unnecessary and cruel. That argument is gaining broader support, as declawing, in particular, has come under fire. While the surgery—which many vets say is the equivalent of toe amputation—will usually keep a cat from scratching the furniture, it may cause other physical and behavioral problems, according to veterinarian Jean Hofve, ranging from lameness and joint stiffness to behavioral issues such as reclusiveness and biting.

In keeping with these concerns, the American Animal Hospital Association now recommends that its members inform clients about the risks of nonvital surgeries and the alternatives. "A lot of vets still feel they should do what the client wants," says Teri Barnato, national director of the Association of Veterinarians for Animal Rights. Many vets fear losing clients or having animals abandoned.

If you're considering a cosmetic or convenience procedure, ask your veterinarian if he'd perform the surgery on his own pet. And weigh the alternatives—instead of declawing, you could get a scratching post and keep your cat's claws trimmed. Another humane alternative: vinyl nail caps called Soft Paws, which were developed by a vet (go to *www.softpaws.com* for more information).

7 "GO AHEAD AND SUE— IT'LL HURT YOU MORE THAN IT HURTS ME."

When Marc Bluestone's dog Shane died after being treated for seizures at All-Care Animal Referral Center in Fountain Valley, Calif., Bluestone decided to sue. In a precedent-setting ruling, a jury awarded him $39,000 for malpractice, claiming he and his dog had a "special and close relationship." (All-Care appealed the ruling, to no avail.)

But that's an exception—suing a veterinarian is at best a dodgy financial undertaking. The reason is that under the law, pets are considered property, says Ireland Moore, the animal lawyer in Oregon. More often than not, that means court awards are for the straight market value of the pet, which could be as little as $10 for your beloved mutt. Meanwhile, suing a vet is likely to be an expensive undertaking.

If your pet becomes the victim of a medical mishap, know that your legal recourse is anything but guaranteed. "It's not always the most economically smart thing to do," Moore concedes.

8 "THE KEY TO MY THRIVING PRACTICE? LOCATION, LOCATION, LOCATION."

While a referral is probably the best way to select a veterinarian, many people pick one simply because the office is around the corner. Indeed, according to the AVMA, only about 11 percent of cat and dog owners choose their vets through referral. That could be a mistake. If you have an aging kitty and the neighborhood vet doesn't have geriatric expertise, it won't be a good fit, says Nancy Peterson, a registered veterinary technician and a spokesperson for the Humane Society of the United States. Peterson adds that in her experience few pet emergencies happened during office hours anyway, nullifying some of the benefits of geographic convenience.

So how best to assess a vet? First, check out the facility. Are the staff friendly? Is the place clean? Look into the veterinarian's educational background, board certification, and record both with the state's medical board and the local humane society. Beyond that, veterinarian Elliot Katz, president and founder of In Defense of Animals in San Rafael, Calif., recommends studying the veterinarian's body language with animals. Make sure she greets animals in a friendly way, approaching them slowly and touching them gently. And if you have a special request, such as wanting to hold your pet when it gets vaccinated, make sure you and your vet are on the same page.

9 "I HAVEN'T THE FOGGIEST IDEA WHY YOUR DOG'S ACTING CRAZY."

The study of animal behavior is a relatively new specialty in veterinary medicine. In fact, the AVMA lists only 38 board-certified animal behavior specialists on its website, compared with 1,675 internal medicine specialists. Yet many pet owners get rid of their cats and dogs, or even put them to sleep, for annoying behavior ranging from barking to eating drywall. Daniel Aja, a veterinarian in Traverse City, Mich., and former president of the American Animal Hospital Association, recalls one client who brought in a St. Bernard to be euthanized because of severe separation anxiety. Once when the owner left the house, the dog jumped through a plate-glass window to chase after him. Aja convinced the owner to treat the pup with antidepressants and had behaviorists on his staff counsel the client on how to work with his dog.

Not all vets will make the extra effort to diagnose a behavior problem, which entails taking a complete medical and behavioral history and spending hours with a pet. What do you do if Champ continues to chase his tail? Ask your vet if he has experience with behavioral issues. If not, request a referral. Or find a trainer through the Animal Behavior College online, at *www.animalbehaviorcollege .com/dog_trainer_search.asp.*

10 *"OUR TECHNOLOGY MAY BE STATE-OF-THE-ART, BUT OUR INDUSTRY REGULATIONS ARE STILL IN THE DARK AGES."*

While veterinarians and animal hospitals are increasingly working with the same level of sophistication as human doctors and hospitals, the regulatory oversight within the field is far less stringent. Under federal law, human hospitals must be inspected, but it's possible for a veterinary hospital to operate for years and never undergo an independent inspection, Aja says.

The American Animal Hospital Association does accredit animal hospitals, assessing them on more than 800 different standards ranging from organization of medical records to diagnostic capabilities. But only about 15 percent of hospitals in the U.S. and 7 percent of hospitals in Canada have been accredited by the organization. Some states, such as California, perform their own inspections on vet hospitals, checking them for everything from outdated drugs to unsanitary conditions. The upshot is that even seemingly petty requirements can have lifesaving results: After a California mandate required vets to have "emergency lighting" on hand, one veterinarian used a flashlight to finish surgery when a blackout hit.

THINGS TO DO

● **When starting the search for** a veterinarian, ask local pet owners for recommendations. If you own a purebred or specialized breed, start by checking with a nearby breed club for recommendations.

● **Don't be afraid to shop around.** Bring Fido in for a consultation at several clinics to compare vets' credentials, personality, office hours, and office cleanliness—then consider fees, payment plans, and whether pet insurance is accepted.

● **To ensure a vet's credentials,** call your local veterinary board and humane society and request a background check. While not all vet boards list disciplinary actions on their sites, they should be able to provide you with info on specific vets when asked.

● **If your vet doesn't offer** emergency medical care, find the closest animal hospital and get your vet's opinion on what facility would best suit your pet in an emergency.

● **Just as important as selecting** the right vet is knowing your pet and monitoring its well-being. Stay informed about common ailments and symptoms, and watch for any change in your animal's behavior that might signal a health problem.

10 Things Your
Nursing Home
Won't Tell You

1 *"WE'RE CARELESS ABOUT THE DRUGS WE GIVE OUT."*

"The primary goal of nursing homes," according to the American Health Care Association, an industry trade group, "is to rehabilitate residents so that they can return to the community." It's a worthy aim, certainly. And many nursing homes—both public and private—do an excellent job of caring for the elderly and infirm. So why is it that so many people not only have a negative view of these facilities but live in absolute dread of entering one? In a recent survey conducted by Prince Market Research, 13 percent of seniors said moving into a nursing home was what they feared most, compared with 3 percent who said death was their biggest fear.

"As scary as what you do know about them is, it's even scarier what you don't," explains Claire Stoffman, who says her own husband died—after just one day in a nursing home—within hours of receiving the wrong diabetes drug. (A spokesperson for the home says it's corporate policy not to discuss patient records.) Indeed, the failure to administer medications properly to residents—and the practice of overmedicating—is a chronic problem critics say is quite common at nursing homes. According to the Health Care Financing Administration, which enforces federal rules affecting these facilities, 13 percent of nursing homes were cited for dispensing unnecessary drugs in 2006, up from 11 percent in 1996.

2 *"WE'RE WOEFULLY UNDERSTAFFED."*

At age 81, Florence Richards was lucky. She had people to feed and bathe her and make sure she stayed interested in the world beyond the Fairfax Nursing Center, in Fairfax, Va. She was lucky, that is, since her daughter, Martha Meserve, was able to hire private-duty nurses to ensure proper care for 11 straight hours every day. The cost? Nearly $4,000 a month out-of-pocket for Meserve—over and above the $5,000 monthly fee the nursing home was already charging. A spokesperson for the facility says it does, in fact, meet appropriate staffing thresholds, but acknowledges that "on occasion, a family member might be asked to hire private-duty sitters."

"It speaks very badly about our system that you have to pay to hire somebody on top of paying for a nursing home," says Elma Holder, founder of the National Citizens' Coalition for Nursing Home Reform, in Washington, D.C. But according to the U.S. Administration on Aging, which tallies nursing-home complaints received by state ombudsmen, understaffing continues to be a major problem. Ideally, says Jeanie Kayser-Jones, a professor at the University of California, San Francisco, and a leading researcher on nursing-home issues, a nurse's aide—the person tasked with providing the bulk of the care, including feeding, bathing, and clothing residents—should be in charge of no more than three people during a meal and no more than six at other times. (At night that ratio can safely go to one aide per 15 residents, experts say.) In reality, however, it's not that unusual to find a lone nurse's aide caring for as many as 30 people.

Not surprisingly, the problem stems from budget issues. In California, for example, just 53 percent of a nursing home's budget typically goes to paying for direct patient care, including nursing costs, notes Charlene Harrington, a professor of sociology and nursing at the University of California, San Francisco. The result is not only too few employees but also low staff salaries (nurse's aides averaged just $10.31 an hour as of 2006) and turnover rates of almost 80 percent a year. As one nursing-home insider puts it: "If you could make the same money flipping hamburgers at McDonald's, why would you do this?"

3 *"MR. AND MRS. SMITH, MEET STICKY FINGERS LOUIE."*

Nursing-home fees aren't cheap— especially for the 20 percent or more of all residents (or their families) who pay the average $6,390 monthly charge out of their own pockets. But there's also often a hidden, hurtful cost to a nursing-home stay: the price of stolen personal belongings. "All nursing homes have some level of theft," says Diana Harris, a sociology professor at the University of Tennessee, Knoxville, who has studied the subject extensively. And it's often a bigger problem than government agencies recognize, since thefts are rarely reported. Cash, jewelry—even wedding rings—and clothes are the most commonly swiped items, says Harris, who points out that nursing homes often unknowingly hire staff with a criminal background. "There are a lot of people working in nursing homes who shouldn't be there," she says. "Some places just take anybody off the street."

How bad is the problem? According to Michigan State Attorney General Mike Cox, an astounding 25 percent of nursing-home employees charged for crimes against residents between 2002 and 2005 already had criminal backgrounds, including retail fraud, drug offenses, and even homicide. The findings prompted Michigan to enhance laws regarding criminal background checks for prospective residential care facility employees. Other states are tightening standards as well. The New York Department of Health, for example, implemented a criminal-history record check program for unlicensed nursing-home workers, in effect since April 2005. Senator Herb Kohl (D-Wis.) plans to take it a step further: He's introduced legislation that would prohibit long-term-care facilities in all 50 states from hiring staff with criminal backgrounds, which could become law by 2011.

4 "WHAT YOU DON'T KNOW ABOUT YOUR CHECKBOOK CAN HURT YOU."

Nursing-home theft isn't just about lifting jewelry from unsuspecting residents. It can also be institutionalized. And with over $138 billion expected to flow into these facilities in 2008, the temptation to skim and scam can be great. In 2007, for example, a grand jury indicted the former business manager at Renfro Health Care Center in Waxahachie, Tex., for allegedly diverting more than $350,000 from residents' trust funds to her own account. That same year in Vermont, the former accounts payable person at Lamoille County Mental Health Services pleaded guilty to embezzling nearly $35,000 from three different residents' accounts administered by the agency. (Both cases were pending at press time; neither Renfro nor Lamoille could comment when contacted.)

And examples like these are just the tip of the iceberg, according to reports by the National Association of Medicaid Fraud Control Units: Nursing-home residents in Ohio, Minnesota, and Mississippi were all victims of institutional theft in 2007. "It's a very disturbing national trend," says Paul Hodge, director of Harvard Generations Policy Program. And with the growing number of nursing-home residents, he says, such cases of institutional fraud are on the rise.

5 "IF IT'S NOT IN THE CARE PLAN, WE'RE NOT GONNA DO IT."

By age 59, Jennifer Means's mother was having difficulty feeding herself.

Huntington's disease had impaired her motor skills, making it hard for her to get food to her mouth and placing her at risk of choking. But that, claims Means, didn't stop the staff at her mother's Kentucky nursing home from simply leaving meals by her bedside and walking away. (Calls to that facility were not returned.)

Though the phrase sounds like sugary brochure-speak, the creation of an individual patient care plan—essentially a blueprint for how nursing-home staff are supposed to tend to a particular resident—is actually mandated by federal law.

The root of the problem, Means says, is that the nursing home never bothered to prepare an appropriate "care plan" for her mother. Though the phrase sounds like sugary brochure-speak, the creation of an individual patient care plan—essentially a blueprint for how nursing-home staff are supposed to tend to a particular resident—is actually mandated by federal law. Unfortunately, according to Means, nothing in her mother's care plan said anything about the need to be fed puréed food by a nurse's aide.

Frequently, a nursing home will make the plans "as pro forma as possible," says Kathy Gannoe, who runs a private ombudsman agency in Lexington, Ky., one of nearly 600 such local entities empowered by state governments to investigate nursing-home complaints. So how to help protect your loved ones? Get involved in both their preliminary health assessment and the development of a care plan right from the beginning. And if you're not satisfied that the plan does enough, call your state's long-term-care ombudsman. The National Long Term Care Ombudsman Resource Center lists contact numbers on its website, *www.ltcombudsman.org.*

6 *"'NEGLECT' IS OUR MIDDLE NAME."*

Ila Swan is still sorry about putting her mother, Rhoda Johnson, in a California nursing home when her mother was in her 90s. There were a host of problems at the facility—as Swan alleged in a civil suit she filed in state court. At the top of the list, she says, was "a gaping hole" in her mother's flesh exposing her hip socket, the result of being left in the same position too long. (The nursing home would not comment on the case, which was later settled for $775,000.)

Such neglect is certainly disturbing, but sadly, it isn't rare. In 2005, nursing-home investigators received some 300,000 complaints nationally, filed by more than 186,000 individuals—the vast majority of whom were either residents or their relatives or friends. The danger, of course, is that staff neglect can lead not only to bedsores and physical discomfort but also to severe dehydration and malnutrition. John Morley, a professor of gerontology at St. Louis University, estimates that

the rate of resident malnutrition varies from about 4 percent in good facilities to perhaps 50 percent at bad ones.

"It's well established that malnutrition is a serious problem at nursing homes," says researcher Kayser-Jones, who testified on the subject before the U.S. Senate's Special Committee on Aging. Following the Senate's public hearings, the Government Accountability Office instructed Centers for Medicare & Medicaid Services to stagger the scheduling of standard surveys to effectively reduce the predictability of surveyors' visits while further investigating this issue.

7 *"SOME OF OUR TACTICS SOUND STRAIGHT OUT OF BEDLAM."*

While the law allows for the use of physical restraints—belts or vests that bind nursing-home residents to a chair or bed to prevent falls and wandering—as a last resort to protect a resident's health or ensure the safety of others, many critics argue it's usually a bad idea. "Research shows that restraints hurt far more than they help," says Sarah Greene Burger, a leading reform advocate and coauthor of *Nursing Homes: Getting Good Care There.* Immobilizing residents through physical restraints not only can make them agitated or depressed, Burger says, but can result in a host of physical problems as well.

The good news is that the use of physical restraints has dropped significantly since the passage of the Nursing Home Reform Act of 1987. According to the Nevada State Health Division, for example, 7 percent of nursing homes in that state received citations for using physical restraints unnecessarily in 2007—a sharp decline from 65 percent in 1996. The bad news is that the practice still goes on. As of June 2007, roughly 5 percent of nursing-home residents across the country had been restrained at some point, according to federal records.

8 *"OUR REPORT CARDS ARE A JOKE."*

How to tell if the long-term-care facility you're considering is any good? Well, you could rely on its health- and safety-standards compliance survey, which, in accordance with federal regulations, is updated annually by a state inspection agency. Nursing homes are checked for things such as unsanitary food conditions and patient neglect, and cited for any code violations.

But watch out, says Michael Connors, former program director for Detroit-based Citizens for Better Care: A clean record may not mean much. Why? Some facilities "prep" for the surveys, he says, by "inundating themselves with staff" during the inspection periods. How do they know when the inspectors are coming to their doorstep? Although technically unannounced, the state surveys tend to occur at predictable times—usually about 12 months after the last one, insiders say. When the inspection's over, notes Connors, "they go back to business as usual."

9 *"FINES? GO AHEAD— GIVE US YOUR BEST SHOT."*

When a nursing home fails to meet federal standards, it's supposed to get fined, right? In reality, the federal government penalizes nursing homes this way so infrequently—"only as a last resort," concedes one government spokesperson—that states are left to implement their own sanctions. But judging from the record of California—which among states, experts say, has one of the better citation records—nursing homes have little to fear. The state assessed $3.6 million in fines during 2006, for instance, but collected just $1.1 million. Why such a poor showing? "There are too many loopholes," says Pat Safford, former outreach coordinator at California Advocates for Nursing Home Reform.

One way to bypass the penalties is through an administrative hearing, whereby a facility can choose to appeal both the type of citation and its accompanying fine. (Of the 211 such hearings held in California in 2006, 191 were still pending nearly two years later.) The Class B citations—for offenses that affect the health, safety, and/or security of a resident and generally carry a fine of less than $1,000—are particularly "toothless," complains Safford. Charged by the state with such a violation, a nursing home need only prove that it "did what might reasonably be expected of a long-term health-care facility" under "similar circumstances"—leaving plenty of wiggle room for interpretation.

10 *"WE CAN KICK A RESIDENT OUT ANYTIME WE WANT."*

It's called "patient dumping": A nursing home decides it can no longer care for a resident—frequently, critics say, because the person requires too much staff attention or is otherwise considered a "problem"—and so it forces that resident out. Anna Mae Washington, a wheelchair-bound Maryland resident, learned of the practice the hard way. Back in 1993, the 82-year-old woman was placed in a van and taken to a guardian's house, without notification, after her nursing facility complained it wasn't being paid. The case, which was investigated by that state's Medicaid Fraud Control Unit, prompted the Maryland legislature to pass the "Anna Mae" bill in April 1995, which imposes criminal penalties for the illegal eviction of nursing-home residents.

Typically, however, the process is more subtle—a resident's family member, for example, might be pressured into

"voluntarily" removing his or her loved one from the facility, says Toby Edelman, a former staff attorney with the Washington, D.C.–based National Senior Citizens Law Center. Such strong-arm tactics are a way of subverting the formal discharge process, she says. And Medicaid recipients, who make up close to two thirds of all nursing-home residents nationwide, are often the targets. While state and federal laws allow nursing homes to discharge residents under special circumstances—for example, if the patient's health improves and he or she therefore no longer requires the facility's care—they generally must provide 30 days' written notice, stating the reasons for the discharge. Even then, residents have the right to appeal.

THINGS TO DO

● **Planning ahead is the best way** to avoid getting stuck in a facility that isn't up to par. You can order or download a free planning kit at *www.longtermcare.gov.*

● **Keep an eye on the ratio** of nurse's aides to patients. There should be at least one aide for every three patients at mealtimes.

● **Don't put too much stock** in a nursing home's health- and safety-standards compliance survey. Instead, ask to speak

with current residents or their family members to get a better read.

● **Before signing on, thoroughly review** a nursing home's proposed care plan to make sure it's not one-size-fits-all.

● **Residents have the right** to appeal any effort by a long-term-care facility to have them discharged. Contact your state's ombudsman for info on the appeal process *(www.ltcombudsman.org).*

10 Things Your
Funeral Director
Won't Tell You

1 *"BUSINESS IS SLOW, BUT MY PRICES ARE HIGH."*

As U.S. life expectancies continue to climb decade after decade, funeral homes struggle to maintain their profits. In most industries, that would mean price wars, but not in the burial business, where consumers often choose providers based on just three criteria: location, family history, and personal recommendations. Knowing that the majority of their customers don't shop around, funeral homes charge for their services accordingly—the average cost of a funeral today stands at roughly $6,850, according to the most recent data from the National Funeral Directors Association. And that's without a lot of fancy extras such as flowers and video tributes. That amount is up 36 percent from 10 years ago, when the average funeral was $5,020.

Looking to protect vulnerable consumers, who are often not at their most savvy when dealing with the burial industry, the Federal Trade Commission put in place the Funeral Rule of 1984, which requires all funeral homes to provide a written price list with itemized fees. Nonetheless, some businesses still don't offer it—or else they exclude simple options such as direct cremation or burial, as well as bundle things consumers aren't required to buy, such as vaults or transportation services.

The best defense? Shop around, or have someone who is up to it do it for you. Specifically, call and request an itemized price list from several funeral homes in your area and choose accordingly.

2 *"CREMATION IS KILLING OFF MY PROFITS."*

Cremation is becoming a steadily more popular practice in the U.S. According to the Cremation Association of North America, the number of cremations increased 5 percent between 2001 and 2005, to 32 percent of all deaths; by 2025, that figure is projected to reach 57 percent. Since cremation can cost up to a third less than the average funeral, this trend is bad news for funeral directors.

To pick up the slack in lost revenue, many funeral homes are promoting extra products and services. While grieving families are often relieved to hear that cremation can include such traditional funereal elements as a viewing and a memorial service, there are some things that are unnecessary or that may be presented deceptively. For example, cremation does not automatically involve purchasing a casket even if you plan to hold a viewing beforehand. (In that case, inquire about renting a casket from the funeral home.) Also, funeral directors who offer the most basic type of cremation are required to disclose your right to buy an unfinished wood box or an alternative container, and are obligated to make such a container available.

3 *"YOU DON'T ACTUALLY HAVE TO BUY YOUR CASKET HERE."*

One of the biggest funeral expenses is the casket. The average price hovers somewhere around $2,000, but many models easily surpass $10,000—and those are the ones you'll likely see on display. Funeral directors are required by law to provide a list of prices for every casket they sell before showing them, but they don't always have every model they offer on hand. If you don't see some of the less expensive models when you're shown the selection, ask about them.

What many people don't know is that you needn't purchase the casket from the funeral home at all. Third-party dealers selling reduced-cost caskets have sprung up in the past decade; caskets are now available for purchase over the Internet, at funeral-supply stores, and even at some Costco locations. Funeral directors are required by law to accept caskets purchased from these outlets, and they cannot legally charge you a fee for doing so. But that doesn't mean some funeral directors don't try to discourage it. When Patricia Anzelmo, a bookkeeper from Stow, Mass., purchased an $1,800 casket for her stepson from Casket Royale, she says her funeral director advised against it. "He tried to put a fear into me that I wasn't going to be happy with it and that it was going to be cheap," she says. "But the casket was gorgeous."

4 *"WE'LL PLAY YOUR HEARTSTRINGS LIKE A HARP."*

When Erin Strout's grandmother died in 1998, Strout's normally frugal grandfather purchased a $14,000 package that was loaded with extras, including the release of a live dove at the burial site. "Neither my grandmother nor my grandfather is really a release-a-dove kind of person," Strout says. Other common pitches include everything from "protective caskets"—metal models that claim to delay the penetration of moisture and can add $1,000 to the cost—to extras like journals and photo frames. Forest Lawn Funeral Home in Goodlettsville, Tenn., offers a silver-plated picture frame, crystal pen, and access to a "grief management library" as part of its "Platinum" package.

Even worse are the questionable marketing practices some businesses use. For example, it's not uncommon for a funeral home to stamp the words "temporary container" on the cardboard box cremated remains are returned in—implying that the family will need to buy an expensive urn. Another trick: marketing optional elements like transportation or steel caskets as part of a "traditional" service. "A lot of people are cowed [by that]," says Joshua Slocum, executive director of the Funeral Consumers Alliance.

5 *"EMBALMING IS OPTIONAL."*

Most people think embalming, the process of chemically preserving a body, is a necessary or even legally required part of the undertaking process. Not true: Embalming is almost never necessary in the first 24 hours and is not required at all in many cases—when you choose cremation or immediate burial, for example, or when plain old refrigeration is available.

If you opt to hold a public viewing, the funeral home may have an embalming policy in such cases. And it'll likely encourage both. "The funeral industry stresses the notion that in order for anybody to come to terms with death, they must see embalmed bodies," Slocum says. "That's malarkey." Funeral directors promote it, he says, not only for the embalming fee, but also because if you're paying for the embalming and beautifying of the body—which can cost up to $1,000—it's easier to sell you a fancier casket.

If your funeral home has such a policy and you're opposed to it, ask if it will hold a private viewing for family members, without embalming. The bottom line? "Don't feel obligated just because it's [considered] normal," Slocum says.

6 *"YOU MIGHT NOT NEED ME AT ALL."*

Despite the common conception, only a few states—including Nebraska, Indiana, and Connecticut—require you to hire a funeral director at all. In most places, it's perfectly legal to plan and conduct a funeral in your own home. While there are no hard statistics on home funerals, "public interest is definitely growing," says Lisa Carlson, author of *Caring for the Dead: Your Final Act of Love.* Experts say the option can make the grieving process more natural. "It allows [people] to feel all their emotions rather than showing up at a building and having to leave an hour later because there's another funeral," says Jerri Lyons, founder of Final Passages, a group that educates consumers about alternative funerals.

That doesn't mean it's easy. When Elizabeth Knox held a home funeral for her daughter nine years ago in Silver Spring, Md., she says the hospital where her daughter died refused to release the body to the family; then she had to call four crematories before finding one that would let the family act as funeral director. Last summer, when she conducted a home funeral for her mother in New Jersey, Knox was erroneously told by state officials that she couldn't transport her mother's body herself. Knox's frustrations prompted her to form Crossings, a nonprofit group dedicated to guiding others through the process. Visit the website (*www.crossings.net*) for information on home funerals.

7 *"PREPAYING BENEFITS ME, NOT YOU ..."*

So-called preneed funeral arrangements seem like a good idea on paper: Customers design their own funeral and pay for it in advance, thus protecting their relatives against escalating prices and having their grief exploited for profit. The cost of the funeral is paid either in part or in full, with a percentage of the total put into a trust or covered via a preneed insurance policy with monthly payments. Sounds like a great idea on paper. But prepaying is often a better deal for the funeral home than for you.

Under the upfront option, the funeral home pockets as much as 50 percent of the payment immediately. If it goes out of business or you change your mind, you won't necessarily get all your money back—and less money earns interest in the trust. Preneed insurance policies, meanwhile, aren't usually refundable, and you may only get pennies on the dollar if you cash out of them. Even worse, if you live long enough, the monthly premiums can end up costing more than the funeral you wanted in the first place.

That's what almost happened to Patricia Cairns, a retiree in Myrtle Beach, S.C. Cairns selected a funeral plan valued at $5,842 and bought an irrevocable insurance policy with monthly premiums of $86.43. "What they never told me was that I had to pay on this until I was 80," she says. By that time, Cairns calculates, she would have paid $10,371.60—almost twice the cost of the funeral she'd chosen.

8 "...AND IT DOESN'T COVER EVERYTHING."

Even if you do prepay, chances are your loved ones will still have to open their wallets, as there are many items commonly found on funeral bills—such as autopsy charges, flowers, and grave opening and closing fees—that can't be included in preneed contracts. Relatives may also get stuck shelling out for the casket, since a model picked out 15 years ago may no longer be available.

It's not uncommon for models to be discontinued, and while there may be a similar replacement found, the price will almost inevitably have increased.

Even worse, a funeral director may claim that a desired casket is out of stock—a convenient opportunity to push for an upgrade. "It's definitely a huge red flag if [you're] asked to buy a more expensive casket" when a preselected model is simply out of stock, says Darrell Simpson, former vice president of Wilkirson-Hatch-Bailey, an independent funeral home in Waco, Tex.—especially when most of the larger casket-manufacturing centers are willing to deliver either same-day or by the morning of the next day.

9 "AT THE CREMATORIUM, ANYTHING GOES."

In 2002 the funeral industry and the general public were appalled by news of decomposing remains found at a crematory in Noble, Ga. The Cremation Association of North America quickly responded by revising a model state cremation law to include certification and training requirements. But in most states crematories are still not required to have inspections or certification.

A class-action lawsuit against the Georgia crematory also asserted claims against several funeral homes for failing to ensure that cremations were performed properly (or, in fact, at all). The funeral homes settled for roughly $36 million, and the crematory later settled for $80 million. To help protect your loved one, the AARP recommends using a crematory that does undergo public inspections and to inquire about the training of the facility's operators. Were they trained and certified by the Cremation Association of North America (CANA)? (Some states require CANA certification.) Is the facility subject to internal inspection as well? Proceed with caution if the answer is "no."

10 "'GREEN' BURIALS HAVE ME FEELING BLUE."

In addition to home funerals, another movement in the funeral industry is burial in "green," or natural, cemeteries—which prohibit embalming, metal caskets, and concrete burial vaults, and generally forbid traditional headstones in favor of smaller, engraved indigenous stones, trees, or shrubs. While the practice is still rare, it has started catching on among the environmentally—and economically—conscious. "There's increasing interest in it," Slocum says. "It's really a return to the way we always used to do it."

In addition to being green, forgoing embalming services and selecting simple wooden caskets can save consumers thousands of dollars. At one green cemetery, Ramsey Creek Preserve in Westminster, S.C., even caskets aren't required. Of course, this is just more bad news for funeral directors. They "don't know what to make of the trend," Slocum says.

THINGS TO DO

• **Don't bother prepaying for funerals**—it can cost you thousands in interest, and if the funeral home goes out of business or you change your mind, you won't get reimbursed.

• **Beware of add-ons** labeled as part of a "traditional" service; they're "traditionally" the way funeral directors run up your bill.

• **Make sure your funeral home** and funeral director are active members of the National Funeral Directors Association (www.nfda.org) or the Cremation Association of North America (www.cremationassociation.org). That means they're licensed and also required to uphold the ethical standards of their field.

• **Funerals can be highly emotional** events for friends and family. One way to draw strength from the passing of a loved one is to personalize the ceremony, using photographs, collages, meaningful quotes, and other materials designed to celebrate the life of the deceased and the way he or she has impacted the lives of others.

CHAPTER 2

Your Children's Education

■ No issue looms larger—or longer—for parents than the education of their children. From preschool through the madness of college admissions, it's all about making the right choices at the right time to suit your kids' needs and help prepare them for the best life possible.

So whether your children are toddlers or teens, whether it's your first kid or your fifth, we're here to help. From "10 Things Your Preschool Won't Tell You," which offers sage advice on what to look for when visiting prospective preschools, to "10 Things Campus Security Won't Tell You," covering the difficult topic of keeping your child safe during those first years out from under your wing, we'll show you how to navigate every turn in the road of your child's education.

10 Things Your
Preschool
Won't Tell You

1 "SURE, WE'RE LICENSED, BUT THAT DOESN'T MEAN WE'RE ANY GOOD."

Most three- and four-year-olds go to preschool these days—a big switch from 1960, when just 10 percent of them did, according to the National Institute for Early Education Research (NIEER). More working mothers and a wide acceptance of the benefits of early education have fostered the growth of preschools. But there's a downside: An alarming number of them aren't very good. "The quality of preschools is highly variable, and overall quality is on the low side," says Steve Barnett, director of NIEER.

One reason: Most state licensing requirements pertain to safety and health rather than quality. That means a school might take extra care to make sure the toilet bowl plunger isn't within a toddler's reach, but it might not require its teachers to have much education. In fact, some states don't require any academic degree to become a preschool teacher.

So how do you find a good preschool for your toddler? One indicator of quality is whether a facility has received accreditation from an outside organization. The largest accrediting body for preschools is the National Association for the Education of Young Children (NAEYC). To find information on that group's requirements as well as a locator for accredited preschools, visit its website at *www.naeyc.org*.

2 "BUS DRIVERS MAKE MORE THAN OUR TEACHERS."

The most pressing problem for preschools is hiring and keeping good teachers. And it's little wonder why. The average annual salary for a preschool teacher is $25,900, less than what a bus driver or a concierge makes, according to the U.S. Bureau of Labor Statistics. And low pay often means short retention of staff: Average teacher turnover at preschools ranges between 30 and 50 percent annually, says NAEYC. And those who do stay may not be well trained.

How can a parent tell if a teacher is a modern-day Mister Rogers? In addition to looking for college degrees in early-childhood development and years of experience, parents should observe teachers at work. Sandra Duncan, former vice president of HighReach Learning, a Charlotte, N.C., developer of preschool curricula, says that good teachers have sore knees because they continually stoop to the child's level to speak to them. Good teachers also know their students well. Brandy Bergman, a mother of two in Westchester, N.Y., says she knew her daughter's teacher was top-notch because she could recount specifics of her daughter's playground conversations. Another factor: having plenty of teachers. NAEYC recommends a ratio of one teacher for every 10 three-year-olds.

3 "LEARNING THE ABCs WON'T PREPARE YOUR TOT FOR KINDERGARTEN."

Preschool used to be solely about sandboxes and finger painting. But more standardized testing in elementary schools, as well as anxious parents who think that learning the alphabet by age four will pave their tot's way to the Ivy League, has pushed academic preparation over more traditional kids' stuff. Once the province of K–12, in-class worksheets and memorization of letters and numbers, for example, are not uncommon in today's preschools. At the end of the day, however, preschoolers may not need as much academics as some parents might think. In fact, education experts say that overemphasizing academics at such an early stage can actually hamper a child's emotional and social development.

The skills kindergarten teachers are really looking for are those that *enable* academic learning, such as following directions or sitting attentively during story time, says Betsy Brown Braun, a child development specialist and founder of Parenting Pathways in Pacific Palisades, Calif. In light of that, she says parents should seek out a preschool that integrates the ABCs into playtime and encourages activities that engage the senses and emotions, which is how

children learn best. A project that includes making lemonade, for example, could also involve lessons about measuring and counting.

4 "DISCIPLINE'S NOT OUR FORTE."

When it comes to discipline, preschools differ dramatically in their approaches, ranging from New Agey time-outs to old-fashioned verbal reprimands, like "Stop running!" One preschool even brands tots with a red sticker if they've had too many outbursts. But ultimately, a child's cognitive and social development is best encouraged through collaboration, discussion, and discovering the hows and whys of their actions, according to the National Association of Elementary School Principals. In other words, discipline is another opportunity to teach—if teachers and schools are willing to put in the necessary time it takes.

For starters, discipline methods need to take into account a child's developmental needs. For example, Braun says that even benign time-outs miss the boat for preschoolers who aren't old enough to contemplate the rights and wrongs of their behavior. A better approach is to stop inappropriate behavior and help the child understand why it was wrong by talking with him about his actions.

Parents should ask preschool directors and teachers if they have a written policy regarding discipline and inquire about what training the school provides its teachers to help implement it. Untrained teachers may simply fall back on the discipline techniques they experienced as children.

5 *"SEPARATION ANXIETY? NEVER GAVE IT MUCH THOUGHT."*

For many toddlers and parents, one of the most significant experiences of preschool is being apart from each other. Yet for some schools, how children and parents separate isn't enough of a priority. "We were told to politely drop our kid off and then haul ass," says Eric Noble, an Orange County, Calif., parent, about his son's preschool's separation policy. "My wife hated it."

The process can be even tougher on the kids. If separation from mom or dad isn't handled thoughtfully, children may act out, regressing in their toilet training or clinging to parents back at home. But there are ways to help smooth the transition. Jill Strauss, former managing editor of *Scholastic Parent & Child* magazine, says some preschools will have a teacher visit the child at home before school starts. During such in-home visits, teachers at Resurrection Preschool in Chicago, for example, will play with the child and invite him to paint his name on an apron the teacher then wears on the first day of school. Debbie Mytych, Resurrection's director, says that once school begins, preschools should allow parents to stay with their child for a period of time and gradually work toward leaving the child alone at school. And depending on the family, that process can take days or even weeks.

6 *"GET READY TO WORK OVERTIME."*

Many cash- and staff-strapped preschools not only welcome parental involvement, they require it. Parents are often prodded to lend a hand, which can mean everything from making snacks for 30 kids at a time to trimming the bushes outside the school's gates. Some preschools go even further, charging a nominal fee, say $100, for parents who want to opt out of bake sales and other extracurricular activities.

But some parental involvement at a preschool is far preferable to the alternative—none at all. If a preschool doesn't have an open-door policy for parents to drop in and visit their kids, many experts say you should seriously wonder why. "It's a huge red flag," says Claudette Pittman, former adjunct professor in early childhood education at Pacific Oaks College in Pasadena, Calif. She recalls a preschool in San Gabriel, Calif., for example, that had a full staff during the morning, when parents dropped kids off, but then let most of the staff go, deeply depleting the ratio of teachers to toddlers.

At the very least, preschools should have a system that enables and promotes communication from parents, whether it's calls to the director or tacking suggestions on a message board. And if schools don't require any parental effort, they should welcome it when it's offered.

7 *"WE SERVE MORE JUNK FOOD THAN McDONALD'S."*

Back in the day, what kids ate in preschool didn't tend to register very high on the list of parental concerns. But with childhood obesity rising and growing concern over the prevalence of food allergies like peanuts, many parents are easing up on the Reese's Peanut Butter Cups and Cheetos at home—even as many preschools continue to serve up plenty of junk food. Despite federal and state nutrition guidelines that require balanced meals, treats like cookies, pretzels, Popsicles, and sugar-coated cereals are still standard snack-time fare at many places.

But more and more preschools are beginning to heed the call for healthy eating and impose nutrition guidelines and snacking policies. Little Village Nursery School in Los Angeles, for example, has a no-sugar rule for its snacks. At other places, special dietary requests from parents will be honored. If a preschool won't meet individual students' needs, then education experts say it should at least address allergy concerns. That means forbidding peanut butter and keeping toddlers from sharing their homemade treats.

8 "WE'RE HARDER TO GET INTO THAN HARVARD."

These days getting your child admitted into a preschool of your choice can be as difficult as getting him or her into an elite college—and that's true whether you live in a big city or not. In urban centers such as Los Angeles and New York, proactive new parents put their newborns on preschool waiting lists. But even in smaller cities and suburbs, the competition for enrollment has gotten tough.

Just how do preschools decide who gets in and who doesn't? Much of the time, it's the luck of the draw. But many preschools are also known to give preference to families with a sibling who's attended or to families who pony up big

donations. And if a preschool is run by a church or a synagogue, members may also get a leg up.

There are sometimes other considerations as well. Since preschools strive to balance their classrooms, a child's gender and even temperament can affect admission. Many preschools want diversity, so race and religion could also play a role. Of course, whom you know counts, too. Julie Bick, a mother in Seattle, says she got her kids into a preschool after friends within her mommy network recommended her.

9 "OUR PRICEY TUITION IS JUST THE START."

Preschool tuition now costs as much as college tuition in many places across America. An all-day preschool in Durham, N.C., for example, can run $7,000, while in Montclair, N.J., it can cost as much as $16,500. But the bigger sticker shock is that tuition is just the start of the money drain.

The number of children a preschool can accept is constrained by the number it can physically accommodate, so revenue growth is limited—but the costs of running the school aren't. Despite low teacher salaries, a significant amount of money a preschool takes in—possibly as much as 55 cents of every dollar—goes toward labor, taxes, and insurance costs, such as workers' compensation, according to Duncan at HighReach Learning. Aggressive fund-raising often fills in the gap, with as much as 20 percent of a preschool's budget coming from annual galas or auctions. In addition, many preschools actively solicit parents for cash donations as well.

For families on a budget, the finances of preschool can leave them with few options. Some schools offer scholarships; there are also cooperative preschools run by parents. Nancy Branka, an Oakland, Calif., mother of two, slashed her costs by nearly 30 percent by joining a co-op preschool. But she found herself donating her time rather than her money—Branka says she put in roughly 12 hours a month to handle the school's finances.

10 *"WE DON'T ALWAYS FOLLOW OUR OWN EDUCATION PHILOSOPHY."*

Most preschools profess to have a guiding philosophy. Some follow specific theories espoused by education pioneers like Maria Montessori. Others buy materials and curriculum plans from education companies. But while they may have a plan on paper, many preschools may not follow it in practice. And while accreditation does offer some guarantee that schools will stick to their program, even that isn't airtight. NAEYC, for example, accredits schools just every five years, leaving plenty of room for slippage.

To make sure their kids' preschool is staying on track, parents should check in on the classroom from time to time, paying attention to how it looks and feels. "A preschool classroom should hum," Duncan says. It should also be designed for children: Artwork should be hung low, for example, where little ones can readily view it. And if the watercolor clowns all look the same, it may mean the teacher has done more of the art than Tommy's inner Picasso. NIEER's Barnett says parents should also check what the daily lesson plans are and whether they include activities their child enjoys. Bottom line: The biggest indicator of whether a preschool is working is if both the child and the parent feel good when they go there.

THINGS TO DO

- **Keep your distance from facilities** that don't have an open-door policy for parents; preschools should welcome communication from parents.

- **Easing your child into the school** may be the best way to help alleviate her separation anxiety. Some schools encourage teachers to visit with new students before the start of the school year so they're a familiar face on day one.

- **A costly tuition might be** just the beginning. One way to get around additional solicitations is to donate your time—say, volunteering as an aide or assistant—in lieu of money.

- **If you have more than** one child near preschool age, ask about a family discount. Even if one is a year or so behind the other, your show of loyalty might earn you some savings.

10 Things Your
School District
Won't Tell You

1 *"LIKE OUR STUDENT/TEACHER RATIO? IT INCLUDES HANK THE JANITOR."*

It's considered Math 101 in the education business: A smaller class size equals a better learning experience for your child. So it's no wonder that school districts are often quick to point to their cozy student/teacher ratios as proof their schools are strictly honor-roll material. But watch out, say experts. Those numbers don't always mean what you think.

Click on the New York State Education Department's website, for instance, and you'll discover that the Pocantico Hills Central School District, a single-school district for pre-K through eighth grade in upstate New York, has a student/teacher ratio of 9-to-1. Impressive, certainly—except for one thing: It isn't true. "We have 20 kids to every class on average," says a spokesperson for Pocantico Hills. Why the discrepancy? Because in many states, there are simply no rules for determining the student-to-teacher stats. "There's only state information, and their numbers are always lower than the real number," says Peter Lisi, former superintendent of Pocantico Hills. "They put in every person, from the school psychologist to the librarian and the gym teacher."

Ronald Danforth, a former associate in Education Information Services for the New York State Education Department, says that the Pocantico Hills number is skewed because it's a tiny district (with around 350 students). That means when you include such staff as remedial teachers—who generally work with groups of one to four students needing extra help—the teacher pool seems comparatively large.

So where can parents get accurate information about the student/teacher ratio at their kid's school? David Paradise, of the Council of Chief State School Officers, a Washington, D.C., nonprofit that offers leadership and advocacy on education issues, says your best bet is to call the school's district office. That way, you can find out what's included in the statistic for that particular district, as well as what has been budgeted for new teacher hires.

2 *"OUR PER-PUPIL EXPENDITURES ARE MEANINGLESS."*

Often the same numbers nonsense goes on with another so-called quality yardstick: per-pupil expenditures. Here the rule seems equally intuitive. More money means better school buildings and supplies, computer equipment, higher-paid teachers—in short, a better education.

Or does it? Consider two New Jersey school districts: New Brunswick City, which spends $13,126 per student a year, and Woodbridge Township, which spends $10,103 per student a year. For the two consecutive school years between 2004 and 2006, about 82 percent of Woodbridge Township's middle school students met or exceeded proficiency in the language arts standardized test, and over 75 percent did so in mathematics. At New Brunswick City, on the other hand, only half the middle school students met or exceeded proficiency in language arts, while 47 percent did so in math. (Richard Kaplan, superintendent for the New Brunswick City School District, says, "I believe we'll be a model for other districts; we're going to soar within a number of years." Woodbridge Township did not return our calls for comment.)

"There's simply no consistent relationship between spending per pupil and student performance," says Eric Hanushek, a senior fellow at Stanford University who has extensively studied the correlation between school spending and student performance. The problem, says a spokesperson for the American Association of School Administrators, is that per-pupil figures don't tell you what the money's actually being spent on: "Some schools have buildings that require a lot of work for upkeep, and that adds to the overall [per-pupil] cost." But frankly, he says, "school systems could do a better job of sharing that fact with communities."

3 "LUNCH MONEY? THAT'S JUST THE TIP OF THE ICEBERG."

The days of eight-cent milk cartons may be as distant a memory as inkwells, but how much has America's free public school system really changed since we were kids? Plenty, it seems. For one thing, it's no longer, well, free. Sure, if you count your property-tax bill, public school never actually was. But today's schools are asking parents to kick in money for things they almost never had to pay for back in the day. Kids at Seattle's Garfield High, for example, fork over a $50 school activity fee to attend sporting events. ("If you do the math, they save a lot of money," says Peggy Jackson Williams, activities and athletic director at Garfield High. "They receive discounts on going to certain games.") And in Arlington, Mass., wannabe football or soccer players have to pony up as much as $290—not including uniform and equipment charges. (Arlington High did not return our calls for comment.)

While it may seem reasonable to ask students to contribute to the cost of their extracurricular activities, many parents are surprised to find themselves nickel-and-dimed for curricular items as well. Utah high schoolers, for instance, are assessed an annual textbook fee and additional fees for courses that require lab work (such as biology and chemistry). And then there's Lafayette Elementary in Washington, D.C., where local parents kicked in the salaries for the art and music teachers—a total of $150,000 in the 2006-07 school year, according to Linda Geen, copresident of the Lafayette Elementary Home and School Association. And it doesn't stop there. "We donate money to the librarian to help update material," Geen says. "We even help with the school's plumbing."

4 *"YOU SHOULD SEE HOW WE'RE SPENDING YOUR TAX DOLLARS."*

In a 2005 audit, the New York State Comptroller's Office identified $3.2 million in misspent funds at the William Floyd School District in Mastic Beach, N.Y. This included a $159,931 unauthorized salary increase for the superintendent and a $24,150 travel allowance for another administrator. And this wasn't the first time: The district had misspent an additional $1.5 million in the past. A spokesperson for the school district says the superintendent has since left the post, "though it was not a result of the audit controversy"; she declined to comment on whether the other employees involved are still with the district.

In response to the audit, the New York State Comptroller's Office sent a report to the school board with recommendations for how the board could better monitor its funds. The truth is that with little state oversight, school boards can often get away with some rather odd budgeting priorities. But it's a more complicated issue than it appears, says Jeremiah Floyd, once the associate executive director for the National

---

The truth is that with little state oversight, school boards can often get away with some rather odd budgeting priorities.

School Boards Association (NSBA). "It's a matter of opinion what constitutes a misuse of funds," Floyd says. "One person's misuse is another person's good discretion."

5 *"SURE, OUR TEACHERS ARE WELL-VERSED—JUST NOT IN THE SUBJECTS THEY TEACH ..."*

Your child's teacher may have studied Spanish for years and mastered the language. "But if the district needs a French teacher, guess what?" says a National Education Association spokesperson. That teacher will be put to work teaching French. Sounds crazy, but the misassignment of teachers happens far more often than you may think. "This is a dirty little secret that's been going on for a long, long time," says Richard M. Ingersoll, professor of education and sociology at the University of Pennsylvania. "It's widespread."

True, good teachers can and do learn on the job and even become wizards in a new area of specialization over time. Nevertheless, "most parents would assume their kid's taking an 11th grade trig class that's being taught by someone who studied math," Ingersoll says. "It's difficult [for teachers] to teach their students subjects they don't know much about themselves." And if test scores are any indication, today's students aren't exactly benefiting from the practice: According to "The Nation's Report Card," sponsored by the U.S. Department of Education, in 2007 roughly 61 percent of fourth-graders and 69 percent of eighth-graders in public schools scored below proficiency in math, while roughly 68 percent of fourth-graders and 71 percent of eighth-graders had substandard scores on reading-proficiency tests.

6 *"...AND SOME AREN'T EVEN LICENSED."*

Lawyers have to pass the bar exam. Doctors must score well on the medical boards. Even beauticians have to prove their body of knowledge before getting a license to cut hair. But not all teachers have to demonstrate their mastery before getting their first teaching assignment. How is it that unlicensed teachers are allowed into the classroom? Normally, with limited or emergency licenses granted when school districts run into labor shortages. "It's scandalous when you think about it, because there's a lot of discussion that we need better-qualified teachers," says Susan Carmon, associate director of the National Education Association. "But instead, we've been going around hiring people who don't meet the standards."

Even Indiana, which is viewed as a national pacesetter in teaching-licensure standards, issues stopgap licensing, called emergency permits. Getting one of these requires only a bachelor's degree and takes into account whether prospective candidates have taken steps to contact whatever governing body is responsible for teacher certification in their field. Just how low is the bar? "The approval ratio is in the 90th percentile," says Ray Graves, the assistant director of teacher licensing at the Indiana Standards Board, who says the state issued nearly 2,000 such permits in 2007. Elizabeth Schurtz, the former director of teacher licensing at the Indiana Professional Standards Board, sees cause for concern: "There's the fear that some

teachers, without the proper training for the first two years, really don't have the necessary skills," she says.

7 *"OF COURSE YOUR KID ACED THE STATE ACHIEVEMENT TEST. WE GAVE HIM THE ANSWERS."*

When students at Staten Island's Susan E. Wagner High School scored well on standardized tests in 2006, parents were obviously pleased—until it appeared that some teachers had tampered with the grades. "It was alleged that various administrative staff, including the principal, directed the faculty to rescore several Regents Examinations," writes David Abraham, assistant commissioner of the Office of Standards, Assessment, and Reporting at the New York State Education Department. In addition, it was alleged that some scores were changed by faculty after the official scoring procedures had been completed. (Representatives of Susan E. Wagner High declined to comment.)

The motive? High test scores don't just mean that schools are doing their jobs well; they often translate into cold, hard cash. Starting with the 2006–07 school year, for instance, New York City has been handing out "rewards," amounting to roughly $30 per student, that can be spent at the school's discretion. Those schools that score As on their Progress Report—intended to help parents, teachers, and principals understand how well they're doing—are eligible for such rewards, according to the New York City Department of Education. Says its website: "Schools that get low grades will also face consequences, such as leadership changes or closure." (Susan E. Wagner

High School earned a B on its 2006–07 Progress Report.)

The problem is widespread, according to David Berliner, a Regents professor in the College of Education at Arizona State University. "What they're doing is tempting people, because higher stakes are involved," he says. "It's the principle behind Enron; it's why athletes take steroids—when the stakes get high, people cut moral corners."

8 "GRADE INFLATION MEANS YOUR KID LEARNS LESS."

Say your child consistently earns As in math, but he got only average scores on his eighth-grade standardized math test. Is your kid just a "bad" standardized-test taker? Maybe. "But more likely, he's just an average math student," says William L. Bainbridge, president of SchoolMatch in Columbus, Ohio. Welcome to the world of grade inflation, where students can get good marks even when they haven't fully mastered a subject. "It's mind-boggling to see how often this happens," says Bainbridge, whose company audits school systems across the country. While looking at some 650 districts nationwide, Bainbridge discovered that roughly 80 percent of them were guilty of grade inflation. The proof: Many schools with students who boasted grade-point averages nearing the perfect 4.0 ranked closer to average on standardized test scores.

The College Board, which administers the SAT, agrees. Since 1997 the percentage of students who report a grade average in the A range (A+, A, A-) has grown from 37 percent to 43 percent, according to a College Board spokesperson. Meanwhile, SAT scores have fallen an average five points on the verbal portion of the test and two points on the math test. The reason for the discrepancy? Grade inflation, says the College Board.

9 "GOT A PROBLEM WITH ONE OF OUR TENURED TEACHERS? TOO BAD."

Bob Nunez was concerned that his son's second-grade teacher "was verbally abusive and demeaning to the kids," he says. "If a child's work wasn't to her liking," claims the Eagle, Idaho, resident, "she'd pull them out of their seat to the front of the room and yell at them in front of the entire class." Nunez first went to the elementary school's guidance counselor, then to the principal. But even after five other parents came forward with similar complaints, school administrators did nothing about the problem teacher, Nunez says. Finally, he and the other parents talked to the district administration. After an investigation, the situation was resolved when the teacher, at her own request, was transferred to another school in the district. Says a district spokesperson, "We acknowledged there may have been concerns, but there was no evidence of wrongdoing."

"It's very hard to get rid of a tenured teacher," says the NSBA's Floyd, "even if they're incompetent." In most states, tenure is earned after a one- to two-year probationary period. Thereafter, districts have to follow a strict procedure before they can fire a teacher. And if that teacher puts up a fight, says Thomas Mooney, a Hartford, Conn., attorney and school-law expert, the district can end up in a costly two- to three-year legal battle. Adding to the difficulty, says

Mooney, is the fact that many parents prefer to remain anonymous when it comes to teacher complaints. If you've got a concern, go to the teacher first; if you feel the issue won't be readily resolved, it's also a good idea to notify (in writing) the principal, the district superintendent, and the school board. In other words, start leaving a long paper trail.

10 *"WE'LL LET ANYONE INTO YOUR KID'S RECORDS."*

The federal Family Educational Rights and Privacy Act (FERPA) legislated that no one but school administrators has the right to peer into your child's private school records—which include everything from grades and standardized-test scores to psychological evaluations—without your (or your child's) permission. But as with any major federal law, FERPA allows for several exemptions, such as cases in which there's an issued court order, or when state or local educational authorities are auditing or evaluating federal- or state-supported educational programs.

Also allowed: Financial-aid sources and offices, as well as organizations conducting educational studies, other secondary schools, colleges, teachers, accrediting organizations—and the list goes on—can likewise examine your child's file without disclosure or your prior consent.

Now, suppose there's an error in that file. Somebody slipped in a bad evaluation that was intended to go into another file, for instance. Or the school psychologist has written an evaluation you don't want the whole world to see. Good luck trying to change or remove it. In fact, unlike the groups above, you may have difficulty accessing your child's entire file, says a spokesperson for the U.S. Department of Education's Family Policy Compliance Office, which investigates complaints of FERPA violations. And even if you do get your hands on it, the spokesperson says, "the process can be difficult." Under FERPA, parents have the right to a hearing if they want to amend something in the file. But if after the hearing the school decides against making the change, there's nothing else the parents can do.

THINGS TO DO

● **Don't be swayed by teacher-to-student** ratios and average spending per student when looking at potential schools. Both stats have little or no correlation with students' performance.

● **Sites like Education.com and SchoolMatters.com** let parents type in a ZIP code, city, district, or school and pull up all sorts of information, including demographics and test results.

● **Students now have the option** to transfer from low-performing schools to ones with better test scores, thanks to the No Child Left Behind Act.

● **Grade inflation may be covering up** areas your child needs help in. To get a gauge on how much she's actually learning, pay attention to her standardized test scores. If they're out of sync with her letter grades, there may be real room for improvement.

10 Things Your
Tutoring Service
Won't Tell You

1 *"WE DON'T HAVE TO STICK TO ANY EDUCATIONAL STANDARDS."*

News of failing schools and the increasing competitiveness of colleges have made education a big concern for parents. To the rescue, perhaps, comes the "supplemental education" business, an estimated $4 billion (and growing) industry that includes private tutors, retail tutoring centers, and test-preparation centers.

While schools must now meet federally mandated standards, these criteria don't apply to supplemental education companies. "You could end up with an excellent tutor who put up a flier at the grocery store, or a crummy tutor from a national organization," says David Hollingsworth, a private tutor in New York City who trained with test-prep powerhouse Kaplan.

To get the best help possible, start with a reliable referral—say, a favorite teacher at your child's school—then focus on credentials and experience. Ask learning centers where they find tutors and if they do background checks; if tutors are certified teachers, that's a good sign. Then get references: Ask past clients if their child's grades went up, if the tutor was reliable, and, most important, if the tutor and child had a good rapport. As

Hollingsworth says, "You need someone who's good with kids."

2 *"OUR RATES AREN'T ALWAYS PINNED TO QUALITY."*

Costs for tutoring can vary wildly, depending on whether your child gets private or group tutoring, and whether he receives it in-home or at a center. "In general, anywhere from $35 to $65 an hour is what you're going to be paying for good tutoring," says Gene Wade, CEO of Platform Learning, a New York City–based firm that develops tutoring programs for public schools. But if you're looking for specialized tutoring, including SAT test prep, or if you live in a big city, the costs can multiply. In Boston, rates can range from $85 to $250 an hour; in New York they can go as high as $500 an hour.

So how do you choose where to send your kid and how much to pay? Steven Shapiro, director of Pinnacle Learning Center, a Canton, Mass.–based tutoring company, suggests word-of-mouth recommendations. "[It's] the best way to find a service you'll be happy with," says Shapiro. "Talk to family, friends, a neighbor, or your child's teacher." As for pricing, tutoring isn't exactly a "you get what you pay for" market. "Some people might buy into that," Shapiro says, but in reality, "you're going to get some places that charge a whole lot and don't do a great job, and you're going to get places that are great for not a lot of money." When in doubt, go for the experienced teacher. And make sure that you understand the company's pricing methodology—beware of centers that require a minimum purchase up front, for example—and cancellation policies.

3 *"OUR 'GUARANTEES' ARE WORTHLESS."*

If you're going to sink potentially thousands of dollars into tutoring for your child, you want some assurance that it will pay off academically. Some companies seem happy to oblige. North American franchisor Sylvan Learning, for one, guarantees that students will improve at least one full grade-level equivalent in reading or basic math skills after 36 hours of instruction or you get an additional 12 hours free. But be careful. The fine print on Sylvan's website (*www.educate.com*), which also touts the guarantee, shows that not all centers have to participate.

Indeed, experts say that guarantees, and even vague promises, shouldn't carry too much weight. "If [a center] says their median SAT score increase is 150 points, what that means is, half the kids are below that and half are above," says Lisa Jacobson, CEO of Inspirica, a tutoring and test-prep firm in Boston and New York City. "But when parents see a number or a grade, that's what they expect."

A better way to measure success is to address specific goals, like improving

studying habits, says Thomas Redicks, former president of the National Tutoring Association (NTA) which offers voluntary certification for tutors (see *www.ntatutor.org*). Also, make sure the center keeps parents informed through regular meetings.

When in doubt, go for the experienced teacher.

4 *"WE AWARD SCHOLARSHIPS— BUT WE'RE NOT UP FRONT ABOUT IT."*

"Nobody says they offer financial aid or scholarships, but they do," says Inspirica's Jacobson. "If you can't afford it, you should ask anyway." Each year, she says, Inspirica tutors volunteer at a variety of schools in New York, but the company also gives a 10 percent discount for families that enroll in 45 hours of tutoring. Pinnacle also offers a 10 percent discount when 32 sessions are purchased.

Andrea Salvador, a Victoria, Minn., homemaker whose son Robert was tutored at a local Huntington Learning Center, received a discount when she purchased his tutoring hours up front. While she still found the cost to be high, the deal reduced the per-hour fee from $54 to about $50. Huntington also offers tuition loan programs through Sallie Mae.

Not surprisingly, private tutors often offer even more room for discounts and negotiation. Jacobson says that she has given discounts herself, based on clients' ability to pay, when she did private tutoring. The important thing for those seeking tutoring to do, she says, "is to always ask. People just don't advertise it." David Hollingsworth agrees but argues that negotiating a discount will go more smoothly when a parent "has a respect for the fact that the tutor is trying to make a living."

5 "WE MAY TEACH ENGLISH AND MATH, BUT WHAT WE REALLY SPECIALIZE IN IS SALES."

Take your child to any tutoring center and she'll be barraged with assessment tests to pinpoint strengths and weaknesses—usually carrying a bill upwards of $150. NTA's Redicks believes that such tests are "absolutely unnecessary" because parents can get that information from their children's school. Many parents, in fact, already receive results from similar state achievement tests in the mail. That's what mom Julie Zemanick, of Excelsior, Minn., discovered when she took her son to a local learning center. After paying $250, she says, "I found out from his school that they do that, and I thought, Gosh, if I'd known, I wouldn't have put him through that."

Learning centers say that those pricey assessments are crucial to helping them determine how many tutoring hours a student needs. But one former Sylvan franchise director says, "The estimate is always high. It's a computerized system that typically [recommends] 100-plus hours." A Sylvan spokesperson says that estimates are "based on each student's individual assessment," averaging at about 72 hours. Regardless, before you agree to have your kid tested, ask which school tests can substitute for some or all of the center's assessments.

6 "JUNIOR NEEDS HELP CRAMMING FOR THE SAT? GOOD LUCK."

Autumn and spring are the hot seasons for college-bound kids to take the SAT and ACT aptitude tests. But don't assume you can easily hire a tutor for help a few weeks or even a couple of months beforehand. Private tutors and test-prep centers book up long before test-taking crunch time. One northern New Jersey mom discovered that the hard way when her daughter wanted to switch tutoring companies while prepping for the SAT and SAT II. When the mother mentioned that she was considering hiring another tutor, the first company declined to continue working with the girl—a mere two months before the SAT II. The test-prep owner "put me in a terrible situation," the mother says, adding that she called several already-booked tutors before finding an available center—which, unfortunately, charged a per-session rate $70 higher than what she had paid before. To help avoid any such problems, she says, a friend of hers went as far as reserving a tutor for when her own eighth-grade son was scheduled to take the SAT—two years later.

"Tutors get booked up early," Inspirica's Jacobson says; nevertheless, reserving two years ahead of time "is overkill." Instead, she recommends booking a test tutor the way you do a summer camp—at least three months in advance.

7 "IT'S CHEAPER TO DO THIS ONLINE."

Tutoring services are no longer touted simply for kids who are seriously struggling in school but also for those who just need a nudge. A growing number of clients are like T. J. Frier, son of Tara Goodwin Frier, who owns a PR firm in Sharon, Mass. She hired Pinnacle Learning Center to help her teenage son raise his B-minus grade in Advanced Placement math. T. J.'s teachers "recommended that he drop back down to regular [math], but our son really wanted to stay in advanced," she says, "so we got him a tutor." After he started private sessions twice a week, Frier was pleased with his progress, saying that T. J. had developed a good rapport with his tutor and his grades were steady.

Even so, NTA's Thomas Redicks says that good students like T. J. can often benefit from peer tutoring at schools, or from free or low-cost online tutoring. "There are a few good services available for occasional help if you have a question," he says. One example is Tutor.com, whose "Live Homework Help" function lets kids connect daily with an online, prescreened, and trained tutor for help with everything from algebra to science. It's free at more than 1,800 libraries across the country.

8 "WE'RE NOT PREPARED TO HANDLE YOUR CHILD'S LEARNING DISABILITY."

Few tutoring centers are equipped to handle students with actual disabilities such as dyslexia or even mild developmental disorders, but parents may seek them out anyway, to diagnose or even "fix" problems the child is experiencing at school. While certain tutors may be adept at recognizing blocks in a child's learning process, it's not a tutor's place to diagnose a disability. If you suspect a problem exists, ask your pediatrician to refer you to a specialist.

If your child has already been diagnosed with a learning disability, look for a tutor who is a credentialed special-education teacher. "You have to ask the company if they actually have an academic tutor who's a learning specialist with degrees, and they usually don't," Jacobson says. Beyond that, says Lynda Covey, a private tutor in Redwood City, Calif., who specializes in disabilities, ask the tutor or center director how he approaches learning disabilities; Covey says that she likes to point out examples of famous people with learning disabilities, such as Albert Einstein, to her students. "If it's handled in a negative fashion, it can be damaging and hurt their self-esteem," she says. Finally, when you ask the center for references, be sure to request them from parents whose children have faced similar hurdles.

9 "WE PROMOTE SMALL-GROUP SESSIONS, BUT ONE-TO-ONE IS BEST."

Many supplemental education centers specialize in small-group tutoring, where two to four students work with one tutor. That's not necessarily a bad thing: A group setting can allow for independent study time, and it can be a lot cheaper. At Pinnacle Learning Center, for example, private tutoring is $65 a session, while a "semiprivate" session, with two students per tutor, is $50.

But at some chain operations, economic factors outweigh individual attention, and your kid may not get his fair share of help—or may just waste time listening to a tutor explain things she has already mastered. "There was pressure to always keep the student-teacher ratio at a certain number—3-to-1 or 2-to-1," says the former Sylvan center director. "We were instructed not to leave one teacher and one student together." Sylvan's vice president of education, Richard Bavaria, defends the company's approach. "Each [student] gets individual attention," he says. Plus, he adds, "a social aspect to learning can make it more compelling."

By and large, however, many experts contend that one-on-one tutoring is more effective than group work. "Research overwhelmingly states that one-to-one tutoring with a structured session is required for students to do better in school," Redicks says.

10 *"YOUR KID WON'T ALWAYS HAVE THE SAME TUTOR."*

Even if your child does go the one-on-one route, it doesn't always mean she'll get personalized care. That's too bad—a good rapport can make the help seem more like fun and less like punishment. In fact, many learning centers can't guarantee that your child will always have the same tutor. Andrea Salvador's son, Robert, received one-on-one tutoring at the learning center he attended, but over the course of seven months, "he probably had five or six different tutors," she says. Sylvan's Bavaria says that the center can't guarantee tutor continuity, and besides, with multiple tutors, kids are exposed to different teaching styles.

To increase your child's chances of success, let the center director know you want a specific tutor and ask about how best to accommodate such scheduling. Otherwise, make sure that all the tutors who work with your child are familiar with his curriculum, and ask centers if they'll meet with your child's teacher to discuss problems and progress. "Schools are always trying new programs," says Lisa Mlinar, former vice president at Huntington Learning Center, "and tutors need to be aware of what those programs are."

THINGS TO DO

- **Often the best place** to find a tutor is through a reliable connection, such as a teacher or another parent.

- **When a learning center** asks students to take an assessment test to enroll, check to see whether any school tests your child has already taken will do. It could save you a hefty assessment fee.

- **Paying for a set number** of tutoring hours up front can lower your bill, but be careful: If the service isn't working, you may not be eligible for a refund.

- **Can't find a tutor** you like in your area? Websites like Etutelage.com and Tutor.com offer sessions online for everything from help with homework to test preparation.

10 Things Your
Private School
Won't Tell You

1 *"WE'RE NOT AS EXCLUSIVE AS YOU THINK."*
As the college admissions game gets more competitive every year, what's a parent to do to help their child get into the school of his choice? You could try cutting back on your kid's TV time or trips to the mall—or you could make a more drastic move, like transferring him from a public school to a private school. If you opt for the latter, you'll be a part of an increasing trend—over 561,000 students were enrolled in K–12 schools affiliated with the National Association of Independent Schools in 2006, up from about 485,000 in 2001.

But just because private schools are becoming more popular, it doesn't mean they've become more selective. While most screen out applicants who can't hack the work, for example, the current economy has led a handful of the more desperate institutions to accept just about any student who can fork over the tuition. The result: Your fast-track child may get slowed down by a bunch of academic laggards.

Or you may run into a situation like that of a Colorado couple who were thrilled when a boarding school for mainstream students in Pennsylvania accepted their daughter despite her history of emotional instability. Two weeks into the school year, the school had second thoughts. "She was asked to leave, and the school wouldn't refund the $30,000 tuition," says Diane Arnold, a Lafayette, Colo., education consultant who helped the parents place their daughter. "It was a very nasty situation."

2 *"SO WE HAVE MONEY PROBLEMS. WHAT START-UP DOESN'T?"*
If you're thinking of sending your child to a private school that's been open only a couple of years, be careful. "They're often fairly dicey," says Gordon Bingham, former executive director of the North Carolina Association of Independent Schools. "Parents should check out the head of school and see if they have experience and standing in the community."

Even the best new schools lack cushy endowments to help them survive the lean times. After being open just three years, Solon Academy in Houston enjoyed a loyal base of parents and a growing enrollment, but was forced to close for financial reasons. The surprised parents managed to save the school in 2003 by forming their own board and raising money to keep the institution from going under until the next round of tuition checks came in. Even still, the school has since shut its doors for good.

Before enrolling your child in a new school, do your homework: Check to see how its expenses compare with its revenue; see if the board is composed of competent business leaders; and find out if it's supported by donations, since few schools can survive on tuition alone.

3 "DON'T EXPECT MUCH GUIDANCE FROM OUR GUIDANCE COUNSELORS."

So your kid got into a tony private school—that means she's a shoo-in for Harvard or Stanford, right? Not necessarily. A lot can depend on the quality of guidance students get from the school's college counseling staff. "I've seen some pretty inexperienced counselors who just didn't know what they were doing," says Christopher Covert, a Carefree, Ariz., educational consultant. Consider the guidance counselor at a top private school in Washington State who was squeezing in college counseling between teaching history classes and coaching athletics. The distractions nearly cost one student acceptance at his favorite school—the counselor wasn't familiar with the student and discouraged him from applying to competitive colleges. Fortunately, the student ignored the advice and was accepted at the school of his choice, Carnegie Mellon. "When it came time for college applications, the school dropped the ball," says the student's father.

Sure, there are plenty of good school counselors out there too. But don't assume that exceptional college counseling at private schools comes with the price of tuition. In choosing a private school, ask about the counselors' credentials. They should have at least five years' experience and spend time visiting college campuses—"at least 25 schools a year," Covert says. And beware of counselors who discourage students from applying to "reach" colleges, those that may be out of the student's range. "Some high schools don't want a student to reach simply because they want to advertise that 100 percent of their students got into their first-choice college," says one education consultant based in Louisiana.

4 "SURE, WE'VE HAD STUDENTS GET INTO YALE—JUST NOT LATELY."

Indeed, many private schools make college placement a pillar of their marketing campaign. Their brochures feature a long list of the prestigious schools at which their grads have been accepted. But don't be dazzled by a laundry list of top-tier institutions. To get a more realistic picture, ask for names of colleges where graduates have actually enrolled within the past three years.

If the main reason you're sending your kid to private school is to better his chances of getting into an elite university, you should know that while many selective colleges do admit private school students at higher rates than their public school counterparts, the gap isn't all that wide. At Duke University, for instance, 25 percent of private school applicants are accepted, versus 23 percent of public school applicants. And the reason for higher admissions of private school students isn't always based on their academic chops. Christoph Guttentag, dean of undergraduate admissions at Duke, says that private school students are likely to be accepted at a slightly higher rate not because they went to better schools academically speaking, but because, on average, they have more "environmental advantages" than public school students. "It's more of an economic factor than an education factor," Guttentag says.

5 *"OUR BULLIES ARE AS BAD AS AT ANY PUBLIC SCHOOL."*

Bullying and verbal teasing have plagued schools since the world's first day of class. But at some boarding schools in particular, rigid social hierarchies can develop that are devastating for those at the bottom of the pecking order. "There are more kids from broken homes with emotional vulnerability attending boarding schools these days, and that vulnerability can be a red flag for other students to start harassing them," says Marcia Brown Rubinstien, a West Hartford, Conn., educational consultant who helps families with boarding school and college placements.

To get the real scoop on a given school's social personality, don't rely on the official student guides offered up at your campus visit—chat with as many students as possible.

One 15-year-old had to transfer out of a pricey New England boarding school after he became the object of endless cruel jokes in the dorm showers—his classmates would pelt him with soap and steal his clothes on a nightly basis. "Even the resident assistant was laughing at him," says Rubinstien, who helped his parents find a new school after the administration ignored requests to keep an eye on the troubled student.

If your child is acutely sensitive to social slights or typically winds up in the role of outcast, he might do better at a smaller boarding school with a nurturing environment—ideally, one that folds lessons on peer respect into the curriculum. To get the real scoop on a given school's social personality, don't rely on the official student guides offered up at your campus visit—chat with as many students as possible.

6 *"YOU MIGHT WANT TO DOUBLE-CHECK OUR CREDENTIALS."*

The International Learning Academy, a private high school based in Naples, Fla., once boasted that it was "fully accredited" by the National Private Schools Accreditation Alliance and the Board of Private Education. Sounds impressive, right? Well, as it turned out, the latter accreditor's then commissioner and current president, Valaree Maxwell, also owned the school. Maxwell says she bought the accrediting association only as a "favor" to its previous owner and that her school was already accredited at the time of purchase. "It's a totally separate business entity," Maxwell says of the association.

In some states, private schools aren't government regulated, but private accrediting associations ensure that schools meet basic standards and live up to their marketing promises. But how can you identify a reputable accreditor? The nation's six major regional accrediting associations are a safe bet: Most schools affiliated with five of these associations are listed at *www.accreditedschools.org*, while those in New England are listed at *www.neasc.org*. Also, many nonreligious schools are accredited by associations affiliated with the National Association of Independent Schools.

7 *"BEWARE OF OUR BOARD. THEY CAN BE PRETTY PUSHY."*

One of the most common reasons schools lose their accreditation is board-of-director shenanigans, such as backdoor deals in which major donors receive favors—a construction contract, for example, or special treatment for a student. Peter Sturtevant, formerly the head of a private school in Maryland who is now a Washington, D.C., education consultant, cautions against schools whose board has too much power over day-to-day affairs. "If the board gets into micromanaging whom to admit and whom to expel, what teachers to hire and to fire, you've got a problem," Sturtevant says. "You need educators at the center of the decision-making, not the board." How to tell whether a board of directors yields too much power? There are a couple of warning signs, says Sturtevant: high turnover for the head of school position; schools that operate like a business, putting too much emphasis on

appearances and fund-raising rather than education; and boards made up mostly of parents, who tend to be too subjective.

But the interference can go both ways: Boards can get pushed as much as they push. In the fall of 2002, Citigroup CEO Sandy Weill admitted that he had talked to a board director at Manhattan's 92nd Street Y about accepting analyst Jack Grubman's kids into its private preschool right around the time that his company was making a million-dollar donation to the institution. The school later said donations do not influence its admissions; still, "sometimes the wealthiest have more influence over the school than they should," says Mark Elgart, CEO of the Council on Accreditation and School Improvement for the Southern Association of Colleges and Schools.

8 *"SOMETIMES OUR 'TOUGH LOVE' METHODS ARE A LITTLE TOO TOUGH."*

When Karen Burnett, a Shepherdsville, Ky., homemaker, discovered that her son Nathan was taking drugs, she paid nearly $20,000 to send him to the Academy at the Dundee Ranch, a private boarding school in Costa Rica affiliated with WWASPS, the Utah-based World Wide Association of Specialty Programs and Schools. "I thought it was a normal school with a behavior-modification program," Burnett says. "What I got instead was a program that used brutality and neglect to break the kids down." According to Burnett, the school employed food deprivation, solitary confinement, and physical restraints to punish students. When she pulled her son out four months into the year, Nathan had dropped almost 25 pounds from his 148-pound frame.

Dundee closed its doors following a 2003 investigation of human-rights violations conducted by PANI, Costa Rica's child welfare agency. But WWASPS continues to service boarding schools, through its Cross Creek programs in Utah. WWASPS's president, Ken Kay, says that parents are made aware of school methods before they enroll their children. "We have 98 percent customer satisfaction," he adds. "But some children lie and manipulate the truth, and their parents buy into this." Loi Eberle, an educational consultant in Bonners Ferry, Idaho, says, "There are some programs that use physical discipline—including a number that have lawsuits filed against them. It's important for parents to find out in advance how a school deals with misbehavior."

9 "OUR EXTRACURRICULARS AREN'T EXACTLY EXTRAORDINARY."

All too often parents assume that when a school hosts a large number of clubs and teams, their kid is almost guaranteed a leadership spot that will beef up her college application. But before you get mesmerized by a school's frills, take a closer look. Boston education consultant Michael Spence contends, for example, that some boarding schools offering a postgraduate year for students use it primarily to pump up their athletic programs. The schools will admit top athletes looking for a little seasoning before heading off to college—and those recruits "could ace your kid out of his spot on a team," says Spence. In one of the more outrageous examples, in 2002 Florida's Heritage Christian Academy was reportedly recruiting and paying the tuition for a number of foreign students in an effort to improve its soccer team, a violation of Florida High School Athletic Association rules. A spokesperson for the school acknowledged the situation, saying they planned to rewrite the handbook "to make sure events like that don't reoccur."

But even if a school offers a rich and accessible assortment of activities for its students, don't assume that participation will necessarily enhance your kid's chances of getting into a top college. "We call that 'big fish, small pond' syndrome," says Jim Bock, dean of admissions and financial aid at Swarthmore College. "There may be some truth that you can do more at private schools, [but] it is put in context."

10 "THAT FIVE-FIGURE TUITION CHECK IS JUST THE TIP OF THE ICEBERG."

It's no news that private schools are expensive. But the actual costs are sometimes much higher than you'd budget for. Many schools saddle parents with burdensome expenses—$500 for books, say, or $2,500 for a laptop—then commence with the donation squeeze. "At many schools there may be an inherent or unwritten understanding that parents are to donate to the school," says Houston educational consultant Lindy Kahn. "Somewhere along the year you'll be asked as part of the fund-raising effort." To avoid nasty surprises, request an itemized list of fees and expenses before you enroll your child in a private school.

Another financial jab: rising tuition rates. The median annual tuition for a sixth-grade private school student reached $15,716 in 2007, compared with $12,318 in 2001, according to the National Association of Independent Schools. Parents hit with an increase they can't afford should explain their situation to the school. "When the school knows your student and wants to keep him, they'll look harder at giving you aid," says Cincinnati educational consultant Nancy Coulbourn Ike.

THINGS TO DO

• **Talking to current and former students** is the best way to get an accurate read on an institution. Schools will probably provide you with some names if you ask, but for an unbiased opinion, try crashing a campus function.

• **Some schools still allow corporal punishment;** be sure to find out about the discipline policy ahead of time.

• **Looking at a newly minted private school?** A flush of outside donations is a good indication it will stay afloat, whereas those that rely solely on tuition have a tendency to fold within a few years.

• **Worried about cost?** Request a list of fees and expenses before your child enrolls to get a better idea of the total tab.

10 Things the
College-Prep Industry
Won't Tell You

1 *"YOUR HIGH SCHOOL COUNSELOR CAN DO THIS JOB FOR FREE."*

Every year hopeful parents across the country employ expensive private college counselors in hopes of getting their kid into the right school. For anywhere from $65 to more than $365 an hour—with two years' worth of help costing as much as $6,500—these consultants would have you believe that their advice is your kid's ticket to her best future. In reality, the counselor at your teenager's high school would probably give you the same advice on the college admissions process—free of charge.

Steve Syverson, dean of admissions and financial aid at Lawrence University in Appleton, Wis., says that hiring private counselors is "something we laugh about in the profession." Syverson knows of a counselor at a private high school in New England who had a student who wanted to go to Dartmouth but didn't do so well on the SATs. The counselor told him to retake the test; he didn't, applied early to Dartmouth, and was turned down. The student's parents then shelled out $3,000 to a private counselor who told the kid—you guessed it—that he needed to retake the SATs. The student did and finally got into Dartmouth.

"There's a batch of parents who think if they pay for advice, it's better advice," Syverson says. And since it's the school counselor and not the independent hire who writes recommendations for college-bound students, time spent with an outside counselor might be better used developing a relationship with the high school counselor to ensure a solid recommendation.

2 *"YES, WE HAVE NO CREDENTIALS."*

If you're expecting the college counselor you hired to have some sort of degree or official credential for the job, think again. In fact, that person may be no more qualified than you are to help your kid get into college. While there are two major national associations for independent college counselors—the Independent Educational Consultants Association (IECA) and the National Association for College Admission Counseling (NACAC)—neither offers formal accreditation, though both require members to demonstrate a certain level of experience.

The only group out there that actually offers certification for counselors is the American Institute of Certified

Educational Planners—which, according to its guidelines, requires a master's degree or higher in a relevant education-related field, five references, and a written exam. But the organization, which has 250 members, concedes that these requirements are, well, flexible. "We're not turning away very many people," says Steven Antonoff, chair of the Commission on Credentialing, noting that a master's degree in an education-related field is not strictly necessary. It's really the counselor's experience that counts, he says, and the exam more than adequately tests for that.

"There are a ton of people calling themselves educational consultants. Most of them don't have educational training," says IECA's Mark Sklarow. "I hear almost every day from someone who says, 'I got my daughter into Swarthmore, so now I want to help others do this.'"

3 "BY THE TIME YOU HIRE US, IT'S TOO LATE."

College admissions is a numbers-driven process: Most schools—especially big, public institutions—weigh most heavily an applicant's GPA during sophomore and junior year and his SAT scores. What this means for your child is that signing up with a college counselor during junior year can have little effect. But that's when most kids seek out help—and counselors, of course, aren't about to dissuade them. Marcy Hamilton, who has been a private college counselor in Greenbrae, Calif., says that most of her colleagues sign up the bulk of their clients as juniors, just after they get their PSAT scores at Christmastime. "By then it's really late," she says.

Ideally, kids should work with a consultant—if they are planning to do so at all—beginning in eighth or ninth grade. Samuel McNair, director of admissions, products, and enrollment at the College Board, agrees that the help many students get is too little, too late. "I really don't think a counselor can take a kid in the fall of his 12th grade and make him a contender," says McNair. "They might be able to package what's already true, but they can't change the facts."

4 "YOUR ESSAY WILL BE SO GOOD, THEY'LL KNOW YOU DIDN'T WRITE IT."

Perhaps the fastest-growing part of the college-prep business is essay help. You'll find numerous websites offering to assist students in focusing and proofreading their essays. And some offer much, much more. Consider EssayEdge.com, which boasts, "Our professional Harvard-educated editors can rework even the roughest draft into an eloquent expression of your unique talents and insights." The company claims to return a student's "dramatically improved essay" within 24 to 48 hours. ("EssayEdge editors do not write essays. Our goal is to help students polish the essays they have already written so that they can effectively communicate their strengths and unique qualities to the admission committee," says an EssayEdge.com spokesperson.)

Don't think colleges won't notice. Dan Saracino, assistant provost of admissions at Notre Dame, can spot a professionally edited essay a mile away. "The essays that are not done in the authentic voice of the student are readily apparent," he says. He recounts an incident where the word "solipsism" was used in the essay of a student who had a verbal SAT score of 500. Saracino concluded that the student either had not written his own essay or had done very little of it.

5 "VISIT COLLEGES? WE CAN'T BE BOTHERED."

One of the most important jobs of a college counselor is to visit colleges. How else will he develop the expertise to really know which school is right for your child? Unfortunately, it seems that such visits are few and far between. Mark Sklarow remembers with dismay the time a parent called to complain about how he'd paid an independent counselor $2,000—and how, in their second meeting, all the counselor did was rip out some pages of a Peterson's college guide and circle a few names. Paul Taylor, regional director at the National Student Clearinghouse, a nonprofit source for enrollment verification, gets the sense that such situations are the norm rather than the exception. Taylor once polled a number of his counterparts and found that independent educational consultants

weren't exactly banging down admissions directors' doors.

The upshot is, too many kids are ending up at schools that are not well suited to their needs. Sklarow has heard the most complaints from students who didn't realize how isolated their chosen college was. "That's because counselors haven't visited campuses," says Sklarow, who says he gets a couple of calls a week from unhappy parents who complain that their counselor must really have known very little or nothing about their child's school.

6 "WE CAN'T GUARANTEE A BETTER SAT SCORE."

SAT preparation has become a given in the college-admissions process and a cash cow for companies such as Stanley Kaplan and the Princeton Review. And while classes, which generally cost as much as $1,099, may help your child get ready for the test by teaching her certain tricks or time-saving strategies, there are plenty of professionals who believe that a motivated, hardworking kid will do just as well without. "A disciplined student can take one of those books or interactive software programs and do well on their own," says Marcia Hunt, director of college counseling at Pine Crest School in Fort Lauderdale, Fla., and former NACAC president.

What's more, kids who sign up for a prep class because they want to retake the test and improve their score are usually disappointed. Martha Moore, retired associate director of admissions at the University of Illinois Urbana-Champaign, saw this over and over again in her 20-

> **One of the most important jobs of a college counselor is to visit colleges. How else will he develop the expertise to really know which school is right for your child?**

plus years of admissions work. "Students who have multiple test scores, most times, do not deviate radically," she says.

Don't think that shelling out even more money for a private tutor is the answer either. Such tutors charge up to $100 or more per hour; the Princeton Review's private classes start at more than $2,800, almost twice as much as its group sessions. "There's absolutely no evidence whatsoever that [private tutors] work," says Bob Schaeffer, public-education director of FairTest, a nonprofit test-monitoring organization in Cambridge, Mass. "Their claims should be viewed the same way as any self-serving advertisement." Counters the Princeton Review's Joel Rubin, "I believe that one-on-one tutoring serves students who need flexibility in scheduling and students who feel they need extra attention or are intimidated in a group."

7 "WE'RE THE ONLY ONES GETTING MONEY OUT OF OUR SCHOLARSHIP SERVICE."

Scholarship scams are nothing new—for years parents have been taken for a ride by companies making false promises of guaranteed tuition funds or scholarship matches in exchange for a "processing" or "application" fee. But there's an even bigger scheme afoot. The Federal Trade Commission is hot on the trail of several companies offering so-called scholarship seminars or one-on-one home visits from a scholarship consultant, all at no cost.

Here's how it really goes: Unsuspecting parents are lured in by the typical promise of information on how to get more scholarship money.

But once they're in the door—or open their door to a consultant—they get the hard sell on additional "financial advice," such as how to shave thousands off their family's expected tuition contribution or how to get more financial aid, and can end up forking over as much as $2,000 for these services. "They justify the higher price by saying they do more than find scholarships," says Gregory Ashe, senior staff attorney at the FTC's Bureau of Consumer Protection. According to Mark Kantrowitz, publisher of FinAid.org, an online guide to financial aid, there are several dozen such seminar companies out there today, up from just one or two about 10 years ago. What's worse, the information you actually get is often of little value. One typical piece of poor advice: Parents should also enroll in college so they can claim a tax credit for more than one person being in school.

8 "ONCE YOU'RE IN THE DOOR, WE WON'T LET YOU GO."

It's not enough that companies are making a killing off SAT prep courses that may or may not help students increase their scores. In the past few years, some test-prep companies have also started foisting admissions counseling on students as soon as they're in the door.

"There are SAT tutors who, once they lure kids in, say they have to stay for help with college admissions," says Marcia Hunt. She says that she receives about 10 calls a year from parents who have gotten such a pitch. Rod Skinner, college counselor at Milton Academy in Milton, Mass., says that he, too, has seen this tactic employed by test-prep companies: "The kid comes in for what is ostensibly SAT prep work, and the company begins to hard-sell admissions counseling," Skinner says.

One of Hunt's former students even told her that he had to lie to his SAT-prep tutor about applying to colleges other than state schools because the tutor would not stop badgering him about helping with the applications.

9 "WE'RE A BUILT-IN HANDICAP."

Any admissions officer will tell you diversity is a priority and that spotting disadvantaged applicants is an important part of their job. So what's the first impression made by a student who has had help from a private admissions counselor? It's certainly not one of disadvantage. Christoph Guttentag, dean of undergraduate admissions at Duke University, admits that the mere whiff of help from an upscale private consultant could be a detriment to your child's chances. Guttentag explains that, as a rule, independent counselors are a privilege of the already advantaged student and that selective colleges struggle against this built-in bias in the admissions process. "We are very aware of this, and we try to take it into account when we're looking at applications," Guttentag says.

Indeed, many schools look with disdain at a student who has tried to package his or her way into college. David Burke, director of college counseling at Pembroke Hill School in Kansas City, Mo., knows this firsthand. At his old job as an admissions officer at Dartmouth, he saw "these fantastically packaged applications with names of Such-and-Such Associates on the cover and with the applicant's name in the window." Recalls Burke, "That gave you a bad feeling right from the outset. Here you are, making a case that you're ready for the nation's finest schools, and you can't even do your own application."

10 "DON'T BELIEVE OUR PROMISES."

As a parent, you may be comforted by a college counselor's promise that he or she can get your kid into Yale. In fact, it's the easiest way to spot a phony. "Nobody can promise admission," says Guttentag. But Leslie Goldberg, a private educational consultant in Hingham, Mass., has seen it happen. "I've seen literature from such consultants," she explains. "It says something about how guidance counselors don't know the students well and only a consultant can guarantee a child admission. It might cite Ivies that their students got into and say that if you work with them they can guarantee connections with these schools." Not only is it not true, she says, it's also "very unethical."

Dan Saracino of Notre Dame has noticed the same problem—as a parent. A father of three, Saracino recalls a letter he received when his youngest was a freshman in high school. "It made false claims, real false claims," says Saracino. "They said, 'We can definitely help your son in preparation for tests and raise his score dramatically, and also help him gain admission to colleges.'" Saracino called the company—only to find that it consisted of just two people whose own kids had gotten into good schools and who then decided, somehow, that they were qualified to become admissions experts. "I immediately saw this as a sham," says Saracino, "but I was concerned for the unsophisticated families who might think, 'Well, I've got to do this.'"

THINGS TO DO

● **High school counselors should be** your first choice for college advice—if they're not able to provide sufficient help, then turn to the private sector.

● **To get the most out of** your college-prep course or private counselor, sign up early—like freshman year of high school.

● **Make sure your private counselor** isn't too hands-on when it comes to the essay portion of the application; essays that appear overly polished or professionally edited are a negative when it comes to college admissions. A good tutor will help applicants brainstorm and effectively organize their essay—not rework it into bad PR.

● **One-on-one tutoring is really only** necessary in certain situations, like when flexible scheduling is needed. In most cases, group tutoring will suffice.

● **Steer clear of any private counselors** who make guarantees or promise admission to certain schools; more often than not, you'll end up disappointed.

10 Things Your
College Financial Aid Office
Won't Tell You

1 *"YOU WAITED UNTIL APRIL? SORRY, WE GAVE YOUR MONEY AWAY."*

At first glance, the amount of financial aid available to students seems like a goldmine. According to education testing and information organization The College Board, students received more than $140 billion in aid during the 2007–08 academic year for undergraduate and graduate study; more than $66 billion came from the federal government alone. Problem is, you'll need a treasure map to find your share. The bewildering aid-application process stumps thousands of families each year, leaving many to pay more tuition than they have to.

Lots of students miss out on aid because of the confusing deadlines for the Free Application for Federal Student Aid—FAFSA—which every applicant must complete to be considered for government grants and subsidized loans. The forms, which are available from colleges and at *www.fafsa.ed.gov,* are reviewed first by the government and then by your student's prospective school. While the deadline on the form is June 30, some schools' individual financial aid deadlines—listed in the colleges' materials but not on the FAFSA forms—are as early as February.

To play it safe, apply for aid the minute admissions applications are in the mail. "Families need to submit their financial aid info as soon as they can after Jan. 1, preceding the student's freshman year," says Barry Simmons, aid director at Virginia Tech. While the forms typically ask for the previous year's tax information—a common reason parents postpone applying until April—it's completely legitimate to estimate tax figures based on last year's return and update them later.

2 *"YOUR ERROR, YOUR PROBLEM."*

If you fail to fill in some key parts of your FAFSA, the central processor will reject your form, sending it back to you and not to the prospective schools, resulting in a potentially costly delay. One error that parents repeatedly make: putting their income and tax information in the student section, or vice versa, which can't be fixed by the machine scanning the form. As a safeguard, Ohio State's senior adviser for economic access, Tally Hart, recommends using the online form at *fafsa.ed.gov;* it will alert you if you leave questions blank and can even recognize some obvious errors—such as household income of $50,000 combined with a $5 million mortgage.

Of course, there are many financial circumstances that can't be fully explained on a FAFSA form—say, if a family member has recently been laid off. In that case, officers recommend writing a letter to a school's financial aid office explaining your family's situation and mailing it off at the same time as your FAFSA paperwork. Just make sure the letter goes directly to the college where your kid is applying. Too many people "send a letter with the FAFSA [to the government office], and it's just destroyed," says Mark Lindenmeyer, financial aid director at Loyola College in Maryland.

3 *"OUR LOW TUITION RATE MEANS LESS FINANCIAL AID."*

Many parents who haven't saved enough for college tell their gifted high school seniors not to consider pricey private schools. Ironically, those colleges may actually be the more affordable alternative. "The more expensive and prestigious the school," says Bedford, Mass., financial planner Tom Brooks, "the more likely it is well-endowed and can meet 100 percent of need," thanks to alumni donation campaigns. "You might be sending your kid to a state school that [for you] costs more than a Harvard or an MIT or a Stanford," Brooks says.

To estimate how likely it is that your preferred schools will give you substantial aid, check a few statistics with the colleges themselves or by using the annual "America's Best Colleges" survey in *U.S. News & World Report,* available at *www.usnews.com* for about $15. Look for two figures in particular: the percentage of undergraduates receiving grants meeting financial need at the college, and its average discount, which is the percentage of a student's total costs including tuition, room and board, and books covered by grants. If they're both 50 percent or better, you can feel assured that your needs will be fairly met.

4 *"YOU'LL PAY DEARLY FOR EARLY DECISION."*

Early-decision admission is a big temptation at elite colleges: Students can apply months before other applicants as long as they promise to attend if admitted. In most cases, the college offers these applicants a better chance of acceptance. But when it comes to getting financial aid, early decision can backfire. Why? Your commitment to attend if accepted means you have less leverage. "If you went to an auto dealership and threw yourself across the hood of a car and told them you would do anything to have that car, you're not in a very good negotiating position," says Linda P. Taylor, a certified college-planning specialist in Agoura Hills, Calif.

If scoring financial aid is your top priority, you're better off skipping early decision and applying with the general applicant pool. That's especially the case if your kid's SAT scores and GPA are above the college median, and she excels in extracurricular activities. If such a student applies in the spring and gets admitted, she'll have a better shot at negotiating a strong financial aid package than if she'd gone the early-decision route.

5 "WE'RE NOT BUYING YOUR PAUPER ACT."

Every year parents are tempted to cheat the financial aid system—trying to look poorer on paper, for example. There are, however, some perfectly acceptable ways to adjust your assets to maximize your aid potential. Step one is to trim any assets held in the child's name—in particular, custodial accounts (UGMAs or UTMAs), up to 20 percent of which the college financial aid system will say should go toward next year's tuition. For assets in the parents' names, the rate is a much lower 5.64 percent. "Technically, parents can't touch UGMAs except for the benefit of the child, above and beyond food and clothing," says Tom Brooks. But "you can use the UGMA to pay for things like summer camp, tutoring, school trips, or a car [for the kid], thus diminishing the account."

If, on the other hand, you're looking to sock away some free-floating cash in your name, you could give up to $12,000 each—any more will trigger the gift tax—

There are . . . some perfectly acceptable ways to adjust your assets to maximize your aid potential.

---

to grandparents or other relatives outside your household, who could then help pay tuition bills; aid officers can't touch their assets. Also, if your kid is still a few years from college, be sure to contribute the maximum to 401(k)s or IRAs. Colleges won't expect you to tap retirement savings to pay your share of tuition.

6 "WHEN IT COMES TO ASSESSING YOUR NEED, WE'RE NOT ALWAYS VERY SYMPATHETIC ABOUT YOUR EXPENSES."

Fortunately for homeowners, the value of your house doesn't get considered in most financial aid formulas. On the flip side, if you're paying a fat mortgage or sky-high property taxes to live in an elite suburb, colleges likely won't be too sympathetic. Here's why: To determine aid, colleges calculate your expected family contribution from your adjusted gross income and assets. They usually don't consider what your actual disposable income is or how cash-strapped you might be after paying the bills. "A moderately high-earning family spending most of its income on housing and other necessities may find that their expected family contribution is difficult or impossible to meet," says Roger Dooley, co-owner of website CollegeConfidential.com.

All is not lost, however. While most colleges do not automatically factor in regional cost-of-living discrepancies, some may if you ask. When writing or speaking to an aid officer during the application process, emphasize "involuntary" costs such as taxes over voluntary ones like your mortgage, Dooley suggests. Your car is normally considered an involuntary expense, but elite schools sometimes ask what kind you own and when you bought it. If your wheels are too new and too swanky, it may be considered voluntary expenses.

7 *"WE'LL LET YOU BORROW MORE THAN YOU CAN AFFORD."*

Vickie Hampton, an associate professor of financial planning at Texas Tech University, knows that being well educated can make you poor. A colleague of hers, she says, racked up more than $100,000 in debt while earning a Ph.D. in English. "There's very little probability of her paying that off in her lifetime," Hampton says. The predicament isn't unique, as more students take on excessive debt to finance degrees that lead to jobs in relatively low-paying fields. Unfortunately, college financial aid offices rarely discourage these decisions.

If your student must borrow, be sure to exhaust the federal programs first. Perkins loans or subsidized Stafford loans—both of which you may be offered after filing a FAFSA—are best; their current 5 and 6 percent rates, respectively, are reasonable, and interest doesn't accrue until the borrower leaves school. The Perkins, which you pay back directly to your school, is the slightly more flexible of the two, offering longer grace periods. Beware of unsubsidized Stafford loans, which your college may offer if your family doesn't qualify for subsidized loans. Although these loans have similar low rates, interest will accrue from the

moment the loan is made, even though payments aren't yet required.

8 *"OUTSIDE SCHOLARSHIPS HELP US, NOT YOU."*

Sure, you're proud of the five scholarships your high school senior won from community groups such as the Lions Club and a local church, but don't be relieved just yet. Unless you weren't counting on any financial aid at all, those scholarships won't make a dent in the total amount you'll owe. Why? Federal guidelines mandate that outside scholarship money be considered a resource in meeting financial need. This means you can't use the scholarship dollars toward your expected family contribution, and the college gets to reduce the amount of aid coming your way. "Many parents mistakenly think their cost will be diminished and then are disappointed to learn that it will actually be the grant [from the school] that is diminished, thus saving the college money and not the family," says Anne Macleod Weeks, dean of academic life at the Oldfields School in Glencoe, Md.

Even so, applying for outside awards can help you, especially if you're looking at a financial aid package that features more loans than grants. Ask your college if it can reduce the loans first, says Patty Hoban, aid director at Willamette University in Salem, Ore. "Secondly, it can reduce work-study, which is need-based." In that case, a few scholarships could still save thousands of dollars in interest and let your student study more and flip burgers less.

9 *"WE WON'T 'NEGOTIATE,' BUT WE MIGHT 'REVIEW.'"*

College financial aid guides have long urged parents to negotiate with aid offices, often suggesting that you bring a better aid offer from a "competing" school to shame them into giving you more money. Tread lightly. Many aid directors hate this tactic. Some schools have strict no-negotiation policies, while others are only a little more approachable. "There's certainly no harm in asking a college to review an aid decision," says Loyola's Lindenmeyer. But "we do not negotiate, and we do not match other colleges."

So how do you request a "review"? When contacting your aid office to discuss your child's package, start by avoiding such words as "negotiate" or "bargain," says Virginia Tech's Simmons, and don't throw another school's financial aid award in an officer's face. Instead, thank him for his hard work and the school's generosity, then follow up by expressing doubt at being able to meet your family's contribution. If you haven't already done so in writing, explain any special circumstances you have, such as recent unemployment, a death in the family, or medical bills. Then directly but politely ask if there's anything the aid office can do to help. Once you've established a rapport with the officer, try casually mentioning that you have a competing offer and where else your student has been admitted. At the very least, aid officers may refer you to outside borrowing opportunities or payment plans.

10 *"THOUGHT FRESHMAN YEAR WAS EXPENSIVE? WAIT TILL SENIOR YEAR."*

Your kid just got her award letter and scored a fat four-year grant covering most of her tuition, with a small loan for the rest. So you're set, right? Not necessarily. Two problems can get in the way. First, the amount of federally subsidized loans a student can borrow increases slightly each year; as a result, your college may expand the loans it offers in subsequent years and downsize grants. Second, many parents and students assume that four-year merit-based awards will keep pace with tuition hikes. That's not always the case. "Not all schools are that generous," warns Willamette's Hoban. Nationwide, the average private college price tag jumped 5.9 percent from last year, with the average cost for resident students now just over $25,000. Assuming a steady 6 percent annual price increase and, say, a constant $19,200 in aid each year, the $6,000 difference you paid on your student's freshman year could grow to $10,745 by senior year.

If your child receives merit-based aid, ask whether the college can adjust it for tuition inflation. And no matter what, make sure your scholar keeps hitting the books. A mediocre GPA can end a merit scholarship faster than roommates can devour a midnight pizza.

THINGS TO DO

● **Apply for aid as soon as possible.** The longer you wait, the more the money pool dwindles.

● **Don't be put off** seeking funding from big-name schools. They're more likely to have the assets to provide full aid to the students they've accepted.

● **If there are unusual circumstances** coinciding with your application, like a parent who's recently been laid off, send a letter explaining the situation to the school, not the FAFSA office.

● **Financial aid offices** have a stricter no-negotiation policy than the U.S. President. But in unusual circumstances—and with some tact—you can probably get a review, which might net you more aid.

● **Parents may also consider PLUS,** a federal Parent Loan for Undergraduate Students, which currently carries an 8.5 percent rate. Find more information on government loans at *www.studentaid.ed.gov.*

10 Things
Campus Security
Won't Tell You

1 *"SAFETY IS NEVER FIRST— AT LEAST WHEN IT COMES TO THE BUDGET."*

Experts agree that colleges have improved campus safety over the past 20 years. Shuttle vans, escorts, call boxes, and electronic ID for dorm access were once standard only at a few schools. And where unarmed night watchmen used to stroll the grounds, today many campuses employ armed security guards with police-academy training. In the post-9/11 era and in the wake of recent high school and college campus shootings, vigilance is at an all-time high, and most students say they feel safe. However, many security experts believe schools still have a way to go.

The first step: allocating more money to campus security. According to Harper College police chief Mike Alsup, colleges tend to earmark about 1.5 percent of their budget for security. "It's the lowest priority for funding, based on the school budgets I've seen," says S. Daniel Carter, VP of Security on Campus, a nonprofit that focuses on crime prevention and victim assistance. Colleges' primary concern is educating students, Carter explains; if money's tight, "they're going to cut the campus police officer, not the professor." Scott Jaschik, cofounder of InsideHigherEd.com, agrees: "There are no Nobel Prizes for safe campuses."

2 *"THERE'S TONS OF CRIME HERE, NOT THAT YOU'LL EVER KNOW ABOUT IT."*

In 1986, 19-year-old Jeanne Ann Clery was raped and murdered in her dorm room at Lehigh University. In court, her parents learned that 38 violent crimes had occurred on campus in the past three years—a fact Lehigh had never disclosed. Subsequently, the Clery Act mandated that all colleges receiving federal student aid must make campus crime information available to students and employees. But more than two decades later, "violations of the act are widespread," Carter says; a recent Department of Justice study found that only 37 percent of schools report sexual-assault crimes in accordance with the act.

One major problem is schools' failure to provide "timely warning" about crimes that could threaten campus safety. A recent example: After Eastern Michigan University (EMU) student Laura Dickinson was found dead in her room in December 2006, the university said there was no reason to suspect foul play—until police later arrested a fellow student for her rape and murder. Turns out top school officials had covered up a grisly crime investigation. In July 2007 university president John Fallon was fired. (An EMU spokesperson could not comment before press time.)

3 *"SURE, OUR RECORDS ARE PUBLIC—SORT OF."*

Despite the Clery Act, even federally funded schools don't have to make available all crime records. Incident reports, for example, may be off-limits. In general, public schools are subject to the degree of transparency that state open-records laws demand. Georgia, however, goes a step further: Anyone—not just students—can access all police reports from both private and public colleges under the state's open-records law. "Schools must provide public reports," explains Atlanta-based attorney Ben Barrett. "Policing is a public act."

Outside Georgia, private schools are another matter. In Massachusetts, for example, incident reports don't have to be open even to students. The state Supreme Court ruled as much last year, after student newspaper *The Harvard Crimson* sued the university police department to provide incident reports on alleged sexual assaults and other crimes. The court reasoned that because Harvard is private, it doesn't have to play by public rules. This is also why private-college crime logs are not as detailed as police logs—"they don't have to put who was involved," according to Mike Hiestand, legal consultant for Student Press Law Center.

4 *"OFF CAMPUS MEANS OFF OUR RADAR."*

Living off campus appeals to college kids on many levels. It satisfies an ever-increasing desire for freedom and independence. There's a taste of "real life" responsibilities: rent, bills, commute, household chores (okay, scratch that one). It even saves parents money. But it can sometimes be all too real for young people out on their own for the first time, since living on private property not owned by the school—whether the apartment is 10 steps or 10 miles from campus—absolves the college of any security obligations. Locks, alarms, adequate lighting—all these issues have to be taken up with landlords.

For their part, most colleges do provide a cursory safety talk during orientation, but they feel there's not much else they can do to protect students who live on their own. What makes life outside the confines of campus so dangerous? Not surprisingly, the majority of off-campus incidents occur between 6 P.M. and 6 A.M., with half the victims reporting they were engaged in "leisure activity" at the time. Translation? Students are often out late at night and are especially vulnerable if they've been drinking, are on the phone, or are

Students are often out late at night and are especially vulnerable if they've been drinking, are on the phone, or are listening to music.

listening to music. Alison Kiss, program director for nonprofit group Security on Campus, suggests that students living off-campus take a greater role in ensuring their own security. For starters, they should stay alert off-campus and keep emergency numbers programmed into their phone, Kiss says. They also need to discuss security with their landlord and find out what measures are in place: "On campus you have school security systems at the dorms, but if you live off campus, you have to have conversations with your landlord about how you're being protected."

5 "WE'RE NOT REALLY EQUIPPED FOR A CRISIS..."

For better or worse, the potential for large-scale disaster is part of the public consciousness. While schools are mindful enough to examine and revamp safety measures, the nature of emergency preparation is reactionary rather than preemptive, says Mike Capulli, vice president of sales at GVI Security Solutions, a provider of video-surveillance security. After the Columbine shootings back in 1999, K–12 school districts woke up to the possibility of worst-case scenarios, Capulli says, while colleges "have been slow to respond."

John McNall, president of BowMac Educational Services, agrees. Administrators have realized for a long time that they need to upgrade emergency plans, McNall says; the Virginia Tech shootings were certainly another "'it can happen here' wake-up call." Christopher Blake, associate director at the International Association of

Campus Law Enforcement Administrators (IACLEA), adds that developing better mass-notification systems via text-messaging is job one. Indeed, by the time Virginia Tech police had e-mailed students that a gunman was on the loose, many were already in class.

6 "... LET ALONE A TERRORIST ATTACK."

Universities don't get money for terrorism prevention and recovery directly from the Department of Homeland Security. Instead, DHS awards money to state administrative agencies that dole out the funds to local jurisdictions as they see fit, often leaving little for college law enforcement. "People forget about campus and public safety. We're not a concern," explains Steven Healy, director of public safety at Princeton University and president of IACLEA.

California, for instance, received over $230 million in 2006 from DHS. But ultimately, the state gave only $1.2 million to three institutions that cover more than 140 campuses: California Community Colleges, California State University, and University of California. "There are lots of applications and very few dollars," says Larry Davis, deputy director of grants management for California's Office of Homeland Security. Where does this leave schools? Largely to their own devices. Marlene Phillips, spokesperson for DHS, says colleges must be "proactive" in ensuring campus safety and should not rely on DHS. "It's a very competitive process," Phillips says. "Not everyone who applies gets what they want."

7 *"WE'RE NOT ALWAYS THE MOST SENSITIVE PEOPLE."*

The college experience has been cast as a period of intellectual growth and personal exploration. But in reality, it's also a time when many young women are victimized. One in eight, for example, will be stalked during their college years, according to Bonnie Fisher, a professor of criminal justice at the University of Cincinnati. Yet few schools go the distance in training campus counselors to help stalking victims or have enough budgeted for round-the-clock protection. And that's when the stalking gets reported.

In fact, 83 percent of stalked female students don't report the crime to police, more than a third of them saying they believe it wouldn't be taken seriously. No wonder: In May a University of Washington (UW) student who'd broken up with a man after he allegedly raped her was denied protection after the ex-boyfriend repeatedly threatened and harassed her. Why? She claims university police told her he wasn't an immediate danger. This came just a month after another UW student was murdered by an ex who then killed himself. Vicky Stormo,

UW's chief of police, says the student lived off campus and "received no threats on campus," so jurisdiction belonged to local Seattle police.

Alison Kiss of Security on Campus says that students need to know what law enforcement body has jurisdiction where, both on campus and in the surrounding community, so they can report problems to the right place. But even then, if students feel they're not getting the help they need, they should seek out a third party, such as a local victims' advocacy group or resource center, for assistance and advice.

8 *"WE'RE TRAINED TO PROTECT THE STUDENTS—BUT NOT THEIR IDENTITIES."*

While students need to watch their wallets, iPods, and other personal belongings, there's one thing they have to entrust largely to schools: personal data. In 22 incidents since Thanksgiving of 2006, 728,497 student records fell into the hands of computer hackers and laptop thieves, according to the nonprofit Identity Theft Resource Center. Indeed, colleges are the second most vulnerable places where your Social Security number and other private data are up for grabs, after government and military institutions. Among the incidents in which hardware was stolen for its contents, the most common on-campus targets were financial aid and professors' offices.

Unfortunately, campus police can do little more than treat such incidents as run-of-the-mill thefts. They don't unleash a dragnet for stolen laptops, and extra manpower is not devoted to areas

> **Students need to know what law enforcement body has jurisdiction where, both on campus and in the surrounding community, so they can report problems to the right place.**

where schools store personal information. Furthermore, hacks and viruses are the province of campus information-technology services; students can only cross their fingers that their school's IT department is up to snuff.

What can parents do? Don't be afraid to ask a college about how your child's identity is being protected, says Linda Foley, founder of the Identity Theft Resource Center, in San Diego, Calif. One red flag: when schools use Social Security numbers for identification purposes rather than issuing a student ID number. "You should only have to give a school your Social Security number for financial aid and maybe once to admissions, that's it," Foley says.

9 "YOUR KID MAY BE BACK NEXT YEAR, BUT WE WON'T."

Retaining campus police staff is a big problem, according to Blake of IACLEA: "It's hard to find people, and it's hard to keep people." Blake explains that sworn campus officers, who have the same training and authority as state police, often leave colleges and universities to work for local law enforcement. The biggest reason: money. Municipal cops receive higher pay than their campus brethren, Blake says. Indeed, the median salary for state and local police officers was $45,500 in 2007, while college and university cops earned $35,000, according to compensation data provider PayScale.

The high turnover rate can adversely affect the quality of safety and campus life. "If you have new staff coming in, it takes time to establish relationships with others on campus," Blake says. "It does have an impact."

10 "NOT ALL STUDENTS ARE TREATED EQUALLY."

Student diversity has been on the university agenda since the 1990s. Nowadays campuses have social and outreach organizations that cater to many ethnic, religious, and sexual-orientation groups. But even though the institutions themselves have become far more sensitive to minority students' needs, gay, African American, and Middle Eastern students, among others, have their fair share of complaints about campus police.

Security at UCLA captured attention in 2006, when an officer repeatedly Tasered an Iranian American student. Witnesses claim Mostafa Tabatabainejad was singled out by guards and asked for ID as he sat using a library computer. When he didn't comply, UCLA police were called in and grabbed Tabatabainejad as he tried to leave the building. As he protested verbally, Tabatabainejad was stunned once and then repeatedly for not getting up from the ground. (A lawsuit was pending at press time, and UCLA spokesperson Phil Hampton says, "We're nearing completion of our investigation.")

Many students also feel hate crimes are given short shrift by campus police. "There's definitely a couple of officers we work with who are really supportive," says John Hellman, former director of Gay, Lesbian, Bisexual, and Transgender Affairs at Boston College. "But it seems like it's all talk." *The Advocate College Guide for LGBT Students* profiles the country's best campuses for gay and lesbian students. Among the most tolerant, it cites Duke, NYU, and Ohio State.

THINGS TO DO

• **Look beyond a school's published crime stats**—which aren't always accurate, experts say—and focus more on the emergency procedures in place. How would the school handle a campus-wide emergency?

• **Ask prospective colleges** about their FERPA policy. Will you be notified if your kid gets caught drinking underage? What if he stops going to class? Some schools contact parents, while others do not.

• **Stress is a safety issue, too.** Ask about a school's wellness center, its hours, and whether counselors are readily available.

• **How to gauge fire safety?** Make sure every dorm room has a smoke alarm, and ask about the frequency of false alarms on campus—too many, and students tend to stop paying attention. Buying your kid a carbon monoxide detector and a small fire extinguisher doesn't hurt, either.

• **Remind your college kids** that dorms are public places—they should keep doors locked to prevent burglaries and avoid broadcasting their whereabouts on Facebook or other social-networking sites.

10 Things Your
College Student
Won't Tell You

1 *"SURE, I'VE CHEATED. WHO HASN'T?"*

Cheating has reached an all-time high on college campuses, with 70 percent of students now admitting to some form of it. Incidents involving unsourced material from the Internet in written work quadrupled between 2000 and 2006, yet 77 percent of students don't consider it cheating or "very serious." "Some students have justified it to themselves," says Donald McCabe, founding president of the Center for Academic Integrity. "They'll say it's the faculty's fault if they're too lazy to stop it."

Mobile devices exacerbate the problem; students can text-message answers to one another or use camera phones to post exams online. SparkMobile, a service from study-guide publisher SparkNotes, lets students send in text-message queries and get crib notes in seconds. But that's just one of many such services: GradeSaver.com grants access to sample essays for $6 a month, while RentACoder.com lets computer-science students outsource homework to India for around $20. The companies say their sites weren't designed to help students cheat, but "it's impossible to police," admits RentACoder founder Ian Ippolito.

2 *"'STUDYING ABROAD' IS ONE BIG PARTY."*

In 2006 Congress passed a resolution dubbing it the "Year of Study Abroad." "We want the next generation of adults to be in touch with their national and global citizenship," says Jessica Townsend Teague, former program manager at the Commission on the Abraham Lincoln Study Abroad Fellowship. But despite good PR, study-abroad programs are often less than rigorous, and underage drinking is rampant. "It's necessary for the image of study abroad to shift from a 'party hearty' experience to a very serious national priority," Townsend Teague avers. It's also a matter of safety: "Students go from being unable to drink legally to countries where alcohol is free-flowing," says Gary Rhodes, director of the Center for Global Education at Loyola Marymount University. "Some students have died while abroad."

Schools are doing their part to protect students, requiring better orientation and urging them to avoid countries deemed unsafe by the State Department. But Townsend Teague advises students to think before they act: "Take a moment to be very sober about what we can and cannot do to rescue a student overseas."

3 "I'D STAY HERE FOREVER IF YOU'D PAY FOR IT."

Brian Bordeau graduated in 2006 from the State University of New York at Binghamton. He says it wasn't a big deal, but admits everyone else thought it was—he'd been in school for seven years. "Honestly, I'd rather come to school again next fall," he says. "I really like it here."

Bordeau isn't alone: Just 53 percent of students enrolled in standard undergraduate programs get their bachelor's degree within five years. Changing majors, transferring schools, and good old slacking off can all result in extended enrollment. One of the obvious downsides is the added financial burden of an extra year or two in school. But there are hidden costs, too. "You lose a lot of money in loan interest and forgone wages by taking that fifth or six year to finish," says Jacqueline King, director of the American Council on Education's Center for Policy Analysis.

If you plan to pay your child's way through college, King suggests setting a firm timetable. When Bordeau was forced to take out loans to pay for tuition during his sixth year, he began to buckle down and hit the books. The final year, "I paid for it," he says. "That motivated me to finish."

4 "COLLEGE LIFE CAN BE HAZARDOUS TO MY HEALTH."

Parents of college students often worry about their children's well-being—and for good reason. The university experience can be marred by physical and mental health issues ranging from anorexia and communicable diseases to depression. But the most serious concern for parents and educators is suicide, which accounts for an estimated 1,100 student deaths each year.

Fortunately, most schools now have counseling and intervention programs, but they differ widely. Some colleges ask those who've disclosed thoughts of suicide to withdraw—a policy that can inadvertently keep students from seeking help. The University of Illinois (UI) has developed another approach: protecting a student's "right to be in school," but requiring those who have threatened or attempted suicide to attend assessment sessions. "If a student says he wants to take his own life, those statements should always be taken seriously," says Paul Joffe, chair of the Suicide Prevention Team at the University of Illinois. The program is aggressive, but it works: UI's suicide rate has decreased by 45 percent since it began 21 years ago and is around half that of other Big Ten schools.

5 "MY RÉSUMÉ ISN'T THE ONLY THING I HAVE POSTED ON THE INTERNET."

Social-networking sites are wildly popular among college students, providing a forum for meeting and chatting with friends, posting photos, and writing about their lives and interests. But search Facebook—as some employers do to screen job candidates—and you'll find photos of underage drinking, partying, and scantily clad college kids. "There are students who work like crazy on their GPA but don't think twice about what they're posting on Facebook," says Lauren Steinfeld, chief privacy officer at the University of Pennsylvania.

College athletes have been particularly brazen. In a 2006 incident involving Northwestern's girls' soccer team, pictures on Webshots.com showed rookies blindfolded and in their underwear performing sexually suggestive acts. The team was temporarily suspended, and some members await further disciplinary action. "It's hard for anyone over the age of 30 to truly understand what is going on at college these days without seeing it for themselves," says Bob Reno, founder of BadJocks.com, a sports-scandal site. And these days, it seems, "seeing it" is just a mouse click away.

6 "JUST BECAUSE I WAS A STRAIGHT ARROW IN HIGH SCHOOL DOESN'T MEAN I WILL BE IN COLLEGE."

The statistics are pretty scary: Each year 2.8 million college students drive drunk, and 1,700 die from alcohol-related injuries. Nearly half a million engage in unprotected sex, and almost 100,000 students are victims of alcohol-related sexual assault or date rape. But alcohol isn't the only substance that's a problem. Use of narcotics other than heroin is back up to record levels among college students, and there's a newer trend causing concern: 29 percent say they have used prescription drugs recreationally. These include pain relievers like Vicodin, which can lead to respiratory and liver failure, and amphetamines such as Ritalin and Adderall, which can result in cardiac arrhythmia and coma—and can lead to harder drugs. Students using these stimulants are 20 times more likely to try cocaine.

Part of the problem is that these prescription drugs are so easy to come by—many college students have prescriptions for drugs like Adderall and Ritalin and are willing to sell them, says Sue Foster, vice president and director of policy research for the National Center on Addiction and Substance Abuse at Columbia University. "Many [of these drugs] are just there for the taking in medicine cabinets across the country," Foster says.

Ironically, while drug use in high school is also up, drinking there is at an all-time low. According to the latest UCLA survey, fewer than half of last year's incoming college freshmen say they drank beer as high school seniors. And while that's surely good news, it remains to be seen whether the trend holds once these students hit campus.

7 "MY GRADES ARE NONE OF YOUR BUSINESS."

Even though parents may have taken their child on campus visits, helped her move into her dorm, and are now picking up the tuition bill, they could be denied access to their child's college records. Want to see if your son failed math? Wonder if your daughter has been ill? Depending on a given school's policy, you may have to get your college kid to sign a consent form.

Some schools grant access to parents of students who are claimed as dependents; there's also an exception permitting disclosure in the case of a medical emergency, such as a suicide attempt or testing positive for tuberculosis. "Nobody should get the impression that anything is absolutely confidential," says Steinfeld, at the University of Pennsylvania. Each school's approach to these exceptions is different, and the policy is usually detailed on the university's website.

8 "I'LL DO JUST ABOUT ANYTHING FOR MONEY."

It's no surprise that college students are strapped for cash, but what they'll do to earn it can sometimes be a bit shocking. Participating in research studies and surveys is one way to earn cash without committing to a steady gig. Fliers advertising participation in an experiment—worth anywhere from $7 to $80, depending on the task and time commitment—adorn campus bulletin boards and psychology department websites. "I have to get my money somehow," says Yale senior Elizabeth Friedlander, who averages three experiments per month—so far including two MRIs.

For an even bigger payout, young women have begun donating their eggs to infertile couples: An "elite" ovum harvested from a healthy female at a top university can fetch anywhere from $10,000 to $35,000. "You'll see ads in all the Ivy League newspapers," says Debora Spar, a professor at Harvard Business School and author of *The Baby Business*. "Some women donate for money, some out of a sense of altruism, and most for a complicated mix of both motives." But the process is relatively new and virtually unregulated. "In other medical fields, we know the long-term effects," Spar says. "Here there's less information."

9 "I'M UP TO MY EARS IN CREDIT CARD DEBT..."

No one said college would be cheap— tuition is up 95 percent from a decade ago at four-year public institutions and 74 percent at private schools. The cost of books and room and board is also on the rise. But many students who graduate with debt have only themselves to blame: Experts say the idea of living within one's means now seems alien to many students and cite growing pressure to keep up with classmates by purchasing expensive clothes, cars, and gadgets. The average college senior now has six credit cards and a $3,200 total balance. (A better idea is for students to begin with prepaid credit cards, to build in control of their spending.)

The effect of mounting student debt is profound: 11 percent of college students frequently pay less than their monthly minimum, which can make it difficult to rent an apartment, obtain a car loan, or even get a job. "Debt strangles their ability to become adults and make good career choices," says Tamara Draut, author of *Strapped: Why America's 20- and 30-Somethings Can't Get Ahead*. In fact, 17 percent of young adults significantly alter their career path because they're so far in the red so early; Draut says that often "the door is locked" to fields like teaching and nursing, since salaries are too low to support young grads carrying heavy debt.

10 "...SO I'LL BE MOVING BACK HOME AFTER GRADUATION."

On graduation day students are ready for the real world, and parents are finally off the hook, right? Not necessarily. Currently, in 13 million households—up 70 percent from 2000—parents are financially supporting children 18 and over, whether they live at home or not. It's a trend that experts don't expect to end anytime soon.

What's more, even working adult children are struggling to make ends meet—and they're moving back home in droves. They're called "boomerang kids," and nearly 11 million homes housed them in 2006, according to MacroMonitor, a market-research program operated by Consumer Financial Decisions. "They're not dependent according to taxes, but they're sleeping on the couch, running up the utilities, and using the ice box," says Larry Cohen, director of CFD. "The nest isn't quite empty."

Experts cite rising rents, the difficulty of finding a well-paying entry-level job, and debt as the primary contributors to this national homecoming. It's not all bad—moving home may give young adults a leg up, since they can use salaries to pay off debt and won't have to jump at the first job they're offered just to pay the bills. "If your parents live somewhere where you can find a job, do yourself a favor and live rent-free for a year or two. It makes a big difference," Draut says.

THINGS TO KNOW

Going off to college is an important step for young adults; indeed, much of what they'll learn on campus extends well beyond class work. Keith Anderson, chair of the American College Health Association's Mental Health Best Practices Task Force, shares his insight about some of the biggest lessons the college experience has to offer students:

● **Interpersonal skills.** The residence hall experience contributes to the development of social skills and an ability to manage conflict. Learning to live well with others teaches students about cooperation and ways to effectively negotiate individual differences.

● **Self-esteem.** Discovering they can be successful both academically and socially in a new and challenging environment boosts students' self-esteem.

● **Delayed gratification.** The average 16-week college semester builds in lessons about delayed gratification—that is, working hard in advance even though there is no immediate pay off.

● **Time management and organization.** Their course schedule and academic workload encourage students to develop better time management, including the ability to prioritize tasks and stay organized—crucial skills for any career track.

● **Self care.** Colleges are increasingly educating students about the value of exercise, nutrition, avoiding drug use, and sleeping well. Schools such as Duke University, the University of Florida, and Cornell University are leading this trend, with programs designed to build awareness and instill lessons on self care that students can take with them as they mature.

Your Home

■ A home isn't just the physical structure you live in, it's an emotional construct as well—a place to make you feel safe, secure, and at ease; a place to recharge; a place to connect with family and friends.

All of which makes its building and maintenance vitally important to your wallet as well as your heart. In this chapter, you'll find concrete advice on a wide range of homeownership issues—from "10 Things Your Architect Won't Tell You," which explains how to communicate effectively to get the house you want, to "10 Things Your Exterminator Won't Tell You," which shows why it's crucial to talk to your neighbors about pest removal. After all, peace of mind is always a smart investment.

10 Things Your
Architect
Won't Tell You

1 *"HAVING A DEGREE AND HAVING A LICENSE ARE TWO VERY DIFFERENT THINGS."*

When Debbie Ford, a La Jolla, Calif., writer, hired an architect to oversee an addition in 2003, she was taken aback when he started ripping out most of her walls, plumbing, and electrical wiring. It was only then that she learned he wasn't licensed—and that most of the gutting was unnecessary.

While Americans may not be buying and remodeling homes as quickly as they were during the housing boom, we are still a nation obsessed with home improvement: Consumers spent roughly $291 billion in 2007 on housing face-lifts, according to NARI, the National Association of the Remodeling Industry, up from $229 billion in 2003. And bringing in the right architect can mean the difference between dream home and disaster area. To ensure the former, first make sure your architect is licensed—and not just someone with an education or background in architecture.

To locate licensed architects, start with the National Council of Architectural Registration Boards (*www.ncarb.org*). Also look for membership in the AIA, the American Institute of Architects, which has its own code of ethics (*www.aia.org*).

Finally, ask for referrals to get a sense of how well an architect works with clients.

2 *"YOU MAY NOT NEED ME AT ALL."*

Hiring an architect can add thousands to the cost of a home-improvement project, which is a lot of money when your project is relatively small—converting a garage to a game room, say, or expanding your kitchen. Architects will argue that they offer expertise that will make any addition, however small, flow better with your house. But many experts say it's often overkill. "If the project is entirely interior to the house, as long as you're not moving windows or adding to the footprint of the house, you may not need an architect at all," says C. C. Sullivan, founder of C. C. Sullivan Strategic Communications, a communications consulting firm for the architecture and construction fields.

The ultimate authority, however, is your local municipality's housing department; some may require architect-stamped drawings in order to get a building permit, while others might let you give your drawings directly to a contractor. For small projects, you may be able to use an interior designer or, if you're doing just one specific room, a kitchen-, bath-, or even basement-design specialist. To find a qualified designer near you, check out the websites of the International Interior Design Association, at *www.iida.org;* the American Society of Interior Designers, at *www.asid.org;* or the National Association of the Remodeling Industry at *www.nari.org.*

3 *"IF I CAN'T READ YOUR MIND, I'LL JUST DESIGN THINGS MY WAY."*

While you can get a good idea about an architect's sensibilities looking at his past projects, it's up to you to make sure what parts of his style you do and don't want to surface in your home. When Janet Kennedy, a health-care professional in Brooklyn, N.Y., was having her brownstone remodeled in 2001, she was surprised to see that a prominent set of new windows had a sleek, modern look when she had assumed they would appear more traditional for her century-old home. The architect, Kennedy says, "never went through with us what the woodwork would be like. It was shocking."

To help avoid unpleasant surprises, talk in as much detail as you can early on about what you envision. David Ashen, an architect based in Long Island City, N.Y., says he encourages prospective clients to "pull a library together of things that inspire them," such as clippings from newspapers and magazines. That "gives me a little bit of a DNA of what the client responds to," he says. Ashen also asks new clients to think hard about how they live

in their home, considering everything from where they like to have morning coffee to how they like to entertain. Finally, if you're part of a couple, make sure that you and your partner agree on aesthetics beforehand so you can present a united front.

4 *"I SEE YOUR BUDGET AS AN OPENING BID."*

When former landscape artist Tom Zavitz bought some property in Montana in 1999, he and his wife decided to build a modest Arts and Crafts–style three-bedroom home with a view of the mountains. They signed up an architect they'd found through a referral from an acquaintance and told him their budget was $200,000. But during weekly meetings over the next six weeks, Zavitz says that he and his wife became increasingly frustrated to see a consistently bigger scale for the project and increasingly elaborate details in the architect's proposed design. "We kept saying, 'This is too much,'" Zavitz says. "But every time he came back [with revisions], his projected budget kept going over, by as much as 50 percent." The Zavitzes ultimately paid the architect $5,000 to end the relationship and found another one, who helped them stay within their budget.

Zavitz says he was much firmer with the second architect about his unwillingness to go over budget. To play it safe, Ashen advises giving a figure 10 to 20 percent lower than you're willing to pay. "Things happen," he says—such as small building glitches, or you may change your mind about details or finishes along the way.

5 "MY PAYMENT PLAN, MY WAY."

Once you decide that you like an architect's basic ideas, you should sign a contract to get the terms in writing. The AIA has a template contract that many architects use, and it covers the size, or "scope," of the project; the homeowner's budget; a time frame for the project; and a payment schedule. Setting the fee structure, however, is completely up to the architect. The traditional amount is based on a percentage of the cost of the job—typically, between 10 and 25 percent of the estimated total construction costs, including design and consultation through the construction process.

Some architects, on the other hand, may insist on an hourly fee, which can run anywhere from $50 to upwards of $200. This fee structure helps architects protect themselves from impulsive clients who ask for endless revisions throughout a project. But even if you don't plan to be wishy-washy, an hourly rate will almost always cost you more. "I strongly advise people not to go hourly," Sullivan says. "Interview another architect."

6 "MY DRAWINGS AREN'T REALLY BUILDER-READY."

Before you can start shopping for a contractor, you'll need your architect's finished drawings. But "finished" can be a subjective term. Tony Crasi, owner of Cuyahoga Falls, Ohio–based building firm Crasi and Co., says that one of the biggest problems in working with other people's architects is that he sees "incomplete drawings, inaccurate drawings, drawings that have no chance of being built for the price the owner would like."

Part of the problem can stem from an architect's lack of construction expertise, but it can also be the result of the homeowner's not knowing what kinds of drawings to ask for. Unless you're doing a very small project, be sure to request "construction-level" or "builder" drawings. Ideally, these should also include "specifications," which describe finishes and quality of workmanship. And discuss as many details with the architect as you can, down to the type of faucets you want in the bathroom. It may add to your fee, but the right drawings make it easier to estimate costs, preserve your wishes—and even determine liability if something goes wrong. "I don't think you can put enough information in a set of plans," Crasi says.

7 "I'M A VISIONARY, NOT AN ACCOUNTANT."

Once you have some contractors' bids in hand, your architect should help you decipher them, spotting possible price inflation or suspicious lowballing. But you shouldn't take an architect's sense of specific prices as gospel. While they can generally make ballpark estimates, "rare is the architect who is on top of what costs are right now," says Bill Kreager, an AIA fellow and a principal with Seattle-based Mithun Architects, "and certainly not what prices are going to be in six months," when construction begins.

Kreager suggests bringing in a contractor, even when you and your architect are just beginning, under what he calls a "negotiated contract."

You pay the contractor by the hour as a consultant—to help estimate price, predict availability of necessary materials and qualified subcontractors, and spot possible building-specific design obstacles—with the option of hiring him for the full job later.

To find good contractors, ask your architect, or even your real estate agent. Another resource is HandymanOnline .com, which can help connect you with licensed and insured contractors in your area who carry at least three good references.

8 "YOUR CONTRACTOR AND I HAVE SOME MAJOR COMMUNICATION ISSUES."

As a rule, architects are interested in aesthetics whereas contractors and builders are more concerned with logistics. So it's only natural that from time to time tensions can arise between them—or worse, they may not be interested in dealing with each other at all. During Janet Kennedy's remodel, she says that problems kept cropping up because the contractor couldn't translate the architect's plans, resulting in misplaced closets, moldings that had to be ripped out and rebuilt, and lots of delays.

To get off to a secure start, try what Tracy Walsh did when she was ready to hire a contractor for a remodel. "We had the architect actually meet [the prospective contractor] before we signed on," says the Brooklyn, N.Y., graphic designer. Happily, the two parties clicked. "We figured it was best to let [the contractor] know up front [the architect] was going to be overseeing this," Walsh says. "If the contractor was going to have a problem, we'd know right away."

9 "ONCE THE BLUEPRINT'S DONE, I'M OUTTA HERE."

The design phase of a home takes an average of about a month, depending on how often the architect and clients can meet to discuss plans. Once construction begins, a good architect should visit periodically to make sure the building is adhering to the design and that corners aren't being cut. Most consumers can "assume the architect will supervise," says Sullivan, but it isn't always the case. In Kennedy's brownstone, she says, "we were the ones noticing that things weren't happening like in the drawing, like when two separate closets were not placed properly."

To avoid problems, check that your contract spells out how often your architect will reappear once construction begins. "At some points he might be there every day, certain times once a week," says Ashen, "and often times on the phone or [making] quick trips." An architect should especially be there to inspect hard-to-undo events, like window installation.

Once construction begins, a good architect should visit periodically to make sure the building is adhering to the design and that corners aren't being cut.

Another way to keep the architect coming back is to structure the payment plan using time as an incentive: Pay a third of the fee up front, another third when most of the documents are done, and the last third when construction is at least substantially complete. Otherwise, Sullivan says, "It's human nature for architects to wander away when you finish paying them."

10 *"A PACKAGE DEAL CAN BE A PACKAGE MESS."*

More and more companies are offering what is known as "design-build" services, meaning that the architect and builder or contractor work for the same company and you pay one fee for both of them—typically, up to 20 percent of construction costs. Such an arrangement "can be a great thing," Sullivan says. But not always. When Barbara and Randy Teach were building a home in Bakersfield, Calif., their builder offered an in-house architect, who helped them tweak one of the development's house plans. But building was delayed by a month because the builders started work using the untweaked blueprint. While Randy Teach blames the builder more than the architect, he says, "You'd think they'd be on the same page."

For a smooth design-build experience, make sure architects and carpenters are truly on staff, and meet with both the design and construction people before you sign on. According to Jerry Levine, president of The Levine Group Architects and Builders, based in Silver Spring, Md., some firms actually outsource the design phase—which entirely defeats the purpose of using a firm that does both. Another good litmus test: Look for firms that call themselves "architecture-build" firms, which by law must employ licensed architects, as opposed to less-qualified designers.

THINGS TO DO

- **Before hiring an architect,** make sure you really need one. Smaller jobs, like turning your garage into a "man cave," probably don't. To assess whether a given job is something better handed to a contractor or even something you could do on your own—ideally, with the help of a handy friend or two—visit *www.doityourself.com.*

- **Hire an architect who charges** a flat rate; getting charged by the hour almost always ends up costing more, according to experts.

- **Flat rates aren't perfect, though.** For an added layer of protection, set your budget 10 to 20 percent lower than what you can afford.

- **Hire a watchdog.** A third-party contractor acting as a paid-by-the-hour consultant can not only spot possible building-specific design obstacles but can also help estimate costs and predict the availability of necessary materials.

10 Things Your
Home Builder
Won't Tell You

1 *"I'LL BUILD YOUR HOUSE ON MARSHMALLOW."*

Population growth and urban sprawl mean there's not much residential land left in many areas these days—and what there is may not be ideal. Shortly after John Duffy and his family moved into their $234,000 home in Highlands Ranch, Colo., long cracks started showing up in the walls and the porch started pulling away from the house. After badgering his builder for the soil report, Duffy learned his lot was a hot spot for potential swell. (Writer Homes, the builder, was ordered to pay Duffy $544,000. John Palmeri, Writer's attorney, says the company offered to fix the Duffys' house, but "they were bent on going to court.")

The Duffy family isn't alone. In fact, a number of homes today are being built on "expansive soil"—earth that swells when it rains—without adequate safeguards. How common is the practice? About 50 percent of homes in Southern California are built on expansive soil, according to Patrick Catalano, founder of The Law Firm of Catalano and Catalano in San Francisco and San Diego, which specializes in real estate and construction defect litigation.

But soil isn't the only issue when it comes to shoddy construction. In October 2007, four hillside homes built in La Jolla, Calif., slipped off their foundations, burying two other dwellings in an alley below, after a landslide that damaged some 111 homes. Catalano, who's representing the owners of 25 of these homes, says that in about 20 percent of cases, the home builder is at fault, since the landslide occurred within 10 years of the home being built. (These cases are pending.)

2 *"I WON'T JUST CUT CORNERS— I'LL SEVER THEM."*

Substandard work has always existed in home building, but the collapse of the housing market and the increased costs of construction are making the problem worse, says Jonathan Alpert, a retired Tampa, Fla., attorney who represented homebuyers. Alpert says he's handled cases in which builders didn't seal roofs, in which two-inch concrete slabs have been used instead of the four-inch slabs specified, and in which sewage pipes have been cross-connected to drinking-water pipes.

In some cases, builders are skipping steps dictated by municipal building codes. In one Sarasota, Fla., gated community called Turtle Rock, four families cut open their houses in 1998 to ferret out the source of some mold growth. What they found, in addition to wet lumber, were several code violations, including missing hurricane straps, which are steel plates that tie the wood frame together and to the concrete base. Says Brian Stirling, the structural engineer hired by the homeowners to investigate, "If we'd had a strong storm, they would have had some serious problems." Like what? "Like losing their top floor." In 1999 the builder, U.S. Home, agreed to buy back the four houses and said it would make county-supervised repairs on 12 others in the subdivision. "We dispute the extent of the problems," says the builder's attorney, Fred Zinober. But by settling the case, he says, "U.S. Home did the right thing."

"It used to be during the housing boom that builders were cutting corners because they were putting things up as quickly as they could stand," Alpert says. Now the issues are inflationary pressures on builders and the need to increase profits. "The cost per square foot for construction is actually increasing while home prices are decreasing," Alpert says, "so that's putting pressure on builders to cut corners."

3 "THIS IS A ROGUE'S INDUSTRY."

Given how complicated it is to build a home, and how serious the implications are if it's done incorrectly, you might expect home builders to answer to rigorous regulatory authority. Think again. According to the most recent survey by the National Association of State Contractors Licensing Agencies, only 18 of the association's 27 member states regulate home builders. And of those member states that do regulate, only 15 require any kind of exam—Arizona and Maryland being two of them—and only 13 require on-the-job experience. Two states, Louisiana and Utah, have continuing-education requirements, but they're the exception.

But greater regulation comes with a price. "Red tape and compliance issues add cost to building a new home," says Carlos Gutierrez, assistant staff vice president for the National Association of Home Builders (NAHB). "And that cost is inevitably passed on to the consumer in the form of a higher-priced home." While he acknowledges that some regulation of the industry is necessary, even welcome, Gutierrez adds that "at a time when affordable housing continues to be a crisis nationwide, governments ought to be careful not to overregulate."

4 "PUBLIC INSPECTORS WON'T CATCH MY SHODDY WORK."

Max Curtis, a Livermore, Calif., private-home inspector, says he hears it all the time from his home-buying clients: "Their builder tells them, 'Why do you need your own inspector? This has been

---

Bottom line: Don't rely solely on the word of a public inspector; hire your own person to inspect the building as well.

signed off on by the municipal building department.'"

Sure, the public inspector is required to check out your new house, but only to ascertain that it's built to code—essentially, that it's safe to live in—not that it is well constructed. "They're just looking to see if that wall is up and painted," says Dwayne Jones, a Memphis builder.

And sometimes they don't even do that well. On one inspection, Curtis found 64 items that the municipal inspector had missed, including a gas water heater lacking flues (without which the heater may leak poisonous carbon monoxide). Bottom line: Don't rely solely on the word of a public inspector; hire your own person to inspect the building as well.

5 *"YOUR WARRANTY MAY BE WORTHLESS."*

Many home builders tout 10-year warranties as protection against future problems. But these warranties are often extremely limited in coverage, particularly after the second year. "It gives people a false sense of security," says Brent Lemon, a Dallas attorney who represents homebuyers. "Most of these basically require that the house fall down on top of you before they kick in." Consider the warranty offered by Denver, Colo.–based Home Buyers Warranty. It lists 71 exclusions and, like many, states that the home must be "unsafe, unsanitary, or otherwise unlivable" to get structural-defect coverage. Em Fluhr, the warranty company's CEO, says, "If [homebuyers] detect any worsening of the situation, they can submit another claim."

The root of the problem with warranties is that builders characterize them too broadly when they say they'll help protect homeowners in a structural problem, says Anne Stark, a Dallas attorney specializing in homebuyer complaints. "Structural-defect coverage often covers only catastrophic failure," Stark says. "Builders will say you've got a great warranty, but then you wake up in the third year with cracks all over your house and you call the warranty company and they say, 'Sorry, it's not a structural failure.'" Some states, like Texas, are aiming to alleviate the problem: In 2003 it created the Texas Residential Construction Commission to help builders resolve disputes without litigation. "We require a warranty whether the builder wants to give it or not, and that warranty needs to meet the minimum level of state standards," says Duane Waddill, executive director of the TRCC. "Even if the builder goes bankrupt, the buyer has additional protection."

6 *"ONCE YOU MOVE IN, YOU'LL NEVER SEE ME AGAIN."*

Even before Denise Burton and her husband closed on their Glendale, Ariz., home, they knew there were problems. Their walls weren't plumb, for example, and there was no framing behind one. Worried about losing their low interest rate, they moved in anyway, with a promise from the builder, Diamond Key Homes, that everything would be fixed once they got in.

It didn't happen. Burton says she made at least a dozen calls to the Phoenix-based builder over a four-month period and sent letters and faxes. Mostly, she says, she was ignored. And when the builder did send workers to her house, Burton says, "they'd make it worse." It took a year for the builder to finally ·make all the proper fixes, she says—and that was only after the state agency that regulates contractors, acting on Burton's complaint, temporarily revoked Diamond Key's license. (Diamond Key declined to comment and has since been acquired by another company.)

Indeed, it's one of the ironies of building a house. During construction, you can't wait to finally get all those construction workers out of your sight. But "once the home is built," says Jason Clark, a consumer advocate focused on home-building issues, "you can't find the builder with a Texas posse."

7 "GOOD LUCK GOING AFTER ME."

Buried in nearly every home-purchase contract is a clause that reads something like this: "Any dispute that arises between the builder and the purchaser will be decided in binding arbitration." Most buyers sign on the dotted line, not knowing that they have just waived their right to take their builder to court. "Arbitration is being sneaked into those contracts, and nobody knows what it means until it's too late," says Dennis K. Drake, a San Antonio attorney who represents homebuyers.

What's wrong with arbitration? Well, for starters, arbitrators are less likely than juries to award treble damages—or three times the amount they lost—say construction-industry attorneys. Also,

though arbitration costs have significantly declined in recent years, it's still expensive. First there's the filing fee—which, for a homebuyer's claim under $75,000, is $375, if administered through the American Arbitration Association (AAA)—plus the added expense of a lawyer. Often, "it's so prohibitively expensive that consumers may find they just don't want to pursue a claim," says Drake.

In addition, construction-industry attorneys say that the fact that builders are the "repeat customers" in arbitration means there's a greater chance they'll be favored. If a builder regularly nominates the American Arbitration Association, for example, that builder may be in front of AAA 10 to 12 times a year, versus the homeowner's one time. For that reason, some construction-industry attorneys recommend using retired judges or arbitrators instead.

"The builders do put arbitration clauses in their contracts, but it's the homeowner that files the complaints," says Robert Meade, senior vice president of the American Arbitration Association. "We get 130,000 cases a year, and less than 300 of those are homeowner cases, so the dollar amount is meaningless to us."

8 "YOUR HOME WON'T LOOK LIKE THE ONES WE TOURED."

It's easy to be impressed with the model home your builder shows you. Who wouldn't love the lush curtains and intricate crown moldings? Unfortunately, the house you buy may not have the same flourish or feel as the model. Few decorative touches are standard, and builders are notorious for using sneaky design tricks to make model homes more attractive, such as putting in scaled-down furniture to make rooms look bigger.

Maria Lo Bianco, a buyers' broker in Springfield, Va., admits to playing this game in her previous job as a builder's marketing executive. "If I know it's a small foyer, my challenge is to get the buyer's eye off it so he has no idea how small it is—until he goes to settlement and can't fit his furniture," she says. "If the dining room is visible from the foyer, I might do an exotic color design there and leave the foyer plain." Showing a home in its best light is one thing, but some practices are downright deceitful. Builders, for example, will often plant grass where the driveway would go to make the lawn look bigger, according to Alan Fields, coauthor of *Your New House*.

Bottom line: "If you think you're getting the model home," advises Tim Carter, a builder and syndicated columnist, "you'd better be writing down language in the contract that says it's going to be exactly like the model."

9 "I HAVEN'T BUDGETED ENOUGH FOR DECENT LIGHT FIXTURES."

It sounds like a reasonable practice—rather than specifying every item for a house, a builder will set cost allowances for things such as light fixtures or carpeting. That way the buyer gets to pick out what he wants. The trouble is, many builders use allowances as a bidding strategy, lowballing the cost to keep the total price down and land the contract.

> The trouble is, many builders use allowances as a bidding strategy, lowballing the cost to keep the total price down and land the contract.

When author Fields and his wife bought their house back in 1990, he says their builder gave them a $500 allowance for all their light fixtures. That sounded great—until "we walked into the store and were just floored by the prices," he says. The couple shopped for discounts but still ended up spending double that amount on lighting.

Jones, the Memphis builder, says that lowball allowances are common in his region. Today the usual range is roughly $1,000 to $1,500 for light fixtures in a three-bedroom house, but the real bill is probably going to be more than double that. "And that's for cookie-cutter fixtures," Jones says.

10 "YOU MAY WIND UP SEEING DOUBLE."

It's no surprise that if you buy a tract house, you'll eventually come across a carbon copy, probably in your own neighborhood. But you don't expect that to happen when you've ponied up for an "exclusive" design. Nonetheless, "we see 'custom builders' offering standard floor plans on their websites all of the time," says Ralph Hudson, owner of Florida-based American Builders

Network, a resource for consumers looking to connect with home builders. "So often the exteriors and elevation are the same, but the interior is slightly modified."

In most cases, if an architect makes an exclusive design for a home, that design is licensed to the builder and the builder has the right to use the design for one specific project and nothing beyond that, explains Jay Stephens, vice president and general counsel at the American Institute of Architects. If that builder turns around and executes that design for other houses down the road, legal recourse is warranted: "If a design is copyrighted, you'll ultimately have to bring it to court," says Gutierrez of NAHB.

Though difficult, it is possible to take preventative measures. If a homeowner has a contract directly with an architect, Stephens suggests asking him to include a clause that states that the design will not be replicated.

THINGS TO DO

● **Cost allowances suggested** by the home builder for items such as carpeting are often much lower than what you should expect to spend. To be safe, double them when drawing up your budget.

● **Construction-industry attorneys** recommend using an independent arbiter (builders who are frequent customers of one arbitration association may get the home-field advantage there). To find an independent arbiter in your state, e-mail the National Arbitration Forum, at *neutral@adrforum.com*.

● **If the model home you're shown** is your dream house, make sure it's in the contract that the one you're buying is exactly like it. Model homes are often full of subtle touches—such as crown molding and top-quality doors—to make interiors look bigger, nicer, and more inviting.

● **Once your home is complete,** public inspectors don't look for how well it's constructed, just that it's built to code. For an independent eye, hire your own inspector to go over the builder's work *(www.ashi.org)*.

10 Things Your
Real Estate Broker
Won't Tell You

1 *"YOUR OPEN HOUSE IS REALLY JUST A NETWORKING PARTY FOR ME."*

Hire a real estate broker to sell your home, and one of the first things he'll likely suggest is hosting an open house so that potential buyers can casually check out your property on a weekend afternoon. But while open houses are promoted as a great way of finding a buyer, a National Association of Realtors study found that their success rate is a mere 2 to 4 percent.

No matter. Holding an open house serves another important purpose—for the broker. "It gives him a database of clients," says Sean McNeill, an independent real estate broker based in New York City who says that he doesn't like open houses, preferring to match clients with appropriate buyers. "At open houses, you get all kinds of people walking in. Some are [trying] to see how much they should sell their own places for; others just want to get a look at what's out there." All are perfect pickings for a broker looking to increase his roster of buyers and sellers. "Think about it," McNeill says. "The broker is devoting a couple hours of a weekend. He won't do that unless it helps him in a big way." But it doesn't necessarily mean that a seller should forego an open house altogether—says McNeill, "It's still a real good way to showcase your house."

2 *"MY FEES ARE NEGOTIABLE."*

Brokers like to make it sound as if their fees are engraved in stone, but that's rarely the case. During the housing bubble, for example, as the number of brokers sharply increased, so did the competition for listings—one broker says he lowered his fee by a full percentage point just to give himself an edge. But even in the wake of the recent crash, you have a good chance of negotiating a better deal—that same surplus of brokers is still out there competing for even fewer listings, giving you something of a leg up.

The broker we spoke with, who asked not to be named, says that sellers should always shop around for better terms and has some suggestions for the best conditions to induce brokers to lower their fees: "If somebody's willing to commit to me for selling one place and buying another," or "If you're in a particularly desirable neighborhood with a house that will bring a lot of traffic" for an open house. And with a lot of smaller brokers, he says, "all you need to do is ask and they'll lower the commission."

3 "THINK YOU'VE HAD NO OFFERS? ACTUALLY, THERE'VE BEEN SEVERAL."

Legally, the broker you hire to sell your home is obligated to tell you about all offers that come in. In reality, some do not. Perhaps he thinks the offer is insultingly low for you, but more likely, "the broker thinks it's too low for his own purposes," says McNeill. "He wants to hold out for a bigger commission." Another possibility is that there's an outside broker (or "co-broker") circling your house, and the primary broker is waiting for one of his own clients to make an offer so he can keep the full 6 percent to himself.

"You must be clear with your broker that you want to be informed of all offers," McNeill says. "Otherwise, you may be leaving him to make decisions that you should be making." Check the listing agreement drawn up when you hire the broker; if the promise to disclose all offers isn't listed explicitly, insist that it be added.

4 "I'M NOT OBLIGATED TO KEEP MY MOUTH SHUT FOR YOU."

You spot your dream house as you're driving through a neighborhood and call the broker listed on the "for sale" sign. That's how a lot of buyers stumble on a broker—who, in turn, happily shows you other houses, asking about your needs, laughing at your jokes. It's easy to get loose-lipped and forget whom you're dealing with: someone else's agent. "Legally, brokers are obligated to provide their sellers with any information that can help them get the best prices

for their homes," says Stephen Israel, president of Buyer's Edge, a Bethesda, Md.–based company that represents homebuyers. "If you tell the broker that you're willing to pay $500,000 but want to offer $450,000, they'll pass that on to the seller. They have to."

Also, some brokerage companies encourage prospective buyers to get preapproved for loans. While that can make a buyer more attractive to a lender, it also tells a broker whether a buyer can afford a $600,000 house when he's trying to haggle on a $400,000 property. "When somebody asks for [a preapproval], find out who they're representing," says Israel, acknowledging that such details can short-circuit your negotiating leverage. "If they represent a seller—or someone in their office does—they shouldn't have it. The broker may tell you she will be impartial, but how can she be?"

The bottom line: You need to hire your own broker. "The only safe way to go about it is to have an agent who represents you," Israel says.

5 "SOMETIMES I FORGET WHOSE SIDE I'M ON."

The past 15 years have seen the proliferation of the buyer broker, agents who are supposed to work strictly in the buyer's interest, helping him get a fair price on a home as well as avoid pitfalls along the way. Unfortunately, things don't always unfold so nicely. While buyers may think they're getting a broker who isn't commission-hungry, many buyer agents are just that: They usually get about 3 percent, the same amount any broker typically earns when he gets involved with another agent's listing. "Buyer brokers are sometimes too focused on closing the sale and getting that commission," says Max Gordon, an Overland Park, Kan.–based real estate broker and attorney, so it's often in their best interest to see you pay as high a price as possible.

Even worse, some brokers who call themselves buyer advocates are actually working for companies that also represent sellers. "Brokerages offer bonuses to buyer agents if they sell an in-house listing," says Israel. A good way to get a broker who has no such conflicts of interest: The National Association of Exclusive Buyer Agents. Its website (*www.naeba.com*) can help you find a buyer agent near you who pledges to help you get the best deal possible and has no ties to sellers' agents; many even work on a fee structure rather than on commission.

6 *"I KNOW ZILCH ABOUT ZONING."*

Real estate agents love to suggest big ideas to prospective buyers—say, removing trees to enhance a view, or even squeezing a rental unit out of a roomy garage— meant to happen once the deal is done and they're out of the picture. But just because it sounds like a good idea doesn't mean it's legal.

"We had a client who bought a dilapidated house with a beautiful piece of property on a marshland," recalls New York City–based architect Mary Langan. "The broker told him that he could fix the house up however he wanted, insisting that this was a sleepy little town where nobody would care what he did." Langan says that the client built a $15,000 shed in

the backyard, took down some trees, and had some of the marshland filled in— only to have the town insist he put things back because of environmental zoning regulations. The moral of the story: Before you buy into your broker's creative thinking, check with your local zoning commission about what you can and cannot do on a given piece of property.

7 *"I WON'T LET TERMITES— OR PESKY INSPECTORS— KILL A DEAL."*

If a broker is selling a house, you figure he knows the place pretty intimately—after all, he talks a good game about the new kitchen, the big closets, the heated garage. What you need to worry about, though, are the home's features that he keeps to himself. Steve VanGrack, former chairman of the Maryland Real Estate Commission, says, "We have had cases where [brokers have] been deceptive about termites and flood damage."

You'd figure that the home inspector, who comes to check out the place before you close the sale, might notice those things. And he probably will—if he's not in cahoots with the broker. "Realtors give potential homebuyers lists of home inspectors," says S. Woody Dawson, a structural inspector and owner of Dawson Inspections in Connecticut. "Those are people who will rubber-stamp the house" in return for repeat business. As one who works outside those lists, Dawson says that he sometimes butts heads with overly controlling brokers. "One time I had a broker tell me that unless I told her the results of my inspection—which is confidential between myself and my client—she wouldn't let me get up on the roof," Dawson says. "I got out my ladder and told her that unless she was big enough to stop me, I was going up there—she wasn't big enough." For information on where to find your own home inspector, see item No. 4 in "10 Things Your Home Builder Won't Tell You," on page 94.

8 "I SOMETIMES FORGET I'M NOT A LAWYER."

Most states strictly regulate the contracts used in real estate transactions, stipulating the use of boilerplate agreements that offer little room for creativity—but some brokers can't keep their clause-adding instincts in check. "I see [brokers] pushing the envelope all the time with amendments and addenda," says Gordon, the Kansas broker and attorney. "They draft language that can have consequences without really understanding it, but they want to keep the sale going."

For example, Gordon points out, it's fairly common for "a transaction to close on one day but possession doesn't happen until a later date, in which case the buyer rents the house back to the seller for those days." Gordon also warns that issues of responsibility for the house often require more than just a couple of lines from the broker's pen—he says, for example, that if a clause is worded improperly, you, the buyer, could end up liable for damage done by your "rental tenant." Same goes for purchases of non-real estate items (such as patio furniture) and owner carryback (in which the seller provides some of the financing). "In both cases payment terms might not get spelled out

clearly," Gordon says, "and can result in one party taking advantage of the other."

Whether you're the buyer or the seller, it's probably worth the legal fees to get the offer contract reviewed by your lawyer before you sign.

9 "MY WEBSITE IS A DEAD END."

Considering that 77 percent of house hunters look on the Web, according to the National Association of Realtors, sellers might assume that using a broker with a site can help make a sale happen. But some brokers' sites are better than others, and you need to look beyond a well-designed home page to figure that out.

One common flaw: posting houses that sold long ago. While the mistake can be simple negligence, others think that it's a bait-and-switch-style ploy. "It brings people in, but it gets them upset when they find out that the property's [gone]," says Frank D'Ostilio, Jr., sales manager for Coldwell Banker in Newton, Conn. "If a broker has to advertise properties that are already sold, it tells you that he doesn't have enough inventory to keep his [roster of houses] full."

Aside from checking up on its prominently placed listings, prospective sellers should also make sure that a site is easy to navigate. And Roger Lautt, a Chicago-based broker with Re/max Exclusive Properties who has his own site, recommends using a broker who "keeps himself relatively high on the search engines." Lautt says he pays a Webmaster to make sure this happens for his site, which is linked with Realtor.com, Yahoo, and the Re/max site.

Another important feature of a good real estate site: community information. It's "one of the big things a broker should have on his site," Lautt says—schools, recreation facilities, commuting options, maps, all of which "attracts people who are thinking of moving to the community."

10 "YOU CAN PROBABLY DO THIS WITHOUT ME."

Brokers like to create a lot of mystique about selling homes, insisting that the process is complicated and best left to professionals. Not so, say homeowners who have sold their homes themselves (about 20 to 25 percent do so each year). William Supple, publisher of the sale-by-owner real estate magazine *Picket Fence Preview* and author of *How to Sell Your Own Home,* says that "properly priced

and advertised, a house sells itself." Supple adds that sellers should plant a yard sign and post online ads for the property on local sites aligned with print publications (call current advertisers to see if a site is effective).

When it comes to the negotiations between buyers and sellers, Supple thinks brokers and their commissions tend to just get in the way. "Usually, the haggling occurs over a 5 to 10 percent difference," he says. "And that is more or less the broker's cut of the sale price. You don't need him." Just be sure you price your home well. The way most self-sellers hurt themselves, Supple says, is in setting either an unreasonably high or tragically low asking price. "Hire an independent appraiser for $200," he suggests, "and he will tell you [the parameters of] what to charge."

THINGS TO DO

● **When it comes to finding a buyer,** open houses have only a 2 to 4 percent success rate. List your home online instead: Nearly a third of buyers say the Internet was their first stop for house-hunting.

● **Thanks to the dampened real estate market,** it's easier than ever to negotiate lower commission fees with a broker—it's as simple as asking.

● **Looking for an independent appraiser?** You can find one at *www.appraisal foundation.org.*

● **House-hunting yourself?** You might want to enlist the services of a buyer agent. Real estate brokers work for the sellers; having an agent on your side can help. Find one at the National Association of Exclusive Buyer Agents *(www.naeba.com).*

10 Things Your
Home Inspector
Won't Tell You

1 *"YOUR IDEA OF A HOME INSPECTION ISN'T NECESSARILY THE SAME AS MINE."*

You've found the home of your dreams. But cautious consumer that you are, you want a home inspector to take a look at it before you buy. That way, you'll be forewarned about any defects or problems, right? Not necessarily. A home inspector's job is to conduct a visual examination of the physical condition of the house and certain systems within it. The key word here is "visual." That means home inspectors don't have to remove carpets to make sure the floors aren't warped, for example, or drill into walls to check for insulation.

Sure, they'll eyeball your water system for observable leaks or plugged-up drains, but don't count on them to check the septic tank or underground pipes. "They probably won't catch everything," says a spokesperson for the American Society of Home Inspectors (ASHI), a professional organization with 6,000 members whose guidelines have been adopted as the industry standard. "They're looking for major defects—electricity that's not grounded, air-conditioning or heating systems that are operating in an unsafe manner."

Amazingly, the eyeball rule applies even to the roof. ASHI says its member inspectors must "observe" the roof, but it doesn't say they actually have to go up there. Even some veteran home inspectors think that's nuts: "To inspect a roof you need to be standing there with your eyes next to it," says Wayne Falcone, owner of Accurate Home Inspection Services in Wayne, Pa., and a former ASHI president. "You can't see anything from the ground." Falcone recommends asking an inspector how he checks the roof before ever hiring him. If he won't go up, for whatever reason, find someone else.

2 *"TRAINING? WHAT TRAINING?"*

As a rule, who do you think faces more stringent licensing requirements, manicurists or home inspectors? (Try again.) While many home inspectors have years of experience that make them experts at what they do, the only credential some can boast is an ad in the yellow pages. In fact, 18 states still have no regulations for home inspectors, and even those that do don't always require much in the way of training.

So if you can't rely on licensing credentials, what should you look for in a home inspector? "I strongly recommend that people hire an inspector with a college degree in either engineering or construction management," says Alan Fields, coauthor of *Your New House,* but finding someone with strong references and years of experience, he says, is equally important. And while ASHI accreditation is no guarantee, the group's members do have to pass two technical written exams and have 250 inspections under their belt.

3 *"I'M MORE LOYAL TO YOUR REAL ESTATE AGENT THAN I AM TO YOU."*

Christopher Eliot was all set to buy a 60-year-old house in Raleigh, N.C. The one thing holding him back: Part of the floor sagged so badly that there was a gap between it and the dividing wall. When Eliot mentioned this to his real estate agent, she quickly recommended (and even paid for) an engineer at the local home-inspection company to check it out. Not surprisingly, the engineer pooh-poohed the damage, saying it was merely a matter of jacking a structural beam into place with a crowbar, and the sale went through. Eliot soon discovered that termites had eaten away at the beam's interior, leaving only three-eighths of an inch of solid wood.

Since many prospective homebuyers are new in town, they naturally turn to their real estate agent to recommend a home inspector. Not a good idea, says Bill Sutton, owner of Bay Colony Home Inspection Consultants in Milton, Mass. Home inspectors often rely on real estate agents for referrals, so it's not hard to figure out where their allegiance lies. "As a result, they'll often sugarcoat the inspection," says Sutton. How to avoid

getting caught in the middle? Get a referral from a disinterested source: a friend, your real estate attorney, or an agent who's not involved in the sale.

4 *"OH, YOU WANT A REAL HOME INSPECTION. WELL, THAT'S GONNA COST YOU."*

The checklist for a standard home inspection, which costs around $300, may seem to cover all the basics—but watch out: Even ASHI-approved inspectors aren't required to look for problems with kitchen appliances, fire and lawn sprinkler systems, septic systems, lead paint, radon gas, smoke detectors, (noncentral) air conditioners, pests, and geological and soil conditions. These "extras" nearly always cost—you guessed it—extra.

Still, if the house you're considering isn't connected to city water and sewers, for example, it's essential to inspect the septic system. (Some states, such as Massachusetts, require it.) And depending on your location, you may also need geologic or seawall testing. "At the very least, everyone who's buying a house should do radon and pest inspections," says consultant Sutton. And for a price, of course, home inspectors are willing to comply. "As a courtesy to the clients, we'd subcontract specialized inspection techniques, including septic tanks, wind- and flood-damage potential, noise advisories, et cetera," says Sam Roberts, a former home inspector from North Augusta, S.C. "We called it 'Survey Plus.'" So what does the plus mean to your pocketbook? Add anywhere from $75 for a radon check to $2,500 for geological testing to the baseline price.

5 *"NEW HOUSE? NEW EXPERIENCE FOR ME."*

When Jim and Joan Nestor hired a home inspector to check out their newly constructed house in Lawrence Township, N.J., they thought they were really going the extra mile. What could be wrong with their brand-new home? Plenty, as it turned out. But you wouldn't know it from the home inspector, who found only a missing toilet and grading problems (meaning having to do with the level of the land) on the west side of the house. By the time January rolled around, the Nestors discovered those were the least of their troubles: They had virtually no heat in the bathrooms and other rooms on the house's periphery. It seems their entire duct system was undersized. Further investigation found missing beams, hemlock substituted for Douglas fir, and inadequate insulation. "I really didn't know anything about building a home," says Jim Nestor. "I thought I was getting some protection by bringing someone through."

Part of the problem, explains author Fields, is that many home inspectors simply have limited experience with new construction. (Of the 7.5 million homes sold in 2006, only about 1 million, or roughly 14 percent, were new.) What's more, inspecting a newly built home can be tricky. Says Fields: "You don't have the benefit of the kind of telltale evidence that long-term problems reveal."

6 *"I DON'T GUARANTEE MY WORK."*

For many prospective homebuyers, a thumbs-up from a home inspector is the last bit of reassurance they need before they sign on the dotted line. That can be a mistake. A home inspection is merely a snapshot of a house's condition at a given moment, say experts. It's not a prediction for when a system (a boiler, for instance) might fail or when a structural component might fall apart. As Bill Libby, of AAA Code Home Inspection in Arlington, Mass., explains it: "I guarantee everything I look at on the day of inspection. The following day, anything can happen."

So how can homebuyers protect themselves? "Be there during the inspection to help make sure the home inspector checks all the mechanical systems and does a thorough job," says Fields. "And if the inspector flags something, consider bringing in a specialist to take a closer look at it."

7 *"WHY WOULD I WANT TO HAVE INSURANCE?"*

When Pamela Kantor called HomeData Inspection Systems to ask about checking out the house she was thinking of buying in Old Tappan, N.J., the company sent her a brochure claiming it had professional liability insurance, along with other testing and evaluation certifications. Reassured, Kantor signed up. After the inspection, the company gave her a bare-bones report with nearly everything marked "average," so she closed on the house. It wasn't long, though, before problems began to surface: cracked and warping floors, inadequate support girders, a structurally unsafe garage. But when Kantor complained that her home-inspection report should have mentioned these problems, she got a shock: The company didn't have insurance.

Many home inspectors agree that it's important to carry general liability insurance that covers them if, say, their ladder accidentally falls through a plate-glass window. But they're hardly unanimous when it comes to errors-and-omissions insurance—E&O, for short—the malpractice or professional liability coverage for home inspectors. E&O covers home inspectors who are proved negligent in their work—if they sign off on a heating system, for example, when the house has no furnace. About 68 percent of ASHI's 6,000 members have E&O coverage, according to the society. Concedes an ASHI spokesperson: "While some see E&O as a marketing advantage, others see it as an invitation to a lawsuit."

8 "BUILDING CODES AREN'T MY JOB—OR MY PROBLEM."

It's a rare homebuyer who knows the finer points of his city's or county's building code. But, hey, that's what hiring a home inspector is for, right? Well, not quite. Just ask Elaine Arabatzis. Arabatzis hired a home inspector (one recommended by her real estate agent—see item No. 3, above) to investigate a Boca Raton, Fla., house she was about to close on. The inspector dutifully pointed out a few things that needed fixing: A drain was clogged; the air-conditioning filters needed to be cleaned. But what the inspector failed to report was that a family-room addition to the 27-year-old, three-bedroom house had been constructed improperly—with just one electrical outlet in the entire room,

short of what the code required. When Arabatzis complained, however, the company told her they hadn't been hired to inspect for code compliance. And indeed, the home-inspection report clearly states that the company is not responsible for code compliance.

Nevertheless, facing an estimated $30,000 repair to bring the addition up to code, Arabatzis felt she hadn't gotten what she paid for and sued Florida Home Inspection Services (which has since gone out of business) and the home inspector who wrote up her report. Responds Jody McFarland, the FHIS inspector, "I feel for the lady, but our report clearly stated we weren't doing code compliance. That's not our job." (Three years later the parties reached a confidential settlement.)

9 "I'VE BEEN KNOWN TO CAUSE MORE DAMAGE THAN I FIND."

David Booth, owner of Britannia Building Consultants in New Port Richey, Fla., tells the story of another Florida home inspector who turned on all the faucets in a 1920s house to check the drains, then went outside to do an exterior examination of the house. Forty-five minutes later he noticed water pouring out the front door. Rather than take responsibility for his carelessness, the inspector noted in his report that the house had a "drainage problem."

"It's inevitable that you're going to damage a house sometimes when you inspect it," Booth says. "We're checking 200 items." He notes that home inspectors are often accused of damaging woodwork, and light fixtures and window panes are particularly vulnerable. True, a thorough house checkup requires hands-on poking and prying—and a little cosmetic damage is a small price to pay for knowing what shape your dwelling is in. But a good inspector should pay for the damage he's caused—or, says Booth, at least repair it. "I figure it's both good practice and good PR," he says.

10 "DISCLOSURE LAWS MEAN NOTHING TO ME."

Thirty-four states have laws on the books that require sellers to fill out property disclosure forms, pointing out any problems their house may have at the time they put it on the market. Other states, such as Massachusetts, make it illegal for real estate agents to withhold any known structural or system problems from potential buyers. But strangely enough, home inspectors often ignore these disclosure forms when they survey a house. Indeed, two we spoke with say they consciously avoid reading them.

Why? One reason, claims Pennsylvania inspector Falcone, is that the information on the form might prejudice his judgment, causing him to look for one problem instead of keeping an open mind. In addition, he says that it's unwise to trust the sellers to disclose what they know. "I don't believe the information people say on [the forms]," Falcone says. "If they did what they were supposed to do, you wouldn't need home inspections."

THINGS TO DO

• **Home inspectors recommended** by your real estate agent don't always have your best interests at heart. Instead, ask an agent who isn't involved in the sale of your home for a recommendation.

• **Not every state requires** home inspectors to be certified. When searching for one, check for a college degree either in engineering or construction management. Or visit the American Society of Home Inspectors at *www.ashi.org*.

• **Home inspections don't take into account** the long-term prospects of the systems—like, say, your duct work—they're checking. For extra protection, ask your inspector what might cause problems down the road, then bring in a specialist.

• **Some home inspectors will avoid** reading property disclosure forms so their judgment won't be affected. That doesn't mean *you* shouldn't read them and double-check the listed problems with the inspector after he's done his job.

10 Things Your
Home Insurer
Won't Tell You

1 *"WE HAVE OUR OWN CASTE SYSTEM."*

Sam Mayer, a physician in suburban Chicago, had insured his home, car, and life with Metropolitan Life Insurance Company for 10 years without ever filing a single claim, until a damaged roof and a burglary led to two legitimate claims totaling $3,000. Mayer promptly installed a new home-security system. But instead of giving him a discount, the company dropped Mayer from its preferred coverage, citing his "claims history," and instead offered him its standard carrier at a higher rate—even though his risk profile hadn't really changed.

("Homeowners insurers may sometimes offer a change in conditions of coverage of a consumer's policy at renewal in order to continue to offer a policy to that individual whose risk profile has increased," says a MetLife spokesperson. "This often occurs when a customer files more claims than average in a short period of time.")

Indeed, almost all insurance firms slot their policies into different categories, based on a variety of factors, including your credit score and the location of your home. But even if your risk profile doesn't change in any substantial way, you might still be shifted from a company's preferred carrier to its more expensive counterpart, says Jim Davis, retired public-information director at the Texas Department of Insurance. "If you're not in the preferred carrier, ask why," urges Davis. Your agent—or even the insurance company itself—may be able to move you into a more favorable slot. Also, it's worth shopping around. A home that may be considered "high risk" for a small regional carrier could actually be deemed "preferred" by a bigger outfit such as State Farm.

2 *"ANYTHING OUT OF THE ORDINARY MAKES US REALLY NERVOUS."*

Everyone knows that if your home is near the water or in an earthquake-prone area, insurers will shun you. Regulators can't do much about that. But some insurers use illegal underwriting guidelines to "red line"—the industry term for "discriminate against"—certain groups or locations. For example, agents say they often get memos identifying undesirable ZIP codes or reminding them to stay away from couples who are having problems in their marriage. Bob Hunter, director of insurance for the Consumer Federation of America (CFA), describes his "favorite" memo from a company advising its agents: "Before writing a policy, drop by the house after work hours and see if the owner is sitting on his porch in a T-shirt and drinking beer."

If you think you've been discriminated against, raise a fuss—like the elderly woman who was purchasing a home with a companion. She was denied coverage due to "an additional nonrelative listed as the named insured," even though all other information was acceptable under company guidelines, according to the agent's report. The woman contacted an attorney as well as the American Civil Liberties Union. The response: The insurance company said it had made an error and immediately offered coverage.

3 "ONE WRONG MOVE AND WE'LL DROP YOU ..."

As insurance companies tighten their belts, they're getting to be even more particular about whom they'll cover and whom they won't. You could potentially file just one claim and get tossed out, or you may not have to file a claim at all to have your coverage terminated. And once you've been dropped, very few insurers will want to touch you. "Insurance companies are cold and hard," says independent agent Michael Grace, of Baton Rouge, La. "They believe that if you get hit once, you'll probably get hit again."

That's what Mike Martin discovered when his Labrador took a nip at an appliance repairman and his insurance company paid out a claim. When his policy came up for renewal, he was shocked to learn that he was being dropped. Martin, a Maryland financial

planner, says he spent the next couple of weeks frantically calling up insurance agents to get a new policy. But since dog bites are a red flag for insurers, he was frozen out. Alarmed by his lack of coverage, the company holding his mortgage forced Martin to join a special "insurance pool," which cost five times as much as his original policy. It wasn't until he filed a complaint with the Maryland Insurance Administration that he got his original policy reinstated.

"I've seen people being discarded by their insurers for reasons much less ominous than a dog bite," says the CFA's Bob Hunter. Some will drop you if you start an at-home business, while others will label you too risky if you've missed a credit card payment or two.

4 "... ESPECIALLY NOW THAT BIG BROTHER IS WATCHING."

Privacy? Not so easy to hang on to in the information age. When it comes to home insurance, companies now have access to their own version of a credit report that reveals all sorts of information about you, sometimes even including past behavioral patterns. The most pervasive source of information is called the C.L.U.E.® report, short for Comprehensive Loss Underwriting Exchange, which enables insurers to check the claim history of both the homeowner and the property being purchased in order to assess the risk of loss.

Insurers contend that they need such services to weed out dishonest customers who attempt to hide their claims history. But the problem is, even when you have had legitimate claims in the past, you're guilty until proven innocent, says Linda Ruthardt, former commissioner of insurance for Massachusetts. Once a person has been branded a high-risk applicant and rejected by one insurer, others are not likely to provide coverage.

5 "WE'RE MORE SECRETIVE THAN THE CIA."

Here's a little test: Call your insurer and ask how many claims it would take for the company to drop you or deem you "risky." Chances are you won't get much of an answer—even if your insurer has written guidelines, it's under no obligation to share them with you. And when an insurer doesn't have written guidelines, its decisions can border on the arbitrary. "It could take some middle manager glancing at the company's loss records to decide that the cutoff should be lowered from three claims to two claims," says Ron Sundermann, an independent agent in Cedar Rapids, Iowa. And agents won't get a bulletin to notify them of the change, so they have no way of advising a client on whether to swallow the cost of a $1,000 roof damage or pass it along to the insurance company and be penalized for it.

Sundermann learned the hard way: Over three years, a customer with a stellar record filed four small, perfectly legitimate claims totaling less than $5,000 and was dropped by his insurance company. When Sundermann pleaded his customer's case, he was reminded that it was the frequency of his customer's losses, not the severity, that made all the difference. The lesson? Filing one big claim may well land you in less trouble than four small ones—all the more reason to get a large deductible and pay for the smaller claims out of your own pocket.

6 "YOU'RE PAYING TOO MUCH FOR YOUR POLICY."

When it comes to your home, the last thing you want is to be underinsured. But could you actually be overinsured? It happens a lot, regulators contend. And when it does, it's often the mortgage lender's fault. For instance, a bank may require that your insurance cover almost the entire value of your home, including the land—which doesn't make a lot of sense, because land doesn't burn down—when what you really want to cover is just the house.

If you think your rates are higher than they should be, ask your insurance agent to come out and assess the home and try to come up with a more reasonable number.

If you're like most homeowners, your policy's rate gets raised every so often to account for inflation. But read the numbers carefully: Your rates may be quite a bit higher than the actual inflated value of your home. Insurers also inspect homes every so often to check on any additions. But that doesn't mean they get the last word—Jim Davis's insurer jacked his premium way up after inspecting his house. But by challenging the inspector, Davis brought down the home's valuation by several thousand dollars. "They were factoring in an uncovered porch area," scoffs the retired Texas insurance official. "That's an open space, not an area that would need replacing." If you think your rates are higher than they should be, ask your insurance agent to come out and assess the home and try to come up with a more reasonable number, says the CFA's Bob Hunter. Also, if you know the square footage of the house, speak with a builder and ask what it would cost to rebuild a home like yours—that's the amount that should be used to determine your insurance premiums.

7 "YOU'RE PROBABLY COVERED FOR A LOT LESS THAN YOU THINK."

Rick and Anne Morrissey of Indian Hills, Colo., were sitting quietly in their living room one day when they heard a tremendous crash in the backyard. Rushing outside, Anne was shocked to see that two giant elk had come along and demolished their children's swing set. They were even more shocked when their Allstate adjuster called—damage by animals isn't covered by most insurance, and it's only one of the many surprises you might discover in the fine print on your policy.

That's also why after Hurricane Katrina even homeowners with flood insurance found that none of the personal belongings they'd lost in the storm were covered. Thomas Martin, the founder of national advocacy group America's

Watchdog, lost $300,000 in personal belongings when a nearby levee broke and everything on the first floor of his home—including jewelry, computers, and flat-screen TVs—was destroyed by "a toxic soup of sewage and oils." Had he known to take out the Federal Emergency Management Agency's supplemental contents coverage in addition to his flood policy, Martin says some of his destroyed valuables would have been covered.

Among the most commonly misunderstood parts of any policy are the ways it handles missing objects, says David Thompson, an independent agent in Vero Beach, Fla. If you drop a piece of jewelry down the drain, for example, it's generally not covered, but if you leave it by the sink in a public place and it's not there when you return, most policies will treat this as a theft and reimburse you for the loss.

8 "WE LIKE SOME OF OUR AGENTS—AND THEIR CUSTOMERS—BETTER THAN OTHERS."

Insurance companies will tell you that any authorized agent is a good agent. But in truth, they play favorites—giving preferential treatment to those who generate the most business, have customers with the fewest claims, or both. And they offer them elite status: State Farm, for instance, includes its preferred agents in the President's Club.

Why should you care? Because buying through one of these favored agents can pay big dividends to consumers. The chosen few tend to have increased flexibility on pricing and, more important, greater leeway on underwriting guidelines. For instance, American International Group (AIG) used to insure boats that travel only up to 50 miles per hour. But when Baton Rouge, La., star agent Michael Grace took on a client with a speedboat, he managed to convince the firm to underwrite it.

The special treatment applies to claims as well. Says Sean Mooney, chief economist at Guy Carpenter & Co., a global firm that advises insurance companies about risk: "When a claims situation comes up, [a preferred agent means] you have a friend in your court." Other advantages preferred agents enjoy: They may have an easier time retaining someone who has had claims and would otherwise be canceled, and they can often get their clients moved from a company's standard carrier to its preferred one.

9 "WE'RE BIASED AGAINST OLDER HOMES."

You have your eyes set on a beautiful period home built in the 1940s, with original slate roofs and fluted ceilings that looks like something out of *Architectural Digest*. Sounds lovely—now try getting insurance. Insurers are increasingly clamping down on "mature" homes, even when they're only 30 or 40 years old. "In Texas, a 1953 house is considered ancient," says Yvonne Darrah of Austin, Tex., who called at least 10 insurance companies before she could find one that would insure her 32-year-old home at a reasonable rate. "We were desperate," she says.

Even if you do get insurance for your older home, you may not get the best kind. Some companies won't sell "guaranteed replacement cost" policies—coverage that will pay whatever it takes to restore your home exactly as it was—in neighborhoods where property values are declining or where the property is old. You could end up with coverage that's limited to only a few risks. Or you might be offered "cash value" coverage—these policies will only cover the cost of replacing what's damaged, minus depreciation. "If you had a kitchen that was built 20 years ago and it's destroyed, the cash value is no help," says Mary Griffin, former insurance counsel at Consumers Union.

10 "YOU NEED TO CHECK UP ON US—AND IT'S EASY."

Insurers may not be the most forthcoming companies in the world, but thankfully, you can find out a lot about them. Your first stop ought to be your local library, where you'll find ratings reports from agencies such as A. M. Best, Moody's, and Standard & Poor's.

You might be surprised at what you can get from your state's insurance department as well. Texas and Missouri, for example, have websites with information on the latest rates in different areas and tips on how to file a complaint. If nothing else, a phone call to the state will let you know what other consumers think of your insurance company. "We can't recommend agents or companies, but we can certainly tell you the number of complaints filed this year," says a spokesperson for the Nevada Insurance Commissioners Office.

THINGS TO DO

● **Before signing on with an insurer,** contact your state's insurance department to check for any complaints your prospective provider has received.

● **Big-name insurers** like State Farm and MetLife might be more apt to give you preferred coverage than their smaller counterparts. Shop around before committing.

● **Be sure to keep updated photos** and/or video footage of your possessions. It will help itemize and verify your losses in the case of theft or fire.

● **Rates are often raised for inflation,** but make sure you're not suddenly paying more for, say, a recent addition like a patio that doesn't require insurance.

10 Things Your
Moving Company
Won't Tell You

1 *"WE'LL HIJACK YOUR STUFF."*

The moving industry packs in nearly 55 percent of its business during the summer months, but often leaves a trail of frustrated consumers in its wake. The Department of Transportation receives up to 4,000 household moving complaints annually, mostly about loss and damage, poor service, or overcharging. The Council of Better Business Bureaus, meanwhile, reports that complaints about movers jumped from nearly 3,800 in 1997 to more than 9,200 in 2007.

Just ask Spyro Malaspinas, a victim of a botched move. He says that Nation Van Lines, which he hired to move his belongings from Austin, Tex., to Chicago in January 2003, hiked his bill from an estimate of $1,050 to nearly $4,300. The movers, according to Malaspinas, said his goods measured 500 cubic feet more than anticipated. When Malaspinas threatened to call the police, the drivers made off with his possessions, which he estimates were worth $47,000. Despite an FBI investigation and the March arrest of Nation owner Eli Peretz by the FBI for alleged crimes with another moving company, Malaspinas wasn't thrilled with the final results: He only got back around $25,000—and never saw his belongings

again. The experience was "paralyzing," he says. "It's not like somebody stealing your wallet; they have stolen everything you've got." (Peretz's lawyer did not return our calls; Nation Van Lines has since gone out of business.)

2 *"WE'RE POPULAR, ESPECIALLY WITH THE FBI."*

Eli Peretz wasn't the only mover rounded up by the FBI in March 2003. The feds indicted a total of 16 moving companies and 74 operators, owners, and employees on various charges following a two-year investigation called Operation Stow Biz. "It is the most significant crackdown that we've done," says a spokesperson for the FBI's Miami division, whose undercover agents posed as potential customers to trap movers committing fraud, money laundering, and other acts. Among those indicted were 20 officers and employees of Sunrise, Fla.–based Advanced Moving Systems. The charges in the 60-count indictment include fraud, extortion, false documentation, and "inflating the price of the move and, thereafter, withholding delivery of . . . goods until [customers] paid the inflated price."

Too bad Patrick and Tammy Runion didn't get advance word of Advanced's alleged practices. The couple booked the company for their move from Toledo, Ohio, to Lake Forest, Calif. Patrick says that Advanced movers locked their stuff in storage in Chicago when he refused to pay an additional $500 because the load's weight had been miscalculated by a driver. "We were so stressed and frustrated" by the ordeal, says Patrick, who eventually paid $1,000 to find the storage space. Attempts to contact Advanced officials were unsuccessful, and the company has since gone out of business. According to the FBI, 10 of the indicted employees are listed as fugitives; the other 10 have pleaded not guilty to charges as of press time.

3 "DON'T MESS WITH US; WE'RE VIRTUALLY UNTOUCHABLE."

While the FBI sting did manage to take some bad guys out of play, Robert Julian, bureau chief for the Economic Crimes Division in Ft. Lauderdale, Fla., doesn't think "consumers should breathe easy." Scammers are tough to stop. Local police hesitate to get involved in moving disputes because they're considered civil matters, and while the FBI will investigate complaints involving interstate moves, getting property back is not its priority.

There are also federal laws to contend with that, historically speaking, have tended to protect moving companies more than consumers. It used to be, for example, that while dissatisfied customers could sue their moving company for goods lost in a move, they stood very little chance of recovering even their basic monetary value, let alone winning any punitive damages on top of that amount. But the advent of the Safe, Accountable, Flexible, Efficient Transportation Equity Act in 2005 has given consumers and the federal government more authority in going after scofflaw movers; it "has helped the agency greatly in curbing abuses" in the industry, according to a spokesperson for the Federal Motor Carrier Safety Administration (FMCSA). Today movers are being held liable in a way they never were before for at least replacing the value of lost items—so long as the customer opted for full-value protection for their belongings in the initial moving contract. For more information, visit the FMCSA's website at *www.protectyourmove.gov.*

4 "SOMEONE WILL DELIVER YOUR STUFF—IT JUST MIGHT NOT BE US."

In June 2002, Carole and Doug Stowers contracted with Elite Van Lines to transport the contents of their three-bedroom house from Palm City, Fla., to Bailey, Colo. Nothing unusual there, right? Guess again. Elite then subcontracted the job to other companies for the cross-country trip. The Stowers were shocked when Majesty Moving & Storage pulled up to their new home with only half their possessions and didn't know what had happened to the rest—after all, they hadn't loaded the goods.

Beware: In the hectic summer months, a mover might get so busy that it asks another company to help out with a job. That's fine, but the consumer should be notified in advance of the deal. A spokesperson for the American Moving and Storage Association says, "For a completely different company to show up at your house with no prior arrangements, that is totally unacceptable." No need to tell Carole Stowers that. She shelled out $5,375 to Elite—the original estimate was $1,700—to get all her possessions back. "We almost went bankrupt trying to save our furniture," she says. (Both Majesty and Elite have since gone out of business.)

5 "HOW MUCH EXPERIENCE DO OUR MOVERS HAVE? AT LEAST A DAY OR TWO."

Even if one company does handle your entire move, don't assume that the movers who show up are actual employees of that company. Moving companies have been known to hire day laborers plucked off the streets on moving day. Peter Drymalski, investigator for the Montgomery County Division of Consumer Affairs in Maryland, says for smaller movers, "That's probably the rule rather than the exception, because they often don't have regular crews." The problem is that inexperienced workers are more likely to damage possessions.

Similarly, many moving companies contract with independent truck drivers—a concern if the mover arrives in an unmarked rental truck. That's a red flag, indicative of a fly-by-night operator with limited fixed assets—who would be difficult to go after in court. Swing by the company's offices before you choose a mover. If the company doesn't appear to have its own trucks, do yourself a favor: Cancel the job.

6 "OUR PRICING POLICIES ARE WACKO."

Moving can test even the most time-conscious planner. For instance, it may be tempting to bypass getting an in-house and written estimate from a mover, opting instead to save a few minutes with a telephone or online estimate. But if you take the shortcut, be prepared to get burned. Tim Walker thought he'd caught a break when he booked a mover online who gave him a lowball quote of $1,800 for a Virginia to Nevada move. But once his goods were on the truck and measured in cubic feet, Walker says, the price was jacked up to $5,012. He could pay only the original amount, so the movers held his belongings until he ponied up the cash six weeks later.

With an in-house estimate, you're likely to get a more precise idea of the cost. But you also need to consider how the mover is reaching that estimate—is it by total weight or by cubic feet? Go the weight-based route, if possible. That will at least entitle you to witness all weighings. Also, it's pretty easy to check your bill to see if you've been overcharged. Simply divide the total weight by the number of items. If the average amount per item is more than 35 to 45 pounds, there's cause for suspicion. The trouble with cubic-foot pricing is that actual charges could depend on how the mover packed your items.

7 "EXTRA FEES AND CHARGES? YOU CAN COUNT ON IT."

Understand this: There are many ways for movers to squeeze extra dollars from customers. Besides charges for accessorial services, movers have been known to levy exorbitant fees for such things as packing supplies. Sound petty? Sure, but they can add up. According to the American Moving and Storage Association (AMSAS), you can knock off some of these costs by packing your own nonbreakables, but movers may be reluctant to take responsibility for items they didn't pack.

There are also charges related to the specific circumstances of a move. You might get dinged for a "long carry," when the distance the movers have to haul your belongings from their truck to your door exceeds a certain limit; this is often applied in cities, where movers can't always secure parking directly in front of a residence, for example. Then there's the "flight charge" for having to lug goods up and down stairs in the absence of elevators.

"You just have to make sure you know all of these costs up front so you're not surprised at the end," says a spokesperson for the National Endowment for Financial Education, a nonprofit dedicated to promoting financial security and education. "If you start to incur these separate charges that weren't estimated before, you're going to have sticker shock."

8 "WE'VE NEVER MET A SCHEDULE WE DIDN'T IGNORE."

Thinking of moving during the last 10 days of June, July, or August? Think again. Those are the busiest moving days of the year. Still, moving companies will often overbook just to keep you from taking your business elsewhere. Consider what happened to Jenna Callahan. She was scheduled to move from Boston to West Chester, Pa., in July, but the movers never showed up. "I lost a lot of time and sanity," she says.

But it doesn't only happen at peak times. In January 2002, Tyrone Kelley was set to move from Stoughton, Mass., to Las Vegas, but the movers didn't arrive until 6 P.M., seven hours late. Says Kelley, "It's a common tactic to arrive after business hours so that it's too late for you to find another moving company." He wishes he had, because U.S. Movers charged him more than double the estimate due to allegedly wrong weight calculations. They also locked his stuff in storage when he didn't have cash to pay for the job. It took three months to persuade the local police to serve a search warrant on the storage facility so he could reclaim his stuff. U.S. Movers' executive vice president, Tom Timen, denied the weight was false, saying Kelley had more than twice the number of items listed on the estimate. "All we asked was to be paid for the services he agreed to," Timen said in 2003. U.S. Movers has since gone out of business.

9 "SURPRISE! OUR INSURANCE ISN'T WORTH MUCH."

Remember Carole Stowers? When she and her husband finally got their belongings back from Elite Van Lines, much of her furniture was battered and broken. The insurance adjuster from Crawford & Co. estimated $13,642 worth of damage. But little good that did—she was entitled to just over $2,000 recompense. The reason? A mover's liability coverage, known as "valuation," doesn't work like a typical insurance policy. For interstate moves, standard valuation limits the carrier's liability to no more than 60 cents per pound, and it's often less for in-state moves. So if your 50-pound plasma screen TV gets smashed, you'll collect just $30.

The AMSA estimates that one in five moves involves a claim for damage. That said, you're better off getting some real protection—say, through a rider on your homeowner's insurance. At the end of the move, look over your possessions carefully before signing a receipt. If you sign and later discover a huge dent in your Chippendale dresser, the mover will point to the receipt as proof that the dresser was fine when he dropped it off.

10 *"WE CHANGE ADDRESSES AS OFTEN AS OUR CUSTOMERS DO."*

James Balderrama called the Federal Motor Carrier Safety Administration (FMCSA) in June 2001 to register a complaint about his belongings being seized by a mover. Good idea. Too bad he didn't get a return call until 10 months later. The agency, a Department of Transportation division that oversees safety, licensing, and regulation of trucks and buses, has only eight full-time investigators to police roughly 4,000 companies.

With so little manpower, the FMCSA lacks the muscle to rein in rogue movers. The agency fined 117 carriers in 2007 at an average amount of $13,000 per carrier—chump change for an industry that brings in $10 billion annually. And companies that do get censured often remain defiant. "Typically, they will not pay the fine; instead, they close down and reopen under a different name," says an FMCSA spokesperson. Until regulators toughen up, take the FMCSA's advice: "Educate yourself before you hire a mover. Once you hire one, most of the time it's too late for us to do anything to help."

THINGS TO DO

● **Get at least three written,** in-home estimates—show the carrier everything that will be transported, including items in the basement, attic, and sheds. Pass on any carrier willing to provide an estimate over the phone or the Internet.

● **Avoid a large down payment**—anything over $100. If a carrier asks for that much or more, you have reason to be suspicious.

● **If you're moving from one state** to another, you have certain federally protected rights, such as the option to request guaranteed pickup and delivery dates. For more information, visit *www .protectyourmove.gov.*

● **How much should you expect** to pay over the original, nonbinding estimate? No more than an additional 10 percent. In fact, any more than that is illegal.

● **Experts say you can expect** to save anywhere from 5 to 15 percent if you move in the off-peak months—typically October through April, when kids are in school.

10 Things Your
Interior Designer
Won't Tell You

1 *"MY QUALIFICATIONS?*
MY GOOD TASTE, NATURALLY."

Remember the days when you could very well expect to find a real treasure, say, a $20 Eames chair, at a garage sale? That was before the home-improvement craze of the past decade. Now everybody and his mother fancies themselves an interior designer—sometimes literally. The fact is, there are scant regulations defining what constitutes an interior designer or decorator. In most states, anyone with a flair for picking curtains can start charging for their efforts; in only 26 states are there rules about the exams, education, and professional experience a person must complete before legally calling himself or herself a licensed, registered, or certified interior designer.

Of course, you may not care about such credentials if all you want is to hire the same person who made your neighbor's living room look fabulous. Advanced training, however, covers materials, safety, and code issues that can have a major impact on your home. Hiring someone who doesn't have that knowledge "can result in anything from material that allows slip-and-falls in bathrooms to kitchen appliances that are beyond the house's electrical load and can cause a fire," says Bruce Goff, a Reno, Nev.–based interior designer with the firm Domus. So do your homework. First, see what your state requires by checking out the International Interior Design Association's website, at *www.iida.org/custom/legislation/statelg.cfm*. Then visit the American Society of Interior Designers' referral site, at *www.interiors.org*, for a list of qualified designers in your area.

2 *"I'LL DECORATE IN MY STYLE,*
NOT YOURS."

Christine and Dan Cleary, of Shorewood, Minn., thought they did everything right when they hired an interior designer. They talked to him about their needs, budget, and style preferences—his were contemporary, hers a bit more traditional. But neither of their tastes was reflected in the proposal, which had a distinctly trendy bent. "I told him I wanted drapes; he came back with blinds. I told him we wanted a Persian rug; he showed us a very plain rug," Christine Cleary says. "What it came down to was that he wanted to sell us the furniture in [the firm's] showroom. He wasn't going to go to other stores to find furniture to match our taste." The Clearys severed ties with the designer and were reimbursed all but $250 of the $1,000 retainer they'd paid.

Indeed, "Designers have the reputation for doing their own style over and over," says Beth Whitlinger, an interior designer in Rancho Santa Margarita, Calif. Or they may stick too close to what's "hot." If you want to keep your decorating options open, when hiring, look for a portfolio that shows a variety of styles. "Specializing in one thing means they don't know how to do anything else," Whitlinger warns. And you'll have better luck with a designer with whom you have a good rapport—one reason to set up an early face-to-face meeting to compare opinions on, say, pictures of rooms you've clipped from magazines.

3 "I'LL REDESIGN YOUR BUDGET ALONG WITH YOUR ROOMS."

Unless you're careful, an interior designer may treat your budget like a swatch of discarded fabric. "Designers assume that budgets don't include things like their fees and taxes," Whitlinger says, adding that they likely regard that number as the amount they can spend on furnishings and finishes alone. That's why you should explicitly tell your designer that the amount you're willing to spend includes everything: furniture, fees, sales tax, delivery, installation, the works. "Have the designer give you a proposal with everything itemized before anything is started," Whitlinger says. "That way you get a breakdown of how every penny is going to be spent."

Leslie Curtis, owner of Leslie Curtis Antiques & Design in Cape Cod and Los Angeles, adds another tip: Collect a folder of looks you like—fabric swatches, photo spreads from decor magazines, paint colors—and show it to your designer before you get started. He should be able to tell you the price range you're looking at, given certain brands, or suggest looking for cheaper alternatives.

4 "YOU HAVE NO IDEA HOW MUCH THAT SOFA REALLY COSTS."

When you pick out new furniture with a designer, chances are that she will order it from a trade showroom at a discounted, "to the trade" price—in between wholesale and retail—then add the markup for her time and service. Some designers have been known to charge up to 100 percent commissions over that base price, says Elizabeth Franklin, creator of The Franklin Report, which lists and rates designers in select areas, including New York City, Connecticut, Los Angeles, Southeast Florida, and Chicago (see *www.franklinreport.com*). But you might not know you're being charged that much, since bills often bare just one lump price.

While most designers charge commissions of between 33 and 50

Collect a folder of looks you like—fabric swatches, photo spreads from decor magazines, paint colors—and show it to your designer before you get started.

percent, Franklin says, "Ask your decorator where he or she falls." If you shop with your interior designer, be sure to ask what pieces in the showroom cost, says Celeste Cooper, design consultant for The Orpin Group, a residential and commercial interior design firm in North Easton, Mass. Anyone not willing to quote you net, or to-the-trade, price "is not a professional," Cooper says.

5 "MY HOURLY RATE WILL MAKE YOU SEE RED."

When Catherine Lynn needed her San Francisco home redecorated, she used the same California-based design firm that had handled her home in Kona, Hawaii, four years earlier. Much to her shock, the prices had skyrocketed. The firm's billing practice had changed, from a flat fee plus 30 percent product commission to an hourly rate plus commission. The result, she says, was a bill for $48,000 more in fees than she'd paid for the first, similar-size project. While Lynn admits that the hourly rates were described in the contract, "It never occurred to me that I would be paying $75 an hour for office assistants to place my orders, check orders, and send mail."

A better way to go is to ask for a fixed fee. To calculate a fair price, consider that a room typically takes about 20 hours of designer work to complete, and hourly rates can range anywhere from $75 to as high as $225. "A fixed design fee is a better deal for clients," says Deborah Wiener, of the Silver Spring, Md., firm Designing Solutions. "If I'm paid by the hour, I don't have as much incentive to get it right [the first time]."

6 "SHOP AT THE RIGHT STORES AND YOU'LL PAY LESS FOR DESIGNERS."

Just because you don't want to spend upwards of 50 grand on your living room doesn't mean you can't hire an interior designer. National retail chains such as Bloomingdale's, Ethan Allen, and Robb & Stucky, along with some independent furniture stores, offer the services of trained designers at excellent rates. At Ethan Allen, for example, design service is free with a purchase—whether you spend $100 or $10,000. Meanwhile, over at Bloomingdale's what's offered and how much it costs (generally $750 to $2,500) varies by location, as does minimum purchase ($10,000 in White Plains, N.Y., versus $25,000 in Manhattan, for example). The designer will also help order nonstore products such as tile and curtains.

Sounds great, but before you sign on, make sure your in-store designer has membership in a trade organization such as ASID or IIDA to ensure that you're working with a trained pro and not simply a glorified salesperson. Just like any hire, ask the designer for referrals, and get fee and purchase requirements in writing.

7 "USING MY CONTRACTORS WILL COST YOU."

When it's time to lay new tile or paint your kitchen, your designer will likely recommend his "preferred" contractors—folks whom he trusts to do the job. But taking these referrals can often be more costly than finding a contractor yourself, thanks to the hidden referral fees, or kickbacks, that designers often get from their preferred contractors. For instance, if a painter normally charges $500 for a job, he may charge you $550 when it comes through a designer, then pass that extra $50 back to the designer.

"We thought we would have better luck getting contractors through a designer," says Heather Wagner, of Colorado Springs, Colo., who was doing a living room makeover. Her interior designer charged a 15 percent "contractor management" fee, she says, then repeatedly booked appointments with contractors who didn't accommodate Wagner's and her husband's schedules. When the Wagners dumped the designer and called the same tile and woodworking contractors themselves, they ended up saving $1,200.

Hidden referral fees are against ASID's ethics code, so ask your designer up front about his policy. Plus, to see where a preferred contractor's prices fall, "Call three different [contractors] and get quotes," advises Michelle Byers, an interior designer in Rockford, Minn.

8 "DON'T RUSH ME—OR I'LL HAVE TO CHARGE YOU."

If you want your dining room redecorated in time for the holidays and it's already October, designers have two words for you: good luck. Not surprisingly, the preholiday season is a busy time for the industry, but so is spring, as clients anticipate summer visitors. That means interior designers don't have as much time for your project, and compounding the problem, furniture delivery anytime tends to be "excruciatingly slow"—up to nine months, says Celeste Cooper. "Most

designers prefer not to be up front about it because they're afraid you won't end up purchasing [the pieces]."

Worse, even if a designer can do your job at what he considers a quicker than normal pace, it won't come cheap. Rush fees, FedEx packages—all such costs are passed on to a client. "I don't think designers are always good about saying, 'I can do it, but you'll wind up paying another 30 percent,'" says interior designer Deborah Wiener. So before the project begins, ask whether your time frame is realistic and what rush fees may be incurred. Better yet, postpone your project until winter or summer. Wiener says she has cut her rates by as much as 25 percent during slow periods in December and January: "I would gladly give a better rate to someone who says, 'You can start the day after Christmas.'"

9 "CUSTOM ORDERS MEAN YOU'RE COURTING DISASTER."

Thanks to economics and industry consolidation, there's less "standard stock" furniture on showroom floors these days. As a result, "custom" furniture is becoming more prevalent, whether it means choosing different upholstery than what's on the showroom model or, says designer Michelle Byers, "being able to say, 'I want [that sofa] 96 inches,' as opposed to 98."

Either way, custom orders can create trouble. If your shortened sofa still won't fit in your study, or if specialty-ordered chocolate chenille looks more like latte, tough luck—once the product has passed the manufacturer's inspections, it's unlikely you can return it. To avoid such problems with custom orders, interior designer Bruce Goff says he makes his clients sign off on every step of the process, from the initial sketch to samples of the finish, fabric, or yarn, which are called "strike-offs." For rugs, he recommends that clients buy a sample corner. At about $250, Goff says, "It's the cheapest insurance you can get."

10 "IF I BOTCH YOUR PROJECT, GOOD LUCK GETTING REPARATIONS."

Janet Mitchell says that a few years back she and her husband, Jeff, had to pay an extra $10,000 to get new furniture delivered to their San Juan Capistrano, Calif., home after their prepayments evaporated under their designer's

care. The Mitchells subsequently filed complaints with IIDA and the California Council for Interior Design Certification (CCIDC), and later received a letter of apology from the designer, carbon copied to the CCIDC.

Letters of apology, of course, won't get your money back. If the designer doesn't have insurance, and many don't, you may not be able to recoup your losses in court. So when you hire an interior designer (or contractors, for that matter), ask to see a certificate of insurance. Even better, have your name added to the designer's and contractor's policies as an "additional insured" so you're protected against any claims of worker's compensation or liability. That way, if someone gets hurt working on your home, you have some measure of protection.

THINGS TO DO

● **Finding an interior designer** who reflects your personal taste is key. Discuss your favorite themes and color schemes with prospective designers to get a feel for whether your style and preferences match or clash.

● **Fees can vary greatly.** Discuss the budget and a payment plan—a fixed fee is generally your best bet—and get it in writing.

● **Seek credentials from an organization** like the American Society of Interior Designers *(www.interiors.org),* not only

for reliability reasons but because these designers are more likely to adhere to safety-code and space-planning issues.

● **If you're on a budget,** steer clear of your designer's "preferred" contractors for jobs like tiling or painting, since they often come with referral fees. Finding your own contractors is often more cost-effective.

● **If it's too much** to splurge on a professional interior designer, consider retail chains like Williams-Sonoma Home, which offers design services free of charge.

10 Things Your
Landscaper
Won't Tell You

1 *"MY SPRAYS ARE REAL KILLERS, ALL RIGHT."*

Sure, you want your lawn to be as green as Yankee Stadium's outfield. But does your landscaper need to poison it in the process? Gloria Megee knows what harm grass-protecting pesticides can do. Several years ago, after a landscaper had sprayed pesticides on the yard of her Arlington, Va., housing development, Megee's bichon frise, Monique, started to nibble the grass. Seconds later the dog was vomiting; she would experience seizures throughout the night. Monique eventually became riddled with skin cancer and tumors. The cause? Megee's vet blamed it on the pesticides. "The poor dog's paws were totally raw from walking on sprayed grass," says Megee.

Indeed, research has linked pesticides to Parkinson's disease, Hodgkin's disease, and liver cancer. One of the major culprits in insecticide poisoning, diazinon—once an active ingredient in Ortho and Spectracide, among many other pesticides—was so dangerous that the Environmental Protection Agency banned it from all household and gardening products in 2004. But a spiffy lawn and long-term health are not mutually exclusive. Rather than chemicals, some landscapers now use bug-eating birds,

kelp spray, and insects that prey on vegetarian pests, the ones that harm trees and plants. Says Steven Restmeyer, a landscaper who has practiced such techniques: "When landscapers deal with pesticides, they deal with liability and health issues, and they are replacing the natural process of the soil microbes that feed the plants."

2 *"DON'T EXPECT A REFUND IF YOUR GARDEN CROAKS."*

A month ago your landscaper planted new shrubs in your front yard. They looked great—for a day. Now they're dry as a wheat field. The landscaper blames you for failing to water them enough, and you blame the landscaper for buying bush-league bushes. Who's right? It doesn't matter—the plants are dead, and don't expect your landscaper to cheerfully reimburse you.

Jeff Herman, the owner of a landscaping company in Fair Lawn, N.J., says landscapers get no money-back guarantee from the nurseries on the plants and shrubs they buy for homeowners. "They figure that the landscaper ought to know what he's doing," Herman says. Still, that doesn't mean your landscaper can't provide you with some protection.

While you'll have little chance to get a refund on such things as rose bushes (they're prone to bugs) or ground cover (ivy, for instance, which will die quickly if not watered), you should demand some kind of payback from the landscaper if it's obvious you properly cared for the plantings. "Show your landscaper the grass around the dead plant," says Hugo Davis, former president of the Kentucky Nursery and Landscape Association, a trade organization for landscapers and nursery owners. "If it's green and thriving, well, then you did all the watering you needed to do."

3 "I'M NOT QUALIFIED TO DO THE JOB, BUT THAT WON'T STOP ME."

Michael Torquato wanted to take advantage of the well behind his new home in Port Charlotte, Fla. So he hired a landscaper to build an irrigation system that would provide fresh, free H_2O, but the plan quickly sprung a leak when the landscaper ended up connecting the irrigation system to a city water pipe—a maneuver a city inspector later told Torquato was illegal. Torquato's big mistake? Hiring a landscaper to do work he wasn't licensed for. (In this case, he should have had a well-driller's license.)

Licensing regulations involving landscapers differ from state to state. Still, with jobs that result in water running underground—with the potential to flood your basement in a big and costly way—James Hsu, executive director of the New Jersey State Board of Architects, offers this rule of thumb: "Unlicensed landscapers should not do anything involving grading or drainage." And don't be swayed by reassuring words without the paper to back it up. "Some landscapers tell clients, 'Don't worry, I'm capable. I can take care of this,'" Hsu says, when "often, it's impossible to tell what they're capable of."

4 "MY BUDGET GROWS LIKE A WEED..."

How much fine print can there be in a contract with a landscaper? You'd be surprised. In ant-size lettering you'll find the kinds of clauses that can raise an annual landscaping bill by 25 percent. For instance, you may be obligated to pay maintenance and upkeep costs, such as a $300 spring-cleaning fee or extra charges for the trimming and disposing of excess growth on bushes. And these types of add-ons may be applied at the landscaper's discretion without your prior approval.

Why not include the charges up front, maybe even in the big print? "They're trying to make extra money without the [customer] being aware of it first," says Jeff Herman. He tries to avoid confusion by sending out fliers that keep his customers informed of work that needs to be done. Many competitors, he gripes, "don't even give the customer a chance to turn down the service."

5 "...BUT MEANWHILE, I'M REAPING BIG SAVINGS."

If you want a deal on bulbs, plants, and topsoil, go shopping with your landscaper. He'll know how to trim the bill. "Nurseries have a secret code for landscapers on the price tags," says one

New York–area landscaper. "There'll be 10 numbers, and I know which ones to look at to decipher the professional price, usually around 30 percent off of retail." He says he then regularly charges customers the retail price for the plants and pockets the savings.

Some landscapers are known to be even more enterprising. "Fly-by-night landscapers go out, steal plants, and then plant them in other people's yards," says Mary Ellen Burton, whose family-owned business in Frederick, Md., has been selling plants since 1929. "We had $8,000 worth of plants stolen from a model home," Burton says. "I guarantee [they're] in somebody's yard."

6 "ALL PLANTS ARE NOT CREATED EQUAL."

There are some very good reasons you hire a landscaper to keep your garden looking like Versailles: You don't have the time or the know-how to do it yourself. And crooked landscapers thrive on your ignorance. "Less-than-reputable people will do whatever they can to get by," says Hugo Davis.

One trick he says some landscapers favor: planting fast-growing bushes that are less expensive than slow-growing bushes, but will later require more care and labor from the landscaper. Also, instead of planting high-tech trees engineered to repel insects and resist diseases, they'll simply plant a cheaper, old-fashioned version—a distinction you won't notice until the tree becomes riddled with fungus.

What can you do about it? Not much, according to Davis, who admits that even

he can be tricked by look-alike plants. "It's similar to buying a car and being told that it gets 22 miles to the gallon," he says. "You won't know that for sure until you've owned the car for a while." All the more reason to choose a landscaper with a good local reputation.

7 "I DON'T ALWAYS FINISH WHAT I START."

Deborah LaBate hired a landscaper she'd found in the yellow pages to plant trees and bushes around her Florida home. Before taking the job, the landscaper wanted $1,000 up front, $1,000 when the job started, and $2,000 at the job's completion. Sounded legitimate—until she gave him the initial $2,000. "I didn't see him for a week," LaBate says. "He'd tell me it was too cold to work, that it was raining, that the ground was too wet to dig—anything to keep from working on my yard."

You might suggest that she file a suit. Bad idea. "You can't prove fraud or deceit, because these guys start the job seeming like they intend to finish," gripes Erin Mullen-Travis, licensing manager for Charlotte County, Fla.'s building construction services. "The way to protect yourself is to get job parameters in writing and parcel out the payments very carefully. If somebody asks for a 50 percent deposit, that should throw up flags." A more agreeable figure is 30 percent.

Mullen-Travis says that if you do run into a snag with a landscaper, consider going to small-claims court—"especially if money was given and no work has been done," she says. "Under any law, that is theft." Or just do what LaBate did. "I relentlessly called the landscaper—every day," she says. "Finally, he came back, and I told him, 'Finish the job, this week, or I'll become your worst nightmare.'" The threat worked. LaBate says she now has the best lawn in the neighborhood.

8 "WHAT I'M DOING WON'T NECESSARILY MAKE YOUR HOME MORE VALUABLE."

Debby Bright, a real estate broker in Gilroy, Calif., estimates that homeowners can recoup 150 percent of their landscaping costs when they sell. But there's a hitch: You need the right landscaping. Oleander bushes, for example, look great, but they're poisonous and a turnoff to botanically knowledgeable house hunters.

Bright's ideas for home enhancements include trees that block noise and shrubs that create a sense of privacy; you don't want just a large, house-exposing lawn. While Bright points out that lattices and high hedges are more appealing than brick-and-cement walls, one quaint touch to avoid is climbing ivy. "It attracts roaches and termites," Bright says. "You'll think your landscaper's ivy is very nice until you are about to sell your house, you have a termite inspection, and wind up spending $8,000 to resolve the pest problem."

9 "MY WORKERS CHUG YOUR BEER WHEN THEY SHOULD BE MOWING YOUR LAWN."

A man in Arizona claims that his landscaper stole pills from his medicine cabinet. A Tennessee woman says she left a group of landscapers home alone, then later discovered that they'd gone down to her basement to drink her beer and play eight ball on her pool table. Because the landscaping profession generally has a low barrier for entry, homeowners need to be particularly vigilant in checking references and finding out about a company's track record.

Mary Ellen Burton says be wary of so-called pickup truck landscapers. These nefarious gardeners often affix magnetic signs to their trucks as identification rather than using the more permanent painted-on logos. Their inexperience can do lasting damage. Burton says these landscapers will commit such mistakes as applying too little mulch to soil or planting a tree too deeply. She has even seen landscaped homes with Leyland cypress planted near the front door— a major foliage faux pas. "Typically, Leylands are used as a screening plant," says Burton, but if you plant one too close to the house, "in two years it will grow to be as tall as your entryway."

To avoid such foul-ups, make sure the landscaper has liability insurance—about $1 million is a reasonable amount of coverage—and vet him through the Better Business Bureau.

10 "IT'S MY FAULT THE NEIGHBORS HATE YOU."

You're relaxing on a crisp autumn afternoon, planning to do nothing more than catch the Cowboys–Giants game on TV, when suddenly, your couch time is blasted to pieces by the roar of a leaf blower. Suburbia's equivalent of Black Sabbath practicing in your basement, leaf blowers can pump out 75 decibels of rumbling, high-pitched noise.

How bad can it get? Enough to prompt the passage of a few rules and ordinances in towns where neighbors have gotten fed up with the unrelenting racket. The gentle people of Palo Alto, Calif., for instance, banned the use of gas leaf blowers in residential areas in 2005 and have set limits on the hours when electric leaf blowers can be used (9 A.M. to 5 P.M. during the week). Since then, "Leaf blowers cannot be used on Sundays or on any holidays—and that goes for electric ones and gas blowers that are only allowed in commercial areas," says a spokesperson for the Palo Alto police department.

THINGS TO DO

• **To find a good landscaper,** start by asking neighbors or friends with well-manicured lawns for a referral. Then ask prospective landscapers to see a portfolio of their work.

• **When determining a fee,** don't start out by announcing your budget. Lay out your vision for your landscaped yard first, and get an estimate in writing—your money will go further that way.

• **Communicate your lifestyle and expectations** to your landscaper as specifically as you can. Do you want a garden that looks beautiful when you're entertaining guests on the patio, for instance, or one that bears up under foot traffic from three kids and a dog?

• **Don't try to fight Mother Nature**—stick with plants that thrive naturally in your region. To that end, choose a landscaper who has a lot of experience working locally with the climate, light, and soil conditions of the area.

• **Not satisfied with the work?** Many landscaping companies will offer another visit, free of charge—if you ask for it.

10 Things Your
Cleaning Service
Won't Tell You

1 *"WE'RE AS GOOD AS OUR WORD. AND THAT'S NOT VERY GOOD."*

It used to be that hiring someone to clean your home was strictly for the superwealthy. But over the years, as more women have entered the workplace, the practice has become commonplace even among middle-class households. Bill Griffin, president of Cleaning Consultant Services, a Seattle firm, also cites more recent trends for the growth of the industry, including increased concern over microbes and infectious diseases such as avian flue. Today, there are an estimated 30,000 cleaning-service companies out there, ranging from self-employed housekeepers to nationally franchised chains. Unfortunately, there's no way of knowing what you'll get until it's too late, since anyone "with a spray bottle, rag, and business card" can call himself a housecleaner, Griffin says.

How to vet prospective services before hiring someone to clean your home? Visit the Association of Residential Cleaning Professionals' (ARCP) website at *www.arcp.us* for consumer FAQs on this burgeoning industry (click on the "Consumer Education" tab). Also, before pulling the trigger, ask for five references from customers who have used the service for at least six months.

2 *"WE'RE MORE ABOUT A QUICK CLEAN THAN A THOROUGH JOB..."*

In an effort to hit several houses in one day, many housekeepers move through homes like whirling dervishes. That can lead to inattention to detail, loss of property—or just substandard cleaning. Stephanie Warner, an information technology specialist in Atlanta, knows that well. One time, she says, a speedy housekeeper threw away a very small but brand-new GPS device for Warner's Palm organizer; the maid denied any wrongdoing. "I don't think she stole it, because I don't think she knew what it was," Warner says. Other times the maid just took extreme shortcuts, says Warner: "Some days she would [only] spray lavender around the room. That's not cleaning."

While service standards vary widely, all firms should promise a reasonably detailed checklist: That means wiping down every surface in the bathroom, for example, including scrubbing the tub, toilet, and sink, as well as cleaning the bathroom counters and mopping the floor with cleaners. Also, to ensure those standards are kept, ask for employees who have been with a company for at least six months. Because housecleaning is a transient business, staff turnover tends to be pretty high, according to Griffin.

3 *"... THAT IS, IF OUR WORKERS EVEN KNOW WHAT THEY'RE DOING."*

Since she works 60-hour weeks as public-relations director at Atlanta's Four Seasons Hotel, Marsha Middleton hired a cleaning service to reduce her hassles at home. But in one year, she says she's gone through five cleaners. One swore she could iron, Middleton says, but "when I said, 'This is what needs to be ironed,' she started shaking like a leaf." The maid admitted to her that she lied to get the job and was planning to call over her brother as soon as Middleton left.

While it may seem like an obvious prerequisite, not everyone in house-cleaning has real skills. Before you sign on with an agency, you should ask what kind of training it offers employees. At Ann Arbor, Mich.–based national chain Molly Maid, for example, new employees go through a two-week training class, then an average of four days practicing in "test" homes before they start working with clients. At the very minimum, according to Perry D. Phillips, Jr., founder of ARCP, a company should offer at least three days of intensive training to new hires, which should cover such topics as the latest equipment—microfiber mops, for example, rather than string mops—and protocol, such as what not to use on marble or wood floors.

4 *"THE FIRST TIME'S GOING TO COST YOU."*

The average price range for a service to clean a four-bedroom, three-bath home every two weeks is $80 to $170, according to industry experts. However, if you've never used a service before, an agency may insist on an initial "deep-clean" of your house. That can mean wiping down the inside of a refrigerator instead of just the handle, or moving a couch to vacuum underneath it—all of which can jack up the price for the initial job by two to three times the typical fee.

For some companies, though, the initial fee is just a ploy. Such cleanings can run upwards of $300, says Griffin, if companies think that's the only time you'll be using their service. It's perfectly fine to request to skip the preliminary deep-clean and go straight to the standard service. If an agency balks at that request, Griffin says, you're better off eliminating it from your list of prospective cleaners. Plus, once you're using the service, don't shrug it off if you come home to find that a subpar job was done. The key here is to speak up fast—many agencies will revisit a home the same day but may excuse their sloppy cleaning as the dirt that's accumulated in your house over the past 24 hours.

5 *"YOU'RE LETTING A BUNCH OF STRANGERS IN YOUR HOUSE, YOU KNOW."*

Consumers typically leave their key—and their otherwise unoccupied home—in the hands of trusted housekeepers on the day of a scheduled cleaning. But there are horror stories, such as the one about a San Francisco–area woman who was stabbed to death a few years ago by a carpet cleaner. How can you feel comfortable about who's entering your home? First, make sure the agency has cross-checked a worker's documentation to verify his or her true identity. Then, at a minimum, confirm that the company runs background checks to look for felony and misdemeanor convictions for the past seven years. It also helps if an agency reviews each applicant's credit history, as well as prior employment and previous judgments against him or her.

Unfortunately, background-check services such as LexisNexis-PeopleWise aren't always available for homeowners looking to suss out a self-employed housecleaner. In that case, contact your state's attorney general to ask what kind of background checks are available in your state. Some have their own bureau of criminal identification, which can run checks for a small fee, but the subject of a check must consent first.

6 "WE'RE BONDED—FOR WHAT THAT'S WORTH."

Background checks notwithstanding, in the event that a housekeeper steals from you, you're likely to see little or no reimbursement for your loss. While most housekeeping agencies are bonded—typically enabling them to offer $50,000 in property damage or loss protection—taking advantage of that coverage is an uphill climb. "Getting bonded means absolutely nothing" for a cleaning service, says ARCP's Phillips. "It just means that [if an employee is] arrested, tried, and found guilty, then the bonding company will pay for a customer's property. But they have to go through all of that first." If no one is arrested, it's a cleaning-service employee's word against yours.

What to do, then, if something disappears and you feel certain that it was stolen? Your best bet is to file a police report immediately in order to start the process early. A good preemptive defense, beyond background checks, is to give preference to companies that use cleaning "teams," in which two to four cleaners, including one supervisor, come to your home at the same time to divide tasks. Not only does that make your cleaning more time-efficient, but also, employees are less likely to steal or be careless under a supervisor's watchful eye.

7 "SORRY, THAT DOESN'T QUITE TRANSLATE."

Linda Arroz, a Los Angeles–based image and fashion expert, likes her twice-a-week housekeeper. There's only one problem: a total lack of communication. Over the past year, since Arroz hired the self-employed Spanish-speaking housekeeper, the language barrier has caused several mistakes—from assuming anything in a spray bottle was Windex to tossing a Mongolian fur jacket in the dryer and having it shrink to a quarter of its original size. "That was probably a several-hundred-dollar loss," Arroz says.

Arroz has grown to tolerate her maid's mistakes, but many homeowners wouldn't be so forgiving. Short of hiring a translator, you can request an English-speaking maid from the service you're using, but getting one may not always be easy, since the majority of workers in the housekeeping industry today are immigrants—as much as 60 percent just at Molly Maid alone. Indeed, it's another good reason to use companies that clean in teams, where at least one person speaks English fluently. Another good tactic: Call the service with special requests the night before, and have supervisors relay them to its housekeepers before they arrive at your home the next day.

8 *"SURE, I'LL WORK UNDER THE TABLE—BUT YOU'RE THE ONE WHO PAYS IF WE GET CAUGHT."*

It's tempting to slash your cleaning costs by forgoing the bigger cleaning services and hiring a self-employed housekeeper. Indeed, self-employed cleaners typically charge roughly $12 to $25 an hour—pretty cheap compared with the big or franchised services.

But those cheaper fees can be deceptive. If you pay an individual $1,500 a year or more in cash wages, you're usually required to pay that person's Social Security and Medicare taxes, which will add about 15 percent to your tally; you may also need to pay state taxes or even federal unemployment taxes. Bottom line: Paying an individual $15 an hour for, say, four hours a week can amount to a yearly wage of $3,120, plus taxes upwards of $500.

Of course, the easy way out is to pay a maid in cash under the table, which many people do. But if you get caught, you'll likely owe the IRS back taxes, and if you've knowingly employed an illegal worker, you could face penalties of $2,000 or more. On the other hand, if you use a service that hires maids illegally, penalties will fall on its shoulders and not yours.

9 *"IF I GET HURT IN YOUR HOUSE, WE'LL BOTH BE IN PAIN."*

Mary Knox came home one day last summer to find an ambulance in her driveway. As it turned out, her housekeeper had fallen while jumping over the garage door opener's electronic beam and had broken her hip, requiring surgery. Fortunately for Knox, the housekeeper had Medicare, which paid for 80 percent of the surgery, and supplemental insurance picked up the rest. But you can't count on being that lucky. Homeowner's insurance policies cover some, but not all, workers who enter your home. You could tack on an umbrella policy to your existing homeowner's plan, but some don't kick in until your losses are high—say, $300,000 on a $1 million policy.

If you have a cleaner who comes regularly and doesn't work just for you, make sure to get a written agreement that states she's an independent contractor and that you are not responsible for her taxes, Social Security, or workers' compensation insurance. It's safer, however, to use a service that carries a few key forms of insurance. For starters, look for general liability, which covers damage to a home or homeowner and typically ranges from $300,000 to $2 million. Most important, though, is making sure the service has workers' compensation, which covers any injuries a worker may sustain while on your property and pays for lost wages so that an employee won't be tempted to sue you.

10 *"WE DON'T ALWAYS MAKE UP FOR OUR MISTAKES."*

Many bathroom-cleaning products contain acid, which can permanently damage certain surfaces. Especially marble, as Jeff Campbell, owner of the

Clean Team, a cleaning company in San Francisco, knows all too well. Two years ago one of his employees destroyed a customer's marble countertop when she washed it with an acid-based product. Campbell says he accepted full responsibility, paying a team of marble refinishers $5,000 for repairs.

But not every service will do the same, whether it's acid on your counter, bleach on your carpet, or a piece of broken furniture. Whereas larger companies are likely to pay for seemingly minor damage—say, broken dishes—they are often technically able to absolve themselves of responsibility for franchisees if they choose to do so.

While you can always sue a company, it's easier and cheaper to try mediation first and then arbitration. You can call on the Better Business Bureau, which handled 700 complaints against cleaning services in 2006. Initial mediation is always free, and at most local bureaus, arbitration is as well. Disputes are typically resolved within 60 days, and most are legally binding. You can find a bureau near you at *www.bbb.org*.

THINGS TO DO

● **Choose a certified cleaning service**— you can find one at *www.arcp.us* or *www.arcsi.org*—and ask for references. Also, make sure a prospective service conducts criminal background checks before hiring, then request that the same person clean your home every time.

● **Clarify your expectations** before the first visit by discussing a checklist of tasks and places within the home that you'd like to have cleaned. Cleaning services don't typically do porches, decks, or garages, for example, but it may be possible to work something out if you bring it up ahead of time.

● **Choose a provider** with a service or satisfaction guarantee. That way you'll get an additional visit, free of charge, if the service falls short.

● **Don't worry about cleaning supplies;** leave that to the pros. If you're concerned about the products being used in your home, ask to see a material safety data sheet, which spells out the chemical make-up and safety issues regarding cleaning products. If you'd prefer environmentally friendly products, seek a green cleaning service, or discuss providing your own supplies.

10 Things Your
Exterminator
Won't Tell You

1 "I'M A FAN OF GLOBAL WARMING!"

Experts agree, it's a great time to be in the pest-control business. Tighter restrictions on pesticides, changing weather patterns, and the emergence of treatment-resistant insects and regional epidemics have converged, creating a perfect storm for exterminators in many parts of the country. And it's spraying the business with cash: According to the National Pest Management Association, bug zapping has grown into a $6.7 billion industry, up 28 percent since 2000.

Two issues in particular seem to be driving growth, according to Austin Frishman, an entomologist and industry consultant. Recent temperature increases seem to allow pests to thrive in an ever-extending geographical area, Frishman says. Case in point: fire ants as far north as Virginia. Even more important, he says, are the movement and migration of people; travelers can bring new kinds of pests into the country, while population shifts have trended toward the Sun Belt states and other areas where insects thrive. The number of pest-control firms is now over 19,000, up more than 7 percent since 2000, and is expected to continue to rise. "There's a lot of business opportunity," Frishman says.

2 "BEDBUGS ARE BACK—AND I HAVE NO IDEA HOW TO TREAT THEM."

One day in the summer of 2006, Ellyn Sullivan awoke to find itchy welts all over her skin. Her doctor was mystified, but with some online research, the Brooklyn, N.Y., publishing assistant discovered to her horror that she had bedbugs. "I didn't even know they existed anymore," she says. Indeed, the fabled bloodsuckers are making a comeback. In New York City, bedbug complaints from renters more than doubled in 2006, to 4,638, and according to the National Pest Management Association, nationwide complaints rose 71 percent from 2000 to 2005.

Among household pests, bedbugs are particularly insidious. They can test your sanity—"I felt like they were all over me all the time," Sullivan says—and they're extremely difficult to get rid of. "There's nothing tougher than bedbugs," says Phil Cooper of Cooper Pest Solutions in Lawrenceville, N.J. "And very few [exterminators] know how, or are willing, to do it right." Proper treatment isn't cheap—up to $500 a room—and often requires multiple visits. But lowballing the job isn't recommended. "With sleep on the line," Cooper says, be prepared to "pay through the nose."

3 "YOU CAN'T SUE ME— MY CONTRACT'S IRONCLAD."

When Elizabeth Allen of Ponta Vedra Beach, Fla., discovered that termites had seriously damaged her house despite a lifetime guarantee from Orkin, she wanted to sue. The contract was supposed to cover repairs, but the damage was so extensive that the house had to be bulldozed. What's worse, litigation was out of the question, thanks to a clause in the contract limiting her to binding arbitration; Allen did get a cash award (which she can't disclose) but feels the process didn't favor her. "It was brutal," Allen says. "I felt I couldn't have justice." (Orkin says this litigation "is not indicative of the way Orkin does business.")

Termites are responsible for an estimated $5 billion in property loss per year, so being aware of your legal rights before signing with a pest-control firm is key. When cases do go to court, as was the case for Allen's neighbor, Collier Black, the damages can be huge: He walked away with $4.6 million. "There's a reason these companies go to such lengths to avoid lawsuits," says Pennsylvania entomologist Thomas Parker, who has consulted on nearly 550 disputes between clients and pest-control providers.

Termites are responsible for an estimated $5 billion in property loss per year, so being aware of your legal rights before signing with a pest-control firm is key.

4 "EITHER I'M NOT USING ENOUGH JUICE FOR THE JOB..."

The pesticide industry has come a long way since Rachel Carson's *Silent Spring* led to the ban on DDT in 1972, and the industry is creating new products all the time. Problem is, they aren't cheap. Thanks to strict regulation from the Environmental Protection Agency and the Department of Agriculture, it now costs roughly $100 million to develop a new pesticide, according to Frishman. And while most exterminators buy and use the right stuff for the job, some have been known to skimp once a contract's been signed. A classic example: termite pretreatment for homes under construction, says Steven Dwinell, president of the Association of Structural Pest Control Regulatory Officials. "It might cost 40 cents per square foot to treat a foundation," he says, "but the contractor offers five cents. Whoever wins that bid isn't using pure juice."

In some cases exterminators have been known to mix milk into white-colored pesticides, like that used to treat termites; in others they might use a different product than promised. The best defense is to pick a reputable service: Ask for references, and interview a few firms before hiring one.

5 "...OR ELSE I'M USING WAY TOO MUCH."

In 1996 the Trimpers of Rotterdam, N.Y., had their house treated twice for termites—only to suffer serious health problems later. "They used enough pesticide for a warehouse," says Bruce

Trimper, who blames his and his wife's ills—including two miscarriages, chronic headaches and fevers, and fatigue—on fumes that lingered in their house for a year and were so strong that friends found it unbearable to visit. The Trimpers took legal action against Terminix and received an undisclosed cash settlement: "We got some money, but now our health is wrecked forever." (Terminix wouldn't comment on the case but said it works "diligently to meet the needs of our customers and provide them with the best service and protection available.")

Pesticides are "highly dangerous poisons" that have been linked with everything from autism to memory loss, says Kaye Kilburn, a toxicologist specializing in chemical exposure. Don't rely only on an exterminator's word about their safety; do your own research. One great resource: the National Pesticide Information Center (1-800-858-7378), which answers specific questions about everything from rat poison to mosquito spraying.

6 "IF YOUR NEIGHBORS DON'T HIRE ME, TOO, THIS TREATMENT IS WORTHLESS."

Pests have no respect for property lines. Indeed, many people get infested directly from their neighbors—or vice versa. Cockroaches, fleas, rats, and even bedbugs can move from home to home with ease. Dan Suiter, an entomology professor who does community-based fieldwork, says he's measured Argentine ant trails 350 feet in length, more than enough to go from one house to another, while carpenter ants can crawl 150 feet. As a result, he

says, treating one home doesn't really solve the problem, as ants, thriving next door, will return once your "ant-proof halo" wears off.

The problem, Suiter says, is that "the whole business model of pest control is treating individual properties." Some parts of the country are experimenting with neighborhood treatment for ants, including a fire-ant-specific program in Louisiana. For those in a hurry to kill off mobile pests, it's important to talk to your neighbors—whether or not they seem to have a problem. Offer to split costs or organize a blockwide effort. "If the whole neighborhood doesn't cooperate, everyone will have the same problem," says Wayne Cowart, a Georgia-based industry consultant.

7 "WE'LL SPRAY EVEN WHEN YOU DON'T NEED IT."

Speaking of ants, more than 20 species afflict American homeowners, swarming into dwellings and, in the case of carpenter ants, burrowing through structural wood, making them the top property threat after termites. And while they can be a horrible problem, most aren't active in areas with a true winter. That doesn't seem to stop many exterminators, however, from pushing contracts for monthly year-round treatment, a level of care critics say has an upside for only one party: the exterminator. Quarterly spraying is usually more than enough— "unless you live in South Florida," says Frank Meek, technical director at Orkin.

"Good pest control is detective work, not brute force," says entomologist Parker, who advocates the "six-pack-and-a-lawn-chair method" of observational pest control. In the case of ants, they generally use a single point of entry into a house, following a chemical trail. Placing a small amount of ant-killing gel in the path of that trail, ensuring the poison is brought back to the colony, is far more effective than generalized spraying. "Most cases don't require overkill," Parker says.

8 "I'LL BUNGLE YOUR HOME INSPECTION—BUT YOU'LL PAY FOR IT."

There's nary a bank in the land that will approve a mortgage without a presale termite-damage check, making such inspections a top source of revenue for the pest-control industry. In theory, the extermination company is responsible for any preexisting, or "old," damage not caught during inspection, yet buried in their contracts is tricky language that can make it difficult to win a claim. Since such problems can take a while to become evident to a new homeowner, pest-control firms often argue the damage is "new," making it a matter of a consumer's word versus an expert's.

That pretty much sums up the experience of Carla Virga, of Yuba City, Calif., who says a Terminix inspection on her new home missed $20,000 in damage, including a gaping hole in the roof. Virga filed a claim, and Terminix sent out a manager, who agreed there was damage, Virga says, but refused responsibility and would not repair it. Virga sued (her contract didn't bind her to arbitration), but the case was thrown out for lack of evidence. "I got nothing but frustration

for something that wasn't my fault," she says. (Terminix declined to comment, saying its "guarantee ensures that if any issues arise, we will work to resolve the issues to our customer's satisfaction.") Industry consultant Cowart explains that since these inspections are for visual evidence of damage only, it's important to be present during the process. In addition, if you're the buyer, ask to pick your own inspector, and pay for it yourself, which reduces the possibility of a conflict of interest.

9 "I'M NOT ABOVE PREYING ON YOUR VULNERABILITY."

We understand: The last thing you want to think about after spotting some creature skittering across the floor is homework. But that's exactly what you should do. Spend some time online to research the critter in question so you'll be prepared when talking to exterminators. Then don't call one, call several, and have them perform an inspection, giving you a written estimate of what they plan to do and how much it'll cost.

Also, contact the local Better Business Bureau to see if there are any complaints filed against the company you prefer. And most important, says Michael Weisburger, president of the nation's largest pest-control insurer, check credentials, because the extermination industry is plagued with fly-by-night operators. "It definitely attracts some crooks," he says. Any legitimate operator will be state-certified and have proof of insurance; top-quality operators will also have an entomologist on staff and certify every field technician.

10 *"YOU REALLY DON'T NEED TO CALL ME FOR EVERY BUG YOU SEE."*

While serious, chronic infestations like bedbugs or termites demand professional help, you can often treat "nuisance" pests, including roaches, beetles, and rodents, yourself. Start by keeping your kitchen crumb-free and removing sources of water. When shopping for chemicals, eschew contact-kill sprays in favor of residual products like dusts and gels, which insects walk through or ingest, then take back to share with their pals.

For rats and mice, exterminators agree that snap- and glue-traps, placed under the sink or in the basement, are more effective and safer than highly toxic rodenticides. "It's not personal. They're just looking for food," says exterminator Cooper. "If you make conditions inhospitable, they'll look somewhere else."

THINGS TO KNOW

Here are the five most common home infestations, according to the National Pest Management Association, and how to prevent them:

1. Ants. Store food in sealed containers instead of leaving it exposed, and trim outdoor shrubs so that branches are not touching the house.

2. Termites. Remove any wood touching soil near your home, such as scrap wood under decks. Store firewood away from the house, and refrain from excessive watering of plants near the foundation of your home.

3. Cockroaches. Where possible, eliminate food and water sources inside your home—keep sinks and countertops dry, and put food away as soon as possible.

4. Mice or rats. Seal any holes in the wall that are large enough to fit a pencil through, and keep an eye out for signs of rodent droppings.

5. Spiders. Reduce humidity in damp spaces, which draws other insects that spiders view as a food source; clean and remove spiderwebs regularly.

10 Things Your
Plumber
Won't Tell You

1 *"THERE'S AN OLD PLUMBER'S ADAGE: 'AN OUNCE OF PREVENTION COULD COST ME 5K.'"*

Water is the single most common cause of household damage, according to a nationwide analysis by Safeco Insurance, a Seattle-based homeowner's insurance company. From 2002 to 2004, 30 percent of home water-damage claims resulted from appliance failure and another 62 percent from faulty plumbing systems. The biggest culprits: water heaters and washing machines. And repairs are costly. Safeco found that American households with water damage spent an average of $5,000 for each episode in that same period.

Some easy cautionary measures, however, can lessen the risk of water damage and dramatically reduce your reliance on plumbers. First, take stock. Make a checklist of your home's water-based appliances and equipment—water heaters, washing machines, sump pumps—and note any wear and tear, especially on appliance parts (washing machine hoses, for example). Water heaters have a life expectancy that is hard to predict, so check yours monthly for puddling and follow all maintenance guidelines to a T. There might not be an immediately visible problem, but tanks can rust on the inside, leading to a rupture.

2 *"I'M NOT REALLY A PLUMBER."*

Al Booker, a college administrator in Newark, N.J., decided to hire a handyman on a referral from a friend when he needed to install kitchen plumbing. "He came in and said he could do everything," Booker says. While laying pipes, Booker says, the worker damaged the kitchen floor and compromised the safety of the structure by cutting into the joists. Booker ended up hiring an experienced plumber to finish the job, paying twice.

A wide swath of the plumbing industry is made up of handymen, guys with tools and a little plumbing know-how. While some of these Mr. Fix-its are competent, many, as Booker learned, are not. The best way to minimize your risk is to hire an experienced plumber. Ideally, one who's licensed, meaning he or she has demonstrated basic competency in written and hands-on exams and, in many states, assisted on a minimum number of jobs. Licensed plumbers are required to abide by state regulations governing how the work is done and to follow local safety and building codes; they're also more likely to carry liability and workers' comp insurance. In states without licensed plumbers, your next-best bet is a licensed plumbing contractor, or at least someone who belongs to a plumbing trade organization.

You can insist that a licensed plumber or plumbing contractor be present on the job, either working or, at the very least, to supervise.

3 "MY LESS-EXPERIENCED UNDERLING WILL BE OVER IN A MINUTE."

Risa Hoag, a public-relations firm owner, says she was surprised when much of the work in a new upstairs bathroom in her Nanuet, N.Y., home was done by people other than the plumber who gave her the initial estimate. According to Hoag, that plumber, hired by Hoag's contractor, visited the home and assessed the job. But when it came time to do the work, he showed up with an apprentice—who neglected to cap a radiator line, which eventually flooded and ruined the ceiling of the kitchen below. "No one checked [the apprentice's] work, and we had to rip out a new ceiling," Hoag says.

It's common for plumbers to bring apprentices on a job; in fact, it's a required part of the licensing process for trainees. But while in many states a licensed plumber is supposed to supervise, that doesn't always happen. The best way to protect yourself is to negotiate personnel at the outset. Most plumbing companies, whether individually run or larger operations, have multiple jobs going at once, so it's common practice to send

employees or even trainees along with (or instead of) the guy whose name is on the side of the truck. But you can insist that a licensed plumber or plumbing contractor be present on the job, either working or, at the very least, to supervise.

4 "I DON'T DO CLEANUP."

Plumbers will often rip up a wall to look for the source of a leak. Some will alert you to this ahead of time; others won't. Many plumbing problems are hidden, requiring walls, tiles, and floorboards to be removed. And while a little demolition is hard to avoid, many plumbers won't repair the damage they've made, arguing that if the plumbing has been fixed their work is done. "You should always consider whether the job includes the repair of the house structure and cleanup," says Marc Edwards, a professor of civil engineering at Virginia Tech, who specializes in home-plumbing engineering.

If your plumbing job is part of a renovation, chances are your general contractor will be responsible for repairing anything that was altered for access. But to be certain, draw up a contract for any job (assuming it's not an emergency) stipulating that the plumber will provide a damage estimate.

And when possible, hire a neatnik over a chaos machine. After the disaster in their home, Risa Hoag and her husband found a new plumber whose "truck was meticulous," Hoag says. "He showed up with his own drop cloths and covered everything: rugs, hardwood floors. He kept the holes he made to a minimum, and he was immaculate."

5 *"WITH A TRUCK THIS SIZE, YOU'D THINK I'D BE WELL STOCKED. THINK AGAIN."*

The truck of a well-prepared service plumber should have enough basics to handle most common emergencies: copper tubing, faucet parts, replacement hoses, rubber washers, fittings, and standard tools. "You want to solve as many problems as you can in the one visit, so the more well-stocked you are, the better your chances," says Billy Silk, a licensed plumber and owner of Silver Spring, Md.–based Master Plumbing & Mechanical. But it's common for plumbers to reschedule an appointment because they're missing a part.

A good plumber should ask questions when you call the problem in so he'll know what to bring in the first place. If he doesn't, ask him what he'll need and whether he has it. Requirements can change dramatically if the job is more than just a service call—part of a renovation, for example, or at an older home. Then it's even more critical that the plumber be up on specific requirements or special parts needed. In some cases, a plumber may ask the client to obtain specialized fixtures or aesthetic items beforehand. "If the client knows what he wants and likes, or if a designer has gotten something before, he probably can get it faster than I can," Silk says.

6 *"THIS LOOKED SO MUCH EASIER IN THE DIAGRAM."*

Hiring a licensed plumber assures a customer of a basic level of experience. But it doesn't guarantee that he or she can handle absolutely anything that comes up.

Several years ago, a client hired Harvey Kreitenberg, a Los Angeles–based licensed plumber, to install new fixtures made by a German manufacturer. "I wasn't familiar with the products, so I asked him to give me one of each of the various fixtures to play around with," Kreitenberg says. The client agreed, and Kreitenberg spent a few days testing the fixtures before starting the job. "I admitted my ignorance, and they appreciated it," he says.

Be aware that even the best-intentioned plumber can get flummoxed; it doesn't always mean that he or she isn't qualified. Recently, there have been a number of innovations and changes in water heaters, for example, and there are many more toilet varieties than there once were, with different kinds of flushing mechanisms. If you have a special problem, or have fixtures or plumbing that are somehow out of the ordinary, say so up front. That way, the plumber will know if he needs to bring another expert to the job or needs a little extra time to brush up.

7 *"EMERGENCY? YOU'RE TENTH IN LINE."*

Robert Pedersen and his wife arrived at their summer home in East Marion, N.Y., one weekend several years ago to find a large puddle of water in front of their hot water heater. It took several weeks, numerous voice-mail messages, and a rising tide in the basement they say, before their plumber visited the house. But Pedersen, a retired pharmaceutical executive, was reluctant to call anyone else. The home, built around 1910, has intricate plumbing and piping issues, and "he knows the house really well," Pedersen says.

While an unresponsive plumber might seem like a sign of a shoddy operation, it can also be the sign of someone in demand. Because so many plumbers are mediocre, good ones tend to be consistently booked. If you find someone you like, it may be worth the wait, especially if your home is old or complicated. Tell the plumber you don't mind waiting for a house call, but you'd like your phone calls returned promptly. He may be busy, but he'll appreciate the loyalty and will want to keep your business.

8 "MOVE YOUR SINK? LET'S NOT AND SAY WE DID."

A plumber may tell you that moving certain fixtures—transferring a sink to a new spot in the bathroom, for example—can't be done. But despite a few exceptions, such as moving a toilet, which is admittedly complicated, in most cases it's doable, says Beaufort, S.C.–based architect Jane Frederick. It just requires some extra parts and a willingness to spend a little more time and money on a job.

When faced with a reluctant plumber, spend a few extra minutes asking him to explain why your wishes aren't possible; inquire about the special parts that might be required. If, for example, the reason he cites against moving a bathtub is the distance between the tub's drain and a pipe, the problem may be fixed by rerouting the piping or relocating a fixture, Frederick says. If your plumber says specialized parts are necessary, offer to find and pick them up yourself, and agree to reschedule the appointment. A demonstrated willingness on your part to

help out a plumber with a more involved task gives him the incentive to tackle the job. So will your willingness to pay a little extra for the additional steps required.

A general rule of thumb: If the room you're making changes to is on the first floor or in the basement, moving any appliance will likely be easier. First floors tend to have a crawl space underneath, offering easy access to the plumbing, and in basements pipes are often exposed, making work easier.

9 "JOB'S ALL DONE, AND YOU'RE GOOD TO GO— THEORETICALLY SPEAKING."

A few winters back, TV writer-producer James Percel wanted to convert the attic in his suburban New York home into an office. Since there were two pipes jutting up from the floorboards, he thought he'd be able to heat the room by attaching a radiator and tapping into his home's steam heating system. The owner of a plumbing company recommended by his real estate broker agreed and sent one of his employees to do the job. It was only after the rest of the room was finished that Percel says he discovered the heating system didn't work. It turns out the pipes weren't the right type for steam heat, but the plumber had never tested them to find out. "I'd just presumed he'd tested the pipes and checked for steam," Percel says. "That seems so basic that I wouldn't even think to ask."

But that's exactly what you have to do. It may seem illogical—you've hired an expert to handle the problem, right? But many plumbers assume it's the client's responsibility to double-check that existing parts work before making changes. Another lesson here: Ask who's doing the work. Percel says the plumber was not the owner of the company—the person he says he'd spoken to about the job and whom he thought he was hiring.

10 *"I COULD'VE WALKED YOU THROUGH THIS REPAIR OVER THE PHONE. BUT, HEY, THERE'S NO MONEY IN FREE ADVICE."*

Contrary to what you might think, there are many plumbing emergencies a homeowner can handle on his own— especially with a little advice from a pro. Silk, the Maryland plumber, says that a good plumber should be willing to talk through a problem with a customer on the phone. Local plumbing-supply shops, he says, can also offer guidance and tips for simple repairs such as a leaky faucet or a shower-head replacement.

John Rendahl, a sales associate at Rosen's Plumbing Express of Burien, in Washington State, says many customers visit the store solely to ask how to fix something themselves. "We'll coach our customers on how to repair a faucet or even a toilet," Rendahl says. He recalls one customer who came in wondering about a problem with a 35-year-old Kohler lowboy toilet that wouldn't stop running. Rendahl opened up a parts book, looked up the valve for that particular toilet, and, based on the problem the customer described, recommended that he replace the tank ball. The customer bought the ball and went home to make the repair himself.

THINGS TO DO

● **Angie's List** *(www.angieslist.com),* a popular home-service rating site, will point you to the best plumbers located in your area.

● **In an emergency,** you may not have time to shop around. Even so, don't compromise on the minimum credentials: membership in a local or national trade organization, and a license if your state requires one for plumbers (visit *www.hometips.com/ articles/contractor_licenseboards.html* to find out).

● **Once you've settled on a plumber** you like, consider entering into a plumbing-service agreement with him if he offers it. These agreements usually involve routine inspections, priority service during emergencies, and discounts. Another big plus: someone reliable becoming well acquainted with the plumbing in your home.

● **Prevention is key.** For information on how to keep your plumbing in good shape, ask your plumber, or go to *www.phccweb.org* and click on "Find a Contractor" for home-maintenance tips.

● **If you purchase plumbing materials** on your own for a project that your plumber will work on, be sure to consult with him about what to buy. If you have a flare for exotic fixtures, show them to your plumber before he begins work.

10 Things Your
Contractor
Won't Tell You

1 *"MY LICENSE IS LAUGHABLE."*

When you hire a general contractor to come build an addition onto your house, you probably assume you're getting someone who has spent years learning his craft, giving him the proper credentials to saw a hole in the side of your den. In reality you could be getting a madman with a toolbox who answers to no one. That's because only 27 states have any state-licensing requirements—and where regulations do exist, they vary. In California, one of the stricter states, aspiring contractors must have four years' experience, prove their financial solvency, and pass a written exam to become licensed, whereas in South Carolina, they need only two years' experience along with an exam and submission of financials. Maybe the disparity helps in part to explain why the Better Business Bureau received 1.1 million inquiries in 2006 from people seeking "reliability reports" on specific contractors—to ensure they were trustworthy enough to hire—ranking them third among industries for that request, according to the Council of BBBs.

So how should you shop for a contractor? Ask for and check references, of course. One good resource is Handyman Online (*www.handymanonline.com*), a referral service that can connect you with contractors in your area who are legitimately licensed, carry liability insurance, and have at least three references. And Tom Pendleton, owner of McLean, Va.–based consulting firm The House Inspector, offers this advice: "Close to 95 percent of home-improvement contractors go out of business or change their name within three years" due to consumer complaints or mismanagement, he says, "so you want a contractor who's been in business under the same name for more than three years."

2 *"OUR CONTRACT FAVORS ME . . ."*

When it's time to sign on the dotted line, most contractors will present you with a boilerplate agreement based on one created by the American Institute of Architects. It lays out the job's details, including its scope, materials to be used, and a payment schedule. Not surprisingly, according to Mark Levine, coauthor of *The Big Fix-Up*, a consumer guide to home remodeling, some contractors will set up a schedule that puts your payments ahead of the work. "When [a contractor] has received 50 percent of the money for

25 percent of the work, that's when he stops showing up as often," he says.

Levine suggests a plan such as paying 10 percent down, 25 percent when plumbing and electrical work are done, 25 percent after cabinets and windows are finished, and 25 percent for flooring and painting. "And don't hand him the last 15 percent on his final day," Levine says. "It's called 'retainage,' and you should keep it for 30 extra days just to make sure everything is working the way it should." In addition, if the job is big enough— say, $50,000 or more—Levine suggests investing in four hours of attorney fees to devise a contract that includes a fair payment plan, with retainage, and stipulates that disputes will be settled through arbitration (the quick and easy way to do it).

3 "... SO I CAN TAKE YOUR MONEY AND RUN."

Mark Zarrilli decided to enhance his Wall, N.J., home by putting a new cobblestone-like path around his swimming pool. It was an $11,000 job, and he paid $7,000 up front to the contractors—supposedly for materials. "They brought somebody in to do the preliminary brickwork, then played a duck-and-run game for three months," says Zarrilli. "They'd tell me the truck broke down, the wife was sick, the cement company couldn't deliver. I'll never get my money back." Zarrilli took the dispute to the Monmouth County Prosecutor's office, who charged the contractor with theft by deception. (The contractor eventually pleaded guilty.)

Mark Herr, former director of the New Jersey Division of Consumer Affairs, calls this alleged scam "spiking the job," and it's one of the worst possible outcomes when you've signed a contract that includes a front-loaded payment schedule. "By completing a little bit of the work, they can face only civil rather than criminal charges," Herr says. You might get sucked into such a scenario if your contractor tells you—like Zarrilli's did— that the up-front cash is for materials. "Typically," says Herr, "that happens because the guy needs to pay up front for goods since he has no credit, probably because he screwed up somewhere else." Your preemptive strategy: Offer to have the materials delivered to your house and to pay for them C.O.D.

4 "BARGAINS DON'T EXIST IN MY WORLD."

Before hiring a contractor, you'll probably solicit various bids. If one comes in much lower than the others, it's natural to think you've lucked out, but that's not necessarily the case, says Lisa Curtis, former director of consumer services for the Denver district attorney's office. Because of the fixed costs of materials and labor, a stunningly low bid is a red flag.

Common tactics include starting a job based on a bargain-basement price, then telling the customer that the work is more complicated (and more costly) than originally thought. Then there's the contractor who quotes a price that includes windows he knows are subquality; once the job is under way, he'll present his client with what is clearly a better window and talk him into upgrading. "Ultimately," Curtis says, "you may pay more than you would have with a reputable person who started off at a reasonably higher price."

5 "I'LL BE BACK WHEN I DAMN WELL FEEL LIKE IT."

So you found yourself a good contractor. Terrific—but here's the bad news. When contractors are busy with multiple jobs, as the best in the business inevitably are, you can pretty much expect the schedule for completing your job will go out the window. "If the contractor's got too many jobs going," says Pendleton, "the workers might only be in your house for two hours when they should have been there all day."

One way to guarantee that your job won't stretch to Wagnerian lengths, he says, is to hire a contractor with a lead person or project manager, "a working supervisor who is on the job from beginning to end." If the job drags, the contractor still has to pay that person, so it "becomes in the contractor's interest to finish the job," Pendleton says.

6 "YOUR LAST-MINUTE CHANGES ARE MY RETIREMENT FUND."

Steve Velasco, now a project manager for a Southern California civil engineering firm, once worked as a carpenter on a residential job in which the homeowner, just after the house had been fully framed, pointed to a peak in the roof and casually asked, "Wouldn't a window be nice there?" As Velasco recalls, "The architect told us to go ahead and do it, and suddenly, he had spent $10,000 of the homeowner's money." Why so much? Because making changes in the middle of construction is the most

expensive way to proceed, since work has to be undone and redone to accommodate the new plan. Indeed, Baker has described "while you're at it" as "the four most expensive words in the English language."

Architect Richard Hornberger advises that you spend time on the front end devising a plan, then commit yourself to living with it. And if you need to make a change, do it the way architects do: "Give the contractor a proposal request, in writing," he says. "Then, in writing, you get back a change order that lays out what will be done, how much it will cost, and how much additional time it will take."

7 "IF IT LOOKS GOOD, I DON'T CARE IF IT'S DONE RIGHT."

Unless you have X-ray vision or the time to spend days watching your contractors in action, all you may ever know about your job is whether it looks good in the end. Evelyn Yancoskie, director of consumer affairs for Delaware County, Pa., knows of at least one family in her area who got a new roof that, indeed, looked just fine. But the roof was lacking a key element: an ice shield, a three-foot-wide rubber lining that's crucial for a roof in this part of the country. "The contractor figures that nobody will miss it anyway," says Yancoskie. "But if you get a cold winter, any water that gets into the gutters will freeze, back up onto the roof, and go underneath the shingles. Without a shield, the ice under the shingles melts and leaks into your house."

Contractors may also cut corners by skimping on insulation, but packing it with care so that it looks filled in; leaving out plumbing lines and pumps that give you hot water fast; and using low-quality wood, but laying it beautifully so that you don't notice. "Guys will use substandard plywood, shingles, siding," says Mark Herr. "In situations where homeowners aren't likely to ask what's going on, contractors use subpar materials." Or just do a subpar job.

What can you do to prevent this sort of behavior? Check with your state's department of consumer affairs to see if, like New Jersey, it requires its contractors to be registered—meaning they're insured, must use certain approved language in contracts, agree to list specifics about materials being used, provide start and end dates for a project, and generally operate with full disclosure about their practices. "Registration [with a state board] is really key legal protection for consumers," says Jeff Lamm, a spokesperson for the New Jersey Division of Consumer Affairs. Otherwise, you should always get multiple estimates on a project, and never settle on a contractor without checking references carefully.

8 *"I DELEGATE TO NOVICES."*

Mark Herr recounts the tale of a family that wanted their kitchen redone in time for Easter. One night before the holiday, a subcontractor was sweating to install the garbage disposal. When asked why the job was giving him so much trouble, the worker replied, "When they showed me this morning at Home Depot, I thought I understood." The story points out a big problem: It's not just your contractor you have to worry about but also the subcontractors whom he hires to do

the actual work. "You need to know in advance who the subcontractors are," says Herr. "You can't let the contractor sub anything out without your permission."

Mark Levine suggests taking things a step further: Visit homes in which your contractor's carpenter has done the finishing work, and if you like what you see, get it in writing that that particular guy will be hired. "Look to see if there are tight joints in the molding, if cabinets are screwed into the walls rather than nailed, if margins between doors and frames are even all around," advises Levine. "Those are signs of a good finish carpenter, and they serve as a litmus test. A general contractor who has a real pro doing his finish carpentry is probably hiring real pros to do other stuff as well."

9 *"IF I COME KNOCKING, YOU'RE BETTER OFF NOT ANSWERING."*

Courtney Yelle was in his Bucks County, Pa., yard raking leaves when a gleaming pickup truck pulled into his driveway. Yelle says that a clean-cut workman emerged and told him it looked as if his driveway needed to be repaved—which, Yelle admits, was the case. But before he would commit, Yelle, former director of Bucks County Consumer Protection, said he'd need a written estimate along with the worker's phone number and address. The guy said he'd leave it in the mailbox, according to Yelle, then backed out of the driveway and disappeared forever.

Yelle says that the "worker" was a seasoned scam artist who approaches people's homes offering to do jobs at bargain-basement prices, often on the premise that he has leftover materials from a nearby project. In reality, if he does the job at all, he'll do shoddy work with low-grade materials, says Wendy Weinberg, former executive director of the National Association of Consumer Agency Administrators. While it sounds like common sense to be suspicious of solicitors, clearly these curbside con artists can be convincing: Lisa Curtis estimates they bilk homeowners out of $20 million per year in Colorado alone.

10 *"I'M AN ENVIRONMENTAL DISASTER."*

Say you have a contractor in your home, replacing those ugly acoustic tiles that have covered the rec room ceiling for 20 years. Early into the job he realizes that the tiles contain asbestos. If he's responsible, he'll insist that the poisonous materials be taken out by a licensed asbestos-removal contractor. This will take time and could cost you thousands of dollars; if he's less than honest, he'll ask for an extra few hundred bucks to do the job himself.

The problem with the latter solution: Even if the contractor doesn't make a mistake and release particles of cancer-causing dust into the air in or around your home, the long-term repercussions are serious and may have legal consequences—for you. Contractors who aren't licensed to deal with such materials can't dispose of them at licensed (and, thus, safe) facilities, says Ross Edward, a spokesperson for the Massachusetts Department of Environmental Protection. If hazardous materials aren't disposed of properly, they could leach into soil and ground water. And if your contractor gets caught dumping toxic materials this way, you may be liable, since the pollution came from your property. "These days," says Edward, "the homeowner has just as much responsibility for the environment as any factory owner."

THINGS TO DO

• **Before hiring a contractor,** get the names and numbers of satisfied customers who are willing to vouch for his work—and don't be afraid to ask to see what's been done in person.

• **Learn how to avoid getting scammed.** Never hire someone who shows up at your door soliciting work, and never offer to pay in full up front. For more information and tips, visit *www.ftc.gov/bcp/*

• **Inspect your contractor's work regularly.** It's much easier and faster to correct something while the work is still in progress than it is weeks or months down the road.

• **Make sure the provisions** of the contract you sign suit your needs and interests. You can find out more about contracts at *www.hometips.com/home_probsolver/ hpso2/good_contract.html.*

10 Things Your
Home-Security Firm
Won't Tell You

1 "A LITTLE HOME SECURITY GOES A LONG WAY."

It's official: We live in a society increasingly obsessed with the technology of safety. According to *Security Sales & Integration* magazine, Americans spent $17.5 billion on electronic security systems in 2000; by 2006, that amount had climbed to $25.9 billion. Yet crime in general, and burglaries in particular, have been steadily decreasing.

As comforting as it may be to have an elaborate alarm system—the average home-security package costs about $1,500 for installation and equipment, and about $25 a month to monitor—the reality is that you can deter most break-ins much more cheaply. "Criminals take the line of least resistance," says Steve Kirby, president of Edward R. Kirby & Associates, a full-service investigative agency in Elmhurst, Ill. "If they were hardworking, industrious people, they wouldn't be criminals."

Lighting works wonders. Merely keeping the boundaries of your house ("perimeters" in security lingo) well lit—perhaps with motion-sensor lights, which cost less than $100—will discourage most burglars. But since the majority of home break-ins occur during the day, when people are away at work, experts suggest a few additional precautions. Keep hedges trimmed low to minimize hiding space around the house, and make sure there's a good, strong lock installed on every door. But perhaps the best deterrent, Kirby says, is "a barking dog. Most burglars aren't going to screw with that."

2 "THE COPS CAN'T HEAR YOUR ALARM."

Think your alarm will ring right in your local police station? Forget about it. Sixty-nine percent of today's home-security alarms ring in a so-called central station, where monitors will phone your house, ask for a code word, and notify the police if you don't respond. That central station can be anything from a boiler room downtown to a concrete bunker in another state, and it may or may not be manned by your security company.

Some of the bigger firms, such as ADT Security Services, run their own central stations. But many others don't directly monitor their customers' alarms; rather, they contract the job out to third-party central stations, which are wired with alarms from companies all over the country. One of the biggest of these third-party stations, Monitronics International, in Dallas, handles more than 500,000 accounts around the clock.

Not thrilled with the idea of having your alarm ringing 2,200 miles away at a company you've never heard of? You should be concerned. For one thing, a feel for local conditions might come in handy when your life is at stake. "I have heard of some pronunciation problems from remote central stations," says Jason Knott, former editor of *Security Sales*. "Imagine someone in Poughkeepsie trying to pronounce 'La Cienega.' The LAPD's going to go, 'What the hell is that?'"

3 *"THIS SYSTEM IS MORE TROUBLE THAN IT'S WORTH."*

More and more people are buying home-security systems. But are they actually using them? Pat Upton and her husband, Bob, decided to install a system with integrated fire and temperature alarms in their summer house in Bridgehampton, N.Y., because of the insurance discount it brought them. But Upton found the installer's instructions incomprehensible. "It was just one giant run-on sentence— 'and if you want to move this you punch that.' My husband and I glazed over," she says. After a month in their new house, the Uptons still hadn't turned the thing on.

Steven Greenberger, associate dean of faculty and professor at DePaul University College of Law in Chicago, came to the conclusion that he could live alarm-free for good. Greenberger had an ADT system in his Evanston, Ill., home and paid the monthly monitoring fee; then it dawned on him that the only thing the system did was cause his brother-in-law to trigger false alarms. He now thinks

the industry is a racket. "You sign people up once, you give them nothing, and you've got this income stream forever," Greenberger says. "All you've got to do is have some Homer Simpson waiting for the alarm to go off."

4 *"THE LOCAL POLICE HATE US."*

If you have an alarm system installed in your home, one thing is certain: You will trigger false alarms. This is, of course, a nuisance in itself. But the real problem is that police departments know it. "We get several false alarms a night," says Lieutenant Pasquale Guido of the Santa Monica, Calif., police department. Most crime-prevention officers estimate that 95 to 99 percent of all alarms are false. "It's a huge, huge problem," says Norma Beaubien, former president of the False Alarm Reduction Association, which seeks to help public safety officials reduce false alarms. She adds that more than 90 percent of the 36,751 alarm calls her department received in 2006 were false alarms. The cost to the department: $1.4 million.

In some locales, the police have responded by fining homeowners for repeat false alarms. Evanston, Ill., for one, allows residents three—after the third, it's $100 a pop, and after 10, the fee rises to $300. The Santa Monica police come down even harder: After two false alarms, they'll charge you $337 for each additional response. And in Montgomery County, Md., officers will not respond at all to the homes of those who have failed to pay fines for previous false alarms.

5 "WE'LL TRY TO SELL YOU EXPENSIVE GADGETS YOU DON'T REALLY NEED."

Security experts and police generally agree that an effective home-security system contains both perimeter and interior sensing devices. Each system can each include some impressive-sounding gear. Perimeter alarms might have magnetic or plunger contacts; foiling, vibration, or shock detectors; and window screens that hold concealed alarm wire for perimeter alarms. And interior alarms might involve pressure mats, photoelectric beams that cast infrared light, heat sensors, and motion detectors. But just because all these gizmos are available doesn't mean you need every one to have a sound security system.

Pat White, a former Schaumburg, Ill., police officer, argues that once the doors have been protected and motion sensors installed in key areas like staircases and hallways leading to bedrooms, a house is pretty well set. Still, many homeowners plunk down money for glass-break alarms on their windows, for example—but if motion sensors cover the key areas of the house, White says, you're "duplicating protection." What about security cameras? Steve Kirby scoffs at the notion that any but the wealthiest homeowner would need them. "That's not something that's necessary, but there certainly are paranoid people out there," he says.

6 "OUR RENT-A-COPS ARE VERY LOW-RENT."

Many home-security firms offer some kind of guard service along with alarm monitoring. Some drive company-owned "patrol" cars, and some even carry weapons. Yet in spite of the high level of responsibility of their jobs, these guards can hardly be said to represent the cream of the labor crop. Guards have been known to loot mailboxes for credit cards and cash, and in one extreme but notable case, a guard who had recently gotten his license and job, in spite of not having worked in years, went on a shooting spree in 1998 and killed two residents at a Florida condominium.

According to the U.S. Department of Labor, the median hourly wage for a private security guard was $10 in 2006, which put it slightly below that of a janitor ($10.78). And it's a career path that often attracts applicants who, for one reason or another, could not secure better-paying work on a police force. Most states require that security guards be licensed, but in California, for example, you need only be 18 years old, have $101 for the application fee, and submit to 40 hours of training. The state does run a criminal-background check—though only to see if you have a criminal record in California—and sends your fingerprints to the FBI, where they are checked against a national database of felons.

7 "GETTING PAST OUR ALARMS IS TOUGH—UNLESS YOU HAVE A PAIR OF SCISSORS."

William Daley learned that an alarm system does not provide absolute protection—even for a well-heeled member of Chicago's first political family. Daley, the brother of Mayor Richard Daley, was cooling those heels in Washington, D.C., in January 1997, awaiting confirmation as U.S. commerce secretary, when burglars entered his house on the northwest side of Chicago and made off with fur coats and silver. Their trick: They circumvented his alarm simply by cutting some wires.

That was over 10 years ago, but the same problems that enabled the break-in remain. The standard home alarm is transmitted over a telephone line, and getting around it requires little more than the ability to figure out where the line is and the skill to handle a good pair of wire cutters. Most alarm companies now offer some sort of backup protection, which typically consists of a radio or cellular device that notifies the central station your line has been cut. But these backup systems can cost a lot more—around $500 extra—which is probably why only 19 percent of all alarmed houses in the U.S. currently have them, according to a survey by *Security Sales*.

8 "I USED TO SELL BASEBALL CARDS, BUT NOW I DO THIS."

There are somewhere between 10,000 and 11,000 alarm companies in the U.S., according to the National Burglar & Fire Alarm Association in Bethesda, Md. And though the industry is dominated by a handful of big players such as ADT, Honeywell, Brink's, and Westec, smaller companies abound. Walter Pendleton runs one of them—the Shaton Company—from his house in Cos Cob, Conn., with a staff of four. He charges $1,000 to $1,500 for installation and alarm equipment and an $18 monthly monitoring fee. The central station is situated, conveniently enough, right in his basement. Back in 1991, when Pendleton's

house burned down and thus shut down his entire operation including all alarm monitoring, he jumped into action to get things running smoothly again. "We were down for a day, but our customers knew about it immediately," he says.

But not all small operators are as on the ball as that. Since regulation is scant and varies from place to place, almost anyone can find somewhere to set up a home-security business with little oversight. Plano, Tex., for example, requires only that alarm systems be registered with the police and charges outfits a $35 yearly fee, along with a $35 registration fee. Shaker Heights, Ohio, police, on the other hand, require each company to certify by letter that it has conducted a background check on each of its employees. Sounds more like it— except that, for the most part, says Chief Walter Ugrinic, they'll take the company's word for it.

9 "WE'LL KEEP YOUR NEIGHBORS UP AT NIGHT."

Some home-security systems include a "local alarm," that is, a bell or siren that rings inside or outside your house. And though many systems combine the local alarm with a central-station linkup— meaning someone on the other end is monitoring things—with each home alarm system averaging two false alarms a year, the likelihood of irritating your neighbors runs pretty high.

Just ask Kathleen Schneider of Hudson, Fla. One summer night a storm caused a blackout in the Tampa suburb. When power returned, it triggered the alarm system of an empty house across the street. The "very loud" ringing kept up for 22 hours, Schneider says, and people three blocks away could hear the earsplitting peal. "Neighbors were calling the sheriff," Schneider says. "Nobody could do anything." A "for sale" sign stood on the house's lawn, and the windows bore stickers giving the number of a monitoring company. But when neighbors tried to call, they found that the number had been disconnected—and sheriff's deputies refused to enter the house because it showed no signs of a break-in. The siege finally ended the next afternoon, Schneider says, when two men from the neighborhood mounted an extension ladder to the alarm box and managed to silence it.

10 *"IF YOU HAVE A PET, WE MIGHT BE WORTHLESS ."*

Alarm companies often claim that Fido won't set off the system. But as recently as 2007, 23 percent of false alarms were attributed to pets, according to trade publication *Security Sales & Integration*.

Darren Lew, a cinematographer in Brooklyn, N.Y., knows this all too well. When he purchased a system from ADT for his new house, he says he was assured that the motion sensors could be adjusted to keep the movements of the family pet from triggering the alarm. Nevertheless, Lew says, his cat, Handsome, managed to set it off twice right away, and after ADT returned to his house to readjust the motion sensors, "then it was set off four times a day," he says.

"These are pet-sensitive motion detectors," says an ADT spokesperson. "They're new enough that there are still some bugs." Indeed, once ADT adjusted the sensors yet again, Lew says, they seemed at last to be working properly.

THINGS TO DO

• **As you think about ways** to secure your home, take your lifestyle into consideration. Children, pets, and the climate you live in should all influence the features of any security system you install.

• **Remember, there are ways** of securing your house without resorting to an alarm system. Motion-activated floodlights around the perimeter of a home can scare burglars away, and metal pins fixing windows shut can make it impossible to force them open.

• **Do your homework when shopping** for a company to install an alarm system. The National Burglar & Fire Alarm Association ensures that its members employ only certified technicians: You can find a list of the association's members at *www.alarm.org*.

• **Once you have a good** installation company, be sure to find an equally professional monitoring service. The Central Station Alarm Association provides a list at *www.csaaul.org*.

• **To prevent racking up fines** with false alarms, you may want to look for a monitoring company with a "two call" policy. That means when your alarm goes off, they'll call your cell phone if no one answers at your house and let you decide whether to call the police.

Your Money

■ The stock market woes of 2008—and before—have taught us many lessons. By far, one of the most important may be this: the practitioners whom we pay to help take care of our money can be an awful lot like doctors—happy to speak with authority, but less thrilled to be questioned.

This chapter addresses the ins and outs of optimum financial stewardship, offering tips and information on how best to manage your money. "10 Things Your 401(k) Provider Won't Tell You," for example, offers guidance on handling your retirement savings in an uncertain world, while "10 Things Your Charity Won't Tell You" advises you what to look out for when donating your hard-earned money. We can't hope to answer every question, but we believe we can help get your financial life on track—and keep it there.

10 Things Your
Tax Preparer
Won't Tell You

1 "A BIG NAME DOESN'T ALWAYS MEAN BETTER SERVICE."

Roughly 135 million Americans file tax returns, and of those, two thirds pay for help. While solo acts like CPAs and so-called enrolled agents have plenty of clients, almost 20 percent of taxpayers go through a big franchise like H&R Block, Jackson Hewitt, or Liberty Tax Service to get their refund—in 2007 costing an average $2,255 per return. Problem is, tax preparation and advice depend on the preparer, and in a system of franchises, that means thousands of seasonal employees and limited quality control.

The results can be dangerous. When staffers from the Government Accountability Office (GAO) went undercover to get returns done by the big chains, they found "nearly all of the returns prepared for us were incorrect to some degree," according to the report. Worse yet, recently filed lawsuits allege that the owners of 125 Jackson Hewitt franchises cost the government $70 million in tax fraud and created an environment "in which fraudulent tax-return preparation is encouraged and flourishes," according to the Department of Justice. Jackson Hewitt says it stands behind its compliance procedures as well as its nationally standardized educational curriculum.

2 "YOU WOULDN'T BELIEVE WHAT I GET AWAY WITH."

As of 2008, complaints about tax preparers, including allegations of inaccuracies and returns that weren't filed on time, were up 80 percent in five years, says the Council of Better Business Bureaus. But when it comes to the IRS policing problem preparers, "the lifeguard is asleep," complains Sen. Chuck Grassley (R-Iowa), who took the agency to task for inaction in 2007. (The IRS had no comment.) Less than 1.5 percent of returns get audited, and while that may pacify nervous taxpayers, audits are the primary way to catch bad tax pros. The GAO found that a year after it reported poor preparers by name to the IRS, the agency had failed to audit a single one.

Professional organizations, like the American Institute of Certified Public Accountants (AICPA) and the National Association of Enrolled Agents, pack even less of a wallop because they often wait for the IRS to act. Then the AICPA will strip membership and report bad accountants to the relevant state-licensing group, says Tom Ochsenschlager, the association's VP of taxation. How to find out if your CPA has been disciplined? Visit the agency's website at *www.aicpa.org/TheCPALetter*.

3 *"YOU MIGHT BE BETTER OFF WITHOUT ME."*

Maybe you're hiring a tax preparer because you've got better things to do with your weekend or numbers make you dizzy—more power to you. But if you're hiring a pro because you think he's smarter than you, think again. On average, tax preparers make more mistakes, and costlier ones, than Josie Taxpayer does. According to a study of IRS data, 56 percent of professionally prepared returns showed significant errors, compared with 47 percent of those done by the taxpayer. And audited taxpayers who used preparers owed an average of $363, while those who filed themselves owed $185.

Of course, tax preparers often see more-difficult returns, which could lead to more errors. But the bottom line? "For one W-2, mortgage interest, and a couple of kids, TurboTax is just fine," says Kerry Kerstetter, an Arkansas CPA. If, on the other hand, you're attaching a schedule for self-employment income or capital losses, consider getting help. And even then, if a return is made complicated by a one-time event—say, the birth of a child or the acquisition of a rental property—you might need only one year's worth of advice. "If nothing changes, you should be able to copy it from year to year," says Ochsenschlager.

4 *"WHAT ARE MY QUALIFICATIONS? WELL, I'M REAL GOOD AT SUDOKU."*

Every April, Sen. Grassley calls IRS officials before the Finance Committee to grill them on taxpayer protection. He's increasingly concerned about unethical, unlicensed tax preparers and what he calls "sharks in the water." "Anyone can call himself a tax preparer," Grassley laments. Many do. There's no mandatory national licensing, and Oregon and California are the only states that require tax pros to take a test. That means as many as 600,000 tax preparers are unregulated, according to the National Taxpayer Advocate, the taxpayer assistance wing of the IRS. Some may set up shop in a local real estate office, but many work for the big chains.

Translation: There's no universal standard for qualification. Licensed preparers, who are usually CPAs or enrolled agents, are tested and must meet ongoing education requirements. Unlicensed preparers do neither. In general that's fine—no harm, no foul. But in the worst-case scenario—say, a tricky audit—only a pro with a license (or a lawyer) can represent you before the IRS.

5 *"IF IT'S FEBRUARY, YOU'RE ALREADY TOO LATE."*

A savvy tax pro may be able to cut your tax bill or juice your refund. But don't expect to find one come Feb. 1. From that point through April, tax pros are generally too busy to talk to new clients. So if you don't already have a preparer lined up by the time you actually have your W-2s in hand, "you're not going to get good service," says Frank Degan, an enrolled agent in Setauket, N.Y. "In the fall, though, tax preparers will give you their full attention." That means you should be talking to tax preparers in October and November. They'll have time to answer questions, look over your old returns, and suggest changes.

Not only that, but talking to a tax pro in the fall means you still have time to plan. If you wait until you have all your W-2s, you've locked in all your income for the year. But in the fall a good preparer can help you figure out ways to manipulate your income by increasing your 401(k) contributions, deferring a bonus until the new year, or taking taxable losses. Wait until spring, and a professional can help you make small decisions, like whether to itemize or think about different deductions, says Bob Scharin, an analyst with Thomson Tax and Accounting, but you've lost most of your flexibility.

6 "YOU HIRED ME, BUT YOUR RETURN IS BEING DONE BY SOME GUY IN PEORIA."

Some accounting firms have begun outsourcing return preparation, says Rich Brody, a University of New Mexico accounting professor. That means your data might be sent out of state or to a local H&R Block, since the chain contracts with CPA firms to do returns. Either way, your accountant isn't obliged to tell you, as long as your account is being outsourced domestically. (The IRS ruled in January 2008 that tax preparers are required to tell clients if their return is being prepared outside the U.S.) "It's very scary," Brody says.

Indeed, transmitting Social Security numbers, names, addresses, birth dates, and account numbers electronically makes some people uneasy. For while the origins of identity theft are often hard to

pinpoint, says Beth Givens, director of the Privacy Rights Clearinghouse, returns contain so much "in one bright, shiny package—that's a great gift to the identity thief."

The number of outsourced returns is still small, but they're becoming increasingly common. An overseas company can process a return overnight for as little as $50, much less than a CPA's hourly rate. CCH, an organization that provides such services, estimates that 240,000 returns will have been outsourced in 2008—up 20 percent from 2007.

7 "TAXES, SHMAXES—LET ME SEE WHAT ELSE I CAN SELL YOU."

The real money in tax preparation has nothing to do with 1040 forms and W-2s. For the big-chain preparers, as well as your local accountant, the register really lights up only when they persuade you to take a loan, open a retirement account, or buy insurance. Chances are you don't need what they're selling, but the sales pitch may blur the issue. GAO staffers reported that when they visited the big-chain tax preparers, loans were described as "options" or "bank products"; on one visit a customer was asked to sign a loan application without being told what it was.

Worse, these extras can do more harm to consumers than good: More than 80 percent of those who opened an "Express IRA" at H&R Block, for example, paid more in fees than they earned in interest, according to a lawsuit filed by the New York attorney general. (H&R Block says most Express IRA accounts opened between 2001 and 2005 have yielded "positive net tax savings benefits and interest earnings," even as the company "has lost money operating this program.") CPAs, too, are in the sales game, ever since the AICPA allowed members to sell insurance products. When commissions can be $20,000, says Terry DeMuth, an insurance wholesaler in California, "it's easy to get greedy."

8 *"IF I SCREW UP, I'LL PAY UP."*

Worried about an audit? H&R Block and Jackson Hewitt are happy to ease your mind—for a price. Both offer the option of buying a souped-up guarantee that promises to cover any back taxes you owe, plus interest, fees, and penalties. Here's what they don't say: You don't need the extra protection. If it turns out you owe back taxes, the big chains' basic (read: free) guarantee already covers fines, penalties, and interest. Many CPAs and enrolled agents will do the same; they often have insurance for that very purpose. Just be sure to ask about it before one does your return.

But what about the back taxes? True, they could amount to a bigger expense than the fines and penalties, which may be why some chains can sell that extra guarantee. But H&R Block and Jackson Hewitt will cover you only up to $5,000 and exclude the most complicated returns. If you're tempted, know there may be an unintended consequence: If someone pays your taxes, the IRS considers that taxable income. In other words, if you buy the guarantee and H&R Block ends up paying your back taxes, expect to get a 1099 next January.

9 *"TAX PREPARATION IS AN ART, NOT A SCIENCE."*

A recent law tightened penalties for tax preparers who play fast and loose with the tax code, taking far-fetched positions because they know 99 percent of returns never get audited. That said, for anyone with a complicated or unusual financial life, there's still lots of wiggle room, says Kerstetter, the CPA: "It's about 10 percent black, 10 percent white, and everything else is in the middle."

Chances are good you have room to maneuver if you have income in a category the tax code treats flexibly—you're self-employed, for example, or own rental property. Ditto if you've earned big capital gains or incurred high or unusual medical expenses. In short, Kerstetter says, if you're attaching a schedule to your return, a good tax preparer will pay for himself.

Now, that may mean raising a red flag with the IRS, and a good preparer should explain if he's taking risky positions, says Fred Giertz, of the National Tax Association. If you can't stomach the specter of an audit, you'll want a pro to err on the side of caution. And think twice before paying someone to look for loopholes if your income picture is relatively simple. "If you've got one W-2, you don't need someone fancy," says Kerstetter. "There's not a lot we can do for you."

10 *"YOU COULD FIND A MUCH BETTER DEAL IF YOU'D ONLY SHOP AROUND."*

There's no standard price for doing taxes. Some preparers charge by the hour, others by the form; either way the cost depends on where you live, the complexity of your situation, and the qualifications of your tax pro. Consider this: The average H&R Block customer pays about $150; a CPA may charge 15 times that. Jay Adkisson, a California lawyer who specializes in helping people protect their assets, says, "People rely too much on word of mouth; they don't shop prices." If they did, they might be surprised. A licensed local pro may not cost much more than a national chain. Nadine Smith, an enrolled agent in Florida, charges by the form, and a simple return could cost just $200—not much more than what you might pay at a big chain.

Even among franchises, prices vary. The return that cost $90 to prepare at one big store was more than three times that amount at another, according to the GAO study. To be fair, it may be hard to know what your return will cost before the preparer actually spends time on it. Ask for estimates using last year's return—that'll give you a point of comparison to find the best price.

THINGS TO DO

● **Protect yourself against bad tax preparers.** Hire a licensed enrolled agent or a CPA with a good record. Find enrolled agents at *www.naea.org*, and vet CPAs at *www.aicpa.org/Consumer+Information*.

● **Ask your preparer what protection** she gives against fines and penalties. Many will cover them even if they offer extra protection—for, say, back taxes—for a fee.

● **Get started early.** Meet with your tax preparer in the fall so she can tell you what to do before the end of the year to minimize your tax bill.

● **Shop around.** Preparers charge widely different rates; a qualified local pro may not cost much more than the big chains.

10 Things Your
401(k) Provider
Won't Tell You

1 *"WE'RE MAKING A MINT ON YOUR 401(K)—EVEN IF YOU'RE NOT."*

Thanks to a growing awareness of the need to prepare for retirement, the number of 401(k) investors has soared in the past decade, to more than 50 million from 28 million, according to Cerulli Associates. But that torrid growth also left millions of investors in the lurch when the market crashed in 2008 and the value of their plans sank, in some cases dramatically. However, in a practice known as revenue sharing, 401(k) providers still got a cut of the expense ratio on the funds in the plan to cover day-to-day administrative costs, regardless of the performance of those funds.

But the gravy train may be coming to an end, as these and other fee arrangements in 401(k)s are drawing attention. Companies, which have the legal responsibility to ensure reasonable fees, are facing lawsuits on the issue, and the Labor Department is mulling new disclosure rules. ING Group, for one, recently moved to resolve an investigation into complaints about past retirement-plan fee-disclosure practices with Eliot Spitzer, who began sniffing around 401(k)s back when he was New York's attorney general. "Plan costs will become more transparent," says Matt Gnabasik of retirement-plan consultancy Blue Prairie Group. "Anytime you have more transparency, it tends to lower fees."

2 *"YOU'RE BUYING WHOLESALE, BUT WE'RE CHARGING YOU RETAIL."*

When it comes to your 401(k) plan, you shouldn't be paying the same fees for a fund that you would if, say, you bought it on your own. But in reality, you might be. Here's how it works: Asset managers sell mutual funds in different share classes, each of which has a different fee structure. From the most expensive to the cheapest class of funds, the range can be as much as a full percentage point, says Yannis Koumantaros, chief pension consultant at Spectrum Pension Consultants. That works out to an extra $1,200 a month in retirement for a 30-year-old with $50,000 in his plan and contributions of $3,000 annually. "You're talking about a difference in your quality of life at retirement," Koumantaros says.

What plans have the highest fees? Usually, those with the fewest investors. Small plans are expensive to run, so they often have to accept costlier fund classes.

But your employer can renegotiate for cheaper options as the plan expands: Those holding between $10 million and $30 million per asset class should lobby for institutional funds, which are cheaper on average than traditional mutual funds.

3 *"NO ONE IN HIS RIGHT MIND WOULD BUY THESE FUNDS— GIVEN A CHOICE."*

Confused about why your 401(k) doesn't offer the top funds? That's because your asset manager may not have them in each category—it might offer stellar large-cap stock funds but mediocre small-cap picks. And providers may charge extra for better alternatives from other sources. "If you see some lousy funds from the company that's providing the plan, that's probably why," says Russel Kinnel, research director at Morningstar. Another issue: Funds need to be big enough that they don't get swamped by the influx of 401(k) money, but for mutual funds, size is often a handicap. Take Fidelity's Magellan, the poster child for asset bloat. The fund is a mainstay of 401(k)s, but has frequently underperformed the S&P 500. It closed to new retail investors in 1997 but continues to accept 401(k) money. The current manager has revamped the strategy, but only time will tell if Magellan can return to its former glory.

As a 401(k) investor, it's also wise to find out whose job it is to do the fund picking at your company. Often, it's a hired hand in human resources likely more schooled in recruitment than in investing. If that's the case, Kinnel suggests asking your company to put someone knowledgeable in charge of the plan or even hire a consultant for the job.

4 *"OUR 'TARGET-DATE FUNDS' MAY MISS THE TARGET."*

In the wake of the 2006 Pension Protection Act, many 401(k)s offer "target date," or "life cycle," funds as their default option. These funds devise an asset allocation based on when you think you'll retire and become more conservative as that date nears. Target-date funds are supposed to address the worst mistakes 401(k) investors make: investing too conservatively or too aggressively, or not rebalancing.

But the recent market crash shows that not all target-date funds are created equal. Among the funds designed for people retiring in 2010, some had as much as 65 percent in stocks; others had as little as 25 percent. Some of the more aggressive funds lost almost half their value in 2008—a hefty blow for anyone planning to retire in a year. The fund companies say target-date funds are designed to carry an investor through retirement—30-plus years past the date on the fund—and that most investors need stocks' higher average returns to avoid running out of money. Target-date funds can be helpful, but as with any other fund, it's important to know exactly how they're investing before trusting them with your nest egg.

5 *"WE OFFER TONS OF INVESTMENT OPTIONS. TOO MANY, IN FACT ..."*

When it comes to picking funds for your 401(k), the more choices the better, right?

Wrong. A recent survey from the Profit Sharing/401(k) Council of America shows that, on average, 401(k) investors have 19 fund options, but with more than 10 to 12, "the average participant goes into paralysis," says Rick Meigs at 401khelpcenter.com. Indeed, academic research draws a direct link between "choice overload" and poor investment decisions: For every 10 funds added to a plan, the probability participants will invest nothing in stock funds goes up significantly. The result: cash- or bond-heavy portfolios unlikely to yield enough for retirement.

According to Emir Kamenica, assistant professor of economics at the University of Chicago Graduate School of Business and coauthor of the study, there is no magic number. Instead, he suggests that plans offer a handful of core funds including a money market, bond index, domestic equity index, and international equity index, with extra choices for those who want them. "Nobody will be worse off by allowing investors who are more sophisticated to select from a wider range of options," Kamenica says.

6 "... BUT YOU STILL AREN'T DIVERSIFIED ENOUGH."

The two most popular holdings in 401(k)s are stable-value funds and company stock, says Pam Hess, senior retirement consultant at Hewitt Associates. And "neither is appropriate." Stable-value funds protect your savings but, by design, don't take enough risk to create as much return as bond or stock funds. Young workers in particular should not have big chunks of their 401(k)s in them. As for company stock, many planners will tell you not to put any of your retirement money there. Your company pays your salary and provides health benefits, so you already have enough exposure there. What's more, you never want the bulk of your portfolio in one stock. But despite having watched companies like Enron crumble, employees with 401(k) plans still put 22 percent of their holdings in company stock, on average, and one in five participants holds more than half of his balance there.

If part of your 401(k) match is in company stock, sell it; it should never compose more than 10 percent of your portfolio. A target-date fund or mix of large- and small-cap equity, international investments, and fixed income is a wiser way to go, Hess says.

7 "IF YOU QUIT YOUR JOB, YOU'LL HAVE TO PAY TO KEEP YOUR 401(K) HERE."

A Hewitt study shows that 32 percent of people who quit their jobs wind up leaving their 401(k)s with their old companies. Maybe that seems easier than hassling HR for the paperwork involved in transferring a 401(k) to an IRA. But chances are, you're paying for it another way. Some employers foot an upfront fee for costs associated with running your plan while you work for them, but an increasing number are pulling the plug once you're off the payroll, says Cook Street Consulting's Sean Waters. This may or may not be clear to employees. "It's not like you get an invoice saying, 'Hey, you owe me $40 a year now,'" Waters says. It makes a case for consolidating your various 401(k)s, because that cost will only increase for those who have multiple plans. "It doesn't make sense to have 401(k)s all over the planet," Waters says.

Often, the simplest solution is to roll them over into your current plan. What if you love your new job, but hate the shoddy funds offered for your 401(k)? Consider an IRA rollover, which means a separate account with an extra set of fees, but also the flexibility to pick the investments you want.

8 "YOU'D BE BETTER OFF IN A ROTH 401(K)—TOO BAD YOUR PLAN DOESN'T OFFER IT."

In a traditional 401(k), taxes on your investments are deferred until you begin withdrawing your money in retirement. With the increasingly popular Roth 401(k), however, you pay the taxes up front, then make withdrawals tax-free. Granted, the Roth isn't for everyone. But if it's the right choice for you, you'll likely be disappointed to discover that your company doesn't offer it—only 5 percent of plans do.

Since Roth 401(k)s first appeared on Jan. 1, 2006, the primary obstacle to their rollout has been the fact that they were supposed to disappear after 2010. Now, thanks to the 2006 Pension Protection Act, they're permanent—but retirement plans have yet to catch up to the legislation. Companies cite other reasons, like administrative complexity, for not offering Roth 401(k)s out of the gate, according to a Hewitt study conducted before the new ruling.

Remember that a 401(k) plan is about having the most money possible in your pocket during retirement. If your plan doesn't include the Roth and you think it's the best option for attaining your goal, ask your benefits department why and what steps employees like you can take to get one. The logistics are their problem.

9 "YOU WANT TO SEE SOME OUTRAGEOUS FEES? TRY A VARIABLE ANNUITY 401(K)."

Insurance companies that run 401(k) plans often package them as annuities. It's the common format for small plans and 403(b)s, which are geared to teachers, professors, and employees of nonprofit organizations. It's also an expensive one. The insurance company slaps a fee on top of the expense ratio you pay for the mutual funds in the annuity. In return, plan participants can get some type of insurance benefit, like principal protection or the opportunity to annuitize their income stream at retirement, says Michael DeGeorge, the general counsel for the National Association for Variable Annuities.

To be fair, insurance companies have the clout to haggle successfully with asset managers for lower expense ratios on the underlying funds. That said, the combined total of the expense ratio and the insurance fee will still be higher than the cost of other plans. All fees should be explained in the prospectus, but critics of the annuity structure complain they're not often broken out in quarterly statements. Instead, the provider quietly deducts its fee from the total return on your fund. Unless you study the prospectus, you may never notice.

10 *"YOUR NEST EGG COULD BE A WHOLE LOT BIGGER."*

In truth, 401(k) plans are getting better. As lawmakers and regulators continue to scrutinize fees, some providers are offering participants access to a more attractive suite of investments and refunding money to plans when expenses exceed costs and a set profit. That said, it's still hard for 401(k) investors to grasp how a small difference in expenses can make a big one for their retirement. Consider this: Brent Glading of the Glading Group, who used to sell 401(k) plans for Merrill Lynch and Dreyfus but now negotiates better plans for company clients, typically can shave 0.20 to 0.40 percent off a plan's expenses. That doesn't sound like much, but it can translate into $100,000 per employee over 20 to 30 years.

THINGS TO DO

● **Don't flail about in the dark.** Take advantage of educational opportunities offered by your employer, and be sure to ask plenty of questions.

● **Always contribute at least enough** to your 401(k) to receive the largest amount your employer will match.

● **Check up on your portfolio regularly.** Changes in the relative value of your investments may throw off your asset allocation; if this happens, redistribute your money accordingly.

● **Make sure your portfolio** isn't too conservative, especially if you're young. A (carefully chosen) target-date fund will manage risk for you by paring down on any potentially volatile holdings as you approach retirement.

● **If you switch jobs,** roll over your assets to an IRA. Otherwise, you risk paying fees to your former employer or losing track of the money. Find out how to make the switch at *www.401khelpcenter.com*.

10 Things Your
Bank
Won't Tell You

1 *"WE'RE IN SURVIVAL MODE."*

Banks may still be a safe place to stash your cash, with the FDIC now insuring up to $250,000 per depositor. But after years of lending money to just about anyone with a pulse, the industry is paying a steep price. Losses on bad loans issued during the credit bubble could top $1.4 trillion, according to the International Monetary Fund. With their balance sheets in tatters and stock prices in the gutter, some of America's biggest banks have been forced to merge to survive. And even with the U.S. government infusing money into the system to get banks lending again, "the days of easy credit are gone," says Greg McBride, senior financial analyst with Bankrate.com.

Customer service also seems to be a casualty of the credit crunch. With less money coming in, many big banks are cutting jobs, closing branches, and scaling back their call-center operations, says Mike Moebs, a bank industry consultant in Chicago. Moreover, employees left on the job now have to handle more customers and may have less flexibility to ease up on fees for overdrafts or other services. "Customer service is waning at the big banks," says Moebs. "It's a downward spiral."

2 *"OUR FEES WILL ONLY GO UP."*

Don't look now but punitive fees—for overdrawing your account, say, or using a competitor's ATM—are increasing. The average ATM service charge doubled between 1998 and 2007, and overdraft fees brought in $17.5 billion in revenue in 2006, up from $10.3 billion in 2004, according to the Center for Responsible Lending. Rubecca Hegarty, a married mother of three in Woodridge, Ill., says she often pays upwards of $100 a month in overdraft fees to Chase, since, like most banks, it changes the order of purchases so that large debts get paid first—increasing the likelihood of incurring fees on smaller purchases. JPMorgan Chase says it does this because big payments like a mortgage are more important to consumers, so they get priority.

Revenue from penalties can be addictive for banks, says Harvard Business School Professor Gail McGovern, but "They're going to face problems from

After years of lending money to just about anyone with a pulse, the industry is paying a steep price.

angry customers, which leads to big call-center bills, employee dissatisfaction, and turnover."

3 *"WE CHANGE OUR INTEREST RATES ALL THE TIME."*

Regardless of what your credit card agreement says, you can never be sure how much interest banks will charge you. For example, nearly all cards have a default rate—as high as 30 percent—which banks apply when you've done something wrong, usually after two late payments in 12 months. But some banks have cut that to one, says Curtis Arnold, founder of CardRatings.com.

Banks can also change the terms of your agreement, raising rates when they like (though you can opt out and pay off the balance at the old rate as long as you never use the card again). Bank of America did that recently, upping many cardholders' rates from 10 or 12 percent to 27 percent or more, even though they'd done nothing wrong. "There's no clarity on what criteria can lead a bank to raise interest rates," says Robert Manning, director of the Center for Consumer Financial Services at the Rochester Institute of Technology. "It's a black box." A Bank of America spokesperson says the company periodically reviews the credit risk of its accounts and adjusts rates accordingly, adding that in the past year 94 percent have had no increase.

4 *"COLLEGE CAMPUSES ARE A GOLD MINE FOR US."*

Students are the customers of the future, and banks are increasingly courting them,

sometimes right on campus. More than 120 universities have cut deals with banks to issue student-ID cards that are also ATM and check cards. Schools can make millions from these deals, sometimes even taking a small cut of individual purchases.

Students are also a hot market for credit card issuers; banks will make private deals with alumni associations to get contact info for students, parents, and ticket buyers to university athletic events. Card companies cut deals to set up booths on campus, and Chase even inked a deal with Facebook to display ads and set up a Chase group on its website.

The problem? Mounting credit card debt among college kids, for one. "Universities don't negotiate on behalf of students," says Manning. "They're negotiating the best deal for the university." A spokesperson for the National Association of Independent Colleges and Universities says don't blame schools—banks would market to students anyway, and universities at least try to get the best rates they can for students.

5 *"IN DEBT? THE COURTS WON'T HELP."*

Since the late 1990s, banks have been including mandatory arbitration agreements in their contracts for many of their products, including auto loans, checking accounts, home-equity loans, and credit cards. Such agreements prohibit you from suing and instead require you to use an arbitrator—someone picked by the arbitration firm named in your credit card contract to hear the dispute and decide the outcome.

While these clauses were originally designed to thwart class-action suits, the banks have also been using them for debt collection, says Paul Bland, an attorney with consumer-advocacy group Public Justice. There are even times when consumers, often victims of identity theft and unaware of the debt, aren't present when awards are handed down against them.

A recent suit against an arbitration firm brought by the San Francisco city attorney noted that arbitrators ruled in favor of banks in 100 percent of the 18,045 California cases brought against consumers from January 2003 through March 2007. "From the consumer perspective, it's a nightmare," says Bland. If a bank brings arbitration against you, hire a lawyer and request a hearing—in person.

6 "WE'RE EXCITED ABOUT YOUR TRIP TO EUROPE, TOO!"

It's not bad enough that the dollar is hovering near historic lows against most major currencies, but when you travel overseas, every transaction comes with big fees attached. Take out cash from an ATM in London, and you'll get hit with a foreign-transaction fee, plus a fee for using a competitor's ATM. All told, it can cost up to $7 just to withdraw $200. Credit card purchases aren't much better. Visa and MasterCard each charge 1 percent of the purchase for converting currency. And the issuing banks may take another cut, which can bring the total to 3 percent of your purchase price, says CardRatings.com's Arnold. "If people don't travel overseas very often, they just

The best thing to do is see which of your cards charges the lowest overseas-transaction fee.

don't think about it," he says.

The best thing to do is see which of your cards charges the lowest overseas-transaction fee. If you travel a lot, Arnold recommends a Capital One credit card, which charges no overseas-transaction fees (even refusing to pass on Visa and MasterCard's 1 percent fee to customers). Also, ask your bank about partnerships with foreign banks. Bank of America, for example, partners with Barclays Bank, saving its customers $5 per withdrawal from the latter's ATMs in the U.K.

7 "FOR ALL THE FINE PRINT, WE DON'T DISCLOSE VERY MUCH."

Bank documents come loaded with small type, detailing terms and conditions. But good luck finding out exactly what you're signing up for when you open an account. In 2007 the Government Accountability Office (GAO) sent investigators to see how well banks explained their fees and other conditions to potential customers. Though banks are required by law to make this information available, the GAO found that one third of the branches it surveyed didn't provide the required information. Worse, more than half didn't have any fee information on their websites.

Nessa Feddis, senior counsel at the American Bankers Association (ABA), questions the report's methodology—

banks failed the test if investigators waited more than 10 minutes for the information—and defends the lack of data online. Banks are afraid of leaving old, inaccurate information on their site if terms change, she says. But without details on fees, consumers can't make educated choices. "Banks are not complying with the law," says Ed Mierzwinski, consumer program director with the U.S. Public Interest Research Group. "People need more information so they can shop around for the best deal."

8 *"YOUR MONEY MIGHT BE BETTER OFF ELSEWHERE."*

Banks offer lots of ways to earn interest on your money—among them, simple savings, CDs, money-market accounts, and IRAs. But they don't always yield the best return. In early 2009, the average savings account, for example, was paying about 0.5 percent interest. But even in this low-interest-rate climate, you can do better—3 percent or more—if you shop around. "It pays to be a free agent," says Bankrate.com's McBride. "There is tremendous disparity in the returns available."

Banks have been expanding into other financial services for a decade or more, including comprehensive wealth management and financial planning, brokerage services, even insurance. The well-off customers who use these are a bank's most profitable; they keep the highest balances and are less sensitive to fees, says Maryann Johnson, senior vice president of wealth market management at the ABA. That's something to remember when you talk to a bank's investment advisers: Many are paid a commission on investment products, says Certified Financial Planner Craig DuVarney, meaning they often go for the easy sale. "They don't have the harder discussion about estate planning, tax bracket, and liquidity," says DuVarney. Johnson sees it differently; she says banks take a more holistic approach and that their wealth managers serve much the same purpose as financial advisers, with bonuses for not only sales but also dollars invested, new clients, and even customer retention.

9 *"WHEN IT COMES TO BANKS, SMALLER IS SOMETIMES BETTER."*

Banks have been consolidating like crazy over the past decade. In 1990 the top 10 banks controlled 25 percent of the market; by 2008 they controlled half. This gives customers of large banks vast networks of free ATMs and branches across the country. But it hasn't been entirely good for consumers, says Arthur E. Wilmarth, Jr., a professor at George Washington University Law School. Though big banks offer many conveniences, they can come at a price: high fees. In 2006 the 10 largest banks generated 54 percent of revenue from fees and service charges; by contrast, the 10 smallest banks generated just 28 percent from those sources.

Not only do big banks bring in more fee income but they also pay out less interest. According to FDIC data, smaller banks generally pay higher interest on savings accounts and other products. For example, in 2006 the 10 largest banks paid an average 1.87 percent in interest for savings accounts, while the smallest banks paid 4.37 percent. "The largest banks are no longer worried about being undercut on price," Wilmarth says.

10 *"YOUR ONLINE ACCOUNT INFO ISN'T NECESSARILY ACCURATE."*

Online banking has changed the way people handle their finances. They can pay bills online, transfer funds, track payments, and get a more detailed view of their bank account than ever before. Unfortunately, it may not always show the proper balance. With electronic transactions, ATMs, check cards, and direct deposits, banking has gotten more complicated.

ATMs and online bank statements will show deposits available before the money is actually in your account. Using your debit card at a gas station or to reserve a hotel room, for example, can put a hold on funds. Some merchants may be slow to send in charges. And banks can sit on deposits—an out-of-state check may take up to five days to clear.

Add to that the constant reordering of debits, and your account balance can quickly become a moving target—hard to track accurately day to day. "Banks use different algorithms to process payments than what you see online," says Harvard's McGovern. "It gives you a false sense of security."

THINGS TO DO

● **Ask your bank or credit card provider** if it offers temporary purchase numbers for shopping online—they're one-use-only numbers designed to keep your actual card number private.

● **At *www.bankrate.com* you can choose** the term length for a CD and get a list of the best and most current interest rates.

● **Want better treatment?** Consider consolidating all of your accounts at one bank to be eligible for more of its services. You'll also have more leverage to negotiate little things, like an overdraft fee, that could come up over time.

● **Before signing up for a credit card,** go to *www.cardratings.com* for an analysis of the major providers plus user forums to see what the card's current customers have to say.

10 Things Your
Credit Card Company
Won't Tell You

1 "WE'RE JUST WAITING FOR YOU TO SCREW UP."

Many things can bump your credit card interest rate into the red zone, but nothing faster than what's called "universal default." You can make all your credit card payments religiously and for a long time, but fall behind on your electric bill and, suddenly, you're a deadbeat—who will be charged accordingly. Rates can change on short notice, from low and reasonable to up to 35 percent.

Card companies claim that what they're doing is managing risk. Consumer groups disagree, since many people in universal default aren't deadbeats by any reasonable definition. Say, for example, you're disputing a charge on a medical bill or waiting for an insurance snafu to resolve itself. If a billing clerk kicks it to collections, you're in universal default. Or suppose your credit score drops—a common event that may be entirely unrelated to your bill-paying behavior. That's also likely to push your interest rate higher.

The best way to avoid the problem is the most obvious: Pay your bills on time. Bankrate.com, a consumer-lending education website, further advises that if you have a disputed bill, resolve it before it reaches collection status.

2 "WHEN IT COMES TO IDENTITY THEFT, WE'RE PART OF THE PROBLEM."

Identity theft victim Tony Sciulli of Santa Barbara, Calif., says it started with a forged credit application—a $3,000 balance was mysteriously transferred to a new card in his name, followed by a ready-made check billed to one of his other cards. What can you do to avoid this sort of low-tech thievery? Buy a shredder, and minimize the credit applications coming to your house by registering at OptOutPrescreen.com.

But paper solicitations are only the tip of the iceberg. As Internet security expert and author Bruce Schneier warns, "Data about you is not under your control." He points to examples such as the May 2005 case involving Bank of America and Wachovia, in which a man posing as a collection agent paid bank employees for customer data in New Jersey. The banks notified customers their data may have been compromised and offered to help watch their accounts for suspicious activity. (The man, Orazio Lembo, pled guilty in March 2007 and was sentenced to five years and a $20,000 fine.)

But John Hall, a spokesperson for the American Bankers Association, insists that banks have "Pentagon-level security." His advice: "Monitor your accounts. Protect your passwords and your computer."

3 *"YOUR CHILDREN ARE OUR FUTURE."*

It wouldn't surprise most parents to know that their college-age kid can get a credit card. After all, university students, however financially dependent, are adults whose earning years are just beginning, making them "good risks" for creditors. What parents might not know is the fact that card issuers are now taking that reasoning a step further: "The big trend is marketing to high school students," says Robert D. Manning, author of *Credit Card Nation* and a professor at the Rochester Institute of Technology.

Manning says that most parents don't realize how early a child's name, address, and other information can turn up in the databases used by credit card companies to market their products—or that kids as young as 16 can get cards without parental permission. "[Credit card issuers] know that if a kid gets in trouble, usually the parent will pay," he says.

What can parents do? Protect your child's information, and assume that all requests, however legitimate, will land

---

What can parents do? Protect your child's information, and assume that all requests, however legitimate, will land it in a database somewhere.

---

it in a database somewhere. Gift cards, for instance, may offer protection if lost or destroyed—but they require personal data. Manning and other experts advise teaching teens about credit well before they get their first cards and monitoring their spending as they learn to use them.

4 *"OUR 'FREEBIE' REWARDS ARE ANYTHING BUT."*

In the hypercompetitive credit card marketplace, rewards are a way for banks to target big-spending niche audiences—frequent-fliers, for instance. But these programs often come with hidden catches, such as exorbitant interest rates and high annual fees, so it's important to do your homework. "[A rewards card] doesn't make financial sense for just anyone," says Manning, of the Rochester Institute of Technology.

Before signing on, figure out how much you'll have to spend to earn the incentives from a given card. If the math works out to anything less than one penny earned per dollar spent (or a mile per dollar, in the case of mileage cards), then you could do better.

Also, be sure to look for the rewards that best suit your needs. For example, if you want an abundance of options, from retail goods and services to charitable donations, American Express's Membership Rewards cards let you accumulate points at the rate of a penny per dollar spent—double that at gas stations and drugstores. Or if it's air miles you're after, the United Mileage Plus Signature Visa is one card that stands out from the pack, with its 1-mile-per-dollar ratio and host of travel benefits, including upgrades.

5 *"DEBIT CARDS SHOULD COME WITH A WARNING: 'USE AT YOUR OWN RISK.'"*

A few summers ago, Vicki Jacobson's college-student son, Craig, was coming home from a European vacation. Arriving at the airport, unable to speak Italian and his available cash growing short, he attempted to pay for his taxi ride with a debit card. The driver ran the card three times and a credit card once, but it was unclear after each pass whether the transaction had gone through. Finally, anxious about catching his flight, Craig paid with his dwindling euros and left Italy behind. You can probably guess what happened: He was charged for that taxi ride three times on the debit card and once on the credit card. And that's when the fun really started —months after the incident, the credit card charge was nearly resolved, but they were still unable to make any headway on the three erroneous debit charges. "It can just be very difficult to penetrate the system," Vicki Jacobson says.

Why so much trouble with the debit card transactions? Well, debit cards resemble credit cards in all visible ways, but have fewer protections for the consumer. Some debit cards offer purchase protection—meaning you can replace a damaged item within 90 days—but many do not. And although unauthorized transactions, like the three charged to Jacobson's son, are supposed to be refunded by the issuer, banks are less motivated to speedily resolve cases involving debit cards than credit cards. Why? Debit cards draw on a checking account, meaning they're essentially checks in plastic form. Credit cards, by contrast, constitute a loan—meaning it's the bank's money, giving it more reason to protect it.

6 *"PAID IN FULL? NOT NECESSARILY."*

Banks generally calculate interest charges in one of two ways: based on average daily balance or on something called two-cycle billing. The latter, which more card issuers are now adopting, penalizes customers who carry a balance, even if it's only on occasion.

Here's how it works: Say you start your month with a zero balance and charge an amount that you don't pay off in full at the end of the month. If your card uses the average daily balance method to calculate interest, you are charged nothing for the month you made the purchase, and interest only for subsequent months in which payment is outstanding. With two-cycle billing, interest charges begin with the day you make the purchase.

Banks defend two-cycle billing as correcting the true interest charges for credit card purchases. Ron Brooks, at National City Corp., says it's a way to make sure card users pay interest should they suddenly go from being "transactors" (those who pay off every month) to "revolvers" (those who carry a balance).

One way to avoid the issue is to stay away from cards that use two-cycle billing to calculate interest charges and stick with those that go by average daily balance. Unfortunately, it's not a permanent solution: Your card provider can switch to two-cycle billing with just 15 days' notice, so you'll have to keep checking.

7 "WE'RE ACCEPTED ANYWHERE ON THE GLOBE, BUT OUR EXCHANGE RATES ARE FROM PLANET RIP-OFF."

In recent years plastic has all but replaced the traveler's check as the preferred method for making purchases abroad. Credit cards are widely accepted overseas, and they can be used in ATMs all over the world to dispense cash in the currency of whatever country you're visiting. But beware of hidden charges. Some banks have recently raised the rates on currency conversion from 1 percent to 3 percent. On top of that, ATM usage has its own fees attached.

Consumers Union recommends studying your cards' policies on foreign-currency purchases before you leave home, then adjusting your spending accordingly. Cards issued by smaller banks, for example, may have lower fees, as do certain brand-name cards. American Express, which has long positioned itself as a card for travelers, charges a flat 2 percent.

8 "WE CLOSE EARLY ON PAYMENT-DUE DATES."

Card statements are crystal clear about what day your payment is due, but they're not so forthcoming about what time on that due date. Some banks have triggered consumer complaints by setting a 9 A.M. deadline on the posted payment date—essentially, before the mail arrives.

Chi Chi Wu, an attorney with the National Consumer Law Center, says that a number of class-action lawsuits have succeeded in getting most banks to push back their payment deadline to 2 P.M., the traditional banker's closing hour, a time by which most mail delivery is complete.

Even so, a spokesperson for the American Bankers Association (ABA), is unsympathetic, saying bills are due upon receipt and that banks spend a lot of money giving consumers options like paying by phone, paying online, and automatic bill pay. "I just don't understand why late payment is still an issue for people," she says. "Pay your bill on time. It's easy."

She has a point—if you can't allow plenty of time for U.S. mail delivery, you can always take advantage of an online or pay-by-phone option. And if you're really in a pinch, another alternative is to send your payment overnight, worth it if it means avoiding a $30 late penalty. But if you go that route, check the promised time of delivery—the standard end-of-business arrival might not do the trick.

9 "OUR WHIMS ARE LEGALLY BINDING."

You may think you've signed up for a credit card with terrific incentives, a low APR, and just the right mix of perks and fees to suit you. But don't get too comfortable. Your card issuer can alter the terms of your once-perfect agreement at any time, as long as it provides you with advance written notice—of as little as 15 days. "The biggest secret in the credit card industry is, they're very thinly regulated," says Wu, of the National Consumer Law Center.

Consumer groups report that this practice is a particular pet peeve with credit card holders, and for obvious reasons. But an ABA spokesperson takes a stab at defending the practice. "A credit purchase is an unsecured loan. It's the riskiest sort of lending we do, which is why it's expensive. The banks have to protect themselves." She adds that since credit card lending is a highly competitive marketplace, unhappy customers are almost always able to seek alternatives.

How can you protect yourself from being blindsided? In short, vigilance. "Pay attention to all the mail you get from your credit card company," Wu urges, "even if it looks insignificant."

10 "GO AHEAD AND EXCEED YOUR CREDIT LIMIT—WE LIKE THAT."

Contrary to popular belief, a purchase that puts you over your credit limit won't necessarily be declined. But you might wish it had been, since it could bump your interest rate into the stratosphere.

Lea Barker, a data-entry clerk in Oakland, Calif., found that out the hard way when she exceeded the limit on her Visa card—and her interest rate skyrocketed to 29.9 percent. The sudden increase was among the factors that ultimately pushed her into credit counseling and a debt-management plan. "I have to find another $1,000 a month to dig my way out," Barker says. "I'm looking at a second job."

Adding insult to injury, banks often levy a so-called overlimit fee against maxed-out cardholders—roughly a $30 penalty every month your balance remains above the credit limit. An ABA spokesperson says that "consumers would rather deal with the fee than the embarrassment of being declined." But consumer advocate Travis Plunkett, of the Consumer Federation of America, is having none of it. Overlimit fees, he contends, are simply another way for banks to make money at the expense of the unwary. "If [banks are] willing to accept charges [over their cardholders' limits]," Plunkett says, "then they should accept the profit that comes from the increased interest charges" and leave it at that.

THINGS TO DO

● **Pay your bill on time** every month to avoid credit problems, penalty fees, and hefty hikes in your interest rate. Ask your card company what your payment options are; most allow you to pay over the phone or online at no charge.

● **If you lose your card** or want to cancel your account, keep a written record of correspondence with your card company. It could come in handy if there's a dispute.

● **Avoid going over your credit limit.** If you're planning to make a big purchase, call your card company ahead to request that it raise your limit. You can also sign up for free e-mail alerts about your balance, if they're offered.

● **Worried about all those** credit card offers landing in the wrong hands? For $10 to $15 depending on your state, you can freeze your credit—meaning no new cards can be opened in your name. The drawback is, if you want to open your credit back up for a big purchase like a car or a home, it's another $10 to $15. Contact one of the three big credit agencies—Experian, TransUnion, and Equifax—for details.

10 Things Your
Money Managers
Won't Tell You

1 "YOU MAY HAVE MORE INVESTING EXPERIENCE THAN I DO."

A surplus of newly minted fund managers flooded the financial world during the late-1990s bull market, when fund companies were scrambling to train talent and launch new funds. Those young turks were eager to seize the opportunity to build themselves a name.

Consider Ryan Jacob. At age 28, he was running the Kinetics Internet fund, which averaged 206 percent gains in 1998 and 1999. Riding that success, he went solo and started the eponymous Jacob Internet fund, and after pulling in $200 million from investors, took such a beating in the tech collapse—a 95 percent plunge—that the fund ended up as the next-to-worst performer for 2001. As its manager gained experience, the fund did better: Over the next five years, it outperformed the S&P 500 by 11 percent. But it seems Jacob is still on a learning curve—when the market crashed in 2008, the fund tanked again.

The moral of the story: Look for an experienced stock jockey at the helm when choosing a mutual fund. Currently, 911 of the 3,095 domestic equity funds have managers with an average tenure of two years or less. And their inexperience shows—funds run by managers with an average tenure of two years or less did worse than the S&P 500 in 2008.

2 "I'LL BEAT THE MARKET— SOMEDAY."

Whether a fund is run by a rookie or a graybeard, it's tough to find money managers who consistently beat the market. That's not so bad when the market is up and your fund is up a little less; it's worse when the market is down you're down more. Yet many underperforming managers are able to hang on to their jobs. Fred Reynolds, for one, has been at the helm of the Reynolds Blue Chip Growth fund since 1988, even though it has, on average, lost money annually for the past five and ten years. (To be fair, it held up better than most funds in its category during the 2008 market crash.)

Such terrible returns "make it tough to argue in favor of active management," says Mercer Bullard, who runs shareholders' rights group Fund Democracy. "Index funds are a better option." Perhaps. But before investing in any fund, dig deeper into its record. Start by going to SmartMoney.com and have a look at the "Snapshot" pages of the fund you're interested in—you'll get information there beyond the typical one-, three-, and ten-year periods.

3 *"I'VE NEVER REALLY RUN A HEDGE FUND BEFORE."*

Once reserved for the super-rich, hedge funds today have become a way for a wider spectrum of investors to avoid crummy mutual fund managers. Assets in hedge funds reached over $2 trillion in March 2007, according to HedgeFund Intelligence. One reason for the surge is the influx of traditional fund managers eager to start or join new hedge funds because they offer substantially better pay. In 2006, 66 percent of hedge fund managers earned 1.5 percent or more of assets, and 80 percent made 20 percent of any portfolio gains annually.

But there's a downside to the trend for investors: Hedge funds are attracting some managers with little experience (and few scruples) in using the funds' sophisticated trading techniques, such as short selling and merger arbitrage. Since 2000, more than 10 hedge funds have been accused of misrepresenting their returns or strategies. "Hedge funds can be dangerous," says Tim Curtiss, former COO at Wall Street Investor Relations, which advises companies' investor relations departments. "There are no regulators looking over [managers'] shoulders."

That isn't likely to change anytime soon. In December 2004, the SEC tried to pass a rule requiring stricter reporting standards for hedge funds, but the U.S. Court of Appeals for the District of Columbia overturned it in June 2006.

4 *"THE NAME MIGHT BE THE SAME, BUT A NEW MANAGER MEANS A WHOLE NEW FUND."*

Today's savvy investors do their homework and make sure to find out who's at the helm before investing in a fund, but with high fund-management turnover—more than 4,000 funds saw management changes between 2000 and 2004, according to Morningstar—the manager you get when you start investing might not be there by the time the prospectus arrives in the mail.

Even if the new manager has a proven track record, it doesn't mean your fund's going to prosper. Harry Lange had 18 years of fund-managing experience, nearly 10 running Fidelity's Capital Appreciation fund, where he consistently beat the S&P 500, before taking over Fidelity's Magellan in 2005. How did this seasoned pro perform? In 2006, his first full year on the job, the S&P 500 more than doubled the performance of Magellan—16 percent versus 7 percent. Since then the sailing has been a little smoother, but for investors it was a bumpy transition to say the least.

A new manager often brings a change in style, and you should see if that style still fits with your investment plans, says Gary Schatsky, a CPA in New York. "When the person at the helm goes away, you should reassess your investment," he says.

5 *"I LIKE TO LOOK BUSY."*

Stocks weren't created to be traded like baseball players in a rotisserie league. But try telling that to some fund managers. "A lot of managers trade through positions just to show they're doing something," says Bullard. "The high turnover is a symptom of a problem. Managers have short-term outlooks."

He has a point. The average domestic stock fund flips through 97 percent of its holdings in less than a year, letting taxes eat into gains. Just look at Security Alpha Opportunity. At first glance it appears that the Bill Jenkins-managed fund has done a fairly good job of beating the S&P 500, but the fund's stocks are traded 10 times as often as those in the average domestic stock fund. Adjust the portfolio for taxes, and Security Alpha Opportunity's roughly 9 percent gains in the three years leading up to 2008 fall to just under 3 percent. (We could not reach Bill Jenkins for comment.)

6 "IF YOUR FUND'S BOARD OF DIRECTORS IS SHADY, YOU'RE IN TROUBLE."

Didn't know your fund even had a board of directors? You're not alone. These days *corporate* boards attract plenty of attention—investors want to know what they make, how much they pay company executives, and how they're protecting stockholders from fraud. But mutual fund boards, which watch over more than $11 trillion of investors' money, wield more power and influence—and receive much less public scrutiny.

That can be a real problem, says Mercer Bullard, president of shareholder-advocacy group Fund Democracy. Bullard points to the series of scandals that have plagued

the mutual fund industry over the past decade, and he places a good portion of the responsibility squarely at the feet of fund directors. "All suggest a systematic breakdown in board oversight," he says.

The good news for investors is that things are starting to get better. The SEC is trying to tighten rules about who can serve as a mutual fund director. A raft of lawsuits threatens to hold directors liable for high fund fees. And Morningstar, the widely followed fund-research company, has changed the way it assigns its influential "stewardship grade," giving higher marks to boards that are more independent of the fund's management.

7 "I'VE GOT WAY TOO MUCH ON MY PLATE."

Obviously, fund managers aren't just looking to make money for investors. Their pay is affected not only by their performance and experience but by the amount of money they manage. "It may be in a manager's economic best interest to take on more than he can handle," says Jon Zeschin, former president of the Founders mutual fund family who now runs Essential Advisors, an investment advisory firm. And performance can suffer.

Consider Elise Baum. After a few good years running Merrill Lynch Mid Cap Value, she took over a second fund, the Small Cap Value and Global Technology. Since then Mid Cap Value—which has been renamed BlackRock Mid Cap Value Opportunities—has fallen to the bottom quarter of its Morningstar group. "We do not believe a manager should deviate from a fund's investment strategy due to market volatility," says a Merrill Lynch spokesperson. "One or two quarters is not an accurate measurement of overall performance."

To avoid getting short-changed by an overwhelmed fund manager, ask the fund company how many portfolios—mutual funds and separate accounts—your manager runs. Also, find out how much money he or she runs in all those portfolios and how much is flowing into the fund you're interested in. Then you'll have a better idea of how important your portfolio is to the manager.

8 "MANAGED ACCOUNTS ARE A TERRIFIC INVESTMENT— FOR ME."

Managed accounts have become increasingly popular investments in recent years. Assets in these accounts more than doubled between 2002 and 2006, to $806 billion, and they're continuing to grow, according to the Money Management Institute. Yet for all their seeming appeal, the question remains, who really benefits from these accounts—the investor or the money manager?

Like mutual funds, managed accounts are professionally managed portfolios with specific investing objectives. Unlike with mutual funds, you actually own the stocks in the portfolio, so you won't owe capital gains taxes unless you sell those stocks. But if you think a customized portfolio means you'll get a lot of personal attention from the manager, think again. Denise Farkas, chief investment officer of Sigma Investment Counselors in Michigan, says managed accounts often rely on computers

to construct a model portfolio and duplicate a manager's moves in dozens, even thousands, of accounts. Managers, on the other hand, get a nice boost by "overseeing" these funds: They earn 1.5 to 2 percent of assets per year, versus 1.5 percent for running a stock mutual fund.

9 "I'M AS SUSCEPTIBLE TO A GOOD SCAM AS ANYONE."

Is a personal money manager better to work with than a stockbroker? Brokers earn commissions on everything they sell you, which critics say prompts them to push products. On the other hand, money managers typically charge a fixed percentage of your assets—usually about 1 percent annually—to manage them. Their mission: to find ways to increase both your earnings and theirs.

Sounds legit, but heads up: Your manager may not be churning your account, but he can still harm it with silly investments or fall prey to fraud. That's what happened to hundreds of investors who collectively lost $35 million in Tampa Bay, Fla., back in 2001. A network of local money managers recommended bonds from Evergreen Securities and Worldwide Bond Partners that promised 10 percent annual yields if investors kept their money tied up for five years. The problem? The bonds were bogus. Evergreen's founders ended up pleading guilty to securities fraud in 2002.

To avoid getting taken, you can check out any investment your money manager recommends by contacting the Securities and Exchange Commission (SEC) or your state securities office to see if the product is registered.

10 *"I RARELY PAY FOR MY MISTAKES."*

The Financial Industry Regulatory Authority reported that there were 3,238 new arbitration claims filed by investors against their brokers or brokerage firms in 2007. But that doesn't necessarily mean that many of these disgruntled investors will be vindicated. In reality, "investors have very few options," says Joseph Borg, director of the Alabama Securities Commission.

But it's not always a dead end to seek arbitration. You may have a suitability claim, for instance, if your manager puts money in speculative investments when you've clearly indicated you wanted only conservative products. Tracy Pride Stoneman, a securities lawyer in Westcliffe, Colo., won a settlement for a client who'd lost $300,000 after a manager invested in high-risk mortgage derivatives despite orders by her client to invest only in government bonds. Whatever your grievance, to help your case against a money manager, Stoneman recommends keeping detailed records of all your transactions, including notes of phone conversations and in-person meetings.

THINGS TO DO

• **Once you've invested in a fund,** keep track of the people managing it. If the person at the helm changes, check out the new guy's record and reassess your investment.

• **To find out who's running a given fund** and for how long, go to *www.morningstar.com* to read the manager's bio and look into how well other funds she's managed in the past have done.

• **Before hiring a personal money manager,** confirm that he's registered with the SEC or your state securities office and has a clean record. You'll find a database of all state and federally registered investment advisers at *www.adviserinfo.sec.gov.*

• **Make sure that any product** your manager recommends is safe by checking to see if it's registered with the SEC *(www.sec.gov)* or your state's securities office (find yours at *consumeraction.gov/security.shtml*).

10 Things Your
Financial Planner
Won't Tell You

1 "I GOT THIS GIG ON A WHIM."

There's a huge market of consumers out there desperately seeking financial guidance—especially in the wake of the 2008 market crash. And a wealth of advisers are eager to serve them. In the early 1990s, only about 25,000 people called themselves financial planners, according to Boston-based research firm Dalbar, but by 2006 that number had climbed to around 650,000. Part of the reason for the boom is that anyone can present themselves as a financial planner—one of several generic titles for someone who provides advice to clients about how best to handle their money. (As opposed to money managers, for example, who actually manage your accounts.) And since there's no required training or experience necessary, why not hang out a shingle and tap into the profit?

But it can get even trickier than terminology—many of those seeking to provide you with financial advice are actually trying to sell you something. Bank-employed pitchmen are often called "personal financial consultants," for example, while insurance salesmen may present themselves as "financial advisers." Indeed, "The bulk of people who market themselves as financial advisers

are salespeople," says the Consumer Federation of America's director of investor protection, Barbara Roper.

How can you be sure you're hiring a qualified pro? You can start by narrowing the field to one of the 56,000 Certified Financial Planner licensees out there (visit *www.cfp.net*). In contrast to run-of-the-mill planners and advisers, CFPs *do* have to meet specific requirements: Their license means three years' minimum experience and passing a comprehensive 10-hour exam. Next, grill candidates on how much real planning they've done. Wind Lake, Wis.–based CFP Jim Cantrell says he's met advisers who claim to have 10 years' experience, "then you find out that they became a planner only a year ago and spent eight years as a bank manager."

2 "I'M A JACK-OF-ALL-TRADES AND MASTER OF NONE."

James Eccleston, a Chicago-based securities lawyer, recalls a client of his who met with disaster when a financial planner failed to advise him about the tax ramifications of exercising stock options. Instead, the planner convinced the client to buy a second home, Eccleston says, using the stock as collateral for the mortgage, "and the coffin was sealed, because this was a 100-percent position in Cisco." When Cisco stock tanked during the tech-bubble fallout, the client's portfolio plunged, from $1.7 million to about $5,400. He was forced to liquidate all his shares and take a $100,000 second mortgage on his primary home to meet margin calls—then got whacked with a $400,000 tax bill.

A good financial planner should work alongside outside professionals—accountants, lawyers, insurance brokers—to offer you the best service. However, at some firms, like the one Eccleston's client used, the planner tries to do everything himself. Beware. "If they're claiming that they have the expertise to do it all, I would seriously question that," Roper says. Like tax planning, estate planning poses great risks, says Eccleston, since flaws might not show up until the client retires or dies. His advice: Double-check anything your financial planner says about taxes or estate planning with a lawyer or CPA.

3 "I HAVE GHOSTWRITERS DRAW UP YOUR PLAN."

So you met with a planner, outlined your goals, and left feeling that your financial future was in good hands. It might come as a disappointment, then, to learn that this wonderful planner won't be finishing the job. Outsourcing financial plans to a secondary firm or freelancer is a growing trend, especially among big firms, enabling planners to spend more of their time wooing new clients. "It's the current corruption in financial planning," says John E. Sestina, cofounder of the National

Association of Personal Financial Advisors. But when a plan is done by outsiders, Sestina says, the information gets stale; there is less intimacy and more room for error. "You can't act on issues as soon as they crop up," he says.

And don't assume the planner will offer up this detail without prompting, says Sherry Rhoades, a Plano, Tex., certified financial planner who says she doesn't outsource. "[There's] no need for the client to know."

4 "I'M A HIGH-PRESSURE SHILL IN DISGUISE."

The majority of financial planners work on commission, which doesn't mean they're bad people but can make for some bad financial planning. When Laguna Hills, Calif.–based Certified Financial Planner Scott Dauenhauer worked at a few big-name brokerage firms during the '90s, he says he was constantly being pushed into selling the firm's proprietary—and often poorly performing—mutual funds, variable annuities, or wrap accounts. "We got pressured to sell them because the payout was higher," says Dauenhauer. "But there was no talk of whether it was right for the client."

To avoid such conflicts of interest, shop for a planner through the National Association of Personal Financial Advisors (*www.napfa.org*), a strictly fee-only group (no charge-backs, kickbacks, trails, or other hidden commissions) with more than 1,700 members. NAPFA planners have to sign an oath stating that they'll never receive commissions and promising to put their clients' best interests first. Along with having three years' experience, they must take 60 hours of continuing education every two years and submit sample plans for review by other NAPFA members.

5 "AM I 'FEE-ONLY' OR 'FEE-BASED'? UM, LET'S NOT SPLIT HAIRS."

As the public's suspicion of commission-driven planners has grown, so has the market for "fee-only" planning—in which financial planners charge for the advice they provide but don't get any commission on the products they sell. The popularity of the approach has inspired some financial planners "to clothe themselves in the 'fee' word," says New York–based CPA and former NAPFA Chairman Gary Schatsky. Indeed, more than 40 percent of certified financial planners now call themselves "fee-based," which means that they charge you an upfront fee *and* collect commissions on products they recommend, according to the Certified Financial Planner Board of Standards.

According to the most recent statistics from the CFP Board, fee-based revenue for registered representatives had climbed to roughly 33 percent of total revenue in 2004, versus 10 percent of total revenue in 1996—and the trend is still going strong. To be sure that your "fee-only" or "fee-based" planner is true to his claims, ask for a written breakdown of fees, especially those associated with each investment product, suggests Virginia-based CFP Randall Kratz. "If someone doesn't have what he makes in writing, I wouldn't work with him," he says.

6 "ONCE I'VE DONE THE PLAN, I'M OUTTA HERE . . ."

Financial planners like to give you the sense that they'll be with you every step of the way through important financial decisions. But in reality, many clients find that a once-attentive planner becomes increasingly elusive as time wears on. When Kratz worked for a financial advisory firm several years ago, he says he adopted more than 1,000 clients who had been discarded by colleagues, usually because they no longer produced adequate income to keep their planners interested. "Typically, the first year was an intense relationship, but clients complained that they stopped hearing from the adviser after that," he says. The reason? The commissions had dried up—a lot of products, especially insurance products, are based on one year of commissions before they drop off, says Kratz.

To avoid a shutout, ask prospective financial planners at the interview stage how often you should expect to be in touch. A good reply, says Coupeville, Wash., Certified Financial Planner Kathleen Cotton, is about four times in the first three months to hammer out a plan, then at least once or twice a year after that.

7 ". . . ESPECIALLY IF YOU'RE NOT SO WELL-TO-DO."

The past decade has seen a big push among planners to target high-net-worth clients, and many planners today have a minimum asset requirement—typically $100,000. Considering that, according to the 2004 Census by the U.S. Census

Bureau, American households have a median net worth of about $44,000, that leaves a lot of folks out in the cold.

Luckily, middle-class clients do have some alternatives. The Garrett Planning Network (*www.garrettplanningnetwork .com*) is a ring of 260 planners across the nation who work primarily with the $100,000-and-under income set, charging hourly fees for periodic advice. Similarly, John Sestina has his own network of 20 planners scattered around the U.S.; he says they can even handle some clients entirely over the phone (*www.sestina.com*). "There's a large influx of middle-class retirees that have assets that need to be put somewhere, so more and more companies are trying to tap into this market," says Percy E. Bolton, committee member of the Certified Financial Planner Board of Standards and founder of Pasadena, Calif.–based Percy E. Bolton Associates. "There are two waves of change today—the planners that are going after the super-rich and those that are going after the middle- and upper-middle-class clients."

8 "CONFUSED? THAT'S THE POINT."

Many clients meet with planners only to leave with more questions than answers. "It's like going to the doctor—you think you understand when you're there, but then you walk out and think, What was it they said?" says Madeline Moore, a Portland, Ore.–based financial planner. Unfortunately, this confusion is often used to manipulate you.

Sherry Fabricant and her husband, of Plano, Tex., started investing $120,000

with a financial planner at an area brokerage firm at the end of 1997. The planner told them that withdrawal of funds before a five-year period would incur a sliding fee (5 percent of assets in the first year, 4 in the second, and so on). However, not only did the planner put them in high-fee funds without their understanding but he didn't explain that with any additional investment transaction, the five-year restriction would begin anew. "Recently, we made a huge sell and a huge purchase," says Fabricant, "and it wasn't explained that our five years would then start over."

Ask plenty of questions and write down the responses, and if you don't get straight answers, move on.

How can you protect yourself? Ask plenty of questions and write down the responses, and if you don't get straight answers, move on. "Remember, they work for you," says Sestina. "So if you never understand what they're saying, fire them."

9 "IN FACT, I DON'T EVEN UNDERSTAND YOUR PLAN."

There's a plethora of computer software today designed to help financial planners with clients' asset allocation, cash flow, retirement planning, and so on. These tools make for quick results, but they can also cause problems—especially when planners don't understand how the software works.

When Scott Dauenhauer worked at one major brokerage firm, he and his colleagues churned out boilerplate documents that, he says, all looked alike and usually had glaring mistakes— everything from a wrong age (which can render the entire plan wrong) to a misunderstanding of the client's goals. The danger was that most of his fellow advisers had little training in planning, "so you have a document that's probably wrong and an adviser who can't tell you why," Dauenhauer says.

Cotton suggests that you quiz your planner about any computer-generated plan to make sure he really understands it. You could ask, say, whether the software assumes a flat rate of return on investments or how it deals with taxation issues. You can also test your CFP's plan against the free service at Financeware.com, which analyzes plans using real stock market returns—and is therefore more realistic than the flat rate used by most planners' programs.

10 *"GOOD LUCK BUSTING ME FOR MALPRACTICE."*

Since the financial-planning industry is so loosely organized, it's not surprising that there are no firm regulations regarding consumer grievances. The CFP Board enforces a code of ethics, "but given the limitations of a voluntary certification program, it's kind of after-the-fact

enforcement," says Roper. So what can you do if you get cheated? If your planner, like most, holds a securities license, you go to FINRA, the Financial Industry Regulatory Authority. But be prepared to wait. Although the majority of arbitration cases are settled in around six months, if your case goes to a hearing, it could take up to 16 months to get a decision.

Quiz your planner about any computer-generated plan to make sure he really understands it.

Even then, there's no guarantee you'll get a favorable outcome: In 2007, only 37 percent of investors who had a hearing recovered any money. Also, since arbitration can cost between $15,000 and $50,000, it makes sense only if you've lost more than $30,000. If you're out less than that, start by writing a formal letter of complaint to the supervising manager, then write one to FINRA, the Securities and Exchange Commission, or your state securities regulator. You're unlikely to get any money back, says Eccleston, but the adviser might face disciplinary action. Even better: Protect yourself in advance by checking out a prospective financial planner's record. The SEC lists client complaints and regulatory violations on its website (*www.adviserinfo.sec.gov*), where you can also get details on both SEC- and state-registered planners.

THINGS TO DO

● **Hire a qualified planner.** "Certified financial planners" and members of the National Association of Personal Financial Advisors must meet professional and continuing-ed requirements. Find one at *www.cfp.net* or *www.napfa.org*.

● **Hire a "fee-only" planner**—that is, one who doesn't get paid commissions by investment companies to hawk certain products. All NAPFA members are fee-only.

● **What to ask a prospective planner?** Find a list of useful questions by going to *www.cfp.net/learn* and clicking on "How to Choose a Planner." NAPFA also offers a diagnostic, at *www.napfa.org/tips_tools/index.asp*.

● **Financial planning isn't just for the wealthy.** The Garrett Planning Network *(www.garrettplanningnetwork.com)* is a consortium of 260 planners that cater to the middle class.

● **Make sure your financial planner's** firm is in good standing and hasn't been investigated for misconduct. You can look it up at *www.adviserinfo.sec.gov*. The SEC is updating the site to include listings for individuals as well.

10 Things Your
Estate Planner
Won't Tell You

1 *"YOU PROBABLY DON'T NEED ME."*

Let's face it: Estate planning is scary. Not only does it involve protecting your hard-earned assets but it makes you think about that most dreaded of topics—your own mortality. That's one reason why many of us run to an estate planner when it comes time to write a will.

But the fact is, you might not need any help. "The overwhelming majority of estates don't trigger the federal estate tax," says a spokesperson for the Internal Revenue Service. In fact, as of 2009 you must be worth at least $3.5 million when you die to pay tax at all. If you fall below that—and don't have any complicated estate issues—you probably don't need a lawyer to draw up a will for you. Instead, you can use software like Quicken's WillMaker Plus (around $45 at Amazon. com) and dispense with the whole task in a single afternoon.

2 *"ESTATE PLANNING ISN'T ACTUALLY MY THING."*

What does it take to call oneself an estate planner? Not much, it turns out. Some estate planners are financial planners. Others are CPAs. Many are lawyers. But none of those titles guarantees an intricate knowledge of estate planning. "If you have a $50 million estate and you ask a lawyer if he does estate planning, the answer you'll get 100 percent of the time is an enthusiastic 'Yes, I do,'" says Tony Fiorillo, a former financial adviser.

Robert N. Sacks, chairman of an American Bar Association estate committee, says that you should stick with a lawyer who specializes in estates. The ultimate badge of competency: membership in ACTEC, the American College of Trust and Estate Counsel, an invitation-only national organization. (You can search ACTEC attorneys in your area at *www.actec.org.*)

3 *"I'D LOVE TO BE YOUR EXECUTOR—IT'S A GREAT WAY TO MAKE SOME EXTRA MONEY."*

Who should execute your will once you're gone? It's a tricky question, especially for parents who don't want to favor one child over another but who also aren't crazy about the idea of entrusting the job to the son who just depleted his 401(k) for a new Miata.

In your time of indecision, you may find your estate planner offering to take the job. A generous gesture? Not likely. Executors often pull in hefty fees. "It guarantees future employment or retirement money," says Stephen McDaniel, former president of the National Association of Estate Planners and Councils and a certified estate planning specialist in Tennessee.

In California, for example, where executor fees are based on an estate's size, a $1 million estate would pay $23,000 to the executor. Many people give the job to family members, who often refuse payment. But an estate planner stepping in to do the job will understandably want to pocket the profit.

4 "YOU DON'T NEED A LIVING TRUST."

Living trusts have been a favorite estate planning tool of the past decade, and it's easy to see why—they allow your estate to transfer property and assets outside the clunky probate process, saving your heirs time and money. Overzealous planners love them too, since setting one up can boost their bill. "I've had several clients who had gone to an estate planner and were pressured into setting up a living trust," says John Huggard, an estate planner and author of *Living Trust, Living Hell: Why You Should Avoid Living Trusts.* "It drove the cost of a basic estate plan from $500 to $3,500."

While the prospect of a long probate can be enough of a deterrent to justify the cost of a living trust, that's becoming less the case. David Scull, a probate attorney in Bethesda, Md., says that over the years many states—including "almost everything west of the Mississippi"—have simplified their probate processes. Two exceptions: If you live in a big city or own

property in two states, probates can still be tedious. But in most cases, he says, "If the executor is organized, it's possible to do a $10 million estate in minutes."

5 "I MAKE MORE MONEY IN INSURANCE THAN ON PLANNING YOUR ESTATE."

John Scherer, a certified financial planner who was once a Northwestern Mutual Life insurance agent, recalls working with a client in need of estate planning. Scherer referred him to an attorney, who charged about $7,500 to draft a will. Then, in order to fund his estate-tax liability, the client considered buying life insurance—a policy Scherer predicted would put about $10,000 in commission in some lucky agent's pocket.

Given the financial incentive for selling insurance, it's no wonder so many estate planners have managed to muscle their way into the insurance business as well. Despite the obvious conflict of interest—planners who sell insurance have an incentive to recommend it—it is a lot easier than it once was for planners to do both. That's because many states have rewritten their laws so that certified public accountants who pass a state exam and are sponsored by an insurance carrier can sell insurance products and collect a commission when doing estate planning.

It's a requirement that the financial incentive be disclosed, but apparently, many planners aren't complying with the rule. It's a "huge" problem, says attorney Jay Adkisson, who runs Quatloos.com, a website that tracks financial scams. He says his site has received dozens of e-mails from people complaining that their CPA or attorney pitched life insurance but didn't mention a commission. "If someone says, 'I'm going to help you with estate planning' and a product is a central point in the presentation—run, don't walk," advises John Olsen, an estate planner in St. Louis.

6 *"MY CUSTOMER SERVICE STINKS."*

The tax code gets a major revision about every other year, and people's lives change constantly. Yet some clients are lucky if they ever hear from their estate planner after the initial meeting. Part of the reason is that many estate planners started practicing years ago, when the idea of maintenance was a foreign concept: Back then people changed jobs less often, moved investments less frequently, and, frankly, amassed wealth less quickly, says Kathleen O'Blennis, an estate planner with Polsinelli Shalton Flanigan Suelthaus PC in St. Louis. Today, "planning is an ongoing issue," she says.

But don't take it for granted that your planner will hold your hand once your initial plan is in place. Cautionary tale: O'Blennis once had a client who, under a previous planner, sold his home and

> **"If someone says, 'I'm going to help you with estate planning' and a product is a central point in the presentation—run, don't walk."**

failed to get the new home transferred into the existing trust. O'Blennis says she managed to salvage the trust, but it cost the client thousands of dollars. "If I were looking for a planner," she says, "I'd ask what they're going to do to help me maintain this thing once the animal is born."

7 *"YOUR PUSHY SISTER IS YOUR PROBLEM."*

Sure, estate planning is primarily about money, but it's also about family and their complicated relationships. But good luck finding a planner who knows something about both. "[Planners] are so entrenched in the tax game that they forget about how the estate plan will ultimately impact the family after a death," says Mike Smith, a court-appointed guardian of estate disputes and chief deputy clerk in the Northern District of Georgia.

Things can get especially dicey when a family limited partnership is involved. This estate-planning tool, which lets people slash estate taxes and protect assets from creditors, divides ownership of the assets among family members. The general partner makes all the decisions, while the limited partners simply reap financial benefits. Sounds simple in theory, but that's not always the case in reality. Gerald Le Van, an estate attorney and family-business consultant, has worked on a handful of family limited partnerships that he says were headed toward litigation because the siblings just couldn't get along. His advice is to anticipate problems early. Lesson No. 1: "Siblings will take orders from parents, but not from each other," Le Van says.

8 "I'M IN BED WITH THE BANK."

You might not know it, but your planner may have other relationships that could affect your estate. Take the case of management consultant Edmund McCormick, who appointed Bankers Trust as corporate fiduciary of his $37 million estate. After McCormick's death back in 1988, Bankers Trust appointed the law firm White & Case to represent the estate through probate. As it turned out, White & Case was also a Bankers Trust attorney, meaning that the estate had no unbiased legal representation, says Patrick Hanley, spokesperson for Edmund McCormick's widow, Suzanne.

Things turned litigious when, according to Hanley, White & Case failed to go after two of the estate's coexecutors who were allegedly involved in the embezzlement of $232,000 from the estate. To Hanley, the reason is clear: Such a lawsuit would have been embarrassing for Bankers Trust, which failed to catch the problem early. In 1998, Suzanne McCormick and her family filed objections against the bank with the Surrogate Court in White Plains, N.Y., alleging mismanagement of the estate and breaches of fiduciary duties; she lost the case. To add insult to injury, White & Case was paid $250,000 out of the estate for its services. (White & Case declined to comment; the lawyer representing Bankers Trust says that White & Case acted without bias.)

Despite the outcome of the case, McCormick's situation serves as a cautionary tale for anyone with a complicated estate. "The banks and lawyers are having collusive relationships," says Standish Smith, founder of Heirs, a nonprofit organization in Villanova, Pa., that helps beneficiaries with complaints regarding trusts and estates. "It's hard to figure out if the lawyer is working for the client or the bank."

9 "GO AHEAD AND SUE ME— YOU WON'T WIN ..."

In some cases, the mistakes of an estate planner are caught early. In most situations, however, your planner's blunders won't surface until long after you're gone. And that can create big problems if your heirs want to sue for malpractice. "The key witness is dead," says Bruce Ross, an estate planner and trust lawyer in Los Angeles.

Generally speaking, beneficiaries have two main hurdles in estate-executor malpractice suits. The first is statute of limitations. The death of the parent begins the statute clock running, oftentimes causing it to expire before problems come to light. (Statute of limitations rules vary by state.) The second hurdle is privity, a contract law that prohibits a third party (in this case, a beneficiary) from suing a party in the original contract (for example, an executor). It works like this: If a car dealer sells you a lemon, and you in turn sell it to your neighbor, the neighbor can't sue the dealer, because he's one step removed.

So what options does a beneficiary with a beef have, if any? If an estate planner who makes a mistake is also a lawyer with malpractice insurance, beneficiaries may have a shot at getting their due. "If a lawyer says he's a specialist, he's held to a higher standard," says Ross. Indeed, most states have relaxed their privity law precedence and some, led by California, have even written into the legal code the liabilities held by lawyers who act as estate executors.

10 *"…BUT THINGS MIGHT BE CHANGING."*

Texas, which long upheld a strict interpretation of privity, is another state that has recently pried open the door to estate planner malpractice suits. In a landmark 2005 case, the state Supreme Court found in favor of a petition filed by Kristen Terk Belt and Kimberly Terk Murphy, joint executors of their father's estate, to take to trial law firm Oppenheimer, Blend, Harrison & Tate, of San Antonio, for legal malpractice. The two daughters had hired the law firm to draft a will and advise on asset management, which they claimed the firm failed to do adequately by neglecting to protect the estate's assets with simple tax planning.

What green-lighted their suit in the face of the state's strict privity interpretation was the fact that the sisters were not just beneficiaries but also executors of their father's estate. This case led the way for Texas and other states as well to begin holding lawyers accountable to an estate after the death of the parent, whether or not these lawyers served as the estate's executor.

In light of the trend, a good attorney will suggest that beneficiaries also act as executors to help protect their interests, but many lawyers continue to write themselves into the estate plan as the sole fiduciary, even after "most states have put regulations on attorneys acting as sole fiduciaries," says Dominic J. Campisi, chair of the ABA Malpractice Committee of Real Property, Probate and Trust Law. Some states, like Massachusetts, have a long history of assigning law firms as executors, and attorneys aren't given an incentive to discuss other options.

THINGS TO DO

We talked with Debra Schatzki, president and CEO of Weiser Capital Management, a New York City–based accounting firm, to get some tips on estate planning:

● **Before you meet with an estate planner** ask yourself: "If I died last night, what would I want to happen? What would I want to give to whom?" That will help you get started.

● **Make sure the estate planner** you hire is an attorney who regularly does estate planning, not someone who does it once or twice a year.

● **Most people don't know** the real value of their estates. The best way to find out: make an inventory of everything you won, and hire an appraiser.

● **Complex estate?** Having some additional professionals, like certified planners and accountants, at the table with your estate planner will make sure every angle is covered.

10 Things Your
Charity
Won't Tell You

1 *"OUR FAVORITE CHARITY IS THE FUND-RAISER WE HIRED."*

Fund-raising expenses are an inescapable fact of life for charities. But in recent decades, as the competition for donations has heated up, many have turned to full-time professional fund-raisers for help. That often means less of your money reaches the cause you're trying to support. In 2003, for example, the American Institute of Philanthropy, or AIP, disclosed that between 1987 and 1995, VietNow, a charity aimed at helping disabled Vietnam vets, allowed its commercial fund-raiser, Telemarketing Associates, to keep more than $6 million of the $7.1 million raised in revenue. Daniel Borochoff, president of the AIP, says the charity still spends more than 85 percent of its revenue on fund-raising expenses today. (VietNow did not return our calls for comment.)

Then there's the Children's Wish Foundation. According to a report by California's attorney general, the charity made no money on a 2005 fund-raising campaign and actually ended up owing the fund-raiser, Facter Direct Ltd., almost $12,000. (A spokesperson for Children's Wish says the attorney general's report presented a "distorted picture" and neglected to take into consideration the "value of a donor's lifetime of giving.")

Sadly, these are hardly isolated cases. According to a 2005 California Department of Justice report, "Historical figures show that a campaign conducted by a commercial fund-raiser returns, on average, less than 50 percent of the contributions to the charity. The rest is retained by the commercial fund-raiser as a fund-raising fee." Indeed, of the 600-plus charities the California Department of Justice surveyed, almost half received 30 percent or less of the intake. How to avoid filling the fund-raiser's coffers instead of the charity you're donating to? Look for charities that keep their fund-raisers' cut below 35 percent. To find them, you can request a charity-rating guide by sending a check for $3 to the American Institute of Philanthropy, at P.O. Box 578460, Chicago, IL 60657.

2 *"WE TRY TO HIDE OUR FUND-RAISING COSTS."*

If you want to know what percentage of a charity's income gets spent on fund-raising, you could always ask the charity itself. But don't count on a straight answer. Under the rules set by the American Institute of Certified Public Accountants (AICPA), charities may, through a bit of creative accounting known as "joint-cost allocation," label some fund-raising costs as "program expenses"—just so long as there is some educational material included with the request for funds.

As Congress has recently noticed, some charities stretch the definition of "educational." That's why Richard Chapin, founder of Help Hospitalized Veterans and the Coalition to Support America's Heroes Foundation (CSAHF), was called to testify on Capitol Hill recently. If you checked both his organizations' websites, you would see that each claimed a majority of its funds go toward program expenses, more than 90 percent in the case of CSAHF. But Congress found otherwise. After reviewing the charities' financial activities over a three-year period, the Committee on Oversight and Government Reform reported they'd spent a meager 25 percent on services for veterans. The rest went to fund-raising, management, and education. Why the difference in numbers? Congress didn't consider the cost of "educational" mailings as a benefit to veterans. "In all honesty, I don't know too much about Congress or about what their thinking is, and where they're getting their numbers from," says Thomas John Palmer, general manager of CSAHF. "The IRS and the AICPA are our guidelines."

A good guideline for you is the American Institute of Philanthropy (AIP)(*www.charitywatch.org*). Its reviews of various charities highlight what gets reported as program expenses versus that amount minus direct-mail, telemarketing, and solicitation costs.

3 *"OUR WATCHDOGS HAVE SOME MAJOR BLIND SPOTS."*
Charity-watchdog groups can be very helpful when you're trying to evaluate where your donations are really going. But unfortunately, they can't see everything. The BBB Wise Giving Alliance, for instance, rigorously evaluates the finances of more than 1,200 groups, but it doesn't cover many local charities, where the majority of the $295 billion in donations went last year. Try to get specific information on your local United Way chapter, for example, and you won't have much luck—the Wise Giving Alliance tracks only the national organization.

Charity Navigator, which evaluates more than 5,000 charities including local ones, also does full evaluations on a similar number of groups, but it tends to base much of its data on Form 990, which all charities must file with the IRS. Form 990 is the return used by tax-exempt and nonprofit groups when filing to the IRS; it lays out an organization's financial activity over the past year, specifying revenue sources and various operational expenses, among other things. Sounds pretty straightforward, but these forms are not foolproof sources—according to AIP President Daniel Borochoff, Form 990 "isn't as scrutinized [by the IRS] as it ought to be." Another problem is that not everything that should get reported does. "There are charities that don't fill out the entire form," Borochoff says. "They just leave some things blank, and they get away with it."

Then there is the one task that none of these groups performs: impact studies. In fact, no one scientifically analyzes charities' effectiveness—that is what they accomplish toward the goals they've set. How to give wisely in the face of less than satisfying data? Fred Lane, a professor at the Center for Nonprofit Strategy and Management at Baruch College in New York, recommends a DIY approach. "Pick a field and volunteer in it," he says. "Give your money to the group that you know from experience is good."

4 "YOU MAY NOT BE GIVING MONEY TO THE GROUP YOU THINK."

You sympathize deeply with breast-cancer patients and decide to mail a check to a respectable-sounding cancer charity. But beware, you may end up donating your hard-earned money to the American Breast Cancer Foundation, rated "F" by the AIP, which spent 87 percent of its earnings on solicitations with an educational message, rather than the "A"-rated Breast Cancer Research Foundation, which devotes more than 85 percent of its funds to research and which you've probably heard good things about.

Are charities deliberately attempting to confuse you with similar-sounding

---

Your best bet for getting your money where you want it to go: Scrutinize a potential charity carefully—including its exact title versus others in its field.

---

names? Probably not. While there may be isolated cases of startup organizations trying to profit from the popularity of an already established charity, "Sometimes," says Borochoff, "it's a genuine case of there not being enough words in the dictionary." Your best bet for getting your money where you want it to go: Scrutinize a potential charity carefully—including its exact title versus others in its field.

5 "YOUR SPARE CHANGE IS GOING TO THIEVES."

Whether they're candy "honor boxes," wishing wells, or plain old tin cans, those ubiquitous countertop collection boxes you see around so many checkouts are often not what they appear. In most cases, the charities aren't getting all the money people drop into the container; rather, they're renting out their name to for-profit vendors for a flat fee or a small percentage of the intake in exchange for posting the charity's logo.

How much does the advertised charity actually get? "You could be talking about 1 percent or 2 percent of the take," says Steven Arter, former president of the National Association of State Charity Officials. And sometimes they get nothing at all. In 2006, Missouri's attorney general filed a lawsuit in Camden County Circuit Court against a man for falsely presenting himself as a representative of the Armed Forces Children's Education Fund—a charity seeking to help the children of American soldiers killed overseas—when he and an accomplice sought to install fund-raising candy-vending machines in stores in several counties in Missouri. (The case was settled in 2006; the accused paid fines both to the charity and to the state of Missouri.) According to a spokesperson for the Missouri Attorney General's Office, it wasn't an isolated case. "From time to time, we'll see similar scams," he says—like the one recently in which "a bunch of guys were placing bogus collection boxes for the Special Olympics in various supermarkets, and they were just pocketing the money."

Most charity watchers agree: Go ahead and toss in your spare change if you want to, but don't expect it to be doing much for the cause. "If you're serious about helping the charity," says Daniel Borochoff, "then get out your checkbook and write them a check."

6 "OUR BOARD MEMBERS ARE TOO BUSY TO CARE."

Just as in big business, a charity's board of directors is one of the keys to successful management. But all too often a board seat is considered a less than serious job, and as a result, some charities' boards are more rubber-stamp assemblies than active oversight committees.

One of the most famous cases was the 1992 scandal at United Way, in which the organization's executive director was forced to resign following allegations of nepotism, graft, and fantastically bloated expense accounts—charges he denied. But United Way has since learned its lesson, revamping its board and instituting a number of management changes, including new internal auditing procedures, a code of ethics, and new expense accounting.

Even today there is little federal oversight in the nonprofit sector. "The

most important regulation of any nonprofit group is self-regulation," says Baruch College's Fred Lane. "We have to rely on the boards for that." But boards aren't always up to the task—in its 2007 Nonprofit Governance Index, nonprofit consultant BoardSource reported that nonprofit "boards do not understand their role very well," based on evaluations by chief executives and board members. The underlying issue, says Linda C. Crompton, president of BoardSource, is the demand on members' time. "People are busier," she says. "It's becoming increasingly difficult for boards to get the kind of commitment that is needed to do a good job."

7 "WE'RE MAKING MONEY OFF YOUR NAME AND ADDRESS."

Trying to save the planet? Then you should know that giving to your favorite charity may be an invitation to having your mailbox clogged with junk. That's because mailing lists are the currency of the direct-mail trade, and it's common for charities to share their lists with other nonprofits—or even sell them to commercial businesses.

Greg Fox, former president of CFF Direct, a direct mailer for the Cystic Fibrosis Foundation among other charities, estimates that most charities have "rented" their lists to commercial companies at least once.

How to stem the tide? While you can visit the Direct Marketing Association's website (*www.the-dma.org*) and ask to be kept off mailing lists, the best way may be to include a note with your donation requesting that your name not be sold to any other groups. "It's a matter of good business sense," says Bob Tigner, general counsel to the Association of Direct Response Fundraising Counsel. "You honor the reasonable requests of your supporters."

8 "IF WE CALL YOU, DON'T ANSWER."

One of life's most annoying sounds is a ringing telephone just as you're about to sit down to dinner. Still, it's hard to be rude and hang up on someone who's phoning on behalf of a good cause. That's part of the reason why charities use the phone so much. "It's a little bit less expensive" than mailing, says a spokesperson for the BBB Wise Giving Alliance, "and it's effective."

But unless it's an organization you know calling, charity-watchdog groups are unanimous on this point: Don't agree to give any money right away to a person or group who solicits you by phone. At minimum, ask the caller to send you some written material first. If the group is legitimate, it'll do it; if it's a scam, you'll never hear from it again. Says Robert Bothwell, former executive director of the National Committee for Responsive Philanthropy: "A charity that has lies to tell doesn't want to put them in print."

9 "WE'RE ROLLING IN CASH."

Some charities are actively taking in funds but not spending them. The reason: They have hoarded so much of their previous fund-raising cash that they can't use the new money. Currently, roughly 36 of the 500 charities tracked by the American Institute of Philanthropy have cash reserves that could keep them running at current operational levels for more than three years without any other revenue coming in.

The Shriners Hospitals for Children, for instance, has cash reserves and endowments estimated by AIP at $8.9 billion. That means the group could dip into its savings and distribute just as much money as it does now for 12 more years without raising another cent, says Dan Borochoff, president of AIP. "Shriners doesn't charge for any of its services," says Keith Gardiner, corporate director of finance. "We have to be assured that over time we can provide continuous care to our in-need population."

John Melingagio, public relations director for Boys Town, another well-known charity with relatively modest cash reserves—just under $10 million—says that these figures often represent more than just untapped cash. "That's our net asset figure, which is all of our property, everything—home shelters, buildings, our hospitals," Melingagio says. "We're doing charitable work, and it's helping us do that more effectively—if the agency's budget changes because of the economy, if it's all gone, how are we going to care for the kids?"

10 "BEFORE YOU WRITE OUT THAT CHECK, YOU'D BETTER CALL YOUR ACCOUNTANT."

Here's a suggestion you can take to the bank: Don't count on charities to give you good tax advice. "It's not that they're trying to harm you," says Carol R. Caruthers, once a charitable-deductions specialist. "Some of these organizations are stretched so thin that they don't have tax experts. If they make a mistake in their advice, you pay the penalty."

Part of the problem is the ever-changing tax code. It used to be, for example, that if you donated more than $250 to a charity, your canceled check did not count as proof for a deduction—you needed a full-fledged receipt. But starting in 2007, a full-fledged receipt is required for *all* deductions. "You need a receipt for everything," says Jeffrey Schnepper, author of *How to Pay Zero Taxes*.

One area to be especially careful about is the appraisal of expensive appreciable gifts. "If it's a significant sum, we recommend that you get two appraisals and average them," says Caruthers. And remember that even if the charity goodheartedly offers its services, IRS rules strictly forbid it. Instead, have the assessment done by an experienced independent appraiser whose fee is not based on the value he gives to the item.

THINGS TO DO

- **To find a charity** that interests you, check out *www.give.org*, *www.charitywatchdog.org*, or *www.charitynavigator.org*.

- **Don't give money to a charity** you've never heard of. Ask for some printed information, or check with the AIP to make sure it's legit.

- **Instead of donating loose change** to countertop collection boxes—from which only 1 to 2 percent of the money goes toward helping the cause—give to the charity directly.

- **Even with some well-known organizations,** your donation might largely be helping to foot the bill for advertising or the charity's next fund-raiser. Visit the American Institute of Philanthropy at *www.charitywatch.org* to see where the money goes.

- **Giving out your name and address** to charities could open the junk mail floodgates. Include a note with your donation saying you'd prefer to be kept off any mailing lists, and if that doesn't work, contact the Direct Marketing Association at *www.dmachoice.org*.

- **To take advantage of the tax breaks** that come with donating money, make sure you get a detailed receipt for your contributions.

CHAPTER 5

Goods & Services

■ *SmartMoney*'s mission has always been to help consumers make informed choices about their money, whether they're saving or spending it. In this chapter, we deal with the latter by taking a look at the goods and services sector of your budget.

In "10 Things Your Cable Company Won't Tell You," for example, we help you untangle the knot of programming packages and bundled-service options, while "10 Things Your Ticket Broker Won't Tell You" offers up the best (and worst) ways to score tickets to the big game. Whatever the industry, we strive to ferret out the best and latest strategies for extending your discretionary dollars.

10 Things Your
Cell Phone Service
Won't Tell You

1 *"OUR COVERAGE AREA HAS MORE DEAD ZONES THAN A CEMETERY."*

If you find yourself bored at the beach or ballpark, try this time killer: In a 60-second span, count how many people are using their cell phones nearby. The number will stagger you—and it's sure to keep rising. Consider that by the end of 2005, the most recent year for which stats are available, there were 213 million cell phone users in the U.S., more than double the number in 2000, according to a Federal Communications Commission report.

But quantity doesn't mean quality. Busy signals. Sloppy service. Static. Problems that have long plagued cell phones persist even with higher penetration. Take New York City, for example, the largest cell phone market in the country. In the vicinity of the city, there are still nearly 200 "dead zones"— areas of heavy interference, frequent dropped calls, and failed connections— according to the office of Sen. Charles Schumer (D-NY). The major reason: Service providers have oversubscribed usage and overwhelmed their networks with call volume. Schumer has proposed legislation that, if passed, will require the disclosure of dead zones.

But New Yorkers aren't the only ones contending with inadequate cell phone service. In 2003 the California Public Utilities Commission fined Cingular Wireless $12 million, finding that the company had provided shoddy service while locking customers into long-term contracts. Says a Cingular spokesperson, "To say we would intentionally sign up customers for service in areas we know we don't have coverage is preposterous." Cingular appealed the decision and lost; the company has since agreed to refund approximately $18.5 million in early-termination fees collected from former customers from January 2000 through April 2002. Less than ideal service is absolutely still an issue, says Allen Nogee, a principal analyst at In-Stat, a market research firm. "There are very few areas where you don't have any coverage, but many where you have marginal coverage," he says. "And that's a problem."

2 *"DON'T EVEN BOTHER BRINGING YOUR PHONE ABROAD."*

Service issues don't stop at our borders. Since 2000, when domestic carriers AT&T Wireless and T-Mobile switched over to the Global System for Mobile

Communications, or GSM, network—the same type used in Europe—subscribers to those services have been able to bring their cell phone with them overseas. In theory, that is. Dharm Guruswamy knows the reality. In 2003 Guruswamy confirmed with AT&T Wireless that he would be able to use his phone while traveling in Amsterdam. "They explained how much it would cost—about a dollar per minute—and told me it was set up," says Guruswamy. But when he arrived in Amsterdam, the phone didn't work. "This was unfortunate," says an AT&T Wireless spokesperson, but "the problem could have been caused by any number of things."

Perhaps, but Guruswamy is hardly alone when it comes to foreign service troubles. Sprint Nextel, Verizon, and Alltel phones won't work at all overseas, and T-Mobile requires you to buy a prepaid SIM card at one of its foreign dealers. Overseas service is getting better, though, according to Jeff Kagan, an independent telecom analyst. "It's better than it was," he says. "Ten years ago it was terrible, and it's going to be much better in five years."

3 "YOU CAN'T ALWAYS DEPEND ON YOUR CELL PHONE IN AN EMERGENCY."

In 2001, Karla Guiterrez was trapped in her car after it barreled into a Miami canal. She dialed 911 on her cell phone, but emergency services could not locate her before she died. Sadly, not much has changed since then. The list of tragedies occurring because the 911 system can't locate cell phone callers keeps growing, and the possibility for more calamities persists.

Currently, carriers are required to connect calls to 911 almost immediately. But up to one third of the emergency calls made on cell phones still don't go through, according to a spokesperson for the Public Safety Bureau. Fortunately, carriers, working with local emergency agencies, are mandated to have precise location technology in place by 2012. That will enable them to locate cell phone users almost immediately, as long as there is a signal.

In the meantime, the National Emergency Number Association, a nonprofit organization that provides national coordination on 911 services, has put together an interactive map that shows local areas' wireless 911 readiness. Find it at *nena.ddti.net*.

4 "OUR BILLS MAY CONFUSE YOU—BUT YOU STILL GOTTA PAY 'EM."

Chip Gracey knows what it's like to feel duped by his cell phone provider. Back in 2002 the Rockland, Calif., resident thought he had signed up with a wireless company for a $99 service plan giving him 900 minutes a month during the day and unlimited usage at night and on weekends. But when he opened his next bill, Gracey was shocked to discover that he owed the company $653. Turns out the provider's plan gave him 900 minutes a month *total*. When Gracey called customer service for help, he says he was told, "There's nothing we can do."

It's not just billing miscues that you should look out for. Hidden fees are another major issue for cell phone users. Sprint Nextel, for instance, adds a

"Federal Programs Cost Recovery" fee as well as a "USA Regulatory Obligations & Fees" to its bill. But a lawsuit filed by the Missouri attorney general's office in St. Louis Circuit Court contends that these fees are a way for carriers to tack on extra expenses to your bill. The lawsuit was settled in July 2003, before Sprint and Nextel merged. Today, Sprint Nextel still honors the agreement to use clearer and more explanatory language in mobile-phone plan advertising and in billing statements sent to cell phone customers in Missouri.

Furthermore, the Cell Phone Consumer Empowerment Act of 2007 prohibits carriers from levying any fees, apart from the basic service charge, not expressly authorized by federal, state or local regulation. Such changes seem to be making a difference with consumers: Complaints to the FCC regarding billing and rate problems actually declined 13 percent from 2002 to 2007.

5 "OUR SMART PHONES ARE GETTING JUST A TAD TOO SMART FOR SOME PEOPLE."

Send photos. Get e-mail. Surf the Web. The advertisements promoting these services can be enticing. But the reality of today's smart phones often falls short of the promise. In fact, of all the electronic products returned after 2007's holiday season, smart phones ranked No. 1, with 21 percent of smart phones purchased being returned, according to a survey by the Opinions Research Corporation. "The inability to understand the product setup process was cited as the primary reason consumers returned their smart phones,"

said Kevin Wood, senior technology analyst at Opinions Research in a statement released with the survey.

"It's not just that the software and experience of the device itself can be complicated," says Charles Golvin, a principal analyst at Forrester Research. "They also require some considerable synchronization with your computer. It's a pretty far distance from the experience most people have with a mobile phone today." The iPhone and BlackBerry have made a lot of strides in making smart phones more user-friendly says Tole Hart, an analyst at Gartner Inc., a research and advisory firm. Still, it takes a reasonably savvy user to get the most out of a smart phone, he says. If you're not among the comfortably digital, you can always ask for a tutorial at the store where you purchase your smart phone—retailers are happiest when their returns are kept to a minimum.

6 "OUR VOICEMAIL ISN'T 100 PERCENT RELIABLE."

Business travelers, beware: Your voicemail messages may be getting lost in transit. In 2006, 6 percent of cell phone complaints were about voicemail, according to J. D. Power and Associates. Why? Often the problem lies with the carriers' network software. Unlike old-school landline answering machines that store messages on audiotape, cellular voicemail is kept in cyberspace. In order to reach your phone when you check in, it has to navigate a nationwide Web of networks. Most of the time, the system works just fine, but when you're outside of your home region, voicemail can easily get lost in space.

Kirk Parsons, senior director at J. D. Power and Associates, knows the problem firsthand. When traveling in Los Angeles on business, "the voicemail icon didn't show up on my phone," he says. He realized only when he returned home that a half-dozen business calls had come in. Be alert: Avoid missing messages when traveling by checking your voicemail even if you don't see an icon.

7 "PAY-AS-YOU-GO DOESN'T REALLY PAY OFF."

Don't want to sign up for a one- or two-year contract? Another option is a pay-as-you-go cellular phone. With such prepaid carriers, you purchase a handset and airtime up front, adding more value via credit card as needed. But this type of service can have its own set of problems. For example, Christine Bohac tried TracFone, the leading prepaid service. Even though Bohac used her phone only a few times, within a week the Chicago resident blew through all her $20 worth of airtime.

How come? As a TracFone spokesperson explained to us, the company indicates in all its promotional material that roaming costs extra. But according to Bohac, "My phone was always in roaming"—even when she was at home. TracFone's terms and conditions says that even if you're using your TracFone in your home calling area, roaming can occur if there's a high volume of callers in the area, if your carrier's signal is too weak, or for other reasons.

Besides roaming problems, many prepaid phones hit users with exorbitant

Be alert: Avoid missing messages when traveling by checking your voicemail even if you don't see an icon.

fees—about 30 cents per minute. "Generally the price of prepaid service is going to be a little higher than when you sign a contract," says Tole Hart. The charge is worth it if you use the phone only for emergencies; just don't get hooked on the convenience.

8 "FAMILY PLANS AREN'T ALWAYS SO FAMILY-FRIENDLY."

Text-messaging revenue is expected to top $1.4 billion in 2009, according to Gartner Inc., largely thanks to the nonstop thumb typing of America's teens. How much texting do kids these days actually do? According to Jupiter Research, 60 percent of teens ages 15 to 17 send and receive more than 30 text messages a month. At up to 20 cents a text, sent and received, that level of usage can quickly add up to big charges. And with nearly three out of four teens on a family wireless plan, that means those big charges are getting paid by the parents.

Kids use text messaging very much the way they use Instant Messaging on the computer, "just to say, 'hey,'" says Charles Golvin, a principal analyst at Forrester Research. "The carriers have done a pretty good job recognizing that this is a pain point for parents." Indeed, service providers have taken steps to put a cap on teens' excessive text-messaging spending. For example, unlimited text-messaging can be added to family plans for between $15 and $30 a month, depending on your carrier. Of course, another option is to make them get their own plan and pay their phone bills themselves.

9 "WE'LL HOLD YOUR PHONE HOSTAGE."

When the FCC mandated number portability back in 2003—that is, the ability to take your cell phone number with you when you switch carriers— consumers everywhere breathed a sigh of relief. Up until that point, providers used to hold cell phone users captive in their contracts by the threat of having to change their number should they take their business elsewhere. But now that you can take your cell number with you wherever you go, cell phone companies have come up with a new stumbling block—your cell phone.

Since cell phones are traditionally associated with a particular carrier, the assumption has been that you can only use it with that carrier, says Jeff Kagan, when in fact, "it's not that the phone is incompatible with other carriers, it's being blocked." But things are changing. Some companies are making it easier to transfer your cell phone to a different carrier. T-Mobile, for example, will provide you with an unlocked SIM card after 90 days, which allows you to use your phone with another carrier. Sprint Nextel and AT&T, on the other hand, will unlock your phone after you've fulfilled the terms of your contract. You can thank the Cell Phone Consumer Empowerment

Act of 2007, which called upon the FCC to study the practice of locking phones, prompting carriers to take preemptive action.

10 "LEAVING US IS GONNA COST YOU."

Many cell phone users, even if they're unhappy with their plan or provider, don't switch services for one simple reason: early-termination fees. Ending a contract before it runs out can cost you up to $200, depending on your carrier. And good luck trying to find out what exactly the fee pays for. It seems that every carrier has a slightly different story. AT&T's customer service agreement says that the company's termination fee is "not a penalty, but rather a charge to compensate your failure to satisfy the Service Commitment on which your rate plan is based." T-Mobile, on the other hand, justifies it as "a reasonable estimate of our harm."

"Early-termination fees are really just an attempt by companies to keep consumers in a program that may or may not be meeting their needs," says a spokesperson for Sen. Jay Rockefeller (D-WV), who helped propose the Cell Phone Consumer Empowerment Act to Congress. One of the things the bill calls for is limits to early-termination fees— which moved AT&T, T-Mobile, Verizon, and Sprint Nextel to introduce plans to pro-rate early-termination fees in new contracts starting in early 2008. Only Alltel hasn't announced changes to its policy yet, but a spokesperson there says the idea is currently under review.

THINGS TO DO

• **Traveling abroad with your cell phone** can be costly, thanks to roaming fees. For a cheaper alternative, check out Cellular Abroad, at *www.cellularabroad.com*. The company rents out cell phones for overseas use, and its rates almost always beat the U.S. carriers'.

• **In many cases,** when a carrier changes its contract—say, by raising the cost of text messaging—subscribers have two weeks to opt out of the plan without paying early-termination fees. How to know if you're eligible? Check your contract for a "material adverse change" clause.

• **For extra security,** buy yourself a phone with a built-in global-positioning system, such as the iPhone. That allows authorities to track your whereabouts even if you can't get a strong enough signal to dial 911.

• **If you switch carriers,** you may be able to take your phone in addition to your number: AT&T and T-Mobile phones are compatible.

10 Things Your
Cable Company
Won't Tell You

1 *"DEREGULATION IS A JOKE— BUT IT'S PROBABLY NOT AS FUNNY FOR YOU."*

For years the cable business had acted like a typical monopoly, providing less-than-ideal customer service, skyrocketing prices, and little choice of service. Then along came the Telecommunications Act of 1996, which opened the door for competition and promised weary cable customers relief at last. Too bad that relief never came. Nearly four years after the bill was passed, a mere 286 of the 30,000 U.S. cable markets were being served by more than one provider, according to the Federal Communications Commission. And in the FCC's most recent report, in 2005, not much had changed; only 294 out of about 33,000 U.S. cable markets were served by more than one provider—meaning that for all the effort to create change, few customers today are being served by the smaller providers that generally offer better deals.

The lucky few who live in markets with more than one cable company to choose from pay about 17 percent less than those in single-provider markets, according to the FCC. "The Telecom Act was meant to generate more competition, resulting in lower prices for cable TV customers," says David Butler, formerly of the Consumers Union, a Washington, D.C., consumer-watchdog group. "We have seen just the opposite—more mergers, less competition, and rising prices for customers."

Meanwhile, the only real alternative to cable—satellite television—has its own issues. While subscribers have been lured with the promise of competitive prices and more programming, about 8 percent of satellite customers still subscribe to cable television, since most satellite services cannot carry local broadcasters' signals, which cover events like city council meetings and high school football games. And satellite service delivers only one channel to a household at any given time—unless users purchase an extra set-top box for each TV, which may cost up to $69 apiece.

2 *"WE RAISE PRICES RECKLESSLY ..."*

Perhaps you've accepted the fact that cable prices move in only one direction—up. But what's really shocking is how quickly they rise. The average price increase for cable service in 2005, the most recent year for which data is available, was more than 5 percent, and from 1995 to 2005, cable rates nearly doubled, according to the FCC.

Will things get better? Not likely. The cable industry has been undertaking a massive upgrade of existing wiring in order to beef up its offerings of services like high-speed Internet access and local phone service—all of which will cost you. "The cable industry is constantly updating its infrastructure to provide consumers with better service," says Brian Dietz, vice president of communications at the National Cable & Telecommunications Association, and the increase in prices is designed to help cover those costs.

3 "...AND MANIPULATE THE DIAL."

Even as prices increase, it seems that the programming choices cable companies offer are somehow more limited. With the most popular channels intentionally divided into different tiers, consumers often must buy several packages of programming to get all the channels they want, says Mark Cooper, director of research for the Consumer Federation of America. "They're not giving consumers the full à la carte choice," Cooper says.

Cable companies that also own a lot of programming—like Time Warner, which owns HBO, CNN, and TNT among other channels—especially benefit from these package deals. "Only a portion of subscribers are going to watch, say, ESPN," says Chris Murray, senior counsel at Consumers Union. "Meanwhile, ESPN gets paid a certain amount for every subscriber, so the customer ends up subsidizing content he doesn't watch," Murray says. A spokesperson for Time Warner Cable says, "The tiers of channels are determined ultimately by viewer popularity, and we offer tiers that we feel will satisfy customers."

4 "BUNDLING YOUR SERVICES CAN END UP COSTING YOU MORE."

Increasingly, consumers are getting bundled telephone, cable television, and high-speed Internet service from one provider for an average price of $100 per month. Sounds like a great deal, especially when it can shave hundreds off the amount of money spent on telecom and TV per year. But it doesn't make sense for everyone, says John Breyault, research director for the nonprofit Telecommunications Research and Action Center in Washington, D.C. "Most bundled packages are based on an all-you-can-eat model," he says, adding that the majority include unlimited local and long-distance calling, for example, which some customers won't use. "Many consumers will find that they're able to save money by buying services individually that more closely meet their needs."

Another thing about these cable-phone-Internet bundles, also known as "triple play" packages, is that they can be complicated and sometimes misleading—especially when they're advertised through special promotions. For starters, it's important to know when the offered deal expires. Time Warner, for example, offers New York City residents a triple-play package for $89.95 per month. But after the first 12 months, the monthly fee jumps to $114.95—something you wouldn't notice unless you did some digging. (A spokesperson for Time Warner Cable says, "It's a promotional deal. We want you to try our service because we believe in it. To get you to try it, we offer a discounted price, and later, the real price.")

Fortunately, there are some good triple-play deals out there, which is why it pays to shop around. Packages vary from provider to provider, so Breyault recommends doing your homework to find the one that best fits your individual needs. In addition, pay careful attention to the fine print, which should spell out early-termination fees and any additional charges.

5 "WE WANT TO CONTROL THE INTERNET THE WAY WE CONTROL YOUR TV."

In October 2007, an Associated Press test revealed that Comcast had deliberately blocked Internet users from sharing files online. In the AP test, computers that were connected to the Internet via Comcast cable modems would not let users send the King James Bible from one location in the U.S. to another using the file-sharing program BitTorrent; however, computers with other connections, including Time Warner Cable and Cablevision, had no problem sharing and uploading the text. (A Comcast spokesperson says that the company doesn't "block access to any websites or online applications, including peer-to-peer services like BitTorrent.")

Industry experts say that Comcast was blocking internal content because the BitTorrent application potentially competes with the company's video

service. And there are fears it could be the start of a push by cable companies to control content on the Internet. "We hope we'll continue to have an open Internet," says Murray, of Consumers Union, "but the dinosaur seems to be gnashing its teeth and not wanting new technologies to thrive or survive."

6 "OUR FIBER-OPTIC CABLES ARE A REAL EYESORE."

Cable companies have invested over $110 billion in infrastructure, according to a spokesperson for the National Cable and Telecommunications Association. But in a move to install fiber-optic cable throughout cities, they're littering neighborhoods with ugly new power lines. Take San Leandro, Calif. Since the winter of 2007, Comcast and AT&T have been competitively racing to install fiber-optic lines there. The results: Black cables roughly 2 inches thick are hanging below utility and phone lines, which are much thinner and less obtrusive by design. In addition, the companies have tacked big black canisters onto telephone poles. "You know, when you walk through your home and find a spiderweb," says San Leandro councilwoman Joyce Starosciak, "that's what the cabling looks like—thick black spiderwebs around your neighborhood."

Starosciak says the cables have a negative impact on the neighborhood and could potentially lower property values in the future. A spokesperson for Comcast says its cables, which have 190 different strands of fiber in each one, are the "standard" thickness for fiber-optic networks. AT&T says it's not aware of any complaints regarding aerial wires in that area and that there are several other providers included on those lines.

7 "WE'RE SO GOOD AT MAKING EXCUSES THAT WE START TO BELIEVE THEM OURSELVES."

Every year when cable prices go up, cable providers rush to justify their rate hikes. Programming costs have increased, they tell us. They're investing heavily in infrastructure to upgrade cable lines. And when all else fails, there's always inflation to blame. But these excuses are often false or vastly exaggerated, according to Murray. "If increased programming costs was the whole story, then cable companies should let TV viewers who want new programming buy it and pay for it, rather than having the programming fall on the backs of all consumers," he says.

Then there's high-speed Internet. After years of investing in infrastructure, cable companies are justifying rate hikes by saying they're providing a menu of consumer-friendly applications and rolling out higher bandwidth that increases speed. At Cox Communications, for example, they're offering customers "faster speeds, greater online security and enhanced features to make their lives easier," says a company spokesperson. "We're continually looking at new features requested by our customers, including larger mailboxes, more online storage and applications like Cox Rhapsody music."

The cable companies "are telling Wall Street that high-speed Internet is the most profitable part of the bundle," Murray says. "And they're telling consumers that costs are going up. They can't have it both ways." But some companies say that's not

true. Cablevision, for one, denies price increases on its Internet service: "For all of our customers, high-speed Internet cost has declined, and speed has increased," says a Cablevision spokesperson.

8 "WE CAN'T HANDLE CUSTOMER SERVICE."

After the FCC insisted in the mid-1990s that the cable industry do something about its dismal customer service, companies began promising such things as on-time installation and service calls. The move was so revolutionary that the National Cable Television Association, the industry's trade group, trumpeted it as "one of the most comprehensive customer-service programs offered by any industry."

Just don't mention that to Ray Lucas. Lucas, who works for a computer-services company in Gaithersburg, Md., called customer service because his Comcast cable Internet access had mysteriously stopped working. During the month-long ordeal of getting his service restored, Lucas says he made at least 10 calls to customer service, often waiting nearly an hour on hold. And despite the fact that he was given a "referral number" designed to ensure that each new representative would have access to documentation of his previous calls, he says he still had to start at square one with each new customer-service rep. A spokesperson for Comcast says the company has "reduced the hold times since then."

Cable companies aspire to become one-stop communications providers, offering everything from cable TV to local phone service. But you might want to think twice about relying on an industry with such a dismal service record for all your telecom needs. "Consumers have much higher standards for phone service and Internet," says Ken McEldowney, executive director of Consumer Action. "Unless it's the Super Bowl, they're willing to tolerate outages for cable, but not for their phone or Internet. This makes them feel cut off from the rest of the world."

9 *"WE'RE GOING TO PUMMEL YOU WITH ADVERTISING."*

For years cable companies have been boasting about all their cool high-tech features: More high-definition programming, extensive On-Demand offerings, cable DVR that provides easy recording and even classified ads available on-screen. But beware. As you give your cable company more and more information about your viewing and shopping habits, it's going to become more and more likely to make you the target of advertisers.

Take real estate company Re/max International, for example. During a two-month campaign in 2007, the company used technology that tapped into data from cable set-top boxes to find out how many homeowners were watching home-improvement shows and to see what other cable channels those viewers were likely to watch. After finding that home-improvement enthusiasts were also inclined to watch auto-racing programming on Speed channel and the TNT series *Without a Trace,* the company promptly placed ads on those shows. Re/max International says the pilot program was conducted on a local scale

but did not comment on whether it has plans to roll it out on a national level.

"The digital revolution has a dark underbelly," warns Gene Kimmelman, vice president for federal and legal affairs at Consumers Union. "A lot of these bits include personal information about viewing habits and interests that are easily transformed into marketing materials. It's a whole new realm for blitzing the public with advertising." It will also help cable companies sell advertising time. "That's the biggest piece of revenue," says Josh Bernoff, vice president and principal analyst at Forrester Research.

10 *"WE PROMISE MORE HIGH-DEFINITION PROGRAMMING THAN WE DELIVER."*

The availability of high-definition television has been steadily growing: Today about 90 percent of U.S. homes can access HDTV via cable. Unfortunately, HDTV programming isn't keeping up. According to a recent *Consumer Reports* survey, 70 percent of cable and satellite subscribers said the availability of high-definition content was average or poor. Bottom line: Viewers aren't getting enough channels in high definition.

Some cable companies offer basic digital packages, for about $15 to $20 per month, which provide only the major broadcast networks in HD. Premium movie channels in high-definition can run the bill up by as much as $100 a month. Still, selection is limited: "Stations were slow to roll out HD content, cable operators have resisted carrying content, and now there's this complete mishmash of analog and HD," says Cooper, of the Consumer Federation of America. "Not everything is available in HD, and the consumer can't count on or find out what is or isn't. It's a complete mess."

THINGS TO KNOW

With the cable industry in rapid evolution, we asked Kyle McSlarrow, president of the National Cable & Telecommunications Association, for his take on what cable television will look like five years down the road. Here's what he predicts:

● **Interactivity.** Thanks to new software currently under development, viewers will have the ability to play games, shop, and check e-mail through their TVs.

● **Virtual reality.** The cable industry is going to lead the way with the next generation of lightning-fast broadband—which will enable virtual reality as well as 3-D viewing on home screens.

● **Connectivity.** More customers will able to transport video programming among different TVs and video devices throughout the home.

● **Off-site control.** Customers will be able to manage video programming and services away from the home—for example, setting DVRs from a phone.

10 Things Your
Utility Company
Won't Tell You

1 *"DEREGULATION BENEFITS US, NOT YOU."*

Back in 1996, when state lawmakers passed an electricity deregulation law, they promised a 20-percent cut in consumers' energy bills by April 2002. Instead, California experienced trouble meeting consumer demand, resulting in rolling blackouts, and by 2001, consumers were facing an average 40-percent rate hike. Since then 23 other states have experimented with deregulation. But today only 14 of those plus the District of Columbia are still deregulated; eight others, including California, have suspended restructuring.

In many states, deregulation— essentially, opening the market for multiple providers of electricity and allowing consumers to choose from among the options for service—has resulted in sharply higher rates, since a competitive marketplace no longer guarantees that utility companies will make a profit. In 2006, for example, there was a 72-percent rate increase in Maryland and a 50-percent increase in Illinois. This comes as no surprise to some. "Deregulation is all about what's good for big business," says a spokesperson for the Safe Energy Communication Council, a policy organization based in Washington,

D.C. "It's never been about what's good for residential consumers."

How to push back? Keep complaining, urges Maine-based consumer-affairs consultant Barbara Alexander. "Only the state's public-service commission can spot a lot of complaints," says Alexander, "and they need information from customers to do that."

2 *"WE HAVE NO IDEA WHAT YOU REALLY OWE."*

So you spent last month turning out lights and fussing with the thermostat— and your utility bill still broke $500. The culprit may be an "estimated bill," which utilities in many states are allowed to send out every other month. It's clear why utilities favor estimates. "They're trying to save money by not sending a reader out to your home," says David Kolata, executive director of Chicago Citizens Utility Board. "There are workforce reductions and utility companies are trying to increase their profits, so sometimes they skimp."

But such shortcuts are error-prone: Back in 2000, San Diego consumer group Utility Consumers' Action Network, or UCAN, studied estimated bills (issued by San Diego Gas & Electric, or SDG&E) and found a 170-percent increase in errors over the prior four years. An SDG&E spokesperson says the company used more estimates during that time due to a shortage of meter readers and the fact that "we no longer go into yards with rottweilers." And a spokesperson for UCAN says the problems that caused SDG&E's misreads have since been adequately addressed.

But errors in estimated bills are still very common. They can run up to 50 percent higher than what they should be, according to UCAN, but they're usually corrected within one or two billing cycles. The solution: Read the meter yourself. Then if you receive an inflated estimated bill, call the company and ask for an accurate meter reading.

3 "YOU'RE BANKROLLING OUR RISKY VENTURES."

If you live in a deregulated state like Texas or New York, your utility might not charge you just for energy. Customers in these states often help utilities pay for "stranded costs," or projected losses incurred after deregulation. In California, for example, consumers paid over $20 billion to cover stranded costs before the state suspended restructuring.

Meanwhile, utilities have had a history of rolling the dice on side projects. In Ohio consumers paid $7 billion to utility company FirstEnergy in 2001, which in turn spent $4.5 billion of that on a merger with New Jersey utility GPU. (A FirstEnergy spokesperson says it was a stockholder acquisition, not a customer acquisition, and that the merger was beneficial for long-term rate stability and service restoration.)

"Utility companies have spent years looking for more excitement and higher returns," says Mark Cooper, director of research for the Consumers Federation of America. And, indeed, many of them have gotten more risk than they'd bargained for, he says: "There's a tendency to think the grass is greener someplace else, especially if you have the cushion of guaranteed customers and revenue."

4 "SURPRISE! YOU'VE SWITCHED COMPANIES."

Some gas and electric utilities have taken a cue from phone companies, switching consumers' providers without consent. Often you won't know you've been "slammed" until a strange (and sometimes higher) bill arrives in the mail. Fort Lauderdale, Fla.–based utility Total Gas & Electric, for instance, agreed to pay $200,000 in penalties for switching gas companies on thousands of unsuspecting New York customers. Former New York Governor Eliot Spitzer, who was the state's attorney general during the time of the case, says the company charged more than the promised rate and failed to tell consumers they could cancel. A company statement maintains that TG&E did nothing wrong and "conducts its business at the highest ethical level."

In many states, like California and Georgia, slamming is illegal. A spokesperson for the Georgia Public Service Commission suggests calling your utility provider if you suspect this has happened, and then contact your public service commission. Only after the commission is made aware of the situation can it follow up with legal recourse.

5 "YOUR CONTRACT IS MEANT TO CONFUSE YOU."

In deregulated markets, where each company plays by its own rules, a utility contract "can start to look like a cell phone contract," says former Consumers Union senior policy analyst Janee Briesemeister. Prices are sometimes based on a "market index price," which by definition can't be determined in advance. That leaves customers with very little sound information on which to base their choice. Consider northern Illinois, where folks can choose their gas supplier. "There's a lot of confusion about the way pricing is structured, as well as a lot of misleading marketing," says Kolata, of the Chicago Citizens Utility Board. "Too many companies are unclear about their pricing policies, and a lot of people feel like they've been ripped off."

How can you do your best to choose between utility providers without special insider knowledge or, for that matter, ESP? Start by comparing pricing policies. Some companies charge a flat rate per unit no matter how much energy you use, while others may increase the unit rate with usage (a nightmare if you run the air conditioner when only the cat is at home). It's helpful to do your research ahead of time and read your contract completely, Kolata says, and "if there's anything that you simply can't understand, you should be skeptical."

6 "WE'LL DISCONNECT YOU IN A HEARTBEAT."

Skyrocketing prices have left many people struggling to pay their energy bills. Often the utility company's response is to try to turn off the juice, refusing to negotiate a payment plan or failing to recognize consumers' rights. "They see disconnection as the ultimate collections tool," says Briesemeister. But in most states, customers have a right to written notice of the termination, a hearing if the charge is disputed, and protection from disconnection if there is serious illness in the household.

Unfortunately, that doesn't always happen. Regulated public utility company SDG&E issued a final notice to Santee, Calif., retirees Hugh and Rose Relaford despite the fact that both of them have been hospitalized repeatedly for pneumonia, diabetes, and other ailments. "I'm on the phone for two hours a day trying to get someone to help," says the Relafords' daughter, Brenda Hunt. "But I get zilch." A spokesperson for SDG&E says they've since implemented "a whole lot of backstops to prevent such a thing," including lower rates and special vouchers for the 14,000 customers that fall into the "medically sensitive" category.

7 "WE'RE MANIPULATING THE MARKET."

The Enron debacle of 2001 revealed accounting records that showed its traders were routinely manipulating electricity prices during the West Coast's energy crisis. And it hasn't stopped there—in 2006 two traders at the hedge fund Amaranth Advisors were accused of manipulating the price of gas futures. Thanks to the so-called Enron loophole— a provision inserted into commodity legislation that allowed the electronic trading of energy commodities to be conducted without oversight—these traders were able to make highly risky bets and manipulate the market. Not only did this lead to the fund's failure, but homeowners nationwide ended up paying higher gas prices.

After U.S. Senators Carl Levin (D-Mich.), Dianne Feinstein (D-Calif.), and Olympia Snowe (R-Maine) fought to close the Enron loophole, the Senate unanimously approved the measure in December 2007. But it's still a work in progress. "There's a lack of oversight in the natural gas markets, so the consumer ends up paying higher prices," says Kolata. "Is it supply and demand? Not really. There are other factors that no one really knows."

8 "FEDERAL REGULATORS ARE IN OUR CORNER."

How many utility regulators does it take to screw in a light bulb? More than you can afford. The Federal Energy Regulatory Commission (FERC) is supposed to regulate the wholesale electricity market, but consumer advocates and industry groups argue that the commission isn't doing its job. According to a February 2008 report called "Consumers in Peril," by the American Public Power Association, "the centerpiece of FERC's new wholesale electric regulatory policy . . . has been especially problematic." Indeed, the development of wholesale markets operated by regional organizations, or RTOs, has driven up prices.

FERC's regulatory record is "spotty at best," says a spokesperson for consumer advocacy group UCAN. "It's far more lax in overseeing utilities than most state commissions"—which is why many utilities turn to it to get their expenditures approved. "FERC is overly generous with rate-payers' money, while failing to effectively monitor the electric markets," the UCAN spokesperson says.

9 "WHEN IT COMES TO THE ENVIRONMENT, WE'RE OFTEN TALKING A BETTER GAME THAN WE'RE PLAYING."

In light of concerns over climate change, more utilities are presenting themselves as environmentally friendly. Southern California Edison, for example, states in its "Environmental Commitment" policy on its website that the company seeks "solutions that solve environmental problems without creating new ones." And their green efforts are particularly attractive to the public: According to a 2007 IBM survey, two thirds of consumers polled said they're willing to pay more for power sources that have lower greenhouse gas emissions. But underneath the brochure-style hype, most utility companies are still big polluters. "There's so much more that utility companies can be doing," says a UCAN spokesperson. "They want to build new coal plants; they're trying to export pollution instead of reducing pollution by building transmission lines; they're relying on fossil fuels—there's just a whole laundry list of things they can be doing that they're not."

Indeed, one of the worst offenders are coal-fired plants, which produce 48 percent of the nation's electricity and are a big source of smog-inducing nitrogen oxide. Many of these facilities profited from a grandfather clause exempting them from clean-air requirements adopted in the 1970s. To see the U.S. Environmental Protection Agency's Toxics Release Inventory, a database that contains information on nearly 650 chemicals managed by industrial and federal facilities in each state, visit *www.epa.gov/tri*.

10 *"OUR CONFUSION WILL LEAVE YOU IN THE DARK— LITERALLY."*

It's one thing for cost-cutting utilities to make economical decisions when it comes to repairs, but blatant disregard for equipment analysis can mean cascading power outages. In a report on the blackout of August 2003 that affected the northeastern U.S. and Ontario, Canada, the U.S.–Canada Power System Outage Task Force identified the number one reason for the power outage as "inadequate system understanding." Several plants in Ohio were offline for repairs or maintenance,

but FirstEnergy didn't notify neighboring control areas and their coordinators about it. "FirstEnergy was not doing so because the company had not conducted the long-term and operational planning studies needed to understand those vulnerabilities and their operational implications," states the Task Force. Translation: They weren't prepared for a crisis.

This problem is nothing new. Following prolonged outages in New Jersey during a 1999 heat wave, the state's utility board probed electric company GPU and found that it had delayed replacing failed transformers for two years. "We recognize that we fell short of expectations," says a GPU spokesperson. According to consumer-affairs consultant Alexander, the likely reason repairs aren't being done is that utilities are saving their money to invest in more-profitable ventures, such as buying plants in other markets, then selling the power at deregulated prices.

THINGS TO DO

• **Know exactly how much energy** your home uses and learn how to become more energy-efficient by doing a "home energy audit." Visit *www.energystar.gov* to get started.

• **Learn to read your meter** so you can spot an inflated bill and request an accurate reading. Your utility provider's website should offer information on how.

• **If your utility company** has been switched on you without warning, it could be illegal. Call the company to ask what happened, but also notify your state's

public service commission in case legal action is necessary.

• **If your home is part** of a deregulated market, you have choices when it comes to utility service. Be sure to read contracts carefully, and compare pricing policies to see which provider best suits your needs.

• **If your bills keep skyrocketing,** think about producing your own power. Solar panels can be an expensive investment but should last 30 years or more. Find out more at *www.ucan.org*.

10 Things Your
Dry Cleaner
Won't Tell You

1 "YOU MAY NEVER SEE THIS SHIRT AGAIN."

By the end of winter, you're itching to swap your wool for shorts and T-shirts. But before you send those sweaters to the dry cleaner, realize this: You may never get them back. Dry cleaners have a knack for losing your stuff. According to the Council of Better Business Bureaus, lost items is the top complaint against dry cleaners, making up 20 percent of all grievances against them. (Damaged items, including pieces of clothing returned with mysterious stains or missing buttons, was the second most common complaint.)

Lenore McIntyre knows all too well. In July 2002, she was hung out to dry after Ireland Cleaners, in Richmond, Va., lost three of her tablecloths, valued at $800. For more than two weeks she called the cleaner looking to get reimbursed. When the store manager finally offered her $100, McIntyre told her, "That won't pay for it." According to McIntyre, the manager replied, "Well, this is all I can do," and hung up. McIntyre later sued Ireland Cleaners in Chesterfield County Civil Court and won a judgment for $820 plus legal fees. Ireland Cleaners paid over $900 in total.

Ron Berry, former senior vice president at the Council of Better Business Bureaus (BBB), says disputes over lost items "are where we have the swearing matches. If a dry cleaner acknowledges he lost it, he has to pay for its replacement." Berry suggests that when you drop off a garment, be sure to ask for a receipt indicating what you had cleaned. It will help your case against a dry cleaner.

2 "YOU WON'T GET MUCH FROM US EVEN IF WE RUIN YOUR FAVORITE SWEATER."

At least if a cleaner loses your item, he's supposed to pay the full amount so you can get a new one. But say your blazer comes back with a slash in one arm. You'd want it replaced, right? Well, that doesn't wash with dry cleaners. For damaged goods, the industry standard is to offer the item's depreciated value as listed in the *Fair Claims Guide*, published by the Drycleaning & Laundry Institute (DLI), a Laurel, Md., association (formerly known as the International Fabricare Institute), which represents more than 10,000 owners of dry-cleaning businesses. The problem is, you won't get much.

Skirts, shirts, cotton suits, and silk dresses that are just over a year old and in average condition before the damage are valued at 40 percent of the replacement cost; a five-year-old wool blazer in average condition gets you 15 percent. On the other hand, if an item is deemed an heirloom—say, a couture Chanel suit or an antique Persian rug—you can get back its market value. But that treasured sweater Grandma knit for you? In the eyes of the DLI, it's worth the same amount as one you bought off the rack at the Gap. As the *Fair Claims Guide* puts it, "'Sentimental value' . . . is subjective and is ruled out as a valid consideration."

3 *"GOOD LUCK PROVING THE DAMAGE WAS OUR FAULT."*

In cases where you and your cleaner can't agree on who's at fault for damaging an item, the cleaner will probably suggest this solution: Send the item to the DLI, which will analyze it and then determine who's to blame for the damages. Sounds like a plan—except it's unlikely your cleaner will be found at fault. Of the 13,000 items that the DLI tested in 2001 (the latest data the organization would provide us with), cleaners were held responsible just 11 percent of the time, while the manufacturer was at fault in 45 percent of cases and the consumer 35 percent (the other 9 percent is unknown). Why the lopsided score? "If a dry cleaner knows he

---

Over the past 10 years, the number of dry-cleaning operations in the U.S. has grown by about 50 percent, to roughly 30,000 businesses.

---

messed up, he's not going to send it in," says Lorraine Muir, manager at the DLI's garment analysis lab.

Ralph Warner, an attorney and executive publisher of legal-advice website Nolo.com, questions the impartiality of the DLI, whose funding comes from dry cleaners. Warner has seen cleaners use the DLI reports as supportive evidence in court cases. "It's a trade association," Warner says. "They want to sell it as expert opinion, but it's not unbiased opinion."

4 *"WE CLEAN YOUR CLOTHES WITH KILLER CHEMICALS."*

Over the past 10 years, the number of dry-cleaning operations in the U.S. has grown by about 50 percent, to roughly 30,000 businesses. That's great news if you like convenience, but not if you worry about the environment. PERC (short for perchloroethylene) is the chemical used to dry-clean your clothes, and this toxic substance is classified by the International Agency for Research on Cancer as a probable human carcinogen. In fact, the National Institute for Occupational Safety and Health found that dry-cleaning workers they studied over a 36-year period were 25 percent more likely to die from cancer than the general population.

But you don't have to work at a dry cleaner to be exposed to PERC. Cindy Stroup of the Environmental Protection Agency says that at least half of the national priority sites for toxic waste cleanup are partially contaminated with PERC. And even though the EPA has increased rules in recent years to prevent PERC dumping, violators still abound.

In 2003, Michael Rosenberg, owner of Avenue Cleaners in Naugatuck, Conn., pleaded guilty to illegally disposing of PERC in a wooded area, thereby polluting water wells. He was sentenced to 18 months in jail. "There is no doubt that there is significant health and environmental risk with PERC," says Stroup. But Jon Meijer, a vice president at the DLI, stands behind PERC. "It's been used safely and continues to be used safely," he says.

5 "WE COULD HELP THE ENVIRONMENT—BUT THAT WOULD BE A REAL HASSLE."

It may defy logic, but water can be used to clean dry-clean-only clothing. The process, though, is hardly catching on—there are currently about 80 wet-cleaning facilities in the whole country. "Cost is an issue," says the DLI's Meijer. "Wet cleaning requires far more labor, and you tend to need a lot more space." Meijer adds that wet cleaning is effective on only 40 percent of clothing. But the EPA's Stroup classifies such claims as "baloney." She contends that "virtually everything that can be dry-cleaned can be wet-cleaned."

Peter Sinsheimer, director of Occidental College's Pollution Prevention Education and Research Center, would certainly agree. A test he conducted with several dry cleaners in Southern California showed that wet cleaning lowered an operator's costs by between 17 and 51 percent, and garments and other items came out as clean as when dry-cleaned. (Costs to the consumer stayed the same.) "We've shown you can do this," says Sinsheimer. Meijer doesn't buy the results, though. "You can't wet-clean garments 100 percent," he contends.

6 "WE'RE MASTERS OF THE OLD BAIT-AND-SWITCH."

The sign on a Dallas dry cleaner's window caught Eric Kaindl's eye: Laundered shirts—79 cents. But Kaindl got the real eye-opener when he picked up the three shirts he had dropped off. The cleaner charged him $1.50 per shirt. Why the price hike? Because, Kaindl explains, they were uniform shirts for work, despite the fact that the sign spelled out no such exceptions. "They just said, 'If you want your shirts, this is what you've got to pay for them,'" Kaindl says.

Edward Johnson, president and CEO of the Better Business Bureau for the metro Washington, D.C., area, warns that dry cleaners' deceptive advertising practices can come in different forms. For instance, the "meet or beat" gimmick is one in which a cleaner claims he'll match or beat a competitor's price. The hitch: Only after the cleaning, according to Johnson, do you find out that you'd needed a copy of the other cleaner's price list to qualify for the price cut. In such cases, consumers have little recourse but to pay the bill, says Johnson—and then find a different cleaner.

7 "WE TAKE NEW BRIDES TO THE CLEANERS."

So your daughter is walking down the aisle soon? Jonathan Scheer, a gown preservationist in New York City, says that all too often clients ask him to restore wedding dresses that have been damaged when dry-cleaned. Unfortunately, he can't always save the keepsake, as Meredith Jowers Lees learned.

In the fall of 2002, Lees brought her $2,800 white silk satin Amsale gown to Watkins Cleaners in Birmingham, Ala., a wedding gown specialist, hoping to have a large stain removed. When she went to pick up the dress, though, Lees says it was yellowed, torn, and still stained. "You cannot replace something that has that kind of sentimental value," she says. But store owner John Watkins, who did not charge Lees for the work, contends that he did not mishandle the dress. "We told her at the beginning it was a risk," he says. "The dress was very much damaged when it came in."

A bride's best move, Scheer says, is to thoroughly research the cleaner first, and have a "low tolerance for risk, because the danger is, the dress will be ruined."

8 "LADIES GET SPECIAL TREATMENT. WE CHARGE THEM MORE."

Wedding gowns aren't the only way female customers get starched by their dry cleaners. Even when a woman brings in the same type of garment as a man—say, an oxford shirt—she's often charged more. How much more? In a sampling of New York City businesses, we found cases where dry-cleaning a woman's shirt cost twice as much as it did for a man's shirt. "Gender-pricing has been going on for years," says the BBB's Berry.

The DLI's Meijer explains that women's shirts often cost more to clean due to machinery, not male chauvinism. Women's generally smaller sizes often don't fit the machines that clean men's shirts. That means they have to be cleaned by hand, and hence the higher cost. Berry remains skeptical. "For something that's common to both sexes, it's hard to see why there's any price difference," he says.

9 "OUR CUSTOMER SERVICE STINKS."

In 2006 the Better Business Bureau logged 4,455 complaints against the dry-cleaning industry, making it the 34th-worst offender among the 1,000 businesses for which the BBB tracks complaints. That's a 7 percent increase from the previous year. There's an even bigger wrinkle: When it comes to resolving complaints in good faith or to the customer's satisfaction, dry cleaners have an unusually low settlement rate: 48.9 percent in 2006, compared with the BBB's average settlement rate of 72.5 percent. "It's not the initial problem but the lack of follow-through to solve the problem that spurs people to file complaints," says Jeannette Kopko, a senior vice president of the BBB serving Dallas and northeast Texas.

Tosha Walden knows what it's like to get put through the wringer. Despite multiple calls and visits, she could never reach Faye Strong, the owner of Strong Cleaners in Macon, Ga. (which has since gone out of business), to discuss how her off-the-shoulder top had come back with the elastic stretched out. Finally, she wrote Strong a letter. In response, Strong fired back that she was "utterly shocked" Walden had planned to wear her outfit to "any place other than to bed," and that "the loss of your business is a welcome event." Only after Walden filed a complaint with the BBB did she receive a $30 check from Strong, who still snidely wrote in the memo area, "To get rid of Tosha Walden." Strong did not return our calls for comment.

10 *"WE IGNORE WHAT THE COURTS TELL US TO DO."*

As Lenore McIntyre discovered, there's no guarantee small claims court will clean up your dry cleaner's mess. Even if the judge rules in your favor, it can be difficult for you to get your money. For dry cleaners who fail to pay voluntarily, as in McIntyre's case, you can either have a law enforcement official go to the cleaner to get your money or directly withdraw it from a cleaner's bank account. But getting a withdrawal can be tricky. Tom

Gallagher, president and CEO of the BBB of Central Virginia, says many dry cleaners operate under a number of names. "It could be that the dry cleaner buys another dry-cleaning shop that has a good reputation and they want to maintain loyalty," he says. For whatever reason, it often means cleaners have bank accounts under multiple names, making it difficult for you to claim your money.

Jenise Arnao, a senior court clerk at the Kings County Courthouse in Brooklyn, N.Y., says she sees at least two cases a week involving dry cleaners. In most instances, Arnao says, the plaintiff wins. But that's hardly a victory. "It's hard to collect," Arnao says, due to the name issue. Plaintiffs often have to file multiple times to get a match, usually giving up after several tries.

THINGS TO DO

● **Hold on to your receipt,** and make sure it lists exactly what items were cleaned—it's the first step toward being compensated for a lost or damaged item.

● **Pricing can be unpredictable**—it usually costs more to clean a woman's shirt than a man's, and it could cost extra if a stain turns out to be difficult to remove. Ask your dry cleaner for an estimate, and request they call you before doing anything that would hike your bill.

● **If your dry cleaner asks you** to sign a customer release form, take it as a warning that they see potential for damage to your item. These forms tend to bear weight in

court—meaning if anything goes wrong, you could be out of luck.

● **Though the chemical widely used** to dry-clean your clothes is a classified toxin, it's still defended as safe by the dry-cleaning business. If you have environmental or health concerns, you can search businesses in your community to see if they have been cited for releasing toxic chemicals, at *www.epa.gov.*

● **There are now several established** eco-friendly alternatives to dry cleaning, such as wet cleaning, and even more in development. Find more information on different methods, at *www.greenerchoices.org.*

10 Things Your
Warehouse Club
Won't Tell You

1 *"YOU PAID YOUR DUES? GOOD, NOW GET IN LINE."*

More than 100 million Americans now shop in warehouse clubs including BJ's, Costco, or Sam's Club each year. That's 50 million more than in 2002. The attraction? For the annual membership price of $35 to $100, discount hunters can spend their weekends stocking up on 36-roll packages of toilet paper and nuclear-canister-size boxes of detergent. Too bad they also spend plenty of time doing anything but shopping.

Michelle Wilkes says she usually waits in lines of no less than 15 minutes on the weekend at her Lake Zurich, Ill., Costco. There are often four to five shoppers ahead of her at the register, she says—and that's despite what Costco CFO Richard Galanti claims is a company-wide checkout policy of "no more than one in line and two behind." What further frustrates Wilkes is that her store never has all its registers open. "I have never seen it fully staffed," she complains. Galanti agrees that "There's nothing worse than having half the 20 registers open. Shame on us."

2 *"YOU'LL NEED A HARD HAT WHEN YOU SHOP HERE."*

Heads up: Warehouse clubs are notorious for letting products drop on unsuspecting customers. In 1998, a woman in Cincinnati was hit by five 38-pound containers of kitty litter while shopping in a Sam's Club. She sustained head, neck, and shoulder injuries. And during the summer of 2001, a woman shopping in a Maryland Sam's Club barely avoided serious injury when a sofa fell from a shelf.

Plaintiff attorney Jeffrey Hyman says injuries often occur when unsecured merchandise slips from shelves, either because a store employee stocking an adjacent aisle accidentally pushes it or because another customer is trying to take down an object. Hyman says that despite the accidental nature of the incidents, "If you know you have a problem and you know you have a dangerous condition, you need to fix it." A Sam's Club spokesperson insists: "Our shopping environment is very safe. But when something like that happens, it causes us great concern." The company, he adds, tries "to put in safety rules to prevent anything from happening."

3 *"OUR CREDIT CARD WILL BURN YOUR SAVINGS AWAY."*

Since Sam's Club honors only the Discover card, Mastercard, and debit cards, many shoppers decide to get a Sam's Club personal credit card. But before you sign up, beware: The standard card comes with a 23.15 percent APR, which is about nine percentage points higher than the current average for variable credit cards, according to Bankrate.com.

Worse, once you sign up for the Sam's card, you may find your phone ringing off the hook with eager telemarketers. Unless you opt out by calling a toll-free number or mailing in your request, the privacy policy on Sam's Club's credit card application says your information can be made available to "third parties, who are interested in offering special products or services to you" —precisely the folks you want calling you at dinnertime. A spokesperson for GE Money, which services the Sam's Club card, denies the use of telemarketing for any product cross-selling, saying, "What we have the right to do and what we do are two different things."

4 "JEWELRY EXPERTS TRASH OUR GEMS."

Survey the landscape at a Costco or BJ's. There are stacks of cornflakes, mountains of mayonnaise jars, and . . . diamonds. Diamonds? You bet. A jewelry counter is now standard at most club stores. BJ's even offers a diamond appraisal guarantee. The $1,800 band you fell in love with at BJ's, for instance, comes with an appraisal certificate stating that it's valued at $3,730. Not even Tiffany offers that.

BJ's says it has a simple explanation for why it can guarantee the value of its gems despite the discounted price: bulk. A BJ's spokesperson says that because the store purchases jewelry in volume from dealers, it can provide "tremendous savings" to its members without skimping on quality. There's just one problem: Jewelry experts say the stores' appraisal guarantee is sketchy at best. As Edwin Baker, a former executive vice president of the American Society of Appraisers, puts it, "If the clubs consistently sell an item for $1,000, then it's obvious the market value of that item is $1,000, not $1,500." Joyce Jonas, jewelry appraiser on the PBS series *Antiques Roadshow,* agrees. She calls the guarantees "misleading. You're not dealing in the kinds of goods that could ever be appraised for more than what they're selling it for."

5 "YOU'LL LEAVE WHEN WE TELL YOU TO."

Ed Fritz and his family had just finished shopping at a warehouse club in northern California. As Fritz got to the store's exit, an employee stopped him and said, "I have to check your receipt." When Fritz declined to show it (he says he wanted to safeguard his credit card number), the employee grabbed his cart and then his arm to prevent him from leaving. Once Fritz freed himself, he headed to the parking lot, followed by six other employees. As one of them took down his license-plate number, Fritz was told never to return to the club. "I said, 'After this treatment, I never want to come back here,'" he recalls.

That may be an extreme example, but as club members have long known, it can often be a hassle just leaving a warehouse store. You'll wait for one of the club's employees to inspect your receipt, a procedure that will usually add several minutes to your outing. Obviously, when you join a club, you agree to follow its rules. But why such scrutiny? Galanti says that at Costco the review helps make sure "the right price is on the right items" and "is a measure of inventory security." While warehouse stores do have the right to check your receipt, Washington, D.C., attorney Donald Temple, who specializes in retail discrimination law, says employees cannot cross-check it with the items in your cart.

6 "WE HAVE MORE ANIMALS THAN A SMALL ZOO."

Warehouse stores don't advertise having pet departments. But looking through health-inspection reports, you'd sometimes think they did. Between 2000 and 2002, two Sam's Clubs in Maricopa County, Ariz., were cited for having birds in the rafters and nesting under the bakery display. And in September 2002 the Georgia Department of Agriculture fined a Sam's Club in Atlanta $80,000 when more than a dozen mice were found in the store. They'd been snacking on food and leaving behind their droppings.

A Sam's Club spokesperson assures us that "the problem is taken care of now." Although she can't comment on the Arizona cases, she says, "At all times one of our [top] priorities is to maintain a safe shopping environment for members. If there are birds in the club or rodents, we work as fast and diligently as we can to get them taken care of."

7 "TRY OUR WEBSITE. IT WILL TRY YOUR PATIENCE."

So you went to the trouble of joining a club store—forked over the annual dues and then endured the long lines—all in the name of saving a few bucks. Well, you could have avoided the crowds and possibly even saved some money by shopping online. Costco's website, for example, features everything from laptops to patio furniture. But unlike shopping at the store, you don't have to be a member to buy items from the site; you're simply charged an extra 5 percent. Which is the better deal? All told, you'd have to buy about $1,000 of merchandise before the nonmember surcharge equaled the cheapest membership fee—and that's without considering the price of gas.

But online shopping comes with its own set of hassles. First, shipping costs could eat up any potential savings. Rachel Caspi of Bethesda, Md., ordered six items from the Costco online pharmacy for a total of $78.10. When she was charged $26.50 for shipping—or 34 percent of the total purchase—she ended up canceling her order. Then there are the logistics of placing orders online. Paul Cohen, a Valley Cottage, N.Y., resident ordered two PCs online from Costco: The first arrived on schedule, the other was MIA. Only after two weeks of repeated calls to Costco's customer-service department—which at one point could not even trace the missing PC—was his order fulfilled.

Costco's Galanti admits that "there will be mistakes made. When we find out there has been a problem, we fix it as best as we can to the customer's satisfaction."

Still, he adds, "I've had friends e-mail me saying they ordered something and it never showed up or they had a problem."

8 *"THAT WARRANTY IS VALID— IN ITALY PERHAPS."*

Ever hear of the "gray market"? Your club store has. The term refers to merchandise that was designated by the manufacturer for distribution in another country but ends up being sold in the U.S. Club stores are often big buyers of gray-market products, either because the goods are priced cheaply or because the manufacturer will not sell directly to the store.

Unfortunately, the warranties that come with gray products don't have to be honored in the U.S. Bret Diamond found that out when he purchased a Seiko diver's watch at his local Costco. It was $75 less than he had seen it for in other stores, but he had to pay more than $100 to have it repaired when the watch stopped working three and a half years later. His five-year warranty was not valid because the watch was gray-market merchandise. If Diamond had known that, "I never would have bought it," he says.

Club stores are often big buyers of gray-market products, either because the goods are priced cheaply or because the manufacturer will not sell directly to the store.

---

9 *"YOUR BACKYARD WOULD MAKE A BEAUTIFUL WAREHOUSE."*

In addition to the demand of cost-conscious shoppers, club stores keep blossoming (at a clip of more than 20 new ones per year) because civic leaders see them as a way to encourage development and jump-start the local economy. But opponents of the buildup contend that politicians take short-sighted measures to gain these quick hits. Al Norman, an activist and editor of SprawlBusters.com, says, "Unfortunately, local officials hand over a rezoning without much scrutiny because they think this means jobs and taxes."

That's what Donald and Sophie Mason believe happened in South San Francisco in the late 1990s. The Masons figured that by virtue of the city's General Plan, a 15-acre plot near their home could be developed only for high-density housing. The city council, though, changed the plan to allow for retail development. The Masons and members of their group, the Concerned Citizens of South San Francisco, say the change was made specifically to lure a Costco to the area. They forced a referendum to approve the changes; to the Masons' disappointment, voters okayed them. The store opened in 2001, and ever since, the traffic near the Masons' home has been, according to Sophie, "an absolute mess."

10 *"YOU'D BETTER LIKE WHAT WE LIKE."*

Warehouse membership may have its privileges, but it doesn't provide much variety. The most mammoth clubs carry only 4,000 to 7,000 different products, one tenth of what your average supermarket stocks. A BJ's spokesperson admits that what customers see in stores is "an edited selection of top quality. So you might not find 30 laundry detergents, but you're going to find the top laundry detergents."

The thing is, warehouse clubs have mastered how to make their aisles look more varied than they are. "Clubs like to rotate items during the year to keep the shopping trip exciting," says Christie Briggs, a senior research analyst at AMR Research, a business research firm. "This means that an item a member is fond of could be gone the next time they go." That's what got Suzy Neal so annoyed. After a year of buying Wow potato chips at a Sam's in Albany, Ga., Neal one day couldn't find the item. Only after she filed a complaint with PlanetFeedback.com, a Web outfit that acts as a middleman for written consumer complaints, did Sam's restock the chips.

THINGS TO DO

● **In addition to low prices,** a membership at a warehouse club may include services like roadside assistance for emergencies or discounts at the gas pump. Check with your club to make sure you're getting the most out of your membership.

● **Joining a warehouse club** doesn't have to mean more telemarketers calling during dinner. When you sign up, specifically request that your information not be passed on to a third party.

● **Tired of waiting in line?** At SamsClub .com you can register for "Click 'n' Pull" and preorder your purchases for in-store pickup at a separate checkout. Ask your club if it offers a similar option.

● **Looking for a product** you saw on the shelf last week, but now it's gone? Speak with a manager about getting the item back on the shelf, or visit the club's website, where there's often a larger variety of products available.

● **Check with your warehouse club** to see if it has an electronics trade-in program. At Costco and Sam's Club, you can get a store gift card in exchange for things like old laptops and LCD screens.

10 Things Your
Lawyer
Won't Tell You

1 *"I DON'T NECESSARILY KNOW THAT MUCH ABOUT THE LAW."*

Ask an attorney about anything outside his niche, and odds are he won't know much. Teacher Marie Karim learned that when she decided to sue the New York City hospital where she had developed an infection and a hernia during exploratory surgery in 1999. Karim hired Sheri B. Paige because her mother had once consulted the Norwalk, Conn., lawyer about collecting a debt. Karim says Paige assured her that she had experience with medical malpractice cases.

More than a year later, Karim says she discovered that Paige had virtually no such experience and that she hadn't even filed the suit. Worse yet, the statute of limitations had run out. "I wanted to kill her," says Karim, who got $325,000 from Paige's insurance company in 2002 with assistance from a specialist in legal malpractice. Paige denies all wrongdoing and blames the entire mess on Karim. But in November 2002, a Connecticut lawyer grievance panel found probable cause to believe that Paige was guilty of misconduct, and she was disbarred in 2005.

Moral of the story: Karim should have hired an expert in the area of law she needed—someone who does almost nothing but medical malpractice. You can find specialists in the lawyer directory Martindale-Hubbell, available in any library or online at *www.martindale.com,* or at the FindLaw website (*www.findlaw.com*).

2 *"I WON'T TAKE YOUR CHUMP-CHANGE CASE."*

Just because you have a strong legal case doesn't mean a lawyer will take it on—not if it's bad for his bottom line. That's especially true with claims involving securities arbitration, usually against brokers who have churned clients' accounts or put them in unsuitable investments. (Most brokers require their clients to agree to arbitration when opening an account.) There were 3,238 of these cases in 2007, down from 4,614 in 2006, according to FINRA Dispute Resolution, the largest securities dispute resolution forum in the world.

Trouble is, lawyers involved in this growing field generally refuse to handle claims of less than $100,000, because smaller cases generate small fees. Henri Draznin, a retired customer-service rep, found himself in just such a bind. He couldn't find a lawyer willing to help him recover the $9,000 he'd lost in high-yield bonds, which his broker had put him into without mentioning they were risky for a retiree. It seemed that Draznin was out of luck, until he found a legal clinic at New York's Pace University Law School, where students supervised by Professor Barbara Black (who has since moved on to the University of Cincinnati) helped him file an arbitration claim, winning him $4,046 in February 2003.

Short of finding a law school clinic eager to help you, what can you do? Visit the website of the Public Investors Arbitration Bar Association (*www.piaba .org*) to get the name of a lawyer in your area who's experienced in securities. If you like him and want to work with him, try offering him a little more than his usual percentage—say, 43 percent, rather than 40—to sweeten the pot.

3 *"I'LL CHARGE AS MUCH AS YOU'LL LET ME."*

Most lawyers can charge for their services in a variety of ways: a flat fee; an hourly rate, typically $250 to $450 per hour; or a percentage of the award, usually either one third or 40 percent. Which is best for you? If your case is simple, with losses of less than $50,000, a flat fee is best. It gives the lawyer an incentive to solve the problem efficiently. If, however, you're filing suit for personal injury, employment discrimination, or malpractice, you're generally better off paying a percentage. These cases are typically more complicated, with many variables involved. The incentive here is to get as much money as possible, fast, and if your attorney fails, you won't be stuck with a big bill. Have him take his

fee after expenses, to keep administrative costs down. Avoid paying a percentage to settle an estate or for a divorce or real estate deal, though. A $1 million closing or divorce is no more difficult than a $500,000 one, so why pay more? In these cases, a flat-fee arrangement is best.

If you have a strong civil suit, your best bet may be a hybrid fee: an hourly rate if the lawyer can solve the problem in a few hours, switching to a percentage if it takes longer or he has to sue. A Fortune 500 company executive hired Kansas City attorney Bert Braud to handle a sex discrimination case in 2001, and the lawyer was able to wrest a six-figure settlement out of the employer in about 15 hours. His fee was $2,000 instead of the more than $33,000 the executive would have paid had he charged a percentage. If a lawyer resists such a deal, tell him you need to interview a few more attorneys before you decide whom to hire. He'll likely come around.

4 *"YOU COULD WIN YOUR LAWSUIT AND STILL WIND UP WITH NOTHING."*

Expecting a bundle from a big lawsuit? Don't start spending it just yet. You may be shocked to learn how little you'll actually get to keep. Lawyers may not like to mention it, but federal taxes—at rates of 18 to 35 percent—can easily wipe out most of the money you win in civil lawsuits; bodily injury cases are the only exemption. Some "winning" plaintiffs even wind up in the hole.

Realizing that such grim victories chill business, members of the National Employment Lawyers Association

(NELA) began prodding Congress to stop taxing discrimination awards and settlements, which often take the biggest hit. Their lobbying efforts helped the passage of the American Jobs Creation Act in October 2004 with a provision that exempted plaintiffs from having to pay taxes on the attorneys' fees portion of their earnings. "It was a partial victory," says NELA Executive Director Teri Chaw. "But there's still some way to go."

5 "YOU JUST MIGHT BE BETTER OFF WITHOUT ME."

Many of the things lawyers do, you can do for yourself, provided you have the time and inclination to learn how. You can write your own will, for instance, if you have a relatively uncomplicated estate. A good place to get help is legal software publisher Nolo (*www.nolo.com*), whose Quicken Lawyer 2008 Wills, for example, sells for $40.

For issues that are too complicated to be handled without some legal assistance, an interim step between going it alone and hiring a lawyer is working with a paralegal. Depending on the state, these professionals can handle living trusts, bankruptcy petitions, real estate closings, and uncontested divorces—often for just a few hundred dollars. The only things paralegals can't do are give legal advice and represent you in court.

Before you sign on, though, look for experience and expertise in a particular field. It's also nice—but not essential—for the paralegal to hold a degree or certificate from one of the 800-plus training programs in the U.S. (258 of them approved by the American Bar

Association) or be deemed a registered paralegal by the National Federation of Paralegal Associations or a certified legal assistant by the National Association of Legal Assistants.

6 "BY THE WAY, I NEVER WIN."

So your attorney has plenty of experience in his field—but has that been as a winner or a loser? How you find out depends on the situation. If you're hiring him to defend you against a criminal charge, ask him if he has ever worked in the prosecutor's office and for how long, because that's where the best criminal defense lawyers typically get their training.

Also, for any court case—criminal or civil—you want to know how many cases he's actually taken to trial in the past five years. Experts say even five or six can be plenty if at least one win is a case similar to yours. On the other hand, if a lawyer says his cases usually settle, that's a bad sign. A guy who's known for always settling probably isn't prone toward driving a hard bargain. "It certainly helps if the defendant knows [a lawyer] is ready

---

If a lawyer says his cases usually settle, that's a bad sign. A guy who's known for always settling probably isn't prone toward driving a hard bargain.

---

to go to court," says Braud, the Kansas City, Mo., litigator, who has taken more than 40 cases to trial.

7 "I'D LIKE TO GET TO KNOW YOU—A WHOLE LOT BETTER."

For years lawyers in most states weren't legally restricted from sleeping with their clients. And many did. In fact, an issue of the *Columbia Law Review* in the early 1990s noted that sexual relations between attorneys and their clients were the legal profession's "dirty little secret." Around the same time, a University of Memphis survey revealed that nearly 20 percent of attorneys nationwide admitted that they or a lawyer they knew had had an affair with a client. But things have started to change. Since 2002, when the ABA weighed in on the issue, stating that lawyer-client sex is generally unethical but that it's up to each state whether to adopt a ban on the practice, 29 states including Arizona, Colorado, and Connecticut have either added or proposed adding a new provision prohibiting lawyers from having sexual relations with their clients unless a consensual relationship existed before the lawyer-client relationship began.

Beyond doing a basic Google search of your attorney, which is free, you can also carry out a background search through commercial sites like *www.knowx.com*.

So what's the big deal if it's two consenting adults? Lawyer-client flings, especially in divorce and family law cases, can warp the lawyer's judgment, prompting him either to prolong a dispute or sacrifice the client's interests to end it faster, says Texas Wesleyan University law professor Malinda L. Seymore. The client may also submit to a lawyer's sexual advances in the belief that if she does, he'll do more to help her keep her home and children.

That's what Plantation, Fla., lawyer Steven W. Effman told two female clients to entice them to engage in sexual activity in his office, according to the women's sworn testimony. Not only did Effman fail to deliver on his promises, these clients say, but he actually had the nerve to bill at least one for their trysts. The Florida bar filed a complaint against Effman in 2002, and a court suspended his license for 91 days. Effman insists his affairs were consensual and denies making promises or billing for sex.

8 "OKAY, SO I'VE MADE SOME MISTAKES IN THE PAST. GOOD LUCK DIGGING THEM UP."

How do you know whether the lawyer you're working with is a good egg or not? Trying to learn whether a lawyer has a record of ethics violations or even just a bad reputation can be an exercise in futility. For starters, the American Bar Association does keep a database of known ethics violators online, at *www .abanet.org*. But the ABA database relies strictly on voluntary reports from state bar counsels, and it costs $10 per name to search.

You could also try calling the bar counsel in the appropriate state—you can find yours listed at *www.nobc.org*. But that can also be a dead end, unless the attorney has been suspended or disbarred; some states may report that a lawyer is "in good standing" even if she has had lots of complaints or worse. Beyond doing a basic Google search of your attorney, which is free, you can also carry out a background search through commercial sites like *www.knowx.com,* which charges a fee that ranges from $10 to $100 to check the disciplinary records of a given lawyer.

9 *"WANNA SUE ME? OOPS—YOU SIGNED THAT OPTION AWAY."*

Most lawyers are competent and ethical. But what if yours messes up? Can you sue him? Not if you agreed to submit disputes to arbitration, where the rules of law and evidence don't always apply and you'll have the right to neither a jury nor perhaps even to appeal. Many lawyers insert compulsory arbitration provisions in their retainer agreements, which isn't unethical, according to the ABA, provided that the agreement doesn't insulate the lawyer from liability and the client understands what it means. Such a clause should be a warning for you to take your business elsewhere.

Inventor Walter R. Fields says he didn't realize he was giving up his right to sue when he hired Maslon Edelman Borman & Brand, a large Minneapolis law firm, to sue the builder of his mold-infested $1.2 million house. Disappointed when he lost his case, Fields tried to sue Maslon Edelman for malpractice, claiming among other things that the firm had failed to submit evidence of the mold in time. But in 2001 a Minneapolis court refused to hear the case because of an arbitration clause in Fields's retainer agreement. Fields also came up empty after arbitrators rejected his claim and two courts upheld the arbitration. As Fields puts it, Maslon Edelman "won hands down." (Maslon Edelman denies malpractice, claiming the mold was a side issue, and defends the arbitration clause, saying that Fields had weeks to review the agreement with a lawyer before signing.)

10 *"EVEN IF YOU CAN SUE ME, YOU WON'T WIN."*

It's mighty tough to nail a lawyer for malpractice. Some 71 percent of malpractice claims from 1999 through 2003 closed without the client's receiving any payment from the lawyer's insurance company, and only 6 percent netted more than $50,000, according to a 2003 American Bar Association survey, the most recent data available.

Why is it so hard? For one thing, only a fraction of lawyers even carry insurance, so collecting is a long shot. Plus, to win your case, you have to prove that the lawyer failed to perform but also that your suit would have turned out differently had he done a better job. Hard to do, since a legal issue is seldom a slam dunk, even if the lawyer does everything right.

Fortunately, there are lawyers who specialize in malpractice cases against other lawyers. "The best way to go about it is to get a referral from someone you trust," says James Keeney, a Sarasota, Fla., lawyer who represents securities investors in arbitration and litigation against brokers, dealers, and firms. "And make sure he or she is board-certified."

THINGS TO KNOW

Lawyers today are specializing in everything from outer space to cyberspace. Here's a quick rundown of four of the most common specialties and when you'll need them:

- **Family law.** More commonly known as divorce lawyers, they're the ones you turn to when the magic's run out. They're also your child-custody and adoption go-to guys. Find one at the American Bar Association's website, at *www.abanet.org/family*.

- **Personal injury law.** Get nicked in a fender bender? These specialists know how to get those medical bills covered by the responsible party. At *www.findlaw.com* you can search for lawyers by topic.

- **Entertainment law.** Contract negotiations, trademarks, and copyright issues are the realm of expertise here. Contact an entertainment lawyer when you've finished your Oscar-worthy screenplay.

- **Bankruptcy law.** When the chips are down, and we mean all the way down, these are the guys to talk to. They'll help you get your debt paid and make way for a fresh start. You can find one at the American Bankruptcy Center's consumer site: *consumer.abiworld.org*.

10 Things Your
Ticket Broker
Won't Tell You

1 *"WE THRIVE ON YOUR CONFUSION."*

In recent years you might've noticed that the options for buying tickets to concerts, sporting events, and theater have been expanding. First there are the venue box offices and event promoters, which sell seats directly to the public. Next comes what's called the primary market, including giants like Ticketmaster that contract with venues and promoters to sell seats at their events. Finally—and this is where things get really confusing—there's a growing secondary market for reselling tickets, including sites like StubHub (a Craigslist-style marketplace where people can sell tickets they've bought) and Onlineseats .com (which buys tickets for resale to the public).

The primary market is still the most common way to get tickets; it brought in $21 billion in 2007, versus $5 billion for the secondary market. But by 2012 the latter is expected to double its sales, according to Forrester Research. The problem is, the resellers' market is the Wild West of ticket sales, rife with opportunity as well as scam. And most folks don't even know there's a difference between primary and secondary sellers, says TicketNews.com

publisher Crystal Astrachan. The upshot: When buying tickets, what you don't know can hurt you.

2 *"YOU MAY BE BETTER OFF BUYING TICKETS THE OLD-FASHIONED WAY."*

A major reason for the growth of the secondary marketplace is the fact that people are willing to pay big bucks to see their favorite artists or teams perform. According to Forrester Research, three out of five consumers paid more than face value when buying tickets online through a secondary seller. Right now ticket prices simply aren't set as high as what they're worth on the open market, says Sucharita Mulpuru, a retail analyst at Forrester: "That's why you have a second market." Take the Super Bowl. Tickets to the 2008 game went for an average $3,540 on StubHub, versus $700 and $900 at face value.

The recent relaxation of antiscalping laws in 44 states—including big ticket issuers like California, Nevada, and New York—has contributed as well, basically providing a free market for resellers. But that's not necessarily a good thing for consumers, says Mulpuru, who warns that eventually the primary market will catch

Stick to the box office or Ticketmaster when possible, until the ticket industry sorts itself out.

up and start charging more. "That's where this is all headed," she says. So what's the safest route for consumers? Stick to the box office or Ticketmaster when possible, until the ticket industry sorts itself out.

3 *"YOU'VE GOT SEASON TICKETS? KA-CHING!"*

The secondary market has been a boon to season-ticket holders who want to sell their seats for a profit. Sean Pate, corporate communications head for StubHub, estimates that 60 to 70 percent of sports tickets on the site are from season-ticket holders. But there's an important variable when it comes to price: Is the franchise any good? Seats for the Boston Celtics, one of the hottest teams in the NBA in the 2007–2008 season, went for an average $97 on StubHub, a 48 percent increase over average face value, according to Team Marketing Research. But owners of Miami Heat seats, one of the league's worst, were lucky to break even, Pate says.

The real money is in NFL tickets, says secondary reseller RazorGator's CEO Jeff Lapin. Resale prices for football can easily be double, triple, or, in the case of the Green Bay Packers, four times face value. If you happen to own season tickets to the New England Patriots, note that the team allows only face-value resale to people on its waiting list. "We state clearly that the reselling of tickets is a revocable offense," says a Patriots spokesperson. But that hasn't stopped the flow of tickets. "They're one of our bestsellers," says StubHub's Pate.

4 *"OUR MOTTO: 'IF YOU CAN'T BEAT 'EM, JOIN 'EM.'"*

Ticketmaster, the largest ticket seller in the world, sold an estimated $8.3 billion worth of tickets in 2007, roughly 40 percent of all ticket revenue in the primary market, according to Mulpuru. But with the secondary marketplace on the rise, Ticketmaster has hedged its bets by creating its own fan-to-fan ticket-reselling platform, TicketExchange, and purchasing TicketsNow, the third-largest online reseller. "Ticketmaster has intentionally tried to vilify the secondary market for years, making it seem like an underground black market," says Pate. "But buying TicketsNow validates the growth and future of the secondary market."

The result? Sean Moriarity, president and CEO of Ticketmaster, says the move "will allow us to provide a safer, more reliable and efficient resale experience." Indeed, Ticketmaster's new involvement in the secondary market has introduced more consumer protection there. But make no mistake: "You've got to be very, very careful when buying tickets for big-time events," says Stephen Happel, professor of economics at Arizona State University. "Make sure the fine print says you're guaranteed a ticket."

5 "BROADWAY TOURISTS ARE SUCH EASY MARKS."

Out-of-town visitors to the Great White Way are often the least-savvy ticket buyers—especially when they go online. Some have shown up at venues with tickets bought from secondary brokers for more than three times their face value when seats were still available from Telecharge.com or the box office, according to Alan S. Cohen, director of communications for trade association The Broadway League.

Part of the problem is the size of Broadway's theaters, which have from several hundred seats to 2,000—tiny compared with sports stadiums or amphitheaters. While there are fewer seats, the same number of brokers are snatching up tickets for the hottest events, jacking up prices. Another factor is the falling dollar, which has spawned an influx of international tourists to New York. According to The Broadway League's annual report, show attendance by foreign visitors rose almost 40 percent from the 2006 to 2007 season. So what's your best bet for scoring seats? Cohen suggests the theater box office or primary source *www.broadwaytickets.com*. If you don't mind the line, you can also get up to 50 percent off tickets at one of the TKTS discount booths in New York.

6 "'SOLD-OUT' IS USUALLY A BIG FAT LIE."

Surprised that a 13,000-seat venue can sell out within minutes? So were the angry moms who tried to buy tickets to Hannah Montana's Kansas City, Mo., concert in September 2007. It turns out they had

a reason to be furious: Only 4,000 seats were made available by promoter AEG to the general public on the initial on-sale date. (An AEG spokesperson says that's because the stage design wasn't set yet, and it wasn't clear what seats would be obstructed.) Of the rest, 4,000 tickets went to fan-club members; 1,600 went to various promotions, sponsors, and comps; and the remaining seats were made available after the stage design was set.

"Events are never truly sold out," says Pate. Even when an event is listed as such with Ticketmaster, for example, there's still a chance for you to snag tickets from a primary source. Check back often as the date draws closer, since some of the outstanding tickets should eventually become available. Unfortunately, there's no rhyme or reason to how many seats will pop up or when, and it varies by event. But you can always try the secondary marketplace—if you have the stomach for it.

7 "THIS INDUSTRY IS A MAGNET FOR SCAM ARTISTS."

The online portion of the secondary market for tickets is expected to top $4.5 billion in 2012, so it's no surprise that opportunists are trying to claim their piece of the pie. Complaints about ticket brokers to the Better Business Bureau jumped 149 percent from 2002 to 2006. One of their biggest cons: advertising seats as located in a good section when they're actually in the nosebleeds.

Industry experts say the best way to protect yourself against fraud in the secondary market is to use a reputable resale platform, like StubHub, or a direct reseller, such as Ticketmaster's TicketExchange. And pay with a credit card or via a system like PayPal; it means added protection and maybe even your money back should there be a problem with your tickets.

8 *"OUR COMPUTERS KNOW HOW TO CHEAT THE SYSTEM."*

If you've ever bought tickets from Ticketmaster, you might wonder why you're asked to retype a wonky string of letters as part of your order. It's actually a vital security measure that prevents automated computer programs from gobbling up all the tickets to an event. But even that's not enough to keep the pros from gaming the system. In 2007 Ticketmaster sued RMG Technologies, claiming it provided software that circumvented security and allowed brokers to cut to the head of the virtual line. The case is still pending, but RMG President Cipriano Garibay maintains the company did nothing wrong. "Ticketmaster underestimated the efficiency of our system," he says.

Even when everybody plays by the rules, it still seems secondary brokers are winning out over consumers. It's a matter of sheer volume: There are at minimum 1,000 secondary brokers out there, each of which may have anywhere from one to 100 people working for them whose job it is to score the maximum number of tickets for any given event as quickly as possible. How to play against the pros? Think like them. Be poised and ready at the keyboard the precise moment tickets go on sale, and hit the purchase button the minute the sale begins.

9 *"WHAT YOU SEE ISN'T NECESSARILY WHAT YOU'LL GET."*

Tickets to see the Dave Matthews Band at the Tweeter Center in Mansfield, Mass., on June 24, 2008, were scheduled to go on sale to the general public on March 29. But oddly enough, on March 20 there were already 195 tickets available on the TicketsNow site—even though the brokers advertising there didn't actually have those tickets yet. "It's the same thing that happens with every big concert," says Mike Joliat, marketing director at brokerage site SelectATicket. com. "As soon as it's announced, brokers list tickets even though they don't have them." ("The tickets on our site are owned and supplied by over 800 different licensed ticket brokers," says a TicketsNow spokesperson. "They have to deliver that ticket at that price. These folks that we let list on our system know what they're doing.")

The practice is "very unethical," says retail analyst Mulpuru. "It's done to assess whether there's a market for the particular event and how hard the brokers should pursue the tickets." Case in point: Lawn seats to the Dave Matthews concert listed on TicketsNow prior to their on-sale date ranged from $65 to $225, notably higher than their $40 face value. "All they're doing is guessing what they think they can sell the ticket for," says Professor Stephen Happel. "The prices start out real high, then as the event gets closer, prices start to come down."

10 *"STREET SCALPERS MIGHT BE YOUR LAST HOPE."*

Ticket-starved New York Giants fans who made the trek to Arizona to watch their team play in the Super Bowl in February 2008 had the chance to get a big discount on tickets if they were willing to wait until the day of the game. Faced with the possibility of getting nothing for their tickets, street scalpers were selling seats for $1,000 that they had originally wanted $2,600 for. "It's open trading on game day," says Happel. "Your best bet is to go an hour before the game and take your chances. You can typically get tickets for face value or less."

Of course, there are always risks involved with buying tickets curbside. Steve Arena found that out firsthand when he bought three tickets for $900 outside the FedEx Forum for him and his two sons to watch a University of Memphis basketball game. When they got to their seats, the real ticket holders informed them they were the third or fourth group to show up with the same bogus tickets. Arena and his sons opted to roam the halls watching the game on the screens and standing in the aisles until someone asked them to move. "Counterfeit tickets are always going to be a worry," says Marianne Jennings, professor of legal and business ethics at Arizona State University. "However, from our experience, it's more of an issue online than it is on the street."

Bring your ticket vendor's customer-service number with you to the event. If there's a problem—say, someone sitting in in your seat—you'll have a better chance at resolving the problem right then and there.

THINGS TO DO

● **Bring your ticket vendor's** customer-service number with you to the event. If there's a problem—say, someone sitting in your seat—you'll have a better chance at resolving it right then and there.

● **To ease your worries about** buying tickets online, TicketNews posts weekly rankings of the top primary and secondary online sellers every Wednesday, at *www.ticketnews.com*.

● **Worried about doing business** with an unfamiliar broker? A good rule of thumb is to get someone on the phone and ask about the guarantee policy. If they don't have one, don't buy.

● **If you're buying** from a secondary seller, you won't know the exact seat location until after the purchase is made. However, before buying, you can look up the venue and assess its general location, at *www.ticketnetwork.com*.

10 Things Your
Florist
Won't Tell You

1 "PRICE GOUGING ON VALENTINE'S DAY? YOU BETCHA!"

If you're among the estimated one third of Americans who send flowers on Valentine's Day, then we don't have to tell you that a dozen roses cost more in early February than at any other time. While florists blame it on growers and growers blame it on demand and the weather, retail prices spike roughly 30 percent in the weeks prior to Valentine's Day. At New York City floral shop Shields Warendorff, for example, a dozen red roses that sold for $85 normally were marked up to $125 in early February 2008.

How to get the best deal? While there's no way of avoiding inflated holiday prices completely, it helps to place your order at least a week in advance. That's because prices can creep even higher for those who wait until the last minute; florists receive more than 50 percent of their Valentine's Day orders on Feb. 13 and 14. And think outside the box: A dozen shorter-stem roses, for example, will be less expensive than the long-stem variety, says Jennifer Sparks, spokesperson for the Society of American Florists. Mixed bouquets, such as a few roses interspersed with some imported orchids or an assortment of California mixed flowers, are also better deals.

2 "THE INTERNET MAKES IT EASY TO ORDER THE CRAPPIEST, OVERPRICED BOUQUETS ..."

Cameron Barrett wanted to send a bouquet to his wife, so he typed "NYC Flowers" into a Google search window. He found a listing for "Urban Florist" and chose a $30 bouquet. His "same-day delivery" arrived four days later; the flowers were nearly dead. To add insult to injury, the fiasco cost Barrett $45.35, including a miscellaneous charge of $4.17 and a $1.36 "foreign transaction fee," since his order was processed in Canada.

What gives? Third-party "order gatherers" with little experience in the floral industry are posing as local florists online. They purchase pay-per-click Google or Yahoo ads that automatically insert whatever city is being searched to make themselves appear local, then pass orders through a wire service and on to florists for a kickback: a 20 percent commission fee, plus a $6 to $8 rebate from the wire service. For every $70 bouquet ordered this way, roughly $45 makes it into the hands of the florist filling the order.

How to spot these poseurs? Never believe claims like "family owned and operated" and "we have a branch in that city" without checking, says a FloristDetective.com spokesperson.

3 "... EVEN FROM THE BIG-NAME FLOWER SITES."

When ordering flowers online, if you think sticking with familiar names will, um, nip the added-fee problem in the bud, think again. Even some floral giants like Teleflora, FTD, and 1-800-Flowers .com tack on an additional "service charge," since they, too, pass on their orders to local florists. And that's not the only cut being taken as your order runs the gauntlet of helping hands.

For example, while Teleflora's $12 fee includes service, delivery, and wire-service charges, as much as 27 percent of the list price of your arrangement never makes it to the florist. It means that even with some of the biggest names in the industry, ordering online "may reduce the quantity of flowers, and the quality will only be as good as the florist that's filling your order," a FloristDetective.com spokesperson says.

Does that mean there's no good way to order a bouquet online? Of course not. But be prepared to spend more on

Be prepared to spend more on an Internet order than you would for a comparable bouquet at a flower shop.

an Internet order than you would for a comparable bouquet at a flower shop. And stick to the top-rated vendors, such as Calyx & Corolla (*www.calyxandcorolla .com*) and Hallmark (*www.hallmark.com*).

4 "OUR ARRANGEMENTS LOOK NOTHING LIKE THESE PHOTOS."

They say a picture's worth a thousand words, but the photos of arrangements shown to customers by networked florists are often meaningless. Indeed, the canned images online and in catalogs aren't always accurate representations of what you're getting for your money. For one thing, they often aren't relayed to the florist filling the order, and when they are, substitutions are more the norm than the exception.

With long-distance orders, some retailers may take advantage of the fact that their customers rarely see the final product and the recipients hardly ever complain. "But if you sent yourself flowers and they arrived looking different than the pictures you ordered from, you would blow the whistle," says George Staby, of the Perishables Research Organization.

Indeed, even when you visit a local shop and choose a bouquet from, say, an FTD guide, the translation won't always be note perfect. "If for some reason they were out of red roses, a florist might replace them with a dark pink," says FTD floral designer Michael Skaff. "We do like-substitutions for color and value." Your best bet: Find out from the online florist whether a local outfit is filling the order, then call the local florist directly.

5 *"OUR DELIVERY TIMES ARE, UM, FLEXIBLE."*

When Alan Meckler, CEO of Jupitermedia, ordered flowers for his wife and mother two days before Mother's Day, he received e-mail confirmation from FTD almost immediately. On the morning of Mother's Day, he got a gracious call from his mom in Florida thanking him. But by noon Meckler's wife in New York still hadn't gotten her flowers. He called FTD and reached a rep who promised delivery by day's end. But the holiday came and passed without his wife's ever receiving flowers.

Late delivery is the number-one complaint about the floral industry, and not getting the delivery at all is number two, according to the Council of Better Business Bureaus. Although some florists hire extra drivers and trucks for the heavy-traffic holidays, timely arrival isn't always guaranteed. It helps to call a local florist at least a week in advance instead of ordering online. While a small shop may stop taking orders once it reaches maximum capacity—generally two to three days before a big holiday—online brokers often don't know how much the various florists they tap can handle, says Gary Reed of the Independent Florists' Association.

6 *"THESE FLOWERS WILL BE HALF DEAD BY THE TIME THEY ARRIVE."*

Scott Brown arrived at his great uncle's funeral with a bouquet of roses he'd bought at a local florist. But by the end of the day, after he'd handed them off to his great aunt, they were already drooping.

What determines the longevity of flowers? Buds are greatly affected by how they're handled before they reach consumers. Have they been transported at the proper temperature (about 32 degrees Fahrenheit) during the average weeklong trek from grower to distributor? You'll never know. But visiting a bricks-and-mortar flower shop means you can check on refrigeration and product placement, both good indicators of life expectancy. Flowers should never be stored near produce (especially apples, which emit a hormone that damages blooms) or cash registers (where air temperature is typically elevated). Also, avoid sidewalk displays, as exposure to car exhaust can decrease vase life.

Some retailers now mark their flowers with sell-by dates. If there's no sticker, ask for a vase-life guarantee, suggests Amy Stewart, author of *Flower Confidential*. Most florists will replace blooms that don't last at least five to seven days after purchase.

7 *"OUR BUDS ARE FREAKS OF NATURE."*

As if dousing flowers in fungicide to pass inspections at Miami International Airport weren't disturbing enough, more growers are breeding their own buds in laboratories and mass-producing the most marketable flowers in factories. They're handpicking their favorite qualities and breeding them into future generations to create the "perfect" flower. Unfortunately, flowers produced to withstand three days in a box without water during shipment lack some of the finer qualities, such as delicacy and scent.

Fragrance is especially limited, since it is closely tied to the production of the hormone ethylene, which shortens the life of a bloom. "We desperately want flowers to smell good, but as flowers are bred to have longer vase life, scent is compromised," Stewart says.

If you want flowers that aren't so altered that they've lost their scent, you might consider buying from a small niche of distributors who sell flowers nationally from their own gardens. Visit BonnyDoonGardenCo.com, for one; owner Teresa Sabankaya grows her signature posies in the Bonny Doon region of the Santa Cruz mountains in California.

8 "OUR SOFTWARE IS KEEPING TABS ON YOUR LOVE LIFE."

Online retailers have been using data-analysis software to better understand their customers' purchasing habits for quite some time now, but recently, they're admittedly less generous when it comes to offering discounts to their most frequent shoppers. At 1-800-Flowers.com, for example, a marketing team maintains profiles of all 28 million of its customers to keep a running history of whom they're sending gifts to and how frequently, what items they're selecting and for what occasions, and how far away they're shipping them. Sales representatives, trained to know how to guide a conversation and push specific additional products based on the caller's profile, are also well aware of the category of consumer each caller falls into. "We have a segment of customers that we call 'just because' shoppers. They'll send gifts for

no particular reason; they're givers," says Aaron Cano, vice president of consumer knowledge for 1-800-Flowers.com. "When we have a promotion like 10 percent off, they won't get that e-mail. They'll get 'Tell someone you love them today' instead."

Want to avoid being typecast and missing out on the best deals? Start a new account with a different e-mail address to cover your consumer tracks. That way, you'll get any enticement deals returning customers aren't privy to.

9 "THE BIGGER THE EVENT, THE MORE WE'LL NICKEL-AND-DIME YOU."

When planning for a large gathering such as a wedding or bat mitzvah, florists are often just as unsure about the price as you are until well into the process. Karen Perry, owner of The Master's Bouquet in Bakersfield, Calif., which services more than 100 weddings and big events each year, says that she offers "ballpark figures" during the initial consultation meeting, but that many variables affecting cost often don't come into play until later. For example, flower arrangements for a recent wedding originally estimated at $2,000 ended up costing a total of $5,000, Perry says, after the clients added centerpieces for the reception and asked for some additional upgrades.

Knowing what you want ahead of time helps, since last-minute changes can factor heavily in the billing for big orders. Prices can be kept in check more easily when clients communicate their budget up front and ask for an itemized copy of the bill from the start, says Walter Fedyshyn, vice president of the American

Institute of Floral Designers. Another tip for trimming costs: Opt for flowers that are in season, like asters or zinnias in the summer and carnations or lilies in the winter.

10 *"THERE'S NO GOOD SHORTCUT TO ROMANCE."*

Considering the emotional weight tied to the act of giving flowers, convenience isn't always the best route. That's because a trip to your local florist and dealing one-on-one with a trained professional can translate into a better experience overall. "Once your florist gets to know you on a personal level, extra attention may be given to your order," says David Coake, of trade publication *Florists' Review*.

Rori Pierpont, owner of Castle & Pierpont Floral Design in New York City, does just that with her customers. "Asking about furniture or artwork in the home plays a huge role in finding out more about a person," Pierpont says. And her customers back her up: "These flowers are about the story that's told through the arrangement; every story is different and personal," says regular customer Miriam Perl.

When sending flowers long-distance, the best results often come from speaking with a local florist and having the order filled via a trusted, networked shop in the recipient's town. Sure, the Internet is fast and easy, but when it comes to giving flowers, the smart money often means taking the path less convenient.

THINGS TO DO

- **A good florist asks questions** about what you're looking for and even the decor in the recipient's home; they should also be able to make suggestions, according to the Society of American Florists. For more ordering advice, go to *www.aboutflowers.com*.

- **Beware: Some firms posing** as local florists aren't. To find out if the one you found online or in the phone book is truly local, call and ask for directions to their shop.

- **To keep costs down,** especially around the holidays, opt for flowers in season.

- **To get the most from your flowers** for as long as possible, keep an eye on the water in the vase. If it turns yellow or gets cloudy—a sign of bacteria—replace it as soon as possible.

10 Things the
Pet Industry
Won't Tell You

1 *"I'M A BREEDER, ALL RIGHT—OF HEALTH PROBLEMS FOR PETS."*

All Ellen Szalinski wanted was a German shepherd puppy. What she got, after buying Bravo for $650 from a breeder, was a four-pound, nine-week-old dog loaded with parasites and health problems. "As a consumer, I was an idiot," says the publications manager for Chicago's Children's Memorial Hospital. The breeder had promised that the puppy would bulk up in a few weeks, but two years and about $5,000 later, Bravo had already undergone knee surgery and been treated for cartilage abnormalities and ruptured ligaments. "For what I spent, I could have made a down payment on a condo," Szalinski says. When Bravo died in 2005, a heartbroken Szalinski had spent $12,000 on his care over seven years, including seven surgeries.

Poor nutrition and care during the first few weeks of life, while a puppy is still at the breeder's, can cause sickness for months or even years to come. You can increase your odds of getting a healthy purebred by choosing breeders who use the services of OFA, the Orthopedic Foundation for Animals, an organization that tests everything from thyroids to kidneys to hips; and you can learn about specific breeds' health issues on OFA's

website, *www.offa.org*. Also, ask breeders for a trial period in which to assess the pup's health and temperament. If you're not satisfied, you can return the dog for a full refund. A breeder who says no likely doesn't stand behind his animals.

2 *"YOUR CAT'S FINE, BUT YOUR WALLET WILL NEED A TRANSFUSION."*

It's midnight, your Siamese suddenly falls violently ill, and your regular vet's office closed hours ago. Going to an emergency animal hospital may not be your best move, says Jeff Werber, who owns the Century Veterinary Group in Los Angeles. Why? Bad-apple clinics can play on owners' anxieties, charging hundreds of dollars for nonemergency X-rays, blood tests, and overnight stays.

Before you find yourself in such a situation, establish an emergency plan. If possible, choose a vet affiliated with a veterinary hospital accredited by the American Animal Hospital Association, which will have passed voluntary on-site reviews in 19 categories, from surgery to continuing staff education. You can find one near you at *www.healthypet.com*.

Meanwhile, keep in mind that "80 percent of animal 'emergencies' that happen after hours are not life-threatening," Werber says. Before hightailing it to any 24-hour emergency clinic—remember, even good ones charge extra for off-hours visits—he suggests paging your vet. Often a phone consultation is sufficient for your pet's regular caregiver to assess the "crisis" and advise whether Smokey needs to go to the kitty ER.

3 "READY FOR YOUR ANNUAL CASH-DRAINING?"

Annual checkups for your pet should include a head-to-toe exam, along with vaccines where necessary and lab work for older pets. Such visits can cost upwards of $150, which is within reason when they include the right mix of care. But many veterinarians will try to tack on additional fees for such things as superfluous tests on a pet's blood and urine. Also, veterinarians and researchers debate the necessity of giving vaccines such as parvo and distemper annually.

How can you avoid getting overcharged? When it comes time for an annual visit, ask the clinic to fax or e-mail an estimate, and be prepared to discuss whether your pet needs all the vaccines suggested, especially if it stays indoors. You might also want to ask about reduced rates on exams for additional pets; some vets offer discounts. Or go elsewhere; organizations such as your local animal shelter, humane society, and pet-supplies store often provide services for a fraction of what a private-practice veterinarian will charge. Some maintenance care might be even worth doing yourself—in particular, teeth cleaning. High-tech pet toothbrushes

that slip over a finger, such as Four Paws PetDental Finger Toothbrushes ($5.99 at *www.petco.com*), are much easier to run over a pet's teeth than traditional pet toothbrushes.

4 "WE CAN 'INSURE' THAT YOU'LL LOSE MONEY."

In 2006 pet-owning households visited veterinarians 193 million times, according to a study by the American Veterinary Medical Association. With the boom in pet-care services and veterinary specialists, as well as advances in veterinary techniques in recent years, animals are undergoing more extensive and costly procedures to fix what ails them. That's driving more owners to invest in pet insurance. In 2007 Americans spent an estimated $195 million on pet insurance premiums; that's an increase of 21 percent from 2006.

Unfortunately, pet insurance woes can be similar to human insurance woes. Premiums can run as high as $6,000 over a pet's lifetime, according to *Consumer Reports,* and preexisting conditions such as epilepsy, untreated hip dysplasia, or even old age can make your pet ineligible for coverage. And even if Sparky does qualify for a basic plan, reimbursements

Even without insurance ... you may have recourse for big-ticket expenses. Many vets, if you ask, will negotiate a weekly or monthly payment plan.

can be paltry, in the neighborhood of $10 per checkup.

If you shop well, however, pet insurance can sometimes be worthwhile. Emergency or surgery insurance plans cover large expenses for minimal premiums—often less than $10 a month, which isn't bad when you consider that procedures for accidents or cancer treatment can easily run north of $3,000. Premier Pet Insurance (*www.ppins.com*) and Petshealth Care Plan (*www.petshealth plan.com*), for example, offer low-cost programs that cover up to $8,000 a year in emergency care. Even without insurance, though, you may have recourse for big-ticket expenses. Many vets, if you ask, will negotiate a weekly or monthly payment plan.

5 "GO AHEAD AND SUE ME. YOU'LL GET CHICKEN FEED."

Did your vet make a big mistake with your pet's care? You're not alone. More owners are suing their vets for negligence than ever before. A few states, such as Oregon and Colorado, have recently introduced legislation allowing owners to sue for emotional loss and other issues, potentially pushing claims into the six-figure range. But since animals are currently deemed property under almost all state laws, owners can generally be compensated only for the market value of a pet—which means zippo for your beloved ex-stray.

James Wilson, a veterinarian and lawyer from Yardley, Pa., recommends drafting an account of your experience and asking your vet for an in-person meeting. If he agrees to use a mediator

before further action is taken, most of the time a satisfying agreement can be reached, saving both parties time, money, and emotional turmoil. Wilson estimates that if pet owners tried this route first, 75 percent of pet malpractice suits would not be pursued.

6 "WE'LL GIVE YOUR POOCH MORE THAN JUST KENNEL COUGH."

No doubt most kennel operators are well-meaning animal lovers who've turned their passion for pets into a benevolent business. But since the industry is largely unregulated, kennels can vary widely in their standard of care. When Beverly Dame brought home her cocker spaniel, Wesley, after 12 days at a kennel near her home in Vermont, he had an open wound on his rear leg and was unable to climb stairs. Subsequent treatment cost her $231—on top of the $169 kennel fee. While the kennel owner denies any wrongdoing, he admits that grooming, not boarding, is the kennel's main business. Indeed, kennels don't have to pass accreditation standards, nor are they rigorously monitored in most states. Inspections are left to local officials and can be spotty at best, so the impetus is on owners to find a safe and appropriate facility for their pet.

How can you know whether your pet will be housed in cramped, unhealthy conditions or put up in four-star luxury? Ideally, you should pick one of the few kennels that not only are members of the American Boarding Kennels Association but also have been accredited by the group. Such kennels must comply with

200 strict standards, including providing an area where dogs can be exercised at least three times per day. You can find such kennels at *www.abka.com*.

If there are no ABKA-accredited kennels in your area, tour any facility before booking your pet there. Also, ask what health concerns pet supervisors are trained to detect—runny noses or urinary problems, for example. And inquire about warranties: Many kennels offer warranties in their contracts, sometimes at extra cost, that will reimburse vet costs for injuries a pet sustains due to negligence on the behalf of the facility.

7 "I'LL TRAIN YOUR DOG, EVEN THOUGH I HAVEN'T BEEN TRAINED MYSELF."

Because all owners want a well-behaved pet—and some fear their dog may attack someone—many people fork over as much as $300 an hour for obedience lessons, only to wind up with a dog who does little more than sit and stay. Part of the problem is that anyone can call himself a dog trainer. "You'll find trainers in pet stores, but sometimes you'll discover they were a cashier last week and then they read a book on training," says Babette Haggerty-Brennan, head trainer for Babette Haggerty's School for Dogs in Palm Beach, Fla.

To avoid getting an inept or inexperienced trainer, look for someone who has graduated from a program, such as the one conducted by the Association of Pet Dog Trainers (*www.apdt.com*). Also, ask how many years of experience the prospective trainer has—training the family dog as a teenager doesn't

count—and how many dogs he's worked with professionally. Then ask for client references.

8 "BEFORE WE EXAMINE YOUR PET'S HEAD—HOW ABOUT YOU FIRST?"

In 2002 Melinda and Mark Ligos paid $1,200 to have a sock removed from their dachshund's intestines. Fed up with Ruckus's penchant for eating household items, they hired a "pet psychologist" to stop the destructive behavior. For the New Jersey couple, the experience was a big flop. "We paid this psychologist $50 an hour basically to teach our dog to sit and stay," Melinda Ligos says. "When it became obvious that she couldn't prevent Ruckus from eating things around the house, she suggested we feed him carrot shavings 'because he obviously needed fiber.' We were so embarrassed that after 30 minutes we gave her $50 and told her she could leave."

For pets who are exceedingly aggressive or suffer from severe separation anxiety, animal psychologists have been known to help—provided they're legit. True animal behaviorists, whether they're also veterinarians or not, are certified through either the Animal Behavior Society (*www.animalbehavior.org*) or the American College of Veterinary Behaviorists (*www.veterinarybehaviorists.org*). Most have advanced degrees or have completed course work in animal behavior studies.

But before dialing a pet shrink, you might want to try a less sophisticated alternative first. Putting a dog in day care two or three times a week for $30 a day, for example, might give your pet the physical and mental outlet it's looking for and alleviate separation anxiety. Choose a center much as you would a kennel. Vets and certified trainers can give referrals, but you should pay a visit beforehand to see that it's clean, that animals are under control as they play—no more than 15 at a time—and to verify that the center has a policy against aggressive dogs.

9 *"GOURMET FOOD, CHOW, SAME DIF."*

That expensive gourmet dog food that promises to make Sparky's coat glow? You'll find roughly the same ingredients in your grocery's bargain-basement brand. That's because almost all pet food comes from the same source: animal by-products that people don't eat.

While most vets agree prescription foods for animals with special needs are in a class by themselves, they admit that choosing food for a healthy pet is mainly a financial decision. "The most expensive doesn't mean the best," says Los Angeles veterinarian Jeff Werber. Be especially wary of diet foods, which are generally packed with added fiber to make pets feel full. Cutting back on regular food is a good way to achieve the same weight loss, Werber says, as long as owners supplement it with vitamins—Pet-Tabs, a multivitamin, runs about $15 for a 60-count bottle.

As a general rule of thumb, look for pet foods tested and given approval by members of the Association of American Feed Control Officials, an industry watchdog group that sets standards for animal-feed manufacturing.

10 *"AS YOUR PET WALKER, I MAY WALK ALL OVER YOU."*

Former New York City attorney Charlotte Reed came home from work early one day not only to find her dog walker ignoring her two dogs, Katie and Kidder, but also blaring music as he danced in front of a mirror in Reed's new $700 dress from Saks. "I walked in, and he stopped midway through a twirl," Reed says. The incident infuriated Reed so much that she left her law career shortly thereafter to form Two Dogs & a Goat, a pet-walking and -sitting company in New York.

Pet owners with demanding jobs increasingly rely on walkers and sitters, but selecting a good one can be daunting. For starters, look for someone certified by the National Association of Professional Pet Sitters or Pet Sitters International, which offer training in animal first aid, pet behavior, and diet and exercise routines; you can search their listings at *www.petsitters.org* and *www.petsit.com.* Second, check references and ask your walker or sitter about backup care should he become ill. Finally, don't put your pets—and your home—in the care of anyone without proof of insurance. The minimum plan should cover $1 million and include both your animal and your home.

> ## As a general rule of thumb, look for pet foods tested and given approval by members of the Association of American Feed Control Officials.

THINGS TO DO

● **When buying a dog from a breeder,** don't be afraid to ask for a trial period with a new pet to assess its health. That way, should your vet find something serious, you can return the animal for a refund and find a new breeder.

● **Another option: adoption.** Many shelters will provide free pets to a good home, often with the animal's full medical history. Get more information and a list of shelters at *www.aspca.org.*

● **Obedience training isn't a licensed** profession, so ask for references and years of experience before signing your dog up. Visit the Association of Pet Dog Trainers at *www.apdt.com* for help finding a good trainer, or ask your vet for a recommendation.

● **Want to give your pooch** a taste of the good life? At PamperedPuppy.com you'll find links to luxury services, product reviews, and even pet-friendly hotels.

10 Things Your
Mail Delivery Service
Won't Tell You

1 *"THERE ARE FEW GUARANTEES COME THE HOLIDAY SEASON."*

When the holidays roll around, all the major mail and package delivery services recommend that you plan well ahead for shipping. In fact, the United States Postal Service suggests that if you mail anything after Dec. 13, you use its Priority Mail service rather than sending it regular parcel post to ensure timely delivery before Christmas. That's a good reason to consider one of the private delivery companies, right? Maybe, but you won't get much protection should they fail to make the holiday deadline or if there's a mistake in delivery: United Parcel Service and DHL both suspend money-back guarantees on their most economical services during the peak season—roughly Dec. 11 through Dec. 25.

Over at FedEx, things aren't much better. The overnight promise doesn't apply to FedEx Ground and Home Delivery services starting seven calendar days before Christmas. (At UPS and DHL, money-back is a no-go on ground deliveries during roughly the same period—and don't forget to add in the surcharges for Saturday deliveries.) Your best bet, especially after Dec. 20, is USPS's Express Mail, which keeps its one- or two-day guarantee and will even deliver on Dec. 25.

2 *"IT'S HARD TO COLLECT ON OUR SO-CALLED INSURANCE."*

When Sean McDonald, a small-business owner in Lake Elsinore, Calif., used FedEx to ship 800 individual promotional signs to automobile dealers in 2003, 34 of them were cracked on arrival. McDonald says he wasn't concerned, though—he'd bought coverage on each package for its estimated worth of $300. But after faxing written claims to FedEx within its 15-day deadline and receiving compensation for only one sign, McDonald stopped payment. He says FedEx threatened to sue him for nonpayment on his account, but once their lawyers got hold of it, they reached a settlement out of court in which FedEx paid McDonald $18,000. "Unless you stick to your guns, you'll never get the payment," McDonald says. (FedEx says it doesn't comment on specific cases.)

The problems McDonald experienced aren't unique to him or to FedEx. You may have difficulty getting a delivery service to pay up when a package is damaged—the fine print of terms and conditions protects companies from many incidents that can happen while a package is in transit. Often the delivery service can claim the packaging was insufficient—not enough padding, for example.

But the reality is that you may not ever need to buy coverage when using private carriers. With UPS and FedEx, for example, all consumer packages are covered up to $100 automatically. Beyond that amount, and for other services, you likely already have coverage for shipped property under your homeowner's insurance. Just be aware that a high deductible on your policy could diminish any reimbursement you might expect on a lost package.

3 *"JUNK MAIL IS OUR BREAD AND BUTTER."*

It's true that the only surefire way to have your mail forwarded when you move is to fill out the USPS's official change-of-address form. But once you do, don't be surprised when you start getting even more junk mail and direct-marketing pitches along with your bills and magazines. While the USPS says it doesn't sell new address information to direct marketers, it does charge a licensing fee of $175,000 per year to third-party companies that are hired by direct marketers to take their old direct-mailing lists and revise them—using the change-of-address information provided by the USPS. The USPS says that licensing its National Change of Address (NCOA) database to these so-called list cleaners saves the U.S. Postal Service money in returned mail and forwarding mail costs. Besides, the official line goes, it's not really up to the post office to differentiate between junk and legitimate mail. "We do this because the customer has told us they want to get their mail at the new address," a spokesperson says.

Fortunately, it's possible to sidestep the NCOA database and still get your mail forwarded without the extra junk. Just fill out a temporary change-of-address form indicating that you'll be back at your old address in a year. The postal system forwards first-class mail only up to a year anyway, and "temporary" address changes don't get stored in the NCOA database.

4 *"PRIORITY MAIL ISN'T OUR BIGGEST PRIORITY."*

The United States Postal Service advertises its Priority Mail as a two-day delivery, but paying $4.60 to send an important envelope this way may not be better than simply slapping on a first-class stamp. According to the Postal Regulatory Commission, an independent agency, 27 percent of packages and letters sent via Priority Mail take more than two days, while regular first-class mail takes one to three days.

A USPS spokesperson says Priority Mail is a "convenient, reliable, and affordable service that does not claim to include a guarantee," and that unlike its competitors, the Postal Service doesn't add fuel or weekend surcharges. Indeed, you'll pay more for express delivery through private carriers: For example, a package weighing one pound or less sent from New York City to Philadelphia via FedEx's two-day service costs about $16—but unlike the USPS's Priority Mail, in most cases, it comes with a money-back guarantee.

5 *"WE DON'T ADVERTISE OUR BEST DEAL FOR SHIPPING."*

Media Mail service—known as "book rate" until 2001—has been around for years, but few people use it because it isn't well publicized down at the local post office. Why not? Because Media Mail is primarily used by business customers, according to a USPS spokesperson. But anyone can—and should—use it to mail books, films, printed music, sound recordings, manuscripts, or computer-readable media including CDs and DVDs. Just be sure that's all that's in the package: To be shipped using Media Mail rates, a package cannot contain advertising or a letter to Mom, and the maximum weight is 70 pounds. Indeed, if a postal clerk is suspicious of a box or envelope's contents, he can open it for inspection.

While Media Mail delivery can be a little on the pokey side—up to nine days—it can sometimes take as little as two days. So it's a great deal as long as you're not on a deadline to return those Tom Clancy books you borrowed from your brother. How good are the savings? Mailing 20 pounds of books using Media Mail from New York to California costs $8.59, compared with $23.98 for shipping them standard Parcel Post.

6 *"YOUR LOST PACKAGE IS PROBABLY SITTING IN A WAREHOUSE SOMEWHERE."*

Where exactly does undelivered mail go? "If I knew, then it wouldn't be lost," quips one delivery-service spokesperson. "Can I get back to you about that?" That's roughly the same response Jing Cao says she got after she shipped two pieces of luggage through UPS from Pennsylvania to her new home in Minnesota in 2003—and she never did track one of them down. UPS finally sent Cao a check for $100 plus shipping costs, since all items sent through the company are automatically insured up to $100. That was little solace, though, when Cao remembered that she had tucked her engagement ring into the lost bag's pocket. "We went to a pickup center to talk to a supervisor, who thought maybe the labels came off," Cao says. "She said there was a warehouse somewhere where lost shipments go, but she didn't know how to contact it."

A UPS spokesperson confirms that the company does have an "overgoods" warehouse for packages that are undeliverable—usually because a label has been lost or destroyed. Cao's experience is unusual in that 70 percent of items held there are eventually delivered or picked up. FedEx and USPS have similar facilities, where they hang on to undelivered goods for three months—often longer for "personal or family-type" items and some tech equipment—and

> **While Media Mail delivery can be a little on the pokey side—up to nine days—it can sometimes take as little as two days. So it's a great deal as long as you're not on a deadline.**

USPS for 30 days to a year. After that, items are destroyed, donated to charity, or sold through auctions.

Your best hope for recovering a lost package, experts say, is calling customer support and requesting a search on the service's warehouse database, which lists detailed descriptions of packages' contents. Meanwhile, cover mailing labels with clear tape, and label the inside of the package as well. "We'll open a box before it ends up at the warehouse," a UPS spokesperson says, "and look for any information that might help us figure out where it's supposed to go."

7 "IF I'M AFRAID OF YOUR DOG, I WON'T DELIVER YOUR MAIL."

According to the USPS, 3,184 letter carriers were bitten by dogs in 2006, meaning an average of 10 dog bites per delivery day. For that reason, the USPS will stop mail delivery to your home if the carrier feels threatened by your pet. And if he believes your dog just might come after him while he's next door or across the street, he can refuse to deliver mail to your entire block. Until the situation has been fixed to the postmaster's and mail carrier's satisfaction—usually meaning that your dog is restrained while the letter carrier is working—everyone involved must pick up their mail at the local post office. Try explaining that to the neighbors.

In the event of an actual incident, your mail carrier can also sue you. As the dog owner, "If you don't have homeowner's or renter's insurance, you could be responsible for footing the entire claim" for medical bills and damages,

says Todd Peterson, a personal-injury lawyer based in Portland, Ore., who has represented delivery people attacked by dogs. "[One] letter carrier I represented had a quarter-inch scar on his calf from a dog bite," Peterson says. "He sued the dog owner and won $8,500."

Think posting a "beware of dog" sign will protect you? Think again, says Peterson; your best bet is obedience training for little Cujo or confining him to a back room while you sign for packages. USPS also recommends that dog owners make sure children don't accept mail directly from a delivery person, as a dog may see the transaction as a threatening gesture.

8 "WE PLANT SPIES AT YOUR LOCAL POST OFFICE."

Does the line at your local post office always seem long? The problem may be exacerbated by a "mystery shopper" or two, undercover USPS employees planted in line to make sure clerks do enough suggestive selling. According to PostalMag.com, an online magazine for postal employees that is not officially affiliated with the United States Postal Service, clerks are told to ask all customers five questions, ranging from how fast they want their mail delivered to whether they need services such as delivery confirmation. While USPS confirms that such questioning is required, a spokesperson says, "The Mystery Shopper program [helps] customers make better-informed decisions."

While few consumers enjoy fending off extra sales pitches, folks on the other side of the counter don't much care for it either. "I've always felt uneasy about how unethical this program is," one window clerk wrote to PostalMag.com. "The only benefit to the customer I see is a reminder that they need stamps or occasionally insuring a package. On the whole, however, the barrage of questions is so irritating to customers that many of them walk up and say, 'Just mail it!'"

To get the best deal for your package—and avoid extra time hearing out extra offers—check out the USPS website, *www.usps.com,* where you can price different mailing methods beforehand. And to avoid the line completely, you can use the Automated Postal Center machines in your post office's lobby. These do-it-yourself systems will weigh your mail, price it, and print the appropriate postage.

9 *"THERE'S A CHEAPER WAY TO SEND PACKAGES ABROAD— BUT IT'S A SECRET."*

Sending a three-pound holiday gift to your pen pal in France using USPS's standard airmail, Priority Mail International, will cost you $28—unless you know the secret to making it cheaper, and USPS may not be telling. That's what one New York City Little League coach learned when he was shipping a package to a friend in Switzerland. The postal clerk told him that if he used another service, First Class International, it would be about $7 cheaper; the package would also get to its destination about as quickly—6 to 10 days. The next time the coach had a package to send overseas, he says he couldn't remember the cheaper service's name, and when he asked the

clerk what it was, she said she couldn't help him. A month later yet another clerk tipped him off to the First Class International secret but cautioned him not to tell anybody because the rate might be raised if word got out.

A USPS spokesperson called the customer's situation "isolated," adding that clerks are required to offer services that match customers' needs. Even so, you're better off checking *www.usps.com* ahead of time. If an item can fit in an envelope, you can save even more money—First Class International items sent in the Flat Rate envelope cost $9 to Canada and Mexico and $11 to anywhere else in the world.

10 *"ELM AVENUE IS REALLY ELM STREET. THAT'LL BE $10."*

Keith Kimmel makes a living in South Bend, Ind., buying and selling political T-shirts and books over the Internet, so shipping is obviously a key component of his livelihood. A big thorn in his side is UPS's $10 "address correction fee." For instance, Kimmel says, "I wrote 'Drive' instead of 'Boulevard'"—his customers and correspondents don't always supply their full street names on orders—"and although the ZIP code and everything else was correct and the driver was able to deliver the package, they still charged me." Out of frustration, Kimmel launched a website (*www.unitedpackagesmashers.com*) that allows other similarly disgruntled customers to share their stories.

UPS stands by its address-correction fee, as does FedEx, which charges up to $10; both offer address-checking services on their websites so that such mistakes can be avoided. "That's a legitimate cost to us," a UPS spokesperson says. "I would love to show people what our employees go through trying to correct an address" after packages get bounced back to a UPS center. "We actually resort to combing through phone books," he says.

THINGS TO DO

Mail delivery has come a long way from the days of tying parcels to pigeons. To make sure you have a higher success rate than our forefathers, we spoke with Joanne Veto, consumer advocate at the United States Post Office, to get some tips on how to make sure your package gets from point A to point B as efficiently as possible:

● **Make sure the address is complete.** The biggest holdup in mail delivery is when an address is missing a boulevard, street, avenue, road, or apartment number.

● **If you're not sure** of the proper ZIP code, you can check at *www.usps.com*.

● **Don't worry about international rates** when sending mail to the troops overseas. All mail delivered to military installations around the world gets shipped at the domestic rate.

● **When sending more than one item** in a box, wrap them separately. Shake the box; if the contents rattle around, you need to use more cushioning, such as foam peanuts.

● **It helps to write "Fragile"** in large print on the box if it contains items that might break, and "Perishable" if it holds food or other items that could spoil during shipment.

10 Things Your
Jeweler
Won't Tell You

1 "THERE'S NO SUCH THING AS A DIAMOND SALE."

Your local jewelry store is advertising a "blowout sale"—what better time to buy the diamond bracelet that seemed too pricey around Valentine's Day, right? Bad news: True sales don't exist, at least not with diamonds, says Matthew Hart, author of the book *Diamond* and former mining editor for trade publication *Rapaport Diamond Report*. "If [a true sale] ever happens, that's the end of the diamond business."

Why? The retail world's diamond supply, he says, is carefully orchestrated by De Beers. Based on the perceived demand of consumers, the mining cartel, which controls 65 percent of the world's rough (or uncut) diamond supply, either chokes back supply or increases production. For instance, in 2000 De Beers was selling about $500 million worth of rough diamonds at each of its regular sales; in 2002, when the market cooled, it sold $300 million. Strategically manipulating sales helps ensure that the market is never oversaturated and prices never plummet.

Though De Beers has staunchly maintained for years that it does not control market pricing, it agreed to pay $295 million in a class-action lawsuit that charged it unfairly monopolized the diamond trade and broke antitrust and consumer-protection laws. (A judge issued an order approving the settlement in May 2008. At press time, appeals had been filed contesting the approval and thus postponing resolution of the settlement.) "Nothing is more important to De Beers than consumers' confidence in diamonds," says a spokesperson for the company. "Consequently, while we don't accept the allegations, we took the step to settle and put all outstanding legal matters behind us."

So what exactly does it mean when a diamond is advertised as "on sale"? Often, according to Hart, a stone cut in less-than-perfect proportions. "You pay for what they throw out," he says.

2 "YOUR 'PERFECT' DIAMOND HAS HAD A FACE-LIFT..."

Thanks to science and technology, the brilliant-looking diamonds in your jeweler's case aren't all necessarily what they appear to be. They could be "fracture-filled," for instance, referring to a treatment in which visible cracks are filled with a glasslike substance, making a stone appear more expensive than it is. The treatment usually isn't guaranteed to last, because if the stone ever gets repaired using heat, the filler can ooze like jelly in a doughnut. You'll get better quality with "Bellataire" diamonds, which have undergone a high-pressure, high-temperature treatment that whitens the color, increasing their value dramatically.

It's fine to go with an engineered stone—as long as you know what you're getting. And they should cost less than the all-natural goods. But unfortunately, some aren't marked accurately or priced accordingly. To establish that your diamond is legit, make sure there's a return policy before you buy, then take the piece to an independent certified appraiser; you can find one in your area through the American Society of Appraisers, at *www.appraisers.org*.

3 "...AND THESE EMERALDS, SAPPHIRES, AND RUBIES HAVE ALL GOTTEN DYE JOBS."

By the seeming bounty of them available at any jewelry store, you wouldn't guess that natural-colored stones are an increasingly rare commodity. But the truth is that few truly stunning ones are found these days; deposits are either depleted or are producing inferior rocks. The result: The rainbow of gems at your jeweler likely consists of rubies, emeralds, and sapphires that have been treated with a variety of techniques such as heating or oiling to make them look more vibrant.

Not that there's anything wrong with that—again, as long as you know what you're getting. "But the average salesperson doesn't volunteer that information or know themselves," says Antoinette Matlins, a gem expert and author of such books as *Jewelry & Gems: The Buying Guide.*

"Unless you read the [fine print] on the sales receipt, the average consumer thinks that's the way the stone came out of the earth." Before you buy, ask if the stones have been treated, and make sure you get documentation attesting to their status. As always, an outside appraisal is a smart move.

Another route is to ask your jeweler to order one of the excellent alternatives to expensive natural-colored stones— tsavorite garnets instead of emeralds, for example, or red or blue spinels in lieu of rubies or sapphires. They're brilliant without any treatment and usually much cheaper. "In fact," Matlins says, "a red spinel is the centerpiece of the Imperial State Crown in London, which for centuries was believed to be a ruby."

4 "THERE'S BLOOD ON THIS STONE."

The diamond industry has been working to clean up its act in recent years, after human-rights advocates estimated in 2002 that as many as 1 in 10 diamonds sold at the time was a "conflict" stone, meaning it came from a country where the diamond trade used slave labor and funded warlords who routinely killed innocent civilians. Then in 2003, the U.S. introduced the Clean Diamond Trade Act, a law designed to stop the trade of "blood diamonds" through participation in the Kimberly Process Certification Scheme. KPCS, as it is popularly known, is an internationally recognized process that aims to prevent conflict stones from entering the rough-diamond market, thus assuring consumers they're not financing war and human-rights abuses. And the effort has paid off—more than 99 percent of diamonds in the market are now conflict-free.

But there's a new concern when buying diamonds today: the environment. If your conscience calls you to seek out an earth-friendly alternative to traditionally mined diamonds, then laboratory-created ones—introduced in 2006 and available from companies like Adia Diamonds, LLC—offer a guilt-free alternative.

5 *"THOSE PRETTY JEWELS DISPLAYED ON MY WEBSITE? THEY'RE NOT FOR SALE."*

You buy your books on Amazon and your airline tickets on Orbitz, so why not purchase a diamond on the Web? Because it's often tough to be certain that what you see on the screen is what you're actually buying. Cecilia Gardner, executive director and general counsel of the Jewelers Vigilance Committee in New York City, routinely comes across sites that use standard photos to represent their goods. "Very often it's a generic picture of a diamond ring, and then you wind up with something very different," she says. To make matters worse, some sites' return policies are problematic, while other sites "sort of disappear" after the sale, says Gardner.

Is there any way to buy a diamond online without getting duped? Look for a return policy that allows you a full refund within a reasonable time frame, Gardner says, and for lab reports that include full disclosure of a piece's characteristics—such as clarity, size, and color for gems—as well as any treatments that have been done. In late 2001 the Federal Trade Commission sent letters to 16 of the 21 largest Web jewelry sellers advising them to post more information about stone enhancements. "If you see no information about treatment," says Gardner, "I wouldn't buy at that site."

6 *"YOUR AUNT HILDA'S PEARLS MAKE A LOUSY INHERITANCE."*

The key to any pearl is the nacre, or lustrous coating that covers the nucleus. Unlike natural pearls—which make up a very small percentage of the market and are virtually all nacre—a cultured pearl is a bead surrounded by nacre. But the majority of cultured pearls sold today "have such a thin [nacre] coating that in a small period of time, the nacre will peel, then chip, and be worthless shell beads," says Matlins. She particularly advises against pearl bracelets and rings that sell for, say, $150 around Mother's Day and graduation: "They're tantamount to flushing your money down the toilet." Even in a fine-jewelry store, Matlins estimates that 30 to 40 percent of the pearls won't hold up from generation to generation.

How can you tell the good from the bad and the potentially ugly? "The luster of the nacre is something the eye can detect," says Matlins, and the thicker the nacre is, the more luster. "I don't mean a surface shine; I mean a glow that seems to emanate from the core." Avoid pearls with a coating that seems transparent or chalky, and stay away from those that seem to blink at you when you roll a string of them across the table, Matlins says. "That's your nucleus showing through." You can also rub a pearl gently against your tooth—a good pearl's nacre will feel slightly gritty, while a cheap pearl with thin nacre will create a smooth sensation.

7 *"I REPLACED YOUR DIAMOND WITH A NIFTY NEW CZ."*

Carole Parrish, a Tahlequah, Okla.-based spiritual adviser, wanted to have her grandmother's gold and diamond ring reset in a more modern style. She had the piece appraised, then found a small local jeweler willing to use her redesign. But after the work was done, Parrish realized that some of the stones were chipped. When she had the piece reappraised, she learned that some of the diamonds had been switched for lesser stones—one was even replaced with cubic zirconia (CZ). When Parrish's jeweler wouldn't replace the broken and fake diamonds, she sued and was awarded $4,827; that prerepair appraisal made her case.

Although stone switching doesn't happen every day, some experts say you're not paranoid to wonder what goes on in the jeweler's back room. Joyce Jonas, president emeritus of the American Society of Jewelry Historians, says that antique pieces featuring stones in high demand—such as late-18th-century Old Mine or 19th-century European cuts—have been particularly targeted. "People often didn't know what they had, and they brought it in to be fixed," Jonas says. "The fakes were so good, you didn't know the difference." Though stone switching still occurs, consumers today are much savvier about potential scams, and it's easier to take protective measures. Jonas advises getting an ID number lasered onto your best pieces by a jeweler you trust or the Gemological Institute of America (*www.gia.edu*). The GIA can also run an identification report on your stone that serves as a virtual fingerprint in case it goes missing.

8 *"IF IT LOOKS OLD, I'LL CALL IT AN 'ESTATE PIECE.'"*

Unlike most jewelry, "estate pieces"—the designation currently given to those crafted between 1890 and 1960—often prove to be good investments, since they're increasingly hard to find and can come back into vogue. But not everything advertised as such is the real deal. Take the platinum "Edwardian" engagement rings that are all the rage these days, admired for their intricate engravings and highly detailed mountings. All too often, Jonas says, jewelers might pawn off a slightly newer ring—crafted of white gold because platinum was needed for the World War I effort—as Edwardian, whose dates span from 1890 to about 1914.

Even true oldies aren't necessarily goodies. Many antique pieces have been revamped, which diminishes their value. For instance, "You don't want to buy a [gold] piece that has been repaired using lead solder," Jonas says; it cuts the piece's value in half and eventually eats through the gold. That's why, along with the requisite outside appraisal, it's important to get things in writing: in this case, when and where the piece was made; its condition; the type of metal or stones, and whether they've been treated; and whether the stones are the original gems.

9 *"YOUR WARRANTY IS PRETTY WOBBLY."*

Many jewelry stores sell extended warranties for their merchandise—typically, from a few dollars to a few hundred—to cover defects and damages for a year or two. But the wording is often so vague, says Tom Adelmann, former assistant vice president at Neenah, Wis.– based Jewelers Mutual Insurance, that "it wouldn't surprise me one bit if customers leave the store thinking they're protected if anything happens to the jewelry." In reality these warranties usually cover only a "partial loss"—like when a stone gets wobbly in its setting—but not a total loss.

What people also don't realize is that for not much more than the price of a warranty, you can often buy a separate insurance policy or an endorsement to your homeowner's or renter's policy that will cover the piece much better. You'll be protected against all kinds of loss, from theft to death by garbage disposal. Another tip: For family heirlooms or pieces you almost never wear, make their primary home a safe-deposit box and they can be even cheaper to insure.

10 *"I'M MORE THAN HAPPY TO HAGGLE WITH YOU."*

Bum-diamond sales aside, you can find deals in a jewelry store—just don't expect merchants to advertise. Jewelry stores play "pricing roulette," says Ken Gassman, a Richmond, Va., jewelry industry analyst. "The only place where you'll see more negotiating is a used-car lot."

In today's soft market, Gassman says, it's common to be rewarded with a 10 to 20 percent discount or an extra piece of merchandise if you ask. It's also a good time to "buy up," or put the cost of an older piece toward a bigger item. Colored gemstones such as opals and topazes tend to carry the greatest margins, Gassman says, while you're less likely to get a discount on wristwatches, which carry the smallest markup in the store.

But timing is everything. The deals dry up a month before Valentine's Day and Mother's Day, respectively, and you'll need to do your Christmas shopping by Oct. 31. Another option: "You can wait until two weeks before Christmas, when retailers panic," says Gassman, "but you don't know what you'll find on the shelves by then."

THINGS TO DO

We asked Patrick Davis, a professional independent appraiser based in Los Angeles, for some tips on buying a diamond. Here's what he says:

- **"Jewelers like it when shoppers** don't know how quality relates to value. Unless you're planning on eloping, you should do your homework before buying a diamond." Go to *www.pricescope.com* to learn about "the four Cs" of diamond appraisal: Clarity, Color, Cut, and Carats.

- **Of "the four Cs,"** Davis says jewelers rank cut the most important. "An ideal cut is one that produces the greatest light return, which affects a diamond's brightness, brilliance, and dispersion."

- **Despite the risks,** there are some good bargains for educated shoppers online. "Sites like BlueNile.com and Diamonds .com are offering the best prices right now." Diamonds bought over the Internet should come with a 30-day guarantee; make sure the purchase is protected by your credit card, and get it appraised.

10 Things Your
Retailer
Won't Tell You

1 *"FORGET COMMISSIONS. OUR STAFF GETS KICKBACKS."*

Plenty of retail sales staff are open to negotiation on prices, but sometimes clerks have hidden agendas you might not know about. Consider "spif"—special promotion incentive fee—a selling incentive that leads sales staff to heavily favor one brand over another. "Spif is a direct commission from the manufacturer," says a retail salesman from New York, who asked not to be named and who says he has received spif for selling electronics, appliances, and even cars. "The higher the spif"—which can run as much as $100 on a TV, for example—"the more you want to move the product," the salesman says. "The customer just thinks you're focusing on the product you think is best."

How can you distinguish good advice from a commission-driven sales pitch? "When you're making a large purchase, make sure you're communicating to the salesperson what it is you need," says Daniel Butler, vice president of retail operations at the National Retailer Federation. "If you feel they're steering you towards something that doesn't meet your needs, find someone else in the store to help you."

2 *"THAT SALESMAN DOESN'T ACTUALLY WORK HERE."*

You're walking the aisles of your local electronics store, when a clean-cut fellow in a blazer walks up and offers to help. He's a sales rep, sure. But he might not work for the retailer you're shopping in. Companies such as Hewlett-Packard, for example, sometimes hire marketing firms to provide in-store salespeople who are there to "offer information" about a specific brand or product. These hired guns may or may not identify themselves as such, says Peter Breen, director of content for the In-Store Marketing Institute, a retail marketing strategy association, making it hard to distinguish them from eager on-staff sales associates.

How to spot the company man? "If somebody seems too aggressive about one brand, ask him who he's working for," says Breen. A Hewlett-Packard spokesperson says his company's reps "help customers identify the best solution for their needs" and wear shirts with identifying logos.

3 *"IF YOU KNEW OUR RETURN POLICY, YOU MIGHT NOT SHOP HERE."*

If a retailer told you up front that all returned or exchanged items would be levied with a 10 to 15 percent "restocking fee," would you shop there? Maybe, maybe not. And perhaps that's why some retailers—mostly electronics stores—downplay such policies.

Stores justify restocking fees by saying they deter customers who use products before returning them. But if retailers' motives are that straightforward, why do so many keep quiet or even seem to hide their restocking-fee policy? If you're lucky, "there might be a sign at the return counter," says Mark Ferrulo, former director of the Florida Public Research Group. "Other stores print it on the back of your receipt, but by the time you see it, you've already paid." Your best bet: Ask about return policies and restocking fees before you make an electronics purchase.

4 "OUTLETS ARE A FRONT FOR CHEAPER GOODS."

Discount clothing outlets may have started as a way for chain stores to unload lingering items, but they have become so popular that these days designers often create secondary lines—with, say, cheaper fabrics—specifically for the outlets. The outlets will then mix these straight-to-discount garments with last season's leftovers and pieces with slight defects.

How can you tell the difference? Look at the price tag. "If the tag has 'compare at' [followed by a price], it may have been made specifically for the outlet," says Randy Marks, author of *Outlet Bound: Guide to the Nation's Best Outlets*. If, however, it says "original price" followed by the lower outlet price, "you can assume the store has sold items like this one at the original price."

5 "WE'LL SAY ANYTHING TO LURE YOU INSIDE."

Nobody expects advertising to be completely aboveboard, but some large retailers are making it hard to believe in the most seemingly straightforward ads. Back in 2000, for example, the Federal Trade Commission charged Delray Beach, Fla.–based Office Depot with false advertising—in particular, for hawking dirt-cheap PCs but neglecting to mention that buyers had to sign up for $800 worth of Internet service as part of the deal. (Henceforth, Office Depot agreed to include such caveats in its ads; the company had no comment when contacted.) And Kmart raised the ire of Target with its "Dare to Compare" campaign in 2001, which allegedly misreported competitors' prices. (Kmart has since voluntarily dropped the campaign; it also had no comment.)

How leery should consumers be when it comes to retail advertising? "Most retailers don't want to risk their good reputation with customers over an ad," says Daniel Butler. "But if something looks too good to be true, do some research and comparative shopping."

6 "OUR GIFT CARDS TAKE AS MUCH AS THEY GIVE."

Whether you see them as terrific stocking stuffers or the ultimate gift-giving cop-out, gift cards have invaded our culture. Retailers love them because they're a cash cow, bringing in $97 billion in 2007, a 16 percent increase from 2006. What's even better—from a retailer's perspective—is the fact that about 10 percent of the total value of cards purchased in 2007 went unused, mainly due to expiration dates, maintenance fees, and good old forgetfulness.

But in some cases, gift cards can lose their value even through no fault of the consumer. For example, Sharper Image announced it was suspending the acceptance of gift cards in February 2008 after it filed for Chapter 11 bankruptcy. The retailer backtracked a month later, saying it would continue to accept gift cards—but only as long as the total purchase was twice the value of the gift card. "People have to realize that gift cards were never intended to be savings vehicles; they're meant to be used," says Brian Riley, a senior analyst at TowerGroup. "The best thing you can do when you get a gift card is go spend it."

7 "THAT DRESS HAS BEEN AROUND THE BLOCK."

It's bad enough when a cheapskate customer buys a high-priced cocktail dress, wears it, and then returns it. But what about when stores are party to putting used garments back on the rack?

It can and does happen. High-end department stores around the country maintain studio-services departments, which rent out designer garments for photo shoots, under the assumption that the barely used garments can then be sold to the public. But used pieces often come back "sweaty and wrinkled," says Stefan Campbell, a fashion stylist based in New York City. "So the store dry-cleans them—if it's a good store." How can you tell when a garment has been worn before? Look for clues: pinholes in the back (used to attain that cinched-in look

for photographs) and handwritten (as opposed to the original, printed) price tags. You may also notice makeup or deodorant smudges on the garment.

8 "COUTURE ISN'T EXACTLY A SUREFIRE INVESTMENT."

Could a designer purse really have "growth potential"? That's what some salespeople would have you think. "I've heard retailers telling customers that an item [might become] collectible," says Cameron Silver, owner of Decades, a Los Angeles–based vintage-clothing boutique.

While it's nearly impossible to play fashion's futures market, it can happen. Nobody, for instance, could have guessed that Gucci handbags from the 1970s would become collectible—purses that sold for $55 originally can go for around $220 now—but it happened after the brand's recent resurgence. Looking for the next hot issue? One decent bet today, Silver says, is a Hermès bag, particularly the "Kelly" bag, which starts at $8,000. "Twenty years from now it will definitely be worth more," Silver says.

9 "CLOTHING DESIGNERS HAVE NO BUSINESS MAKING HOUSEWARES."

Just because a designer makes beautiful clothing, don't expect his skills to transfer to anything else he chooses to create. These days fashion designers of every stripe are rolling out all manner of crossover goods—Armani towel rack, anyone?—trying to cash in on the lucrative housewares market. But not all these products are up to snuff.

In particular, Evan Lobel, proprietor of New York City's Lobel Modern antiques shop, isn't impressed with designer-affiliated furniture. "Fashionistas send their people around to shops like mine so they can see how the proportions are done on mid-century furniture, and then they copy it," Lobel says. "That may be the way fashion is done"—knocking off garments made by competitors and predecessors—"but furniture is different." Don't buy it; the originals, even as antiques, are better made and often less expensive than these new look-alikes, Lobel says.

10 *"BRAND LOYALTY IS SUCH AN ANTIQUATED NOTION."*

Okay, so nobody assumes that Elizabeth Taylor concocted the formula for White Diamonds perfume in her basement. But the degree to which big companies will sell off their names should make you think twice about brand loyalty.

Even telecom giant AT&T is guilty: All its brand-name phones are manufactured by VTech, known for talking kids' toys. "When a product is well licensed, consumers rarely know [the difference]," says Seth M. Siegel, vice chairman of the Beanstalk Group, a licensing company that handled the AT&T deal. Ironically, VTech makes its own line of phones in addition to its AT&T branded models—which they look awfully similar to and are often cheaper than. (A spokesperson for VTech admits the phones have very similar features.) "Wherever there's a brand, there's a cheap imitation," says Tracy Mullin, president of the National Retail Federation. "It's up to the consumer which to buy, and in some cases the imitation might be better than the branded product."

THINGS TO DO

We spoke with Tracy Mullin, president of the National Retailer Federation, to get her take on what the retail industry will look like moving forward:

● **Shop from your phone.** "Mobile technology is going to play a huge role in the near future. It's already big in Asia. Consumers will be able to shop and purchase items instantaneously from their cell phones."

● **Micromarketing.** "Retailers already collect a large amount of data about their customers; expect them to utilize that to customize marketing to specific individuals."

● **A global marketplace.** "There's already an influx of foreign retailers finding their way to the U.S. Expect that to lead to a large European and Asian influence on American culture."

● **Consistent pricing.** "Today retailers have three channels to reach the consumer: the store, the Internet, and catalogs. With price changes a constant, retailers have had a hard time keeping all three channels on the same page; that won't be a problem in the future."

10 Things Your
Antiques Dealer
Won't Tell You

1 "BE NICE AND I'LL LOWER THE PRICE."

If you like to shop for antiques, then you probably also like to haggle over prices. After all, you may not even know what you're looking for when you walk into an antique shop, but you probably know one thing—that the dollar amount on the price tag isn't always what the dealer actually expects to get. For most buyers, though, the negotiation is shrouded in one mystery: Just how much wiggle room do I really have?

Lincoln Sander, an antique dealer in Redding, Conn., explains that dealers generally have what's called a "trade price" —that is, an amount for which they will sell the item to another dealer, a known collector, or a regular customer. The discount can be significant—often as high as 20 percent—and most dealers build it into their markup when pricing an item. What you may not know is that the trade price could also be available to you as a first-time customer. The dealer may, for example, offer you the special price if he sees the potential for building a relationship with you, Sander says. But you might also get it just for being pleasant and not so presumptuous in your negotiating. "Ask in a nice way," Sander advises, "with the idea that you might or might not get the price." Pat Garthoeffner, a dealer in Lititz, Pa., agrees that manners go a long way. "Never make an offer [by saying] 'I'll give you . . .' or 'Can you take . . .?' That's just insulting," she says. The phrase that makes her most likely to give customers a break? "I think the best thing to say," says Garthoeffner, "is 'Do you have any room . . .?'"

2 "NEED AN APPRAISAL? DON'T LOOK AT ME."

Congratulations, you're an antique dealer! Want to call yourself an appraiser, too? Go right ahead. In fact, of the 30,000 to 50,000 people in this country who say they're personal-property appraisers, just 10 percent are professionally trained, according to the International Society of Appraisers. The reason is that appraisers are completely unregulated, with no educational or licensing requirements. "Anyone can hold himself out as an appraiser of fine arts, antiques, or whatever, and can even obtain accreditation," says Marshall Fallwell, Jr., an antique appraiser in Nashville. And those dealers who do boast of their appraisal credentials are not necessarily well trained. "Your pet cockatiel could be a member in some of these [appraisal] organizations," says Irene Austin-Gillis, an appraiser in Providence, R.I.

Even the four biggest and most respected groups that offer credentials to appraisers don't have the most rigorous standards for admission. In fact, just one, the American Society of Appraisers, requires its members to pass a test on a specific area of appraisal expertise—Oriental rugs, say—before gaining entry. The remaining three test the bulk of their members only on general appraisal standards and practices. Says Paul Dewees, president of one of them, the Certified Appraisers Guild of America, "Our test is general, primarily because the type of work our members do is usually not high-end appraisals. Our members are trained for the everyday estate sale."

But the problem isn't just that many dealers can't give you an accurate appraisal. It's also that they shouldn't. Austin-Gillis says that you probably shouldn't seek an appraisal from anyone affiliated with an antique store or gallery. "Only someone who's not going to buy or sell the property will give you its true value," she says. Your best bet? Do your research and educate yourself, says Patricia Hefner, treasurer of the International Society of Appraisers. And seek the help of a reliable dealer (they do exist). Look for someone who

---

"Only someone who's not going to buy or sell the property will give you its true value."

---

is willing to educate customers and who works toward cultivating relationships, not just turning a quick profit.

3 "EVEN I'VE BEEN DUPED BY FAKES…"

If you're a regular on the flea market circuit, you know that there's no shortage of reproductions out there. "If it's repro-able, they're doing it," says Pat Garthoeffner, adding that she was once at an "antique" show where there was a rug on sale for $1,200 that she had bought at retail store T.J. Maxx for $36.

The trouble is that even some professional dealers can't tell the difference between a fake and the real thing. Donna O'Brien, a dealer in Brownsville, Tenn., admits that she was taken earlier in her career when she purchased what she thought was an authentic Qing Dynasty figurine for $100. "Since then, I've been in stores in Memphis and seen the exact same piece," she says. "And when you see six of them sitting on the shelf, that's a dead giveaway." And O'Brien is pretty sure she's not the only dealer who's been had. "I'm in good company," she says. "They say even the experts at Sotheby's have been fooled."

Part of the problem is that the word "antique" covers a lot of ground. There's furniture, jewelry, art glass, and the list goes on. Any buyer who expects her dealer to be knowledgeable in too many areas is dreaming. Says Gary Espinosa, vice president and director for the auction house Bonhams & Butterfields, "A person who can answer a question on any object is a person you should stay away from."

4 *"...SO YOU SHOULD DEMAND A GUARANTEE."*

Given that you can't count on your dealer to be certain of what he's selling you, the last line of defense is a written guarantee. But not every dealer will be willing to provide one. Sander says that your request might be met by a suspect dealer with resistance or a simple "no"; just as likely, the dealer may try to hedge his bets by saying, "That's what I believe the piece to be." In that case, caveat emptor.

As a buyer you should demand more, say the experts. "A dealer should be 100-percent willing to describe the condition in full and guarantee things," says Leigh Keno, a dealer in New York who is known for his appearances on the PBS series *Antiques Roadshow.* A true guarantee, he adds, should include a detailed description of the item, when it was made, and what parts, if any, have been repaired or replaced. Armed with that documentation, you can be sure you'll get a full refund if the item turns out to be something other than what you—and your dealer—thought it was.

5 *"MY RESTORATION WORK IS A DISASTER."*

If you're buying something used, repairs are usually a good thing, right? Not when it comes to antiques. Many types of repairs can seriously reduce an item's value. Not only that, you may need to look closely to detect any artful touch-ups. For Lyn Fontenot, author of *Antique Furniture: How to Tell the Real Thing From the Fake,* it was the early morning light that tipped her off. While delivering a lecture in Puerto Rico, she stopped in

an antiques shop and found what she thought was a very special piece—a 16th-century Italian wood carving. Intrigued, she asked the dealer to send the carving to her hotel room so she could examine it more closely the next day. When she did, she found that about half the carving had been replaced and some of the wood cuts were made by a modern saw.

While the repairs may have made the piece look better, they had the opposite effect on its value: Untouched, the piece would have been worth about $7,000, notes Fontenot; with the repairs, its value dropped by roughly 60 to 70 percent. Even a simple cleaning can make a big difference. When looking at wood furniture, for instance, be sure to ask specifically if anything has been done to the surface, since a cleaning that improves a piece's finish could strip away much of its value. Keno points out that a piece of 18th-century furniture that has been overly cleaned could see its value cut from $100,000 to $20,000 as a result.

6 *"ANTIQUES AREN'T ALWAYS SUCH A GOOD INVESTMENT."*

While a turbulent stock market may lead you to seek the safety of investing in a piece of well-built furniture, be forewarned: The bulk of what's for sale in the antique market is not going to appreciate at any dizzying rate. "I don't think that people should be buying antiques as investments," says Lincoln Sander. But what about those people you've heard of who made money buying high-quality antiques? For the most part, they've held on to their purchases for a very, very long time. "I think that the people who have done well from a financial point of view are those who bought [antiques] with the intention of never selling them," Sander says. "They bought them with the idea that they would take them to the grave."

While you may not need to take it that far, don't expect to turn a quick profit either. "In the vast majority of cases, you're going to need to keep a collection together for probably at least a minimum of 10 years," says Kyle Husfloen, editor-at-large of *Antique Trader* magazine, and maybe "up to 25 years or more, to see any important escalation." Most of all, be aware that an item's value will ebb and flow with its popularity. "If you invested in Beanie Babies," says Rudy Franchi, a collectibles appraiser who makes regular appearances on *Antiques Roadshow,* "you would be up to your ass in them now."

7 *"NOT HAPPY? I'LL GIVE YOU YOUR MONEY BACK."*

No businessperson wants to be sued. But for an antique dealer, the prospect is particularly unpalatable, since most are sole practitioners in a business where reputation reigns supreme. Antique dealers "live by their reputations," notes John Collins, Jr., a rug dealer in Newburyport, Mass. "No one wants unhappy customers." All of this adds up to one truth: If you think you've been had by a dealer, don't throw in the towel, even if you failed to get a written guarantee.

Marshall Fallwell, Jr., has been called on dozens of times to do appraisals for clients who have bought "antiques" that turned out to be fakes. And in every case, he says, those who have gone back to the questionable dealer with an appraisal in hand have gotten their money back. Yet despite this incredible success rate, Fallwell still finds that some clients who have been taken just "go off and lick their wounds." Don't be one of them. "I think they see having gotten nailed as an indictment of their own taste," Fallwell says. "Somehow if you have the taste and money to buy those things and you get a fake, that means that you really don't have that much taste. And that, of course, is absurd."

8 *"I'M IN CAHOOTS WITH YOUR INTERIOR DECORATOR."*

Remember that rosewood cabinet your decorator said would be fabulous for your living room? Well, it's possible that she had another motive besides making your home look its very best. It's common practice for an interior decorator to offer to do your antique shopping for you, either recommending that you buy a specific piece from a certain dealer or simply going out and buying it for you. And especially when the decorator and the dealer have an established relationship, the decorator in many cases will earn a commission for her trouble.

Some in the business consider "commission" a generous description of said payment. "Do decorators get kickbacks from antique dealers? Oh, my goodness, all the time!" exclaims one New England appraiser. The trouble is that such an arrangement sets up an inherent conflict of interest, putting the decorator in a position to benefit financially from buying certain pieces from certain dealers. As a result, you should make sure that your decorator discloses any such payment arrangements—before the shopping begins.

9 *"I DON'T ACTUALLY SELL ANTIQUES."*

There's no question that public interest in antiques has gone up in recent years. "Everybody and his kid brother now has a tax number and is a professional dealer in old stuff," Fallwell says. But, he adds, what they're selling often isn't antique, "because there aren't that many antiques left." So what exactly makes a piece an "antique"? Contrary to what most people think, the term isn't simply synonymous with "old." In fact, it's generally accepted that to qualify as antique, an item must be at least 100 years old. And by that definition, the 1930s art deco desk you just shelled out for doesn't qualify.

The trouble is that dealers know most shoppers aren't aware of the distinction. Armed with that knowledge, many will overuse the word "antique" to get buyers inside the shop, where much of what is being sold today should really be referred to as "collectibles"—that is, stuff that's less than a century old whose value has been enhanced by widespread interest— or "vintage"—a catch-all marketing category that covers anything roughly 30 years old or more. So why don't dealers simply change their wording? Because "If the sign in front of the shop said 'collectibles,' people probably wouldn't go in," says Garthoeffner, the dealer from Pennsylvania.

10 *"I'M THE ONE WHO'S BECOMING AN ANTIQUE."*

As with most things, the Internet has totally changed the nature of the antique business. Whether you are looking to buy that last dish to complete your collection or unload a Queen Anne chair that you're tired of, you're no longer confined to doing business with your local dealer. The Internet allows a skittish buyer to educate himself without being at the mercy of the dealer and also links up a huge community of buyers and sellers in a quick and seamless way. Sites like PriceMiner.com and Artfact.com provide reams of information for buyers who just want to know a little bit more before they plunk down their credit card. And, of course, there's always eBay, which, because of the enormous amount of traffic it gets, is often the perfect venue for those trying to sell their wares for top dollar.

David Amer, a collector of "pre-casino" Atlantic City memorabilia, knows just how valuable the Internet can be. After spending five or six years schlepping from shop to shop looking for a few specific items to round out his somewhat obscure collection, Amer had great luck in just two weeks after posting a listing online. His greatest coup? Finding silverware from the now-defunct Ambassador Hotel, where his mother worked as a pool attendant decades ago. "There was a slim chance in hell that I would have walked into the right antique store" and found that, Amer says.

THINGS TO DO

How do you tell if Grandma's hand-me-down throw rug is worth anything? We checked in with Karen Keane, president of Boston auction house Skinner Inc., to get some tips on how to spot the gems in your attic and what to do with them:

• **Take your antique** to one of the larger auction houses, like Sotheby's or Christie's, to have it appraised. They offer appraisals for free and have the best specialists.

• **Listen to your friends**—if they're always saying "I really love that painting hanging over the fireplace," it could be a sign that it's worth something.

• **Be very cautious** about selling to someone who appraised your antique. A public auction is the best way to assure that you're getting a fair price.

10 Things Your
Headhunter
Won't Tell You

1 *"I'LL PLAY YOU FOR A SUCKER."*

Headhunters come in two flavors. "Retained" executive search firms, such as blue-chippers Korn/Ferry International or Heidrick & Struggles, charge a company up front to locate candidates for client openings. "Contingency" search firms, on the other hand, get paid by employers only if they place a candidate. The payoff? For both, around a third of your first year's salary.

Charging the candidate for a search is verboten. The Association of Executive Search Consultants, which represents 253 retained firms worldwide, expressly bans the practice. But there are headhunters out there who still try to bill candidates thousands of dollars for "career services," thus potentially snaring fees at both ends. Industry bible Kennedy Information's *Directory of Executive Recruiters* has been known to screen out new applicants who squeeze job candidates for fees, and plenty of other firms doing the same thing don't even try to get listed. There are also numerous online ventures that charge the candidate, and not the posting companies, for the privilege of trolling through their jobs databases. But as John Sibbald, head of a St. Louis management consulting firm and author of *The New*

Career Makers, puts it: "You shouldn't have to pay a cent to find another job."

How can you determine whether your headhunter is on the up-and-up? Ask up front. "It would be highly unusual, if not unethical, for either a contingency or retained recruiter to ever charge a fee to a job seeker," Sibbald says.

2 *"THERE'S A LAWSUIT IN YOUR FUTURE."*

Lawyers must love the job-search industry. Why? Because any given job move has the potential to embroil your former employer, your new employer, your search firm—and even you—in a fireworks display of legal writs. Company-to-company lawsuits over talent pilfering, for example, have become almost commonplace: *Wal-Mart v. Amazon.com, Nortel Networks v. ONI Systems, Nike v. Gap,* and so on. And how do these affect the job candidate? Such a suit could hold up your appointment, or even block it altogether, especially if you signed a noncompete agreement and are jumping to another firm in your field.

More chilling are lawsuits that try to block appointments even if there are no noncompete clauses. Famous attempts include Federated Department Stores' suit against search firm Herbert Mines Associates for poaching Matthew Serra, who left to become CEO of Foot Locker in November 1998. Herbert Mines was accused of "tortious interference"—that is, enticing Serra to break his contract. Only after two and a half years of litigation did the parties agree to settle their dispute without any payment exchanged. Like many such lawsuits, the attempt to block the candidate from making the job leap wasn't ultimately successful—but even a slam-dunk case means a long-term headache for the job candidate who gets stuck in the middle.

3 "I MAY BE HEADED FOR EXTINCTION."

If you're a rising star, recruiters are going to want you all to themselves. And, indeed, an exclusive relationship with the right recruiter who knows you well can lead to fantastic job offers, the right corporate fit—and, of course, commissions in the recruiter's pocket.

But before you invest all that time and energy with a headhunter, take heed: He may be going the way of the 8-track tape. Websites such as BountyJobs.com, 6FigureJobs.com, and Netshare.com have been compiling databases of $100,000-plus earners and matching them directly with companies, a task previously the sole domain of retained recruiters. It's faster, and it's financially alluring—no middleman, no hefty fee.

For its part, 6FigureJobs.com says it's seeing the shift away from recruiters gain momentum "month by month": Whereas the site's subscriber ratio was 60/40 recruiters to companies back in 2000, these days it's more like 33/67. "We think the math just makes that inevitable," says a spokesperson for 6FigureJobs.com. "You can save yourself a lot of money by using smart research and using the right mix of sites."

4 "I'M NOT ABOVE WASTING YOUR TIME."

You may be excited about an upcoming job interview your headhunter just set up, but don't break out the bubbly just yet. The reality is that you may be considered "filler." That is, the recruiter doesn't think you're a good fit for the position but sends you to the interview anyway. "That sometimes happens with difficult searches," says former Santa Monica, Calif.–based headhunter Marijo Bos. "The recruiter can't find enough candidates, and so they talk this person into interviewing, because it's an upset client."

To mask the fact that you're a square peg being pitched for a round hole, your résumé might even be tweaked by an overzealous recruiter who's stretching for a fit. This tactic revealed itself to an automation engineer for a South Carolina industrial equipment manufacturer who was lured to an interview by a lavish job description—and found that his CV had been altered almost beyond recognition: "I said, 'What is that?' The interviewer said, 'This is your résumé.' I said, 'No, it's not.'" The job candidate says that the recruiter had changed the format of the résumé completely, as well as the way he had listed his jobs and skills. "They only wanted to emphasize the things that matched the job description, so they could have an identical fit," he says.

5 "I'LL SEND YOUR RÉSUMÉ EVERYWHERE—EVEN IF YOU DON'T WANT ME TO."

Since contingency firms get paid only if they place a candidate, the temptation is to carpet-bomb hundreds of companies in hopes that something pans out. The result: Your information could be spread far and wide by recruiters eager to make a commission or traded with others who might do the same. It could even end up in the lap of your current employer. "You should know who it's going to and for what position," says Dudley Brown, retired former head of Irvine, Calif., startup staffer BridgeGate. "If an agency's reluctant to do that, it should be a real warning sign."

Even if you're careful, you might still get burned. Ask Michael Greiche, an auditor at a Wall Street financial firm, who had insisted on prior permission—but didn't get it, as he found out when he approached a potential employer earlier this year. "They said, 'Your agency sent your résumé here.' I said, 'I never gave permission for them to send it here,'" Greiche says. "Sure enough, I found out two days later they also sent it to two other firms without my permission."

If multiple agencies are sending in your résumé, a company might decline to hire you simply because "it looks like you don't know what you're doing," warns Brown. Or it might not want to get involved in a nasty fee dispute between competing headhunters who are pitching the same person—even if you're the perfect candidate.

6 "I HAVE NO IDEA WHAT YOU DO FOR A LIVING."

When it comes to technology, too many recruiters still don't know what they're talking about. To be sure, many firms now offer sector-specific high-tech placement services. But there are plenty of headhunters who are just trying to get by. They might be up on the latest tech buzzwords, for example, but that doesn't mean they're savvy about e-commerce. At the very least, it can mean a waste of time and effort spent chasing the wrong job. Worse, if you took the word of a clueless recruiter, you could be looking for another job as soon as you start. "I'm in technology, so a lot of what I do is a little obscure," says Mark Aurora, an electrical engineer for Motorola in Austin, Tex. "You can list all your qualifications and give them a résumé, but they don't understand what it's about."

It doesn't happen only in tech jobs, either. Tony Scott, now president of Silicon Valley executive search firm ChampionScott Partners, was once an up-and-coming banker who was contacted by a headhunter he says knew nothing about banking: "I asked him, 'What was your background? Did you work in banking?' 'Nope, I was an undercover cop for the DEA. Before that I was on the marine patrol for the Chicago police. I was the guy that fished bodies out of the water.'"

7 "WE'RE TOO BUSY TO WORRY ABOUT YOU."

One big dilemma with headhunters: When the market's in trouble, there aren't enough jobs for candidates; then, when the market recovers, recruitment firms overbook themselves, meaning clients don't get enough or the right kind of attention. The top five international search firms made $2.47 billion in 2006, according to the most recent figures from search consultants Hunt-Scanlon Advisors. And that means "too many assignments to actually give the detailed personal attention that people want," says Tony Scott.

Another consequence of a firm's scrambling on too many searches at once: Your file might be offloaded onto a junior person. This happened to Tim Hu, a Cheyenne, Wyo., systems analyst. Bounced around between reps, he ended up with a green staffer who "didn't quite understand what was going on," Hu says. The result: Hu was placed at a financial-services firm with a far more buttoned-down corporate culture than he had been looking for. He left soon afterward.

8 "I MAKE PROMISES I CAN'T KEEP."

In a tight job market, recruiters and the high-tech companies they represent often offer perks they can't deliver. Just ask Derek Barrett, a database administrator who was placed at a Los Angeles billing-software company. He says he agreed to a lowball salary because of the gold-plated training program he was promised. "The headhunter and the hiring manager specifically outlined which software packages the company was going to do formal training for," Barrett says. "But it never did come."

Recruiters will also sometimes paint a far rosier picture of a job than is actually the case. And that could lead to some very bad career decisions. "You have to think of your job as if you're buying a car: You wouldn't take the salesperson's advice," says a spokesperson for Hunt-Scanlon Advisors. "Do your own due diligence, so you can compare and contrast with what the recruiter tells you."

9 "YOU DIDN'T HIRE ME—BUT I'M OUT PITCHING YOUR RÉSUMÉ ANYWAY."

At the lower end of the headhunter food chain, recruitment tactics can get a little fast and loose. In the case of a desperate firm—one whose agents are engaged in what ChampionScott Partners' Tony Scott calls "glorified telemarketing, saying or doing anything to close a deal"—the recruiter might pitch you without having ever met you or even spoken with you about the job.

So how do these firms find out about you? The Web, naturally. Headhunters have grown increasingly savvy when it comes to navigating job-hunting sites like LinkedIn or Monster. Often they'll manually search these sites, where they may come upon your résumé and add it to their own candidate pool—without your ever knowing about it. In addition, member profiles for LinkedIn will often come up in Google searches with a high page rating if the user has chosen to let their profile be "publicly viewed," a LinkedIn spokesperson explains.

Fortunately, there are ways to limit the possibility of your résumé landing in the hands of a dicey headhunter —especially if you're posting it for networking purposes, rather than to find a new job. Many sites offer contact and privacy settings that you can fiddle with. A spokesperson for LinkedIn also suggests typing the phrase, "If you're a headhunter, please do not contact me," directly in your online profile.

10 *"THIS JOB WILL SELF-DESTRUCT IN THREE MONTHS."*

Don't expect headhunters to tip you off about a possible merger or downsizing. Even if they know, they won't tell you—sometimes because they're legally required to stay mum, and sometimes because it's just not in their job description to air a company's dirty laundry. After all, recruiters work for the companies, not you.

Take Marijo Bos, who, in her headhunting days, helped recruit a slew of people to website provider GeoCities, including then CEO Thomas Evans. The firm was later snapped up by Yahoo, and

Evans and company had to find work elsewhere. "The devil's really in the details, in terms of the kind of agreement you sign when you go in," says Evans, now CEO of Bankrate.com. "Change-of-control provisions or termination provisions—those are the things you should negotiate. So if you do get acquired, you have protection in terms of your equity and your stake in the company."

But such stories aren't always about $4.6 billion acquisitions. Sometimes they're about imminent corporate meltdowns of which the candidate hasn't been apprised. "We hear cases of executives leaving good jobs to go to another company, and three months later that company announces horrible earnings or a downsizing or bankruptcy," says a spokesperson for Kennedy Information. "But it's not the recruiter's responsibility to point out the problems that might exist within a client company."

THINGS TO DO

Now that you know what your headhunter isn't going to tell you, here are some ideas on what you should tell your headhunter, courtesy of Peter Felix, president of the Association of Executive Search Consultants:

● **The first thing to ask:** "Do you have an exclusive mandate to handle this assignment?" If they don't, they probably don't have the ear of the client, and you don't want your details being bounced around without knowing whom they're going to.

● **Find out as much about** your prospective employer as you can. If the headhunter is being cagey about it, they might not

know very much about the job, and no job description should set off immediate alarms.

● **If a company likes you,** they may move quickly to make an offer. But hold on—you should be comfortable with the answers to these questions first: "Why is this job vacant?" "Does the company have a history of success?" "What are the promotion prospects?"

CHAPTER 6

Food & Drink

■ Eating and drinking may be two of life's simple pleasures, but people keep finding ways to charge more for it. Even casual dining places, like "gastropubs," can set you back some serious money. And it's not just restaurant meals: With fancy appliances and organic ingredients, cooking at home has become pricey as well. Nonetheless, we're here to help you maximize the pleasure of all things culinary while keeping an eye on your wallet. In "10 Things Your Restaurant Won't Tell You," for example, we'll tell you how to spot the best value on the menu, while "10 Things Your Supermarket Won't Tell You" offers up our recipe for food-shopping success. If you're more apt to be playing host, "10 Things Your Caterer Won't Tell You" will help you take care of the business of feeding your guests so that you can relax and enjoy the event. Bon appétit!

10 Things Your
Bartender
Won't Tell You

1 *"IT'S MY WORLD; YOU'RE JUST DRINKING IN IT."*

Back in the day, bartending was all about consistency and service. From the humblest watering hole to the fanciest hotel bar, bartenders knew how to mix a repertoire of classic cocktails just right every time, and the customer came first. Today, not so much. Ray Foley, author of *Bartending for Dummies*, says a growing number of the 500,000 working barkeeps in the U.S. are following the lead of celebrity chefs, hoping to make their mark with their own signature drinks. Sure, that means an explosion of creative cocktails dressed with such exotica as cucumber shavings or lavender foam. But good luck if you're in the mood for an old standard such as a sidecar.

The upshot? A lack of consistency, for one, says Tony Abou-Ganim, who created the Bellagio's cocktail program in Las Vegas. "I can go to the same bar, order the same thing from three different bartenders, and get three different drinks," he says. Even worse is customer service. Some bartenders have flipped the old equation, Foley says, putting 30 percent into pleasing customers and 70 into showcasing their personality: "The prime thing we're losing in the bar business right now is service for the customer."

2 *"YOUR TOP-SHELF PRETENSIONS ARE MONEY IN MY POCKET."*

From wild-berry-infused vodka to the latest in Herradura tequila, liquor companies continue introducing high-end spirits as the consumer thirst for luxury goods trickles down to beverages. Sales of the most expensive brands of vodka, rum, tequila, and scotch rose 21 percent in 2007, while those of the cheapest grew by just 3 percent, according to the Distilled Spirits Council. But Tony Abou-Ganim warns, "A higher price doesn't always mean better quality." He notes, for example, that many bars now use lime-flavored powder in their cocktails, which can dilute subtler notes in an expensive spirit.

Another concern: scams involving "short pouring" and brand substitution that have ridden the luxury-spirits wave, according to Robert Plotkin, a beverage-management consultant. Say you order two premium cocktails. The bartender might pour only half a shot of alcohol into each—but he'll charge you for two, ring up just one, and pocket the difference. Or you might be charged for a premium Cadenhead's rum that's actually a basic Bacardi. Your best defense: Sit at the bar, where you can see your drinks being made.

3 "BAR TABS ARE FOR SUCKERS."

While visiting New York City a few summers ago, Chris Romanowski started a tab at ESPN Zone for his family and friends. But once the air hockey ended and they paid the bill, they saw they'd been charged for 21 drinks despite having ordered only 13. Romanowski contested the charges and eventually got his money back. (Susan Abramson, regional marketing manager for ESPN Zone, says the Times Square establishment is under new management and that "we try to make sure [our guests] are satisfied at all times.")

"My advice would be to not run a tab," says Plotkin, who after 20 years behind the bar notes, "It's really easy to inflate tabs." For example, a bartender might give a buddy a free bottle of Heineken, then bury the charge in your bill, especially if you're with friends or getting tipsy and not keeping track of who's ordered what. One of the most common ploys, according to Elizabeth Godsmark, coauthor of *Controlling Liquor, Wine & Beverage Costs,* involves billing you for a round without breaking it down into separate charges. If you'd still rather run a tab than pay for drinks one at a time, be sure to get a receipt that specifies the number and cost of each drink.

4 "IT'S ALL ABOUT THE BOTTOM LINE—DOWN TO OUR CHOICE OF GLASSWARE."

Between 20 and 30 percent of booze served in a bar never gets paid for, due in large part to bartenders' overpouring their spirits. But management is cracking down and working every angle to curb this practice. In 2005, for instance, a study published in the *British Medical Journal* found that when bartenders were asked to free-pour a shot of liquor, they dumped an average 20 percent more into a short, wide tumbler than into a tall highball glass—even though they knew each held 12 ounces. And these weren't amateurs; they had, on average, nearly six years of experience. According to Brian Wansink, the Cornell University professor behind the study, bartenders are subject to an optical illusion that makes them gauge volume based more on the height of a glass than on width.

The industry jumped on the data: Immediately after the study was released, many bar owners and industry publications began advising managers to choose taller barware to save money while giving guests the impression they were getting more. So next time you want a stiffer drink at no extra cost, ignore what your eyes tell you and insist on a short glass.

5 "FAST SERVICE DOESN'T NECESSARILY MEAN GOOD SERVICE."

Much the way fast-food places use the three-minute rule, some bars now require that drinks be mixed, poured, and at the table within a certain time frame. And while you might enjoy faster service that way, it doesn't guarantee great-tasting drinks. In fact, it could mean the opposite. Clear cocktails, like the classic martini, should always be stirred carefully to achieve the right level of chill, says cocktail specialist Ted Haigh. But "bartenders are under pressure to make things faster," which is why "shaking has become ubiquitous."

Some drinks take so long to make that bartenders try to deter customers from ordering them. When Heather Leonard, a former bartender from New York City, used to muddle lime juice, mint, and sugar for a mojito, she'd often hide it below the counter. "Once everyone sees you're making a mojito, they want one," she says. "And after 30 minutes, you're four customers deep." The emphasis on speed can also lead to carelessness. In a rush, bartenders sometimes skip the tongs and jam barware into the ice machine—risking broken glass in your drink. So when a bar seems busy, you might want to order your liquor neat.

6 "THIS BAR IS FILTHY."

Most bars offer dim lighting for atmosphere—but it can also hide a lot of hazards. Slippery floors, sticky countertops, and lemon wedges strewn about the floor are among the most common problems undercover investigators find in bars, according to Gwen Lennox, CEO of Keeping Tabs, which conducts independent evaluations for bar owners. Nightclubs frequented by twentysomethings tend to be the worst, she says, but it's not always easy to spot problems, such as open bottles of alcohol that haven't been cleaned or covered between shifts, thus encouraging the buildup of dust and germs.

Bars and taverns are just as susceptible to spreading food-borne illnesses as restaurants, warns Dean Peterson, director of environmental health for San Mateo

County in California. Indeed, health-inspection reports for establishments connected to a bar cite all sorts of violations, ranging from dirty floors to lip-stained tumblers. One North Carolina inspector even found black-slime mold in an ice machine—though it might not make you sick, it "would be kind of repulsive to have in your drink," says Frances Breedlove, food sanitation section chief for Wake County. So what types of bars have a better track record? Those tied to restaurants, says Bonnie Nasset, operations manager at Keeping Tabs.

7 "RESTAURANTS ARE A TERRIBLE PLACE TO GET A GOOD DRINK."

Restaurants are a tough business. The majority of new establishments close their doors within the first three years, and only 30 percent last 10 years. One way to up the chance of turning a profit and running a successful restaurant is to secure a liquor license as soon as possible, since owners can expect to earn up to 40 percent of their profit from alcohol. To further milk every drop of their drink sales, restaurants are micromanaging and automating their bartending wherever possible. By using so-called liquor-control systems, all a bartender needs to do is push a button to fill up, say, a pitcher of beer, thus saving time and controlling the pour to the letter; it even allows workers to serve another customer while the machine pours the next drink.

In a climate like this, "anyone can pretty much bartend," says Tara Clark, general manager of a restaurant and bar located just outside Atlanta, as long as they have a friendly personality. "If people don't get a great martini, as long as you can hold a great conversation, they'll forget about the drink," she says.

8 "I DON'T KNOW DIDDLY ABOUT WINE."

You'd think a bar would be the perfect place to order a crisp chardonnay. Think again. Experts say bars tend to minimize their wine offerings because the bulk of their sales comes from spirits or beer. Some bar managers and their staff know so little about wine that they leave it up to distributors to develop their menu, even though these salespeople might get rewarded with free trips or other incentives to push certain brands, says Ty Wenzel, author of *Behind Bars: The Straight-Up Tales of a Big-City Bartender*. That's why it's not uncommon for bars to limit their list to a single red and a single white offering. In fact, Wenzel says one trick she used to clear out old stock at her own bar was to pass off the house wine—a cheap cabernet—as a more exotic shiraz or syrah. "I couldn't believe they couldn't tell the difference," she says.

One way around the issue is to ask your bartender to show you the bottle and pour the wine in front of you. Also, keep in mind that if bottles are stored near a hot kitchen or displayed on a shelf where natural light can strike them all day, their contents can oxidize or begin to spoil, rendering even a decent wine undrinkable.

9 "YOUR DRINK COSTS WHATEVER I SAY IT COSTS."

When Alexandria Steppe wants a Corona from one of her favorite clubs in Asbury Park, N.J., she doesn't always know how much it's going to cost: During a recent visit, her beer was $4 when her boyfriend ordered it, then $6 when Steppe ordered one from the very same bartender later that night. What's more, there are three different bars in the club, and she's discovered that the bartenders in the back charge less for drinks than those who work closer to the front of the house. "I don't think it's fair, but there isn't much I can do about it," Steppe says.

While it's not uncommon for bars to feature certain specials like "ladies drink free," many bartenders will go one step further, charging different rates to different people, particularly if a patron appears drunk. "What it usually means is that the bartenders are playing fast and loose, and they're probably not putting all of the money into the register," says Lennox. The best way to avoid getting overcharged? Ask for a receipt, or if that's impractical, ask to see the drinks menu. If you note a discrepancy, speak to the manager.

10 "UNLESS YOU'RE USING A WALKER, EXPECT TO BE CARDED."

There's little logic when it comes to getting your ID checked these days. Some bartenders seem to have no qualms letting underage drinkers run rampant, while others wait to see what a person orders before they ask for identification. A toasted-almond cocktail, for example, is often popular among teens, while folks who order a scotch on the rocks are typically assumed to be of drinking age.

Then there are the places with tougher rules, where no one who appears under the age of 40 is allowed a drink until they've flashed their license. So no matter how old you are, or appear to be, carry your card at all times.

Even so, policing has become so strict at some places that even a valid ID isn't good enough. Back in 2006, while waiting for a pool table at a Dave & Buster's in Arcadia, Calif., 29-year-old Jason Flores ordered a few rounds of vodka tonics with his friends. Once a table opened up and the optometrist started carrying his drink toward it, he was stopped and accused of having a fake ID. Flores spent nearly half an hour trying to convince the management otherwise—going so far as offering to have the police come over and authenticate his ID. In the end, the group was given permission to stay at the pool table, although no one was allowed to order or drink any more alcohol. Flores says this was after they had already paid for their drinks and tipped the bartender. Manager Steve White says he doesn't recall the situation, but notes that the bar hews close to the letter of the law, "which is extremely strict" when it comes to checking ID. Cards can be considered suspect if they are cracked or torn or if the laminate has been peeled back.

THINGS TO KNOW

Walking into a posh bar can be a little intimidating, so we asked Jeff Garcia, a bartender at the Four Seasons New York, for some tips on ordering:

• **When the customers start pouring in,** the best way to get the bartender's attention is with eye contact or a raised hand when they're looking in your direction. If that isn't working, a simple "hey" will do the trick as well; just don't go overboard.

• **When choosing from the wine list,** Garcia says you should never be afraid to ask for a recommendation—and a sample—from your bartender.

• **Of all the cocktails,** it's the martini you should really splurge on. Because you're basically just drinking the gin or vodka, you'll appreciate the smoother flavor of a top-shelf spirit.

• **Since the bartender has no idea** how well you're going to tip until after he serves you, it's easier to establish a rapport through good manners and kindness. It also helps to be a repeat customer.

10 Things Your
Restaurant
Won't Tell You

1 *"IT'S MORE ABOUT THE FLASH AND FLAIR THAN THE FILET MIGNON."*

As any restaurateur will tell you, going out to eat is never just about the food; it's about the overall experience. At legendary Aureole Las Vegas, for example, spandex-clad "wine angels" climb up and retrieve bottles from a 42-foot-tall spirits tower. The thinking behind the spectacle: "Anything that gets patrons' attention will get them to spend," says restaurant designer Mark Stech-Novak.

Indeed, facing tough economic headwinds, restaurants are working every available angle to maximize profits. Even fast-food outlets get into the game, setting up a high-stimulation environment for customers—"it encourages faster turnover," says Stephani Robson, senior lecturer at the Cornell School of Hotel Administration. "Specifically, the use of bright light, bright colors, upbeat music, and seating that does not encourage lolling."

Although seemingly innocent, even menus are rigged. "We list the item that makes the most profit first so it catches your eye," says restaurant consultant Linda Lipsky, "and bury the highest-cost item in the middle."

2 *"EATING HERE COULD MAKE YOU SICK."*

The 2006 E. coli outbreak that started at a New Jersey Taco Bell and sickened more than 60 people was likely the fault of contaminated lettuce. But food-borne illness isn't the only cause for concern: In a separate December incident, several hundred people in Indianapolis got sick after eating at an Olive Garden where three employees tested positive for the highly contagious norovirus. (Olive Garden says that the source of the outbreak has yet to be determined.)

"You don't call out [sick] unless you're on your deathbed," says freelance chef Leah Grossman. Indeed, according to a recent study, 58 percent of salaried New York City restaurant workers reported going to work when sick; the number is even higher for those without benefits. "A lot of poor, transient people work in restaurants," says Peter Francis, coauthor of industry exposé *How to Burn Down the House.* "They're not giving up the $100 they'd make in a shift because they're sick."

How can you protect yourself? Check inspection results, which are often posted online by local departments of public health. Or just visit the restroom; it "tells you everything you need to know about a restaurant," Francis says.

3 *"OUR MARKUPS ARE RIDICULOUS."*

It's no secret that restaurants enjoy huge markups on certain items: Coffee, tea, and sodas, for example, typically cost restaurants 15 to 20 cents per serving, and pasta, which costs pennies, can be dressed up with more expensive fare and sold for $25 a dish or more. At a fine-dining restaurant, the average cost of food is 38 to 42 percent of the menu price, says Kevin Moll, CEO and president of National Food Service Advisors. In other words, most restaurants are making roughly 60 percent on anything they serve.

It's not all gravy, though. Restaurants keep only 4 cents of every dollar spent by a customer, says Hudson Riehle, vice president of research and information services at the National Restaurant Association. The remainder of the money, he says, is divided between food and beverage purchases, payroll, occupancy, and other overhead costs.

Given the slim profit margin, many restaurants rely on savvy pricing to create the illusion of value. Putting a chicken dish on the menu for $21 will make a $15 pasta dish, where the restaurant is making a big profit, seem like a bargain, says Gregg Rapp, owner of consulting firm MenuTechnologies.net. So how can customers get the best value? Often the real deals are some of the most expensive

Often the real deals are some of the most expensive items on the menu.

items on the menu. A dish like prime rib, for example, gives you the most bang for your buck, says Rapp, since it costs the restaurant over half the menu price to prepare it.

4 *"BIG BROTHER IS WATCHING YOU … EAT."*

No one likes having their every move scrutinized, but that may be just what's happening at your favorite restaurant. Cameras are popping up everywhere, from four-star eateries to the place where you grab your lunchtime sandwich. At historic Randy's Steakhouse in Frisco, Tex., where checks average $45 to $50 per person, co-owner Don Burks has installed 12 cameras around the premises. Of those, two pick up activity in the dining rooms and two are aimed at the bar. "We've had customers stand on chairs to try to take out a camera," Burks says. "But the cameras aren't even pointed at them; they're pointed at the wine rack." Their primary purpose: deterring employee theft.

At some restaurants, however, the cameras are indeed trained on the tables. At New York City's four-star Daniel, for example, four closed-circuit cameras monitor the dining rooms, offering a bird's-eye view of every plate. "It's about maintaining a quality of service," says Daniel spokesperson Georgette Farkas. "With the cameras the chef can tell when each course needs to be plated and served." So much for that romantic dinner for two.

5 *"THERE'S SOMETHING FISHY ABOUT OUR SEAFOOD."*

Even when you pay top dollar for a seafood

dish, you might not get what you're expecting. About 70 percent of the time, for example, those Maryland crab cakes on the menu weren't made using crabs from the Chesapeake Bay, says James Anderson, chairman of the Department of Environmental and Natural Resource Economics at the University of Rhode Island. Because of high demand, crabs are often from other eastern states or imported from Thailand and Vietnam. (Look closely at the menu: "Maryland-style" crab is the giveaway.) It's a matter of opinion about whether that means poorer-quality crabs, says Lynn Feglcy, biologist for the Maryland Department of Natural Resources. But it certainly smacks of false advertising.

There's also the problem of outright substitution—inexpensive fish, such as pollack, getting passed off as something pricier, like cod. How widespread is the problem? In 2006 the *Daytona Beach News-Journal* sent fish samples to a lab to prove that 4 out of 10 local restaurants were pawning a cheaper fish as grouper. The same lab also checked seafood from 24 U.S. cities and found that, overall, consumers have less than a 50/50 shot at being served the fish they ordered.

What can you do? Ask where the fish comes from. "If they're not sure if the fish is from Alaska or Asia, I order the beef," Anderson says.

6 "RESERVATION? WHAT RESERVATION?"

When Timothy Dillon, 34, showed up at new Chicago trattoria Terragusto for his friend's birthday, he wasn't expecting a wait. He'd made a reservation for four, then called the day of to confirm and add one more. The restaurant told him no problem, but when the party showed up, they were met with a long wait. "After almost an hour of standing by the bar being ignored, we ended up leaving for another restaurant," Dillon says. Terragusto says it was its first week open: "We were probably working out a lot of glitches," says a spokesperson.

As Dillon discovered, a reservation isn't a guarantee. "Overbooking is almost a necessary evil," says John Fischer, associate professor of table service at the Culinary Institute of America. Restaurants calculate their average no-show percentage for any given night, then overbook the restaurant by that much, hoping it will come out even. How to avoid Dillon's fate? It's considered poor taste to offer a tip before you're seated, Fischer says, so if it's your first time, inquire politely after 15 minutes. But go ahead and slip the manager or maître d' $10 or $20 on the way out; it should ensure you're seated promptly next time.

7 "OUR SPECIALS ARE ANYTHING BUT."

"I'm very careful about ordering my food," says Rick Manson, owner of Chef Rick's restaurant in Santa Maria, Calif. If he orders oysters, Manson says, he'll offer multiple dishes on the menu that use oysters, "to make sure I use every one of them." Nonetheless, countless variables can leave surplus ingredients at the end of the day—which often become tomorrow's special. "It could be the chef legitimately wants to try out something new," says Stephen Zagor, founder of consulting firm Hospitality & Culinary Resources.

"But it could also be something nearing the end of its shelf life that needs to get out of the kitchen."

How can you tell a good special from a bad one? Watch out for "an expensive item used in a way that's minimizing its flavor," Zagor says, such as a lamb chop that's been cut, braised, and put into a dish where it's a supporting player. Pastas, stews, and soups containing expensive meats are also suspect. "There's an old saying in the restaurant industry," says David A. Holmes, VP and director of Out East Restaurant Consultants. "'Sauce and gravy cover up a lot of mistakes.'"

8 "THERE'S NO SUCH THING AS TOO MUCH BUTTER."

Think that salmon fillet you ordered for dinner is good for you? Think again. Many restaurants load even their healthiest fare with butter and other calorie-heavy add-ons. Restaurant meals average 1,000 to 1,500 calories, says Milton Stokes, a registered dietitian and spokesperson for the American Dietetic Association. That's roughly two thirds of the daily average calories recommended by the USDA. And according to a recent study, women who eat out five times a week consume an average of 290 additional calories per day.

While most Americans assume that fast food is the worst offender, similar fare at casual sit-down restaurants can be even more caloric. The classic burger at Ruby Tuesday, for example, has a whopping 1,013 calories and 71 grams of fat. The McDonald's Big Mac, with its 540 calories and 29 grams of fat, seems downright diet-worthy by comparison. "We butter our hamburger buns," says Julie Reid, recently retired vice president of culinary and beverage for Ruby Tuesday, "so we tell people if they're looking to cut calories, they shouldn't eat the bun." If that sounds less than appetizing, try splitting an entrée with someone, or order an appetizer instead of a main dish.

9 "NICE TIP—TOO BAD YOUR WAITER WON'T GET IT."

Just because you tip your waitress 10 bucks, it doesn't mean she's going home with that money. More than likely, she'll have to pass on some of it to the people who helped her serve you: The bartender might get $2, and the busboy $3 to $5. It's called a tip pool, and it's becoming standard practice in many restaurants. "It happens often that if someone leaves a voluntary tip [for their server], a significant portion of that money is going to other people," Zagor says.

According to federal law, only employees who customarily receive tips—waitstaff, hosts, bartenders, and bussers—can participate in the tip pool. But sometimes management takes a cut. In 2006 waitstaff from the Hilltop Steak House in Saugus, Mass., won $2.5 million in damages after complaining that managers dipped into their tips.

Mandatory gratuities are also divvied up. At high-end restaurants such as New York City's Per Se and Napa Valley's French Laundry, both owned by chef Thomas Keller, the practice is called service compris. "The 20 percent service charge is clearly stated on the menu, and it's equally divided among the staff," says a spokesperson for both restaurants.

While the tip pool is designed to foster a team environment among workers, for customers it means something else entirely—that your gratuity isn't specifically rewarding the waiter or sommelier who provided you with exemplary service.

10 *"YOU MIGHT NOT WANT TO EAT HERE ON A MONDAY."*

If you think that Monday, when restaurants tend not to be crowded, is a great time to eat out, think again. "You're being served all of the weekend's leftovers," says Francis, coauthor of *How to Burn Down the House.* Most kitchens prepare food on a first-in, first-out basis, meaning whatever is oldest gets served first. It's a way to ensure that everything on the menu is as fresh as possible.

The system works great most days, but it can run into a little glitch over the weekend. Distributors typically take Sunday off and make their last deliveries Saturday morning—which means that by Monday, any food not used over the weekend could be three to four days old. And it will be served before the same ingredients arriving in Monday's delivery.

What to do if you wish to dine out on a Monday? Ignore your instincts and go to a place that's perpetually crowded. "If you are open 24/7 and busy all the time," says New York–based chef Lucia Calvete, "all your ingredients are fresh all the time."

THINGS TO DO

● **Making reservations online isn't just convenient**—it might save you money. Free restaurant reservation sites like DinnerBroker.com can get you up to 30 percent off your meal when you book through them.

● **Worried about cleanliness?** Check the restrooms. According to experts, they're a microcosm of the overall condition of a restaurant.

● **You can eat out** and still eat healthy: Go to *www.healthydiningfinder.com* for nutritional tips and restaurants searches by ZIP code.

● **When ordering fish,** ask the waiter where it comes from. If the Alaskan salmon you think you're ordering is from Asia, you might want to stick with pasta.

● **Have theater or movie tickets** and want to get in and out in a hurry? MenuPages .com lets you browse complete menus of restaurants in such cities as New York, Chicago, and Philadelphia from home, so you can select your dishes before you get to the restaurant.

10 Things Your
Butcher
Won't Tell You

1 *"I'VE NEVER TOUCHED A BAND SAW OR EVEN HANDLED A SIDE OF BEEF."*

Being a butcher is a lot different than it was 25 years ago. Back then skilled meat cutters used their muscle to break down whole carcasses and their know-how to ensure that no scrap was wasted. Today butchers are more often found behind the meat department counter at one of the large grocery chains, where their skill set—and salary—has been reduced to accommodate the demands of big business. Their main job now is to cut up smaller pieces, known as primals, into individual portions, as well as to shape and tie roasts, and to grind meat for sale. The upshot: Many butchers don't know a whole lot about the meat they're hawking—where it comes from or basic information about varying cuts, preparation, or cooking time.

So where do you go if you want to know how to butterfly a leg of lamb? Look for an old-fashioned, owner-operated butcher shop. Or visit an upscale market, such as Whole Foods—Theo Weening, the chain's national meat coordinator, encourages untrained staff to enter a two-year apprenticeship program, and each year meat department personnel are taken on educational outings to organic ranches.

2 *"NO SPECIAL ORDERS."*

Many meat departments don't even have butchers anymore. Thanks to an innovation known as "case-ready" meat, staff are often little more than glorified stock handlers. Case-ready meat is prepackaged in plants and delivered to vendors ready for sale. The industry contends that prepreparation helps prevent contamination, enhance quality control, and lower prices. And while that may be true, it also means fewer choices for consumers. Staff at chains that rely on case-ready products are not trained to alter cuts. What you see is what you get—you can't ask for a boneless rack of lamb, for example, or an extra-large sirloin—and what's in stock is probably going to be cut and sized based on what moves.

Among the monster chains, Wal-Mart has led the way—its supercenters have carried only case-ready meat since 2001. Fortunately, not all stores are on the case-ready bandwagon. High-end and specialty grocers are the exception. At New York–based Dean & Deluca, for example, breaking down a carcass is part of the job interview. "We have highly skilled people because that's what our clients expect," says Bill Lettier, vice president of retail operations. The bad news is, you can expect to pay a premium for the privilege of choice.

3 *"THE REAL MONEY'S IN PREPARED FOODS— MARINADES, KABOBS ... KA-CHING."*

"Don't take a butcher's advice on how to cook meat," Andy Rooney once quipped. "If he knew, he'd be a chef." Perhaps. But more and more butchers now spend as much time preparing meat as cutting it—often at a premium. Wegmans, for example, offers marinated pork tenderloins and chicken cutlets. Recently, the chain's Dulles, Va., store was selling straight pork tenderloin for $5.39 a pound, while a honey-mustard-marinated version of the same went for $7.29 a pound. That's too much for many people, even those who hate to cook, like Bonnie Cohen, an international business consultant in Washington, D.C. "Even I, who am both lazy and nondiscriminating, find the prepared kabobs and other meats are a waste of money," she says.

But markups aren't always so obvious. At Whole Foods, for example, oven-ready chicken and beef kabobs in various marinades or a New York strip steak in a smoked chipotle sauce cost the same as nonmarinated cuts, but a preshaped, seasoned ground-meat patty can run

---

More and more butchers now spend as much time preparing meat as cutting it—often at a premium.

20 to 75 percent more than the regular stuff. Prices vary widely by region and depending on the cost of beef, so compare carefully.

4 *"YOU THOUGHT FAT WAS BAD; WAIT'LL YOU GET A LOAD OF THE SALT CONTENT."*

Americans' obsession with leaner meats has had an unwelcome consequence: Cut out the fat and you cut out the flavor. "Choice" beef, the grade most commonly found in supermarkets, has less marbling than it did 30 years ago— a result of breeding initiated in the 1970s to respond to health concerns over fatty meats. To counteract the lack of flavor, most processors get around the problem by injecting beef, pork, chicken, and turkey with saline, which often reaches 15 percent or more of the purchasing weight.

Meat processors argue that customers want preseasoned foods, which taste better and save cooking time. (These additives also add shelf life.) Critics counter that so-called enhanced meats and poultry are mushy and salty. And most customers are outraged when they realize what they're getting: "I paid for one quarter of a pound of salt water when I bought a two-pound pack of chicken breasts," seethed New Yorker Amanda Bernard. But for many people, money is the least of it. Enhanced meat can be risky for those who need to watch their salt intake. The good news is, it's relatively easy to spot enhanced products, which are required to carry an ingredients-and-nutrition label listing the "solution" used to enhance the meat.

5 *"YOU ARE WHAT THE ANIMAL EATS."*

Americans are consuming more meat than ever. In 2005 we averaged more than 200 pounds of meat and poultry per person, up from 178 pounds in 1970. In order for the industry to turn a profit on the low prices Americans have come to expect, most livestock are kept and slaughtered on factory farms, where animals eat corn- and soybean-based feed—a good portion of which is often radically different from what the animal would consume naturally. For example, poultry feathers and manure are acceptable ingredients in cattle feed, according to the Food and Drug Administration. Poultry may also be fed meat and bone meal ground down to an inexpensive, protein-rich powder that encourages fast growth.

This practice can be dangerous to humans. According to the most recent data from Consumers Union, the publisher of *Consumer Reports,* between August 1997 and March 2004, 52 companies were forced to recall products for violating federal rules protecting feed from infectious "prions," the proteins believed to cause mad-cow disease. So how can you avoid contaminated meat? For starters, buy organic, which prohibits feed containing animal by-products. And for information on food safety, visit *www.notinmyfood.org.*

6 *"THIS BEEF'S 'ALL NATURAL'— WHATEVER THAT MEANS."*

Surely "all natural" meat is a good option? Not necessarily. According to the U.S. Department of Agriculture, the terms "natural" and "all natural" on a meat label in no way reflect how the animal was raised or what it was fed; "natural" means only that producers have introduced no colors or additives to the meat after processing.

Other labels are equally misleading. To qualify as "free range," according to the USDA, chickens must be given access to the outdoors only in the most technical sense: The door to the pen must be open for five minutes each day. Whether the birds actually go outside, or for how long, is irrelevant. "If you want to pay twice as much for essentially the same product, go right ahead," says a spokesperson for the National Chicken Council, which represents the largest chicken producers and processors. "There really is no difference."

7 *"IT'S NOT EXACTLY SPICK-AND-SPAN BACK HERE."*

Is your meat department sanitary? Taking a look at store cleanliness may be the only way to tell. Though inspection records are public information, *SmartMoney* had to file a Freedom of Information request to review state reports. And no wonder. According to the New York Department of Agriculture, 25.5 percent of the state's supermarkets were cited in 2004 for a critical deficiency involving insect, rodent, bird, or vermin activity that could have caused contamination, while 7.5 percent were cited for unsanitary equipment services. Another 1 percent of stores were slapped on the wrist for employees failing to wash their hands.

Your best option: Buy meat in stores where you believe sanitation is taken seriously. Then develop a relationship with the butcher or meat department personnel, and express any concerns.

8 "'GROUND BEEF' IS A EUPHEMISM."

John Montana, a Boston executive, is a gourmet cook, but sometimes he just wants a burger on the grill. When the mood strikes, Montana doesn't buy any old ground beef. Instead, he selects a raw cut and asks the butcher to grind it on the spot. "That way, I know what I'm getting," he says. Excellent idea. Ground beef, especially that found in processed foods such as sausage and pizza toppings, is often extracted by a process called "advanced meat recovery" (AMR), where carcasses are fed to a machine that strips soft tissue from bone. Consumer advocates warn that AMR increases the risk that spinal tissue—which can carry mad-cow disease—could be included among the processed meat. The American Meat Institute counters that the spinal cord is removed from all carcasses before being stripped. Meanwhile, the first case of mad-cow disease in domestic-raised beef was discovered in Texas in June 2005.

But that's not the only worry with ground beef. It's also a bacteria magnet. During the grinding process and packaging, it's exposed to air that is rife with harmful bugs including listeria, staphylococcus, and salmonella. It's so difficult to prevent infection that the USDA okays ground beef with 7.5 percent incidence of salmonella bacteria, versus just 1 percent for raw cuts. Most experts agree that's a reasonable level as long as meat is cooked to an internal temperature of 160 degrees, the temperature at which most pathogens are destroyed. The problem is, that's well beyond the popular medium-rare.

Our best advice: Find a butcher with a dedicated grinder for beef—you don't want any pork or chicken mixed in—and have your beef ground at the store. Then cook your burgers medium-well at least.

9 "THESE PORK CHOPS COULD COME FROM ANYWHERE."

After Canada confirmed cases of mad-cow disease in 2003, consumers suddenly became interested in the origin of their meat. But it's not often easy to tell. Meat from Argentina, Australia, and Canada, among other places, is available in supermarkets, bearing a USDA stamp.

It's not only Canada that's of concern: In 2003 consumer-watchdog group Public Citizen warned that many overseas inspection systems certified by the USDA do not meet core requirements of U.S. law. Brazil and Mexico, for example, violated U.S. rules that meat be inspected by independent government officials, yet these countries have retained their eligibility to export. The USDA's zero-tolerance policy for contaminants including feces and urine has also been repeatedly violated by Australia, Canada, and Mexico. A USDA spokesperson says that inspections have been modified to spotlight higher-risk products. "We have a very rigorous system of importation and certification," he says. "We continually do audits to ensure that overseas food-safety systems remain vigorous." To date the industry has defeated country-of-origin labeling. So stick to domestic meat, locally raised if possible.

10 "TAINTED MEAT SLIPS THROUGH THE CRACKS ALL THE TIME."

In 2001 Barbara Kowalcyk's young son died after eating a burger she prepared from meat infected with Escherichia coli. The strain that killed him was identical to the E. coli found in meat recalled that summer by meat processor American Food Groups. But Kowalcyk can't be sure that's where it came from, since recalls are voluntary.

How do you know if the meat you're buying is okay? Code numbers on every package of beef sold can be cross-referenced online with those of contaminated meat, posted at *www.fsis .usda.gov.* But few consumers are going to hit the Internet every time they throw a steak on the grill. The reality is that the system is imperfect, and tainted meat does slip through the cracks. In 2005 there were more than 24 recalls of meat due to dangerous levels of pathogens, including listeria, E. coli, and spinal-column remains of a cow over 30 months old.

Your best defense remains prevention. Freeze or refrigerate meat as soon as possible after buying it, and thaw it in the refrigerator, not on the counter. Cook meat thoroughly; the meat can be a little pink but the juices should be brown, not pink or red. Place cooked meat on clean plates, and never reuse dishes that have been in contact with raw meat. Finally, serve immediately, or keep meat hot.

THINGS TO KNOW

We caught up with American Culinary Federation President John Kinsella to get his thoughts on the top cuts of meat:

- **8-ounce filet mignon.** When you're buying meat, look for speckles of fat in the muscle. That's where the flavor comes from. If your filet doesn't have any fat in it, it's going to be tough.

- **24-ounce porterhouse.** In the old butcher meat markets, the guys who used to transport the beef around were called porters. Whoever hauled the most meat every week was given this steak—which

consists of filet and New York strip—as a bonus, hence the name.

- **16-ounce T-bone.** This steak should never weigh more than a pound; it has less fillet on it than a porterhouse.

- **10-ounce New York strip.** Just a terrific piece of meat. It's the same as the meat you'd find on the porterhouse or the T-bone, but unattached to the bone.

10 Things Your
Farmer's Market
Won't Tell You

1 "YOU MAY NOT SHOP HERE, BUT YOUR TAX DOLLARS SUPPORT OUR MARKET."

Farmer's markets aren't just quaint hallmarks of rural America; they've become de rigueur resources for many consumers of fresh produce. Over the past decade, the number of farmer's markets in the U.S. has more than doubled, to 3,700, as consumer demand for local and seasonally fresh food—as well as the push for new outlets for struggling farmers—has stoked growth. So have your tax dollars.

Since the early 1990s, the Agricultural Marketing Services division of the USDA has been actively spawning new markets, providing feasibility studies, architectural designs, and marketing gewgaws such as farmer's market coloring books. The support comes out of the government's desire to assist smaller farms.

While it's tough to pin down exactly how much tax revenue goes to farmer's markets, many do receive some federal, state, or municipal support in the form of grants, subsidized administrators, or marketing, according to the USDA. One perk for consumers: As part of its promotion of farmer's markets nationwide, the USDA keeps a detailed, state-by-state listing of them at *www.ams .usda.gov/farmersmarkets/map.htm.*

2 "OUR PRODUCE IS A MITE PRICEY."

Decades ago farmer's markets sprouted up in cities to combat the suburban flight of grocery stores and to supply low-income residents with inexpensive, fresh produce. These days, though, many farmer's markets cater to the urban elite. "The idea that you can get food cheaper at a farmer's market is ancient history," says Al Courchesne, owner of Frog Hollow Farms in Brentwood, Calif. Courchesne's organic peaches fetch $3.90 a pound at markets in the Bay Area, over 30 percent more than conventional peaches cost at supermarkets on the West and East coasts.

Why the premium? Small farmer's market growers often can't compete with the prices of major grocery chains, which have become ever more cost-competitive in the age of Wal-Mart and other big consolidators. Farmers also say the price is more than compensated for by quality. Supermarkets choose fruit and vegetable varieties for their ability to survive thousands of miles of transportation. Supermarket fruit is also picked well before it's ripe, Courchesne says, a process that allows it to last longer, but that has the side effect of lessening the sugar content that makes vine-ripened fruit sweeter.

To get the real deal, frequent markets that bill themselves as "producer only." And get to know the farmers.

3 *"THESE 'LOCAL' TOMATOES HAVE MORE SKYMILES THAN DEREK JETER."*

A spokesperson for the Arizona Department of Agriculture says farmers eager to make a bigger profit have been known to buy produce wholesale, say it was from their land, and take the markup at market. And some farm stands have been known to bring in fruit and vegetables from other regions and sell it as "locally grown."

While few farmer's markets have the resources to police the pedigrees of peaches and plums, some states and larger markets employ tougher policies than others. Greenmarket, which operates farmer's markets at 44 locations in New York City, requires vendors to grow produce within a 170-mile radius of the city and demands that farmers file detailed crop plans. If a farmer shows up with two trucks of corn from a single planned acre, inspectors know those ears aren't homegrown.

To get the real deal, frequent markets that bill themselves as "producer only." And get to know the farmers. Ellie Josephs, a die-hard market-goer in Venice, Calif., says she knew one vendor well enough to tell when he was pawning off second-rate fruit and saving his premium goods for another market.

4 *"YOU DON'T KNOW FROM RIPE FRUIT."*

Fire-engine-red apples and oranges round as softballs all stacked in pristine pyramids down at the local supermarket have trained consumers to expect perfect produce. But farm-fresh fruits and vegetables come in all colors, shapes, and sizes. "People aren't used to vine-ripened produce," says Randii MacNear, head of the California Federation of Certified Farmers' Markets. Ultrafresh produce can be more perishable as well. It took Portland, Ore., resident Ev Hu several pints of moldy strawberries to realize she needed to eat her farmer's market berries within a day.

Fortunately, there are some handy tips to guide you through the stands. No. 1: Look for fruit with broken skin from bird pecks. Vance Corum, a former farmer's market consultant based in Vancouver, Wash., says birds know which fruit has the highest sugar content. Other gems: A fresh artichoke will squeak when you rub it with a finger; a green bean should stick to your clothes when it's fresh.

Some markets are helping to educate city dwellers online—the West L.A. Farmer's Market & Community Fair in Los Angeles posts fact sheets on its website, such as "Asian Vegetables 101." And many fruits, vegetables, and herbs have national boards that host sites on how to pick and cook fresh produce.

5 *"A LITTLE DIRT ON OUR CARROTS DOESN'T MEAN THEY'RE ORGANIC."*

Fresh doesn't mean organic. Ever since the USDA implemented the National Organic

Program over five years ago, farmers who claim they're organic are required by law to meet uniform standards for growing produce without synthetic pesticides and fertilizers. But few farmers, even those at folksy farmer's markets, are certified organic. "As a general rule, most produce at farmer's markets is conventionally grown," says Anthony Piccola, an organic tomato farmer near Austin, Tex.

Nationwide, only 9,000 farms out of 2 million have certification, according to the Organic Farming Research Foundation in Santa Cruz, Calif. But some farmers do claim they're organic when they're not, Piccola says. They might also use terms such as "natural" or "hormone-free" to imply organic status.

How does a shopper know whether a farmer is truly organic? You can start by asking. Chicago resident Barbara Aitcheson passed on apples at her local market after the vendor told her they were sprayed with pesticides. For a more objective source, go to *www.localharvest.org* to locate organic farms in your area as well as find information about the various kinds of organic status.

6 *"OUR CROWDS ARE WORSE THAN MONDAY MORNING RUSH HOUR."*

Open-air markets began as folksy alternatives to jam-packed supermarkets, a place where shoppers could stroll in the sunshine and leisurely chat with farmers. Many still are. But numerous others have become mosh pits for foodies, drawing crowds that rival those at rock concerts. During peak season on a Saturday, nearly 60,000 people shop at Greenmarket's

Union Square location in New York City. "You have to push people aside and squeeze under their legs to get to vendors. It's stressful," says shopper Necmiye Onder.

And the crowds aren't just relegated to big cities. In Madison, Wis., the Dane County Farmer's Market surrounding the state capitol building draws more than 20,000 people each week. Market manager Larry Johnson says the foot-traffic flow has had to adapt to the throngs. "People move in a counterclockwise direction around the capitol," he says. "If you don't, you get run over."

So how do you beat the masses? Go early. Serious shoppers arrive at the Dane County market at 6 A.M. Or shop online. Many farms such as Frog Hollow in Brentwood, Calif., have websites (*www.froghollow.com*) and will ship fresh produce directly to the consumer.

7 *"THESE DAYS EVEN SUPERMARKETS SELL CACTUS LEAVES."*

Farmer's markets pride themselves on offering unique products, but grocery stores have become far more specialized and competitive. The lollo rosso lettuce at your local farmer's market can now be found in convenient salad bags at supermarket chains. Even Wegmans sells regional specialties such as cactus and jicama.

Traditional supermarkets are even borrowing farmer's market techniques, slicing open apples for consumers to sample, stocking organic produce, and buying locally. Daytona Beach, Fla., resident Geraldine Schwartz, for example, buys local tomatoes at her Winn-Dixie supermarket. "People are demanding it," she says.

However, you'll still find more variety at most farmer's markets. There are about 14 different types of meat, including emu and ostrich, offered at the Dane County market in Madison. If the produce at your local farmer's market starts to look too familiar, get to know the vendors and let them know you'll be first in line to buy their next batch of Suncrest peaches.

8 "CONVERSATION? DON'T MUCH CARE FOR IT."

Though talking with vendors about the ins and outs of the produce is part of the appeal of an outdoor market, on the whole, farmers aren't generally a bunch of Chatty Kathys. For many, the only contact they have with groups of people is on market day—and most farmers like it that way. What's more, all the work it takes to get to market would make anyone a tad grumpy. Life for the small farmer entails long hours of back-bending work; it's not uncommon to rise at 2 A.M. and drive five hours to sell at urban markets. "I'm not about to entertain anyone," says vendor Piccola.

Still, realizing that a smile goes a long way toward selling a zebra tomato, Piccola says he has become far more convivial and now tries to get to know his customers one-on-one. Other farmers are attending seminars to learn how to be more consumer-friendly. In Caruthersville, Mo., farmer John Hutchinson has counseled new vendors on the finer points of salesmanship. And consultant Vance Corum has traveled to Moscow, Idaho, to lecture farmers on market-day etiquette—advising them to wear a clean shirt, for example, and avoid loitering on the back of their pickup trucks.

9 "OUR SAMPLES ARE ABOUT AS SANITARY AS A BOWL OF BAR NUTS."

Everything from apple slices and goat cheese to caramel corn gets doled out at farmer's markets. But with so many shoppers fondling bowls of orange sections, these freebies can be a breeding ground for bacteria. "Who knows whose fingers have been in there?" says Ellie Josephs from Venice, Calif., noting that she steers clear of free samples.

To cut down on food-borne illnesses such as salmonella and E. coli, farmer's markets have rules about dispensing samples. Some states regulate this area, too. California, for example, requires farmers to wash knives with bleach and set out toothpicks to pluck berries from trays. But it's difficult for market managers to maintain these policies, says MacNear, of the California Federation of Certified Farmers' Markets. For that reason, many markets are forgoing sample grazing altogether. If you're queasy about a farmer's freebie tray, ask the vendor for a whole piece of washed fruit to taste.

10 "FRESH? ABSOLUTELY. CLEAN? NOT EVEN CLOSE."

Fruits and veggies at farmer's markets are fresh. But that doesn't mean they're ready to eat. "The produce and fruit [at farmer's markets] are not sold as ready-to-eat or cleaned beforehand," MacNear says. While farmers who sell produce to supermarkets typically flush-wash it for at least 15 minutes, reducing the potential for cross-contamination with bacteria found in fertilizers and on farmers' hands, vendors heading for open-air markets typically don't hose down their wares.

Supermarkets also have other systems in place to protect produce. At chains such as Whole Foods, Wegmans, and Wal-Mart, "Third-party audits are done to ensure the supply chain is as safe as possible," according to Meg Major, fresh food editor for *Progressive Grocer,* an industry publication. "This is a pretty common practice for retailers these days."

New York-based grocery chain Pathmark employs its own sanitarians, who routinely inspect its fruit and vegetables to guard against food-borne illnesses, says a company spokesperson.

Farmer's market shoppers should never eat fruit or vegetables before washing them. Market-goers also should wash their hands after handling samples or attending other farmer's market events. In August of 2002, 82 people got sick after visiting a sheep and goat exhibit at an Oregon County fair, where they came into contact with bacteria surrounding the animals. The incident resulted in the state's largest E. coli outbreak.

THINGS TO DO

- **Farmer's markets are a great place** to get fresh produce. You can find a state-by-state listing of them at *www.ams.usda.gov/farmersmarkets/map.htm.*

- **Ultrafresh produce, like fresh-picked strawberries,** isn't going to last as long the stuff you buy in a store. So shop accordingly.

- **Look for "producer only" farmer's** markets, where vendors can sell only food they've grown themselves. Otherwise, you might be getting store-bought produce sold at a markup.

- **Terms like "natural" and "hormone-free"** don't necessarily mean the produce is organic. Ask the vendor if you're unsure.

- **Produce bought at a farmer's market** is almost never ready to eat. Make sure you wash any fruits or vegetables before consuming.

10 Things Your
Caterer
Won't Tell You

1 *"DID I MENTION THIS IS MY FIRST TIME?"*

As any stressed-out host can attest, planning a social event of any scale is hard work, be it a small cocktail party or a formal wedding. With the time constraints of daily life—those related to work, family, and other commitments—on the increase, more and more people are turning to the pros for relief. By some industry estimates, there are now more than 30,000 specialty caterers doing business in the U.S.

But that figure leaves out smaller operators who may not be listed in phone books and professional directories, a group International Caterers Association former president Linda West describes as "selling sandwiches out of the back of the Volvo," which could include thousands more outfits. And since anyone can call himself a caterer, that means a huge disparity in the level of service, skill, cleanliness, and general professionalism you might find out there. The best way to choose a caterer you can trust? Word of mouth, West says. Talk to people in your area whose opinions you trust; even better, ask anyone who has held a catered event you've enjoyed. And when speaking to a potential caterer, be sure to request— at least three references.

2 *"YOU COULD PROBABLY DO THIS A WHOLE LOT CHEAPER."*

Most full-service caterers like to handle everything from the food and the alcohol to the coat check. They say this makes things easier on the host, but it's also more profitable for them. There are some easy ways to save money, though—starting with buying your own liquor. Some caterers charge above-retail prices on alcohol; if you buy it yourself, you'll pay roughly half their price. Even if your caterer then charges you a $2 to $5 corkage fee per bottle, the savings can still be significant—especially if your retailer accepts returns of unopened bottles, which many do. A word of caution: Liquor laws differ by jurisdiction; in some areas it's illegal to provide your own alcohol at a catered event, so check first.

You can also save big by renting your own supplies—if your caterer will allow it—such as tables, chairs, or dishware. You'll save on the markup, which can be as much as 30 percent, and you can still ask your caterer to handle the setup.

Finally, be flexible about the date. If you hold your event on a Friday, Sunday, or even midweek, you can save up to 15 percent, says Michael Roman, president of Catersource, a support and education organization for caterers.

3 "YOU MAY NOT WANT TO KNOW WHAT'S IN MY SECRET RECIPE."

There was a caterer in Indiana, who has since passed away, famous for his sweet-and-sour meatballs. People begged him for the recipe, but he kept it closely guarded. And for good reason: The meatballs came frozen from a restaurant-supply house, and the sauce was doctored with such secret special ingredients as grape jelly.

Ingredients can become an issue when it comes to caterers and their dishes, many of which include surprising—and not always healthy—additions. If you have any special requests such as vegetarian offerings, be sure to let your caterer know, and ask to review lists of ingredients. Food allergies are a more serious concern. Fort Wayne, Ind., catering chef Marla Cohen recalls a four-year-old at one event who was allergic to peanuts and touched a plate that had held chicken satay: "Her bottom lip swelled up just like that." Cohen called an ambulance and the child was fine, but anaphylactic shock can be deadly. Most people with allergies know what foods to avoid, but if any of your guests has such a condition, it's vital to tell your caterer in advance. Some troublesome ingredients—like peanut oil—may be hidden in preparations.

You can save big by renting your own supplies—if your caterer will allow it—such as tables, chairs, or dishware.

4 "THAT STAGGERING DRUNK WANTS ANOTHER ROUND? NO PROBLEM!"

Alcohol gets almost any good party flowing, but serving it in your home presents potentially dangerous situations. Liquor concerns "are a very hot issue in catering today," says Catersource's Michael Roman, who adds that hosts often expect bartenders to cross the line by serving minors or by continuing to serve guests who've already had too much to drink.

Giving alcohol to underage or obviously drunk guests is illegal, and if something goes wrong, you're the one who could be held liable. "This is something that's up to everyone to enforce," Roman says. "The host should back up the bartender." Such situations require diplomacy and finesse, so ask for experienced bartenders—and ask the caterer to keep a watchful eye. Linda West, owner of Houston-based Mélange Catering & Special Events, hands out taxi vouchers to anyone whose level of impairment seems questionable. The vouchers include next-day returns so guests can pick up their cars—sober. An added safeguard: While you may pay much more for it, if you do purchase the alcohol through your caterer, you are generally covered by the caterer's liability insurance.

5 "THIS SPREAD WILL EASILY SERVE 50 . . . DIETING MODELS."

A host's worst nightmare is running out of food. Dallas event planner Jennifer Fenimore recently handled a wedding where she was promised food for 50. Forty-two guests showed up, and they still ran short. "I wish I had known what the caterer considered a portion size," she says. "The only thing that didn't run out was the mashed-potato martini bar"—a station featuring mashed potatoes in martini glasses, with a variety of toppings—"and that's only because we had the wrong size of martini glasses. They were too small."

Experienced caterers know that some groups eat more than others, but they should never run short. If you expect your guests to be served a full lunch, be sure to tell your caterer. If a finger-food buffet will serve as a light meal at your reception, make that clear, too. On the flip side, if your budget is limited, don't skimp on portion size. Former Chicago caterer Adrienne Battin once had a client who was expecting 18 for lunch and wanted her to serve a buffet with just 18 shrimp. "I told her that I wasn't going to stand there like a police officer and tell anyone who took two to put one back," Battin says. "If you can't afford shrimp, don't serve it."

6 *"YOU WANT TO KNOW IF THINGS WILL GO SMOOTHLY? HIRE A PSYCHIC."*

Timing is critical in the success of any social affair: A cocktail hour that's going well should be extended, but not by too much, or your guests may overdo it and be unable to fully enjoy dinner. One of the most important roles of a caterer is to help ensure that things go smoothly by finessing the pace of an event. A good caterer should keep things moving along on schedule, but should also be flexible. Late-arriving guests to a sit-down dinner

can be accommodated by a longer appetizer course, for example.

But even the best-laid plans can be disrupted by the unexpected snafu. Battin once handled a home wedding reception where the portable ovens she'd brought couldn't run without shorting out the host's electrical system. A neighbor was nice enough to lend his portable generators, but without them the entrée might have been Chinese takeout.

Experienced caterers schedule walk-throughs when they're planning to cook at an unfamiliar facility and carry such unusual kitchen equipment as socket testers and oven thermometers. If your caterer doesn't ask to see your facility first, request that he pay a visit—or consider going with another caterer.

7 *"YOUR LEFTOVERS WILL FEED MY FAMILY FOR A WEEK."*

You paid for all that food, but you may not be entitled to the leftovers. You'd assume that, just as in a restaurant, it's your right to have all the leftovers returned to you, wrapped for takeout. But more and more catering companies today are enforcing strict leftover policies, primarily to avoid lawsuits that could arise from, say, seafood that has been left sitting for too long before getting packaged as a leftover.

But even in cases where the catering company does allow customers to keep leftovers, you might not see any of them. "At one company I worked for, the cleanup people walked off with the leftovers," says Battin, whose client had been expecting to find food in her refrigerator the following morning. It was probably a misunderstanding, but it cost her company, which then had to compensate the client. Of course, you may not want the leftovers. Newlyweds, for instance, may be leaving on their honeymoon the day after their reception and don't particularly want to come home to two-week-old food.

If none of your relatives or guests are interested in taking home slightly wilted hors d'oeuvres, consider gifting them to your caterer—Battin says she often parcels them out to service captains, security guards, and other support staff as an extra gratuity of sorts. Another option: Ask your caterer if he works with an organization that accepts leftovers for the needy.

8 "I HOPE YOU LIKE PIERCINGS. MY WAITERS HAVE MORE HOLES IN THEIR HEAD THAN SWISS CHEESE."

Food service attracts a wide range of workers, from career professionals to moonlighting artists. And while it may be cool for artists to sport pierced eyebrows on their own time, you have a right not to have to look at them at your event. If you don't want to see piercings, for example, or green hair or tattoos on your servers, tell your caterer up front. In turn, it's the caterer's right to accept or not accept a job based on those requests.

You can be as specific as you like: Roman of Catersource says he once had a hostess ask him not to use any waitresses who were well-endowed. "She said, 'My husband and I are having problems,'" Roman recalls. He complied with the request. "Don't be afraid to ask

for something—anything is negotiable," he says. (Not entirely true: Race and ethnicity are off-limits.)

You're free to dictate a dress code for the servers, too, within reason, though any special outfits—if you're throwing a costume party, for example, or a corporate event and want the servers to wear T-shirts with logos—are your responsibility. Otherwise, simple all-black, all-white, or black-and-white attire is considered standard.

9 "YOU SAY 'BUDGET'; I SAY 'GUESSTIMATE.'"

Many a host has spent hours on end fine-tuning the menu, shaving costs here and there to fit a strict budget, only to be surprised by the bill at the end. That's because many caterers neglect to calculate tax and gratuity charges in their estimates, add-ons that can easily boost a final bill by as much as 25 percent. "If I say I can pay $100 [per guest], I don't want to get a bill for $125," says Linda Cauiola, an event planner in Scottsdale, Ariz.

Tax and gratuity figures can vary widely; you can expect to pay as much as 22 percent for the latter. Ask whom it will cover: Often the gratuity may include wait staff, security guards, captains, and any other service people employed by your caterer. You're not required to tip more on top of it, but you may want to: It's not uncommon, for example, to give a little extra to captains or the wait staff. (Valet parkers are tipped at the guest's discretion.)

But to avoid any surprises, tell your caterer you want to see an inclusive budget, and ask specifically about tax, gratuity, and any potential extra charges. "If they get quiet, you have a problem," Cauiola says.

10 *"OF COURSE YOUR EVENT WILL BE UNIQUE. BUT WE'RE PRICING CHICKEN KIEV TO MOVE THIS WEEK."*

All hosts want their party to be memorable, and for the right reasons— not because theirs was the last in a long line of mini-quiche and vegetable-plate receptions this season. "I tell banquet managers all the time, I don't want the same thing they're serving at Company Y's function," Cauiola says. "But it happens—because they're lazy."

Caterers should keep up with trends but also have original ideas that can work within your budget. One result of the recent explosion of home-entertaining TV shows, books, and magazines has been an increase in creative ideas and widespread availability of gourmet ingredients, often at reasonable prices. So there's no excuse anymore for banquet-style chicken cordon bleu.

To ensure that your event is unique, Cauiola advises micromanaging: Check and recheck menus and event orders, ask questions, even peek into chafing dishes before guests arrive to make sure the salmon you requested is there and cooked the way you want it. "You have to be able to trust your caterer," she says. "My clients don't want a refund or an apology. They want their dinner to go well."

THINGS TO DO

● **One of the best ways** to find a good caterer is still word of mouth. Even so, check other references; you might want to ask prospective caterers if they have an event coming up that you could stop by and observe for yourself.

● **Trust your instincts.** In spite of good reviews, if you don't get a good feeling from a prospective caterer, find someone else.

● **If an Internet search** is more your style, try *www.localcatering.com,* where you can submit detailed information about your event and interested caterers in your area will contact you with a quote.

● **If you're the hands-on type,** you can save yourself some money by purchasing the optional items in the catering package— like alcohol and other beverages—and handling them yourself.

10 Things Your
Health Food Store
Won't Tell You

1 *"'ORGANIC' ISN'T JUST ANOTHER WORD FOR 'HEALTHY'..."*

What comes to mind when you hear the word "organic"? Despite the fact that the U.S. Department of Agriculture laid down standards in 2002 for what does and does not constitute organic food, consumers still seem to be confused. In a 2005 survey sponsored by Austin, Tex.–based Whole Foods Market, 72 percent of respondents said they believe organics contain more nutrients than conventional food. In fact, evidence for extra nutrients in organics is debatable.

So what does organic really mean? Produce is grown without the use of most synthetic pesticides, genetic modification, irradiation, or fertilizer made with synthetic ingredients or sewage sludge. Organic meat comes from livestock that has never been treated with antibiotics or growth hormones and has been given organic feed free of animal by-products.

Though the Food and Drug Administration monitors conventional produce to ensure that pesticide levels aren't toxic, it's the cumulative effect of small amounts that concerns some people. The Environmental Working Group compiles a list of "dirty dozen" produce that retains the most pesticide residue according to FDA and USDA tests. You can see the list, which includes apples, strawberries, and potatoes, at *www.foodnews.org.*

2 *"...BUT THE LABEL'S STANDARDS ARE CONSTANTLY UNDER FIRE."*

No sooner did the federal organic standards get implemented than food producers began to lobby Congress for changes weakening the regulation. In one notable case, after Georgia chicken producers reportedly balked at the standards, they convinced Rep. Nathan Deal (R-Ga.) to add a rider to the 2003 Omnibus Appropriations bill allowing them to label chickens raised on conventional feed organic if organic feed was more than twice the cost of conventional feed. Organic activists and trade groups objected, and the rider was repealed in April 2003.

Around the same time, Alaska's two senators sponsored an amendment to a wartime bill, opening the door for wild-caught seafood to be labeled "organic"—a boon for Alaska's wild salmon fishery. The problem? Organic standards are meant to deal with farming, and organic advocates argue it's impossible to know how wild seafood has been fed or maintained. Indeed, wild shark and swordfish can contain such high mercury levels that young children and pregnant women are advised not to eat them. For more details on wild seafood safety, check out the EPA's advisory at *www.epa.gov/ost/fish* or visit *www.environmentaldefense.org.*

3 "SOME OF OUR PRODUCTS AREN'T AS ECO-FRIENDLY AS THEY SOUND."

As the demand for organic products has grown, a number of other eco-labels that imply health or environmental purity have also proliferated. Their true meanings range from the application of standards stricter than the USDA's organic rule to kinda-sorta organic to anything but organic—adding another layer of confusion when you're shopping.

For example, "Biodynamic," a label created by a consortium of farmers, shares many of the same principles as organic but has even stricter rules. On the other hand, "Food Alliance Certified," a label created by the eponymous Food Alliance—a nonprofit that believes "organic isn't a complete solution"— is aimed at "helping farmers reduce pesticide use and toxicity over time," according to a company spokesperson. Make sense? Not really. "Consumers are caught in a marketing war that's meaningless as a whole," says Alex Avery, director of research at the Center for Global Food Issues, a think tank that supports modern high-yield agriculture. To find out what's behind any confusing label, head to *www.greenerchoices.org.*

4 "HEALTH FOOD DOESN'T HAVE TO EAT UP YOUR ENTIRE PAYCHECK."

Organic and health-oriented foods generally will cost you more than conventional foods. Some of the biggest differentials exist in meat and milk: Organic milk typically costs as much as 50 to 100 percent more than conventional milk, while organic meat can cost two or even three times more, according to an Organic Trade Association spokesperson.

But there are plenty of ways to minimize costs in health food stores. Buy from that old hippie standby, the bulk bin, where you can save on staples such as cereal, pasta, and flour. Or consider joining a local co-op, where you exchange a little volunteer time for big savings, or a community-supported agriculture—or CSA—program, in which you pay a farmer up front for an entire season's worth of produce. (To find one near you, go to *www.csacenter.org.*)

James Brundage, an administrative assistant at a PR firm, joined his local co-op in Brooklyn, N.Y. "I used to buy most of my food at Whole Foods," he says. "Now I buy it all at the co-op, and prices are about 30 to 50 percent cheaper." As for the co-op's requirement that members put in about three hours of work per month at the store, Brundage says he finds it "only mildly annoying. Everyone is so friendly, the time passes quickly."

5 "OUR SUPPLEMENTS ARE A MYSTERY WRAPPED IN AN ENIGMA."

Dietary supplements are a booming business in this country, with sales of about $17.5 billion in 2007. Since the fallout surrounding the FDA's ban of ephedra years ago, many consumers have already learned that manufacturers of these supplements don't have to submit evidence of effectiveness, since they don't make overt claims of curing or preventing a particular disease. Indeed, there are few controls to make certain that supplements even contain what they claim to. "Assume that nothing is guaranteed [about content] or the appropriate dosage advice," says Ron Buchheim, deputy health editor at *Consumer Reports,* which has tested numerous supplements since 1995. Though the products are more consistent these days, "We still sometimes find significant variation" in the concentration of the active ingredient, he says, "sometimes more than 20 percent outside the amount on the label."

Right now testing by independent labs is the best way to ensure that your vitamins or supplements are at least reliable. Before buying, check out how the product rated on the website ConsumerLab.com, which tests a wide range of supplements for identity, potency, and purity.

6 *"TAKING OUR ADVICE MAY BE HAZARDOUS TO YOUR HEALTH."*

Don't assume that health food store employees are experts on their products, especially supplements. In 2003 the journal *Breast Cancer Research* published a study in which investigators went undercover to 34 health food stores and asked about recommendations for supplements for their fictional mother,

diagnosed with breast cancer. The stores suggested 33 products, none of which has sufficient evidence of effectiveness. Of the 10 employees who asked which prescriptions the mother was taking, only 8 mentioned that the drug tamoxifen might interact with the natural remedies.

Though this particular study focused on a small group of stores in Canada, it was modeled on similar research that drew the same conclusion. "Every study we've seen has found the same thing"—that the health advice dispensed by clerks is "usually in a range of 50 to 100 percent wrong," says Stephen Barrett, a retired psychiatrist who runs the website at *www.quackwatch.org.* "Imagine going to a doctor with [that] batting average." The majority of health food store workers have no scientific training, he points out. If you are interested in trying dietary supplements, check with your doctor about any adverse interactions with your prescribed medicines.

7 *"ENHANCED FOODS CAN BE TOO MUCH OF A GOOD THING."*

Though many people exercise caution when downing supplements in the form of pills, it's easy to forget that we may be overloading on certain nutrients by regularly consuming the "enhanced" foods sold in health food stores. Soy is the perfect example: Due to an FDA-approved health claim that soy protein lowers LDL—or "bad"—cholesterol and preliminary evidence that other soy components known as isoflavones may reduce symptoms of menopause, soy is a popular additive to foods. Products such as bread, juice, and sports bars are often enhanced with added soy protein, sometimes including isoflavones.

However, "There are more and more studies showing that isoflavones [may not] have the greatest effect, that you may need to have the whole bean," says an American Dietetic Association spokesperson. On top of that, some researchers worry that consuming high quantities of soy isoflavones may even have adverse health effects, including contributing to thyroid problems in some situations. If you think adding a large amount of a particular nutrient to your diet would be beneficial, consult with your doctor just as you would about a medication.

8 "THINK THERE'S NO JUNK FOOD HERE? THINK AGAIN."

Gone are the days when the most sinful thing in a health food store was carob chips. Today plenty of dietary pitfalls lurk in the aisles: banana chips fried in coconut oil; vegetable crisps, which are essentially fried potatoes flavored with small amounts of vegetables; and so-called enhanced waters, which add sugar and "literally pennies worth of vitamins" to plain water to create what's basically a glorified soda, according to Bonnie Liebman, director of nutrition at the Center for Science in the Public Interest. "The problem is, these foods have an aura of healthfulness," she says, in part because they are sold in health food stores.

To really know what you're getting, you need to read labels on packaged food just as closely in a health food store as you would in a regular grocery store.

Look out, for example, for seemingly low-cal foods that actually contain several servings per package. Liebman says she found a giant "high-energy" cookie that contained only 140 calories per serving—but each cookie constituted four servings. Also watch for prepared vegetarian foods that are high in saturated fat—more than 4 grams per serving—from added butter, cream, and palm kernel or coconut oil.

9 "WE MAY UNDO THE BENEFITS OF ORGANICS."

Participants at nearly every stage of food production—seed vendors, farmers, and processors—must be approved by independent certifiers in order for the final product to be labeled "organic." However, for the last link in the chain, the retailer, certification is optional except in organic food preparation areas.

Why does it matter? In a store, with so many foods commingling, the potential for contamination with nonorganic substances can be high, argues Cissy Bowman, an Indiana-based organic produce farmer and a USDA-accredited certifier. Some problems: nonorganic produce stored above organic, where residues can drip onto the food below when misted with water to stay fresh, or worse, simply mixing up conventional and organic produce that look virtually identical. Chemicals used in an uncertified store—everything from cleaning agents to rodenticide—may also wind up in the food.

Fortunately, organic certification does seem to be catching on among retailers. Whole Foods Market has had all its retail operations certified organic, as have many independent stores, such as the Wedge Co-op in Minneapolis. If you don't see a certification seal posted at your local health food outlet, ask the manager how the store prevents contamination of organics.

10 "ORGANIC SHAMPOO? DON'T WASTE YOUR MONEY."

Walk into almost any health food store and you'll see so-called organic cosmetics and personal care products that are often much pricier than their traditional drugstore equivalents. But shoppers should understand that there are no national USDA standards for organic cosmetics.

Many products create an organic halo by calling themselves "70 percent organic." Right now that 70 percent can include "organic hydrosol," essentially a tap-water-based extract of an organic plant. "Shampoo and lotion are usually well above 70 percent water anyway," says Craig Minowa, environmental scientist for the Organic Consumers Association, which is opposed to counting added water in hydrosols toward an "organic" total. "So you can have a product labeled 'organic' that's exactly the same as if you went into a Wal-Mart and bought a conventional product with the same synthetic cleansers and preservatives."

How to know what you're getting? When considering an "organic" personal-care product, check the ingredient list. If the first entry is hydrosol—sometimes called "organic hydroflorate," "organic plant extracts," or "floral water"—it's probably being counted toward the total.

THINGS TO DO

● **Stick to stores that clearly label** and separate organic and nonorganic food. When placed together, there's potential for residue from nonorganic produce and other products to contaminate the organic.

● **A lot of health food products** claim to be eco-friendly as well as good for you. Visit *www.greenerchoices.org/eco-labels* to enter product information and get a breakdown on how green it really is.

● **Just because it's natural** doesn't mean it's healthful. Many natural herbs can cause unpleasant or even dangerous side effects. Always check with your doc before taking a natural supplement.

● **Health food and health care** should work together—consult your doctor about making the right changes in your diet to maximize your health and well-being.

10 Things Your
Supermarket
Won't Tell You

1 "OUR 'SPECIALS' ARE ANYTHING BUT."

Do you tend to pick up a supermarket circular when you walk into your store, hoping to cash in on the weekly sales? Well, attention shoppers: They can be a bad deal. "Shoppers don't bother to compare the price when they have a coupon," says Arun K. Jain, a marketing professor at the State University of New York at Buffalo. "So supermarkets use them to unload products that are more expensive than other brands."

Some markets even raise the price on items during the week store coupons for them will be appearing in newspapers and circulars. "The regular retail prices fluctuate, making the discount seem larger for some sales," says one ad department employee at a large supermarket chain.

Also, beware of misleading in-store "sale environments," used to promote certain items—often highlighted by a cardboard display and handwritten signs announcing the price. Despite the fanfare, it might not be such a great deal after all. "People think it must be a special deal," says Jack Taylor, a professor of retailing at Birmingham-Southern College in Birmingham, Ala. "But in reality, it's the same price as always."

2 "EVERYBODY PAYS A PRICE FOR OUR 'LOYALTY' PROGRAM."

More than 50 million Americans use supermarket loyalty cards that entitle them to special in-store discounts. Who foots the bill? Those customers who refuse to join. "The whole point is to give the best shoppers something special, and you have to pay for that out of something," says David Diamond, former president of emerging business for Catalina Marketing, the St. Petersburg, Fla., company that handles many supermarket card programs. "It used to be that everybody got Rice Krispies for, say, 79 cents. Now they're available to anyone for 89 cents, but the best shoppers get them for 49 cents," Diamond says.

Even if you do join, you'll pay in another way—with your privacy. Consider the case of Robert Rivera, who slipped on a carton of spilled yogurt in his local supermarket in Los Angeles, shattering his kneecap. Rivera filed a lawsuit against the store (which was later dismissed by the judge for lack of evidence), and during a discovery session, Rivera says, a lawyer for the store threatened to air his buying habits. "He said they had information that I buy a lot of alcohol," Rivera says. "I shop at lots of different stores in the chain. There's no way they could have known that unless they used my club card information."

Sounds far-fetched? Not according to Tim Duffy, a consumer advocate in Los Angeles. "They know if you drink, have hemorrhoids, or practice safe sex," Duffy says. "I tell people, Unless you're using the card to cash checks, give them a fake name." Luckily, your supermarket will usually play along—Safeway, for example, allows members to sign up merely as "Safeway Customer."

3 "OUR STORES MIGHT MAKE YOU SICK..."

You'd naturally be horrified to find roaches, rats, or other critters in your kitchen, but those same vermin may be running amok in your grocery store. A 2007 New York State Department of Agriculture and Markets report, for example, found rodents, birds, or bugs in the aisles of almost 15 percent of supermarkets. At an Albany, N.Y., Sam's Club, an inspection turned up rodent-gnawed chocolate bars, 500 samples of mice droppings, and six dead mice in aisle 13. (A Sam's Club spokesperson says that the store has "taken extensive steps to correct the problem.")

And while the bugs and rodents present an obvious health hazard—flies can carry E. coli on their legs and bodies—the pesticides that stores use to fight them can be even worse. "We've seen people go in and spray pesticides [and] actually contaminate the food," says Joe Corby, director of the Food Safety and Inspection Division of New York's Department of Agriculture and Markets.

How can you tell if your supermarket is really safe? Good supermarkets employ a food-safety manager to ensure that foundation entrances are sealed and food shipments are inspected before they hit the shelves—the best ways to prevent vermin from getting in. One red flag: old, faded stock. A failure to rotate products properly gives insect eggs that have snuck in with grain products time to hatch and create an infestation.

4 "...AND IF THEY DON'T, OUR EMPLOYEES WILL."

Vermin aren't the only cause of harmful bacteria at your supermarket. "Employee practices are probably the number-one cause of cross-contamination," says Joseph Reardon, director of the food and drug protection division of the North Carolina Department of Agriculture and Consumer Services. Who's to blame? In part, the workers themselves. But management also shoulders plenty of the responsibility. "The hours budgeted for cleaning are constantly under

---

Good supermarkets employ a food-safety manager to ensure that foundation entrances are sealed and food shipments are inspected before they hit the shelves—the best ways to prevent vermin from getting in.

---

barrage by management, and it's hurt food safety," says Carl Lafrate, president of ProCheck Food Safety Consultants, a Baldwinsville, N.Y.–based firm that designs food-safety programs for grocery chains. Ten years ago "meat departments were cleaned every four hours," Lafrate says. "But now they've cut that out." Indeed, in a published 2004 survey of U.S. supermarkets, the FDA found more than half of deli workers didn't properly wash their hands and that 42 percent of meat department employees failed to keep surfaces sanitized.

To see how your store scores on cleanliness, request a copy of its most recent health inspection report. In most jurisdictions, inspections are handled by the department of health, consumer affairs, or agriculture.

5 "FEDERAL GUIDELINES ARE OPTIONAL."

While the FDA regularly issues a food code to suggest good safety practices, it's merely a recommendation—the federal government has no authority in the matter of supermarket inspections. Not surprisingly, few of the 3,000 regional inspection authorities update their local regulations to match the current food code, and states tend to follow suit: Only 18 of the 56 U.S. states and territories have adopted the FDA's 2001 food code, while just 5 have adopted the more recent 2005 code. The result? Utter inconsistency.

Among the suggestions the FDA makes: Cold foods should be kept at 41 degrees or lower. Sounds reasonable, but most states set it at 45 degrees. And

where the FDA says grocery stores should be given a maximum of 10 days to correct health violations, Vermont, for one, gives its stores a full month to comply.

Not all states are so lax; some enforce codes even stricter than the FDA's. California, for example, is famous for its stringent supermarket regulations, says Sarah Klein, food safety attorney for the Center Science in the Public Interest. But even where local laws reflect high standards, they're not always enforced. "Most states require annual inspections, but that's often not taken seriously," says Lafrate. "In a lot of states, inspections are generated only on a consumer-complaint basis"—a good reason for shoppers to file a complaint if a store appears subpar.

6 "'FRESH' IS A RELATIVE TERM."

What do supermarkets do if the steaks don't sell fast enough and start to look a little grungy? Some will grind them into hamburger meat. And if the chicken is past its "sell by" date? Others will slap a new label on it. What might surprise you is the fact that these supermarkets are not doing anything illegal. Except for regulations pertaining to baby food and infant formula, there are no federal laws mandating product dating in supermarkets. In most states a retailer may legally sell foods beyond the date on the package as long as the product can be considered unspoiled and safe to eat. Even repackaging is allowed.

The FDA does require that where dates are provided, they be accompanied by an explanatory phrase. But chances are those phrases won't reveal much about the actual condition of the kielbasa in your cart: A "sell by" date simply tells the store how long to display the product, while a "best if used by" date can suggest when the product will lose its peak flavor or quality. Only an expiration date can be used by the supermarket as an indicator of whether food is still safe to eat. Not that you're likely to find one—in the majority of states, no type of freshness dating on food is required at all. How to ensure what you're buying is fresh? Let your senses do the work. Pay attention to color and appearance, says Klein. And above all, give the food a good sniff. If it doesn't smell right, don't buy it.

7 "WE LIKE TO PLAY HEAD GAMES."

Shoppers who stick to a prepared list are few and far between—and they're a supermarket's worst enemy. So how do stores capitalize on most people's tendency to stray? For starters, by playing soft music in the aisles, inducing you to relax and spend, says Richard Rauch, a marketing expert who has consulted for supermarket chains. Some stores, he adds, even use special mood-enhancing lighting that filters out higher frequencies in the visible light spectrum, producing only relaxing colors such as blues and purples. "It slows your pace and gets your mind to slow down," Rauch says. "Using lighting to create an atmosphere is not an unusual tactic; most of the larger, more sophisticated stores use it."

But sight and sound aren't the only senses grocery chains use to entice spending. Ever notice how good the bakery smells? There's a reason those ovens are always running full blast. "Studies show the smell of baking bread drives people bonkers," says Jain, the SUNY-Buffalo marketing professor; the scent drives up sales all over the store. A spokesperson for the Food Marketing Institute, a retail association, denies the widespread use of such tactics. "We haven't encountered these things," he says. "Retailers want to offer the best value, quality, and selection. That's what drives sales."

8 "OUR PRODUCT OFFERINGS ARE RIGGED."

So your local supermarket stopped carrying your favorite brand of potato chips? Don't assume it was discontinued. More likely, the manufacturer refused to fork over its "slotting fee"—a payment to the supermarket in return for shelf space. Many manufacturers gladly pay such fees in order to score primo shelf space at eye level, where a product is most likely to attract attention.

But other kinds of slotting fees stifle competition, hurt consumers, and hold smaller manufacturers over a barrel. Among the worst: "pay to stay" fees—regular payments the manufacturer makes if it wants to sell its goods in the store. It's an issue that many small manufacturers quietly accept for fear of angering the powerful supermarket chains. So great is the fear, that at a 1999 Senate Small Business Committee hearing on the issue, some small manufacturers testified wearing hoods and using voice scramblers to conceal their identity.

The Food Marketing Institute says that slotting-fee profits are passed to consumers as lower prices. But Nicholas Pyle, president of the Independent Bakers Association, disagrees, saying that those fees force bakeries to increase wholesale prices by passing on business costs to consumers—thus canceling out any in-store savings. "Otherwise," Pyle says, the bakeries "couldn't survive."

9 "BUYING IN BULK ISN'T ALWAYS THE BEST IDEA."

Most of us have spent enough time in supermarkets to think that we know how to work the system to get the best deals, and buying in bulk is often at the top of a shopper's list of tried-and-true ways to save. And while bulk purchases often do represent significant savings—often 25 percent or more on items like oatmeal and trail mix—it's not always the right choice. "It's been drilled in consumers' minds that when you buy larger packages, they're cheaper," says Jain. "Sometimes it's true, but many times it's not." In fact, some supermarkets, having caught on to the way shoppers think, will jack up bulk prices. How to avoid overpaying? Always compare the unit price of items to see if you're actually saving money by buying bigger.

But even when the price is right, buying in bulk isn't always the most practical strategy or the best idea, especially for processed foods like cookies and candy, as well as big cans of coffee beans. "Buying coffee in bulk is often cheaper, but not a good idea," Jain says. That's because the quality of roasted coffee diminishes over time, and a

household can only consume so much in a given day. Jain suggests asking yourself how much of an item you'll realistically use and how frequently before hitting the checkout line.

10 "OUR SCANNERS ARE A SCAM."

While supermarkets were among the first retailers to adopt price scanners, many stores still can't seem to use them right. A 1998 FTC study of supermarket scanner systems found that roughly a fourth failed to earn a passing grade, and a few chains overcharged customers on more than 1 out of 12 items. Have things improved since then? Not according to consumer advocate Duffy. "It's still a problem," he says, "but it's not with the scanners—it's human error and negligence, generally." Error comes into play, says Duffy, when the wrong prices are put into bar codes or when pricing doesn't get updated.

The most common errors are made on sale items, adds Jerry Butler, a former field supervisor with the North Carolina Department of Agriculture's Standards Division. Store management fails to enter the sale price into the system, and the product gets scanned at the original price.

Duffy suggests that shoppers avoid getting overcharged by jotting down prices and watching the register as you get rung up. "What I tell people to do is, Take your shopping list, leave enough space to pencil in the price, then compare it to your receipt when you get it," he says. "That way, if there's any egregious difference you'll know right away."

THINGS TO DO

● **Leave room on your shopping list** to jot down the advertised prices of your purchases so you can notify the cashier if something gets rung up incorrectly. Some stores, including A&P and Waldbaum's, will give you a discount if there's a pricing error.

● **Does it seem like your** supermarket's always tinkering with its layout? Good—frequent changes in displays and product location are a way to avoid insect and vermin problems.

● **Can't trade in those name brands** for generics but still want to save? Before heading to the supermarket, check the manufacturer's website—it may have its own promotion going.

● **Supermarkets tend to put** the most expensive items at eye level—so you might have to search the top and bottom shelves to find the cheaper brands.

● **Burning away your savings** on groceries at the pump? You can eliminate the price of gas from your grocery budget by ordering food online and having it delivered. Amazon.com, for example, offers free shipping on many items once your tally reaches the required amount.

10 Things Your
Wine Merchant
Won't Tell You

1 *"YOU'RE PAYING FOR PRESTIGE, NOT TASTE."*

Cruise the aisle of your local wine store. Take in the various vintages, and imagine the taste of a fine old Bordeaux on your palate. But before you grab that special bottle, notice the dizzying degree to which wine prices can vary, even for offerings that seem extraordinarily similar. Take, for instance, bottles of Mondavi Pinot Noir 1997 and Benton-Lane Pinot Noir 1998. They both come from the West Coast of the U.S. Their tastes are difficult to discern from one another. But then look at the price: The Mondavi, which sells for $110, costs twice as much as the $54 Benton-Lane.

What is such a price difference really about? In a word, prestige. "Expensive wines command high prices because they are produced in limited quantities or come from very specific geographic regions," says Vic Motto, a wine industry consultant with Motto, Kryla and Fisher in California's Napa Valley town of St. Helena. Motto cites the well-known Opus One—a joint venture of Robert Mondavi and Rothschild—as an example. Opus One's 1980 cabernet sauvignon sells for a whopping $300 a bottle. "How much better is that than a $50 wine?" asks Motto. "Probably not three times as good.

But it's scarce, reliable, and prestigious." According to a spokesperson for Opus One, that is pretty much the point. "I'd have to ask [Motto] which $50 bottle of wine he has in mind," he says. "Will it have the cachet, the imprimatur of the Rothschild and Robert Mondavi families? No."

2 *"OUR LABELS ARE MISLEADING."*

Seeing the words "Napa Valley" on a wine label is reassuring. The area is known for its first-rate grapes, and many of the best American wines originate there. That explains why California wineries like to have their products associated with the region—even if the grapes were grown someplace far away. Such was the case with a wine called Napa Ridge, which is actually made from grapes grown in central, rather than northern, California. Similarly, CK Mondavi, owned by a member of the famed wine-growing family, slapped references to the Napa Valley all over the labels of its wines, which are produced from grapes grown elsewhere in California. In 2000 a California judge fined the California-based Bronco Wine Co., makers of Napa Ridge, $750,000, and CK Mondavi

$300,000 over a labeling complaint. And in 2005 a ruling went into effect making it illegal to use a geographical name on a wine label unless 75 percent or more of the grapes in the wine come from that region. A 2006 law extended the ruling to include wines labeled as being from Sonoma.

The folks at CK Mondavi see the issue more benignly. "It was just a reference to where the winery was located, and it was originally okayed by the Bureau of Alcohol, Tobacco, and Firearms," says John Garaventa, former brand manager at Mondavi. "Apparently they changed their mind." Bronco Wine says, via a written statement, that in part "this was one of those notorious 'gut and amend' bills that started life as one thing and got hijacked to serve a special interest"—namely Napa Valley grape growers.

3 "OUR FAVORITE WINES AREN'T NECESSARILY THE BEST . . ."

You're sitting in a restaurant, perusing a wine list loaded with unfamiliar names, and so you ask your waiter for assistance. He immediately suggests an offering, smiles, and tells you that it's one of his personal favorites. What he doesn't tell you is why. "Some wine companies offer incentives to waiters who move their products," says Anthony Bourdain, chef-at-large for Les Halles' three locations, host of the Travel Channel's *Anthony Bourdain: No Reservations*, and author of the bestseller *Kitchen Confidential* about the ins and outs of the restaurant business. "Wine salesmen spend a lot of time in their customers' restaurants," Bourdain explains. "They give away fancy corkscrews, signage,

cute outfits, free cases." In other words, it's often in the waiter's best interest to push one wine over another, even if it's not the best value.

In some cases, the benefits may be too alluring to pass up. "I know of one waiter who is ferociously selling a not very good wine," continues Bourdain. "The vintner maintains a château in Portugal, and the waiters who sell the most bottles of his wine get invited to stay there. I understand that the place is a Portuguese equivalent of Hef's pad."

4 ". . . BUT YOU WON'T NOTICE ANYWAY."

Back in 1999 a group of British wine critics were challenged to try five wines, four of which were defective in some way, and as one of the participants, Richard Neill, wrote in London's *Daily Telegraph*, "Thirty of the assembled tasters didn't get a single correct answer [as to what was wrong with each wine], and not one person managed to get all five right." The results of the test do beg the question: If the experts can't tell the good from the bad, what chance does an amateur oenophile have?

Tim Kopec, wine director for the restaurant Veritas in Manhattan, reveals some sure signs that you have been handed a bad bottle. "When you smell the wine, you are looking for a flaw," he explains, adding that you should at least hope for an agreeable, pleasant scent. If the wine smells like wet cardboard, Kopec explains, that means the wine has been "corked"—that is, become infected with a spore from the cork. If it smells acidic, like vinegar, the wine is spoiled.

You should also be sure to aerate the wine with a swirl before tasting it. What if you're still not sure whether or not the wine is flawed? Says Kopec: "Ask the sommelier [or waiter] to have a taste and give you his opinion."

5 "STAY AWAY FROM MY WINE OF THE WEEK."

Ever wonder why on certain trips to the wine store, various bottles are being offered at bargain-basement prices? Sometimes wines are on sale because merchants have gotten particularly good deals on them. But often there are other motivators at work. "Some places will push a wine because they have it in stock and it's not moving," explains Al Hotchkin, former owner of the esteemed New York City wine store Burgundy. Hotchkin was recently at a wine tasting where one of the star attractions was a French white wine. The people hosting the tasting bragged about having purchased the wine for about half its going price. After drinking it, Hotchkin realized that it was heavily reduced for good reason. "The wine tasted old and tired," he says.

You should also be skeptical about those handwritten shelf tags that promote various wines—you know, the ones that promise a "velvety finish" and a "hint of blackberry"—as they may be little more than sales gimmicks. "Hopefully, those cute things written that adorn the shelves were written by the wine merchant *after* he tasted the wine," says Hotchkin. "Less good is when the store copies it from a reputable review. The third possibility is something that I'd rather not think about." What does he imagine it might be? "Creative writing."

6 "THE BEST REGIONS OFTEN MAKE FOR THE WORST DEALS."

If you really wanted to get serious about wine, you'd spend some time traveling through obscure towns in France, checking out underappreciated wines from boutique growers. But because few wine lovers have that kind of time or money, they often find themselves at the mercy of liquor store sales staff who tend to play it safe by pushing familiar wines from familiar regions—and it doesn't hurt if they're on the expensive side. Robert M. Parker, who publishes the bimonthly newsletter *Wine Advocate* and is an editor at *Food & Wine* magazine, cites the much-touted Burgundy Chambertin vineyard as an example. "Three wines that come out of there are stupendous, six are good, and the rest range from mediocre to undrinkable," he explains. "Yet they all sell for $150 to $300 per bottle. You're paying for a legendary vineyard with a mythical reputation that often disappoints."

Fortunately, it is possible to find good wines from little-known regions for bargain prices. That's exactly what Kermit Lynch does for a living. Lynch is a Berkeley, Calif.–based wine importer who spends half the year scouring the French countryside for unknown wines. Most recently, Lynch has had a lot of luck in the South of France. Some of his favorites? A white varietal from Domaine de la Done for $7 and a sauvignon blanc from Domaine du Salvard for $9.

7 "WE'LL SHIP YOU THE BOTTLES, BUT YOU MIGHT NEVER GET THEM."

The Internet seems like a fabulous resource for wine—especially for hard-to-find bottles produced in limited quantities. Unfortunately, Internet wine retailers may or may not be able to deliver to where you live, legally speaking. In a hangover from the days of Prohibition, many states' laws prohibit wine from being shipped across state lines—there are currently just 30 states where you can legally and unquestionably receive such a shipment. (To see where your state fits into all of this, go to *www.wineinstitute.org*.)

While Internet retailers have different ways of dealing with the problem, some just ignore it; that is, they'll ship you wine wrapped in brown paper, regardless of what the law says. No harm, no foul, right? Not necessarily. The feds can seize illegally delivered wine, explains John Hinman, managing partner at Hinman & Carmichael, a San Francisco-based law firm that specializes in alcoholic beverage law. "You do run the risk," he says. In Maryland, for example, "there have been a number of wine seizures, which tend to strike during the holiday season."

8 "YOUR WINE HAS BEEN SPIKED."

Because all wine essentially looks the same, the label goes a long way in guiding you toward what you want to drink. When something is identified as, say, cabernet sauvignon, that's what you expect to be drinking. But what if the label also promises that the wine includes "natural flavors"? You might assume that means other grapes. Nope. In fact, the most likely mystery ingredients are fructose, water, and alcohol.

How do winemakers get away with spiking their product? Because the laws state that while all the grapes present in the wine must be named, the specifics of any additives do not need to be listed. Karen Ross, president of the California Association of Winegrape Growers, is outraged by the laxity of the law. "It's a rip-off to consumers," she says. Ross also doesn't like its inconsistency of wine-labeling rules: Winemakers get fined when they "put less expensive grapes in with, say, their zinfandel grapes" without making it clear to consumers, she says, but when they acknowledge that so-called natural flavors are mixed in with a known varietal, they're allowed to do it, "even though you have no idea what you're drinking."

9 "WINE IS A ROTTEN INVESTMENT."

As with all limited commodities, the value of a wine grows when demand exceeds availability. That is the idea behind investing in wine futures, fancy financial instruments that allow you to buy wine years before it is produced, at a discounted price. Then, the theory goes, you will wind up with a case of wine poised to grow in value as it ages to perfection.

Really, though, wine futures are only great to buy if you want the wine to drink, since they guarantee you an allotment of the wine in question. As an investment, "it's pretty risky," acknowledges Jake Sobotka, a financial adviser for Joshua

315

Tree Imports in Duarte, Calif., who is also an avid wine collector and a frequent purchaser of wine futures—though only for vintages that he knows he'll want to drink. "Yes, 1990 was a great year for Bordeaux, and you could have made a 50 percent return on your investment," he says. "But if you bought Bordeaux futures for 1992, '93, '94, '97, or '98, you actually overpaid in relation to what the wine sold for when it was released."

10 *"IGNORE THE REVIEWS I'M TOUTING."*

Wine reviewers are everywhere, in upscale food magazines, in every newspaper, and on the Web. Merchants, of course, use this to their advantage, scouring the wide field of critics to find reviews that will best help them to promote the wines they most want to sell. But don't be fooled. Those in the food and wine industry put limited stock in most of the reviews, and you should do the same. Only one reviewer is regarded as being completely beyond reproach and stunningly consistent: Robert Parker, whose bimonthly newsletter accepts no advertising. "Robert M. Parker is the god," says Anthony Bourdain.

Upon hearing this adulation, Parker—who is partial to wines that are young and unctuous—points out that he was the first wine critic to "depart from the gravy train of being sponsored for trips and getting [four-star] treatment from the wineries. I pay my own way." Parker also believes that his signature method of giving wines a numerical score (out of 100 points) has created a level of accountability for reviewers who use it. "If you give a wine a 90," he says, "well, it better be a damned good wine."

THINGS TO DO

● **It pays to be adventurous**—some of the best bargains are little-known foreign wines. Don't be afraid to ask your local wine merchant for off-the-radar suggestions.

● **Want to visit some wineries** but don't know where to start? You can plan your own tour of U.S. wineries using *www.wines andtimes.com.*

● **Don't be shy about choosing** the least-expensive bottle of wine at an expensive restaurant—top-tier eateries pride themselves on their wine selections at every price point.

● **Before visiting any winery,** always check in advance to see if you need a reservation.

Gourmet Grocer

1 "OUR DELECTABLES ARE AS SUSCEPTIBLE TO GERMS AS THE SUPERMARKET STUFF."

Stroll through your local gourmet shop, and you'll likely be taken in by the opulent displays: There are baguettes for the grabbing, delicious free samples all over the place, and a salad bar overflowing with fresh fruits and vegetables. It's the kind of stuff you can't wait to taste. Michael Doyle, director of the Center for Food Safety and Quality Enhancement at the University of Georgia, suggests self-control. "I personally would not buy any food exposed to handling," he says, pointing out that these visually appealing delectables may carry germs like salmonella and campylobacter jejuni (the leading cause of bacterial diarrhea in the U.S.). Indeed, Doyle practically shudders at the notion of people "taking samples with their fingers."

Those richly stocked salad bars are probably the worst offenders. Warm temperatures and unsterile prepping conditions can transform a Greek salad into a stomach-turning petri dish. "With some of these salad-bar items, after they're cut, the diseased organisms can grow and increase to dangerous levels," says Joseph Frank, a colleague of Doyle's at the University of Georgia. Even at the poshest gourmet emporiums, he adds, "there are no disease-free guarantees."

And don't count on the stores to do their part. One former gourmet-store employee remembers an ever-changing code, announced over the store's P.A. system, used to warn workers when a health-department inspector entered the premises. "We'd all put on our gloves and make sure the zucchini muffins were wrapped in plastic," she says.

2 "OUR PRICES ARE OFTEN TOUGH TO SWALLOW."

Nobody expects good food to come cheap. But it seems that the gourmet food industry—which was estimated at $59 billion in 2007, a 10 percent increase since 2006, according to market-research firm Packaged Facts—regularly exhibits extreme chutzpah with its pricing policies. Indeed, the comparative cost of items in gourmet stores can be pretty steep. Within a four-block radius of New York City's Union Square, for example, the high-end Garden of Eden Gourmet Market sells a pint of Sharon's Sorbet for around $5.50; at Trader Joe's across the park, it'll cost you more than $3 less. Similarly, a package of four Dr. Praeger's California veggie burgers that's about five bucks at Garden of Eden sells for nearly two dollars less at the Trader. And the list goes on. A spokesperson for Garden of Eden says the store isn't offered wholesale prices that are as low as the consolidated prices offered to big chains. "We bought Sharon's Sorbet wholesale for $2.96 and sell it at about an 85 percent markup," she says. "Dr. Praeger's was $2.61 wholesale and we sell it at about 90 percent markup—but with that comes a very educated and informed staff to help serve customers."

Indeed, the markup at a gourmet prepared-food counter is about the same as at a restaurant. (Raw food costs make up about 30 percent of the ultimate charge.) So what keeps gourmet grocery shoppers coming back? It could be that the much touted "total package" offered at these high-end specialty shops simply "makes shoppers happier," says John Roberts, former president of the National Association for the Specialty Food Trade.

3 "THIS BOTTLED WATER IS ACTUALLY TAP WATER."

Some of the hottest items in any fancy food store are the beautifully packaged bottled waters. In fact, Americans spent some $4.2 billion in 2007 to ensure that they were drinking only the purest. But despite the pleasing presentation, "a lot of bottled water is no better than tap water," explains Adrianna Quintero-Somaini, a senior attorney with the Natural Resources Defense Council in San Francisco.

Consider Aquafina, which sounds vaguely European and sports a label that depicts a mountain sunrise—never mind that this supposedly upscale beverage is actually bottled by Pepsi. Like many

bottled waters produced in the U.S., Aquafina is no more than "purified water" that comes from "municipal sources." Translation: tap water. Which isn't necessarily a bad thing; it's just not worth paying extra for. (A spokesperson for Pepsi says that Aquafina "uses state-of-the-art purification systems, including reverse osmosis and carbon filtration.")

Far more disturbing is the fact that some bottled waters are less healthy than what pours into your sink for free—even potentially dangerous. "Tap water is regulated by the EPA; a lot of bottled water is not," notes Somaini, whose agency spent three years testing more than 100 brands of bottled water. Some were found to contain fecal contamination and even arsenic. And unlike with other kinds of food hazards, those associated with bottled water tend to be hard to detect. "The water can taste fine," says Somaini, "and still be contaminated."

4 "ORGANIC FOOD IS A CRAPSHOOT."

Quick: What's the definition of organic? In many gourmet grocery stores, it might seem like it's nothing more than a synonym for "expensive." Indeed, shoppers generally pay a premium of 30 to 50 percent for the label—which usually means that the farm of origin has been free of pesticides and fertilizers for three years—even though there are few assurances of what you're getting.

Part of the problem is that requirements for being "organic" are far from clear. Even after the U.S. Department of Agriculture set standards in 2002, the labeling is still quite confusing to consumers. In part, that's because even with the standard, the business is not exactly strictly regulated nationwide. "Some farmers are not up to standards and will bounce from [organic] certifier to certifier," says Dennis Blank, editor of *Organic Business News* in Orlando, Fla. As a result, fraud abounds. In one such case, Blank recalls, two executives at a now-defunct Minnesota company called Glacial Ridge Foods pleaded guilty to felonious theft by swindle for deliberately mislabeling nonorganic grains and beans as organic. Unfortunately, Blank says, such practices are not uncommon.

5 "BUYING THE BEST ISN'T ALWAYS WHAT'S BEST."

Many gourmet stores pride themselves on their highest-quality products. But few will tell you that their best and most expensive items are not necessary—indeed, they're sometimes inappropriate—for everyday use. Consider olive oil. The finest can run more than a dollar an ounce, but it's meant to be used only sparingly. "You don't need extra virgin olive oil to fry fish," says Christopher Pappas, president of Dairyland, a distributor of gourmet foods, pointing out that good canola oil—which is far cheaper—actually has a higher burning point and is better suited for the job. "Save the extra virgin to use as a flavor enhancer," he advises. Same goes for high-quality Parmesan cheese. "If you are blending it with four other cheeses or using it to make ravioli, you don't need a $10-per-pound aged cheese," explains Pappas—who makes his living selling this stuff.

But that won't stop grocers from encouraging showy foodies to spend too much on high-end products, only to mix with other ingredients. Case in point: caviar. "Combining Russian caviar with condiments"—such as crème fraîche, hard-boiled eggs, and onions—"is like combining Dr. Pepper with Cognac," insists Mats Engstrom, co-owner of the San Francisco-based distributor Tsar Nicoulai Caviar. What's the difference? "We charge $35 for an ounce of [domestic] paddlefish roe, and the [Russian] sevruga costs $240 an ounce," Engstrom says.

6 "LOOKS CAN BE DECEIVING."

Sure, gourmet food stores make their products look great. But does that mean they'll also taste better? Not necessarily. Consider, for example, "gourmet meat," which is generally marketed as "cryogenically aged." (The term comes from "Cryovac," which is the brand of plastic often used to vacuum-pack the beef.) "This basically means that it was left in its box and wrapping for a week, but not aged the way they do it in a restaurant," says Mark Oppenheimer, a former meat merchant. "It won't taste the same." Ironically, though, it will probably look more appealing. "Many people look at the cryogenically aged meat and think it's a better steak because it looks juicy," Oppenheimer explains. "But once it's cooked and on the plate, this will not be the case."

Cheese, too, can be made to look and smell much tastier than it is. Just about all cheese merchants employ a process called "cheese cleaning," in which the moldy parts are skillfully shaved away in order to maintain the quality and visual appeal. (Hey, cheese is all mold anyway.) But some unscrupulous retailers do it to make fast-fading cheese look fresh. "Let's say that a merchant is buying a blue cheese for $2 a pound that once wholesaled for $6 a pound. By that point, its rind may be slimy, and the cheese might smell too strong," says Roger Soudah, owner of Say Cheese in San Francisco. Some merchants will "cut off the surface of the cheese's exposed sides, and it will look and smell fine for that day," Soudah says. But not much longer than that. "Two days later, well, you'll figure that you didn't eat it quickly enough," he says. A rule of thumb for buying cheese: Soft cheeses go bad more quickly, so buy smaller amounts more frequently. Hard cheeses have a much longer shelf life, so feel free to buy it in larger quantities.

7 "MOM AND POP ARE GOING CORPORATE."

The gourmet food business has become so lucrative that big corporations naturally have moved in on the action. General Mills, for example, acquired organically oriented Small Planet Foods. Even Balducci's, the venerable New York gourmet shop, was bought by private-equity firm Bear Stearns Merchant Banking. So what's the problem? "It's not possible to create a great gourmet store in a corporate framework," says Ed Levine, author of *New York Eats*, a guide to New York City's best markets. "It's not about efficiency or about serving a customer base."

In practice, what this trend means is that less and less food is being cooked in gourmet stores' back kitchens and served up immediately to shoppers. "The big companies feel that they can do [gourmet] just as well as the independent stores, but they won't cook on the premises," gripes Joe Doria, Jr., owner of Grace's Marketplace on the Upper East Side of Manhattan. "You get guys coming in with shirts and ties and wanting to run the store from an office. They don't cook the food; they just want to see so much percentage of profit."

8 "FREE-RANGE CHICKEN ISN'T ALL THAT."

Rocco DiSpirito, executive chef and owner of Union Pacific in New York, has always believed that the organic free-range poultry he serves in his restaurant is worth its high price. And he's not alone: Customers of gourmet food stores regularly pay two to three times as much for free-range birds as they would for a regular supermarket chicken, based on the premise that such high-end poultry is healthier and, more important, better-tasting. So imagine DiSpirito's shock when, in a blind taste test, he actually chose the supermarket chicken over the free-range. "I was surprised that it tasted as good as it did," admits the chef. "It goes to show that you can buy a good supermarket chicken."

Many experts agree that the "free-range" distinction is essentially meaningless. "I don't think free-range chickens are better than regular chickens," says Stanley Bailey, who worked as a researcher and microbiologist specializing in poultry for the USDA research service. Bailey correctly defines a free-range chicken as one "that has an option of going outside." What's more, Bailey notes, free-range chickens—even the organic kind—are probably no healthier than regular chickens. "The antibiotics [added to nonorganic chickens' feed] are at such a very small level, and for the most part they are a class of antibiotics not used in humans," he says. "They should not be harmful."

9 *"OUR CAVIAR IS COUNTERFEIT."*

Mark Russ Federman knew that trouble was brewing when shady-looking guys began offering him suitcases filled with caviar. "After the Soviet government fell, things got wild," says Federman, proprietor of Manhattan's venerable gourmet grocer Russ & Daughters. "People were flooding the market with inferior caviar."

In fact, caviar thieves have devised a particularly cunning rip-off: selling fish eggs harvested from American paddlefish as Russian caviar. (An undiscriminating palate can't tell the difference, though paddlefish is a fraction of the price.) The proprietors of Rockville, Md., importer U.S. Caviar & Caviar were indicted for allegedly wholesaling the mislabeled product to gourmet grocers. (Philip L. Kellogg, an attorney representing the company, declined to comment.)

Federman blames his fellow retailers for allowing something like this to happen: "Many purveyors don't know what they are buying," he says. "And a caviar shortage makes it worthwhile for people to do what they can get away with. It's an equation set up for scams."

> Free-range chickens—even the organic kind—are probably no healthier than regular chickens.

10 *"LIFE IS CRUEL. SO ARE WE."*

No gourmet grocer worth his imported sea salt would be caught without caviar, foie gras, and succulently tender milk-fed veal in stock. But there is nothing appetizing about how the animals are treated in order to yield such delicacies. Consider what it takes to harvest caviar from sturgeon. It's a painful process, notes Bruce G. Friedrich, vice president for People for the Ethical Treatment of Animals. "Massive numbers of sturgeon are pulled out of the water, and their bellies are slit open while they are still alive so the fish eggs can be pulled out," he says.

Over at the Humane Society of the U.S., a livestock specialist voices an oft-mentioned beef about calves that are raised for veal: The animals' muscles are made to atrophy in order to keep their meat tender and white. He also takes issue with the production of foie gras, the duck and goose liver delicacy produced in France, the U.S., and elsewhere. "Ducks and geese are force-fed via 12- to 18-inch tubes down their throats," he says. The tubes, he says, are often attached to pressurized pumps, and the animals are normally fed three times a day for 28 days until the liver swells to 10 times its normal size. In fact, it's the fattened liver that makes it taste so good.

As far as the Humane Society is concerned, "We view the method for producing [foie gras] to be every bit as cruel as, say, kicking a dog," the livestock specialist says. But the processes of producing veal, caviar, and foie gras aren't isolated cruelty problems in industrial agriculture, says Wayne Pacelle, president of the Humane Society. Turkeys, for example, have been genetically manipulated through selective breeding to be obese and heavily muscled to the point that they're incapable of copulating. They also have all manner of hip and leg problems.

THINGS TO DO

● **Buy fresh fruits and vegetables** in season. They'll be much tastier—and cheaper. The Food Network provides an online guide to in-season produce at *www.foodnetwork .com/food/ck_cg_produce_guide*.

● **Try a farmer's market.** There's no middleman, and the food is locally grown and fresh. Visit *www.eatwellguide.org* to find one near you.

● **When shopping at a gourmet** grocery store, you're paying for the expert staff. So don't be afraid to ask questions, let them help you choose products, and use their advice to expand your palate.

● **Gourmet stores often provide samples** and host tasting events. Take advantage of these freebies to experiment and boost your knowledge—but do so with caution. Make sure, for example, that there are toothpicks or disposable forks on hand.

● **If you know what you** want, you'll find gourmet flagships like Dean & Deluca (*www.deandeluca.com*) have fully stocked online stores.

CHAPTER 7

Your Mind & Body

■ Let's face it, life is stressful. And compounding that stress is the constant pressure to make do and keep up through economic good times and bad. So if you choose to spend some of your hard-earned money taking care of yourself, we're here to help.

In this chapter you'll find all the information you need on matters of well-being. If you're a regular at the gym, for example, "10 Things Your Fitness Club Won't Tell You" offers tips on how to get added benefits to an existing membership. If you'd rather get your head together, "10 Things Your Therapist Won't Tell You" will advise you on what kind of therapy to seek and how to find a practitioner of it. We're offering our best advice on attaining better emotional and physical health—after all, you shouldn't have to stress about how to lead a less stressful lifestyle.

10 Things Your
Fitness Club
Won't Tell You

1 *"IF YOU'RE STILL HERE IN APRIL, IT'LL BE A MIRACLE."*

Gym attendance was up 23 percent from 2001 to 2007, to 41.5 million, according to the International Health, Racquet and Sportsclub Association (IHRSA). And most new recruits sign up in January—the busiest month for fitness clubs. That's when well-intentioned souls trying to stick to their New Year's resolutions flood their local gyms, often resulting in long lines at the treadmill, overtaxed gym staff, and towel shortages in the locker room. But it won't be long before the throngs thin; most resolution-makers trip up in the first 90 days, says Alan Marlatt, director of the Addictive Behaviors Research Center at the University of Washington. And indeed, that's what clubs expect. "They bet on it," says Meg Jordan, editor of *American Fitness,* adding that most gyms count on a 20- to 30-percent dropout rate.

In the meantime, there are ways to avoid January overcrowding and make it past the 90-day hump. When selecting a new gym, visit the facility during the time of day you're most likely to attend. If it's crowded, check to see whether waiting lists and time limits on machines are enforced or whether it's a free-for-all.

2 *"DON'T TOUCH ANYTHING— THIS PLACE IS CRAWLING WITH BACTERIA."*

About 80 percent of all infectious disease is transmitted by both direct and indirect contact, says Philip Tierno, director of clinical microbiology at New York University Medical Center and the author of *The Secret Life of Germs.* That makes the gym, with its sweaty bodies in close proximity, a highly conducive environment for catching everything from athlete's foot to the flu.

In swabs of medicine balls, for example, Tierno found samples of community-acquired MRSA—a strain of staph resistant to some antibiotics. "You take your chances," Tierno says. "Anytime you touch a medicine ball or machine, you have to know that your hands are contaminated and should be washed."

What about those spray bottles some gyms provide for wiping down equipment? They may help, Tierno says, but he recommends additional measures, such as wearing long sleeves and pants while working out. Also, bring your own towels, since there's no guarantee that your gym's linens have been bleached or rinsed in clean water. While in the locker room, make sure you wear flip-flops, and avoid sitting nude on any exposed surface.

3 *"WE'RE NOT EQUIPPED TO HANDLE HEALTH EMERGENCIES."*

Almost one third of sudden cardiac arrests outside of homes and hospitals occur in fitness clubs or sports facilities, says Mary Fran Hazinski, a registered nurse and senior science editor at the American Heart Association. Yet most health clubs aren't fully prepared for such crises. That was the case at a 24 Hour Fitness in California, where Nick Pombra, 43, collapsed after running on a treadmill in July 2004. Gym staff tried CPR, but by the time paramedics arrived, it was too late, says Mike Danko, a lawyer for Pombra's family. 24 Hour declined to comment.

While effective CPR can buy time, it won't reset a heart after cardiac arrest. That's where automated external defibrillators, or AEDs, come in. Chances for revival drop as much as 10 percent each minute that passes without proper CPR and defibrillation. But even in states like New York that require gyms to have CPR equipment as well as AEDs and trained personnel in clubs with over 500 members, two thirds surveyed by the attorney general's office in 2005 weren't in compliance. Find out if your club has the right equipment and, equally important, staff trained to use it.

4 *"OUR TRAINERS DON'T KNOW WHAT THEY'RE DOING."*

If you work out at a gym, chances are an on-site personal trainer will try to sell you his or her expertise. And with their Colgate smiles and buff bodies, they must be able to teach you a thing or two about getting into shape, right? Not necessarily.

Trainers need no standard certification, and the credentials some flash require only a quick online course or a fee, says Neal Pire, a fitness-industry consultant and former trainer.

Jonathan Jacobson, a marketing exec with a degenerative disk disease in his lower back, sought out a trainer to design a routine appropriate for his condition. But after following a boxing regimen the trainer recommended, he was left in pain. When his doctor told Jacobson, 35, to stop, the trainer suggested Pilates—which only further aggravated the problem, ending in a slew of medical procedures. "He had certificates and tons of plaques on the wall," Jacobson says. "It's taken about a year to not be in pain every day."

Seek trainers with credentials from respected institutions like the American College of Sports Medicine or the National Strength and Conditioning Association (NSCA)—preferably with some training in sports medicine or phys ed. And consult with your doctor before beginning any fitness regimen. "A doctor will make sure there are no underlying complications and [that] you're ready to engage in physical activity," says Jay Dawes, education director for the NSCA.

5 *"WE WON'T LET YOU QUIT."*

If you think giving up the Ben & Jerry's is tough, try quitting your gym. Trouble canceling membership is one of the top complaints against fitness clubs logged with the Better Business Bureau and states' attorneys general offices. Before Chris Hinkle and his wife moved to North Carolina, they met with the manager at their Gold's Gym in Austin, Tex., to cancel their prepaid membership. They were told a refund check would be in the mail. That was March. After months of unreturned calls, Hinkle contacted the BBB, which also got no answer from Gold's and gave it an unsatisfactory rating. "I was an ecstatic booster of Gold's," Hinkle says. "Now I tell people to never go there." A Gold's spokesperson says the club sends a refund in such cases once it receives proof of a move—documentation Hinkle says the Austin manager didn't ask for in March.

For those paying monthly, calls from collectors or a battered credit score may be the first clue membership was never terminated, says Todd Mark of the Consumer Credit Counseling Service of Greater Atlanta. Follow contract terms to the letter, providing proof of a move or a doctor's note. Create a paper trail, and alert credit agencies about the dispute.

6 "BE SURE TO READ THE FINE PRINT ON OUR CONTRACT."

The devil is in the details, and it's never truer than when it comes to fitness club contracts. Fast-talking reps may offer you a deal you can't refuse, but often that's exactly what you should do. "Sometimes you end up with salespeople trying to make quotas that engage in pressure," says Helen Durkin, head of public policy at IHRSA. Occasionally, this can lead to a glossing over of details. One Bally offer that has elicited complaints on Consumer Affairs' website is a 30-day trial membership with a catch: You must visit the club a minimum of 12 times during the first month to cancel without

penalty; otherwise, you're locked into a multiyear membership. Some consumers complain they did attend the required number of times but that when they decided to cancel, the club had no record of the visits. A Bally spokesperson says the company's policy is to check all members entering the club and record their usage.

Your best defense: Read every word of the contract. Never rely on a suave salesperson's "word" no matter what authority they profess, and don't let anyone pressure you into signing before you're ready—take the contract home and read it overnight.

7 "OUR EQUIPMENT CAN BE DOWNRIGHT DANGEROUS."

Unlike many businesses, fitness clubs do not need a license to operate. Furthermore, although the American College of Sports Medicine and other groups publish guidelines for the industry, they don't have the teeth of the law. "In most cases [the gym] is not a safe place to go because there is little standardization," says Marc Rabinoff, forensic expert and professor of human performance and sport at the Metropolitan State College of Denver.

Take equipment maintenance, for example. Although manufacturers must include instructions with exercise machines, nothing forces gyms to follow them, Rabinoff says. Injuries can result from poorly or improperly maintained equipment, says Cedric Bryant, chief science officer for the American Council on Exercise. Bryant recommends asking to see maintenance and cleaning logs— hallmarks of a good club. Gold's Gym, for one, says it follows manufacturers' maintenance guidance to the letter and replaces equipment every five to seven years. And avoid machines that stick or don't move smoothly.

8 *"EVERYTHING IS NEGOTIABLE."*

Balloons and freebies often signal promotion time at your local gym—most frequently before the holidays and at the start of summer.

Already a member? Jot down these specials and ask for one of them when it comes time to renew your membership. Some gyms will honor the rate months after the posters come down, says Mark, of the Consumer Credit Counseling Service of Greater Atlanta. If you're looking into a new membership, remember that the cheapest deals will likely be those that lock you in for a long time. For example, Bally's flexible plans, including month-to-month memberships, typically cost $5 to $10 a month more than its popular long-term "Value Plan." As for trainers, you might be able to get a break if you decide to share sessions with a friend or two, says Carol Espel, Equinox's national group fitness director.

9 *"IF YOUR WALLET GETS LIFTED, IT'S NOT OUR PROBLEM."*

In 2003, the FBI put out a bulletin about a group of burglars stealing credit cards from lockers of health club members on the East Coast. Since then, there's been no similar FBI bulletin—but that doesn't mean your valuables are safe at the gym. You never know who's lurking around

the locker room while you're sweating away on the elliptical machine. "For so many people, the health club is like a community," says IHRSA spokesperson Brooke Correia. "You feel very comfortable, but there are situations where potential thieves will break into the club and take advantage of that safe atmosphere."

Ben Osbun tried to end 2004 on a healthy note by working out at his local YMCA on New Year's Eve. But the day quickly soured. When the Chicago real estate agent returned to his locker, he found that the padlock had been cut and his cell phone, keys, and wallet were all missing. Only his jacket was left behind; the thieves showed him some mercy since it was December, Osbun says. He adds that the gym staff wasn't particularly surprised by the incident, since petty theft is common in health clubs. Osbun learned his lesson; he now brings very little with him to the gym.

If you do intend to store items in a locker while you're working out, IHRSA recommends using a padlock with a key, which is harder to pick than a combination lock. Good to know—not that it would have helped Osbun any.

10 *"GO AHEAD AND SUE; YOU'LL NEVER WIN."*

Fitness clubs sure do know how to watch their backs, legally speaking. It's nearly impossible to visit a fitness center without signing a waiver that absolves the club of liability—involving everything from malfunctioning machines that cause injury to improper instruction by staff members.

In Michael Stokes's case, it was a defect in the basketball court's floor at his

Kent, Wash., gym that caused ruptured tendons in his knee and shoulder. While a judge found that Stokes may not have known what he was signing, a subsequent Court of Appeals ruling upheld the waiver and dismissed the case, says Mark Davis, a lawyer at Curran Mendoza who represented Stokes.

And that's how it usually goes, since the majority of states' courts tend to side with the gyms on the matter of liability waivers, while only a handful, including those in New York and Virginia, are likely to rule against them. Occasionally, a judge will rule on behalf of plaintiffs in instances of gross negligence, but that bar is set pretty high in some states, such as Washington, Davis says.

Bottom line: Understand that you're taking your health in your own hands when you go to the gym, so you need to watch your back—literally.

THINGS TO DO

● **Ask whether your fitness club** offers a complimentary training session when you sign up for your membership (many do). Though you might get the hard sell on private training sessions, you'll also get to learn how best to use the facilities and equipment your gym offers.

● **For the best results,** work with a seasoned trainer. Ask for credentials from respected organizations like the American College of Sports Medicine or the National Strength and Conditioning Association (NSCA).

● **Not happy with the staff** at your gym? Ask if you can bring in your own trainer. You can find one in your area who has been certified by NSCA at *www.nsca-lift .org/trainers/locator.*

● **Read the fine print.** Know exactly what the provisions of that trial membership are and just how to terminate your membership.

10 Things Your
Personal Trainer
Won't Tell You

1 *"I'M A SPECIALIST—IN MARKETING MYSELF AS A HEALTH EXPERT."*

By 2008 an estimated 91 percent of health clubs offered the services of personal trainers, with some 6.3 million Americans signing up for sessions, up from 4 million in 1998, according to the International Health, Racquet and Sportsclub Association (IHRSA). But the growth fueled competition among trainers, who began offering specialized training in such areas as injury recovery, cardiac rehabilitation, and the condition du jour, diabetes. "There's a real demand for these trainers," says Todd Galati, certification manager for the American Council on Exercise. "More people walking through the door are overweight or diabetic."

And yet not all so-called specialists are properly trained—on the fast-and-loose end of the spectrum, you'll find certification requirements as minimal as a $500 fee and passing an online exam. That worries John Buse, president of medicine and science at the American Diabetes Association, because when exercise isn't done properly, any vision problems and nerve damage in the feet that some diabetics develop could worsen, he says, in extreme cases to the point of blindness or amputation.

2 *"I'LL PUSH YOU TILL YOU COLLAPSE."*

When Richard Thomas of Brooklyn, N.Y., was a trainer at Bally Total Fitness in 2004, he says he witnessed an out-of-shape man in his 40s being worked so hard by a fellow trainer that he practically fainted. "I had to catch him," Thomas says. Sounds extreme, but it's not the only time he says he's seen a trainer push clients too hard to show them how out of shape they are—and thus in need of more personal-training sessions. (Bally Total Fitness declined to comment.)

Given that 37 percent of health club members are beginners, personal trainers are largely catering to the unfit, according to IDEA Health & Fitness Association, a San Diego–based organization for fitness professionals. They're reaching out to seniors as well, since clients 55 years and older constitute one of the fastest-growing segments of gym members, says IDEA's executive director, Kathie Davis. Nonetheless, many trainers are guiding clients with a less-than-gentle hand. "The majority of people that come into the club haven't worked out since their high school gym class," Thomas says. "Then we're told to work them hard. It's dangerous." If you feel your trainer is being too tough, speak up. Remember, you're the boss.

3 "CAUTION: MIGHT NOT WORK WELL WITH KIDS."

One of the biggest trends in fitness today: enrolling Junior in a little one-on-one training. Concerned about their kids' weight and lack of physical activity, parents are increasingly turning to personal trainers at rates of up to $60 an hour. Seventeen percent of personal-training clients—over 1 million total—were between the ages of 6 and 17 in 2006, says the IHRSA; that's a 20 percent increase from 1998.

This niche is growing because our kids are: Roughly 15 percent of American children are overweight, ranging from a high of 22.8 percent in Washington, D.C., to a low of 8.5 percent in Utah, according to nonprofit Trust for America's Health. But not all health clubs have trainers who work well with kids—or even know how to work them out safely, says Davis. Even a good trainer with the wrong attitude can turn impressionable kids off working out.

Bottom line: Be selective. For starters, ask for a trainer with a background in teaching, coaching, or child development, Davis says. And if your kid is involved in a particular sport, requesting a trainer with a similar background can help develop specific muscles and prevent injuries.

4 "BRING A FEW PALS AND I'LL CHARGE YOU HALF PRICE."

Fees for personal trainers can be pretty steep. Sign up for a session with personal-training superstar Jackie Warner of SkySport&Spa in Beverly Hills, Calif., for example, and it could run you about $400 an hour. But there's a way to save in the neighborhood of 30 to 50 percent if you know what to ask for: More than 70 percent of personal trainers offer group sessions at a discount, according to a recent survey by IDEA. Even Warner has been known to offer reduced prices now and again—about 30 percent—when training two to five clients at once.

Though health clubs don't typically dangle the group option in front of you, most personal trainers will work something out if you ask. After all, it's a win-win situation. For a group of three, for example, the average fee of $60 per hour is reduced by half for each client, while the trainer brings in about 50 percent more than he typically makes in an hour. And it could mean a better workout: "There's a lot to benefit from group camaraderie, as long as you don't need a trainer counting every rep you do," says Richard Cotton, national director of certification for the American College of Sports Medicine.

5 "IF I LET YOU USE THE EQUIPMENT, YOU'LL REALIZE YOU DON'T NEED ME."

Does your trainer steer you away from the abs machine, making you do crunches with a medicine ball instead? Trainers are sometimes told not to spend too much time teaching clients how to use the big equipment for fear that once they get comfortable, they'll want to go it alone. That's why trainers might emphasize coordination exercises and rely on smaller props like stability balls, resistance tubing or bands, and balance tools, the three types of gear most frequently used by

"The best trainers serve clients by helping them become independent exercisers."

trainers. This type of "functional training" helps prep clients for popular recreational activities such as tennis and skiing, as well as basic movements like bending down during household chores. But larger equipment also has its benefits; it can bring speedy results in strength-building and help keep weight off.

"The best trainers serve clients by helping them become independent exercisers," Cotton says. He suggests asking prospective trainers how they'll help you get there. A spokesperson for the National Exercise Trainers Association says it encourages trainers to prove to clients there's more to working out than using big machines, in part because of the benefits of functional training.

6 "I LOVE TO GOSSIP— ABOUT YOU."

Word around the gym is that some trainers are sharing personal information about their clients. "It can be as innocent as a trainer talking to another trainer under the guise of asking for advice," says Gregory Florez, CEO of consulting firm FitAdvisor in Salt Lake City. Not so egregious, perhaps. But with more health clubs requesting medical information, which they often then make available to trainers, some clubs have had to crack down on disclosure: "We have

no tolerance at all for gossip," says a spokesperson for New York Health & Racquet Club, explaining that after a written warning, an employee's job is at stake.

Other health clubs are less stringent. Bally Total Fitness doesn't have a company-wide code of ethics by which trainers must abide, but says it's confident its trainers were adequately informed about general ethics during their individual certification programs. "Unfortunately, our industry does not have the same federal regulation as, say, a psychiatrist that risks losing a license if he shares personal information," Florez explains. Before divulging private health information to your fitness club, ensure that it has a strict privacy policy. And think twice before pouring your heart out to your trainer.

7 "I'M JUST AS QUALIFIED TO TRAIN YOU AS, UM, THAT GUY LIFTING OVER THERE."

The personal-training industry is practically swimming in credentials, with more than 70 certifying organizations. "There's so much controversy over certification because there are just so many of them," Kathie Davis says. But whereas some programs demand a broad-based understanding of human physiology, others require much less from their candidates, according to a spokesperson for IHRSA. There's no standardized testing in the industry; applicants often can get away with taking either a weekend course or even just an online exam before calling themselves personal trainers.

How to know what you're getting? Find a list of programs with third-party accreditation from the National Commission for Certifying Agencies at *www.noca.org,* an umbrella group that weeds out lesser training programs. Industry experts point to the American College of Sports Medicine and the National Strength and Conditioning Association as two of the most reputable organizations.

8 *"JUST BECAUSE I'M MORE EXPENSIVE DOESN'T MEAN YOU'LL GET A BETTER WORKOUT."*

Personal trainers charge more depending on their level of experience and how booked up they are, and any fees you pay them are obviously an investment in your health. Nonetheless, a more expensive trainer won't necessarily yield better results. "At the end of the day, it's about behavioral change," fitness consultant Florez says. So safety aside, finding someone who personally motivates you and with whom you click is most important—and that person may not be a top-dollar seasoned veteran. "If he can't motivate you based on your personality style, you're throwing money away," Florez says.

To find the right match, ask for a trial workout session with a trainer before you hire one. Florez specifically recommends a preliminary consultation, which should include no exercise but rather an in-depth conversation about your personality and goals. To evaluate a prospective trainer's ability to produce results, ask questions like, "Have you worked with someone like me before and been successful?" If the answer is yes, request a recommendation from that person.

9 *"ONCE I GET MY BIG BREAK, I'M OUTTA HERE."*

When Patrick Wickman, a scientist for an engineering firm in New York City, signed up for eight sessions with a personal trainer at $70 a pop, he was excited about the prospect of developing a long-term program. And sure enough, says Wickman, the trainer promised to help him reach his goals—only to disappear after five sessions, at which point, Wickman says, he was passed off to other trainers: "The personal touch evaporated."

The personal-training industry has high rates of employee turnover, partially because of low salaries, which average $32,900 for independent trainers and $35,000 for those employed by a health club, according to IDEA. Plus, the flexible nature of the gig attracts those who want to work part-time while following other pursuits, like acting or dance. Unfortunately for you, when your right-hand man lands a call-back audition that conflicts with your next appointment, you're the one stuck rescheduling or settling for a sub. To help avoid future disappointment, ask about your prospective trainer's intentions and long-term career goals, especially if you're interested in purchasing a bigger package of sessions.

10 *"I'M NO NUTRITIONIST, BUT THAT WON'T STOP ME FROM TELLING YOU WHAT TO EAT."*

Personal trainers have been pushing protein powders and meal replacements for years, but now many are playing nutritionist as well. "There's no evidence that nutritional advice or any of these health products are beneficial—or at all necessary," says Ann Albright, dietitian and president of health care and education for the American Diabetes Association. "It's just an income generator, a way to push products."

Not only that, but if you're facing certain health issues, nutritional advice given by trainers can sometimes do more harm than good. "Nutritional supplements, when mixed with other medication and strenuous exercise, can result in injury or even death," says a spokesperson for the American Council on Exercise. Take one of the country's growing epidemics—diabetes. For those suffering from it, "it's crucial that your health care provider knows you're taking nutritional supplements, because it can be dangerous," Albright says.

Buyer, beware: Before agreeing to alter or supplement your diet based on a trainer's recommendations, ask lots of questions, and keep your doctor in the loop, Albright advises. The best personal trainers don't pretend to be health professionals, but they are happy to facilitate an open channel of communication between a client and a health care provider if the situation calls for it, says a spokesperson for New York Health & Racquet Club.

THINGS TO KNOW

You've picked a certified trainer who shares your interests and will motivate you. Diane Vives, a personal trainer in Austin, Tex., and secretary/treasurer of the National Strength and Conditioning Association, has some tips:

● **Your trainer is only as good** as the time you spend doing your own work outside of the session; two or three hours a week with your trainer alone is not going to get you results.

● **You need to communicate** with your trainer and come to an agreement about what your comfort level is. People move at different paces.

● **If you're investing in a trainer,** then you have to invest the time in good nutrition and making lifestyle changes, too.

● **Your workout plan should be** very goal-specific and individualized. It's important to have a short-term and long-term plan.

● **Be engaged and willing** to ask why you're doing what you're doing.

10 Things Your
Yoga Instructor
Won't Tell You

1 *"I JUST STARTED DOING YOGA MYSELF!"*

Yoga is booming: For proof, you needn't look any further than your health club, your cable-TV schedule, or even conventional retailers like Target and Walgreens, where yoga mats and DVDs now share shelf space with household sundries. According to a Harris Poll in 2006, some 16.5 million Americans were practicing yoga—an increase of 5.6 percent from the year before.

The problem is that there's no real standard for how much teacher training is required of instructors, so almost anyone can lead a yoga class. Yes, there are plenty of certification programs around, but they run the gamut from thorough training—like that offered at the Advanced Studies Program at the Yoga Room in Berkeley, Calif., which requires 500 hours of classwork covering such subjects as philosophy and anatomy—to mere weekend workshops.

How, then, to avoid un- or underqualified instructors? Check with the Yoga Alliance, a consortium of yoga schools based in Reading, Pa. (*www.yogaalliance .org*). Although joining the group is voluntary and many perfectly good teachers haven't signed up for its instructor registry, you can check to see if yours has at least attended a YA-approved program, which must require a minimum of 200 hours of teacher training.

2 *"SURE, WE HAVE MATS YOU CAN BORROW—HOW ABOUT A CASE OF ATHLETE'S FOOT, TOO?"*

You've probably seen yoga die-hards heading to class, their telltale yoga-mat bags slung over one shoulder. Yet many studios lend or rent mats to their students, often charging a nominal fee of $1 to $2, so is lugging around your own really necessary? *Absolutely.* "The one thing I'd tell new yoga students is always bring your own mat," says Tim Cowen, a yoga instructor in San Francisco. "Never use the ones at the studio." Even though some facilities do try to wash or disinfect their mats regularly, Cowen says, "I can honestly tell you that most mats don't get sprayed on both sides."

If that's not warning enough, consider Bikram yoga, a popular version that's performed in 105-degree classrooms; the heat is designed to allow muscles and ligaments to relax as much as possible and the body to sweat out toxins. "Sure, it's supposed to be a dry heat," Cowen says, "but with 30 people sweating for 90 minutes? The room's a petri dish."

Our advice: Spend the $20 on your own mat—or go without. The California Yoga Center in Palo Alto, Calif., uses mats only for seated poses, headstands, shoulder stands, and some back bends; all standing poses are performed on wooden floors that get mopped before each class.

3 "YOU'RE NOT READY FOR THIS CLASS..."

A few years ago Kim Rutenberg and her husband began attending classes at Jivamukti Yoga Center, a New York City studio popular with celebrities. They started out in a beginner's class and after a month decided to try a more advanced class. They quickly found they were underprepared. "You go immediately into headstand and some other really tough poses, and we couldn't do a lot of them," says Rutenberg, a marketing executive. The couple didn't get hurt, but no one warned them about the degree of difficulty, she says. (The cofounders of Jivamukti insist the studio recommends that beginning students complete at least three months of its basics program before taking more advanced classes.)

Yoga classes tend to be rated by level of expertise—typically beginner, intermediate, and advanced. But if you say you're ready for an advanced class, chances are no one at the sign-in desk will question you. The best thing to do, says yoga instructor Rickie Milmoe, is "Call the studio ahead of time and say how much yoga [you've] done and ask them which class is most appropriate. Don't try to guess." And be honest about your abilities. After all, you won't learn much if you're in over your head and become too discouraged to continue.

4 "...AND YOU COULD REALLY HURT YOURSELF."

Some yoga poses are universally acknowledged to be risky—in particular, inversions such as shoulder stands and headstands. Since they cause blood to rush to the head and can raise blood pressure, these poses are potentially dangerous for anyone being treated for glaucoma or chronic headaches, or anyone who's recently had a stroke; they're also not recommended for anyone who's more than 30 pounds overweight, since they compress the vertebrae in the neck. Good yoga instructors will caution a class before going into inversions and will keep a careful eye out for anyone doing the pose improperly.

But not every instructor is that careful. Realtor Oonagh Kavanagh was surprised when she switched from a yoga studio in San Francisco that did provide individual attention to each student doing inversions to another, where her new instructors didn't watch her at all. "It was just, 'Up you go!'" Kavanagh says. But it's not always a matter of supervision—often it's your own enthusiasm and ego you need to watch out for. Donna Rich, a psychotherapist in Austin, Tex., recently pushed herself into a hamstring stretch she wasn't ready for and ended up tearing some connective tissue in her foot. "Wanting to show off is dangerous," she says.

5 "I'M JUST HERE TO GET LUCKY."

While many gyms, training schools, and yoga teachers' associations frown on liaisons between instructors and students, with all that bared skin and limber bodies, it's no surprise that this rule sometimes gets broken. It's not always a big deal, but on occasion these matside flirtations have been known to erupt into full-blown sexual scandals. One of the most egregious happened back in 1994 at the Kripalu Center, a well-known yoga retreat in Massachusetts' Berkshires, after its charismatic guru Amrit Desai—who both preached and claimed to practice celibacy—admitted to having slept with students. Desai was ejected and the ashram's reputation tainted.

Serious stuff, but even today many yoga teachers haven't learned that lesson, making some studios as rife with drama as a nighttime soap opera. One New York City woman tells of a recent flirtation with her female yoga teacher that turned into a full-blown affair. She soon found out the instructor was simultaneously involved with two other women at the same studio—one a student and the other another teacher. The woman ended the relationship and warned friends to avoid the instructor. If you suspect inappropriate attentions are being directed at you, you have every right to protest or to find another class.

6 "YOUR GYM IS A TERRIBLE PLACE TO DO YOGA."

Not surprisingly, gyms have jumped on the yoga bandwagon: As of 2006, 66 percent of all U.S. fitness clubs had yoga on their class schedule. But how seriously they take it is another matter. Edward Vilga, a private yoga instructor, once taught at a popular gym. "One day, while my class was in savasana"—a stone-silent, meditative final rest period—"someone came in and started doing leg lifts in the

corner." Vilga asked the intruder to leave, but he says the club's management didn't back him up.

Although most gyms try to hire good teachers, they often don't provide a yoga-friendly environment to go with them. Whereas many dedicated yoga studios discourage arrivals that are more than a minute or two late, at some gyms, Vilga says, "students drop into a class like it's a cocktail party." What's worse, those who roll in late aren't warmed up and often miss critical instructions. Karyn Taylor, a yoga student in Los Angeles, doesn't mind the chaos one bit. She says that blocking out the clanging weights and other distractions at her gym has become an essential part of her practice. "Yoga studios can be sort of surreal," Taylor says. "Give me a real experience, and let me see if I can calm my mind within it." Try yoga both at your gym and at a studio; in the end, it's all about what works for you.

7 "YOU DON'T HAVE TO LET ME TOUCH YOU."

If you have yet to attend your first yoga class, let us be the first to alert you to what otherwise will be something of a surprise: Not only will the teacher give you verbal instructions, he or she will probably want to adjust you manually. In other words, while your bum is raised in the air during the ubiquitous "downward-facing dog" pose, you may suddenly notice a pair of hands on you that weren't there before.

What you *should* feel is a gentle correction or even just a calming touch—according to Yoga Alliance's former president Hansa Knox, adjustments should never try to force you into the perfect version of the pose. Instead, they should help you discover what's right for your individual body. Furthermore, a thoughtful teacher should always tell you that he's going to touch you—and should never do so inappropriately. Not your cup of tea? If you don't want to be touched at all, it's fine to say so, says Knox. "You're always the boss."

8 "YOGA ISN'T A CURE-ALL."

Several recent mainstream medical studies have shown that yoga can help alleviate everything from chronic back pain to asthma. One study even found that people with coronary heart disease who do yoga have fewer angina episodes. But yoga doesn't have all-healing powers, as some high-profile yoga proponents have implied. Bikram Choudhury, for instance, displays prominently on his website testimonials from students who claim his brand of yoga has helped alleviate symptoms of everything from rheumatoid arthritis to anorexia and bulimia.

While yogic tradition has long held that certain poses relieve certain ailments—seated forward bend for sinusitis or headstand for insomnia, for example—not all such claims are supported by hard evidence. "What we do say is that yoga's primary effect is to bring all the body's systems into balance," says Trisha Lamb, former associate director of the International Association of Yoga Therapists in Prescott, Ariz. "Someone with cancer may be helped by yoga, but you should not assume yoga will cure cancer."

Nor will it make you look like Angelina Jolie. Exercise of any kind can increase muscle tone and help you lose weight, but there are some things only good genes—or plastic surgery—can give you.

9 "I TEACH ONLY ONE KIND OF YOGA—AND IT'S NOT THE ONE FOR YOU."

There are dozens of different types of yoga, among them Integral, which include lots of chanting and prayer but minimal physical activity; fast-paced "flow" classes; Iyengar, which emphasizes the alignment of the body and uses props including straps and wood blocks to help students into positions; and hot and sweaty Bikram yoga, which consists of 26 poses done in a room heated to 105 degrees. Which kind is right for you? It depends on what you're looking for—relaxation, say, or a rigorous physical workout.

Trying different classes is the best way to determine the type of yoga that best suits your goals and abilities. Even more important than what kind of practice you choose, though, is how much the teacher inspires you. Yoga instructors have dramatically different styles—some are as authoritative as gym coaches, while others are more touchy-feely. One class with a teacher who lights incense and chants about world peace, for example, might turn you off to the practice altogether. "Different people are drawn to different philosophies of teaching," says Larry Hatlett, director of the California Yoga Center of Palo Alto. The best thing to do is to sample a few classes and listen to your instincts, says Nina Zolotow, a writer and teacher in Berkeley, Calif. "If you look forward to seeing your teacher and to going to class," she says, "you can't lose."

10 *"A LITTLE CLASS TIME GOES A LONG WAY."*

Attending class regularly will keep you motivated and inspired—and regular instruction will help you learn the proper way to hold poses, especially if you are new to yoga. But one of its biggest benefits is its portability: As long as you have a flat surface and enough room to move, you can do yoga almost anywhere.

Indeed, the best instructors will encourage you to establish a home practice—and with fees approaching $20 per class at some studios, you can save a bundle. In his book *Moving Toward Balance,* yoga expert Rodney Yee lays out an eight-week program carefully designed to keep you working happily at home. "For most people, the biggest stumbling block to doing yoga at home is the fear that you're not doing it right," says Zolotow, the Berkeley writer. For the best results, she says, yoga students seeking to practice at home should "listen to your body and use your common sense about what you're capable of."

THINGS TO DO

- **Talk to your instructor and doctor** about any health problems you have before starting yoga. Some conditions may prevent you from fully participating in a class, while others may require simple modifications of moves and poses.

- **Beginners should stick to loose,** modest clothing that allows for easy movement. Don't bother investing in expensive trendy sportswear designed for yoga until you're sure you're going to stick with it.

- **Cultivating a practice at home** between lessons will help you get the most out of yoga. Ask your instructor what you can do outside of class to improve and build on your work.

- **Push yourself, but don't hurt** yourself. Ask instructors which classes are suited to your skill level, and build up to those that may be too difficult at first.

10 Things the
Weight-Loss Industry
Won't Tell You

1 *"YOUR WALLET'S GONNA SHRINK, TOO."*

Losing weight can be tough, as anyone who has ever tried to trim a few inches from their waistline can tell you. So it's no wonder that so many people seek help—often in the form of special regimens or dietary supplements—from a thriving weight-loss industry that has built up around the battle of the bulge. Indeed, according to the most recent figures, Americans spent $58 billion in 2007 trying to slim down. And with nearly two thirds of the population categorized as overweight or obese, the demand remains even in tough economic times. But where there is demand, there are also less-than-scrupulous marketers seeking to make a buck from desperate dieters.

Several New Yorkers found that out when they joined LA Weight Loss Centers, lured by television and newspaper ads promising that dieters could join for "only $7 per week." The reality: Since it wasn't possible to pay as you go, customers had to fork over a yearly fee of $376 in advance. On top of that, they were expected to buy nutrition bars for as much as $28 a week. The New York Attorney General's office investigated and found that the total cost of the program exceeded $800 a year—or more than $15 a week, over twice the price

advertised. After revising its contracts to fully disclose the program's costs, LA Weight Loss agreed to pay a $110,000 fine to settle false-advertising charges.

2 *"WE'RE BIG FAT LIARS."*

Janet Makinen was listening to a Tampa radio station when she heard an ad for Body Solutions with the tempting come-on: "Lose weight while you sleep." Wanting to shed a few pounds, Makinen ordered a bottle of Body Solutions for $48. It sounded simple: Swallow a tablespoon of the fruity liquid before bed (and at least three hours after your last meal), and in a matter of weeks you'll see results. What happened? After two and a half months, Makinen had *gained* six pounds—and was out almost $150. She filed suit in Pasco County, Fla., against Mark Nutritionals—the maker of Body Solutions—alleging false advertising. The company denies the charges, but it has since dropped the slogan "Lose weight while you sleep" from its promotions—and now stresses exercise.

The fact is that most claims made by weight-loss programs are false or misleading. According to the Federal Trade Commission's most recent study of weight-loss ads, published in 2002,

55 percent strain credibility by making such claims as "works three times faster than fasting itself," or "lose up to 2 pounds daily." Says Richard Cleland, an assistant director at the FTC: "The ads are filled with testimonials about amounts of weight that are just physiologically impossible for a person to lose. You just don't lose 30 pounds in 30 days." In fact, the standard disclaimer "results not typical" is one of the few claims that are actually true. "[Weight-loss marketers] highlight the real 'success' stories of those that are atypical, highly motivated, and doing more than what they say they are doing," says a spokesperson for the American Dietetic Association. "Mostly, [the programs] just don't work."

3 "QUALIFICATIONS? HERE ARE MY BEFORE-AND-AFTER PHOTOS."

Although shedding pounds should be motivated by the desire for health and well-being more than the quest for dropping dress sizes, don't expect your local weight-loss center to be staffed with certified nutritionists—as Janine White found out. Looking to lose 80 pounds, White enrolled at a Jenny Craig in Tempe, Ariz. But when White first met her counselor and asked about her qualifications, the counselor did nothing more than show White a photo of how she'd looked before trying the Jenny Craig program herself. Three days later White canceled her membership, complaining that she didn't want to make lifestyle changes that could affect her health without more-credentialed advice. "I was disappointed that the counselors were not medical professionals," she says.

A spokesperson for Jenny Craig says the company does use former clients as counselors, but that they must pass an initial 60 hours of training then take follow-up classes in nutrition, motivation, and stress management. She emphasizes that the program's counselors, especially the 60 percent who were former clients, strive to "pass the inspiration on to others."

4 "OUR DIET ISN'T AS EASY AS WE MAKE IT LOOK."

Despite the ever-expanding market of how-to books, exercise and meal-replacement programs, herbal supplements, and self-help websites all guaranteeing quick and effortless results, losing weight is almost never easy. And for all their promises, these products and regimens often fail to live up to the hype. According to a study published in 2005 by two professors at the University of Pennsylvania, commercialized weight-loss programs such as LA Weight Loss and Jenny Craig demonstrated no scientific proof of being effective. Of the nine commercial programs examined, only Weight Watchers demonstrated effective results, "a mean loss of approximately 5 percent of initial weight," according to the study.

Thomas Wadden, director of Penn's Weight and Eating Disorders center and lead author of the study, explains that weight-loss programs almost never keep track of participants to see how much weight they're actually losing or, just as important, how long they keep it off. Out of the 108 different weight-loss regimens—either published by individual companies or presented in medical journals between 1966 and 2003—that Wadden and his colleagues assessed, only

10 met the study's minimum criteria by including a commitment of 12 weeks or more and some kind of assessment process over the course of one year. Furthermore, most studies tracked only participants who completed the program, making the outcomes best-case scenarios. Bottom line: Most weight-loss programs offer no verifiable proof of success.

5 "OUR 'MAGIC PILLS' OFTEN HAVE LESS THAN MAGIC RESULTS ..."

Fortunately, one of the most dangerous and widely available weight-loss supplements, ephedrine, is no longer on the market. This Chinese herb—also known as ma huang—was banned by the Food and Drug Administration in April 2004 after causing more than 100 deaths between 1993 and 2000, as well as more than 900 adverse reactions.

*Un*fortunately, the latest thing in weight-loss supplements, Alli—although FDA-approved and deemed safe—comes with a slew of bizarre side effects, many of them more embarrassing than harmful. The way it works: Alli uses an active ingredient called orlistat to block about 25 percent of the fat you eat, cutting your calorie intake and thus promoting weight loss. The problem is that the blocked fat, which is never absorbed by the body, can get expelled in strange and noxious ways, including gas accompanied by an oily discharge and frequent or loose stools. The maker of the pill, Glaxo, offers this helpful suggestion on its website Myalli.com: "It's probably a smart idea to wear dark pants, and bring a change of clothes with you to work." (You read that right.) Any way to

avoid the scatalogical unpleasantries and still benefit from the pill? Without a trace of irony, Myalli.com goes on to explain that lowering calorie intake can also lower side effects—not to mention alleviate your need for the pill in the first place.

6 "... AND SOME ARE DOWNRIGHT DANGEROUS."

With the exception of Alli, today's over-the-counter diet pills come under the category of "dietary supplements," meaning they're not technically drugs and therefore don't need to be proven safe before they reach the marketplace. It should come as no surprise, then, that the effectiveness of most of these so-called diet pills is questionable at best. But what you might not know is that the side effects can be serious, ranging from dizziness to high blood pressure, heart palpitations, even heart attacks.

How do such potentially dangerous products end up on the market in the first place? Manufacturers don't have to register with the Food and Drug Administration or get approval before they sell supplements. Instead, the burden is on the FDA to take action against a manufacturer *after* its product has been sold, consumed, and proven unsafe.

7 "WELCOME TO FAT CAMP, KID. GET READY TO STARVE."

Consider yourself lucky if you've never gotten razzed with "fatty fatty two-by-four, can't get through the kitchen door!" Lots of overweight kids can't say that, though—and their numbers are multiplying. The National Center for Health Statistics reports that about 18 percent of children ages 6 through 19 are overweight, or triple the percentage from 1980.

For kids who won't lay off the Big Macs, more parents are turning to camps that specialize in trimming down chubby children with regimented menus and exercise programs. Sounds promising— just beware: "There are camps that are like boot camps," says Melinda Sothern, coauthor of *Trim Kids* and director of pediatric obesity research at Louisiana State University. "The trainers operate from the 'no pain, no gain' mentality." Even when weight-loss camp turns out to be a positive experience, Sothern warns of another problem—what awaits these kids when they get home. Without family participation, campers often return to the same conditions that contributed to their weight problem in the first place.

8 "SURE, THIS SURGERY WILL MAKE YOU THIN— IF IT DOESN'T KILL YOU."

The number of weight-loss surgeries, including gastric bypass—which reduces the size of a patient's stomach and reroutes part of the intestine so that fewer calories are absorbed—is growing at a rapid pace. In 2007 an estimated 205,000 bariatric surgeries were performed, up from an estimated 177,600 in 2006. Unfortunately, these procedures can be dangerous: According to the American Society for Bariatric Surgery, the mortality rate for gastric bypass is 5 in every 1,000 patients. There are also a number of scary complications to be considered, including malnutrition, abdominal infection, and gallstones.

It's one thing when adults struggling with obesity opt for this type of surgery; it's another matter entirely when overweight teenagers want to go under the knife. In an editorial in the medical journal *Pediatrics,* Sue Y. S. Kimm, a professor in the department of family medicine at the University of Pittsburgh, expressed concern that physicians are looking to gastric bypass as an option for young patients. "My major concern is not so much the immediate post-op complications but the long-term complications," Kimm says. She points out that the surgery is known to limit calcium absorption by the body; to perform gastric bypass when the bones are still forming raises questions that have not been fully studied.

9 "FORGET 'LITE' FOOD— JUST EAT LESS."

Something doesn't compute: The sale of food products labeled "lite," "lean," and "better for you" keeps on growing, but then so do American waistlines. According to market-research firm Packaged Food, weight-loss food and beverages raked in over $5 billion in revenue in 2005, up from $3.2 billion in 2001. Even in the junk food aisles, sales of alternatives to high-calorie snacks continue to climb.

So what gives? For one thing, some products aren't telling the whole truth about their ingredients. The Atkins program, for example, which was built on the idea of limiting carbohydrates, upset many of its followers when it was discovered that its proprietary diet products contained more carbohydrates than the labels indicated. (Subsequently, Atkins Nutritionals filed for bankruptcy in August 2005, all but pulling the stops on that diet fad.)

Another problem is misinformation about the science of weight loss. For example, reduced-fat versions of products get marketed as diet-worthy—though they often have the same or even more calories than full-fat versions. And when it comes to obesity and the quest to lose weight, says Dr. Robert Eckel of the American Heart Association, "you have to blame it on calories."

10 *"OUR GUARANTEES MEAN NOTHING."*

You're probably familiar with the Ab Energizer, an electronic muscle stimulator belt that promised "six-pack abs without exercise"—thanks to the product's $8 million ad campaign, complete with money-back guarantee. "If you don't lose at least two inches off your waist in the first 30 days," the ubiquitous infomercial touted, "return it for a full refund . . . no questions asked!" Turns out consumers had more than just questions; the Better Business Bureau says it received more than 500 complaints from Ab Energizer customers seeking refunds.

In the world of weight-loss products, the "money-back guarantee" is routine; indeed, the FTC found that 52 percent of the weight-loss ads it studied contained such promises for results. But as Ron Berry, senior vice president of the Council of Better Business Bureaus, cautions, "Guarantees are only as good as the company behind them." Case in point: The FTC sued the various companies involved in marketing the Ab Energizer, alleging that consumers who sought refunds could not reach a customer-service representative. Ab Energizer marketers and certain retailers paid out more than $2 million in damages.

THINGS TO KNOW

A few tips from Dr. Donald Hensrud, a weight-loss expert at the Mayo Clinic in Rochester, Minn.:

● **"Many people have the attitude,** *Oh, no, I've got to go on a diet!* That's negative and restrictive, and it's going to fail. You have to approach this with a positive attitude."

● **"People are in denial,** [thinking] that if they can just get the weight off, then they can somehow keep it off. That isn't the case; it involves permanent lifestyle changes."

● **"Make excuses to get physical activity** during the day. My secretary's office is down the hallway, and I make it a point to walk down there to talk to her, not to e-mail or call."

● **"Eat a healthy snack** before you go out to eat. If there's a buffet at a party, don't stand by it. If it's going to be a really rich meal, be sure to get in some exercise that day to make up for it."

● **"Be aware that sometimes** other people can try to sabotage your efforts. A spouse or friend can be threatened and a little bit insecure that you're doing this to improve yourself."

10 Things Your
Therapist
Won't Tell You

1 "MY TITLE MAY NOT MEAN MUCH."

If you're looking to start therapy, you know that a psychiatrist (an M.D. who can prescribe medication) or a psychologist (typically a Ph.D.) has probably mastered his discipline. But with many other confusingly labeled providers, you can't be so sure.

The fact that licensing requirements for therapists vary by state doesn't help matters. In New York, for example, psychoanalysts and family and marriage counselors in training are required to practice under supervision and pass an examination before launching into the profession. Sounds about right. But since the state recently revamped its regulations, many "experienced" therapists who trained under less-stringent guidelines were "grandfathered" into certification, via submission of an application and without ever taking the exam, according to Ruth Ochroch, past president of the New York State Psychological Association. And still, she says, the current regulations are inadequate. "Some of these people will be a danger to the public because they won't be trained enough," Ochroch says. "The term 'therapist' is no longer legitimate."

Before picking a therapist, investigate the credentials of any candidate. Get referrals from your primary-care doctor, visit the websites of the American Psychological Association (*www.apa.org*) and the American Association for Marriage and Family Therapy (*www.aamft.org*), or check with a district branch of the American Psychiatric Association (listed at *www.psych.org*). To learn your state's requirements or the status of individual therapists, try your state's licensing and medical boards.

2 "MY FEES ARE NEGOTIABLE."

The more education a therapist has, the more he usually charges. In a comparison of fees by industry newsletter *Psychotherapy Finances,* marriage and family therapists charge around $60 to $90 per session; psychologists, $70 to $100 per session; and psychiatrists, $90 to $150 per session. Rates run even higher in pricey areas such as New York City. If you have only partial insurance coverage or pay out-of-pocket, your bill can run pretty high.

What you might not know is that you can request a reduction in the rate. In fact, some practitioners see it as, well, therapeutic. Christine Ryan, a San Francisco editor, was seeing a therapist who disclosed, two years into treatment, that she would be raising rates. The therapist asked Ryan to think about the increased charge and discuss it later. The upshot: Ryan, who was considering increasing the frequency of her sessions, negotiated a break in the price hike to offset the cost of the added sessions. "She approached it as a learning opportunity," says Ryan. "And it really underscored that this was the right therapist for me."

Another way to save money is to find a therapist who offers a sliding scale of fees based on need or who charges lower rates for hard-to-fill time slots, such as midmorning and midafternoon. And if you're willing to consider a therapist-in-training, you'll really save on sessions. In New York City, for example, training clinics, like those at the William Alanson White Institute (*www.wawhite .org*) and the National Institute for the Psychotherapies (*www.nipinst.org*), offer low-cost psychoanalysis. Universities that offer postdoctoral programs in psychoanalysis are often another good resource for reduced rates.

3 "I DON'T KNOW ANYTHING ABOUT YOUR CONDITION."

If you're suffering from a particular problem, say, anxiety attacks, you'll want to see someone who takes a special interest in treating the problem. A diabetic wouldn't sign on with a lung specialist, right? Unfortunately, some therapists will take on all comers. "Not every therapist is well trained in

every disorder," says Richard Dana, a psychologist in Newton, Mass. "Someone who is referred with obsessive-compulsive disorder may find that his therapist was not really trained in that area." According to Herbert Klein, editor and publisher of *Psychotherapy Finances*, many therapists lost substantial income during the 1990s, when businesses shifted to managed-care insurance. As a result, some practitioners don't feel they can afford to turn away patients.

Talk with your prospective therapist. For confidentiality reasons, he can't provide the names of clients as references. But you can describe your issues or symptoms and ask whether he has worked with patients like you before.

4 "I USE ONE APPROACH—AND IT MIGHT NOT BE THE ONE YOU NEED."

Therapy comes in many flavors. Among the classic approaches, "cognitive-behavioral" focuses on changing the patient's thought and behavior habits, while "psychodynamic" stresses the role of early and current relationships, often with an emphasis on the one between patient and therapist. Then there are the newer, less mainstream approaches. For example, Emotional Freedom Techniques stimulate the body's meridian points, as in acupuncture, and Eye Movement Desensitization and Reprocessing, often used to treat victims of trauma, uses objects waved in front of the eye to reduce stress.

"Different problems need different techniques," says Tina Tessina, a psychotherapist in Long Beach, Calif.

Before starting therapy, ask your provider about his methodology. It's also possible to set up an initial trial period—anywhere from one to several sessions—to see if a given therapist's approach suits you.

5 "I'M JUST A PAWN TO YOUR INSURANCE COMPANY."

Managed-care companies have clamped down relentlessly on psychotherapy, requiring extensive reporting by practitioners and "a lot of time devoted to paperwork justifying treatment," says Daphne Stevens, a clinical social worker in Macon, Ga. What's more, patients tapping their insurance to pay for treatment generally sign a release at the outset giving the managed-care company the right to see their records and discuss aspects of their treatment with the therapist.

Several years ago, Stevens says, she started seeing a suicidal patient who was in the throes of an emotional crisis. After six months of therapy, "the managed-care company started asking when I was going to wrap it up," she says. When she insisted that the patient still required treatment, the insurer said okay—as long as Stevens checked in after every session. Finally, Stevens worked out a fee agreement that allowed the patient to pay out-of-pocket. A less-charitable therapist might have let a patient go untreated.

You can't do much about your managed-care company's access to your files, but you can discuss your concerns with your therapist and ask to see any correspondence he has with your care manager. At least you'll be able to know what's being said about you.

6 "OUR CONVERSATIONS AREN'T NECESSARILY CONFIDENTIAL."

If you think conversations between therapists and patients are always private, they're not. Court decisions have found that the confidentiality of records should be determined on a case-by-case basis. Should you end up in a court case in which you've raised the issue of emotional health, your records can be subpoenaed by the other side. It's common in child-custody suits, for example. "Those records can become part of the legal fodder if parents are divorcing," says Leah Klungness, a psychologist in Locust Valley, N.Y.

In addition, the federal Health Insurance Portability and Accountability Act, which was originally meant to safeguard patient privacy, was amended in April 2003 to remove a patient's right to give consent before certain "covered entities"—i.e., providers, insurers, and health-information clearinghouses—could access his medical records. As a result, confidential information about you can easily be disseminated without your ever knowing.

What to do? Ask to see what's in your records so you know what information could be passed on. While your therapist can't change what he has written, you can ask that he put in positive factors as well, such as your efforts to change.

7 "I'M EVERY BIT AS CRAZY AS YOU ARE."

Therapists generally receive some form of therapy themselves before treating patients. It is a requirement for becoming a practicing psychoanalyst, for instance. But that doesn't mean the person you see is necessarily a beacon of mental health. "Some therapists may have their own set of emotional problems, which, in some cases, could interfere with successful therapy," says Los Angeles psychologist Yvonne Thomas. The real problems arise when a therapist has unresolved emotional issues and takes them out on you. One writer in Santa Fe, N.M., for example, recently saw a psychologist who, she says, came late to every session. When the patient finally called her on it, she says the therapist responded by angrily lashing out. "She told me this is an issue she was trying to work on, and I had no right to criticize her for it," the writer says.

If you feel your therapist is behaving inappropriately, bring it up. Bottom line: "A person should feel comfortable confronting the therapist and trying to have the problem improved," Dana says. If that can't happen, move on.

8 "I'M A DRUG PUSHER … AND IT PAYS."

Antidepressants and other psychotropic drugs have helped millions of people. But they're not right for everyone. Managed-care companies, however, encourage psychiatric consultations, in which patients are routinely prescribed drugs, in part because it's often cheaper than long-term therapy. Meanwhile, more psychologists are moving toward practicing psychiatry, in part because it's so profitable, says George Goldman, a psychologist in New York City. "A psychiatrist can see a patient for 15 minutes, for what's essentially medication management, and get the same fee as a therapist that spends 50 minutes with a patient," Goldman says.

Your best move: Before you start working with a psychiatrist or psycho-pharmacologist, ask him to describe his philosophy about prescribing medication. If he suggests that you go on drugs, ask what the rationale is for the recommendation, how the two of you can monitor the treatment, and whether he has been pressured by insurers. If you don't feel comfortable with his answers, consider getting a second opinion.

9 "I'LL EXAGGERATE YOUR DIAGNOSIS TO GET YOU COVERED."

To qualify for insurance coverage, patients must be given a specific diagnosis, drawn from the Diagnostic and Statistical Manual of Mental Disorders, known as the DSM, published by the American Psychiatric Association. And since the level of coverage may depend on the diagnosis, therapists will sometimes assign a more serious condition when given two similar options—"because then there's the need for more therapy," Goldman says. Indeed, some states, such as California and Massachusetts, allow certain psychiatric disorders to receive a higher benefit level, which is generally assigned to medical visits. "So [therapists] might give someone the diagnosis of 'panic disorder' when the milder 'adjustment disorder with anxiety' may also be appropriate," says Steven Sultanoff, a psychologist in Irvine, Calif.

But an exaggerated diagnosis can have negative implications as well. A diagnosis of depression, for example, could make it difficult to get disability insurance. To avoid diagnosis backlash, discuss the options before you begin therapy. Many practitioners are not inclined to put labels on their patients for a variety of therapeutic reasons but are forced to provide one before insurance companies will cover their services. Pay for your treatment out-of-pocket, and the need for any diagnosis—and certainly for an inflated diagnosis—may disappear.

10 *"I'M GOING TO DRAG THIS OUT AS LONG AS POSSIBLE."*

If your health plan doesn't impose treatment limits, you have more freedom to resolve your problems at your own pace. But you might also find your therapy goes on too long. "Unless you have a serious problem, you should see some improvement within a few weeks and considerable headway in a couple of months," says psychotherapist Tina Tessina. At the same time, don't delude yourself that your last visit signals a cure for whatever sent you there. "These tend to be chronic relapsing conditions," says Darrel Regier, executive director of the American Psychiatric Institute for Research and Education.

Discuss with your therapist how long your treatment is estimated to last. Then set up a schedule for evaluating your progress to determine if it should continue. If you feel things are dragging on without much progress, discuss your concerns with your therapist, and if you don't get a satisfactory answer, consider moving on.

THINGS TO KNOW

Today therapists use a variety of approaches, some of which may be more effective for you than others. Here are five common treatment methods:

- **Cognitive-behavioral therapy:** This common form of therapy focuses on eliminating negative and unhealthy thoughts as a means of changing one's behavior; it tends to be briefer than other forms of psychotherapy and instructive rather than exploratory.

- **Psychodynamic psychotherapy:** This way of working explores the patient's unconscious and focuses on relationships and memories as key to lasting structural change.

- **Family systems therapy:** Stresses the role each person plays in the family unit and patterns among those relationships as a means for instigating change.

- **Art therapy:** Incorporates the making of art in the therapeutic process as a means of accessing experience and emotions that may otherwise be difficult to express.

- **Eye Movement Desensitization and Reprocessing, or EMDR:** This treatment is most effective for patients suffering from deep-rooted anxiety and emotionally distressing memories. Therapists have patients focus on moving objects in order to release negative emotions and associations.

10 Things Your
Spa
Won't Tell You

1 "WANNA RELAX? TAKE A NUMBER."

Americans spend more than $150 million a year on Prozac, but apparently happy pills aren't enough. In search of bliss and a good rubdown, people worldwide flock to spas, making more than 130 million spa visits each year. And while spa brochures dangle such promises as "finding yourself and nurturing your soul," what you're more likely to find are other people, a whole bunch of them in fact—all vying for the very same services you want.

Those crowds mean that it can be almost impossible to schedule appointments for treatments—the whole reason you're there to begin with. When Bernard Burt, a veteran travel writer and coauthor of the book *100 Best Spas of the World*, visited Ancient Cedars Spa at Wickaninnish Inn on Vancouver Island, he found guests scrambling to get the treatments they wanted. "The spa is just too small," Burt says. "They can't keep up with demand." Ancient Cedars manager Miranda Moore admits that the facility is a bit "humble," or "intimate," but explains that it has added a treatment room, bringing the total number of rooms to six.

Jenni Lipa, president of Spa Trek Travel in New York City, does her research to avoid the crowds. "I look at the ratio of spa treatment rooms to guest rooms and the ratio of spa staff to clientele," she says. At a destination spa, one treatment room per 10 guest rooms, or one staffer per guest, is a good sign, according to Lipa: "If a 300-room hotel has only three spa treatment rooms, that's a problem."

2 "THE BROCHURE RATE IS JUST AN OPENING BID."

Everyone knows that spas aren't cheap. The nation's top destinations—including the Golden Door in Escondido, Calif., and the Greenhouse in Arlington, Tex.—will run you around $7,000 a week. But hidden extra costs can jack up your tab even further, and even at a reasonably priced facility. The biggest culprit: gratuities, which are included in the prices at some spas but not at others. "It's appropriate to tip 15 percent for services, and that can add up if you have three $150 services a day," says travel consultant Lynn O'Rourke Hayes.

Another budget-buster: Many spas will try to sell you pricey skin-care products following your treatments. And while you're not required to buy, "They're very pushy sometimes about selling these products," Bernard Burt says. "You're relaxed after a massage and susceptible to suggestion. It's big money for them."

3 *"WE'LL RUB YOU THE WRONG WAY."*

Massages come in a variety of formats these days, from intense deep-tissue work to Reiki, where the masseur barely touches you. When you enter the massage room, you may have no idea what kind you're getting.

Terry Herman, a management consultant and spa industry adviser in Westmont, Ill., thought she was scheduled for a relaxing 45-minute massage when she visited the Heartland Spa in Gilman, Ill. Then the masseur began kneading her so forcefully that she almost cried out in pain. Herman, who has chronic back problems, asked him three times to lighten his touch, but, she says, he seemed too absorbed in his work to notice. "I complained to management, but they didn't care," Herman says. The next day, Herman saw that she was covered with bruises. Mary Quinn, Heartland's executive director, says that although she does not recall Herman's visit, "One of the greatest assets of the Heartland is the way we handle guests." She adds that Heartland's masseurs are certified by the State of Illinois and must complete in-house training, which includes instructions on how to interact with clients.

Herman had a similarly harrowing experience with a facialist at a Chicago day spa. "She broke some of the capillaries on my face," Herman says. "To get them fixed, I would have to get laser surgery." What's a client to do in such cases? "You have the right to ask the therapist to lighten his touch," says Susan Lord, M.D., of the Center for Mind-Body Medicine, an educational institute in Washington, D.C. "If he doesn't listen to you, get off the table right away."

4 *"OUR THERAPISTS AREN'T TRAINED."*

Today there are roughly 14,000 spas in the U.S. alone, generating more than $9 billion in annual revenue—an 18 percent increase since 2003. With so many new facilities opening up, finding enough trained masseurs, facialists, and personal trainers has become a challenge for new businesses. "With so much demand, it's getting harder and harder to recruit people," says Bernard Burt. "Spas have to take what they can get."

Many spas get away with hiring undertrained staff because the rules are lax at best. The International Spa Association (ISPA)—the closest thing to a governing authority for the industry—requires that employees who provide treatment at its member spas meet certain state requirements for licensing (such as completing 500 hours of training and passing a state exam). But thanks to individual state laws, that rule doesn't amount to much. "Many states don't require licenses, and it varies within states," says Anne Bramham, founder of the Bramham Institute, a spa and spa-training center in West Palm Beach, Fla. "It's different all over the country."

If you're in the market for a facial, the ultimate stamp of approval for facialists is certification from CIDESCO, an international school for aestheticians. When in doubt, says Robert Stergas, clinic director for Syracuse, N.Y.'s Onondaga School of Therapeutic Massage, look for massage therapists who have been certified in either New York or Nebraska, since these states have the highest standards for licensing. In both states, a massage therapist must complete at least 1,000 hours of classroom instruction followed by a comprehensive exam.

5 "SOME OF OUR TREATMENTS ARE JUST PLAIN SILLY ..."

New and innovative treatments are continually being added to spa menus, ranging from the bizarre, such as "aura imaging," in which a special camera takes a full-color photo of your "energy field," to the downright goofy, like the "barbecue wrap" at Dallas's The Spa at the Crescent, where a massage therapist slathers you with a mixture of honey, tomato paste, cayenne pepper, and cornmeal.

Do such treatments have any real purpose? A spokesperson for Crescent's spa says that the barbecue wrap "exfoliates and smoothes dry skin, stimulates circulation, and helps rid the body of toxins. And it smells fabulous—you just want to eat it." Dr. Lord isn't impressed. "I can't think of any biochemical reason why these food treatments would be useful," she says.

6 "... WHILE OTHERS ARE POTENTIALLY HARMFUL."

People often turn to spas in search of better health, and many facilities have responded by trying to play doctor, offering such procedures as hormone-replacement therapy and "chelation therapy," which claims to clean out fatty deposits in the circulatory system. Yet only 7 percent of spas are officially designated "medical spas," according to the ISPA.

Spas that don't ask specific questions about your medical conditions or allergies should definitely arouse suspicion. Even some of the most traditional treatments can be hazardous to your health. Twenty minutes in the sauna, steam room, or Jacuzzi, for example, can be dangerous for someone who suffers from diabetes, high blood pressure, or heart disease, says Mary Tabacchi, an associate professor at the Cornell University School of Hotel Administration.

Hydrotherapy, a toxin-purging treatment that involves immersion in alternating hot and cold water, deserves special caution, explains Sara Eavenson, cofounder of the Bramham Institute. "That's the most dangerous and misunderstood treatment in a spa. Anyone getting into a hot bath should be asked if they have a heart condition. Make sure you ask the therapist what kind of bath you should be having and why."

7 "WE'RE NOT EVEN REALLY A SPA."

According to a recent study by ISPA, the number of spas in the U.S. is growing at a rate of 16 percent a year. More than 80 percent of these establishments call themselves "day spas"—meaning no overnight accommodations—and many inside the industry think that term is getting abused. "Everybody calls themselves a day spa," says Hannelore Leavy, executive director of the Day Spa Association, an 800-member group based in Union City, N.J. "They just put a massage table with a curtain at the back of a salon."

To be accredited by the Day Spa Association, a facility must offer a private treatment room for each client receiving a personal service; it should also provide at least four types of massage and four other body treatments (such as wraps and exfoliation, as well as facials and aromatherapy). Leavy says the DSA visits most member spas to check on standards.

Pseudo-spas, on the other hand, can put unsuspecting visitors in pretty weird situations. "I had a friend on business in Chicago who asked the concierge at her hotel about local spas," Leavy says. "She wound up in a massage parlor. She got the massage, but was more stressed out when she came out than when she went in."

8 "NO ONE UNDERSTANDS WHAT WE DO."

Sure, glossy travel brochures often overstate the beauty of resorts and hotels. But in the spa industry, the problem of pumped-up advertising is even more pronounced. Why? Mostly because the industry is so poorly understood. For starters, there's the problem of ever-changing trends (ever heard of "ayurveda"?), plus the fact that there are few travel agents who are up to speed on the industry, making consumers even more reliant on an individual spa's marketing materials. "Travel agents really don't know how to define a spa," says Jenni Lipa, of Spa Trek Travel, who also started up a training program to turn her colleagues into "spa specialists." "Most travel agents haven't experienced a spa; unless you've experienced something, you really can't sell it."

Unfortunately, you can't rely on many spa websites, either; SpaFinder .com and SpaWish.com, for example, earn commissions when consumers book spa vacations through them. (An objective source to check out: TripAdvisor.com, which posts unbiased consumer reviews.)

9 "WE'RE UNDERINSURED..."

With the growth of the spa industry, consistent standards have become an afterthought. Industry associations do exist, but membership is strictly voluntary. The biggest one, the ISPA, represents about 2,700 spas worldwide, but its application process isn't exactly grueling. Members must agree to abide by the association's "standards and practices," which include such bare minimums as clean treatment rooms and staffers trained in CPR. "It's difficult for a trade association to come up with any certification, because the laws vary so much from state to state," admits the ISPA's executive director, Lynne Walker McNees.

Because spas generally don't have anyone looking over their shoulder, most carry inadequate insurance, says Mary Lynne Blaesser of the Marine Agency, which has provided coverage for about 15,000 spas. "In most states, the only insurance spas are required to carry by law is workers' comp," Blaesser says, which is bad news for consumers. Adds Guy Jonkman, publisher of trade publication *Spa Management Journal*, "If [a spa] puts you in a bath that's too hot, they often don't have a policy to cover it."

10 *"... SO IF YOU'RE NOT HAPPY, GOOD LUCK GETTING YOUR MONEY BACK."*

The combination of spotty insurance and almost nonexistent refund policies means one thing for dissatisfied customers: Good luck collecting if something goes wrong. And that applies even for the most egregious mishaps. Leandros Vrionedes, a personal-injury lawyer in New York City, had a client whose day-spa facial turned into a horror show. "The esthetician oversteamed the client and applied the wax immediately after," Vrionedes says. "She wound up taking part of this person's face off—several layers of skin were removed. The spa argued that it was the fault of the product and we didn't have a case. We argued that it was the procedure."

After five years of legal wrangling, the woman received an undisclosed settlement—which, after all was said and done, her lawyer describes as "too low."

Even when a spa does carry insurance, consumers may have a tough time obtaining compensation for injury. "Some insurance companies will fight you tooth and nail," Vrionedes says. Don't assume, though, that you have no case just because of some lengthy waiver you signed when you arrived at the facility. According to Vrionedes, some of these documents will hold up in court, but others won't—especially those that are all-encompassing. If the release "absolves the spa of absolutely everything in the world," he says, courts will sometimes void the agreement.

THINGS TO DO

● **Spas come in many varieties,** from those that stress healthy living and exercise to those that aim to pamper you and cater to your every whim. Evaluate what type is right for you before booking.

● **When looking for a spa,** consider working with a knowledgeable travel agent—she can help you find one that fits your budget and interests.

● **If you're planning your trip** on your own, look for spas that are members of the International Spa Association, which requires all members to hire staff who meet training requirements. To find one, go to *www.experienceispa.com/ISPA/visit,* and click on "Search for a Spa."

● **Once you get to the spa,** communicate any medical conditions you have to the staff, and make sure you participate only in activities that are safe for you.

● **In the mood for a quick jaunt** to the local day spa? Make sure it's sanctioned by the Day Spa Association, which seeks to weed out seedy establishments from its ranks.

10 Things Your
Alternative Healer
Won't Tell You

1 *"I'M NOT A DOCTOR, BUT I PLAY ONE IN MY OFFICE."*

In some ways, the alternative health care industry has come into its own. Physicians endorse meditation. Supplements get recommended for everything from combating aging to fighting cancer. Even some insurers are covering naturopaths and yoga instructors. That's because a number of alternative treatments and approaches have proved helpful for so many. And when used as an adjunct to conventional medicine, that's terrific. But too many patients have come to view their alternative practitioners as trained medical professionals.

Take Dr. William Brown, who's based in Sedona, Ariz. He converses confidently about the bloodstream, capillary cells, and the immune system. He also claims to be able to "accelerate the lymph stream and raise the immune system" through massage, which most physicians believe is scientifically implausible. It's easy to imagine that Dr. Brown is an M.D., but he's not. He's an *N.D.*, a doctor of naturopathy. (He also holds doctoral degrees in nutrition science and religious counseling.)

"We have reflexologists who tell you that what they do [treating ills through foot massage] is better than medicine," says David Thornton, executive director of the Medical Board of California. "And then there are the iridologists who look into your eyes and can supposedly pinpoint what's wrong with you and prescribe vitamins, minerals, and herbs to bring your body into 'alignment.' In most cases, these people may start out believing in what they do, but eventually, it becomes more a matter of making money."

Thornton acknowledges that most of these practices can be done in legal, nonfraudulent ways, but "it crosses the line when these people start telling you that you have certain physical or mental problems that they have diagnosed," he says. "At that point it becomes the practice of medicine."

2 *"DON'T TAKE THIS STUFF IF YOU'RE ON REAL MEDICATION."*

In 2000 some 72 million Americans sought alternative care. Yet less than one third of them told their physicians that they were fiddling with mugwort or valerian. Most problematic, 22 million people took conventional drugs and herbal remedies simultaneously. "Why would you want to tell your doctor something that he will chew you out about?" says Larry Dossey, M.D., executive editor of *Explore: The Journal of Science and Healing.*

Whatever the case, secretly taking medication increases one's risk of experiencing unhealthy interactions between pharmaceutical drugs and herbs, which might be sold without warnings about complications or overuse. Compounding the problem is the fact that bottles of herbal medication are not required to be labeled with ingredients—or even to be consistent in their potency. "There are cross-reactions that could happen between St. John's wort and Prozac," says Wallace Sampson, a clinical professor at Stanford University. Among the few things that Sampson and alternative enthusiast Julian Whitaker, M.D., agree on is the danger of mixing drugs with herbs and the need to keep doctors informed about what you are ingesting. "If the patient were mine," says Whitaker, "I'd be sure to get him off the Prozac."

3 "HYPOCHONDRIACS ARE MY SPECIALTY."

One of the first things that doctors-to-be are taught is that 80 percent of the ailments that induce people to visit physicians require no treatment at all. Sporadic headaches, stomach pain, joint inflammation—such things normally go away on their own. Consequently, doctors tend to spend less time with patients who really don't require treatment. That's why hypochondriacs like alternative healers, who often get most of their information from patient interviews rather than from blood work and head-to-toe physicals. In fact, they'll frequently devote hours to discussing the minutiae of a patient's life. "I went to a homeopath who focused on my dreams for 15 minutes," marvels Larry Dossey. "He spent two hours speaking with me. I left there feeling like a million dollars even though nothing was done to me physically."

Conventional doctors insist that a friendly bedside manner should not be confused with bona fide health care. "For chronic sufferers of pains that may be real or [psychosomatic], this is very rewarding," admits William Jarvis, a professor at the School of Medicine at California's Loma Linda University. "They validate illnesses, imagined and real, that cannot be pinpointed. And when it comes to treatment, these guys have a never-say-die attitude. They will constantly be fishing for positive results." Good for a patient's psyche, perhaps, but terrible for his wallet.

4 "WHEN IT COMES TO HOMEOPATHY, LESS IS USUALLY LESS."

Is homeopathy the greatest underutilized resource in medicine, or sheer quackery? Based on the belief that the healing process will be expedited by ingesting a highly diluted concoction of substances that triggers a patient's symptoms, homeopathy is widely practiced in Europe. However, John Renner, M.D., former chief medical officer for HealthScout.com, voices the general view of mainstream medicine when he insists it's "unscientific and based on an outrageous theory." Adds John Dodes, a

Forest Hills, N.Y., dentist and the author of *Healthy Teeth*, "It's as if you went to the ocean, threw an aspirin in, then came back a month later and drank the ocean water to cure a headache."

Woodson Merrell, M.D., the executive director of Beth Israel Hospital's Center for Health and Healing in New York and an assistant clinical professor of medicine at Columbia University, defends homeopathy, but he disdains doctors who use it as anything other than "early intervention for benign problems that you are making go away faster. Doctors should not use it for serious acute problems or to treat underlying diseases."

Yet many hard-core boosters of homeopathy believe that by diluting the medicine to an infinitesimal degree, its effectiveness multiplies dramatically. It's a theory that dismays Renner. "If a doctor really believes in homeopathy—that the more you dilute something the stronger it gets—that's pretty serious," he says. "It means he doesn't understand chemistry."

5 "JUST BECAUSE I'M AN M.D. DOESN'T MEAN I'M NOT A FLAKE."

Not all alternative-health practitioners have alternative degrees, like the N.D. Health guru Andrew Weil, a Harvard-trained physician, has written that "improper breathing is a common cause of ill health," and like Weil, many M.D.'s have embraced various forms of alternative health care. But some go overboard. "I know a doctor who was an ordinary G.P.," says John Renner. "He had a good bedside manner and was always recommending simple

> ## "It's as if you went to the ocean, threw an aspirin in, then came back a month later and drank the ocean water to cure a headache."

solutions to people, suggesting hot and cold compresses for sinus problems and the like, which can help." But according to Renner, the doctor got excited about "yeast syndrome," in which an allergy to yeast is considered the "cause of everything from fatigue to respiratory illnesses."

How can you be sure that your doctor isn't using alternative remedies to the exclusion of more effective, mainstream treatments? "Pick a physician with hospital privileges, because it means that other doctors have evaluated and accepted him," Renner says. "Be careful of doctors who know everything about everything and have treatments that nobody else—including the American Medical Association—knows about."

6 "MY DETOX DIET IS DOWNRIGHT DANGEROUS."

As the alternative-health-care industry pushes kits and regimens that "purify," "rebalance energy," and even help you "detox emotionally," the detox diet fad is becoming increasingly widespread. Sales of herbal products that claim to cleanse your bowels, liver, and kidneys reached $28 million in 2006, according to market research company SPINS.

But while more people are popping pills, drinking gallons of liquids, and indulging in Korean skin scrubs to help flush out toxins, medical professionals are questioning whether detox is even necessary. The human body is capable of detoxing itself, says Roger Clemens, professor of molecular pharmacology and toxicology at the University of Southern California. "There's no medical foundation or scientific merit to prove that these regiments detoxify anything," Clemens says. "The normal body functions will take care of everything." Furthermore, detox diets can come with an array of harmful side effects, including dehydration, headaches, fatigue, heart palpitations, and feeling faint.

7 "I'M HAPPY TO STEER YOU TOWARD THE REMEDIES I HAPPEN TO SELL."

Imagine your CPA trying to peddle you mutual funds. It would make you wonder about his intentions, just as you should when an alternative healer encourages you to purchase herbal medication directly from him. According to Steven Barrett, founder of the Quackwatch website, "The products are typically sold at markups of 50 to 100 percent."

Worse than the chance of being ripped off is that you may be steered away from a more effective treatment. As M.D.'s Charles Rogers and Richard Lange wrote in the bulletin of the Medical Society of the State of New York, "a window of opportunity for survival may be lost" if patients pass up recognized treatments for "media-hyped" herbs.

8 "TAKE MY MIRACLE MEDICINE WITH A GRAIN OF SALT."

Unlike Food and Drug Administration-approved medications, which have been clinically tested, many alternative treatments are verified solely by anecdotal evidence. "There's no reason why alternative therapies cannot go through the same rigorous tests that all other medicines do," insists Larry Dossey, M.D., executive editor of *Explore: The Journal of Science and Healing*. Stanislaw Burzynski, M.D., of Houston, is lauded in radical cancer-therapy circles as a visionary for his medication—antineoplastons—which he initially extracted from human urine and then used in treatment, claiming it could "turn off the genes that cause cancer growth." Yet Burzynski was unable to agree with the National Cancer Institute on how his drug should be tested. The FDA charged him with a 75-count indictment that ranged from insurance fraud to contempt of court. (He was acquitted of all charges in 1997.)

When a former patient, who wrote about Burzynski pseudonymously in *Health* magazine, called his office to see if charges that he was not cooperating were true, "I was shunned," she wrote, "for asking questions that leaned toward 'the other side.'" A spokesperson for Burzynski replies, "There've been a lot of changes since she was there. Today, every patient is treated either on an FDA trial or pursuant to a special exception approved by the FDA." An FDA spokesperson responds that Burzynski's current trials "can provide evidence of [healing] activity in a variety of tumor types. But these studies are preliminary and could not be viewed as definitive."

9 *"EVEN YOUR TEETH ARE FAIR GAME."*

Like chiropractors, who insist that a bum back causes countless other maladies, some alternative dentists believe that the mouth is the center of the body. They diagnose imperfect bites as the cause of everything from headaches to menstrual cramps. Treatment typically involves filing down teeth and crowning them. John Dodes, the Forest Hills, N.Y., dentist, estimates that he's seen at least 500 people who've gone through this costly, painful, and extreme treatment. One patient of his had the procedure done twice on all 28 of his teeth, at a cost of $700 to $1,000 per tooth each time. When he came to Dodes, his bite was still messed up, and his headaches, for which this treatment was prescribed, persisted.

Some holistic dentists even blame tooth plaque as the cause of ill health, linking it to such problems as respiratory infections and ulcers. Unfortunately, it's difficult to distinguish fact from fiction, since holistic dental care isn't regulated or backed by respected industry associations like the American Dental Association. In fact, the ADA defines "unconventional dentistry" as "encompassing scientifically unproven practices and products that do not conform to generally accepted dental practices." Or as Dodes puts it, "Holistic dental care means getting paid for treating a patient when there's nothing wrong with him."

10 *"THESE TREATMENTS OFTEN ATTRACT THOSE WHO'VE RUN OUT OF OTHER OPTIONS."*

After Suzanne Henig, a former professor at San Diego State University, was diagnosed with cancer and had her diseased thyroid removed, she became understandably panicked. "The first feeling I had was terror," she says. "You suspend your disbelief and look for a magic bullet." Henig pinned her hopes on a treatment that reportedly involved making a vaccine out of her own blood—and, she says now, it ultimately had no effect in treating her illness. In Henig's opinion, "Nobody gets cured of cancer with herbs and alternative medicine."

It's a painful reality: Seriously ill people in search of an elusive cure often pin their hopes and exhaust their savings on unproven treatments. Shark cartilage, herbal vitamins, and flaxseed, for instance, all get touted as cancer cures. Saul Green, a biochemist formerly at New York's Memorial Sloan-Kettering Cancer Center, acknowledges that you'll hear about people getting better with alternative cures, but warns, "These people have temporary remissions, which happen all the time without the treatments. Sometimes it's because they have previously had standard therapies; sometimes it's because of the nature of the disease itself."

THINGS TO DO

● **Good news: You may not** have to look any further than your traditional doctor for alternative health care, since many physicians are jumping onboard. Just make sure you keep him aware of any supplements you're taking to avoid a bad reaction with traditional meds.

● **Before trying an alternative health** remedy, talk to someone who's used it. Ask your alternative practitioner if he has patients who would be willing to talk to you.

● **Want to keep on top** of the latest trends in alternative medicine? The National Center for Complementary and Alternative Medicine offers news and information, at *www.nccam.nih.gov/news*.

● **Even if your doctor** is strictly traditional, he may still be able to recommend a trusted alternative practitioner. Another option is to find a wellness center in your area; check out the directory at *www.alternativemedicinedirectory.org*.

● **The Federal Trade Commission targets** false or unsubstantiated health claims through Operation Cure All. You can find information on how to avoid health care fraud at *www.operationcureall.com*.

10 Things Your
Plastic Surgeon
Won't Tell You

1 *"I TRAINED A WHOLE WEEKEND TO LEARN THIS PROCEDURE."*

With skyrocketing malpractice premiums and the Kafkaesque insurance system, it's little wonder M.D.'s are flocking to the plastic surgery biz. It's easy to get into (legally, any doctor can do it), patients pay up front for surgery, and demand is up: The number of cosmetic procedures increased 59 percent from 2000 to 2007, making it a $12.4-billion-a-year industry.

The best surgeons spend years honing their chops in residencies; by contrast, those hoping to offer a little Botox along with flu shots tend to opt for less rigorous training—like the popular weekend classes at the International Society of Cosmetogynecology, an odd but official-sounding organization that promotes plastic surgery as an extension of gynecology. Its three-day courses cover liposuction and injectables. Empire Medical Training offers an even thriftier nine-hour seminar on lipo—two hours of which are devoted to marketing.

Real plastic surgeons are appalled. "Any licensed physician can put up a plaque and say they do plastic surgery regardless of training, and that's scary," says Roxanne Guy, president of the American Society of Plastic Surgeons (ASPS).

2 *"I MAKE A MINT OFF OTHER SURGEONS' MISTAKES."*

When 35-year-old Kelley Young of Fresno, Calif., looks at her wedding photos, all she can see is her plastic surgery disaster: Young's nose is bent to one side and its tip is misshapen. "Those photos just look ugly, ugly all over," she says. Later, when Young went back to her doctor for a fix, he tried snapping her nose back into place—without anesthetic. A year later she finally found a competent plastic surgeon to fix the problem.

Young is hardly alone. In fact, she's part of a new growth area in the field: fixing botched cosmetic procedures. According to a survey by the American Academy of Facial Plastic and Reconstructive Surgery, one in five nose jobs are corrections of a failed procedure. Stanley Frileck, an associate clinical professor of plastic surgery at UCLA, says that 35 percent of his work is fixing the mistakes of other surgeons. Botched rhinoplasty, face-lifts, and eyebrow procedures are the most common. Not only are these repairs more complex than the initial surgery but they can cost up to three times as much, Frileck says—and the result is never quite as good as a well-done procedure would have been in the first place.

3 "SURE, I CAN TURN BACK THE CLOCK, BUT IT JUST STARTS TICKING AGAIN."

Just because you shelled out $10,000 for a face-lift doesn't mean you're set for life. Even the most skillful work will need some attention a decade or two down the line. Some jobs may require supplemental fillers (compounds that are injected under wrinkle lines in the skin) or minor surgery to tighten up a few sags, while others could call for a repeat of the same procedure. "All cosmetic surgery has a life span," says Richard D'Amico, president elect of the ASPS. "Procedures will not last forever."

Even the most skillful work will need some attention a decade or two down the line.

Surgery to tighten droopy eyelids, for example, often needs to be revisited after a decade, and any work on the lower face will age more quickly than that on the upper face, since the lower face is fleshier and has less bone for sagging jowls to hang onto. Breast implants are the most predictable: Like any foreign objects in the body, they'll eventually be surrounded by scar tissue, which can make breasts hard and painful. That's why every decade or two, depending on the patient, most implants need to be replaced. While 300,000 women receive implants annually, 25,000 have them removed. "It's strictly a function of time," Frileck says.

4 "YOU'D BE BETTER OFF SPENDING THIS MONEY ON A GOOD THERAPIST."

Plastic surgery doesn't make you crazy, but those who have had it, both men and women, are more likely to suffer from psychological problems. Several studies in the mid-1990s found that women who chose to get breast implants were two to three times more likely to commit suicide; other studies have found that 20 percent of plastic surgery patients have undergone some form of psychological treatment.

Up to 15 percent of plastic surgery patients suffer from "body dysmorphic disorder (BDD)," marked by obsessive and exaggerated concern over aspects of one's appearance. It may sound like a convenient diagnosis for our beauty-obsessed culture, but it is a very real, very dangerous condition, says David Sarwer, an associate professor of psychology at the University of Pennsylvania School of Medicine. "At the extreme, people will not leave their home, they're so preoccupied with how they look," Sarwer says. BDD sufferers often seek plastic surgery hoping it will magically transform their lives, and when it doesn't, they may harm themselves. Every plastic surgeon worth his salt asks probing questions to gauge patients' motives, but to date there's no standardized screening tool for BDD.

5 "OF COURSE I'M BOARD-CERTIFIED—FOR WHAT THAT'S WORTH."

A board-certified plastic surgeon should be the best, right? Not always. Because any doctor can perform any cosmetic procedure, and because certification boards are self-regulating, many certifications aren't so telling. The American Board of Laser Surgery, for example, certifies nurses, veterinarians, and oral surgeons in laser surgery—through a take-home written exam. Meanwhile, two different boards certify practitioners of "mesotherapy," the use of injections to dissipate cellulite, although there's little evidence to suggest it works. "To say you're 'board-certified' is meaningless," says Michael McGuire, of the ASPS.

There are some certifications that matter: The American Board of Plastic Surgery is the most rigorous for this specialty and the only certification body for plastic surgery recognized by the American Board of Medical Specialties. Members of the ABPS have completed residencies in both general surgery and plastic surgery and are trained to do all procedures from liposuction to nose jobs. Likewise, physicians with board certifications in either otolaryngology or in facial plastic and reconstructive surgery also have reliable training in procedures above the collarbone.

6 "YOU CAN GET THIS DONE FOR A FRACTION OF THE COST OVERSEAS."

When Janette McNeal decided to get some work done, the Tulsa, Okla., homemaker balked at the $10,000 cost of a face-and neck-lift. McNeal decided to look overseas, and wound up having surgery in Malaysia, where the same $10,000 bought her the face-lift plus liposuction in three areas, a tummy tuck, and an eyelid lift.

It's not for everyone, but "medical tourism" is less risky than it used to be. Since 2000, Joint Commission International, the international wing of an organization that accredits U.S. hospitals, has okayed 110 facilities overseas. Also, private companies that do their own screening have sprung up to guide patients through the process. One of those, MedRetreat, visits each hospital it uses and guarantees that the best surgeons will be on the case.

But medical tourism still has its hazards. It can be tough determining doctors' qualifications, and eager patients may try to cram in too many surgeries at once, requiring a longer recovery and boosting the chance of lethal blood clots, a risk already increased by flying. Travel following surgery can also up the possibility of infection. And if something goes wrong, well, forget a malpractice suit.

7 "I MAKE MY LIVING OFF THE FAT OF THE LAND—LITERALLY."

The number of Americans who lose 100 pounds or more is increasing. But dropping the weight is just part of the process; next comes what's known as body contouring. After a person loses so much weight, his skin does not snap back, leaving folds of excess skin on his thighs, back, torso, abdomen, and neck, which can cause rashes and make fitting into clothes and exercising problematic. In many cases the extra skin must be removed through extreme versions of mastopexy (or breast lifts), tummy tucks, and other procedures. And there are often complications: The remaining damaged skin can die or separate after the procedure, requiring additional surgeries. Despite all the problems, body-contouring surgery is increasingly popular; between 2004 and 2007, the number of procedures increased by 20 percent, to nearly 67,000.

After Michele Fitch, a teacher in Melbourne, Fla., lost 190 pounds, she waited eight years to have the follow-up surgery. She wanted to make sure she could keep the weight off, and she needed to save money—insurance often pays for the gastric bypass, but it rarely covers contouring. First she had skin removed from her arms and chest. Then 10 pounds of skin was cut from her sternum to her bikini line and from hip to hip. Out-of-pocket cost to date: $33,000. And Fitch still faces two more surgeries on her legs.

8 "LONG-TERM EFFECTS? BEATS ME."

More than most other specialists, plastic surgeons are under pressure to compete with one another, and an easy way to get the upper hand is to offer all the latest technology. "There is great pressure for physicians to jump on the bandwagon of a new filler or technique before it is really evaluated," McGuire says. "And their ethics are not too high to begin with."

Doctors are often happy to try new techniques before the long-term effects are known, and in some cases they're performing procedures that already have poor track records. Injecting a person's own fat from other areas into her breasts for enlargement is on its way to popularity again. When this was tried years ago, much of the fat died,

causing unsightly rippling and lumps. But that wasn't the worst of it: The tiny calcifications that resulted from the dead fat were easily confused with tumors and rendered mammograms less effective. While some argue that new techniques and better mammograms have eliminated these problems, McGuire is certain that this rush to the latest and greatest will once again produce disastrous consequences.

9 "SILICONE'S BACK—AND PUTTING MY KIDS THROUGH COLLEGE!"

Fifteen years after the U.S. Food and Drug Administration banned them for elective use and after massive class-action lawsuits bankrupted their manufacturer, silicone breast implants have gotten the green light again. Though there's no conclusive evidence that silicone from ruptured implants causes the problems once associated with it, the FDA is staying cautious, recommending that patients undergo a long list of expensive follow-up tests over the long term. Due to concern about leaks, the FDA has required labeling that instructs those with the implants to get MRIs to check for ruptures after three years, then once every two years after that. Silicone implants should also be replaced every 10 years.

There's no actual mandate for these procedures, and some doctors say that patients won't follow through, especially once they start tallying the bill: The initial surgery can cost between $5,000 and $10,000; MRIs are about $1,500 apiece, and you'll need four over a decade; and the replacement surgery can cost about as much as the original procedure. Grand total: between $11,000 and $16,000 every 10 years.

10 *"THOSE WHO NEED SURGERY THE MOST WILL BENEFIT FROM IT THE LEAST."*

Most people turn to plastic surgery when they feel age has finally caught up with them and nothing else will rid them of that troublesome bulge. But the dirty little secret of plastic surgery is that with many procedures, the more you need it, the less you can expect.

Those who have damaged skin, more common as we age, can expect some serious complications. Skin stretched by weight gain, for example, loses its elasticity; following liposuction it may not snap back into place but hang like an apron over the area that was suctioned.

Because smokers have poor circulation to the epidermis, their skin can die after surgery, meaning months of unsightly scars and possible additional surgery. And procedures such as a face-lift done on sun-damaged skin won't last as long and may result in more-prominent scarring. Likewise, those hoping for dramatic weight loss from liposuction are looking in the wrong place; surgeons say it's meant only to shape a certain part of the body in conjunction with diet and exercise.

Ironically, those who need cosmetic surgery the least—generally, those who are younger and opt for a little tweaking here and there—are going to fare the best. "How well a person cares for themselves throughout life is very important," says Mark Jewell, former president of the American Society for Aesthetic Plastic Surgery.

THINGS TO KNOW

According to the American Society of Plastic Surgeons, Americans spent more than $12 billion on cosmetic surgery in 2007 (the most recent figures available). Of that, roughly $4.9 billion went to the top five procedures:

Type of Surgery	Total # Performed in 2007	Average Cost per Procedure
Breast augmentation	347,500	$ 3,815
Liposuction	302,000	$ 2,982
Nose reshaping	285,000	$ 3,833
Eyelid surgery	241,000	$ 3,134
Tummy tuck	148,000	$ 5,264

Medical & Dental

■ Of all the decisions you make as a consumer, few have the potential impact of those involving your health care. As strained and complicated as the system is today, we depend on our medical professionals to keep us healthy when we're well and make us better when we're ill. And knowing where and how to get that help can make all the difference in the world, both for your own quality of life as well as that of your loved ones.

In this chapter, we take a closer look at the world of health care, with the information you need to make better and smarter decisions, whether it comes to choosing a pharmacist or preparing for an upcoming stay at a hospital. At a time when the health care industry is in a state of flux, it's easy for patients to get lost in the shuffle. We hope to help you and your loved ones stay out of the fray.

10 Things Your
Primary-Care Physician
Won't Tell You

1 *"THEY SHOULD PUT ME ON THE ENDANGERED-SPECIES LIST."*

A good primary-care doctor—someone to coordinate your health care, help choose your specialists, and be the first to diagnose just about any problem—is the key to good medical treatment. But they're getting harder to come by. According to a 2007 study, it took new patients in Massachusetts an average 26 days to land an appointment with one. Why? Fewer med students are going into primary care; interest is so low that the number of primary-care internal medicine residency positions dropped by more than 50 percent in the past decade. "We're not really getting the best and brightest in primary care," says Kevin Pho, a Nashua, N.H., physician who writes the blog Kevin, M.D. "And that's where they're needed."

Cherrie Brunner of Syracuse, N.Y., knows this all too well. She had such trouble finding a new doctor that she stuck with her old one despite problems—when she had blood in her urine, for example, she had to wait a week for an appointment, and the office then tried to cancel. But find a new GP? "I want to," says Brunner. "But when friends say, 'My doctor's great,' he won't take new patients." (Brunner's doctor had no comment.)

2 *"I'M THE PAUPER OF MY PROFESSION."*

One big reason fewer medical students are specializing in primary care is pure and simple economics. In 2006 primary-care doctors earned an average of $171,519. That might sound like a lot to most working people, but it's less than half of what dermatologists made that same year. And the call of more-lucrative specialties is only likely to get louder for today's residents: According to one study, the income of primary-care doctors, adjusted for inflation, actually fell by 10 percent between 1995 and 2003. "Students are not dummies," says Pho. "They graduate with $130,000 in debt; why should they go into primary care?"

The income of primary-care doctors is under such pressure these days because general practitioners are paid roughly $30 to $70 for each patient they see regardless of how long the individual visit. That scale, based on Medicare reimbursements, has changed little since 2000. "Reimbursement for primary care is lousy," says John Ford, an assistant professor at the David Geffen School of Medicine at UCLA. "They put a premium on volume, not on spending time with patients."

3 *"SORRY, YOUR 12 MINUTES ARE UP."*

These days it seems like a visit to the doctor involves little contact with an actual doctor. Instead, most of the time is spent explaining problems to assistants and having blood drawn by nurses. Indeed, doctors have been beefing up their support staff—physician assistants and nurse practitioners—to help them squeeze in more patients. It certainly has been effective; some doctors are able to see 40 patients a day. That's one every 12 minutes. And it doesn't show signs of slowing: According to one survey, the average number of patients doctors saw grew by 7.5 percent from 2004 to 2005.

While this system isn't inherently bad, it can be abused, says Ford. Assistants may have a different philosophy from the doctor, leading them to treat problems differently as well. Communication can break down, causing confusion about medications, and a misdiagnosis by an assistant is always possible. Some doctors do take things to the extreme: In the Massachusetts study, 41 percent of patients had an appointment during which they never saw the doctor.

4 *"I HAWK FOR BIG PHARMA IN MY SPARE TIME."*

Your physician relies on his best judgment when deciding what drugs to prescribe. And influencing that judgment is big business. Market-research firm IMS has found that the pharmaceutical industry spends $7.2 billion a year targeting doctors with ads and sales representatives. That translates into $8,000 in marketing money spent on each of the 900,000

doctors practicing in the U.S. today. "The introduction to pharmaceutical representatives starts as early as medical school, and it never really stops," says Pho.

The real amount is certainly much higher, since these figures include only journal advertising and salaries of sales reps, not their expenses. Drug reps give away pens, cups, hats, and shirts, and buy office staff lunch, all in hopes of nabbing time with the doctor. But that's just the beginning—drug companies know doctors are more likely to take their cues from other doctors, so they sponsor weekend seminars at expensive resorts featuring presentations by physicians. Drug companies pay these docs to give informative talks about medical conditions—for which the company's drug gets pitched as the best remedy.

5 *"SORE THROAT? YOU MIGHT BE BETTER OFF GOING TO THE MALL."*

When Mary Furman got a call from her daughter's school at 10 A.M. one morning, she was sure it was strep throat, but her pediatrician couldn't see the girl until four. Furman decided to try a new clinic she'd noticed at a nearby Wal-Mart; they were in and out with a prescription in under an hour.

Walk-in clinics are springing up across the country. They're run by nurse practitioners, who diagnose simple maladies, like strep throat or flu, and provide prescriptions, medical advice, or referrals if the problem is beyond their scope. These clinics have caught on in part because they're fast and don't require an appointment, says Steven Cooley, a physician and CEO of SmartCare Family Medical Centers in Denver. They're also cheap—less than half the cost of a doctor visit and about 10 percent of an ER visit—and many take insurance.

Today there are about 460 such clinics, but analysts expect the number to jump to 4,000 by 2009. When visiting one, says Jim King, president of the American Academy of Family Physicians, ask to have your records forwarded to your doctor, and be sure to tell him about any medication prescribed at the clinic.

6 "I HATE TECHNOLOGY."

It's almost impossible to imagine anyone doing his job these days without a computer—except your doctor. Although billing and other systems may be computerized, when it comes to medical records, many GPs still prefer pen and paper. New electronic medical-record systems can print out clear prescriptions that are cross-referenced with medical databases to avoid incorrect dosages or dangerous drug combinations; hospitals can access patient histories in case of emergency; and care can be better tracked over time. But as a group, primary-care physicians have been slow to adopt the technology: A recent study found that only 28 percent use these systems. Why? They can cost up to $70,000, and cash-strapped GPs see little payoff.

For most patients the benefits of the technology are huge. It eliminates prescription errors due to illegible handwriting. It ensures that patients get the right dosage. Records won't get lost. It reminds doctors when they need to monitor their patients. And specialists and others can easily forward electronic records to your GP. "I'd seriously consider changing doctors if he didn't have an electronic records system," King says.

7 "YOUR INSURANCE COMPANY IS CALLING THE SHOTS."

These days doctors have more freedom to send you to a specialist or order expensive tests than they once did under managed care. But that doesn't mean the system is mended. For starters, your insurance provider's pool of doctors may lack, say, a great cardiologist, King says. And with increased deductibles, it's often the patient who foots the bill for a referral or an expensive test.

Insurers also still wield the power when it comes to hospital stays, says Jerome Epplin, a geriatrician and clinical professor at the Southern Illinois University School of Medicine; he has recommended that a patient spend four days only to have the insurance company overrule him, refusing to pay for the last day and sticking the patient with the bill. "We are powerless over it," Epplin says. "It's incredibly frustrating." Mohit M. Ghose, spokesperson for America's Health Insurance Plans, an industry trade group, says, "When I hear physicians speaking like this, it tells me that physicians need to be working more closely with plans to understand what the guidelines are."

8 "MY LEGAL HISTORY IS NONE OF YOUR BUSINESS."

Today's insurance plans give patients a wider range of doctors to choose from, but patients don't have any more information to help them decide. "If insurance companies really wanted to bolster patient choice, they would give patients the ability to make informed choices," says Peter Lurie, deputy director of the health research group at Public Citizen. The best information about doctors is off-limits to patients. It's the National Practitioner Data Bank, which state medical boards and hospitals use to do background checks, and it includes information on disciplinary actions and malpractice payments.

To find out if your doctor has been sued, you'll have to go down to the local courthouse, but if your doctor has moved around, you'll get only part of the picture. The best publicly available information is tracked by state medical boards, many of which publish this information on their Web pages. If yours doesn't, you can pay a nominal fee for a report from DocInfo .org, a site run by the Federation of State Medical Boards.

9 "IF YOU'RE OVER 65, I DON'T THINK I CAN HELP ..."

As troubling as things are in primary care, the situation is worse when it comes to treating elderly patients, especially those on Medicare. Doctors who specialize in geriatrics are certified by the American Board of either Family or Internal Medicine, and they're increasingly rare. Right now there is just one geriatrician in the U.S. for every 5,000 seniors, about half of what we should have, according to the American Geriatrics Society.

The problem is that fewer medical students are choosing this subspecialty:

Last year only two thirds of geriatric fellowship programs were filled. That's because treating older patients who have multiple, often complex problems is about the worst way a doctor can make a living. Medicare doesn't compensate much more for a 45-minute appointment with a patient with dementia, hearing loss, and a half-dozen other maladies than it does for seeing someone for a simple checkup. "It is fiscal suicide to go out there and say, 'I am a geriatrician,'" Robinson says. "You get the patients that require the most time that pay the worst."

10 "... UNLESS, OF COURSE, YOU'RE WILLING TO PAY EXTRA."

Unfortunately, the shortage of geriatricians is worsening. As med students shy away from geriatrics, the number of people over 65 is set to grow faster than ever as boomers retire. The American Geriatrics Society estimates that by 2030, there will be a shortage of about 36,000 geriatricians in the U.S., up from 7,000 today.

Though the situation seems dire, there are ways to guarantee qualified care. One approach is to see a good primary-care doctor who is also a geriatrician long before you need one. Epplin says that in southern Illinois, not many doctors accept new Medicare patients, but when their existing patients go on Medicare, they keep them. Other approaches can be costly. In Sarasota, Fla., where Robinson practices, many doctors provide "concierge" service: Patients pay an annual retainer of about $4,000 in exchange for their doctor's cell number and upgraded access. Other physicians in Florida have begun asking patients to pay an annual administrative fee of about $200 or $300 to help them continue to provide individualized care. These pricey options aren't what most people have in mind when they think of health-care reform, but they may be the only way to maintain ready access to a good doctor.

THINGS TO DO

● At *www.healthgrades.com* you can find a list of primary-care physicians by city, including what insurance they accept and average prices for the procedures they perform.

● **When you've narrowed your choice** to one or two doctors, run a check with your state's medical board to get a full physician's profile—which includes any disciplinary action. You'll find a directory of state health boards at *www.fsmb.org* under "Public Services."

● **Make a list of questions** or concerns that arise between visits. It's not uncommon to forget important health issues in the short time you're afforded to actually speak with most doctors, so bring your list with you.

● **Geriatricians are disappearing** just at the time when the aging patient population is peaking. One way to protect yourself down the road: Find a primary-care physician who's also a geriatrician before you need one.

10 Things Your
Hospital
Won't Tell You

1 *"OOPS, WRONG KIDNEY."*

In recent years, errors in treatment have become a serious problem for hospitals, ranging from operating on the wrong body part to medication mix-ups. According to a report from the Institute of Medicine, at least 1.5 million patients are harmed every year from being given the wrong drugs—that's an average of one person per U.S. hospital per day, or roughly one out of the 97,000 inpatient admissions per day into U.S. hospitals, according to 2006 data from the American Hospital Association Research Center. One reason these mistakes persist: Only 10 percent of hospitals are fully computerized, with a central database to track allergies and diagnoses, says Robert Wachter, chief of the medical service at UC San Francisco Medical Center.

But signs of change are emerging. More than 3,000 U.S. hospitals, or 75 percent of the country's beds, have signed on for a campaign by the Institute for Healthcare Improvement implementing new prevention measures such as multiple checks on drugs. As of June 2006 these hospitals had prevented an estimated 122,300 avoidable deaths over 18 months.

While the system is improving, it still has a long way to go. Patients should always have a friend, relative, or patient advocate from the hospital staff at their side to take notes and make sure the right meds are being dispensed.

2 *"GETTING OUT OF THE HOSPITAL DOESN'T MEAN YOU'RE OUT OF THE WOODS."*

A week after Leandra Wiese had surgery to remove a benign tumor, the high school senior felt well enough to host a sleepover. But later that weekend she was throwing up and running a fever. Thinking it was the flu, her parents took her to the hospital. Wiese never came home. It wasn't the flu, but a deadly surgical infection.

About 2 million people a year contract hospital-related infections, and about 90,000 die, according to the Centers for Disease Control and Prevention. The recent increase in antibiotic-resistant bugs and the mounting cost of health care—to which infections add about $4.5 billion annually—have mobilized the medical community to implement processes designed to decrease infections. These include using clippers rather than a razor to shave surgical sites and administering antibiotics before surgery but stopping them soon after to prevent drug resistance.

For all of modern medicine's advances, the best way to minimize infection risk is low-tech: Make sure anyone who touches you washes his hands. Tubes and catheters are also a source of bugs, and patients should ask daily if they are necessary.

3 *"GOOD LUCK FINDING THE PERSON IN CHARGE."*

Helen Haskell repeatedly told nurses something didn't seem right with her son Lewis, who was recovering from surgery to repair a defect in his chest wall. For nearly two days she kept asking for a veteran—or "attending"—doctor when the first-year resident's assessment seemed off. But Haskell couldn't convince the right people that her son was deteriorating. "It was like an alternate reality," she says. "I had no idea where to go." Thirty hours after her son first complained of intense pain, the South Carolina teen died of a perforated ulcer.

In a sea of blue scrubs, getting the attention of the right person can be difficult. Who's in charge? Nurses don't report to doctors, but rather to a nurse supervisor. And your personal doctor has little say over radiology or the labs running your tests, which are managed by the hospital. Some facilities employ "hospitalists"—doctors who act as a point person to conduct the flow of information. Haskell urges patients to know the hospital hierarchy, read name tags, get the attending physician's phone number, and, if all else fails, demand a nurse supervisor—likely the highest-ranking person who is accessible quickly.

4 *"EVERYTHING IS NEGOTIABLE, EVEN YOUR HOSPITAL BILL."*

When it comes to getting paid, hospitals have their work cut out for them. Medical bills are a major cause of bankruptcy in the U.S., and when collectors are put on the case, they take up to 25 percent of what is reclaimed, according to Mark Friedman, founder of billing consultant Premium Healthcare Services. That leaves room for some bargaining.

Take Logan Roberts. The 26-year-old had started work as a business analyst near Atlanta but had no insurance when he was rushed to the ER for an appendectomy. The uninsured can pay three times more for procedures, says Nora Johnson, senior director of Medical Billing Advocates of America; Roberts was billed $21,000. "I was like, holy cow!" he says. "That's four times my net worth."

After advice from advocacy group The Access Project (*www.accessproject .org*), Roberts spoke with hospital administrators, telling them he couldn't pay in full. Hospitals frequently work with patients, offering payment plans or discounts. But to get it, you have to knock on the right door: Look for the office of patient accounts or the financial assistance office. It paid off for Roberts, whose bill was sliced to $4,100—20 percent of the original.

5 *"YES, WE TAKE YOUR INSURANCE—BUT WE'RE NOT SURE ABOUT THE ANESTHESIOLOGIST."*

The last thing on your mind before surgery is making sure every doctor involved is in your network. But since the answer is often no for anesthesiologists, pathologists, and radiologists, what's a patient to do? Los Angeles-based entertainment lawyer and patient advocate Michael A. Weiss repeatedly turned away out-of-network pain-management doctors on a recent visit to the hospital.

We're not suggesting you go as far as Weiss did to save money, but do ask for someone in your network if you're alert enough. If it's an emergency and you're stuck with an out-of-network doctor, call your insurance company to help resolve the issue. If you're having elective surgery, ask a scheduling nurse in the surgeon's office to find specialists in your plan, says South Bend, Ind.–based billing sleuth Mary Jane Stull. And if you know your procedure will be out-of-network, call the hospital billing department to negotiate price and a payment plan. It will likely point you to a patient representative or the director of billing. Once you've dealt with the hospital, then try the surgeon or other specialists involved—some hospitals will back you in those discussions, Friedman says.

6 "SOMETIMES WE BILL YOU TWICE."

Crack the code of medical bills, and you may find a few surprises: charges for services you never received, or for routine items such as gowns and gloves that should not be billed separately. Clerical errors are often the reason for mistakes; one transposed number in a billing code can result in a charge for placing a catheter in an artery versus a vein—a difference of more than $3,900, Stull says.

So how do you figure out if your bill has incorrect codes or duplicate charges? Start by asking for an itemized bill with "miscellaneous" items clearly defined. Some telltale mistakes: charging for three days when you stayed in the hospital overnight, a circumcision for your newborn girl, or drugs you never received. Ask the hospital's billing office for a key to decipher the charges, or hire an expert to spot problems and deal with the insurance company and doctors (you can find one at *www.billadvocates.com*). Their expertise typically will cost up to $65 an hour, a percentage of the savings, or some combination of the two. If you want to be your own billing sleuth, talk to the highest-ranking administrator you can find in the hospital finance or accounts office to begin untangling any mistaken codes.

7 "ALL HOSPITALS ARE NOT CREATED EQUAL."

How do you tell a good hospital from a bad one? For one thing, nurses. When it comes to their own families, medical workers favor institutions that attract nurses. But they're harder to find as the country's nursing shortage intensifies—by 2020, 44 states could be facing a serious deficit. Low nurse staffing directly affected patient outcomes, resulting in more problems such as urinary tract infections, shock, and gastrointestinal bleeding, according to a 2001 study by Harvard and Vanderbilt University professors.

Another thing to consider: Your local hospital may have been great for welcoming your child into the world, but that doesn't mean it's the best place to undergo open-heart surgery. Find the facility with the longest track record, best survival rate, and highest volume in the procedure; you don't want to be the team's third hip replacement, says Samantha Collier, vice president of medical affairs at HealthGrades, which rates hospitals. (For information on specific hospitals, you can visit its website at *www.healthgrades.com.*)

The American Nurses Association's website lists "magnet" hospitals—those most attractive to nurses—and a call to a hospital's nurse supervisor should yield the nurse-to-patient ratio, says Gail Van Kanegan, an R.N. and author of *How to Survive Your Hospital Stay.* She also suggests calling the hospital's quality-control or risk-management office to get infection statistics and asking your doctor how frequently the hospital has done a certain procedure. While reporting these statistics is still voluntary, more hospitals are doing so on sites like *www .hospitalcompare.hhs.gov,* which compares hospitals against national averages in certain areas, including how well they follow recommended steps to treat common conditions, says Carmela Coyle, senior vice president for policy at the American Hospital Association.

8 "MOST ERs ARE IN NEED OF SOME URGENT CARE THEMSELVES."

A 2007 study from the Institute of Medicine found that hospital emergency departments are overburdened, underfunded, and ill-prepared to handle disasters as the number of people turning to ERs for primary care keeps rising. An ambulance is turned away from an ER once every minute due to overcrowding, according to the study; the situation is exacerbated by shortages in many of the "on call" backup services for cardiologists, orthopaedists, and neurosurgeons. Currently, 73 percent of ER directors report inadequate coverage by on-call specialists, versus 67 percent in 2004, according to a survey conducted by the American College of Emergency Physicians.

If you can, avoid the ER between 3 P.M. and 1 A.M.—the busiest shift. For the shortest wait, early morning— anywhere from 4 A.M. to 9 A.M.—is your best bet. If you are having severe symptoms, such as the worst headache of your life or chest pains, alert the triage nurse manager, not just the person checking you in, so that you get seen sooner, says David Sherer, an anesthesiologist and author of *Dr. David Sherer's Hospital Survival Guide.* Triage nurses are the traffic cops of the ER and your ticket to getting seen as quickly as possible.

9 "AVOID HOSPITALS IN JULY LIKE THE PLAGUE."

If you can, stay out of the hospital during the summer—especially July. That's the month when medical students become interns, interns become residents, and residents become fellows and full-fledged doctors. In other words, a good portion of the staff at any given teaching hospital are new on the job.

Summer hospital horror stories aren't just medical lore: The adjusted mortality rate rises 4 percent in July and August for the average major teaching hospital, according to the National Bureau of Economic Research. That means 8 to 14 more deaths occur at major teaching hospitals than would normally without the turnover.

Another scheduling tip: Try to book surgeries first thing in the morning, and preferably early in the week, when doctors are at their best and before schedules get backed up, Sherer says.

10 *"SOMETIMES WE DON'T KNOW HOW TO KEEP OUR MOUTHS ZIPPED."*

Contrary to what you might think, sharing patient information with a third party is often perfectly legal. In certain cases, the law allows your medical records to be disclosed without asking or even notifying you. For example, hospitals will hand over information regarding your treatment to other doctors, and it will readily share those details with insurance companies for payment purposes. That means roughly 600,000 entities that are loosely involved in the health-care system have access to that information. These parties may even pass on the data to their business partners, says Deborah Peel, the founder of Austin, Tex.–based Patient Privacy Rights Foundation.

If you want to access your medical records, you don't have to steal them like Elaine did on *Seinfeld* after she learned a doctor had marked her as a difficult patient. You are legally entitled to see, copy, and ask for corrections to your medical records. For your own "Patient Privacy Toolkit," visit the Patient Privacy Rights Foundation's website at *www.patientprivacyrights.org.*

THINGS TO DO

- **You *can* get an itemized bill.** Call up the medical provider's office at your hospital and ask for one, then check it to make sure it accurately reflects the care you received.

- **Call your insurance carrier ahead** of a hospital stay to ensure that any specialists you'll be seeing are in network and that your treatments will be covered. Also, find out if your coverage requires you to get a referral.

- **Make friends with your nurses!** Their care can make all difference in how comfortable and pleasant your stay at the hospital is.

- **When scheduling surgery,** try to book an early-morning slot at the beginning of the week. Experts say that's when doctors are usually at their best.

10 Things
Hospital CEOs
Won't Tell You

1 *"I'M A CEO FIRST AND A HEALTH-CARE PROFESSIONAL SECOND."*

With 46 million uninsured Americans and major health care reform possibly ahead, the roughly 5,000 CEOs at U.S. community hospitals aren't in an enviable position. In the 1980s, almost all hospital heads held advanced degrees in health administration, but the American College of Healthcare Executives says more than one in four of its member CEOs now has an MBA, which president Tom Dolan thinks has "advantages and disadvantages." One plus: Business savvy sure helps in the $1 trillion U.S. hospital industry.

But along with that have come less welcome changes, like Wall Street–style salaries and perks. Gary Mecklenburg, former CEO of Chicago's Northwestern Memorial Hospital, was paid $16.4 million from September 2005 to October 2006, including a nearly $11 million retirement bonus. A Northwestern spokesperson says the hospital complies with IRS standards of "fair and reasonable" compensation. Cathy Glasson, a nurses union leader in Iowa, says only recently have hospitals internally begun calling patients "consumers" or "clients." "Even that small shift hints at today's business model," she says. "Focus less on care and more on profits."

2 *"JUST BECAUSE WE'RE NONPROFIT DOESN'T MEAN WE'RE GOOD GUYS."*

These days, even nonprofit hospitals have become more entrepreneurial. Executives have all but replaced the nuns who once ran Catholic hospitals, and at least a few facilities have upped prices to several times what procedures cost. What's more, even though nonprofit hospitals get roughly $12.6 billion in annual tax breaks and billions more in government subsidies in exchange for community service, there's no standard for how much free care they must provide. Studies show many hospitals don't give enough free care to equal their tax breaks, and figures they report can be misleading. For instance, many facilities claim the amount they bill for a service instead of what it costs to provide it.

The Service Employees International Union recently criticized Beth Israel Deaconess Medical Center in Boston for reporting bad debt (unpaid bills for which it had already been partially compensated by the state) as charity care, inflating its free-care figure by about 20 percent. A Beth Israel spokesperson says hospital auditors have "never found any cause for concern." And no wonder: The hospital was acting in accordance with IRS regulations.

3 "WHO SAYS YOU CAN'T HAGGLE FOR HEALTH CARE?"

After media coverage about how they often accept lower payments from insurers while charging higher list prices to the uninsured, hospitals are now more open to bargaining. So how can you take advantage? For starters, many facilities have financial counselors who can set up no-interest payment plans or adjust prices based on financial need—all you have to do is ask. Or team up with an outfit such as North American Surgery—which pairs patients willing to pay up front with small hospitals willing to give discounts—and you could save up to 80 percent on common procedures like bypass surgery.

Kelly Proffitt, a 39-year-old teacher in Bassett, Va., knows the benefits of bargaining. In May, when her mother got a $12,000 bill from a hospital after spending almost a week there with

a near-fatal blood infection, Proffitt hired a health-care advocate—a private individual, often with insurance experience, who helps tackle charges. Weeks later, the hospital offered to cut the bill by 80 percent. The advocate "found strings to pull we didn't even know existed," Proffitt says. To follow her example, visit *www.billadvocates.com* to find your own bill bargainer.

4 "IF WE BUILD IT, YOU WILL COME."

The hospital industry is in the midst of a building boom, having spent more than $100 billion on construction from 2002 through 2007, double the amount from the previous five years. Hospital executives argue that they're trying to make patients more comfortable, but critics claim much of the work is unnecessary, "like putting waterfalls in the lobby," says Maggie Mahar, author of *Money-Driven Medicine*. "And that cost trickles right back down to consumers."

What's more, when construction increases the number of hospital beds, doctors tend to fill them and charge accordingly. Researchers at Dartmouth University have repeatedly found that patients with chronic conditions spend more time in the hospital in areas with more hospital beds per capita. And during the last months of life, patients in bed-glutted regions like Miami spend 20 days in the hospital on average, compared with six days elsewhere.

The upshot for patients? "Researchers have never found all that extra care is producing better health outcomes," says Paul Ginsberg, president of the Center

After media coverage about how they often accept lower payments from insurers while charging higher list prices to the uninsured, hospitals are now more open to bargaining.

for Studying Health System Change. "In some cases, outcomes are actually somewhat worse."

5 "WE DON'T LIKE COMPETITION, ESPECIALLY FROM DOCTORS."

Tensions are up between hospital executives and doctors, especially since many physicians have begun opening small outpatient-surgery centers or mini hospitals in direct competition with big hospitals. The CEOs worry such facilities—which often focus on profitable specialties like liver transplants—will shear off the most high-paying, well-insured patients.

Orthopaedic surgeon William Reed has felt the blowback: In 2003, when he and 21 colleagues opened Heartland Spine & Specialty Hospital in Kansas City, Kan., he said the six biggest insurance firms in the area stopped talking to him about adding the facility to their networks. When Reed filed suit alleging tortious interference and civil conspiracy, his lawyers uncovered e-mail showing several large local hospitals had told the insurers they didn't want them working with Heartland. One hospital allegedly said it would drop an insurer that did. Five hospitals settled for undisclosed sums in spring 2008; the one that allegedly threatened to drop an insurer says its contracting uses a "thorough, lawful approach." But says Reed, "They were trying to find a way to choke me right out of business."

6 "IT'S ALL ABOUT PR."

You can hardly log on to a hospital's website without a logo proclaiming it "one of the country's best." Rankings have proliferated in recent years and are now offered by such varied sources as the for-profit firm HealthGrades and magazines like *U.S. News & World Report.* The problem is, consumers still don't know how to assess and research hospitals adequately, says Howard Peterson, managing partner of hospital-consulting firm TRG Healthcare, so "image becomes everything." That's why each year when hospital rankings that factor in the reputation of a facility within the health care community get compiled, "I can't even tell you how many e-mails I get wanting my vote," Peterson says.

How to find reliable rankings? For starters, look closely at what goes into these calculations. For example, a facility may label itself "best hospital" when only one division (say, ophthalmology) has won an award. Among rankers, HealthGrades *(www.healthgrades.com)* bases its ratings on more than 90 individual procedures and lets you access ratings based on mortality or complication rates of patients, as well as data on safety and what the hospital charges.

Consumers still don't know how to assess and research hospitals adequately.

7 "YOU MIGHT BE PAYING FOR THE GUY IN THE NEXT BED."

Hospital CEOs tend to focus on "the mix of privately insured and Medicare patients at their hospitals," says Leah Binder, CEO of industry monitor The Leapfrog Group. And for good reason: Because Medicare reimbursements barely cover the cost of procedures, privately insured patients and their insurers often pay more to compensate. One study by PricewaterhouseCoopers predicted that by 2009, one of every four dollars spent by private insurers would cover such cost shifting. That can lead to some pretty outrageous charges. For example, says consumer advocate Nora Johnson, many hospitals bill about $30,000 for appendectomies when the cost to do the procedure is more like $4,200. (Insurers negotiate prices, usually somewhere between those two benchmarks.) But because it isn't easy to compare prices, Johnson says there are "no checks and balances to keep hospitals from marking things up as much as they want."

Richard Clark, CEO of the Healthcare Financial Management Association, a professional group for hospital CFOs, says it's "frustrating" to hear arguments that pricing is arbitrary, since hospitals painstakingly adjust prices based on the number of patients covered by government programs and on market forces.

8 "OUR MERGERS CAN BE PRETTY MESSY."

The hospital industry has been rapidly consolidating since the 1990s, with more than 100 merger-type deals announced or completed in 2007 alone. What does this mean for consumers? When a hospital buys another one close by, prices can jump more than 40 percent. That's because big chains have more leverage to demand higher rates from insurers, says Robert Town, professor of health policy at the University of Minnesota.

Hospitals say mergers ultimately help them improve quality—they'll spend more on care and less on back-office needs. But the process can cause customer-service snafus and occasionally compromise quality. Hospital consultant Corbett Price says it's "very common" for hospitals to have problems coordinating accounting systems after a merger, which can result in duplicate or flawed bills, for example. And since mergers gobble up competition, some critics say hospital CEOs no longer feel they have to address black marks—like low nurse-to-patient ratios—to compete.

Price urges concerned consumers to talk with their primary-care doctor about changes at a newly merged hospital and make sure the facility remains accredited by checking www.jointcommission.org. Another option: Wait at least three months for the dust to settle before going back to that hospital.

9 "IF IT WERE UP TO ME, WE'D BE DOING MORE BREAST IMPLANTS."

With more hospitals focused on financial survival, many are pushing the most profitable types of care. Nowhere is this trend more apparent than in advertising: A 2005 study of top academic medical centers' ads found that 29 percent of those focused on specific treatments touted cosmetic procedures, while another 38 percent focused on experimental (read:

high-priced) services like deep-brain stimulation for Parkinson's disease.

Critics worry hospitals are becoming dangerously out of sync with the needs of the public. Author Mahar says ERs are often crowded because hospitals don't want to expand this low-profit unit. Poor financials also explain why the U.S. doesn't "have nearly enough burn units," she says, and why more than three-quarters of hospitals don't offer palliative care. Clark says that while a focus on building up profitable parts of facilities is "definitely going on," nonprofit hospitals also focus on "making sure they are still providing the services the community needs while making a hospital financially sustainable."

10 *"WE DON'T LIKE YOU POKING INTO OUR BUSINESS."*

Things have improved in recent years, but consumer advocates trying to make data publicly available on such topics as staph infection rates in hospitals often describe a multiphased process of resistance. "First the executives just flat-out oppose you," says Denise Love, executive director of the National Association of Health Data Organizations. "Then they say they love the idea but begin attacking the data points and methodology."

At HealthGrades, Chief Medical Officer Samantha Collier says she gets calls "at least once a week" from hospital CEOs or their underlings complaining about everything from her methodology to where they fall in the hierarchy of rankings. Granted, hospital execs have some legitimate concerns: For example, there's the issue of whether hospital researchers and raters are properly adjusting data to be easier on facilities seeing the toughest cases and thus posting higher mortality rates. But Mahar says hospitals' stake in keeping the public underinformed is mostly business savvy. "CEOs realize that patients walk away [from the hospital] knowing whether they like the food and the view," she says. "They've got no idea if they actually got good quality health care."

THINGS TO DO

● **Just because a hospital has** a great reputation, it doesn't mean it's top-notch in every specialty. HealthGrades .com gives the 5,000 hospitals it ranks star ratings on how well they perform 32 common hospital procedures, ranging from coronary bypass surgery to total hip replacement, by looking at mortality and complication rates.

● **Want to shop hospital care** like the smart consumer you are? For less than $10 a pop, HealthGrades.com offers reports on prices for various medical procedures that detail average costs based on factors like region, age, and gender.

● **Good care from a hospital** is about more than successful procedures. The Leapfrog Group (*www.leapfroggroup.org*) tracks whether hospitals are adhering to standards that experts say are the best way to shield patients from dangerous and costly medical errors as well as infection.

10 Things Your
Dentist
Won't Tell You

1 *"YOU MAY NOT NEED TO SEE ME EVERY SIX MONTHS."*

If you're like most people, you see your dentist twice a year—just like those appointment postcards in your mailbox say you should. But where did the rule originate? In a comic book written more than 150 years ago—English satirist George Cruikshank's *The Toothache*—and the biannual checkup has been gospel ever since. But it isn't ideal for everyone.

"A six-month checkup means everybody has the same risk for disease, and that doesn't make very much sense," says Douglas Benn, oral and maxillofacial radiologist and professor emeritus at the University of Florida. "If you look at the typical middle-class population, the majority are not at high risk for lots of decay and gum disease; they probably don't need to be seen every six months." A number of studies support Benn's view, finding no appreciable benefit from biannual visits for all patients. Still, a 2005 survey by the American Dental Association (ADA) confirmed 49 percent of the U.S. population reported seeing a dentist within the past six months.

Have a conversation with your dentist about appointment frequency. You may be one of the lucky folks who don't need such frequent checkups.

2 *"THOSE OLD METAL FILLINGS OF YOURS MAY BE LEAKING TOXINS."*

When Rep. Diane Watson (D-Calif.) learned the mercury in her fillings could end up in her blood, she decided to have them removed. But she met with resistance from local dentists who thought it was unnecessary or worried about health risks from dislodging the fillings. Watson ignored their advice and had the work done in Mexico; she's now sponsoring a bill to phase out mercury in fillings by 2009.

Most fillings dentists use today are amalgams, a mixture of mercury, silver, and tin once thought completely stable. But amalgam fillings have been found to leak mercury vapor that can pass into the bloodstream at the rate of 10 micrograms a day—four times what the average person consumes daily in her diet. "There's no question that it's harming people," says Richard D. Fischer, a Virginia dentist, who cites studies where sheep and monkeys given amalgam fillings showed decreased kidney function and traces of mercury in other organs.

To avoid amalgams, you can request pricier resin fillings. But following Watson's lead isn't the best idea: Removal of amalgams can release a surge of mercury if the dentist isn't extremely careful, Fischer says.

3 "I CARE MORE ABOUT YOUR SMILE THAN YOUR TEETH."

Our nation's oral health has improved significantly in recent years. Between 2004 and 2007, for example, tooth decay in children decreased from 25 to 21 percent, and by 2007, 27 percent of adults over 65 had lost all their teeth, down from 34 percent in 2004. Dentists attribute the improvement to such advances as fluoridation and better oral hygiene at an early age.

But healthier teeth mean less demand for traditional dentistry. Hence the booming field of cosmetics: Between 2000 and 2007, membership in the American Academy of Cosmetic Dentistry jumped 70 percent. Indeed, cosmetic dentistry is big business. Ronald Goldstein, cofounder of the American Academy of Esthetic Dentistry, a 142-member invitation-only organization, estimates that of the $100 billion Americans will spend this year on dental procedures, about half will go to cosmetic work. And that figure is only likely to increase.

The potential for profit is turning some dentists into pitchmen—a digital photo and special software can show you how you'd look with whitened teeth or a set of crowns. But before falling for the new you and opting for elective dental work, get a second opinion.

4 "NO HUMAN BEING SHOULD HAVE TEETH THIS WHITE."

Over the past few years, an explosion of tooth-whitening products has hit drugstore shelves, promising brilliant, made-for-TV smiles for all. But some dentists worry that the long-term effects of these chemical whiteners are unknown. "No one quite knows what's being taken off the tooth," says Reg Moncrieff, a New York City dentist. "It's possible that bleaching takes something from the tooth that you might want later."

Most over-the-counter products contain hydrogen peroxide and other bleaching agents; these unstable compounds release oxygen, which whitens the teeth over time. You'll get much faster results at a clinic, where high-intensity light acts as a catalyst when applied to far heavier concentrations of hydrogen peroxide. This route not only costs more (roughly $400), but it also exposes your mouth to more chemicals and heat, which can damage teeth. "The safest technique is the one that takes the longest," Moncrieff says.

Whatever method you choose, check with your dentist first: Certain types of discoloration don't respond well to bleaching and could leave you with a two-tone smile.

5 "WHEN I SAY THIS WON'T HURT A BIT, BOY, DO I MEAN IT."

The American Dental Association says modern dentistry should be painless, but the rise in time-consuming cosmetic work has some patients a little too eager to find ways of coping with hours of discomfort. To make these long procedures less daunting, dentists are using everything in their arsenal to keep patients comfortable, from old standards Valium and nitrous

An increase in the use of sedatives and anesthetics means an increased risk of complications.

oxide to something called "conscious sedation." Introduced nearly a century ago to help women endure childbirth, "twilight sleep," as it's sometimes advertised, involves mixing a tranquilizer or narcotic with local anesthesia. Many patients leave the office with no memory of the procedure.

So what's the problem with avoiding pain? An increase in the use of sedatives and anesthetics means an increased risk of complications, including vomiting, fainting, and prolonged recovery time. "The more you lose consciousness, the more risky it is," says an ADA spokesperson. If your dentist recommends twilight sleep for your next procedure, check to see that he or someone in his office is licensed to dispense anything stronger than laughing gas.

6 "MY EQUIPMENT IS STATE-OF-THE-ART—CIRCA 1985."

"Dentists are creatures of habit," says Richard Hirschland, president of Carestream Health's dental systems business. Perhaps that's one reason they've been slow to embrace the digital X-ray, developed more than two decades ago. Manufacturers estimate that only 15 to 25 percent of dentists have a digital system in their office, and according to a 2004 study in *The Journal of the American Dental Association,* fewer than 12 percent of U.S. dentists rely exclusively on digital radiography.

The benefits are clear: Instead of waiting four minutes for X-ray film to develop, digital systems display your teeth on a monitor in seconds. Your dentist can also use computer tools to search for decay automatically, and if needed, he can email your X-rays to your insurance company for approval.

Despite these advantages, many dental offices have balked at the cost: roughly $10,000 to $20,000 to convert an exam room. Of course, old-fashioned X-rays are fine too, but when you see an endodontist for a root canal, a digital sensor can spare you a lot of unpleasant time in the chair. Luckily, about half of endodontists have gone digital—check ahead to make sure yours is among them.

7 "DID I MENTION THAT WE'LL NEED TO DO THIS AGAIN IN A FEW YEARS?"

When it comes to whitening and other cosmetic procedures, thousands of dollars often buys you only a few years. Drinking coffee and cola may reverse the bleaching process, and normal wear and tear can damage even the most durable crowns, veneers, and bonding. (Hint: Don't chew ice.)

Because porcelain fractures more easily than healthy enamel, porcelain veneers last between 5 and 15 years, according to Goldstein, the cosmetic dentist. "If you're in your 20s, you're going to want to replace them three or four times in your lifetime," he says. If that seems daunting, Goldstein suggests that patients opt for "conservative" procedures, such as fillings, cosmetic contouring, and orthodontics—work that enhances appearance without dramatically disturbing the original structure of the tooth. Trendy "restorative" procedures, on the other hand, such as crowns and implants, often cost up to five times more and are far more likely to compromise teeth, if not replace them altogether.

8 "I'M A BIG FAN OF CONTINUING EDUCATION— ESPECIALLY WHEN IT MEANS A WEEKEND IN VEGAS!"

As new technology emerges, the dental industry must keep up, which is why 49 state boards require dentists to undergo continuing education, anywhere from 15 to 100 hours a year. The problem is that only a small minority of states specify a minimum number of hours of hands-on clinical study. What's more, continuing-education courses for dentists are regularly held on cruise ships and in such scholarly hubs as Las Vegas, where attendance at the for-profit Las Vegas Institute for Advanced Dental Studies has tripled over the past eight years, and Costa Rica, where the University of Florida has been offering courses for the past three years. "Dentists like to bring their families and make a vacation out of it," says a spokesperson for the university's College of Dentistry.

The latest trend in continuing ed, online courses, are sometimes conducted without approval from the ADA. These classes may be run with little or no instructor supervision, nor do they answer to state dental boards. A study of

the issue in *The Journal of the American Dental Association* recommends that states begin monitoring online coursework.

9 "THAT REMINDS ME OF A JOKE I ONCE HEARD IN REHAB."

The choice of a dentist is arguably as important as your choice of a family physician, but trying to distinguish good dentists from bad can be tough. For one thing, consumers have restricted access to complaints made about dentists to their state dental boards: Only complaints that have been investigated and substantiated are available for public scrutiny.

Another worrisome fact—an estimated 15 to 18 percent of dentists are addicted to drugs or alcohol, and a 2002 study of the problem by the ADA had roughly 10 percent of dentists reporting they'd used illicit drugs in the past year. Not exactly a comforting thought with a vibrating drill stuck in your mouth. To address the issue, most states have instituted programs where dentists can get treatment for addiction, temporarily surrendering their license to practice. That's obviously a good idea, but once again, the consumer is out of the loop: Dentists who submit to these programs do so with the promise of no public disclosure in most states.

So where can you turn for help to find a competent, trustworthy dentist? Dr. Oogle (*www.doctoroogle.com*) offers more than 82,000 reviews of dentists nationwide. Looking for a Texas dentist? We found a complaint against one who suggested a patient take out a home-equity line of credit to pay for expensive veneers. Um, next.

10 "YOU THINK THIS ROOT CANAL HURTS—WAIT TILL YOU GET MY BILL."

The skyrocketing cost of health care is an issue of growing concern; what you might not know is that dental treatment is rising faster than other kinds of medical services. A $1,000 dental bill in 1985 would translate into $2,837 in 2006, since dental care has shot up at nearly twice the rate of inflation, according to the Bureau of Labor Statistics, and of all Americans who had at least one dental expense in 2003, the average annual cost was $540, up 41 percent from 1996.

The good news is that 65 percent of employers now offer dental benefits, according to Mercer Human Resource Consulting. But that's not the whole story, as employers are paying less of the tab than they used to: Only 23 percent of policies are fully covered by employers, and average premiums for families have risen about 5 percent per year for the past six years, according to the National Association of Dental Plans.

If you really want to save money on your teeth, take care of them. Experts say decay and gum disease can be prevented to a large extent, so don't forget to floss.

THINGS TO DO

• **We all know that dentists** recommend brushing twice a day with fluoride toothpaste—but technique is important, too. Ask your dentist for tips on the best way to brush and floss to help maintain healthy teeth and gums.

• **Be sure to replace your toothbrush** every three to four months—sooner if bristles are fraying.

• **Feeling overwhelmed? If your dentist** suggests multiple treatments and you're concerned about cost, ask him to prioritize treatments so you know which are most important or time-sensitive, and which can be delayed without serious consequence. Then together, devise a treatment schedule you both can live with.

• **If you have a billing dispute** or complaint and talking the matter over with your dentist hasn't been fruitful, it's time to call your local dental association—they'll advise you on how to quickly resolve the issue, and if necessary, they'll step in.

10 Things Your
Eye Doctor
Won't Tell You

1 *"OPHTHALMOLOGIST, OPTOMETRIST—WHAT DOES IT REALLY MATTER?"*

For years it was as plain as that big "E" on the wall: Optometrists, who have a doctor of optometry degree, checked you for glasses, and ophthalmologists, who are M.D.'s, treated you for eye diseases. But the lines have blurred, so to speak. Over the past two decades, all 50 states have widened rules to allow optometrists to treat many of the same medical conditions that M.D.'s do. In Oklahoma, despite protests from the American Medical Association, optometrists can now perform some surgeries, too.

While optometrists say that their degree now covers all the skills needed to treat eye diseases, many M.D.'s still argue it's no substitute for medical school. Which should you use? A rule of thumb: For regular checkups and problems affecting the outside of the eye, such as allergies or dry eye, an optometrist is sufficient. (Two sites for locating good ones: the American Academy of Optometry, at *www.aaopt.org,* and the American Optometric Association, at *www.aoa.org.*) But if you experience symptoms such as loss of vision or flashing light, or if your optometrist finds signs of a cataract or macular degeneration, it merits a visit to an ophthalmologist.

2 *"HANG ON, JUST A FEW MORE TESTS. PAPA NEEDS A NEW SPEEDBOAT."*

Whether you see an optometrist or an ophthalmologist, most people should get their eyes checked about every two years, according to the American Optometric Association (AOA). A few tests are evergreen: the trusty eye chart, which gives a basic idea of what you can see; a refraction test, in which you look through a machine to determine your exact prescription needs; a cover test, using a paddle, which reveals how well your eye muscles work together; a test for glaucoma; and a "slit lamp" examination and retinal exam, which look for diseases inside your eye.

But some "routine" tests for otherwise healthy patients are probably unnecessary—especially if they're not included in the basic exam fee. A "visual field examination," in which a machine is used to check side vision, may be one such test, says Walter Beebe, M.D., a cornea specialist in Dallas. It can pick up advanced glaucoma or a brain tumor, he says, but unless symptoms or other signs warrant it, the test is probably not necessary. Another potential overkill fee: "photography of the eye." Many doctors will encourage it on the first visit, but, Beebe says, some want to repeat it every time. "It's hard to make a case for upwards of $100 for everybody who walks through the door," he says.

Some "routine" tests for otherwise healthy patients are probably unnecessary—especially if they're not included in the basic exam fee.

3 "THOSE $20 DRUGSTORE SPECS JUST MIGHT DO THE TRICK."

It's a relatively minor but annoying sign of middle age: Small print starts to get a little blurry, making those stock tables maddeningly hard to read. The medical term is presbyopia, a hardening of the crystalline lens, and it's becoming more common as a nation of aging baby boomers start squinting their way through dinner menus.

The solution many people quietly opt for is a pair of those ubiquitous drugstore reading glasses, which help magnify vision for a low-impact $10 or $20, versus 5 or 10 times that for prescription glasses. The problem with "drugstore readers" or "cheaters," says San Diego optician Carter Shrum, is that since they're mass-produced, the magnifying strength is the same for both eyes and is usually centered within each lens. That may be bad for

you if that centering doesn't correspond well with the shape of your face or if, like many people, you have a different refractive error in each eye.

And like any mass-produced product, says Minnesota optometrist Kerry Beebe, some readers are better than others. A good eye doctor can suggest which ones are best for your situation, Beebe says, or he can analyze them "to check that the powers are what and where they're supposed to be."

4 "THESE LENSES WILL MAKE YOUR HEAD SWIM."

If you need bifocals but can't bear the idea of wearing lenses with etched-in lines, you have another option. Progressive lenses offer varied lens strengths like bifocals, but the varying prescriptions are graduated, so they're invisible to anyone but the wearer. Other than cost—$400 or more for the lenses alone—some progressives do have a major drawback: They can be difficult to get used to, causing dizziness, headaches, even teeth grinding as the eyes adjust. When San Diego human resources director Debi Ives first tried them, she got dizzy, had trouble focusing, and lost her balance on the stairs. "I couldn't see where my feet were going," she says.

Adjusting to progressives can take from a few minutes to two weeks or longer; if you experience problems, have your glasses checked to ensure they were ground and fitted properly—a good reason to ask about return and repair policies before you buy. A misplacement of the "near" zone, for example, can make a big difference. When Ives tried progressives again a year later, this time using larger lenses with less variation between zones, she was recoached on "pointing with her nose," rather than shifting her eyes to see different objects. "I've had much more success," she says.

5 "I HAVE ZERO INTENTION OF HANDING OVER YOUR CONTACT LENS PRESCRIPTION."

Since the late 1970s, eye doctors have been required by law to provide you with your eyeglass prescription after an exam so that you can buy glasses wherever you want. It wasn't until early 2004 that they had to do the same with contact lens scripts. Under the new law, a doctor can no longer make you buy your lenses from his office once the exam-and-fitting stage is complete. Char Pagar, an attorney with the Federal Trade Commission, points out that a contact lens prescription still isn't ready for release after an initial exam the way glasses are, but often requires one follow-up to ensure that the proposed lenses are right for you. However, "once the doctor is willing to sell you the lenses," Pagar says, "that fitting is complete."

But not all doctors are readily handing over the scripts. Some, Shrum says, "will lead patients into the dispensing place and hand [the prescription] to a person working there." If your doctor balks at giving you your lens prescription, first remind him of the law; if you still meet with resistance, you can file a complaint at *www.ftc.gov*. In October 2004, the FTC sent warning letters to 25 lens prescribers and sellers who were allegedly violating the rule.

6 "OF COURSE YOUR CHILD NEEDS GLASSES. HE'S SQUINTING, ISN'T HE?"

If your child is straining to see the chalkboard, don't assume glasses are the answer. Unfortunately, too many eye doctors do. A 2004 study by Vanderbilt University professor and pediatric ophthalmologist Sean P. Donahue found that kids were more likely to be prescribed unnecessary glasses if they saw an optometrist or general ophthalmologist than if they went to a pediatric ophthalmologist. Donahue estimates almost one in five kids who wear glasses don't need them. Worse, superfluous glasses may cause headaches or even legitimate vision problems.

A pediatric ophthalmologist is attuned to how kids' eyes develop, says David Granet, M.D., director of pediatric ophthalmology at UC-San Diego. "You have to understand those changes, or you can do the wrong thing." Rather than taking your child to your eye doctor, he says, let the pediatrician examine him during annual checkups and refer you to a specialist if needed; to locate specialists in your area, go to *www .aao.org/find_eyemd.cfm*. If your child ultimately does need glasses, avoid mass retailers and use a shop specializing in kids' glasses, since fitting their frames can be tricky.

7 "YOU CAN GET GLASSES MUCH CHEAPER AT COSTCO..."

Since new prescription glasses can easily cost hundreds of dollars, a good number of savvy consumers take their prescriptions elsewhere, often to mass chains or warehouse stores, looking for a break on price. And more often than not, they get it. According to optical trade organization Vision Council of America, the average price for eyeglasses exceeds $200 per pair: Frames cost an average $117, and a pair of lenses, an average of about $101. But some retailers offer lower prices: At wholesale club Costco, for example, the median price for eyeglasses is more than $50 below the norm.

But what do you give up when you go the megastore route? Some selection, particularly among the higher-end merchandise, more-personalized service, and that's about it. What about shopping for frames on the Internet? Judy Reggio, a stay-at-home mother in Cranford, N.J., was hit with a serious jolt of buyer's remorse when she spotted her brand-new $400 DKNY frames for $100 less on a Web retailer's site. But the truth is, she's better off having paid the extra money. Ordering glasses online can be complicated (do you really want to attempt to measure your own pupil distances?), and the nuances of a well-made pair of glasses are best handled at a bricks-and-mortar store, where you get a hands-on fitting and can more conveniently come back for adjustments.

No matter where you shop for glasses, though, be sure your lenses are ground and fitted by a professional optician. To verify that you're dealing with a reputable outfit, look for technicians who have been certified by the American Board of Opticianry/National Contact Lens Examiners, which requires rigorous testing.

8 "... BUT WHATEVER YOU DO, DON'T SKIMP ON THE EXTRAS."

When Brian Wade, a teacher in Los Angeles, bought new glasses, he got scratch-resistant, polycarbonate lenses and paid $45 extra for an antiglare coating. But a few months later, his lenses were covered with scratches. He took them back to his optometrist and learned that the antiglare he chose was vulnerable to scratching regardless of the quality of lens beneath it. The technology behind coatings has improved a great deal in the past decade, says Janice Jurkus, a professor at the Illinois College of Optometry, but overall, "You get what you pay for." At the very least, look for a one-year warranty on coatings, optician Shrum says.

Frames should be covered for defects for at least 90 days, but ideally, a full year. And paying a little extra, Shrum adds, can reap big rewards. Most vision-care plans, he says, cover a $75 frame, but if you spend as little as $25 more, "you'll get a three-times-better frame." Frames in the $160 to $180 range, he says, are typically made more carefully, with stronger plastic or metal, and hold their shape better. But anything over $250, experts agree, means you're likely paying for style or a designer name.

9 "MY LASER NEEDS A TUNE-UP."

Laser surgery—the most common form of refractive surgery, which alters the eye to correct vision—continues to boom. In 2007 some 1.5 million Americans had a Lasik procedure, according to Jobson Optical Research. While many people are under the impression that the laser surgery known as Lasik is a uniform procedure, in reality, several different companies make the lasers used in the procedure, and not all of them are created equal.

Laser manufacturer Visx, which has the largest U.S. market share, is well regarded by many doctors. But even with the best equipment, surgeons must be consistent in getting their lasers updated regularly to help guarantee safe, precise performance. So when shopping for a laser surgeon, ask doctors how often they have to perform retreatments or enhancements—as well as how often they have their laser upgraded. (In most cases, the answer should be at least once a year.) A good place to check out laser options: the FDA's informational site at *www.fda.gov/cdrh/lasik.*

10 *"NOTHING LASTS FOREVER—NOT EVEN LASER SURGERY."*

Some studies of the newest forms of Lasik put your odds of 20/20-or-better vision at roughly 94 to 98 percent. Still, up to 10 percent of Lasik patients need a follow-up procedure or enhancement. But even with an enhancement, don't count on perfect vision forever. As the eyes age, you may still need reading glasses. Matt Wapner, a lawyer from Hoboken, N.J., had Lasik surgery in 1998, and his vision improved from 20/400 to 20/10—better than perfect. Shortly after, he started seeing halos at night, and within a few years had regressed to 20/40. Wapner has since reverted to glasses. "I see so much crisper with glasses that I've started wearing them all the time," he says.

While new versions of Lasik likely offer better long-term results than that, talk to your doctor about expectations. "If a patient says, 'I want to see as well as I do with glasses and want it guaranteed,' that's unrealistic," Kerry Beebe says. "A realistic expectation is that you'll be less dependent on your glasses."

THINGS TO DO

● **Thanks to a 2004 law,** you aren't obligated to buy glasses or contact lenses from your eye doctor. So shop around— you'll likely find a better deal elsewhere.

● **Check** *www.allaboutvision.com* for tips on where to buy contact lenses or glasses—but don't forget, you'll still need an eye exam at least once a year.

● **Depending on your state,** the role of an optometrist has been expanding to include treatment for minor eye problems. Visit the Vision Center at

www.everydayhealth.com for tips on eye exams and when to see which type of eye-care professional.

● **Lasik eye surgery** is a big decision— but you can get all the information you need, including a checklist for how to prepare, at *www.fda.gov/cdrh/lasik.*

● **When it comes to eye surgery,** you'll want to stick to a specialist and stay away from price shopping. The best way to find one? Ask your primary-care physician or another trusted doctor for a referral.

10 Things Your
Orthodontist
Won't Tell You

1 "I MIGHT NOT REALLY BE AN ORTHODONTIST."

Orthodontic work isn't just for kids anymore; today, people of all ages are looking to build the perfect smile they didn't come by naturally. In 2007, the most recent year for which figures are available, orthodontic specialists treated some 4.6 million patients, according to a study in the *Journal of Clinical Orthodontics*—a 15 percent increase from 1998. The real number is probably even higher, since that figure doesn't include patients who get orthodontic treatment from general dentists. Indeed, there is no law that prevents any dentist from practicing orthodontics, which more and more dentists have been taking on as a way to increase their business and client base.

How to make sure you're seeing a trained orthodontist? Look for a member of the American Association of Orthodontists (AAO), which means she has gone through an average of four years of dental school and a minimum of two years in an accredited residency program. Another good sign: voluntary certification with the American Board of Orthodontics. You can search the organization's website, *www.americanboardortho.com,* for practicing members in your area.

2 "MY FEES ARE NEGOTIABLE..."

Getting orthodontic work done isn't cheap. Minor adjustments, which might require treatment for three to six months, can cost between $600 and $1,500, but the median fee for full-scale treatment is $4,500 for a child and $5,000 for an adult—even as much as $10,000 in pricey areas like New York City. That means if you have only partial insurance coverage or are paying out of pocket, your bill can be pretty steep.

The good news is that orthodontists often offer a variety of payment plans. Many allow patients to pay in monthly installments with no interest, and with some orthodontists, you can negotiate the fee itself. In 2003 Lisa Madsen sought the opinion of two orthodontists when she wanted to correct her bite. She felt more comfortable with the diagnosis of the first, though his treatment was more expensive. "I took the lower quote to the [first] orthodontist and said, 'Can you work with me?'" says Madsen, a stay-at-home mom in East Windsor, Conn. The result: He reduced his price by $300.

Other angles: Some orthodontists will give a discount, usually 5 to 10 percent, if you pay the total in cash or with a credit card at the beginning of treatment. And some have even been known to offer a family discount of $300 per patient after the first one is treated.

3 *"... BUT YOUR FINAL PAYMENT MAY NOT BE SO FINAL."*

Most orthodontists charge an all-inclusive fee, which covers appointments and appliances from the beginning of treatment to the finish. But patients often end up shelling out hundreds of dollars more for broken appliances, retainers, and appointments that extend beyond the scheduled treatment time. Orthodontists can also charge extra for X-rays, molds, and missed appointments along the way.

Just ask Marianne Eagan. After her son finished with braces back in 2000, his orthodontist installed a permanent retainer on the back of his bottom teeth; when it cracked a year and a half later, Eagan, a fitness supervisor at Purdue University in West Lafayette, Ind., had to pay $130 for a new removable retainer. And when the replacement wore down, she had to pay for another one. Her advice: "Make sure you have everything written down in your contract." Also, read the fine print for hidden extra costs—and leave a few hundred dollars in your budget for unforeseen bills.

4 *"MY TREATMENT MIGHT NOT BE THE RIGHT TREATMENT."*

Even orthodontists admit that straightening teeth is not an exact science. There are often clear approaches for common conditions such as buck teeth and cross-bites. But more complicated cases may involve judgment calls—

whether it's necessary to pull teeth, for example, or to perform jaw surgery. The wrong approach could prolong treatment or make the problem worse.

In fact, if you go to two different orthodontists, you will very likely hear two different opinions about how to treat your teeth. If the orthodontist suggests invasive treatment, such as jaw surgery or pulling several teeth to create more space, it's a good idea to seek a second or even third opinion. In some cases there may be a less invasive treatment available— polishing off some of the enamel between teeth, for example, to create more space.

Be sure to inquire about alternative treatments and the possible risks each option poses. And ask the orthodontist if you can see pictures of cases similar to yours that were treated in the same manner. Or better yet, talk to former patients—some orthodontists keep a list of people who have gone through the same treatment and are willing to speak with potential patients about their experience.

5 *"YOUR KID NEEDS BRACES— BUT MAYBE NOT RIGHT AWAY."*

The American Association of Orthodontists recommends that all children see an orthodontist by age seven. Indeed, advocates of early treatment argue that skeletal problems, such as a severe cross-bite or narrow jaw, are much simpler to correct when the jaw is still growing, making a second treatment— often required when patients are in their teens—easier and faster. Orthodontists might also suggest early treatment for severe cases of buck teeth or crowding, for example, on younger kids who feel embarrassed or are teased at school.

But some orthodontists say that not every child should be treated so early. Often, they say, later treatment will still be necessary, which can drive up the total bill significantly. And early treatment doesn't always guarantee easier treatment later on—sometimes adult teeth can grow in ways that create a whole new set of problems. "Kids are such moving targets," says William Gray Grieve, a Eugene, Ore., orthodontist. Early treatment, he says, "may or may not make it easier later on."

If the orthodontist suggests early preventative treatment, ask for a clear explanation of what he intends to do and why it can't wait. Also, assess the maturity of your child. Is she going to be cooperative? Can she handle the discomfort involved?

6 "THERE'S NO GUARANTEE YOUR TEETH WILL STAY STRAIGHT."

Ten years ago, journalist Debbie Michel wore braces for a year and a half to correct her overbite and crooked teeth. After getting her braces removed, she says she diligently wore her retainer for a year but then slowly started lapsing until she wasn't wearing it at all. Eight years later her teeth had shifted so much that she had to get braces again. The second treatment took seven months and cost $1,000.

Since your face and the density of your bones will continue to change over time, some slight movement of the teeth even after orthodontic treatment can be expected. But as anyone who has ever worn a retainer can attest, orthodontists' pleas to patients to wear one often go unheeded, and without the use of a retainer, teeth can very quickly begin to revert to their old positions. Since orthodontists don't offer warranty-type programs, if the teeth do move out of alignment, patients have little recourse beyond getting back in the chair.

To help keep teeth properly aligned, many orthodontists will put permanent retainers on the back of patients' lower teeth, which have a greater risk of shifting. And most agree that to keep teeth in place, patients should wear their removable retainers regularly—almost all the time for the first two to six months after the braces come off, then every night for the rest of their lives.

7 "I DON'T MEAN TO GROSS YOU OUT, BUT SOMEONE MIGHT HAVE WORN THESE BRACES BEFORE YOU DID."

Some orthodontists use professionally sterilized and remanufactured materials that have been worn by other people. Ortho-Cycle, a Hollywood, Fla., company that recycles brackets, bands, and other orthodontic attachments, says it sells its products to U.S. dentists and orthodontists across the country, who in turn can save about 50 percent by using the recycled material.

Still, many orthodontists say that although there is no real health risk associated with the practice, they prefer to use new parts because of the "gross-out" factor. "It's more psychological than scientific," says Terry Pracht, former president of the American Association of Orthodontists. If the idea of wearing used materials bothers you, ask your orthodontist if she uses recycled brackets or other equipment.

8 "BRACELESS OPTIONS ARE TRENDY, BUT THEY MAY NOT BE THE RIGHT CHOICE."

Invisalign, a teeth-alignment system that uses clear, thin, removable plastic aligners to move teeth, debuted in 1999 and has become popular in the past decade for obvious reasons: The system is less noticeable than braces, and treatment typically lasts only 6 to 12 months.

But think twice before going with this option. It's expensive—the national average cost of Invisalign treatment is $5,000—and it's not always the best choice for many patients. Some orthodontists don't recommend it for complicated treatments like jaw realignments or tooth rotations, for example, though Invisalign's parent company Align Technology says that orthodontists and dentists who have more experience are starting to use it for increasingly complicated cases. And while Invisalign is removable, it still takes dedication: Patients have to wear the aligners at all times, except when eating, drinking, brushing, or flossing their teeth.

In addition, many orthodontists still aren't practiced at it. Lisa Madsen, the patient who negotiated her fee, had her heart set on Invisalign, and her primary dentist was ready to prescribe it for her. But when she found out that he had handled only two cases before her, she balked. "I didn't want to be a guinea pig," she says. Madsen sought opinions from

two orthodontists—both of whom said standard braces were better for her teeth.

9 "THIS PROCESS COULD TAKE MUCH LONGER THAN YOU THINK."

How long does orthodontic treatment generally take? Anywhere from six months to three years, and most patients finish within two years. Orthodontists typically set an estimated time frame at the beginning of treatment, but it can sometimes run longer than expected. This inexactitude may be due to a variety of reasons—a misdiagnosis on the part of the orthodontist, a patient's failure to adhere to instructions, or an atypical growth pattern that may cause a teenage patient's teeth or jaws to move differently than anticipated.

When Brian Weiler's son Zac started with braces at age 12, the orthodontist prescribed a straightforward 18-month treatment to correct his crooked teeth and slight overbite. But when one of Zac's adult teeth didn't come in on its own, he had to go through oral surgery mid-treatment. That helped stretch the time frame by four months past the original estimate, costing Weiler some $250 more than he had anticipated. "The whole experience was not pleasant emotionally and financially," says Weiler, of Duluth, Ga. "I felt like I was getting ripped off." Zac's orthodontist blames the extra time on missed appointments and Weiler's delay in scheduling the surgery.

To best avoid such problems, adhere to the orthodontist's instructions. Also, if your child is being treated, ask your orthodontist to do a growth study: Taking

X-rays of your child's hands and looking at the parents' and siblings' jaws can help gauge future growth speed and patterns.

10 *"BY THE WAY, THIS IS GOING TO HURT—A LOT."*

It's no secret that orthodontic treatment can be painful. In most cases, the discomfort goes away two or three days after braces are put on or tightened, but some people are extremely sensitive. Just ask Robyn Perry, a stay-at-home mom in Loveland, Ohio. Seven weeks after getting braces put on, she had lost seven pounds because eating was so difficult. "There have been days when I've been in tears telling my husband, 'I want them off,'" she says.

Soreness can generally be relieved with over-the-counter pain medicine, but you can also ask your orthodontist to tighten the bottom and upper braces at different appointments. Chewing sugarless gum, too, can help bring relief, by stimulating ligaments in the teeth.

Even more painful are lingual braces, which attach to the backside of the teeth and are popular among adults. Lingual braces can tear up the patient's tongue; some also find it difficult to talk and may speak with a lisp for the first month of treatment. Within five days of having lingual braces put on, Javier Avila, a teacher in Brooklyn, N.Y., says his tongue had been scraped raw—and his students often asked him to repeat himself. How bad was it? He called his orthodontist's emergency number and had him remove the braces on a Sunday morning.

THINGS TO DO

● **You can't always predict such** things as broken braces or lost retainers—but you can at least be prepared for the added costs they might incur. Talk to your orthodontist about pricing such contingencies right in the initial contract.

● **For braces-friendly recipes** anyone can enjoy, go to *www.braces.org/fungames/funfacts* or *www.parenthood.com* (type "braces friendly recipes" into the search box).

● **For tips on how to care** for your retainer—and not lose it—go to *www.myretainer.com*.

● **When it comes to payment plans,** you probably have more options than you think. Some offices offer family discounts, discounts for payments in full, monthly payments, and even reduced monthly payments through programs with your credit card provider, so discuss it with your orthodontist.

10 Things Your
Pharmacist
Won't Tell You

1 *"I'M OVERWORKED AND STRESSED OUT..."*

It seems that doctors are prescribing a lot more medication than they used to. In 2007 pharmacists filled 3.8 billion prescriptions, up from 3.3 billion in 2002. Michael Negrete, CEO of the Pharmacy Foundation of California, says that some physicians may actually be prescribing drugs unnecessarily, say for the flu. "It's easier and quicker than explaining to a patient why they don't need an antibiotic," Negrete says.

The upshot is that your pharmacist is probably working harder than she should be—Paul Lofholm, owner of two pharmacies in Marin County, Calif., says his pharmacists fill prescriptions at a rate of 80 to 100 per shift. "Pharmacists are stressed out," says Frederick Mayer, a veteran pharmacist and president and CEO of the Pharmacists Planning Service in California, "and it's getting worse." One side effect is that most pharmacists don't have the time to offer the counseling federal and state law require with each prescription. It's not just a formality—a pharmacist's recommendation for how and when to take a certain medication can go a long way, for example, in helping to decrease some of the adverse side effects of medication.

2 *"...WHICH MEANS I'M MORE ERROR-PRONE."*

At first it was a bit of a mystery: When Daniel Hawkins of Danville, Calif., took the penicillin he was prescribed, he became violently ill. But days later it was discovered that he had mistakenly been given Zoloft, an antidepressant. It may sound like an isolated incident, but it happens all the time. In California alone, there were 433 complaints of prescription error filed with the state Pharmacy Board in 2007. Those inside the pharmacy industry blame such mix-ups on long hours, tough working conditions, and a shortage of qualified personnel.

Another big factor: the increasingly rapid pace of the work. "Things get so busy," Mayer says, "that I have no time to look at the computer screen, or even to look inside the bottle and make sure that the pills I'm giving out are the right ones." Pharmacists are also being asked to spend more time on administrative chores these days, especially those involved with insurance. "Add to that the small things—such as insurance companies only approving 30-day dosages at a time, causing more face time with each patient in the pharmacy, which only adds more to the administrative hassle," says Lofholm. "It's a spiraling effect, which means more distractions open up more room for error."

3 *"I DON'T UNDERSTAND ALL MY MERCHANDISE."*

With so many people taking an interest in alternative medicine these days, most pharmacies sell profitable herbal remedies right at the prescription counter. This setup encourages customers to make impulsive herbal purchases while picking up their prescriptions.

But many pharmacists are woefully uninformed about the complications that can develop when various drugs get taken in tandem. Even if your druggist sees you purchasing, say, the memory enhancer ginkgo biloba as you pick up a prescription for the blood thinner Coumadin, studies have shown that he may fail to recognize that the two taken together increase your risk of internal bleeding and stroke. "It is a problem," says Varro E. Tyler, former professor emeritus at the Pharmacy School of Purdue University. "Herbs get sold in this country as dietary supplements and foods, but they are drugs. And all drugs have interactions."

Many pharmacists are woefully uninformed about the complications that can develop when various drugs get taken in tandem.

"Don't buy dietary supplements, period," says Larry Sasich, chair of the department of pharmacy practice at the LECOM School of Pharmacy in Erie, Pa. "They're not regulated, so you have no idea if what you're seeing on the label is really what is in the bottle."

4 *"MY DRUG-SWAPPING COULD MAKE YOU SICK."*

Pharmacists will sometimes switch up a patient's medication from one manufacturer's make to another without ever asking permission. And most of the time, it's fine. But there are times when this practice can be dangerous, particularly in the case of epilepsy patients and some people on thyroid or heart medication. "Most people can use any manufacturer's version of a product without problems, but there's a small but significant number of people that cannot," says Sandy Finucane, vice president of legal and government affairs for the Maryland-based Epilepsy Foundation. "Unfortunately, we don't know who those people are until after they've experienced the side effects."

Many epilepsy patients in particular have spent years trying to find the right drug and the right dosage to control their seizures, Finucane says, and a drug from an unfamiliar manufacturer can lead to unexpected side effects including seizures, blurred or double vision, or severe headaches. "Because the consequences of having a seizure are so dramatic, we want to do everything we can to avoid this," Finucane says. Her suggestion: All epilepsy patients should inform their pharmacist of their condition and ask to have their records indicate that switching from one manufacturer to another is prohibited. "And if any questions come up, tell the pharmacist to call your doctor directly," she says.

5 "FRANKLY, YOUR PRIVATE RECORDS AREN'T ALL THAT PRIVATE."

While the Health Insurance Portability and Accountability Act (HIPAA), first enacted by Congress in 1996, has helped to better protect patients' privacy over the years by ushering in a host of confidentiality laws, there are still some ways that information about your health and medication history can get disseminated without your knowledge. For example, drug companies are still paying pharmacists to access customers' personal information for consumer marketing so that they can send out refill reminders or information about a new drug brand to patients.

But as the medical profession goes digital—with doctors' sending prescriptions electronically to pharmacists and the use of information exchange networks, which allow doctors, pharmacists, and even nursing homes to access patients' electronic medical records—industry experts are worried that HIPAA may have some troubling loopholes. "The HIPAA privacy rule was written at a time when we weren't aggressively moving towards a networked health-care system, so we have to review that law and strengthen that law to protect consumer privacy," says Leslie Harris, president of the Washington, D.C.–based Center for Democracy and Technology. "If too many people have

access to that database, you've got a big problem."

If you're concerned, ask your physician or pharmacist up front what their privacy policies are and exactly who will have access to your medical records, says Christine Bechtel, vice president of eHealth Initiative, a nonprofit organization in Washington, D.C. Only those who are authorized and authenticated should be able to look at your records, she says.

6 "I CAN BE PRETTY SNEAKY SOMETIMES."

It's certainly not true of all pharmacists, but some have been known to resort to underhanded tricks in order to beef up their profit margins. Jim Sheehan, an associate U.S. attorney based in Philadelphia, experienced this firsthand when he was on vacation in Florida and came down with strep throat. A local pharmacist there inspected Sheehan's prescription for antibiotics from a nearby urgent-care center and offered the following choice: Pay cash for the medicine and get it immediately, or run it through Sheehan's insurance company and wait half an hour since he was from out of state. Sheehan, who specializes in prosecuting health-care fraud cases, had heard of this scam before. "The pharmacist figured that I had no idea of the retail price, and he would have charged me whatever he wanted," he says. Sheehan opted to wait, and lo and behold, the process of checking with the insurance company took only a few minutes.

Other tricks he's come across are equally dodgy. Sheehan says he's seen pharmacists who buy deeply discounted drug samples from doctors then turn around and sell them at retail prices. He also has encountered unethical druggists who will charge a customer her insurance plan's $10 copayment even if the retail price for the drug is less than that.

7 "PAYING OUT-OF-POCKET? THE PRICE OF YOUR PRESCRIPTION JUST WENT UP."

The pharmacy business should be all about uniformity. Go from drugstore to drugstore, and your prescription should have the same name, dosage, and instructions for use. But that's not always the case when it comes to the cost of medication: A recent comparison of pharmacies found little consistency in the price of prescriptions. Why? There are differences in the cost of doing business—rents vary, as do other fixed expenses.

But there's another factor at work, explains Larry Sasich: "The pharmacist has to figure out his break-even point." Among the variables is the percentage of prescriptions filled that are covered by insurance. In pharmacies with a lot of covered customers, the break-even cost is shifted heavily to patients who are paying full price—generally, the elderly on Medicare or the working poor. "Pharmacists can't push around a big HMO," says Sasich, "but they can push around a little old lady."

8 "THIS MEDICATION IS STALE."

Most people don't think that underworld crime figures can come between them

and their Celebrex. Well, they haven't heard of Anthony "Tony Ripe" Civella. In 1991 Civella was convicted of buying $1 million worth of discounted drugs that were supposed to go to nursing homes—where large quantities of medication are purchased at bulk prices and used quickly—but instead found their way to retail pharmacies (at a tidy profit for Tony Ripe). The problem is called "drug diversion." In a typical case, crooked druggists buy diverted medication at reduced prices and in quantities far bigger than they're legally allowed to handle; by the time the last of the shipment reaches consumers, the pills are long out of date.

The big losers in all this are consumers who end up with stale medication that hasn't been properly stored, explains a spokesperson for the U.S. attorney's office in Kansas City, Mo. There's also a secondary price, since in the long run such practices raise the cost to the consumer. "Somewhere the drug manufacturers and wholesalers have to recoup their losses from having discounted drugs going to retail pharmacists," the spokesperson says.

9 "I DON'T JUST SELL DRUGS. I MAKE THEM."

Say your five-year-old needs a medication that comes only in pill form. If you think he'll do better with a liquid, you can ask your pharmacist to make the conversion himself—right there at the store. It's called "compounding"—a traditional practice in which pharmacies combine, mix, or alter ingredients to create unique medications that meet specific needs of a patient—and when done right, it's perfectly safe. But some pharmacists compound drugs that already exist—such as injectable morphine or hormone-replacement-therapy meds, for example—because it's cheaper. "They do that so they can make more money," says Larry Sasich. "Only the dangers get passed on, none of the savings."

The bottom line: If the product is available commercially, you're better off getting it that way. "Pharmacists don't [compound] under good manufacturing guidelines; they do it in the back of their shops," says Sasich, advising that "if you can buy the FDA product, you should."

10 *"YOU CAN GET ANY PRESCRIPTION YOU LIKE ONLINE."*

Go on the Internet to buy medicine, and you'll probably save some time and money. But be careful. While there are many legitimate websites that sell prescriptions, such as RxSolutions.com, there are also countless dubious operations in cyberspace, which tend to specialize in "lifestyle drugs" like Viagra and Propecia. In lieu of requiring a doctor's prescription, these rogue sites offer e-physicals in which you answer questions to determine whether or not you should be taking the medication in question. Not only is this illegal, it's dangerous. "Viagra can kill a man with a heart condition," says Mark Herr, former director of the New Jersey Division of Consumer Affairs. "You should not be buying Viagra online if you do not have a doctor prescribing it."

When purchasing prescription medication online, look for an insignia bearing the initials VIPPS—which stand for Verified Internet Pharmacy Practice Sites—to find reputable sellers.

THINGS TO DO

• **Compare prices at a few pharmacies** in your area before settling on one. Prices aren't necessarily fixed across the board.

• **Even when using a verified** online pharmacist, choose one that lists its phone number—if there's a problem with your medication, you'll have to get in touch with them immediately.

• **Have your pharmacist compound medications** for you only if he's done it before and you trust him—as a general rule, use the FDA product if it's available.

• **Save herbal supplements for specialists,** and avoid impulse buys at the pharmaceutical counter. If you see something you're interested in, make a point of asking your doctor about it at your next visit.

10 Things
Drug Companies
Won't Tell You

1 *"WE'RE OFTEN YOUR DOCTOR'S BIGGEST SOURCE OF INFORMATION."*

It's comforting to imagine your physician sitting behind his desk after hours, carefully perusing reports on the latest drugs. While some still do their research the old-fashioned way, many doctors today get the bulk of their information from drug reps, essentially door-to-door peddlers who push specific medicines. Drug companies are spending between $12 and $30 billion annually selling and promoting their products to doctors, according to various reports. But what's really disturbing is the quality of information they provide. In 1995 a study by the *Journal of the American Medical Association* found that 11 percent of statements made by drug reps were found to be inaccurate and 35 percent of their promotional materials lacked a fair balance of information. "I have no reason to think that the situation is any better today," says Peter Lurie, the deputy director of the Health Research Group at Public Citizen.

Typically, says Allen F. Shaughnessy, doctor of pharmacology and research professor of public health and family medicine at Tufts University, a drug rep gives a 90-second spiel that hits three or four salient points, followed by the classic sales pitch. "Everybody thinks that doctors are coldly logical," says Shaughnessy. "But pharmaceutical reps just keep pushing buttons"—probing for guilt, insecurity, and pride—"until they find one that works. To me, it's outrageous." Jeff Trewhitt of the Pharmaceutical Research and Manufacturers of America counters that "doctors have to be aware of new medicines when they come out." Spreading this awareness, he says, "is the primary role of sales representatives."

To gauge how seriously your physician relies on drug reps, Shaughnessy suggests that you press for details: "Ask him why you are taking the drug he is prescribing, and make sure you understand what he explains." This approach will either get you the information you need, "or else you'll see a physician who blusters and carries on about why you are questioning him," says Shaughnessy. The latter scenario "will show you that he doesn't have a clue."

2 *"HYPE IS OUR FAVORITE MEDICINE."*

Choosing a medication shouldn't be like choosing Pepsi over Coke. But that's very much what's happening, thanks to the drug companies and their ad agencies. With famous faces like Bob Dole, NBA star Alonzo Mourning, Lance Armstrong, and Cheryl Ladd all playing spokesperson for various brands of medication, the companies marketing prescription drugs have learned to harness celebrity star power to help boost their brands.

Blame it on the Food and Drug Administration. When the agency's decision to liberalize drug advertising in the late 1990s allowed direct-to-consumer, or DTC, campaigns, pharmaceutical ad budgets skyrocketed. From 1996 to 2005, spending on DTC campaigns increased 330 percent, according to a 2007 study by *The New England Journal of Medicine.* The money is clearly well placed: A Harris poll has shown that 36 percent of people who take a prescription drug feel that advertising helps them make better decisions about which medications to take.

"It's horrendous," says Brian L. Strom, M.D., chairman of biostatistics and epidemiology at the University of Pennsylvania. "It's directly in conflict with proper therapeutics. But the manufacturers use patients as arms of their marketing departments." It can be dangerous, too. When Olympian Dorothy Hamill appeared promoting Vioxx for her arthritis pain, an excessive number of prescriptions were filled before the drug's heart risks became known.

3 *"THERE'S NO SUCH THING AS A FREE SAMPLE."*

Patients love getting free trial-size medications from their doctors, doctors like giving them away, and drug companies rely on samples to wade new

treatments into the pharmaceutical mainstream. In pushing free samples, drug companies hope that physicians will continue to prescribe the new—and often pricier—medication long after the honeymoon period is over. "A lot of these new drugs are more expensive than the old drugs," says Allan S. Brett, M.D., vice chair of Internal Medicine at the University of South Carolina, "so you often prescribe something more expensive when the previous drug was just as good."

But even more problematic than price is the fact that "what is being sampled is usually the newest product that has less known about its overall safety profile," says Joel Lexchin, M.D., an emergency-medicine doctor and associate chair of the School of Health Policy and Management at York University in Toronto. The good news is that with increasing financial pressure on drug companies to bring these new treatments to market, clinical trials have also increased—47.5 percent from 2000 to 2006, according to CenterWatch, a clinical-trial listing service. But it's still not ideal. "The drugs have generally been tested on between 3,000 and 5,000 people," Lexchin says. "Statistically speaking, you will only recognize what occurs in one out of 1,000 people; you may have a fatal adverse drug reaction that occurs in one out of 5,000 people."

4 *"YOUR DOCTOR IS OUR BOUNTY HUNTER."*

During a 1995 checkup, Thomas Parham's physician focused on the condition of his prostate, which had never bothered him before. The doctor sent the La

Drug companies are lining the pockets of doctors who provide human guinea pigs for their experiments.

Habra, Calif., resident to a research lab, urging him to participate in a SmithKline Beecham study for a prostate drug. Unbeknownst to Parham, the doctor was getting paid for every patient he referred to the study. Parham actually had a perfectly healthy prostate, and his heart reacted so adversely to the medication he received that he subsequently required a pacemaker. (Citing patient confidentiality, SmithKline Beecham declined to comment on the case, but stressed its commitment "to maintaining the integrity and credibility of human clinical trials.")

Facing mounting pressure to bring new medicines to market, drug companies are lining the pockets of doctors who provide human guinea pigs for their experiments. "It's hard for me to believe that this does not lead physicians to consciously or unconsciously encourage patients to participate in studies that are not in their best interest," says David Shimm, M.D., a radiation oncologist at Raleigh Regional Cancer Center in West Virginia. Drug companies also pay doctors anywhere between $500 and $5,000 an hour for speaking at dinners or conferences organized by sales reps, according to Lennox McNeary, a member of the National Physicians Alliance. "I blame the pharmaceutical company for going to my doctor and offering him

such a bounty," says Parham. "It could twist anybody's head. These people were motivated by greed. I'm a human and I was sacrificed like a goddamned lab rat."

5 "YOU'LL FIND OUT ABOUT SIDE EFFECTS THE HARD WAY."

The moderate side effects listed—dry mouth, constipation, blurred vision, and dizziness, among others—made Pat and Ben Christen of Weimar, Tex., feel comfortable about giving imipramine to their seven-year-old son, Cory, to treat his attention deficit disorder in 1999. Tragically, several months later, Cory's heart gave out and he died. Cardiac arrhythmia, a known side effect of the drug, was not listed in the information that the Christens had received from their pharmacist. "We would never have put him on it if we knew that this was a side effect," says Ben Christen. Today, the drug's label lists cardiac arrhythmia as a possible adverse reaction.

Other drugs like Vioxx and Bextra have been voluntarily removed from the U.S. market by their manufacturers after studies showed that patients taking them had an increased risk of heart attack or stroke. How did these medications get federal approval in the first place? Critics point to the drug industry's generous donations to the drug division of the FDA—$400 million in 2007. "You'd have to be living on a cloud to think that the money doesn't have an impact on the FDA's drug approvals or regulation of the industry," said Sydney Wolfe, director of the Health Research Group at Public Citizen, in a statement to the FDA from January 2008.

6 *"WITH ALL THESE COMPLICATED DRUG NAMES, IT'S NO WONDER YOU'RE CONFUSED!"*

A 73-year-old New Jersey woman named Helen McLaughlin went to her local ShopRite supermarket in 1997 and submitted a prescription for chlorpromazine, an antipsychotic medicine. The pharmacist allegedly gave her chlorpropamide by accident, which is used by diabetics to lower blood sugar. McLaughlin, as it happens, was already taking medicine to lower her blood sugar, and the additional drug reportedly set off an avalanche of medical problems that ultimately proved fatal. A ShopRite spokesperson says, "Our position is that there is no causal relationship between her death and the misfilled prescription." (The family eventually sued the supermarket; the case was settled out of court.)

The FDA reviews about 400 drug names a year, through the Office of Postmarketing Drug Risk Assessment. Before a drug's final moniker is settled on, it has to pass an expert panel review, handwriting and verbal analyses, a computer analysis, and overall risk evaluation, collectively aimed at minimizing the risk of sound-

---

How to avoid getting the wrong medication? Check your pills against those represented in an up-to-date illustrated reference book.

---

a-like and look-a-like names. But problems persist: The Institute for Safe Medication Practices estimates that medication errors—including, but not limited to, mix-ups like the ShopRite incident—result in more than 7,000 deaths a year, according to the Institute of Medicine. How to avoid getting the wrong medication? Check your pills against those represented in an up-to-date illustrated reference book, such as *The Pill Book* by Harold Silverman (at press time, in its 13th edition).

7 *"DON'T TRUST ANYTHING YOU READ ABOUT OUR DRUGS ONLINE . . ."*

If you're searching the Internet for information on, say, arthritis, what better place than a site like Arthritis.com, right? Not necessarily. While you will certainly get information there, it will come from Pfizer, maker of arthritis drug Celebrex—not exactly an unbiased source. Similarly, if you're looking to read up on depression, you'll find the site Depression.com is run by GlaxoSmithKline, maker of antidepressants Wellbutrin and Paxil. The problem with these drug-sponsored medical-information sites is that they can easily be mistaken for noncommercial information sources. And even when such affiliations are made clear, the fine line between editorial and advertorial—which can be as subtle as the exclusion of seemingly minor details—becomes even finer when viewed on a computer screen.

But the most egregious misinformation online comes from companies peddling non-FDA-regulated products such as vitamins, minerals, and supplements, according to Brooks Edwards, M.D., of the Mayo Clinic. "The most important thing in evaluating information is knowing where it's coming from," Edwards says. "Sometimes you can tell on the Internet, and sometimes you can't." In 2007 the FDA issued warnings to 180 companies extolling fraudulent diabetes cures, advising them to remove unapproved and illegal drug claims that stand in direct opposition to medical fact.

8 "... AND BE EXTRA CAREFUL WHEN ORDERING MEDS OVER THE INTERNET."

With Americans spending $275 billion on prescription drugs annually, the temptation to shop around online for the cheapest prices can be an alluring option, especially for those who value privacy. But like with most things in life, cheaper doesn't necessarily mean better. In fact, when it comes to buying prescription drugs over the Internet, big discounts might mean counterfeit capsules.

Take Marcia Bergeron, a Vancouver Island native, who in December 2006 was found dead in her house with three types of pills she had purchased online. A coroner ruled that the drugs were laced with extremely high quantities of metal, which led to the cardiac arrhythmia that killed her.

The World Health Organization estimates that 10 percent of the global drug supply is counterfeit, and that Internet-based sales of pharmaceuticals are a major source of these problem meds, threatening those who seek cheaper, stigmatized, or unauthorized treatment. Since website content is unregulated, the FDA's only recourse is to issue warnings to the public about unreliable online purveyors of pharmaceuticals. It recommends that when buying medication online, you do so only from licensed pharmacies located in the United States; also, make sure the site requires a prescription and has a pharmacist available to answer questions by phone. You can find a list of state-licensed pharmacies on the National Association of Boards of Pharmacy website, *www.nabp.com*.

9 "WE KNOW YOUR MEDICATION HISTORY— BECAUSE WE BOUGHT IT."

How do drugmakers know precisely which medicines you take—and how often your doctor renews your prescriptions? Simple. They buy the information from your drugstore. "Whenever a prescription is billed to a third party"—any HMO or benefits-management company—"you've got all of the data to construct a physician's prescribing habits," says Public Citizen's Larry Sasich. "Confidentiality is a myth." In 2006 the American Medical Association made it an option for doctors to keep their prescribing information inaccessible to reps. As of March 2008, just over 9,000 had opted out.

Such information is extremely valuable to pharmaceutical companies, which use it to gauge the degree to which individual doctors are prescribing one medication over another in the same class. Then, in order to stimulate sales, the drug companies offer a wide range of perks to groups of physicians plucked from the drugstores' sales info. Their swag arsenal includes everything from pens and pads to golf outings, steak dinners, and Caribbean trips for "medical conferences"—all of which ultimately contribute to the rocketing costs of medication. "Doctors think of themselves as totally rational," says Allen Shaughnessy. "They get offended when I tell them that they are human and cannot be wined and dined without being influenced."

10 *"WE'RE IN CAHOOTS WITH YOUR INSURER."*

Stephen Fried was in the midst of writing *Bitter Pills*, an exposé of the pharmaceutical industry, when a doctor suddenly switched his uncle from Procardia XL to a similar high-blood-pressure drug called Norvasc. Fried says he found out that "drug companies offer substantial discounts [to health-care managers] if they put all their [appropriate] patients on a particular drug." The insurer then contacts your doctor, he explains, who will usually do what the HMO requests. The problem? "You can have seizures, heart problems, dementia," Fried says. "The only reason to switch drugs should be to enhance your health. But most drug switches are made for dollars and cents."

Even when drugs are in the same class and are designed to treat the same symptoms, they are not necessarily identical. "One drug may not work as well as the other, and it could have a totally different set of side effects," says Raymond L. Woosley, M.D., president and CEO of the Critical Path Institute, a nonprofit that supports the FDA to promote safe medical-product development. "You have to individualize therapy. You can't just pick the lowest-cost drug from a list of drugs in the same class."

THINGS TO DO

● **Ask your doctor why he's prescribing** a certain drug for you. Does he genuinely recommend the medication to suit your needs, or is he simply relaying info passed on from a drug rep?

● **Don't assume a drug** that once required a prescription and is now offered over the counter is any less powerful than it was before. Be sure to read the labels, and talk to your doctor or pharmacist if you have questions.

● **Look into and talk** with your doctor or pharmacist about possible side effects of the drugs you're taking, so you know what to expect and whether you need to change brands or dosage.

● **Be smart: Buy prescription drugs** online only from licensed pharmacies located in the U.S. You can visit the National Association of Boards of Pharmacy at *www.nabp.com* for a list.

● **Need help paying for medication?** Most drug companies offer indigent patient assistance programs, which provide drugs free or at low cost to those who can't afford them. You can also visit the Partnership for Prescription Assistance at *www.pparx.org* to get info on additional prescription-assistance plans.

CHAPTER 9

Your Car

■ The automobile is at the center of American life: According to recent government statistics, Americans drive about 1.7 trillion miles every year, and more than 90 percent of American households own at least one car. No consumer advice book worth its salt would be complete without a chapter on this country's favorite means of conveyance.

Unfortunately, driving isn't as simple as turning a key and pushing the gas pedal. There are a lot of things to consider in buying, selling, leasing, or even renting a car, let alone performing maintenance, staying legal, and staying safe. In this chapter, we cover it all, from what to look out for when shopping for insurance to how to survive a trip to your local DMV.

10 Things the
DMV
Won't Tell You

1 *"IT'S OUR PLEASURE TO CONFUSE YOU."*

It seems like everyone's got a DMV horror story. For Mike Hume, a sports journalist, it came after a move from Connecticut to Virginia, when he headed to the DMV to transfer his out-of-state license. He says it took four visits and roughly three hours of standing in line to get it. The problem? Everything from not bringing enough or the right forms of ID to having his records confused with those of another driver of the same name. After an estimated 20 hours of DMV-related work over the course of a week, Hume finally received his license, and just in time: It was the day before his old one expired. "I consider myself a smart guy," Hume says. "But it doesn't matter. Everyone can be a victim at the DMV." (A Virginia DMV spokesperson says, "We have a high standard for meeting customer expectations, and have a large number who are satisfied.")

Making sense of the DMV is an $11.5 million business for DMV.org, an unofficial guide to state rules and peccadilloes. "DMV.org was created to bridge the gap between consumers and the government," says founder Raj Lahoti. Indeed, the site gets five million visitors a month hoping to ace their next DMV visit.

2 *"YOUR USED CAR COULD BE A TICKING TIME BOMB ON WHEELS."*

Remember those pictures of flooded car lots after Hurricane Katrina? You could end up buying one of those cars today and never know it. In the past five years, the number of flooded cars sold as "used" has doubled nationwide, according to Carfax spokesperson Larry Gamache.

Once deemed totaled, cars are supposed to be sold for scrap. But unscrupulous sellers can buy them at auction, then replace the title at a Department of Motor Vehicles office in another state by fudging the document, saying it's lost, or retitling it in a state that doesn't recognize "flooded" as totaled. The practice isn't just deceitful, it's downright dangerous, says Gamache, as Diane Zielinski found out. She bought her teenage son a used Grand Am thinking she'd gotten a great deal—until the engine exploded as he was driving. "He could very easily have been killed," she says. A Carfax report revealed the car's title had been branded "flooded" after Hurricane Floyd then reregistered in Pennsylvania. If you're buying a used car, Gamache recommends having a mechanic inspect it first. And screen the car's vehicle identification number (VIN) through the free database, at *www.carfax.com*.

3 *"WHEN IT COMES TO CAR THEFT, WE'RE PART OF THE PROBLEM."*

There's another way criminals take advantage of flimsy DMV car records: "VIN cloning," a kind of vehicle laundering. A stolen car's vehicle identification number is switched with that of a junked car, and a clean title is obtained from the DMV. To combat this practice, the 1992 Anti-Car Theft Act authorized the creation of a database, known as the National Motor Vehicle Title Information System, which allows state DMVs to verify a car's title, theft, and damage history before issuing a new title. But 15 years later, only 30 states belong to the network, and those that don't, including California and Illinois, are havens for car thieves and chop shops. "Until all 50 states participate, the system is full of holes," says Rosemary Shahan, of Consumers for Auto Reliability and Safety, a nonprofit consumer-advocacy group.

Car theft costs Americans $7.6 billion a year, according to the National Insurance Crime Bureau. Who benefits? Organized crime, for one. But the stakes are higher than mob money. Perpetrators of the first World Trade Center bombing and the Oklahoma City Federal Building bombing were traced with the help of VINs.

4 *"CONSISTENCY IS THE HOBGOBLIN OF . . . WELL, NOT US, THAT'S FOR SURE."*

Rules that differ by state (and city, and county) may be a problem for law-abiding drivers, but for those looking to slip through the cracks, they're a godsend.

For example, emission checks are required for registration in 13 states and in parts of another 17 states, but not at all in 20 states. And since every state has different plates, says Ashly Knapp, founder of Auto Advisors, a consultancy for car buyers, police can't tell if an out-of-state license is expired until they can see it up close. Some drivers register a car in a state with lower taxes, then drive it in their own state with expired plates. "I'm impressed how many people tell me they get away with it," Knapp says.

Worse are loopholes for drunk drivers. Repeat offenders get listed in the National Highway Traffic Safety Administration's National Driver Register, but records for those with one DUI are often confined to one state— meaning you might get a clean driving record simply by hopping states, says Jason King, of the American Association of Motor Vehicle Administrators (AAMVA). The Real ID Act could ultimately fix these problems, King says, by forcing states to share driving records in a national database.

5 *"YOU THINK GETTING YOUR LICENSE IS A HASSLE—TRY FILING A COMPLAINT."*

Every institution has problems, but the DMV is notorious for its surly service. Newlywed Laura Zhu tried to get a license with her maiden name as her second middle name. When she explained this to the DMV worker at a New York City office, Zhu says the woman yelled at her, "You have to hyphenate if you want two last names!" After speaking with a supervisor and finding out that it is indeed state policy to hyphenate, Zhu says she was sent back to the same window. That's when things got ugly. "Little Miss Doesn't-Want-to-Hyphenate wants a license now," the clerk announced loudly, then proceeded to sing a little tune as she worked: "Anderson hyphen Zhu! Anderson hyphen Zhu!"

The online complaint form Zhu filed about the incident promised a five-day response—but at press time, Zhu said she'd been waiting well over a month. New York State DMV spokesperson Ken Brown insists online complaints usually receive a prompt response and says Zhu's letter must have encountered technical problems. Other ways of filing a complaint include talking with the supervisor or sending a letter to the office manager.

6 "WE'RE JUST AS GOOD AT BREAKING THE LAW AS ENFORCING IT . . ."

DMV employees must deal with the public and handle sensitive information, but unsavory characters can slip through anyway. Consider North Carolina license examiner George Sidbury, convicted in 2004 for assaulting a 16-year-old girl taking her road test, or California DMV instructor Calvin Hoang Cat, who in 2005 pleaded no contest to 29 charges of fondling or talking lewdly to teenage girls and women. But more common are the opportunists, looking to use their position to make a quick buck. New Jersey, New York, Virginia, Connecticut, and California have all uncovered DMV scams in the past 10 years in which employees granted driver's licenses to illegal immigrants for a hefty profit. FBI indictments in a 2006 Oakland, Calif., case identified 10 people in a black-market conspiracy to sell driver's licenses—5 of them DMV employees.

"There's a high demand for valid ID obtained through fraudulent means," says Jason King, of the AAMVA. Fraud is a problem on both sides of the DMV counter, he says, and the fact that so many employees are being caught shows how committed the DMV is to addressing the problem.

7 ". . . AND WE ALL BUT ENABLE IDENTITY THEFT."

Identity theft is the number one crime in the U.S., according to Werner Raes, president of the International Association of Financial Crimes Investigators. The simplest form, mostly used by beginners, is to ask the DMV for a duplicate license in someone else's name. Identity thieves tell the DMV clerk that they've lost their license or that it was stolen, then provide someone else's illegally obtained information. It's a simple con to pull off. As for the victims, there's nothing simple about it—their credit will be damaged as checks start bouncing and new credit card accounts are opened in their name.

Some state DMVs are beginning to take precautions against identity theft, such as checking a database of past photographs before renewing or mailing the completed license to the address provided. Nevertheless, Raes recommends checking your credit report at least once a year to see if there's any unusual activity.

8 "JUST BECAUSE YOU CAN'T SEE DOESN'T MEAN YOU CAN'T DRIVE."

Everybody thinks they're a good driver, but a 2007 study by market-research firm TNS showed that one in six drivers would fail a state test if they took it again. Indeed, most people get their driver's license in their teens and are never retested. One big problem over time is vision, which tends to degenerate, says Richard Bensinger, a Seattle ophthalmologist and American Academy of Ophthalmology spokesperson. Physical impairments, along with macular degeneration, glaucoma, and cataracts can make older drivers less safe behind the wheel, and it's projected that by the year 2025 drivers over age 65 will make up 25 percent of the driving population, up from 14 percent in 2001, according to nonprofit research outfit the RAND Corporation.

When renewing your license, vision-test requirements, like everything else, vary by state. And while the trend is moving toward age-related regulations, according to a 2007 Insurance Institute for Highway Safety report, 24 states still do not require older drivers to renew more often or have their vision tested when renewing.

Bensinger says that he will sometimes make recommendations about license restrictions for his patients, suggesting a person shouldn't be allowed to drive at night or on high-speed roads. But ultimately, it's the DMV's decision. Family members (along with physicians and police officers) can likewise recommend that the DMV check up on someone they think is a danger on the road—though it varies by state whether such tips can be made confidentially or not.

9 "YOUR VANITY PLATE SAYS 'MUG ME.'"

Personalized license plates might seem like a harmless accessory, but they could make you a more likely target for criminals. Why? Because they communicate much more than the written message. "Personalized plates indicate that the person bearing them wants to be noticed," says Phil Messina, a retired New York City police officer and founder of a self-defense school in Lindenhurst, N.Y. "The downside of doing things that tend to 'get you noticed' is that they can get you noticed by the wrong kind of people."

Consumer advocate Tim Duffy agrees, pointing out that plates indicating the driver is a woman or a senior citizen or both—as in "Katie's Grandma"—are especially problematic. Spotting one of these plates in a parking lot, a mugger may hide behind or near the car, waiting for the driver to return. "You don't want to be a victim of a crime," Duffy says, "and you don't want to make it easier for someone to commit a crime."

10 "FAKE ID? WE FALL FOR IT ALL THE TIME."

A driver's license is often considered the default form of identification in the U.S., used to board airplanes, rent cars, and open bank accounts. Yet it's not hard at all to obtain one illegally by taking advantage of the weakest link in the U.S. identification system: the birth certificate.

"I can show 60 to 70 ways to get a birth certificate, either fake or real," says Werner Raes, of the International Association of Financial Crimes Investigators. And as a result, "You can go in and get driver's licenses all day long in this country, in any name you want."

Since the Department of Motor Vehicles also issues alternative nondriver's license ID cards—a real state-revenue booster—the DMV is, in effect, being used as the leading identification verifier in a country where national security is increasingly important and terrorism is an ever-looming threat. Yet it's not their main responsibility. "Their task is to certify that people can operate a motor vehicle," says Raes.

The best solution? Raes would argue that it's national identification cards. But many groups are opposed to the idea, saying the lack of privacy would overshadow the safety and security benefits. Not to mention create another civil service bureaucracy for the public to navigate.

THINGS TO DO

• **To streamline your visit** to the DMV, go to privately owned site *www.dmv.org* beforehand. That way you won't have to wait in line to find out whether you've left some vital piece of documentation at home.

• **To avoid long lines,** get there before 11:30 A.M.—DMV employees go on lunch break the same time you do. Also, avoid Mondays and Fridays.

• **When calling the DMV,** have handy your driver's license number, license plate number, or vehicle identification number. They won't be able to tell you much more than their hours of operation without this information.

• **You could save a few bucks** by renewing your registration or license plate by mail. Check your state's DMV website for details.

10 Things Your
Gas Station
Won't Tell You

1 *"GOOD LUCK FINDING THE BEST DEAL."*

When it comes to gas prices, most stations are branded—meaning the name of a major oil company hangs out front—and must buy gas from their proprietary company. They can't shop around. With a lock on sales, the oil companies charge each station a different price depending on various factors, such as the station's competition and its location. That means a station can pay as much as 46 cents a gallon more than one down the street, and that cost gets passed along to you.

Faced with such instability, Gainesville, Fla., resident Steven King plans ahead: "If I know I'm going out of town, I try not to buy gas so I can fill up after I leave." King says he can save 10 cents a gallon by purchasing gas on the road. You'd be similarly wise to shop around—with prices constantly in motion, the cheapest gas may not be at the same station every time.

2 *"I HATE IT WHEN GAS PRICES GO UP."*

Stations earn on average between 10 and 15 cents on a gallon of gas. Ironically, they earn the least when prices are highest. When fuel climbs, gas stations must shrink their profit margin to remain competitive, meaning they earn less per gallon than usual. But another big cost during tough times is something they can't do anything about—credit card fees, which add up to about 2.5 percent of all purchases. When gas is at, say, $2 a gallon, the station pays credit card companies 5 cents a gallon; when gas hits $3, that fee becomes 7.5 cents—more than half the station's entire average profit. "Those credit card fees are miserable for the gas station business," says Mohsen Arabshahi, who owns five Southern California gas stations.

How do station owners make up for lost revenue? "Prices go up like a rocket and come down like a feather," says Richard Gilbert, a professor of economics at UC Berkeley. For several weeks after wholesale prices drop, stations can earn as much as 20 cents a gallon before retail prices are lowered to reflect the change.

3 *"MY GAS ISN'T BETTER FOR YOUR CAR; IT'S JUST MORE EXPENSIVE."*

Oil companies spend lots of money explaining why their gas is better than the competition's. Chevron's gas, for example, is fortified with "Techron," and Amoco Ultimate is supposed to save the planet along with your engine. But today more than ever, one gallon of gas is as good as the next.

True, additives help to clean your engine, but what the companies don't tell you is that all gas has them. Since 1994 the government has required that detergents be added to all gasoline to help prevent fuel injectors from clogging. State and local regulators keep a close watch to make sure those standards are met; a 2005 study indicated that Florida inspectors checked 45,000 samples to ensure the state's gas supply was up to snuff, and 99 percent of the time it was. "There's little difference between brand-name gas and any other," says AAA spokesperson Geoff Sundstrom.

What's more, your local Chevron station may sell gas refined by Shell or Exxon Mobil. Suppliers share pipelines, so they all use the same fuel. And the difference between the most expensive brand-name gas and the lowliest gallon of no-brand fuel? Often just a quart of detergent added to an 8,000-gallon tanker truck.

4 "IF YOU'RE SMART, YOU'LL PUT THAT DEBIT CARD AWAY ..."

Your debit card might be a convenient way to pay for gas, but it's a no-win proposition. When you swipe a debit card at the pump, the bank doesn't know how much money you'll be spending until you've finished pumping. So to make sure you have the funds to cover the purchase, some stations ask banks to automatically set aside some of your money: That amount can be $20 or more. That means even if you just topped off your tank for $10, you could be out $30, $50, even

$100 until the station sends over its bulk transactions, which can take up to three days. If your funds are running low, you might end up bouncing a check in the meantime—even though you had the money in your account.

Unfortunately, paying inside with your debit card isn't much of a solution either. Many banks charge their customers between 50 cents and $1 for the privilege of using their debit card in any PIN-based transaction. The American Bankers Association estimates only 13 percent of consumers pay these fees, but critics say the practice is on the rise and consumers are often unaware of these charges.

5 "... AND DON'T EVEN CONSIDER APPLYING FOR OUR GAS CARD."

When it comes to gasoline credit cards, a little research goes a long way. The good deals are great, but the bad deals are really bad. Similar to store cards issued through retailers, gas cards are riddled with drawbacks, says Curtis Arnold, founder of CardRatings.com. APRs are high, starting above 20 percent; many don't offer rebates on gas purchases; and they often lack standard protections such as fraud monitoring and zero liability for unauthorized transactions.

What about a Visa or MasterCard affiliated with a gasoline brand like Exxon or BP? They often offer lower interest rates and significant rebates, but limit your ability to shop around. In December 2005, a few months after gas hit $3 a gallon, Justin Andringa of Minneapolis considered a Shell MasterCard with a 15 percent rebate on gas purchases. But the rebate was temporary; he decided to stick with his Citi Dividend Platinum Select card, which gives him a 5 percent rebate on all gas purchases no matter where he buys it. "I'm a college student," Andringa says. "I need to save money." The deals on these cards are constantly changing. So visit CardRatings.com to find updated information.

6 "LOOKING FOR THE CHEAPEST GAS IN TOWN? TRY THE INTERNET."

You can't actually buy gas online, but Web resources can help you find the cheapest fill-up in town. Among them, GasPriceWatch.com and GasWatch.info help people track pump prices. But the most comprehensive of the bunch is GasBuddy.com, which includes a network of 174 local sites, complete with maps and message boards that tally gas price by ZIP code. "People are frustrated by the variation in the price of gas," says GasBuddy.com cofounder Jason Toews, and they're using the Internet to take control.

It has worked wonders for Sue Foust. Every day, as she passes roughly 10 stations on her commute across Tucson, Ariz., Foust makes a mental note of their prices, then posts them on TucsonGasPrices.com, a local affiliate of GasBuddy.com. Then every four days or so, when she needs to fill up, she checks the prices others have posted in her area. It turned out the Shell station she used to frequent is one of the most expensive in the city. Now she fills up elsewhere. "I really do feel like I'm saving money," she says.

7 "IT'S A GALLON WHEN I SAY IT'S A GALLON."

It's hard to know if you're getting all the gas you paid for at the pump. But in some places there's a very good chance you're not. The state or county weights-and-measures department usually checks pumps for accuracy, but in some areas it can be years between inspections. Arizona, for example, has only 18 staff members to check the state's 2,300 stations.

That means stations there can expect a visit once every three to four years, according to Steve Meissner, an Arizona Department of Weights and Measures spokesperson. In 2005, 30 percent of the more than 2,000 complaints the department received were valid, and it levied $167,000 in fines. The good news is that it's often easy to catch the most common problem: Older pumps in poor repair may begin charging you for gas before you've pumped it. Check the meter to make sure it registers $0.00 before you begin and doesn't start charging you before the fuel is flowing.

8 "I MIGHT GOUGE YOU ON A SODA, BUT MY COFFEE'S A REAL BARGAIN."

With margins on gas taking a hit—in 2006, fuel sales made up 71 percent of revenue but only 34 percent of gross margins—stations are increasingly looking to their convenience stores for income. Given that fact, you'd assume the average Kwik-E-Mart to be a terrible place to buy just about anything. But that's only partially true.

Stock that usually sits on the shelf does tend to be vastly overpriced, so if you forgot ketchup on the way to a barbecue, you can bet you'll pay a lot more for it at a gas station than you would at a supermarket, says David Bishop, director of convenience retailing for Willard Bishop Consulting. What about popular beverages? You'll pay more for a 20-ounce soda at a gas station than you would for a two-liter bottle in a supermarket; water and energy drinks similarly tend to have high markups.

But there are bargains to be had: Some high-volume goods, such as cigarettes and beer, are often competitively priced at gas stations. And a cup of coffee goes for a fraction of what you'd pay at Starbucks.

9 *"IF YOU'RE HAVING CAR TROUBLE, YOU'RE IN THE WRONG PLACE."*

The days of the local gas station staffed with a skilled mechanic have all but come to an end. Station owners are swapping car lifts for beverage cases and car washes, anything that brings in a high-volume stream of income and traffic, says Dennis DeCota, executive director of the California Service Station and Automotive Repair Association. The more people who pull over for a soda, the greater the chance they'll top off their tank and vice versa, the thinking goes. Few owners want the hassle of a business like car repair even if it earns the same amount of money as a convenience store.

In addition, repairing cars is increasingly expensive, and the ill will and potential liability from a fix-it job gone wrong are more of a headache than many owners are willing to risk. Today a service station can require $100,000

worth of diagnostic equipment—a significant investment. It's a risky venture with little payoff, says Southern California station owner Arabshahi. In fact, Arabshahi removed the service station from one of his locations after he bought it. "I don't have a service station because I am not a mechanic," he says. "If he messes up a job, then it's my name on there."

10 *"YOU DON'T EVEN NEED GAS TO RUN YOUR CAR."*

Cars run on gasoline—but not all cars need gasoline to run. In fact, 6 million cars on the road today (mostly from U.S. manufacturers and built since 1998) are "flexible fuel" vehicles that can run on E85, a fuel that is 85 percent ethanol and only 15 percent gas. When Minneapolis resident John Schafer bought a car in late 2001, he chose a Chevy Tahoe because it's a flexible-fuel car. Since then he's filled up almost exclusively with E85. The big difference he's noticed: Cars using E85 get about 15 percent fewer miles to the gallon. But it's a drawback he's willing to put up with. "I'm committed to the technology," Schafer says. "With E85, it burns cleaner so it won't pollute as much."

While E85 generally costs less than regular gas, there is some concern that it may grow prohibitively expensive as demand outpaces supply: By 2006 ethanol was not just being used in E85—it also composed 15 percent of every gallon of gas sold. Supplies of ethanol are likely to grow thin, which could drive up the price of E85. And even die-hard Schafer says he won't buy E85 if it starts to cost more than gasoline.

THINGS TO DO

● **With gas prices constantly in flux,** the best way to find the best deal in your neighborhood is to look before you leave the house—on the Internet. Sites like GasBuddy.com and GasPriceWatch .com track prices around the country; you can search by ZIP code for stations near you.

● **If you have a flexible-fuel car,** you can find out where to get E85 near you by visiting the Ethanol Vehicle Coalition website, at *www.e85refueling.com*.

● **Since the U.S. government** closely regulates the quality of gasoline at stations, there really isn't much difference between brands. Translation: Use whatever brand is cheapest.

● **Keep yourself safe at the pump:** Choose well-lit, well-monitored stations. Lock your car doors, and stay alert while filling.

10 Things Your
Rental Car Company
Won't Tell You

1 "WE'RE A TAX MAGNET."

Rental-car customers are paying more, due to an unprecedented slew of taxes and fees. But that extra money doesn't go to the rental car companies; it goes into city and state coffers, where it's used to fund municipal projects. For example, in 2005 car rentals in Arlington, Tex., were hit with a 5 percent tax to help pay for the new Dallas Cowboys stadium. Car rentals get tapped as fund-raisers because local politicians won't feel the repercussions at the voting booth. "They're taxing people who are flying in from someplace else," says a Hertz spokesperson. "These people can't and don't vote locally, so there's no harm for them."

But there's a way for consumers to dodge some of these fees: Pick up your car in town, not at the airport. In 2005 Travelocity found that taxes and fees were 45 percent lower for off-airport rentals. An added bonus, according to Neil Abrams, president of Abrams Consulting, is that you'll save on rates, too: On average, they're $10 cheaper per day in town.

2 "WE TRACK YOUR EVERY MOVE."

Over the past few years, rental agencies have begun to install GPS devices in their vehicles. These units allow companies to track cars that are lost or stolen. But global-positioning technology also lets them know when a renter has been speeding or has taken a car into another state, which may be construed as increasing wear and tear. "Opportunity for a rental car operator to impose geographic limitations was never pitched by GPS sellers, but was discovered coincidentally," says Michael LaPlaca, an attorney who specializes in rental car law.

To date, most companies don't use the technology to impose fines, but it can and does happen. American Car Rental, for example, was charging customers in Connecticut $150 each time they topped the speed limit for two minutes at a stretch, claiming it damaged their vehicles. Connecticut's Consumer Protection Commission deemed the fines excessive, ordering the company to refund penalized customers, and in 2005 the state's Supreme Court affirmed the decision. (American Car Rental has since gone out of business.)

Since then other states, including New York and California, have passed laws preventing rental car companies from imposing such penalties. But some still try to get away with it: In 2006

California's attorney general announced a settlement of over $700,000 in a consumer protection lawsuit against Fox Rent A Car for using GPS to illegally charge customers who traveled outside a three-state area and for forcing customers to purchase liability insurance. (Fox Rent A Car has not returned calls for comment.)

3 "OUR PRICES ARE ETCHED IN SAND."

Trying to find the best rental deal can be frustrating, since rates can fluctuate dramatically from day to day, even minute to minute. "Prices are constantly changing," Abrams says. That's because rental car agencies use something called yield-management technology, which continually adjusts pricing depending on how many cars are available. A sudden rash of cancellations or bookings, for example, can push rates up or down. When we priced an Enterprise rental for a spring trip to Los Angeles, the cost vacillated dramatically: Two hours after we first checked the company's website, the per-day rate for a full-size car dropped almost $8, and over the next week it continued to yo-yo dramatically, with a range of $40. ("There are any number of reasons why the price of a rental car can fluctuate," says a spokesperson for Enterprise. "During weekend specials you may see savings up to 50 percent; renting during the week could cost you more.")

Even the way you book can affect prices. When we called the Avis desk at LAX to reserve a minivan, we were quoted a price more than $150 higher than the amount being advertised

simultaneously on the company's website. Also, online travel agencies like Orbitz or Priceline can have completely different prices. That's why it pays to comparison-shop and check back later to see whether rates have fallen—there's usually no fee to cancel a reservation or rebook at a lower rate.

4 "YOU PROBABLY DON'T NEED OUR INSURANCE."

Most companies make reserving and renting a car pretty simple—until it comes to the issue of insurance. That's where they offer a bewildering array of supplemental coverage, which can easily add $10 to $30 to your daily bill. What the overeager reps won't tell you is that you may already be covered, either partially or completely.

There are two major types of insurance you'll want: a collision/damage waiver and liability. The former covers repair and replacement costs to the car should anything happen to it; the latter protects you from lawsuits if you've injured anyone or damaged property when driving. If you have auto insurance, it usually extends to rental cars, providing both collision/damage and liability, as long as you're on a leisure trip. And many credit cards cover damages to the vehicle but don't offer liability.

As with any type of insurance, it's always more complicated than it seems. "You shouldn't assume you're covered by your credit card," says a spokesperson for the Insurance Information Institute. Check ahead of time with both your credit card and auto insurance providers to see if, when, and how you're covered.

5 "YOUR RESERVATION DOESN'T MEAN BUPKES."

Andy Parker was looking forward to spending his winter vacation exploring the back roads of Aruba. He even reserved a Jeep with Hertz to handle the rough driving conditions. But when he went to pick it up, he was told all they had on the lot was a sedan. "It was a sore spot," says the Buffalo, N.Y., meteorologist, who got stuck with a small Nissan.

As Parker found out, a reservation isn't a guarantee. The rental agreement is contingent on availability. In fact, you're not reserving a specific car model, but simply a class of car. (One exception: Hertz allows you to reserve high-end models in its "Prestige Collection.") What a reservation actually means is that the company is supposed to have some kind of vehicle on the premises for you to rent. So if you get a smaller car than what you reserved, be sure to ask for a rate adjustment. (Parker got Hertz to take 20 percent off his bill; Hertz did not return our calls for comment.)

If the lot is empty, the company is supposed to find you a car even if it means calling another agency and covering the difference. So if the clerk doesn't offer, remind him that the company is liable if you wind up paying more for a rental car elsewhere.

6 "SPECIAL ORDERS ARE OUR BREAD AND BUTTER."

Just like supermarkets, rental car companies bank on getting their customers to do some impulse buying at the checkout counter—where you can now choose from a sizable menu of à la carte amenities and services. The strategy seems to be working: 2007 revenue reached $21.5 billion, a 21 percent increase since 2002, according to *Auto Rental News*.

A spokesperson for the American Auto Association says that a rental vehicle tricked out with extra features could run you $20 more a day. Here's how it breaks down: GPS with turn-by-turn directions costs about $12 a day. Avis and Budget rolled out a service that for a minimal amount each day will let you pay highway tolls electronically—but that fee doesn't include the tolls themselves. And if you want a baby seat for the minivan, add another bill to the pile.

Companies have also begun pushing specialty cars. In 2007 Avis introduced its "Cool Car" collection, which includes the Nissan Altima Hybrid, Cadillac CTS, and Hummer H3. And even low-priced Thrifty has a "Beyond Luxury" collection, offering cars like the BMW 5-series and Cadillac Escalade. "It can be a place to make money," the AAA spokesperson says.

7 "YOU'VE GOT TO DO A LITTLE DETECTIVE WORK TO FIND A GOOD DEAL."

It used to be that better deals were to be had at smaller, independent rental car companies. But with rising energy prices and weakening demand, that's no longer true. In fact, the changing rental car landscape is making it any company's game to pitch a bargain—which means it's more important than ever to shop around for the best deals.

Good to know, since rental car rates—which remained relatively flat after 2000—have begun to rise again. The average daily cost of a rental was $73 in the second quarter of 2008, a 3 percent increase over the year before, according to American Express Business Travel.

So how to find a bargain? Your best bet is to hit the Internet: Expedia.com and Orbitz.com offer reliable online comparison-shopping tools for rental car companies at locations near you. A recent search of Orbitz.com, for example, turned up a $230 weekly rate for an economy-size car from Budget's location at New York's John F. Kennedy International Airport—that's nearly half of what Avis was charging ($458).

8 "WE'RE CUTTING CORNERS ANYWHERE WE CAN."

You may not have noticed, but over the past few years the fine print on rental contracts has been changing, restricting privileges and perks, even for the industry's best customers. For example, in the winter of 2005, Hertz shortened the grace period for returning a car from one hour to half an hour for everyone including its #1 Club Gold members; customers also can no longer return a car after a location has closed for the night without incurring a late fee. (Hertz did not return our calls for comment.)

In another move to cut corners, rental companies across the board have begun making customers liable for damage caused by so-called acts of God, such as hurricanes and floods. Avis and Budget, the last major holdouts on this policy change, have recently added it, even to their frequent renters' contracts. The new rule means it's now up to renters either

to return a car before the natural disaster hits, drive the vehicle out of harm's way, or pay up for the newly developed insurance option to cover this type of damage.

9 "YOU WON'T BELIEVE WHAT WE'RE CHARGING FOR FILL-UPS."

Even when Brandon Harris is in a hurry, he tries to gas up before returning his rental car. When he was on vacation in Costa Rica a few years ago, he had to travel 15 minutes out of his way to find an open station. "I don't think the rates that [rental agencies] are charging are fair," the Chicago resident says. "It's cheaper to do it yourself." Although most car rental companies claim they charge the same for gas as local market conditions, it's really the service charge that jacks up the price: You're paying for fuel plus the luxury of not having to pump it yourself, says an AAA spokesperson, and not filling up the tank can tack on an additional $20 to your bill.

Car rental companies do offer another option: prepaying for a tank of gas at a more reasonable rate so you don't have to worry about finding a station at the last minute. There's only one problem: You're not likely to return the car empty. "Whatever gas you leave in the tank is a donation to the rental car company," the AAA spokesperson says. So unless you're tight for time, it still pays to gas it up yourself upon return. But watch out for gas stations right next to the airport, since they tend to have higher prices. These pumps "make a killing on out-of-towners filling up rental cars," the AAA spokesperson says.

10 *"WE OFFER SOME TERRIFIC DEALS—ON THURSDAYS WHEN THE MOON IS FULL."*

Jay Winger thought he'd found a great deal. He was planning to use a Budget double-upgrade coupon when he rented a car for his Las Vegas vacation. The coupon had been accepted when he made the reservation online, but when he arrived at the rental desk, the agent refused to honor it. Why? At the bottom of the coupon in "really small print," Winger says, it stated that the coupon wasn't valid in all areas— including, as it turned out, Vegas. "There are always certain locations that don't take part in national promotions," says an Avis Budget Car Rental spokesperson. Winger wound up spending about $60 more than he had planned. "Renting a car is really tricky," the Minneapolis native says.

On every rental car company website, there are ads flaunting the companies' latest deals. Not to mention the paper coupons that appear regularly in newspapers. But there are so many rules and restrictions involved that it's often impossible to get exactly the deal that's being advertised. For starters, some require a Saturday-night stay or a minimum five-day rental. Companies also designate blackout days, exclude popular locations like New York and Las Vegas, and reserve the right to terminate any given offer at any time.

THINGS TO DO

● **Shop around—even after you've made** a reservation. Prices can vary from hour to hour and between companies. If you find a better deal after you've already booked, cancel and rebook.

● **Before you sign up** for insurance from the rental company, look into the coverage your auto insurance policy and credit card provide for rentals.

● **Remember to put the name** of anyone who will be driving the rental on the contract, and don't let anyone else behind the wheel—the contract could be voided in the event that something happened while someone not listed was driving.

● **Read your contract carefully.** Does it restrict where you can drive? Does it provide for assistance in the case of a breakdown? Knowing all the provisions will help you get the most out of your rental—and relieve you of any false expectations.

● **Before ever leaving the lot,** inspect the vehicle and note any dents or problems— that way you won't get charged later for damage you didn't cause.

10 Things Your
Auto Insurer
Won't Tell You

1 *"WHEN I SAY THIS IS A GOOD POLICY, I MEAN IT'S GOOD FOR ME."*

In 2004 and 2005, broker commissions landed the commercial insurance industry in hot water with then New York Attorney General Eliot Spitzer. But auto policyholders may be surprised to learn that some of the same issues afflict the car insurance industry. While agents can help you navigate auto policies, some may not have your best interest at heart: The Consumer Federation of America found in 2005 that 14 of the 20 largest auto and home insurers used "contingent commissions" to compensate agents who sold their policies.

Contingency fees come in two types: "steering" commissions for signing customers with a particular carrier, and profit-based commissions, when clients don't file a lot of costly claims. The concern with the former is that unscrupulous agents push certain policies to reap larger commissions; with the latter, they might delay or discourage claims. "It doesn't mean that this happens often," says Consumer Federation of America (CFA) Insurance Director J. Robert Hunter. "Most agents are honest, but if the system provides an incentive, if there's money on the table, well, people do things."

How to protect yourself? Ask about commissions, and have prospective agents explain their recommendations.

2 *"YOU CAN CHALK UP YOUR HIGH PREMIUMS TO OUR LOUSY INVESTMENTS."*

When premiums started to drop in 2004, auto insurers cited fewer drunk drivers and state crackdowns on insurance fraud. But the Foundation for Taxpayer & Consumer Rights (FTCR) offers a different explanation: Executive Director Doug Heller charges that hikes on auto and homeowner's premiums from 2000 to 2003—as well as similar crises in the mid-1970s and mid-'80s—were precipitated by investment losses by the major insurance carriers.

The FTCR studied public investment filings of major insurers and found that between 1998 and 2001, 9 out of 10 shifted their investments from government bonds into higher-risk stocks and corporate bonds. "Insurance companies jumped headlong into the stock market bubble—only to fall hard when it burst," Heller told Congress in 2003. What followed were rate hikes and insurers threatening a pullout from several markets across the country.

The bad news, says Heller, is that it could happen again. In the wake of the subprime crisis and other troubling economic news, it's likely the insurance industry will impose rate hikes in the future. "The rest of America has to tighten their belts when investment opportunities weaken, but insurers just tie the noose around policyholders' necks to keep their income high," Heller says.

3 "SPOTTY CREDIT? THAT'LL COST YOU."

Sara Lapham and her husband, Derek, an engineering technician in Dallas, went through a rough financial patch in 2002, when Derek's paychecks started to bounce. But the worst part was the letter from their car insurer saying that they were being moved to the company's high-risk subsidiary with higher rates because of their credit history—despite the fact that they'd had "no claims, no tickets, nothing," says Sara, a small-business owner.

This practice has been on the rise since the 1990s, when insurers discovered a strong correlation between low credit scores and filing lots of claims. Now more than 90 percent of insurers use credit history in their underwriting, according to the Insurance Information Institute. Although consumer advocates argue that it unfairly penalizes the poor, it can also bite the middle class, says Birny Birnbaum, executive director at the Center for Economic Justice. After all, "80 percent of families in bankruptcy are there because of a job loss, medical catastrophe, or divorce," he says.

Since many insurers do factor in credit history, it's important to get your credit report from each of the three bureaus—TransUnion, Experian, and Equifax—and check them for errors before you shop for insurance.

4 "HOW DO WE SET PREMIUMS? THAT'S FOR US TO KNOW AND YOU TO FIND OUT."

The good news is that, starting in 2004, auto-insurance rate increases began falling off in most states, after having risen steadily for four years. The bad news is that as insurers continue to adopt complex pricing systems, not everyone is seeing savings. Why the disparity? For starters, premiums vary widely by state.

According to a 2007 study from the National Association of Insurance Commissioners, the average yearlong policy in 2005 cost $949—ranging from a low of $664 in Iowa to a high of $1,343 in the District of Columbia. State insurance regulators are in part to blame for the huge price disparity. New Jersey, for example, has long been notorious for heavy restrictions on insurers. Before the Garden State revamped its rules in 2003, many companies claimed they couldn't make a profit and left, thus limiting competition and pushing rates higher.

But what's really muddied the waters are the formulas used to set premiums for individuals. Twenty years ago most insurers sorted customers into four or five pricing tiers, based on where they lived, their age, and their driving record. But over the past decade, hundreds of variables have been added to the mix, including credit history, homeownership, and limits on past policies. And since each insurer interprets these variables differently, it's even tougher for consumers to get a handle on the system.

5 "YOUR REPAIRED CAR MIGHT LOOK AND RUN LIKE NEW, BUT IT'S WORTH A LOT LESS."

As many policyholders know, when the other party's insurer is paying for repairs after an accident, you have the right to opt for original manufacturer parts instead of generic aftermarket ones. But even with the best parts and service in the world, "a fully repaired vehicle will often be worth less as a used car or trade-in than an identical car without the accident history," says J.D. Howard, executive director of iCan, the Insurance Consumer Advocate Network. What many people don't realize is that you're often entitled to collect that difference, known as "diminished value."

But what if your insurer is paying the repair bill? You may be out of luck. While policyholders in Kansas and Georgia can collect diminished-value losses from their own carriers, in most states it's less clear-cut. Illinois's supreme court ruled in August 2005 that policyholders there had no right to collect diminished value from their own carrier.

Luckily, Howard says, it's not a total loss—even if you can't collect diminished value outright, you can probably write it off on your tax return. (Consult your tax adviser.) That's why it's a good idea to hire a postrepair inspector, both to ensure that the work was done properly and to assess diminished value.

6 "TOTALED YOUR CAR? GOOD LUCK COLLECTING ITS FULL VALUE..."

When Mitch Stanley's 1998 Toyota 4Runner was totaled a few years ago, he figured it was worth $12,000 to $15,000. But Farmers Insurance offered the Portland, Ore., nurse $10,100, based on comparable vehicles for sale ("comps," in insurance-speak). Policyholders may be surprised that insurance companies don't get their valuations from such standard sources as Kelley Blue Book or Edmunds.com. Instead, most use claims-servicing companies—the biggest is CCC Information Services—which consult proprietary databases to assess valuation. CCC canvasses dealerships in 250 local markets to build a database of comps that's updated daily, and "we talk to dealers to find out what they're willing to sell the car for," says Mary Jo Prigge, president of service operations. KBB and Edmunds, on the other hand, use transaction data, which is often higher.

But if your car is totaled, you needn't accept your insurer's first offer. Go to Edmunds.com or AutoTrader.com to find better comps, and call the sellers listed on the insurer's report to verify their price. No dice? If it's a matter of $1,000 or more, hire your own appraiser and go through an appraisal-arbitration process.

7 "...AND WE'RE MORE LIKELY THAN EVER TO DECLARE YOUR CAR TOTALED."

Given the haircut you're likely to take when replacing your totaled car, many policyholders would prefer to have repairs covered in all but the most severe accidents. But that's becoming increasingly difficult. According to the trade magazine *Collision Repair Industry Insight,* the percentage of damaged cars declared a total loss by insurers jumped from 7 percent in 1995 to 16 percent in 2003. And as mass-market cars get more high-tech, that number continues to increase—having reached 20 percent in the first half of 2007—since the growing number of electronic components and passive restraints, such as airbags, can make for difficult and expensive repairs.

What constitutes "totaled"? An insurer's rule of thumb is to deem a car totaled when repairs would exceed 70 percent of the vehicle's value, says J. D. Howard of iCan—a threshold easily surpassed with a cracked fender and a few deployed airbags. And if your car's frame is damaged, it can remain a safety hazard even when repaired. But if the damage is limited to a few minor, albeit expensive, components, you can appeal your insurer's decision to total it.

8 *"YOUR MECHANIC WORKS FOR US."*

The auto insurance industry has long relied on direct-repair programs, which function like HMOs for ailing cars, with insurers maintaining lists of recommended repair facilities. In recent years some insurers have taken the relationship a step further; Allstate, for one, bought a nationwide chain of repair shops in 2001.

Whether it's a network of preferred providers or outright ownership, such coziness between insurers and body shops makes consumer advocates nervous. "It lets the insurers take too much control over the repair process," says J. D. Howard. And when you have pressure to keep costs low, he adds, you may start to see "shortcuts" in repairs. But Allstate contends that it offers even more-comprehensive guarantees on the work done in its own body shops than on repairs from its referral network. Owning the body shops "helps enable the insurer to provide competitive rates by creating efficiencies in the claim process and removing incentives for fraud," says a company spokesperson.

More often than not, you have a choice whether or not to use the insurer-recommended shop. So should you? It's convenient, and in some cases policyholders who take their cars there can get their deductible reduced or waived. If you do take the "in-network" route, hire a postrepair inspector to make sure repairs are done properly.

9 *"BRAND LOYALTY IS FOR SUCKERS ..."*

Since 2005, when she began taking on additional responsibilities for her aging mother, Sara Kaul of Bethesda, Md., has been trying to lower her monthly expenses—a big chunk of which consists of car insurance premiums. As a State Farm customer of 20-plus years, she'd watched her rates march steadily upward; as of fall 2005 she was paying $437 for a six-month policy. By calling and checking online quote engines, Kaul was able to shave $82—or 18 percent—off the annual premium with a similar policy from Allstate.

As more insurers adopt elaborately tiered pricing strategies, rates may differ dramatically from company to company and as your circumstances change, meaning it often doesn't pay to stay. You're better off comparison-shopping once a year rather than automatically renewing your policy. Start by getting online quotes from Geico and Progressive Direct, which sell their policies via company employees. (Progressive's site even generates comparison quotes from other major insurers, though you may get slightly different numbers if you check directly with the companies.) Also be sure to ask an independent agent for quotes, as well as from companies like Allstate and State Farm, which use exclusive independent contractors. A study by the Consumer Federation of America found that insurers with lower agent commissions often had cheaper rates.

Worried that lower prices mean poor service? The same CFA study found no correlation between policy price and complaints. You can check complaint statistics at *www.naic.org*.

10 *"... BUT BE CAREFUL SWITCHING CARRIERS— IT COULD COST YOU."*

No doubt you've seen the warnings in your policy that not paying your premiums can cause your policy to be canceled. It might lead you to think that when you want to switch carriers, dropping the old insurer is as simple as stopping payment. Not so. If you don't pay a bill for the next term, chances are your carrier won't simply cancel the policy—it may also report your nonpayment to the credit bureaus. (Most insurers are required to give you a certain number of days' notice before cancellation.) Also, your new carrier will see a cancellation in your history, which could mean you'll pay higher rates or be declined.

To avoid the issue, get the proper documentation. Ask your current carrier for a policy cancellation form, and make sure the timing is right—that the ending date of your old policy coincides with the start date of your new one.

THINGS TO DO

- **Do your homework on possible** discounts. Your teenager's good grades and your LoJack security system, for example, could reduce your premiums.

- **Don't drive that much?** Ask if your insurance provider offers a low-mileage discount.

- **Scrutinize your policy for mistakes.** Many policies are complicated, and an unnoticed error could end up costing you.

- **Insurance companies are increasingly factoring** in your credit score when setting premiums, so avoid surprises by checking out your credit report before shopping for auto insurance.

- **If your car is older** or has significantly diminished in value, consider dropping collision or comprehensive coverage. Do the math—paying extra for this type of coverage may not be worth it.

10 Things Your
Car Dealer
Won't Tell You

1 *"THESE CARS COST ME LESS THAN YOU THINK."*

Haggling over price has always been the most unbearable part of buying a car. But since the advent of the Internet, consumers have gotten a leg up on the process: Car-buying sites like CarsDirect .com and NewCarTestDrive.com will provide you with any car's invoice, or wholesale, price, and consumer-information hub Edmunds.com even lists the invoice price of a car's options. But don't get too comfortable just yet. Critics caution that Internet pricing can sometimes be out of date.

What's more, a practice called "holdback" allows dealers to pay up to 3 percent below invoice for vehicles. Here's how it works: The dealer buys the car from the manufacturer at the invoice price. Then after the car is sold, the manufacturer reimburses the dealer for the cost of keeping it in inventory for 90 days. When a dealer sells the car faster than that, part of the holdback payment becomes pure profit, even if the car is sold at invoice price. "You'll never get holdback money back from a dealer," says Burke Leon, author of *The Insider's Guide to Buying a New or Used Car*. But just knowing about it can help when a dealer whines that he can't meet your price.

2 *"OUR LENDERS AREN'T AS TOUGH AS I'LL MAKE THEM SEEM."*

Car dealers' reputations have been so bad for so long that some will do anything to pass the buck regarding pricing and sales tactics. One common trick: Blame everything on the lender. For example, some dealers who don't want to give you the price you're asking for may tell you that the leasing company requires all deals to be based on the sticker price, says Mark Eskeldson, author of *What Car Dealers Don't Want You to Know*. That probably isn't the case, since lenders can't control a car's price.

Likewise, some dealers will try to sell you an extended warranty, claiming that the lender requires it. Don't be fooled. "I don't think you'll find many mainstream lenders that require that," says Art Spinella, president of CNW Marketing Research, a market-research firm. In its online "Facts for Consumers" report on auto-service contracts, the Federal Trade Commission tells car buyers to watch their back: "If you're told you must purchase an auto-service contract to qualify for financing, contact the lender yourself to find out if this is true." The FTC also says that some people have had a hard time trying to get out of a service contract they signed up for thinking it was a standard requirement for their car loan—another good reason to ask questions before any papers have been signed.

Car shopping on the Internet is saving consumers money— an average of $1,794 per purchase.

3 "YOU COULD PROBABLY GET THIS CAR CHEAPER ON EBAY."

As you might imagine, one of the biggest threats to bricks-and-mortar car dealerships today is direct sales over the Internet. Indeed, nearly one in four consumers looking to buy a late-model used vehicle went online to buy a car in 2007, a 44 percent increase from 2006, according to a report by J.D. Power and Associates. EBay Motors alone has helped consumers sell more than 2 million cars on its website—not surprising, considering that 37 percent of all online automotive minutes are spent on eBay Motors, according to Nielsen Online. What might come as a surprise is the fact that car shopping on the Internet is saving consumers money— an average of $1,794 per purchase, according to J.D. Power.

Dealerships have been slow to catch on to the trend, but "more and more dealers are recognizing the value of promoting their brand on the Internet,"

says Steve St. Andre, president of FordDirect, a joint venture between Ford Motor and its franchised dealers aimed at promoting Internet sales. Indeed, the FordDirect concept seems to be working: Dealers sold 52,000 new cars through the service in 2007, a 73 percent increase over 2006.

4 "THE OLD BAIT-AND-SWITCH IS ALIVE AND WELL."

It's a tried-and-true tactic: You walk onto the car lot, your heart set on a certain model, but immediately, the salesperson starts ticking off all the reasons why that model simply isn't good enough for you. Before you know it, you've signed on for something bigger and better and, naturally, more expensive. Even these days, when car shoppers often show up armed to the teeth with information they've gleaned online—everything from the invoice price of the car right down to the cost of heated seats—dealers still try to steer you into unfamiliar territory, their best defense, says Phil Reed, of Edmunds.com.

That's exactly what happened to Christine Kemp, of Orange, Calif., who got sucked into leasing a $40,690 Toyota 4Runner Limited, despite the fact that she'd been researching lower-priced models for over a year. At a California Toyota dealership that had advertised a 4Runner sale, the salesman immediately discouraged her from looking at the base model. "You don't want that car," Kemp says the dealer told her. "Its engine isn't powerful enough for towing"—a feature Kemp had said was important, since she was getting ready to buy Jet Skis. But that wasn't necessarily true: According to Toyota, the base model 4Runner Limited Kemp was interested in could tow up to 3,500 pounds—easily strong enough to tow Jet Skis.

5 "I'LL GIVE YOU A GREAT PRICE—AND THEN LOWBALL YOUR TRADE-IN ..."

If you're trading in an old car, Leon explains, the dealer's greatest potential for profit lies in giving you the lowest possible value on your trade-in. How come? Most people have no idea what their car is worth, and besides, you're less likely to play hardball on this point when that new car is much more interesting. "They get you involved in loving the new car," Leon says. "And your old car seems kind of punk in comparison, so they 'do you a favor' and get it off your hands." For this reason, Leon recommends always settling on a trade-in price *before* considering a new or even a used car, despite the conventional wisdom of doing it the other way around.

Reed went undercover as a salesman in two Los Angeles-area dealerships and then wrote about it for Edmunds.com. During three months he saw firsthand how much money can be made in used-car departments. One day, he says, he watched a man drive into the dealership's parking lot, scurry over to the used cars, and then rush back to his car. "He said he had just traded in his Chevy Cavalier here," Reed says, "and wanted to know what they were selling it for." The discouraging answer: While the customer had gotten $5,000 for the car, its asking price on the lot was $12,000.

6 "... BUT YOU WON'T KNOW IT, SINCE THE BLUE BOOK PRICE FAVORS ME."

To help prevent a trade-in disaster, some consumers try to suss out their old car's worth beforehand by consulting the *Kelley Blue Book,* long held as the gold standard for used-car prices. But both Leon and Spinella warn that those numbers aren't gospel. Here's why: Kelley Blue Book publishes two different guides, one for dealers, which prints wholesale prices, and one for consumers, which contains retail prices (and is therefore of little help in determining what your car is worth to the dealer). What's more, at Kelley's website, you can look up trade-in figures that, even for a car in excellent shape, are below the dealer's lowest figure (the wholesale price). That means that when a dealer gives you the "best" *Blue Book* value, there's still a built-in profit for him, even if he turns around and sells the car for its wholesale price.

"*Kelley Blue Book* is an industry publication, and its loyalties are less to consumers than to dealers," says Leon. Stephen Henson, executive vice president of sales and marketing at Kelley Blue Book, argues that the spread between trade-in and wholesale values is accounted for by any expenses the dealer incurs in readying the car for sale. Nonetheless, the best way to estimate your car's value, says Spinella, is to look at classifieds ads to see what vehicles similar to yours are going for. Just remember, you won't get that full amount since it's retail.

7 "THE CAR YOU'RE BUYING WAS TOTALED LAST MONTH."

When Annette Sloan bought a used Chevy Astro from a dealer in Overland Park, Kan., she noticed that the interior trim was cracked in a few spots. But she had no idea what an examination by an autobody expert would reveal: The van had once been wrecked. In fact, according to the mechanic, it had actually been two separate vans now welded together with a seam running beneath the carpeting. When Sloan returned to the dealership, she says she was shown a document with her signature on it (which she doesn't remember signing) acknowledging that the dealership "believes the van has had previous paint and metal work." "That's like saying someone who stepped on a land mine has a flesh wound," says her attorney, Bernard Brown. When Sloan later sued the dealer over the defective Franken-van, the case was dismissed due to issues of jurisdiction—the dealer had bought the vehicle out of state.

While Sloan's is an extreme case, such problems are far from rare in the used-car market. The advocacy group Consumers for Auto Reliability and Safety estimates that about 5 million cars each year are totaled, rebuilt, and often sold as if free of damage. The best way to avoid being taken is to have any used car that you're considering buying inspected by an independent mechanic, which typically costs about $100. "Don't even think about paying any attention to Carfax [reports]," Brown says. "It's work, but in five minutes of looking at it, [a mechanic] will let you know."

8 "YOUR CAR LOAN PUTS CASH IN MY POCKET."

Ever wonder why that dealer is so keen on finding you an auto loan, even after you say you can pay cash? He might be sniffing out an extra source of profit. When dealers set up loans, they commonly take the rate offered by the lender, then tack up to two percentage points on top. All or part of that so-called dealer markup is given by the lender to the dealer as a kickback. And dealers aren't required by law to disclose the practice.

The National Automobile Dealers Association (NADA) says that dealers are entitled to a markup for arranging financing. "Because dealers buy credit in bulk and provide the retail infrastructure for serving individual customers, they get lower rates than a consumer would if dealing directly with a bank," says a NADA spokesperson. The problem isn't so much that the markup exists, says attorney Aurora Dawn Harris, but that it's not always disclosed. "Dealers say, 'We'll get you the best deal we can,' and pretend that they're providing you a free service," she says. "And sometimes they're making most of their profit on it."

9 "OUR 'NEW AND IMPROVED' CUSTOMER SERVICE IS A FARCE."

After years of having a terrible reputation for consumer satisfaction, car dealers are now making a collective effort to clean up their act. According to a 2007 survey by J. D. Power and Associates, approximately 61 percent of customers described their sales experience as "above expectations," compared with the 37 percent of customers who said it merely met their expectations.

That's a start, but auto dealers still have a long way to go toward achieving solid customer satisfaction. In 2006, for example, new-car dealers still ranked second among all businesses in overall complaints filed with the Better Business Bureau, behind the cell phone service and supplies industry. And some of the car manufacturers' attempts to inspire better customer service among dealers have turned out to be less than successful. Take, for example, the Customer Satisfaction Index, a set of scores that manufacturers give dealers based on customer surveys. Since carmakers have started looking at the numbers closely, dealers have begun courting customers to achieve better scores—by offering them coffee, cookies, flowers, or even a gift certificate for a local restaurant chain just before they answer the survey.

Reed's advice: Before you visit a dealership, call ahead. If they refuse to answer any questions about prices, urging you instead to "come on down to the lot for a deal," move on.

10 "SURE, LEASING IS A GREAT DEAL—FOR ME."

You may have noticed that many dealers would rather you lease than buy. The reason is simple: Leases generally bring dealerships more profit than sales, even for the exact same car. Why? Consumers tend to know less about leasing than buying. So while 43 percent of car buyers haggle over the car's purchase price, only 21 percent of leasing customers do, according to CNW. Plus, lease customers tend to choose more expensive cars.

So be extra wary if your dealer tries to hard-sell you into a lease. One common tactic, says Eskeldson, is to give customers an "apples-to-oranges" chart comparing payments on a lease versus a loan—quoting a low-interest rate on the lease and a high one on the sale. "If the consumer doesn't know how to calculate his own lease payment," Eskeldson says, "he is ripe for a rip-off."

THINGS TO DO

- **When it comes to shopping** for the best deal, knowing a model's invoice (or wholesale) price is important, since it gives you better bargaining power. Find it online at websites like CarsDirect.com and Edmunds.com.

- **Understanding your options for financing** your purchase can help ensure you get the best deal. Check out the FTC's vehicle financing guide—go to *www.ftc.gov/bcp/consumer.shtm* and click on the

"Financing, Leasing, or Renting" link under the "Automobiles" tab.

- **Do your homework before buying** an auto service contract. The Federal Trade Commission provides a helpful guide—go to *www.ftc.gov/bcp/consumer.shtm* and click on the "Buying a Car" link under the "Automobiles" tab.

- **Before buying a used car,** protect yourself by hiring an independent mechanic to inspect it.

10 Things Your
Car-Leasing Company
Won't Tell You

1 *"NEVER MIND ALL OUR TALK ABOUT MONTHLY PAYMENTS."*

Low, low, insanely low monthly payments! When you walk into a car dealership and inquire about leasing, that's what you're going to hear about. But try to tune it out—no matter what the salesperson might tell you, the most important things to think about when investigating a lease are a vehicle's price, the lease's finance rate, and the car's value at the lease's end.

Here's why. Every lease starts with a sale. That is, the dealer sells the car to a finance company, also known as a leasing company. In return for your monthly payments, the leasing company lets you use the car for a fixed time, and when that time is up, you return the car. Your monthly payments cover the difference between the sale price and the car's value at the end of the lease, plus finance charges and taxes. By encouraging you to focus on the monthly payment, a dealer can distract you from the real question: Are you getting a good price on the car or not? If you can lower the price, in turn you will pay less in monthly payments. So before you sign any lease, know the car's purchase price, its value at the end of the lease, and the finance rate you'll be paying. If you don't like what you see in terms of any of these three variables, this is the time to negotiate.

2 *"DON'T KNOW WHAT WE'RE TALKING ABOUT? GOOD."*

Auto leasing is tricky enough. But it's made even more confusing with jargony terms like "residual value," "lease rate," "capitalized cost," and "capitalized cost reduction." The less you understand the terminology, the more susceptible you are to accepting a bad deal. So to help you figure out what you're agreeing to, here's a glossary of the most important terms you'll need to know to negotiate effectively.

The *lease rate* is essentially the interest rate on the money used to finance the car. It shouldn't be higher than what your bank or credit union charges on new-auto loans. The *residual value* is the estimated value of the vehicle at the end of the lease term. Typically, you can purchase the vehicle at its residual value when the lease is up. The industry's bible for residual values is the *Automotive Lease Guide's Residual Percentage Guide;* you should view ALG's numbers as low-end amounts. *Capitalized cost* is basically the price of the car, plus other miscellaneous charges; it should be well under the manufacturer's

433

suggested retail price. Finally, *capitalized cost reduction* is the amount of money you give to the dealer up front, like a down payment, to lessen your monthly nut. It's negotiable.

Before you sign any leasing contract, contact your attorney general's office and ask if your state's lemon laws apply to leased vehicles.

3 *"LEASING A LEMON WILL LEAVE A SOUR TASTE IN YOUR MOUTH."*

In every state there are "lemon laws" designed to protect consumers from the worst-case scenario—a car that's fundamentally unfixable. But what happens when you lease an automobile that turns out to be just that? Since you're not technically the owner of the car, the lemon laws won't apply in many states. Alaska doesn't cover leased vehicles under its lemon laws at all, and 12 other states—including Colorado, Maryland, and Arizona—offer no guarantees, saying that protection under their respective lemon laws depends on the specifics of given lease agreements and warranties.

Before you sign any leasing contract, contact your attorney general's office and ask if your state's lemon laws apply to leased vehicles, suggests Philip Nowicki, former director of the Lemon Law Arbitration Program for the Florida attorney general's office. Also, make a point of reading your warranty thoroughly. In those 12 states where the lemon laws are not expressly extended to lessees, you're okay as long as the manufacturer's warranty covers you and not just the leasing company.

4 *"WE'LL DRIVE YOUR LIABILITY PREMIUMS THROUGH THE ROOF."*

You may be attracted to leasing by the promise of low monthly payments. But here's something you might not hear about until after you've signed on the dotted line: You'll probably have to buy more insurance for a car you're leasing than one you own. Most lease contracts require a lot more insurance than what's mandated by state law. How much more? Typical among leases is liability coverage of $100,000 per person and $300,000 per occurrence, compared with, say, California requirements of $15,000 per person and $30,000 per occurrence. That can amount to anywhere from a 5 to 25 percent increase in your insurance premium, or upwards of $50 extra a month.

What's more, most insurance companies require that you have the same coverage on all vehicles. So not only will you have to buy more coverage for the leased car, but all your other vehicles will have to match this higher policy. Aurora Dawn Harris, an Orange County, Calif., lawyer specializing in lease-fraud cases, has had clients whose premiums have doubled and even tripled as a result of leasing a car—so much for low monthly payments.

5 "A WIPEOUT COULD REALLY TOTAL YOUR FINANCES."

It's bad enough having your car stolen or wrecked. But if you're driving a leased car, the pain can be even more excruciating. The reason: Lessors usually treat a stolen or wrecked car as a form of early termination. So while your insurance company should pay the leasing company the car's market value, the amount insurance will cover may be a lot lower than what you still owe on the lease financing.

The solution is what's called gap insurance, which covers the difference if your leased car is totaled or stolen, so you don't have to. Most finance companies provide their own gap insurance right in the contract, either by including it as part of the monthly payment or by charging drivers a modest premium for each vehicle leased (typically less than $10 per vehicle). But if you're working with a smaller, independent leasing company, make sure to ask about it.

"It's silly not to have gap insurance in a world of carjacks and accidents," says W. James Bragg, CEO of Fighting Chance, a Long Beach, Calif., auto-pricing information service. "It's a pretty expensive mistake to make." How much should you expect to spend? Art Spinella, president of CNW Marketing Research in Oregon, suggests no more than 1 to 1.5 percent of your monthly payment; if gap insurance costs more, he says, try to negotiate.

6 "KEEP YOUR CAR CLOSE TO HOME—OR ELSE."

Ah, freedom. That's what the automobile is all about, isn't it? The ability to hop in and go anywhere you want? Well, if you've leased a car instead of buying one, you could be in for a shock: A little-noticed provision in many leasing contracts sharply restricts the places you can drive. Some may forbid you from going out of your state or out of the country, or specify that you can do so for only a limited period of time.

For example, buried in Ford's lease agreement is a restriction saying that the lessee cannot take the car "outside the state where first titled or registered for more than 30 days without Ford Credit's written consent [or] outside the United States, except for less than 30 days in Canada." (A Ford Credit spokesperson says that the contract is not designed to restrict the lessee's lifestyle, only to protect the leasing company's interests.)

What's the penalty? If you violate these conditions, you may be considered in default. That means you'll owe the difference between the balance on the lease and the amount Ford can get for the car at auction, plus any mileage or wear-and-tear penalties.

7 "YOU CALL IT AN ODOMETER; WE CALL IT A CASH REGISTER."

Quick—how many miles did you drive last year? Not certain? Neither was Jaclyn Bryant when she signed an auto lease. Like with most lease agreements, her vehicle came with an annual mileage limit. The lower that limit, the lower the depreciation of the lease—and hence the lower the monthly payment. Bryant agreed to 15,000 miles per year, which seemed like a good idea at the time. But the Ardmore, Pa., real estate agent managed to accumulate a total of 84,000 miles on her Volkswagen Jetta GL sedan by the end of the three-year lease. Her penalty for overshooting her limit by 39,000 miles: $5,850.

"This is a common thing," says Ashly Knapp, head analyst at Auto Advisor, a Seattle car-buyer service. Knapp says he knows a man who garaged his car for six months in order to avoid paying a big fine for exceeding his lease's mileage limit. Your best bet? Keep tabs on your odometer. Track how much you drive in an average month and multiply by 12. If you're over the limit, you'll need to go on a mileage diet.

8 "YOUR CAR'S NOT IN GOOD SHAPE UNLESS WE SAY SO."

All leasing contracts require you to return your car in good shape. The problem is, your definition of "good shape" may not match your leasing company's—and guess who's in the driver's seat. How to avoid a problem? A month or two before you're ready to turn in the car, ask the dealer to inspect it for excess wear and tear. If there are any dings, dents, or chips to take care of, you can get them fixed ahead of time rather than have the dealer charge you for them later.

Still, you may be in for a fight. After Robert Bonderman, a consultant in New York, returned his leased Jeep Cherokee with what he believed to be average wear and tear, the leasing company sent him a bill for $450 to replace a damaged windshield. Bonderman says he couldn't believe it—the windshield had seemed fine to him. But when he inquired about this charge, he says the company reported it had found a chip in the glass using an ultraviolet scanner.

9 "THE BEST TIME TO LEASE A CAR ISN'T SO OBVIOUS."

You may think the most expensive time to lease a new car is at the beginning of the model year, when vehicles have just hit the showroom. But that could actually be when you'll get the best deal. Here's why: A number of manufacturers hike their prices three or four times annually, according to vehicle pricing experts at Kelley Blue Book. For example, the 2008 GMC Acadia's retail price was $29,990 in October 2007; as of December 2007, the price had already gone up $480, to $30,470. And the higher the price, the more expensive your lease.

Why do manufacturers do this? Partly because they like to cut prices at the very end of the model year to help rush the late models out the door as the new ones are coming in. The trick is, this supposed end-of-year "price cut" is largely an illusion. Another tactic, growing in popularity since 2007, is manufacturers and dealers removing records of vehicle pricing available online, thus making it virtually impossible to note historical price comparisons.

10 "OUR CONTRACTS ARE UNBREAKABLE."

While it was once true that negotiations were an accepted and nearly expected part of the leasing experience, dealers have been getting stricter in recent years, making it much harder for lessees to wiggle out of anything in the contract. Stories like Terri Knight's—who was able to roll over a $1,650 penalty for exceeding her original mileage agreement into a new lease contract on her 1992 Acura Legend LS coupe—are becoming the stuff of legend. Dealers have begun tweaking lease clauses to make them nearly impossible to back out of, and "if you want to end a lease before it's due these days, good luck," Knapp says. "Once they have your signature, it's like you've signed in blood."

In fact, there's simply "less negotiation and more rigidity across the board," he says. In addition to hiding a lease's conditions in the fine print, for example, often on the back of the contract—far from where your signature goes—dealers now won't even help you out by recommending models with favorable rates of depreciation when it comes time to renew a lease. And there's no grace period once you sign pen to paper. "Ultimately," says Knapp, "you're paying more in total and have less control."

THINGS TO KNOW

Understanding car-leasing jargon can help you know what you're getting into. Here, a few terms that will help you talk the talk:

● **Capitalized cost (aka, cap cost):** The price of the car you're leasing, including options. This is one variable in the calculation of your monthly payment.

● **Drive-off fees:** The fees you pay up front when you begin the lease. These can include the security deposit, the capitalized-cost reduction, and other miscellaneous expenses.

● **Gap insurance:** Insurance that covers the difference between what your standard car insurance policy will cover if your vehicle is totaled or stolen and what you owe your leasing company.

● **Capitalized-cost reduction:** An up-front lump-sum payment made to the dealer to reduce what you owe every month.

● **Lease rate:** Essentially, the interest rate you pay every month on the money used to finance the car. You can translate it into a percentage by multiplying it by 2,400.

● **Residual value:** The estimated value of the vehicle at the end of the lease. The Automotive Lease Guide rates how well vehicles hold their value, at www.alg.com/depratings.

10 Things Your
Mechanic
Won't Tell You

1 *"YOU MIGHT BE IN THE WRONG GARAGE."*

Consumers have three basic choices when it comes to taking a car in for repair. You can go to the dealer, find a department or chain-store franchise like Sears or Meineke, or try an independent mechanic at a service station. Where you should go depends on what type of repair you need. But mechanics in each type of repair shop will try to convince you that they're the best ones for the job.

Clearly, any work under warranty should go straight to the dealer. That's where you'll find some of the best-trained mechanics for complicated jobs such as electric, chassis, fuel injection, and engine work. Because dealer overhead is so high, expect to pay top dollar for any repairs not covered under your warranty. Chain and department-store shops, on the other hand, are often the best deal for more routine maintenance such as oil changes, tune-ups, and brakes. But be sure to go to a chain that specializes in the repair you need—you probably don't want a brake-shop mechanic fiddling with your transmission no matter how much he assures you he can do the job.

Independent mechanics are your best bet for routine repairs such as fan belts, hoses, mufflers, and batteries, though some specialize in more complicated services. Because independents don't have the high volume of a chain shop, they often cost more; nevertheless, consumers tend to like the individual attention and convenience a neighborhood service station can provide. It also may be easier to establish a relationship with an independent mechanic. That's important, because you want someone to get to know the particular quirks of your car. But beware—independents often don't have the diagnostic equipment necessary to pinpoint a major problem.

2 *"MY FANCY CERTIFICATES DON'T MEAN VERY MUCH."*

The National Institute for Automotive Service Excellence (ASE) certifies mechanics in eight specialties, including brakes, electrical systems, engines, and heating and air-conditioning. Although auto mechanics must have two years' experience and pass an extensive standardized exam to become certified, an ASE sticker in your repair shop's window is no guarantee that the work will be done well.

Most repair shops hire both certified and uncertified mechanics. And only 33 percent of ASE mechanics are certified in all eight specialties. That means that when you bring your car in to have an oil leak fixed, a mechanic certified in air-conditioning may be doing the work. He's certified all right, but just not in what you need. Be sure to ask who is going to do the work on your car and what areas that person is certified in. You might also check to see when the certification expires. Mechanics are supposed to go in for a refresher course every five years, but the ASE can't make them take down their stickers if they don't.

In addition, look for repair shops that are endorsed by the American Automobile Association. These facilities must meet rigorous standards and guarantee their work for AAA members. Also, AAA agrees to arbitrate any disputes between its members and approved repair shops.

3 "I MAKE UNNECESSARY REPAIRS ALL THE TIME."

Back in 1979 the Department of Transportation found that 53 percent of the costs associated with auto repair were unnecessary. At the time, that translated into a $26.5 billion loss to consumers. Unfortunately, things haven't gotten much better since. Ralph Nader estimates that because the industry has grown so much, the total loss has jumped to $40 billion. The worst of these phantom repairs are the result of outright fraud. Some scam-artist mechanics have, for instance, been known to plunk a seltzer tablet into a battery cell, causing it to boil over. Or they may squirt oil on your shock absorber to make you think the seal is broken. Then there are the simple, everyday affronts such as the gas-station

attendant who doesn't push the dipstick all the way down when checking the oil, prompting you to buy an extra quart.

The most common problems are overselling and recommendations for unnecessary maintenance, says Dick Sullivan, deputy chief of field operations and enforcement for the California Bureau of Automotive Repair. It's those kinds of dishonest practices that cost Santa Ana–based EZ Lube $5 million in a civil settlement for unfair business practices in December 2007. A two-year investigation by the Orange County district attorney's office "uncovered a pattern of unfair and deceptive business practices at several EZ Lube locations where consumers were being sold unneeded parts and services," according to the DA. As part of the settlement, EZ Lube agreed to pay restitution to anyone with a legitimate claim over the past five years. (When reached for comment, a spokesperson for EZ Lube referred us to a company's press release on the matter, which reads: "It is our goal to make sure all of our customers are protected by the highest safeguards in the industry when they bring their vehicle to one of our stores.")

"Most unnecessary repairs are due to incompetence and the fact that cars are so incredibly complex that often a shop ends up trying a few things in order to solve the problem," says Jack Gillis, author of *The Car Repair Book* and director of public affairs for the Consumer Federation of America. Indeed, when a repair baffles a mediocre mechanic, he or she will probably keep replacing suspect parts until the problem is finally solved. Many of the parts replaced may have nothing to do with the problem, but you'll probably end up paying for them anyway.

4 "SOMETIMES I'LL EVEN CHARGE YOU FOR WORK THAT HASN'T BEEN DONE."

It happens on purpose. It happens by mistake. Either way, it happens a lot. Let's say you drop your car off at the garage to have the fluids, belts, and filters replaced. But the garage is busy, the mechanic who works on your car is a new hire, and the station manager hasn't left very clear instructions. As a result, the belts never get replaced, but you drive away thinking you've got brand-new ones. "This was one of the most common complaints," says Gillis, who spent three years at the Department of Transportation in the 1980s. It still is today.

A good way to avoid the problem of work that was supposed to have been done but wasn't: Ask to see the old parts. Some states, like California, even require mechanics to give you the parts they've removed from your car unless the warranty requires they be sent back to the manufacturer. In addition, Gillis suggests taping to your steering wheel an itemized list of all the repairs you want made. That way the mechanic who works on it—in most cases not the person you talked to when you drove in—will have direct instructions from you.

5 "YOU SHOULD GET A SECOND OPINION—EVEN IF IT MEANS A TOW."

Getting a second opinion is a must for major repairs, since it's a competitive business and prices can be all over the map. Sure, you may have to pay a few dollars more for an extra estimate, but the hundreds you could potentially save by shopping carefully will more than make up for it.

When exactly is it time to seek out a second opinion? A general rule of thumb is that you should get more than one mechanic's take on a repair if you expect to pay more than $200 for it. If your mechanic calls in the middle of a job with a laundry list of additional repairs, that's another good time to seek another estimate of the problem and the cost of fixing it—and beware the mechanic who tries to stop you by saying that he's already taken apart the engine, the transmission, or whatever. If you were able to drive the car into the shop, you should be able to drive it back out for a second opinion.

You also may consider paying around $100, more or less, to get your car checked first at a diagnostic center that isn't affiliated with a repair shop, such as those operated by the AAA. They have no reason to recommend unnecessary repairs, and you'll be armed with important information about your car's condition before you start negotiating with mechanics.

6 "REBUILT PARTS ARE OFTEN JUST AS GOOD AS NEW—AND A LOT LESS EXPENSIVE."

When it comes time to replace a part on your car, you can save a significant amount of money by buying it used. Indeed, a rebuilt part can save you as much as 75 percent over the cost of a new one. But chances are your mechanic isn't going to advertise this money-saving option—often you must specify that you want a remanufactured part, or the mechanic will likely install an expensive new one.

Also, keep in mind that rebuilt parts aren't right for every replacement. They usually work best for alternators, starters, and radiators, and are often guaranteed for less time than new parts.

7 "YOUR CAR IS TOO HIGH-TECH FOR ME."

Automobiles have become incredibly sophisticated over the past 10 years, incorporating technology that Henry Ford never could have imagined. But most mechanics haven't caught up. Jack Gillis says that the industry is experiencing a "big shortfall" of mechanics properly trained in the computerized systems found in most cars today.

This trend has been especially tough on service stations, whose share of the auto-repair market has slipped to about 24 percent, from close to 40 percent a decade ago, according to Hunter Publishing, a Des Plaines, Ill., trade-magazine company. Dealers, on the other hand, are required by most manufacturers to buy the expensive diagnostic equipment needed to pinpoint the source of computer problems. That means their technicians are more likely to be trained in these complicated repairs. But if you don't drive an American car, you may want to go another route. Check out the kind of specialty shops that focus on only one or two foreign makes. Mechanics at these outfits are often as well or better trained than those at the dealer—and they usually charge less.

8 "I MAY SEND YOUR CAR SOMEWHERE ELSE FOR REPAIRS—WHICH WILL COST YOU."

Let's say you're taking your car in for several repairs at once—replacing the battery and headlamps, changing the oil, and repairing the fuel-injection system. Chances are an independent shop won't have the facilities or expertise to do them all in-house, and if so, it may pay another shop to do all or part of the work without your knowledge. In addition to seeming a little underhanded, this kind of auto-repair outsourcing can add significantly to the final price tag on the job, since your mechanic will have to charge a premium for the work he subbed out.

How to avoid the problem? When you take your car in for repairs, be sure to ask if all the work will be done onsite before you agree to anything. If your mechanic tells you he needs to subcontract some of it, simply tell him not to do those repairs and take the car yourself to a shop that can handle the rest of the job.

9 "THE LESS YOU KNOW ABOUT YOUR WARRANTY, THE HAPPIER I AM."

Confusion about your warranty is good for a repair shop. After all, it's not in an independent mechanic's best interest to tell you when a repair is under warranty because if he's mum, he can charge you for it. Dealerships, meanwhile, make little money on warranty repairs, so they're under pressure to get as much nonwarranty work out of you as possible.

The way dealership warranties often work is that if you get the car repaired somewhere else and something goes wrong as a result of that repair, the cost of fixing the problem will no longer be covered by the warranty. So say you get an oil change at a quick-service franchise shop and the mechanic does something wrong that eventually damages your engine; the dealer doesn't have to honor your warranty when your engine is finally repaired. But some dealers like to take it a step further by making it seem as if you have to bring your car to them for *all* repairs or risk losing your warranty protection.

Don't fall for it. Taking routine work such as oil changes, tire rotations, and even your 10,000-mile checkups to the less-expensive chains won't jeopardize your warranty in most cases. Nor will emergency repairs that would normally be covered under the warranty. Just be sure to keep all your receipts, says Gillis. That way, if the dealer tries to claim you

have an engine problem because you failed to get an oil change, for example, you can prove otherwise.

10 "YOU HAVE MORE POWER HERE THAN YOU THINK."

If you feel you've been wronged by an auto mechanic, take heart—there's something you can do about it. First file a complaint both with your state's Better Business Bureau and the attorney general's office. This will help unsuspecting consumers who check on the reputations of potential auto mechanics to avoid shoddy repairmen.

In some states, like California, you have even more recourse—the Bureau of Automotive Repair mediates or investigates each complaint it receives. To check to see whether your state has a similar agency, contact your state highway department. Finally, if your auto-repair garage is endorsed by the AAA, be sure to contact the organization. If your complaint is egregious enough, or joined by others, the outfit may lose the AAA's seal of approval.

THINGS TO DO

● **Warranty's up? Continue to take** your car to the dealer for complicated jobs, such as engine work. Chain stores and independent mechanics are better for routine jobs, like tune-ups and oil changes.

● **Shops associated with AAA guarantee** their work, and if there's a problem, they have an arbitration system in place. Search for AAA shops in your area, at *www.aaa.com*.

● **Not dealing with an AAA mechanic?** Make sure you get a written guarantee on the labor and parts used in the repair.

● **Above all, you want a mechanic** who is familiar with your car. So if it's a new shop, be sure to have a look around when you arrive—are there other cars like yours in for repairs?

CHAPTER 10

Your Free Time

■ Finally, the payoff! You've worked hard and invested wisely, the kids are all taken care of, and you've been eating right and seeing your doctor regularly. Now it's time to cut loose and have some fun.

We know how valuable your free time is, and with that in mind, we've pulled out all the stops to make sure that both your leisure hours and your leisure dollars are well spent. From "10 Things Your iPod Won't Tell You," designed to help you get the most from the world's most beloved and ubiquitous tech gadget, to "10 Things Your Cruise Line Won't Tell You," which offers help on how to navigate the sometimes turbulent waters of the cruise ship industry, there are tips here for revelers of every stripe. We've even thrown in some pointers on how to beat the house in "10 Things Your Casino Won't Tell You."

10 Things Your
iPod
Won't Tell You

1 *"IT'S GOOD TO BE KING—BUT MY REIGN MAY BE COMING TO AN END."*

Since launching the iPod in 2001, Apple has been the undisputed leader in digital music players, owning 70 percent of the market. What has set the iPod apart is not only its hip, user-friendly design but also its companion iTunes music store, the first online audio megamart, offering an ever-expanding catalog of songs for purchase at the click of a mouse. This two-pronged approach has given Apple a huge lead over competitors; so far the company has sold over 120 million iPods and more than 4 billion songs on iTunes. But the iPod's days at the top may be numbered.

At issue is Apple's proprietary format, which up until recently has made iTunes-purchased music incompatible with other non-iPod MP3 players. According to Chris Crotty, former senior analyst for consumer electronics at iSuppli, such closed systems either move toward compatibility or get surpassed by the competition. Apple has seen the writing on the wall—in January 2009, it unveiled its plan to make it easier for consumers to recode music into the more standard MP3 format. Good idea, according to the experts. "Over time the market prefers open systems," Crotty says.

2 *"CUSTOMER SERVICE IS A PRIVILEGE, NOT A RIGHT."*

Customer service isn't what it used to be. According to Ross Rubin, director of industry analysis at the NPD Group, companies across the board are pushing "more self-service" to cut costs. But even so, he says, Apple is "pretty aggressive in terms of the consumer electronics industry." IPod buyers, for example, get just one call to customer service during the first 90 days of ownership; each one after that will cost you. (If you want more phone time, the AppleCare Protection Plan offers unlimited calls for two years and doubles the one-year warranty.)

So where to turn for free help with your sputtering iPod? You can always visit an Apple Store—if you happen to live near one and don't mind the wait. But the Web is the real mother lode of information. For starters, Apple's site offers tons of troubleshooting advice and some quick-and-dirty DIYs. But for more-complex problems, the company has, in effect, outsourced customer service—to its own customers. Sites like iLounge.com and iPoding.com offer tutorials and bulletin boards where users answer one another's questions and explain tricky repairs. And you get to come back as many times as you want.

The Web is the real mother lode of information. For starters, Apple's site offers tons of troubleshooting advice and some quick-and-dirty DIYs.

3 *"IF YOU DROP ME, I'M TOAST."*

You've seen the ads—hip, young people exuberantly dancing with iPod in hand. But the reality is that the device is delicate. Apple's edgy designs "tend to be more attractive, but also more fragile" than other players, says industry analyst Rob Enderle.

At the heart of the iPod Classic, for example, is a tiny hard drive that can stop working if it's dropped or even knocked around. (Fortunately, the Touch, Nano, and Shuffle all use flash drives, which are more resilient.) But it's not only the hard drive that needs careful handling—the screens on these players have been a source of trouble as well. Apple admits some of its Nano iPod screens were faulty, causing them to crack and scratch too easily, but claims the problem affected "less than 1 percent." Patrick Destvet, a New York City psychologist, says it isn't just a Nano problem; the color screen on his new 30-gigabyte iPod Video was scratched up after a month, making it hard to see anything on the device. "Coming from Apple, I didn't expect this," Destvet says.

To protect your iPod, invest in a padded case. Apple sells many, including a leather shell; other good covers include the iSkin Claro and Speck Products'

ArmorSkin sleeves. Visit *store.apple.com* for the best selection.

4 *"WHEN IT COMES TO SHARING MUSIC, WE'RE STILL NOT AS FLEXIBLE AS YOU MIGHT THINK."*

Apple makes it very easy to load your iPod with music—iTunes software is free to anybody who wants it. But once you've filled your player with 40,000 songs, it's not so easy to get them off again. Despite loosening copyright restrictions, Apple doesn't let you move music from your iPod to another computer or other electronic devices, even though it would be legal to do so.

Fortunately, there are ways to circumvent Apple's roadblock through third-party software that allows you to move music from your iPod back to any computer. Among the options, both Mac and PC users can download the affordable Music Rescue from *www.kennettnet.co.uk;* PC users can save a few bucks with iGadget, *(www.ipodsoft.com)*. After downloading the software, you'll be asked to plug in your iPod so the software can pull the music from your player and save it in your iTunes folder.

5 *"MY BATTERY LIFE IS PATHETIC."*

The new iPod boasts a robust battery life of more than 20 hours. But if you look at the fine print, Apple admits on its website that "battery life and number of charge cycles vary by use and settings." The company also warns consumers that you can recharge a battery only so many times before it must be replaced. According to *The Rough*

Guide to iPods, the magic number is 500, depending on use. But according to Enderle, the typical iPod lasts an average of only 300 charges—and it doesn't matter whether the battery is empty or not when it's charged. "A cycle is a cycle," he says.

For a few years Apple simply refused to recognize the problem and recommended that users buy a new player if the battery died. Only after a public outcry—and a class-action lawsuit—did the company develop a battery-replacement program. Now you can send back your ailing iPod and get another for roughly $60, plus shipping. Most likely, you'll receive a comparable used or refurbished unit.

Better to extend the life of the battery you have. Do this by regularly updating your iPod's software. Check Apple's website for the latest version; you can download a free upgrade there. Minimize charging to when the battery is almost drained. And don't charge your iPod in its protective case, where it can overheat and diminish the battery's capacity.

6 "I'M DESTROYING YOUR HEARING."

A major selling point of digital music players is that you can tune out the world around you for hours at a time. But as you crank up your iPod to drown out ambient noise, you could be damaging your ears. According to a study by the American Speech-Language-Hearing Association, at full volume an iPod can generate up to 120 decibels, equal to the sound of a jet plane taking off. At that level you'll begin sustaining permanent hearing loss or tinnitus after just 5 to 10 minutes. The issue is serious enough that a maximum volume setting now comes standard on all new iPods.

"Noise-induced hearing loss is easy to ignore until it's too late," says Pam Mason, an audiologist at the ASLHA. Extended listening at 80 to 85 decibels is safe, according to Mason. Roughly speaking, that means you should turn it down if you can't hear someone talking normally three feet away from you or if the people around you can hear your music. It also helps to invest in a good pair of noise-canceling or noise-isolating earphones. Both types block out ambient sound so you needn't jack up the volume as high.

7 "I'M OUT OF DATE BEFORE I'M OUT OF THE BOX."

In the fall of 2005, small-business owner Peter Quinones wanted to replace his iPod but kept hearing Apple was about to come out with an improved model. "I was in a holding pattern," the Miami resident says. "You don't want to buy something and find out a week later there's a new product." So Quinones waited six months, then bought a video iPod instead of the Nano he'd been considering. His new player worked with the charging cradle in his Mercedes; the Nano wouldn't have.

All consumer tech companies have shortened their product cycles, adding innovative new features to maintain their competitive edge. But with the iPod, Apple seems to be churning out new versions at an unprecedented rate.

"It can be a nuisance for some consumers," says Susan Kevorkian, an analyst at IDC, since some of the older accessories, such as speakers or docks, aren't necessarily compatible with the newer models. Fortunately, Apple has now standardized the docks for the iPod, meaning future models should still work with the one you buy today.

8 "I'VE SPARKED A CRIME WAVE."

You know a product is popular when it becomes a favorite target of thieves. In New York City, an increase in crime on the subways has been blamed on the iPod, as folks sporting the telltale white earphones are being ripped off in record numbers. But iPod crime isn't isolated to urban areas. A number of college and high school campuses have experienced a rash of thefts, leading some schools to ban the device. A spokesperson for the Broward County school board in Florida says that district recently restricted the use of iPods and other electronic devices, citing theft and peer pressure to own these items as distractions to learning.

A spokesperson for the Law Enforcement Alliance of America says the iPod is a favorite among thieves because "it's easy to conceal, it has turnover value on the street, and people are willing to buy one on the black market." Not to mention, they're easy to spot: "The white headphones are a giveaway," he says, "just like flashing a fancy watch." He recommends other earphones and not using your iPod in dicey areas.

9 "WE'LL NICKEL-AND-DIME YOU ANY CHANCE WE GET."

Apple's first fiscal quarter of 2008 was a record-breaker: The company reported new highs for both revenue ($9.6 billion) and earnings ($1.6 billion). Yet even with these impressive financial stats, the company continues to pile on extra fees for owning and maintaining an iPod.

We're not talking about the burgeoning iPod accessories market, such as stylish cases and portable speaker systems. No, Apple has begun charging for standard equipment it once included with the cost of the player. Why? "It keeps retail prices down and drives sales volume," Kevorkian says. Early iPod models shipped with a wall charger and a dock. These "extras" are no longer free. Want to connect your video iPod to a TV? You'll have to buy a cord separately.

Adding insult to injury, should your iPod conk out after the warranty expires, you could end up paying as much to get it fixed as it would cost you to buy a new one—for example, the standard fee for repairs on a Nano is roughly $20 less than the cost of a new one—and that doesn't include shipping.

10 "ONCE YOU GO IPOD, YOU'RE LOCKED IN FOR LIFE."

One of the reasons Apple has been able to dominate the digital music player market until now is that while the iPod can play songs from a variety of sources, music bought online at the iTunes store can be used only on an iPod. That's because the company developed its own format for songs, called Protected AAC, instead of using the widely compatible MP3. Crotty points out that while basic AAC is an open format, the digital rights management software Apple lays over it—called, ahem, "Fair Play"—renders it incompatible with other players. No other company is legally allowed to make a device that can play songs in Apple's format.

The company claims AAC has many advantages over MP3, but the format also serves as the lock on the iPod's closed door—which could lead to its downfall. "They've set themselves up as Apple and the iPod versus the rest of the MP3 market," Crotty says. "Customers may get upset that they can't move their purchased music." The tide is already turning in Europe, which, he adds, "doesn't accept a closed system as a business practice": The French government passed a law in 2006 forcing Apple to allow music on the iTunes store to work on competitors' players.

THINGS TO DO

● **Want to fill up your** iPod on the cheap? You can start with the iTunes store's free section, which includes music tracks and video.

● **Buying a protective case for** your iPod is the best way to guard its hard drive or flash drive from damage and the screen from obtrusive scratches. You can find over 150 options, priced anywhere between $20 and $100, at Apple's online store (*store.apple.com*).

● **To get music off your** iPod and onto a new computer, you'll need a separate program like Music Rescue, available at a reasonable price at *www.kennettnet.co.uk*. Mac users have a free alternative, Senuti, available at *www.fadingred.org/senuti*—a small donation gets you free updates for life.

● **A little known iPod feature** is the ability to set a maximum volume. Choose "settings" from the main menu, then select "volume control."

10 Things Your
Airline
Won't Tell You

1 *"WELCOME TO THE CROWDED SKIES."*

If you've flown much lately, you've probably noticed that air travel feels like rush hour on the subway. Indeed, as airlines get more efficient, they're squeezing more people onto fewer planes. But that's had an unintended consequence: More fliers get left behind. Airlines have always overbooked flights to compensate for last-minute cancellations. But they don't always get the numbers right. And with so few seats open on later flights, fewer folks are volunteering to get bumped. As a result, the number of involuntarily bumped passengers is up, having grown 44 percent between the first nine months of 2005 and the same period in 2007, according to the Department of Transportation.

The silver lining for travelers is that airlines must get involuntarily bumped fliers to their destination within four hours of the expected arrival time or refund them up to $400. The bad news is that the problem isn't going away—airlines are busy developing computer systems to help them rebook bumped passengers. "Instead of fixing the problem," says Tony Polito, an associate professor at East Carolina University who has published several studies on the airline industry, "they are institutionalizing it."

2 *"YOUR HARD-WON AIR MILES ARE WORTH LESS ALL THE TIME."*

Air miles are easy to accrue. You can earn them using your credit card, getting a mortgage, "for anything short of breathing," says Tim Winship, editor at large of SmarterTravel.com. American Airlines, for example, has thousands of "mileage partners" to whom it sells air miles, making its frequent-flier program an important revenue center. And United Airlines' Mileage Plus plan brought in $600 million for the company in 2006.

But as miles flood the market, they're getting harder to use. Joe Lopez, a publications manager in Phoenix, wanted to redeem the 70,000 miles he earned on Northwest—but couldn't find a flight he liked. "It was ridiculous," he says. (A Northwest spokesperson says 50,000 miles will get you a seat on almost any domestic flight the airline offers.) What's worse, some airlines have reduced the shelf life of air miles, while others have increased the amount required for an upgrade. Winship says customers can keep their account current by using a credit card affiliated with the program, which will build miles as they make purchases. You can also redeem a small amount of miles, to keep your account active, on things like magazine subscriptions.

3 *"WE'LL GIVE YOU A GOOD DEAL—IF WE CAN GET SOMETHING OUT OF IT."*

Once in a while airlines do offer serious bargains. Currently, they're doing so in an effort to steer you away from the Expedias and Travelocitys of the world. Why? Airlines pay these online booking sites a fee for every ticket they sell—something they'd rather not do. The upshot: If you're looking for the best deals—anywhere from a few dollars off to savings of 25 percent or more—your first stop should be the airlines' own websites.

The industry is following the lead of Southwest, which long ago pulled its tickets from travel sites. In 2005 it introduced Ding, a computer application that scans for the best fares and regularly updates you on deals. What does Southwest get in return? Loyalty and repeat fliers. "Subscribers to Ding are highly engaged customers," says Anne Murray, senior director of marketing communication with Southwest. "They fly a lot." American recently launched a similar application called DealFinder, which offers big discounts on flights, and other airlines may follow.

4 *"WE LOVE HIDDEN FEES."*

The inflation-adjusted price of an airline ticket has actually fallen since the airlines were deregulated in 1978. But at the same time, fuel costs have risen. How do airlines make up the difference? In part, through additional fees. These fees keep the listed ticket price competitive but boost the total cost to travelers, often at the end of the booking process, when buyers are less likely to change their mind.

The most common is the fuel surcharge, which ranges from $5 to $25 or more. (Southwest hedged against rising oil prices before they spiked; it doesn't have a fuel surcharge.) Other examples of fees: Northwest charges around $15 for an exit-row seat. United now charges approximately $25 each way for checking a second bag. And Allegiant, a small airline that provides services from cities like Missoula, Mont., to the Sunbelt, charges a fee just to book a ticket online—a process that costs the company virtually nothing. Even frequent-flier programs, which are supposed to let you book "free flights," have added fees for things like booking too close to your travel date. "I keep seeing more and more of these hidden fees," says George Hobica, creator of Airfarewatchdog.com. "I get complaints from people all the time."

5 *"CUSTOMER SERVICE ISN'T ALWAYS OUR TOP PRIORITY..."*

A few years back, when Larry Meyer tried to fly from the U.S. Virgin Islands to Florida, he arrived at the airport only to find his flight had been canceled and nothing was available until the next day. "It really rubbed me the wrong way," he says. "They have my number in the computer; you'd think they could call me." Some customers, after enough bad experiences, have started fighting back. Kate Hanni, who was delayed on the tarmac for nine hours in 2006, formed a group that pushed New York State to enact a passengers' rights law, which requires that passengers stuck on a plane for three hours or more have access to such basics as restrooms, food and water, and fresh air.

According to Claes Fornell, a professor at the University of Michigan Ross School of Business, the major U.S. airlines currently have their lowest customer-satisfaction ratings in seven years. "There is collusion in dissatisfaction," he says. "They all offer about the same lousy service." But David Castelveter, spokesperson for the Air Transport Association, which represents the airlines, sees it differently. He says travelers, upset by delays that are often out of the airlines' control, assume customer service is the problem when other factors are to blame. "This is a customer-service-driven business," Castelveter says.

6 "... UNLESS YOU HAVE A LOT OF MILES."

They may be making a lot of customers miserable these days, but if airlines could be said to cater to anyone's needs, it's those of the folks in the top tier of their frequent-flyer programs—heavy travelers, many of whom fly for business and therefore buy the most expensive tickets. "These people get white-glove service," says Henry Harteveldt, a travel analyst with Forrester Research. "[Airlines] really want to cultivate that relationship." These favored flyers get the first crack at upgrades. The reservation center answers their call on the first ring. They often get special bonus-mile offers and free upgrades. And they can use first-class check-in, meaning shorter lines through security and early boarding.

Chuck Guedelhoefer, president of Raths, Raths & Johnson, a structural engineering firm in Willowbrook, Ill., cherishes the benefits he gets from United's top-tier membership program. For one, it makes it easier for him to redeem frequent-flier miles. And because he has so many with United, he always gets seated in the exit row, so he doesn't have to pay for upgrades to business class. "I even get treated better at the ticket counter," he says.

7 "OUR PLANES ARE ANCIENT."

Airline passengers in Europe are accustomed to seat-back entertainment systems with movies on demand and videogames—innovations that seem like space-age fantasies compared with the pull-down screens still so common in the States. That's because after the industry's near collapse in 2001, most major U.S. airlines decided they couldn't afford new jets and stopped buying them. Now our commercial fleet averages 12 years old. And with so many older jets in the air, airlines feel little pressure to upgrade, says Richard Aboulafia, an aviation analyst with the Teal Group.

"An inordinate number of our planes [in the U.S.] are old and inefficient," says Harteveldt. Among U.S. carriers, Northwest has the oldest planes, with an average age of 17 years. (JetBlue and AirTran, by contrast, have the newest fleets, averaging three years old.) It's not that old aircraft are dangerous; they're maintained to high safety standards. But in addition to being dingy and less comfortable for passengers, old planes cause more delays due to last-minute mechanical problems, and they guzzle fuel, a cost that filters down to customers. The situation is only going to get worse, says CreditSights analyst Roger King, since most U.S. airlines have placed few or no orders for new planes.

> **In addition to being dingy and less comfortable for passengers, old planes cause more delays due to last-minute mechanical problems, and they guzzle fuel, a cost that filters down to customers.**

8 *"EVEN WE DON'T UNDERSTAND OUR PRICING."*

Most flights are divided into first class, business, and economy. But when it comes to pricing, there are often up to 200 different price points for seats on each plane. "Ticket pricing is a mix of science, game theory, and art—a three-dimensional matrix," Harteveldt says. The biggest factor, beyond basic costs like fuel and labor, is the competition. Airlines track one another's fares, then try to determine how many business travelers, who generally pay a premium for flexible tickets, are likely to book a flight. On routes with lots of business travelers, seat prices can stay high because airlines know they'll book seats at the last minute. As each seat sells, the prices of others fluctuate. "Domestic fares can change up to three times a day," says Hobica.

But prices don't only go up. If demand from business travelers is lagging, prices may fall as the flight time gets closer. If that happens and the fare drops by the time your flight leaves, you can get a voucher from a number of airlines for the difference—United, Southwest, and Alaska do this without deducting a fee.

9 *"WE'RE AT THE MERCY OF 'LEAVE IT TO BEAVER'-ERA TECHNOLOGY."*

Air traffic in the U.S. has been increasing, but our air-traffic control hasn't changed much since the 1950s. This radar-based system tracks planes as they take off, travel, and land. And while it's reliable, it's not efficient. Planes are routed across the country on a series of highways in the sky, spacing them at least five miles apart for safety. And that's the problem: Because radar pinpoints planes only every 12 seconds, their exact location is never known. "It's like driving a car when you only look out the window every 12 seconds. You can't get close to anything," says R. John Hansman, director of the Massachusetts Institute of Technology International Center for Air Transportation.

The airlines would like to see this system replaced by one based on GPS technology, Castelveter says. That would allow planes to fly much closer together safely, which would help congestion. The main sticking point is how to pay for it—Congress has yet to decide how to fund the change.

10 *"YOU'LL WAIT BECAUSE THE SYSTEM'S BROKEN."*

The year 2007 was one of the worst on record for airline delays: Only 77 percent of flights arrived on time, while 76 percent departed on time. And the antiquated air-traffic-control system isn't the only reason. Airlines routinely stuff more flights into a given time slot than ever have hope of taking off. For example, there's room for 32 to 52 flights to leave New York's JFK airport between 8 and 9 A.M., but 57 are normally scheduled, automatically leading to delays, according to congressional testimony by the National Air Traffic Controllers Association. Newark, LaGuardia, and O'Hare all have similar chronic overscheduling problems. And when bad weather rolls in, delays increase and spread across the country. Fed up, the Federal Aviation Administration stepped in last year, capping flights going in and out of JFK at 83 for peak hours, down from the usual 100. Caps will be imposed at Newark as well.

Even the airlines say it's a necessary temporary step. But the carriers would like more action from the government, including pushing through upgrades of the air-traffic-control system, which would increase capacity at airports. Castelveter blames part of the problem on corporate jets, which take off and land at smaller airports in the region whenever they choose, exacerbating delays. "It's an incredibly complex problem," says Shannon Anderson, associate professor of management at Rice University, one involving aging technology, competing airlines, and private and commercial carriers. "Just capping the number of flights is not going to solve it."

THINGS TO DO

- **Despite the proliferation of discount** travel sites, you'll find the best rates on an airline's own website.

- **Want to keep track** of discounted fares? Sign up with *www.airfarewatchdog.com,* and the free service will e-mail you when prices drop on routes you choose to monitor.

- **Frustrated by advertised prices** that don't represent the full amount you'll pay? Some travel sites such as FareCompare.com display hidden fees when tallying the cost of your tickets.

- **Digital luggage scales**—like the one Balanzza.com offers for around $25—can save you from paying overweight fees that kick in if your bag's over 50 pounds.

10 Things Your
Cruise Line
Won't Tell You

1 "OUR GAIN IS YOUR LOSS."

The Cruise Lines International Association, with 24 member cruise lines and 16,000 travel agencies, represents all the major American cruise lines and accounts for 97 percent of the North American cruise market. Its member ships carried 12.6 million North American passengers in 2007, up 4.6 percent from 2006. But when the industry experiences growth, passengers don't likewise reap the benefits. For example, the average fare on Carnival Cruise Lines rose about 18 percent from 2003 to 2007, according to industry analysts, and since cabins were filling up more quickly than in the past, there were fewer bargains to be had.

How to find the best deal in good times and bad? Oivind Mathisen, editor of *Cruise Industry News,* says, "When a cruise hasn't been selling as fast as it should,

> Savvy consumers also should look for "shoulder season" departures, just before or after holidays, and off-peak in various regions.

[cruise lines] advertise bargains, mainly through travel agents or via mail to past customers." Savvy consumers also should look for "shoulder season" departures, just before or after holidays, and off-peak in various regions: early spring in the Mediterranean, for example, or May or September in Alaska. Transatlantic crossings tend to be better values, too.

2 "OUR ENGINES BREAK DOWN ALL THE TIME."

In 2005, Rex Pierce, a customer-service technician in Fort Worth, Tex., took his wife and three kids on a Carnival cruise departing from Galveston, Tex., for Cozumel and Calica, Mexico. Once on board, they were informed there was a small chance that repairs to the engine wouldn't be finished in time to reach both destinations. Passengers were given the chance to leave but, according to Pierce, were told "they thought they would get it running shortly." Though the ship made it out to sea, it never reached either port. Pierce feels cheated: "We lost five days of our lives," he says.

"Engine problems are very common," says Ross Klein, editor of CruiseJunkie .com and author of *Cruise Ship Blues: The Underside of the Cruise Ship Industry.*

A record Klein maintains on his website shows that in 2007 roughly 5 percent of ships that had to cancel some or all port calls did so because of engine or mechanical problems.

As many disappointed passengers realize too late, they have little recourse. According to Ron Murphy, director of the Office of Consumer Affairs and Dispute Resolution Services at the Federal Maritime Commission, "Almost all tickets allow cruise lines to change itineraries at their discretion."

3 "THIS SHIP IS A HEALTH HAZARD—IT'S JUST CRAWLING WITH VIRUSES."

Cruise ships are an ideal breeding ground for germs: thousands of people in close proximity, eating food made in the same kitchen, inhabiting enclosed spaces that just a few days before housed someone else. In December 2002 the norovirus made waves in the media after a series of outbreaks on Holland America, Disney, and Carnival lines in which hundreds of passengers were infected. Unfortunately, the problem has not disappeared since then. Twenty-three outbreaks (as defined by 3 percent or more of passengers having been diagnosed) were recorded by the Centers for Disease Control and Prevention (CDC) in 2007, down from 37 in 2006. "An increase in norovirus outbreaks in 2006 and 2007 coincided with the emergence of two new strains of norovirus," says Lisa Beaumier, public health analyst for the Vessel Sanitation Program at the CDC.

The CDC posts outbreaks on its website (*www.cdc.gov/nceh/vsp*). But this information accounts for only a portion of worldwide outbreaks, because the CDC monitors only ships that include a U.S. port in their itinerary. Short of not going on a cruise, Beaumier says the best way to stay healthy is to wash your hands frequently and thoroughly with soap and water.

4 "SURE, WE CAN TAKE CARE OF YOUR PLANE RESERVATIONS, BUT YOU'D DO A WHOLE LOT BETTER ON YOUR OWN."

Many cruise lines offer to book customers' airfare, with the guarantee that should there be a flight delay, they'll hold the ship or fly them to the next port. But customers pay a premium for this security. Mike Cordelli, a manager of information systems in New York City, has been on nine cruises and says he has had the cruise line book his plane tickets about half the time, but only after checking other available fares. "You often don't get to choose a flight, you may end up with some fairly lousy connections, stuff like that," Cordelli says. On several occasions he has saved enough money by booking on his own to arrive in a port city a day early and spend the night in a hotel.

A spokesperson for Regent Seven Seas Cruises admits, "Typically, guests can find a better fare on their own." He adds that customers who purchase airfare through the cruise line are indeed entitled to free ground transportation and additional support. But if they want to specify the carrier, route, or schedule, "we charge them the difference"—roughly $100 "custom airfare" fee in addition to the extra cost of the ticket, making for one very expensive security blanket.

5 *"THINK EVERYTHING'S INCLUDED? THINK AGAIN."*

In 2007 Carnival Corp. brought in 77 percent of its cruise-related revenue through fares. The source of the other 23 percent? According to the company's annual report, "on board and other." If this seems like a large percentage for an industry that often claims its packages are "all inclusive," that's because only the basics are covered in the price of most cruises. Mathisen says, "You get most food, entertainment, soft drinks, and coffee. You pay for alcohol, merchandise, for the spa, for pictures. All of these things are optional, but it's hard not to spend money on a cruise because you are a captive audience."

Another significant expense for passengers comes in the form of tips for the staff. Many cruise lines have begun charging a fixed gratuity for restaurant and custodial service, set at an average of $10 per guest, per day. A CLIA spokesperson stressed that the amount varies by cruise line, and that passengers can almost always alter the percentage on request.

6 *"OUR 'GOURMET' FOOD IS ANYTHING BUT."*

Cruise lines are quick to tout the "fine dining" available on their ships, but in most cases the label is a misnomer. "On a few small ships, it's possible to create a dining experience that matches the finest dining ashore," says Deborah L.

Natansohn, former president of Seabourn Cruise Line. "On larger ships, however, the main dining venues will basically be serving banquet-style food." Typically, the kitchen staff knows about how many entrées will be needed, so they prepare that much in advance and finish it when the diners arrive. According to Natansohn, "This is different from what a fine-dining restaurant does, where the dish is cooked to order."

Large ships often provide alternative restaurants that do cook to order, but this special treatment comes at a price—one that isn't included in the cost of the cruise. As Douglas Ward, author of Berlitz's *Ocean Cruising & Cruise Ships 2006,* explains, "It's economics. If you don't charge enough money for your cruises, you have to lower the quality of the food." Ward says the smaller, reservations-only restaurants on the big lines use premium ingredients, but charge up to an extra $30 per person per meal. The bottom line: If eating well is important to you, be prepared to pay.

7 *"WE MAKE MONEY WHILE YOU'RE OFF THE SHIP, TOO."*

Most cruises offer "shopping lectures" before docking in a port and hand out store maps to passengers. This service is usually provided by one of two contractors: The PPI Group and Onboard Media. Both firms promote only stores that pay for ads and pass on a portion of that revenue to the cruise lines. When asked about this arrangement, a Carnival spokesperson said, "It is disclosed to guests in writing that the stores pay an advertising fee."

Once a ship docks, passengers can either explore on their own or join a port excursion, in which they're shepherded via bus to beaches, historic landmarks, and shopping areas. Excursions, which are not included in the cost of the cruise, are a "huge moneymaker" for cruise lines, according to Klein, who says, "One of the biggest ways you can save money is to not get drawn into [them]." Cordelli echoes the advice. While he feels excursions are sometimes helpful, especially in non-English-speaking countries, "It makes little sense to pay the cruise line four or five times what a taxi would cost you to get to a beach on St. Thomas, for example."

8 "OUR INSURANCE? YOU'RE BETTER OFF LOOKING ELSEWHERE."

When traveling abroad, comprehensive medical insurance is a must. Unfortunately, coverage varies greatly from policy to policy: Some plans cover international trips of limited length, while others (like Medicare and Medicaid) provide little or no overseas coverage. Passengers can buy supplementary insurance through their cruise line, but such policies have holes. "As soon as you step off the ship [independent of an excursion], you're no longer covered," Ward says. An outside policy makes more sense and is often less expensive; Ward advises a policy specifically designed for cruises and warns, "Make sure it includes emergency evacuation insurance" in case of a serious medical problem.

Websites like InsureMyTrip.com allow you to compare plans that are often better and cheaper than those offered by cruise lines. For example, at press time, Holland America's medical coverage, included in one of its Cancellation Protection Plans, has a $10,000 illness and $50,000 emergency evacuation maximum, and averages around $160 per passenger (depending on the fare). By contrast, the CSA Travel Protection Plan covers trip cancellation and provides $250,000 in illness coverage and $1,000,000 in evacuation expenses for just over $70. The bottom line: It's worth your time to shop around.

9 "OUR ADS MIGHT SAY CHAMPAGNE AND CAVIAR, BUT EXPECT BEER AND PRETZELS."

New cruise lines are sprouting up all the time, many of which cater to niche interests. But be careful: You may not get the experience you expect. Gina, owner of a logistics-management company in Harquahala, Ariz., who declined to let us use her last name, went on one cruise with Princess Cruises, but "won't ever do another one." She chose Princess for the "upscale experience" and "formal dress code" described in its brochure, but when Gina and her husband arrived at dinner the first night, Gina says many diners were dressed in jeans, shorts, even pajamas. "If I wanted to schlep around in shorts, I'd stay at home," she says. (A spokesperson for Princess Cruises responds: "Her experience sounds atypical. Most passengers are respectful of the dress code.")

Marketing can be misleading. A commercial for Carnival shows a well-dressed couple dancing to smooth jazz, but an Expedia.com review warns,

"People who expect a sophisticated experience probably wouldn't be happy." (Carnival's cruises are geared heavily toward families.) To avoid surprises, do your homework before selecting a cruise—unbiased sites like Expedia and CruiseCritic.com are helpful resources.

10 *"WE'LL GET ALONG FINE— AS LONG AS YOU DON'T HAVE ANY COMPLAINTS."*

In January 2005 Dave Levine and his wife boarded the Royal Caribbean *Grandeur of the Seas* in New Orleans. When his wife became ill and the ship's doctor recommended she disembark at the next port, guest relations staff "made no effort to help arrange transportation" and told Levine he would be charged a $300 U.S. Customs fine if she left the ship early.

When Levine threatened to tell other passengers—and became verbally abusive, according to Royal Caribbean—ship security forced the couple to disembark at Key West. Once home, Levine wrote directly to Royal Caribbean's chief operating officer and was reimbursed for the fee.

Levine was smart to bypass customer service. According to the Better Business Bureau of Southeast Florida and the Caribbean, Carnival and Norwegian Cruise Lines have an "unsatisfactory record" of dealing with customer complaints. While Norwegian has been "responsive" to BBB criticism, Carnival showed "a pattern of no replies to customer complaints and a failure to eliminate the basic cause of customer complaints brought to their attention by the Better Business Bureau."

THINGS TO DO

● **Cruise ships fill up fast,** so try booking three to six months ahead of time to ensure a spot. Since some ships have capacity-controlled fares (the price goes up as the ship fills up), it might even save you money.

● **Shoulder seasons, or the periods** just before and after peak times, typically offer the cheapest tickets. Try the Mediterranean in early spring or Alaska in September.

● **Many cruise lines set up** on-shore excursions for passengers—but that means you'll likely be spending the day with a group from the same boat. For more options, talk to your travel agent—she may know about excursions the cruise doesn't offer.

● **Today there's a cruise for everyone—** from family getaways to romantic trips for two—just don't get them confused. To avoid booking the wrong boat, check out CruiseCritic.com, which features reviews.

10 Things Your
Ski Resort
Won't Tell You

1 *"SNOWBOARDERS ARE OUR BEST FRIEND—AND YOUR WORST ENEMY."*

Alpine skiing has fallen on tough times lately. In fact, since the 2000–01 season, the number of skiers has dropped in the neighborhood of 14 percent, according to the National Ski and Snowboard Retailers Association. Snowboarding, on the other hand, is growing more popular: The number of snowboarders has increased roughly 21 percent in the same period. That means ski resorts have to do whatever they can to attract boarders and keep them on the mountain. But skiers beware: Snowboarders can be hazardous to your health.

Just ask Boston investment adviser Grenville Anderson, who was skiing a beginner trail at New Hampshire's Loon Mountain when he was suddenly knocked over by a snowboarder who also took down an eight-year-old. "I didn't know what had happened. I didn't see anything," he says. When Anderson went to check on the other two, he was greeted with shouts of profanity. "The snowboarder was swearing at me!" he says. "We never even got an apology. We all could have been killed."

Resorts know that mixing snowboarders with skiers means trouble. For one thing, the sports have a completely different rhythm. Also, snowboarders have a blind spot that skiers don't—and a reputation for being rude and reckless. (The typical practitioner is male and falls in the age-range of teen to twentysomething.) But dollars and cents dictate that the resorts let snowboarders rule the mountain: Anderson says that the boarder who crashed into him didn't even have his lift ticket revoked. "I don't know what happened with this individual, but I do know that we're very proactive and we have a fair number of ambassadors on the slopes," says Rick Kelley, Loon Mountain's general manager. "Their function is to deal with people who aren't skiing under control."

2 *"WE FUDGE OUR SNOW CONDITIONS."*

Ever wonder why one ski area boasts 12 inches of "packed powder" while another down the road reports just 4 inches? The reason is that the measuring guidelines set forth by groups like SnoCountry, the outfit that collects and distributes over 800 ski-condition reports from resorts around the world, are merely that— guidelines. And when the honor system rules, abuse abounds.

"Our guys just kind of look at the roof tower and make an estimate," says a spokesperson for Shawnee Peak in Maine. Keith Sutherland, snow-surface supervisor for Waterville Valley in New Hampshire, admits to being less than precise as well. "We try to be consistent," he says, "but it's tricky because you can get 2 inches in one place and 18 in another, so you poke around a bit and come up with a number."

When conditions are outright lousy, most resorts rely heavily on euphemisms. A spokesperson for Jiminy Peak, southern New England's largest ski and snowboard resort, explains it this way: "I say 'thin spots' when there are rocks. I don't use the word 'frozen,' because that sounds like ice, and I never use the 'r' word"—rain.

3 "CLIMATE CHANGE COULD RUN US INTO THE GROUND."

A soft winter can devastate a ski resort. And since all signs suggest that climate change isn't going away anytime soon, ski slopes have responded by heavily bolstering their snowmaking equipment—meaning a huge increase in expenses. "Energy costs for making snow continue to escalate," says Kurt Zimmer, director of sales and marketing for Windham Resorts in the Catskills. "These are expenses that inevitably end up being passed on to customers and make skiing a more costly form of recreation than it already is." Slopes are also cutting corners where they can on staff and supplies—for example, fewer ski patrollers on the slopes with less than fully equipped portable safety kits.

But some resorts aren't thinking only of profit—they're taking measures to "go green" where they can. Nick Bohnenkamp, communications manager for Colorado Ski Country, reports that 12 of the state's 26 resorts offset 100 percent of their energy use with renewable energy credits. Environmental impact statements are run to minimize land damage when resorts install new lifts or add new terrain—Arapahoe Basin, for example, recently opened 400 acres of new terrain and removed only 1 percent of trees. "And it's not just the big guys with large pocketbooks doing their part," Bohnenkamp says. Silverton Mountain, a one-lift resort, purchased a used lift from a neighboring resort and salvaged "handheld radios, furnishings, carpet, bar equipment, ski-patrol toboggans, rope, and bamboo, all headed for the dump."

4 "ONLY SUCKERS PAY FULL PRICE."

Jennifer Sundman has been skiing Colorado's resorts for years. And when friends come to visit her in Colorado Springs, the first place she sends them is to local retailer The Ski Shop, where you can pick up discounted single-day lift tickets. They'll sell you a one-day ticket for Winter Park ski resort for roughly $20 off the on-the-mountain rate, and you'll save about $10 if you want to ski Copper Mountain. "No one I know pays full price for ski tickets," Sundman says.

Sure, navigating the lift-ticket maze can be complicated: Prices typically go up and down half a dozen times each season and up by about 4 percent from one year to the next. But as Sundman's example demonstrates, there are discounts to be had if you're willing to scout them out. For starters: If your looking to score discounted tickets to slopes in the Northeast, visit *www.cheapskiingguide .com*, which offers links to ski deals in nine states, including Vermont, New Hampshire, and New York.

5 *"OUR INSTRUCTORS NEED LESSONS THEMSELVES."*

So you've got snowplowing down, and you really want to try out the moguls. Should you sign up for ski school in hopes of advancing your skills? Linda Legere of North Berwick, Maine, doesn't think so. Her three kids have had their share of lessons throughout New England. And while their instructors certainly ranged in ability, says Legere, lessons generally didn't work out for them—because her kids were often better skiers than their teachers.

Legere's experience is not unusual. According to the Professional Ski Instructors of America (PSIA), the group that sets the guidelines at most resorts, about half its member-certified instructors have only minimal experience. These "Level Ones," as they're called, must be able to do only the simplest of turns. Further, only 25 percent of Alpine ski instructors are certified at the highest level, Level Three, which requires mastery of difficult turns on all types of terrain.

But more often than not, instructors aren't PSIA-certified at all. That's because they don't have to be—anywhere. "There are a lot of transplants who become instructors just to get the free season ticket and enjoy the sun," says Mike Bell, a former ski instructor at Colorado's Steamboat Resort.

6 *"WE'RE BLOWING SNOW— AND A LOT OF HOT AIR."*

Ski resorts are forever bragging about their snowmaking capabilities. Heavenly Mountain Resort in Nevada claims that it's "home of the West Coast's largest snowmaking system," while the website of Maine's Sunday River boasts about the resort's 1,570 snow guns. The trouble is, snowmaking equipment rarely creates first-rate conditions. The weather needs to be quite cold for man-made snow to be any good, says snowmaking consultant Scott Barthold, who designs systems for resorts across the country. "Anything above 29 degrees and you'd be making compromises," he says. "Snow that is made above 29 degrees is not as fluffy. It's more like the consistency of a snowball."

Furthermore, resorts can't possibly blanket the kind of terrain they say they can unless Mother Nature helps them out, says Waterville Valley's Sutherland. "There are very few places that can cover the whole mountain on man-made snow alone," he says. "Conditions have to be ideal for that to happen. And those ideal days don't come along very often—once every couple of weeks, if you're lucky."

7 *"SKIING IS GETTING MORE DANGEROUS ALL THE TIME."*

There's no doubt about it: Skiing can be hazardous to your health. And it's especially tough on the knees. Though the number of debilitating knee injuries among skiers has been marginally decreasing over the past decade, it's not doing so as fast as other ski-related injuries—there were still about 15,000 tears of the anterior cruciate ligament in the 2006–07 season, according to Vermont Safety Research, a company that compiles data on skiing injuries. And the ski resorts shoulder some of the blame.

Part of the problem is that many resorts have made a push toward "grooming" their trails, or removing piles of powdery snow to make the runs smoother and sleeker, explains Jasper Shealy, retired professor emeritus at the Rochester Institute of Technology who studied ski injuries for 30 years. And while groomed trails certainly make skiing more action-packed, Shealy contends that they also increase the chances for knee injuries by making it much easier to ski quickly and aggressively. Another culprit: the promotion of shaped, or "parabolic," skis. "They make it so easy to turn that people who used to confine skiing to the middle of groomed runs are now skiing more aggressively and at higher speeds," Shealy says.

8 *"BEWARE OF SCENIC TRAILS."*

These days many ski resorts are beefing up their offerings of wooded trails. Indeed, beautiful runs that take you through picturesque groves of pine trees offer "that natural ski experience" so many people are drawn to the mountains to experience, says a spokesperson for Killington, a Vermont resort that has added 12 such wooded trails in the past four years.

But there is a substantial downside to communing with Mother Nature on these scenic runs. "The principal cause of death to skiers is impact," says Shealy, noting that there have been approximately 38 skiing deaths across the country per year

for the past 20 years. Of those, he says, the majority were cases in which a skier hit an obstacle—often a tree. ("We don't disclose any information about injuries," says a Killington spokesperson.) If you find you can't resist the allure of wooded trails—and who could blame you—stay alert and try to take it reasonably slow. As for whether to don a helmet or not, the PSIA calls it a "personal or parental choice." Says a spokesperson for the organization, "Snowsports helmets offer benefits and limitations, and we encourage all participants to educate themselves appropriately."

9 *"SO SUE US—YOU'LL NEVER COLLECT."*

Robert D. Ahearn, a personal-injury lawyer in Quincy, Mass., says he has just about given up taking on any ski-related injury cases. Every season he gets 12 to 20 inquiries, and only about 25 percent of those are worth even an initial investigation. Even then "They're not worth pursuing because I know I can't collect on them," Ahearn says. "It's next to impossible." That's because in nearly every skiing state there's a statute indemnifying resort operators from injuries to skiers that result from the inherent risks of the sport. "Unlike amusement parks, where you're strapped into a ride, this is a participant-controlled activity," says defense attorney Peter Rietz, who represents many of the Colorado ski resorts.

Are there any cases that Ahearn might seriously consider? Only the most extreme. "There really has to be some gross negligence on the part of the resort," he says, "like a huge tree has fallen in the middle of the trail and has not been removed." But those cases are tough to come by, Ahearn says, and there are still no guarantees, since any case against a ski resort is "just very difficult to win." Michael Director, a personal-injury lawyer in New York, can certainly confirm that. "The assumption of risk is a major component in the strength of a ski resort's case," he says. "It's a dangerous sport—if you're an inexperienced skier and you find yourself on a slope meant for experts, the resort will claim you didn't belong there."

10 "WELCOME TO ROCKY MOUNTAIN HIGH."

While most people consider hot chocolate the treat of choice while skiing, there are plenty of folks on the slopes who have other preferences—in particular, marijuana. When former ski bum Jerry Larson was a town marshal in Alta, Utah, he says he caught a lot of people smoking pot in the trees and even more lighting up while riding the ski lifts. "I was always taking dope away from people on the lifts," Larson says. "People come up here and think that because they're in the mountains they're free from prosecution."

Why not just a stiff martini? Because pot gives thrill-seeking skiers and snowboarders a "pleasantly altered and controlled high," says research scientist Benedikt Fischer of the Centre for Addictions Research of British Columbia at the University of Victoria. "It's a feel-good substance that makes them more receptive to central experiences, like the things they see around them, the visual experience of being in nature." The problem is that "controlled high" or not, smoking marijuana makes skiing less safe, says a PSIA spokesperson. And there's nothing "feel-good" about a couple of broken limbs and a trip to the ER.

THINGS TO DO

● **Planning your first ski trip?** Search for "ski trip" at www.wisegeek.com, and you'll get a breakdown of things you might not consider but should.

● **Don't pay full price** for a lift ticket. Go to www.cheapskiingguide.com to find the best deals.

● **Look up weather reports** and ski conditions at www.onthesnow.com—so you don't have to rely on the euphemisms resorts tend to use.

● **The majority of instructors** at most resorts have only the most basic training. If you're seeking a challenging lesson, call ahead and ask if there are Level 3 certified instructors on the premises.

● **To get the most for your money,** look for a resort with a loyalty program that offers promotions for frequent visitors. Visit www.snow.com for details about the Peaks Rewards program at five of the largest resorts in the country.

Bed-and-Breakfast

1 *"DON'T BE SURPRISED IF IT SEEMS LIKE WE DON'T KNOW WHAT WE'RE DOING."*

Running a bed-and-breakfast sounds like a dream job for many folks, and plenty are willing to give it a shot. Today there are more than 20,000 licensed B&Bs in the U.S., according to the Professional Association of Innkeepers International (PAII), up from a mere 1,000 in 1980. With guests spending a collective 21 million nights at bed-and-breakfasts last year, according to PAII estimates, many innkeepers often find themselves struggling to manage even the basics, which can turn your dream getaway into a weekend of hassles.

A good litmus test before you book a room is to check whether a B&B is a member of its state or regional association; that usually means it operates within city and state laws, has met all licensing requirements, and carries commercial liability insurance. Most member bed-and-breakfasts also get inspected for cleanliness, safety, and hospitality. To find them, start with the PAII's website, *www.paii.org*, which has links or phone numbers for state and other associations.

Keep in mind, though, that some good, small B&Bs may forgo association membership because of costly dues. As a backup, make sure the inn belongs to its local convention and visitors' bureau or the chamber of commerce.

2 *"OUR REVIEWS ARE BOGUS."*

One way a lot of travelers hunt for a B&B in a certain locale is by using one of some 200 online travel directories, such as BedandBreakfast.com and BBOnline.com. On such sites you can find rates, a short description, and a picture of the property. Bigger directories like them can even let you screen B&Bs for niceties such as, say, fireplaces. Just don't expect to find independent reviews on these sites. Most property descriptions are written by the innkeepers, who almost always pay to be featured. For true third-party reviews, check out *www.tripadvisor.com*, which lists thousands of bed-and-breakfasts worldwide, many of which are reviewed online by former guests. Another good resource: *www.we8there.com*, which has 325 bed-and-breakfast guest reviews.

If you can't find any guest-written reviews, look on the bed-and-breakfast's website. Also, note the size of the property. In cottages with just one or two guest rooms, you're going to feel as if you're staying in someone's home, says Helen Bartlett, a Hot Springs, Ark.-based inn consultant. One quick rule of thumb: If the inn has been running for more than 10 years, even under different management, it tends to be a good property, Bartlett says.

3 "SURE, YOU CAN FIND A LAST-MINUTE DEAL."

Seasoned B&B visitors know that many of the most popular inns can get booked up more than six months in advance. But bed-and-breakfasts may not always be as full as you think. These days, with the growth in last-minute travel, many offer steep discounts to spur-of-the-moment guests. Indeed, you can often get up to 40 percent off for booking the week of your stay.

To find these deals, you're best served by going back to those online directories. BedandBreakfast.com lists "hot deals" every Wednesday, and BBOnline.com shows properties with current last-minute discounts by state. Sometimes the prices are too good to pass up. Micah-Shane Brewer, the founder of Encore Theatrical Company in Morristown, Tenn., paid $150 for a $250 suite with a hot tub at the Christopher Place in Newport, Tenn., by booking a few days before his trip. "I wouldn't have traveled if I couldn't have gotten that deal," says Brewer, who found the special on BedandBreakfast.com.

If your preferred property doesn't show up on any lists and is full for your chosen weekend, don't give up. Just as with restaurants, there are often cancellations, and some B&Bs will call folks on a waiting list to fill rooms.

4 "OUR FIRST PRICE IS OUR WORST PRICE."

Like the rest of the travel industry, the bed-and-breakfast market has been stagnant over the past few years. Business fell 4 percent between 2000 and 2002, according to lodging-industry analysts PKF Consulting, and PAII estimates that the industry has shown minimal gains since 2003. At the same time, though, rates are up, according to PAII, but even so, discounts are still prevalent—and not just for last-minute deals. Many properties will cut their room rates by up to 10 percent, especially for off-season and midweek bookings; weekday corporate rates can even mean 15 percent off for business travelers.

So how do you get a discount? "Just ask," says Erin Bernall, a spokesperson for the California Association of Bed & Breakfast Inns. "Unlike with chain hotels, you have a little bit more leeway." Some B&Bs also offer "frequent guest" specials: free nights, discounts, or perks for return customers. The Chetco River Inn in Brookings, Ore., for example, offers one free on-site dinner for every three nights you stay, while the Magnolia Glen Bed & Breakfast in Inverness, Fla., offers "pillow miles," giving a free night to some second-time guests.

5 "THREE STARS, FOUR STARS—WHO'S COUNTING?"

In the no-brand-names world of B&Bs, independent rating systems, cited in guidebooks or brochures, are very important to both travelers and innkeepers. The most prestigious ratings are those handed out by Mobil (stars),

AAA (diamonds), and an innkeepers' association called Select Registry (a stamp of approval). All three groups rigorously inspect properties and share the results. For 2008, for example, AAA inspected 1,930 B&Bs, evaluating everything from curb appeal to linens.

Unfortunately, some properties have been known to keep promoting years-old ratings. Little changes can hurt an inn's annual score, says an AAA spokesperson. For example, "If a property stopped offering a turn-down service, it could make a difference in its rating." So don't get starstruck: Check the year the B&B's rating was awarded, and ask what has changed since then.

Other properties simply award themselves a rating. Julia's Bed and Breakfast in Hubbard, Ohio, for example, sold itself as the "ultimate four-star Bed and Breakfast experience" in 2004, while it still had a pending application with AAA. "What we're saying," said owner J. V. Ferrara, "is that we have everything that would qualify us to be a four-diamond inn." Julia's did in fact earn four stars from AAA later that year, but not all B&Bs live up to their own hype.

6 "THANK GOODNESS FOR PHOTOSHOP!"

For the last night of their 2001 vacation in New Mexico, Glenn and Andrea Panner booked a night at the Chocolate Turtle Bed & Breakfast, expecting a bucolic setting outside Albuquerque. The inn's website, which pictures the Pueblo-esque inn, advertises the Chocolate Turtle as a place where visitors can enjoy the "relaxed and low-key" environment. But when the Panners pulled up to the property, they say it felt like they were smack in the middle of the suburbs. "There's the Joneses' house, and there's the B&B," Glenn recalls thinking. "You felt like you were staying in a relative's house." Making matters worse, the Panners say that from their room they could hear doors slamming and conversations going on throughout the house.

In some cases, what you see on a B&B's website might be, well, a little different from what you actually get. To avoid being duped, it's best to ask the innkeeper about the B&B and its surroundings before booking. Chocolate Turtle's former owner, Debra Humiston, says that the houses in her area are on one-acre lots and that she's heard no other complaints. "Most people feel like it's very rural," she says. "The houses are not tremendously close together." Chocolate Turtle's new owner, Nancy Renner, adds: "All we've had is fabulous raves from our guests."

7 "WE'RE MORE FLEXIBLE THAN YOU THINK."

Julie Tupker regularly stays at B&Bs while doing ancestry research in the Midwest. On a recent trip, the bed at one inn was so uncomfortable, she says, that she got up in the middle of the night and slept in a wooden chair. "It was the worst mattress I've ever had," says Tupker, a cake maker from Marion, Iowa.

Many inngoers think that because of a B&B's small size, you have to take what you get. Not so. Make your needs known when you book. And to avoid Tupker's fate, test the mattress as soon as you check in. If it doesn't feel comfortable, call the manager before unpacking. Many innkeepers will bring in a bed board if a mattress is too soft or move you to a different room if one is available. But you may have to pay extra for nicer accommodations.

Some travelers avoid B&Bs altogether because they loathe the idea of socializing with strangers in the morning. But even that tradition is negotiable. If requested, a lot of inns will deliver a hot breakfast to your room or arrange for a basket of cold continental-style goods left at your door. Same goes for dietary requests: If you let the innkeepers know when you book, they'll likely let you eschew their famous pumpkin-pie pancakes for, say, a low-carb omelet.

8 "WE'VE SOLD OUT TO BUSINESS TRAVELERS."

To stay competitive in the lodging industry, many bed-and-breakfasts are now marketing to niche groups, offering discounts and packages to seniors and families, and meeting rooms or breakfasts-to-go to corporate visitors. Even so, many people choose to stay at bed-and-breakfasts precisely to avoid the sights and sounds of workaday life.

If that's you, look for properties that forbid cell phones in common areas or that keep groups of travelers separated from other guests. The 1870 Wedgwood Inn in New Hope, Pa., adopted a rule to help prevent large groups from alienating single guests: If more than two couples traveling together want to stay at one of the property's three houses, they have to rent the whole house.

On the other hand, if you're traveling for business or with a family, make sure the inn can actually accommodate your needs. Angela Goddard stays in B&Bs about four times a year while on business, choosing them over chain hotels for their homey feel. But the St. Louis marketing consultant has had trouble getting online—either there's no high-speed access, or she's had to use the innkeeper's own office—and now tells people to contact her by cell phone on such trips. Goddard's advice: "I've had better luck in city locations."

9 "WHEN IT COMES TO CANCELLATIONS, WE'RE SOFTIES AT HEART."

Because bed-and-breakfasts tend to be small—they average 7.5 rooms per property—most do not overbook, unlike hotels, and they count on each guest to show up. As a result, B&Bs take cancellations seriously. Though policies vary, if you don't cancel two to three weeks before arrival, you could be charged a nominal fee, and if you don't give at least 72 hours notice, you could be billed for the entire amount. B&Bs do tend to be more lenient with business travelers—sometimes accepting day-of cancellations—if, that is, you identified yourself as one when you booked.

But if a last-minute illness or another emergency strikes, don't despair. Many innkeepers won't charge guests if the room can be filled—a good reason to check for a waiting list when you book. A spokesperson for BBOnline.com says that although the industry has become more stringent about cancellation policies in recent years, some bed-and-breakfasts still offer gift certificates to customers who cancel.

10 "IF YOU'RE NOT HAPPY, YOU CAN GET YOUR MONEY BACK."

JoMay Schleicher and her husband, David, were looking forward to a romantic night at the Pacific Grove Inn outside Monterey, Calif. But when they arrived, the Schleichers discovered to their dismay that their "ocean view" was a sliver of blue they could barely make out through rooftops and trees. But that wasn't the worst of it: There was also a soda can full of cigarette butts on the balcony, extremely loud plumbing, and sand in their sheets. When the Schleichers asked for some sort of compensation the next morning, the manager refused. JoMay wrote an e-mail complaint when she got home, and the manager replied that they had found no trash or sand when they cleaned the room. "All we wanted was a nice, peaceful, romantic evening," says the Moraga, Calif., homemaker. "And what did we get? It was horrible." (The inn's current manager, who has started since the Schleichers' visit, says she would have upgraded the couple to a new room that night, or offered a free second night or discount the next morning. She calls the treatment they received "ridiculous.")

Many innkeepers are, indeed, willing to negotiate refunds or discounts after a bad experience. If for some reason yours isn't, you can make a claim through your credit card company. Just take careful notes to document your case. Your chances of winning a claim are even better if you pack up and leave as soon as you realize the inn is a bust. And pics of the offending items won't hurt either. You'll have more leverage if you don't receive any of the promised goods and services.

THINGS TO DO

- **If you're traveling internationally,** keep in mind that living standards are going to vary. Be specific about your expectations when you book the room—you might find out that shared bathrooms are considered luxurious in some places.

- **Have to cancel at the last minute** and don't want to pay for lodging you didn't use? Some B&Bs will let you postpone your trip and reschedule for later without charging any additional fees.

- **Do a thorough check** of your room as soon as you arrive—if you report any unsatisfactory conditions to the innkeeper, she'll probably set you up with a new room.

- **Another option for unsatisfied customers:** Go back to your referral source. If a third party helped book your room, they might compensate you for your troubles—or at least suspend their partnership with a bad B&B.

- **The International Bed and Breakfast** Pages offers a comprehensive listing of B&Bs, detailed descriptions, and current discounts, at *www.ibbp.com*.

10 Things Your
All-Inclusive Resort
Won't Tell You

1 "'ALL INCLUSIVE' DOESN'T INCLUDE EVERYTHING."

What could be more relaxing than going on vacation and never pulling out your wallet? That's exactly why all-inclusive resorts are so appealing. But the term "all-inclusive" means different things to different people. At some chains, like Beaches resorts, whose slogan is "the world's only ultra all-inclusive family resorts," you'll have to read the fine print in the brochure to see that recreational activities such as deep-sea fishing and golf cost extra. In Club Med's brochures, you're encouraged to "sit down for gourmet dining without the check" and "order your favorite drink off the top shelf"—only to discover in very fine print that's not including Club Med's mandatory membership fees, which could run you several hundred dollars for a family of four with two teenage children.

A spokesperson for Beaches resorts explains that activities cost extra because they're owned and operated by third-party vendors. A spokesperson for Club Med says that although the resort's membership fee is in fact mandatory, it allows you to use the facilities and dine at other Club Med resorts.

2 "OUR SERVICE CAN BE PRETTY SLACK SOMETIMES."

When Glenn Broderick took his girlfriend away to Sandals Royal Bahamian Resort & Spa, he decided not to hold back. He selected the resort's most expensive room for a week and coughed up more than $10,000. From the outset, though, Broderick, an executive director of gaming for AT&T in San Antonio, Tex., found the staff, well, less than doting. First, a request to have a bottle of champagne and an orchid waiting in their room was flatly denied—despite the brochure's claim that a concierge would be sure that "every wish [was] fulfilled." Then, Broderick says, the service in the resort's restaurants was "miserable." "On four occasions after dinner, I had to wait 20 minutes to a half hour to get coffee and dessert," Broderick says. A spokesperson for Sandals explains that because rooms are sometimes not assigned until check-in, it is difficult to put things in a guest's room ahead of time. As for Broderick's dining troubles, she says, "All of our restaurants are fully staffed. We try to go above and beyond consumers' expectations."

Such tales would not surprise Jack Franchek, founder of consulting firm Franchek Inc. "The purpose of a non-all-inclusive resort is to advertise at a fair price and then sell as much [as possible] to a client once they're on site through good service," Franchek says. "With the all-inclusive, it's exactly the opposite—they promise the moon and then try to deliver as little as possible."

3 "CHARTER FLIGHTS AREN'T EXACTLY THE FRIENDLY SKIES."

In the past, taking a charter flight to an all-inclusive resort was the most common method of transportation—and sometimes the only practical option for more out-of-the-way locations. But with the growth of inexpensive airlines and the convenience of booking flights online, the popularity of charter flights has decreased overall in recent years, giving some resorts even more incentive to offer bargains on their charter flights, especially in the off-season.

It will almost certainly be cheaper, but if you decide to fly charter, you should know some of the limitations. For example, unlike with scheduled airlines, charters seldom rebook you if your flight is delayed or canceled, says Bill Mosley, of the U.S. Department of Transportation. And they don't have to give you a refund until your flight's been delayed 48 hours. Also, says travel columnist Ed Perkins, charter flights usually have narrower seats—and more of them—than commercial aircraft. Ron Kremnitzer, a New York attorney who flew on a charter to the Beaches Turks and Caicos Resort & Spa several winters ago, agrees: "[My flight] was unbelievably cramped," he says. "It was much worse than a commercial coach flight." How bad was it?

The following year, Kremnitzer's family went back to the resort, but they spent $1,500 more to fly American Airlines.

4 "OUR HURRICANE GUARANTEE DOESN'T GUARANTEE MUCH."

Between June and November, the risk of having your Caribbean vacation wrecked by a hurricane multiplies. To compensate, several resort chains have instituted hurricane guarantees. Unfortunately, these policies can be tough to collect on. When Hurricane Jose swept through the Caribbean in October 1999, John Frenaye, who owns travel agency JVE Group in Annapolis, Md., had clients whose vacation at Sandals St. Lucia was ruined. They weren't able to swim in the ocean, indulge in water sports, or even enjoy a walk on the beach. Knowing that Sandals has a "Blue Chip Hurricane Guarantee," which offers a free replacement vacation if "hurricane-force winds (as defined by the U.S. National Weather Service) directly hit the resort while you are a guest," Frenaye called and requested a free vacation for his clients. He says he was denied because the eye of the hurricane had not passed directly over the resort. (Frenaye did end up talking the resort into three free nights for the couple if they stayed a minimum six nights and paid their own airfare—which would have cost them another $2,500.)

A spokesperson for Sandals insists that the company's hurricane guarantee does not require the eye of the storm to pass over the resort. (It does require "hurricane-force winds," however, which she says were not present at the resort during Hurricane Jose.) "We have the most comprehensive program in the industry," the spokesperson says.

5 "YOUR TRAVEL AGENT WILL MAKE A KILLING OFF US."

Travel agents haven't had it easy of late, what with airlines slashing commissions and Internet travel sites stealing market share. But one of the last remaining frontiers of profit for agents is the all-inclusive resort. Since most everything is included, agents end up getting a percentage of your meals, water sports, and drinks—not just air and hotel costs.

The perks don't stop there. Most all-inclusive resorts also give travel agents some kind of extra incentive to send clients their way, ranging from American Express gift checks to barbecues to a free night's stay for every sale they make. "Travel agents are heavily incentivized to sell these vacations," says freelance travel columnist Christopher Elliott.

Some may even push them to the exclusion of all other choices. Says Eric Morrow, owner of Jamaica Inn, a non-all-inclusive five-star luxury resort, "I've had several guests who told me they went to a travel agent and wanted to go to my hotel. [The agents] all say, 'No, no, no, you want to go to Sandals.' They just won't hear otherwise."

6 "WE REALLY WANT TO SELL YOU A TIME-SHARE."

While plenty of big resort chains— including Sandals, SuperClubs, and Club Med—don't sell time-shares, they're big business in certain areas. Almost a third of the hotels in Cancún and roughly 40 percent in Aruba do. And many sell them hard.

Sometimes the sales pitch is so aggressive that you can't even enjoy your vacation. That's what happened to Kyle Larsen, a staffing coordinator from Ottawa, Canada. After being relocated to the Moon Palace in Cancún because of a hurricane, Larsen, who had been staying at another Palace resort, made an innocent inquiry at the guest-services desk about food and entertainment. He was immediately offered a resort tour, only to be dragged into a time-share sales pitch that lasted an hour and a half.

"They were obnoxious, pushy, and very in-your-face," Larsen recalls. Worse, Larsen says that he was treated badly by the resort staff once he made it clear that he wasn't interested. And although the resort clearly wasn't full, management refused his request to stay on at the Moon Palace so that he and his girlfriend wouldn't have to relocate again. "We knew that if we weren't [willing to buy a time-share], we weren't going to get anything we wanted," Larsen says. A spokesperson for the Moon Palace says that the resort's time-share presentations are not mandatory, adding that Larsen's request to stay there could not be granted because convention groups were arriving.

7 "DON'T EXPECT MUCH PEACE AND QUIET."

Increasingly, Caribbean resorts are going after the family market. And while most resort chains clearly describe which locations are for families and which are for adults, some are less diligent. Sofia

Guerra, a travel agent in Oakland, N.J., found herself at one such example when she and her husband went to the Grand Pineapple Beach Resort in Antigua for their honeymoon. During the interval between Guerra's booking of the trip and the couple's arrival there, Allegro Resorts had bought the place and changed it from an adults-only to a family resort. Guerra was never informed. "Here I was on my honeymoon, and there were all these kids with diapers going into the pool," says Guerra. "We were dumbfounded."

Today, Grand Pineapple Beach (which has since been bought by Elite Island Resorts) is still a family destination, but remarkably, more than eight years after Guerra and her husband's unsatisfactory visit there, the resort is still marketed to couples with the slogan "Antigua's most romantic all-inclusive resort playground." Visit the company's website, and there isn't a child in sight. It's only in the small print that the company explicitly says "couples, families, and singles are all welcome."

Even if you're clear on what kind of resort you're going to, you still may have a hard time finding peace and quiet, especially in the summer, during spring break, and around the Christmas holidays—times when all-inclusive resorts tend to teem with kids or college students.

8 "OUR ROOMS DON'T LOOK ANYTHING LIKE THE ONES IN THE BROCHURE."

"Lovely beachfront rooms and lavish suites . . . Sumptuous beds . . . The kind of splendor usually reserved solely for royal couples." That's what Terri Gordon

was expecting when she went to Sandals Royal Caribbean after reading the resort's brochure. But when she arrived, Gordon, an accountant from Kernersville, N.C., was sorely disappointed. She and her husband had upgraded to a so-called Grande Luxe room that Gordon describes as "dingy." "The bathroom fixtures were old and leaky," she says. "There was dirty tile, the toilet stuck, and the upholstery was threadbare. We had stayed in Comfort Inns that were nicer."

"We definitely have different categories of rooms," explains a Sandals spokesperson. "Maybe from looking through the brochure they wanted something a little higher than what they had booked." She adds that Gordon would have been switched to a different room had the resort not been totally booked—and that it offered Gordon two free nights on a future visit as compensation.

"[With brochures], there's a certain amount of puffing that's allowed," says *Trouble-Free Travel* coauthor Ann Shulman. And the law offers little protection, she says. "No court is going to back a consumer if it's not superluxury."

9 "'OPEN BAR' ISN'T AS GREAT AS IT SOUNDS."

Enticed by the idea of unlimited drinks on your all-inclusive vacation? While that may be what you're getting according to the most literal definition, don't set your sights too high. For one thing, resorts that promise top-shelf booze will almost certainly make you ask for it. "I can almost guarantee you," says Terry McCabe, a travel agent in Oakland, N.J., "that when they're pouring you a gin and tonic, they're not pouring you a Tanqueray." And even if some premium-brand liquors are available, variety isn't always a priority. Says John Rachlin, a former Club Med employee: "The clubs have contracts with that country's distributors to serve the most popular local [beer and wine] at meals." Club Med says that it imports its wine from France but that it does contract with local companies to provide almost all the beer at meals.

That's not the only issue. "All you can drink" can mean big crowds at the bar. "The brochures say, 'Drinks are unlimited,' but that's only if you're willing to wait in long lines for the one bartender to serve you," says LeAnna Dinardo, a former administrative director for the Democratic Legislative Campaign Committee, who stayed at Sandals Royal Bahamian a year ago. "We didn't drink that much because of the lines." Sandals' Rivera insists that the bars at Royal Bahamian were fully staffed the week that Dinardo was there.

10 *"WE CAN BE BAD FOR THE LOCAL ECONOMY."*

Think about the way you vacation in Europe or in major U.S. cities: You eat in local restaurants, shop in local stores, take taxis or city buses between one place and another. In short, your money goes to the people who live there. That's often not the case when it comes to big resorts. While they do offer some local benefits, much of the money spent at all-inclusive resorts—especially when they're foreign-owned—ends up elsewhere.

Barry Didato, of the management firm PA Consulting in Laguna Beach, Calif., explains why. "With a very sophisticated all-inclusive mega-resort," he says, "they bring in a lot of their own labor, bring in containers for all their food, and totally manage the entire experience." If you stay at a small, locally owned Caribbean inn, says Didato, every dollar you spend has the potential to recirculate eight times within the local economy. By contrast, a dollar spent at an all-inclusive resort, he says, would recirculate only 1.4 times.

THINGS TO DO

● **Go with a travel agent** on this one—since all-inclusive packages usually end up being cheaper than visiting non-inclusive resorts, you can afford an agent's fees.

● **Describe your dream vacation** to a travel agent, and don't hold back on the details. You'll be spending most of your time at the resort, so you'll want to make sure it suits you.

● **How to spend literally no money** on an all-inclusive vacation? Resist extras provided by third parties, like scuba diving or ballroom dance lessons, which will cost extra.

● **But what if you want** to learn ballroom dancing? Choose trustworthy third-party vendors that have a working relationship with the resort.

● **"All-inclusive" doesn't necessarily mean unlimited**—ask the resort or your travel agent about any limits on things such as room service or the number of times you can eat in the restaurant.

10 Things Your
Country Club
Won't Tell You

1 "WE'LL DO JUST ABOUT ANYTHING TO GET YOU TO JOIN."

You may think of country clubs as untouchable bastions of wealth and exclusivity. While that's still the case with some, the industry as a whole has seen better days. Why don't clubs have the same appeal as they once did? People work longer hours, and the competition for their downtime is fierce. Plus, there are plenty of places to network these days, including upscale gyms. "[Country] clubs are finding themselves in this new position where they have to actively go out and pursue members," says Rick Coyne, an executive director of the Professional Club Marketing Association.

The result: Many clubs are trying to bring in new members by cutting attractive deals. The Santa Rosa Golf & Country Club in Santa Rosa, Calif., for example, offers sliding fees for "young executives" under 40. And the Boca Pointe Country Club in Boca Raton, Fla., provides one- to three-month trial memberships for about $400 per month—no strings. If you don't see a deal at your local country club, that doesn't mean there isn't one. Not all discounts are advertised, so just ask.

2 "WANT OUT? IT COULD TAKE A WHILE."

Quitting your country club can be even harder than joining. Just ask Bob Husband, president of Heritage Golf Group, which owns 15 clubs. A longtime member of three clubs in Southern California (none of which Heritage owns), Husband decided that paying triple monthly dues and fees was too much, and he asked to quit one of the three. That was in 2003; in 2005 he was still No. 30 on a waiting list to leave. The catch: The club requires eight new members to join before any one person can quit.

A waitlist to leave is not uncommon at clubs, where members' monthly fees are the primary source of income. While eight-to-one policies are an anomaly, it's common for clubs to require one new member for each one that quits. But there are some ways around it: Inquire about suspending membership until someone new joins. At the Quail Creek Country Club in Naples, Fla., a member can pay a year's worth of dues, then become inactive until a new membership is sold. And some clubs will refund some or all of the initiation fee, which can be thousands of dollars, upon exit—but you may have to wait for the check until you're out. Kathi Driggs, chief operating officer for the Club Managers Association of America, advises carefully researching a club before joining. "It's a major decision," she says.

3 "JUST BECAUSE WE LOOK POSH DOESN'T MEAN WE HAVE ANY MONEY."

In 2003 members of the Raleigh Country Club in Raleigh, N.C., were shocked when the club filed for Chapter 11 bankruptcy protection. They soon found out it owed about $7 million, much of it for ambitious renovations. An investor came in and rescued the club, but not before members sweated rumors that it was going to be turned into a subdivision. That same year, owners of Hunting Hills Country Club in Roanoke, Va., suffering from a decline in membership, were forced to sell the club's golf course. They leased it back and continued running it, but only by slicing monthly dues and adding hundreds of new members.

Country clubs are businesses, too. How to know if your club, or the one you want to join, is financially sound? Chat with members—the gossipy ones. Look around. If routine maintenance is being ignored, that could be a red flag, says Frank Vain, president of McMahon Group, a private-club consultancy. Sure, the grass has been cut, but is worn carpeting being quickly replaced? Says Vain, "That really is a sign of the underlying financial strength of the club." You can even ask to see the books. Some clubs will let potential members read their annual report.

4 "MEMBERSHIP FEES ARE ONLY THE BEGINNING."

You paid your initiation fee and your monthly dues, but your obligation isn't squared away just yet. About two out of three clubs impose a "food minimum," an amount members are required to spend, which can run $100 a month or more—and alcohol doesn't always count. Between his three clubs, Husband spends about $200 a month on food.

Some clubs also charge extra for services like bag storage, shoe shines, and locker rentals. At Colonie Golf & Country Club in Voorheesville, N.Y., in addition to monthly dues and a food minimum for the restaurant, families pay an annual house fee for storing golf bags, hitting balls on the practice range, and using the putting green. Cart rental is also extra. Many clubs also charge members for big maintenance and renovation projects, and some even divvy up financial losses among members.

How to avoid surprises? Study your contract: Any extra charges must be spelled out (all of the above were). Another strategy is to stay involved—some clubs will put these issues up for a vote, often to all members.

5 "THE PUBLIC COURSE IS JUST AS NICE AS OURS."

Avid golfers used to look down their noses at public courses. But over the past decade, public facilities have been stepping up their level of service and have become competitive with private courses. When Greg Sinner moved to Arizona, he wanted service on par with that of his exclusive private club back in Texas. Instead, he's found what he needs at the Raven Golf Club at South Mountain, a public course in Phoenix. Not only is the price reasonable—$70 to $180 per person per round, and no initiation fees or club dues, as with country club courses—but he can bring as many friends or clients as he likes.

Raven also offers fancy extras, like staffers who wipe down your clubs and provide course conditions. Sinner also likes the fact that he can play at other clubs guilt-free: "If you spend a lot of money on some of these private courses, you don't want to play anywhere else. You can't afford it."

6 "ANY JOE OFF THE STREET IS WELCOME TO GOLF AT OUR CLUB ..."

Is that golfer slowing your game by hogging the seventh hole? He might not even be a fellow member. To raise revenue, many country clubs have begun opening their courses to the public, charging a per-day fee for a round of golf and use of the facilities. The Colonie Golf & Country Club, for example, opened its course to nonmember foursomes in early 2003 and took in an additional $40,000 in fees in the first year as a result. (The club currently limits nonmember foursomes to weekends only.)

If your club allows nonmembers on its course, there are ways to ensure that you get to golf when you want to. At most clubs, reserved tee times are guaranteed, and in the case of walk-ins, a club will almost always give priority to its members. But with more nonmembers playing these days, it doesn't pay to be

spontaneous: Clubs often won't bump nonmembers who reserve tee times a few days in advance.

Bottom line: Consult your club's bylaws. Boca Pointe's, for example, stipulate that its golf course is for members only. Also, see what your options are. ClubCorp, a national chain of country clubs, offers Signature Gold, an enhanced membership program that for a one-time fee of around $3,000 will let members enjoy complimentary golf and dining at 170 clubs and resorts around the country.

7 "... AND DINE IN OUR BANQUET ROOMS, TOO."

Many revenue-challenged country clubs are finding themselves sitting on plum assets, such as sizable ballrooms and catering-friendly kitchens, and realizing that renting out their facilities for big events can bring in big money. For example, a lavish affair can net the Flossmoor Country Club in Illinois around $20,000, which "fills in a lot of gaps," says Tom Gilley, a club member and former president of the board of directors.

Members can rent these spaces too, of course, but clubs often charge nonmembers more. And don't assume members get any special privileges. Event facilities at many clubs are rented on a first-come, first-served basis. "If [a nonmember] books a room first, there's nothing I can do," says Paul Volin, general manager at Boca Pointe Country Club.

How can you avoid going for a quiet dinner at the club and getting turned away—or worse, being seated in an adjacent room, the walls throbbing to the beat of "The Chicken Dance"? Ask about your club's policy on special events. Many facilities have a dedicated party room and will keep the regular dining room open for members, or will send a calendar to members so they're informed about scheduled events in advance.

8 "THAT 'PRO' HELPING YOU WITH YOUR SWING MIGHT BE AN APPRENTICE."

A big perk for many country club members is getting to train or practice with a golf pro. To be considered a "pro," a golfer should be a Class A Professional, which means he or she has successfully completed the Professional Golfers' Association of America's three-level training program. But at many clubs, lessons are given by assistant pros, which is perfectly acceptable— in fact, the golf pro training program requires aspiring pros to clock a certain number of hours working under Class A Professionals.

While many assistant pros can be good teachers, some are, well, greener than the grass on the golf course. Nick Stripling, a former assistant pro at Bolingbrook Golf Club in suburban Chicago, recalls a colleague who was hired when he had just begun PGA training and had never taught a lesson before. "He just played golf in college," says Stripling. (A Bolingbrook rep says assistant pros often give lessons to beginners.)

Tom Gustafson, former executive director of the Southern California Section of the PGA, says pros should have apprentices give them mock

> **Ask about your instructor's training. And if you want your club's seasoned pro, request him or her specifically—but be prepared to pay more, as much as $150 for a one-hour lesson.**

lessons before teaching others. But that doesn't always happen. Ask about your instructor's training. And if you want your club's seasoned pro, request him or her specifically—but be prepared to pay more, as much as $150 for a one-hour lesson.

9 "DON'T LET THE FINE CHINA FOOL YOU—WE'RE NOT AS CLEAN AS WE LOOK."

Country club restaurants are just that—restaurants—and are subject to the same health-department regulations. But there's one difference: Country clubs are big on buffets, often a more fertile breeding ground for bacteria than food served à la carte. And people sometimes get sick.

In one notable case, more than 100 people contracted salmonella poisoning after eating at Brook-Lea Country Club in Rochester, N.Y., in 2002. The club's insurance company later settled claims for an undisclosed amount; John Maggio, former president of the board of the Brook-Lea Country Club, says the club hired a new chef after the incident and worked with the local health department to put additional health-safety procedures in place.

Most clubs are regularly inspected, but be aware that they're held to no higher standard than your local Denny's. And when you can, think about skipping the buffet.

10 "SURE, WE'RE A PRIVATE CLUB, BUT WE'RE ALSO A BIG CORPORATION."

Traditionally, country clubs have been tightly held by a wealthy family or by the club's members. Many still are. But as in so many industries, corporations are gobbling up the more than 5,000 U.S. country clubs and some 16,000 golf courses. ClubCorp, one of the largest

of these companies, owns or operates nearly 100.

Critics say the conglomerates detract from the personality and charm of the country club industry. Big companies running strings of clubs, Vain says, "are going to look at it from the bottom line up." Indeed, when a chain acquires a club, its first priority is often to increase membership, since that's the fastest and easiest way to boost revenue.

But consolidation can sometimes be good for members. Big companies can often afford to operate an unprofitable club, even spend money on improvements, which is something independent operators can't always do. And though membership generally grows when a corporation steps in, membership fees often go down.

THINGS TO DO

• **The best way to get the scoop** on a club is by talking to its members. Luckily, private clubs tend to breed gossip.

• **A club typically reflects** its surrounding community—so if your neighborhood is full of kids but you'd rather your country club not be, try another club in an older community.

• **Check to see if the club** you're interested in is a members' club or a proprietary club—the former gives members the right to vote on policies, while the latter leaves these decisions to management.

• **Ask the club if they offer** transferable memberships. This type of membership allows you to leave at some point before your contract is up, at which point you can sell your membership to a new member for a percentage back, based on the time remaining in your contract.

• **If you just want to golf** or have a place for the kids to go swimming, some clubs offer limited or partial membership tailored to such needs. So don't be afraid to ask.

10 Things Your
Casino
Won't Tell You

1 *"WHEN WE SAY, 'THE HOUSE ALWAYS WINS,' WE MEAN IT."*

Maybe you've had a good night or two at the casino sometime in the past decade, but it's the house that's really hit the jackpot. Visitors gambled and lost more than $34 billion at U.S. casinos in 2006, up from about $17 billion in 1996—not that the casinos are passing much of that growth on to consumers. While the odds always favor the house, some casinos are changing the odds and payouts on table games to be even more in their favor.

Take blackjack. Instead of the traditional 3-to-2 payout—which means a player betting $20 would get $30—some casinos are now paying 6-to-5, effectively reducing the payout by 20 percent. And almost every casino now uses multiple decks, stacking as many as eight in a single sleeve, which makes it harder for gamblers to keep track of which cards have been played. In perhaps the most significant shift, an increasing number of casinos don't allow the dealer to hold on "soft 17," the term for a 17-point hand that includes an ace. Continuing the hand improves the house's odds by about 0.2 percent. It doesn't sound like much, but on a table that sees $100,000 in wagers on a given day, that adds $200 to the house's take.

2 *"THERE'S NOTHING COMPLIMENTARY ABOUT OUR COMP CARDS."*

"Comp" cards have become increasingly popular at casinos in Las Vegas and elsewhere. They work like frequent-flier miles, offering customers a chance to earn free lodging, food, and other extras each time they spend money at the casino. For casinos, the cards are a valuable tool in building brand loyalty, says Gary Loveman, chairman and CEO of Harrah's Entertainment. But the spending bar is usually high for most of the "rewards," and since the games favor the house, odds are a gambler will lose money while racking up points.

On a recent visit to Vegas, *SmartMoney* signed up for an MGM Mirage Players Club card. After 90 minutes on a Treasure Island casino 5-cent slot, we had enough points for a free T-shirt—woo hoo!—but we spent $85 in the process.

3 *"OUR ATM MACHINES ARE THE REAL ONE-ARMED BANDITS."*

While ATM fees are creeping up everywhere, perhaps nowhere are they higher than at casinos, where access to cash is king.

At Atlantic City, N.J., casinos, many cash machines double the average usage fee for most out-of-network ATMs. It's roughly the same at Vegas casinos. And if you want to use a credit card for a cash advance, the fees are even higher: Some machines charge a $2.95 fee and 3.5 percent of the amount withdrawn, while others charge a flat fee ($29 on any withdrawal between $401 and $500, for example). That's anywhere from a 5.8 to 7.2 percent tax on your withdrawal—on top of any interest your credit card might charge.

How to avoid the fees? Obviously, try to fuel up before entering the casino. Or bring your checkbook: Many casinos cash personal checks for free.

4 "SMELL THAT? IT'S SUBLIMINAL RELAXATION."

Taking a cue from retailers, casinos often circulate oils and scents through their ventilation systems to try to put gamblers in a good mood. At 500,000 square feet, the gaming/hotel section of the Mohegan Sun complex in Uncasville, Conn., is the largest scented building in the world. It has more than a dozen different smells circulating within its walls, says Mark Peltier, cofounder of AromaSys, the firm that installed the system. And The Venetian casino in Las Vegas, also an AromaSys client, circulates an array of herbal scents, including lavender, throughout the casino floor.

Why the olfactory overload? It's generally believed that people will stay longer—and therefore spend more—in a place with a pleasant smell, says Peltier. The scents have no known harmful side effects, but be aware that it might be more than just the free drinks making you feel so happy-go-lucky.

5 "NINETY-FIVE-PERCENT PAYBACK DOESN'T MEAN YOU WON'T LOSE A LOT OF MONEY."

Casinos often advertise that their slot machines pay out a very high percentage of the money they take in, 95 percent payback being a common claim. But the numbers can be misleading. Advertising 95 percent doesn't mean that all the casino's slot machines are paying out at that level all the time. While it's true that each slot is programmed to return a percentage of the money players feed into it—anywhere from 83 to 99 percent over a long period of time, says Jeffrey Compton, a gaming analyst at Compton Dancer Consulting—not all pay out the same percentage. So at any given point, some machines pay out nothing while others pay out much of their take. To arrive at the 95 percent figure, casino management simply limits the scope of its claim to a subset of slot machines that will deliver a 95 percent payout.

State gambling regulators will punish any casino they discover advertising a particular payback on its slot machines and returning less. But again, the regulators are looking at a very long time horizon. So don't be fooled by the casino's marketing efforts. If you feed $100 into a slot machine on any given day, there is no guarantee that you will get $95 back.

6 "THE LESS YOU PLAY, THE LOWER WE PAY."

Think you're saving money by playing the penny slots? Think again. Slots and video poker machines with lower denominations have lower payouts than their more expensive cousins. The reason? The house takes in a lot more money on higher-value machines and wants to draw customers to them, says Rick Santoro, executive vice president of asset protection and risk management at Trump Hotel Casino Resorts.

The Argosy Casino in Lawrenceburg, Ind., is typical of many gambling houses in the U.S. In July 2007, for example, Argosy kept almost 12 percent of the $34.3 million that customers wagered at its 345 penny machines. But at its 84 $5 machines, the house kept just over 4 percent of the $52.4 million that was wagered, paying out the balance in both cases. So customers, on average, got a much better payout percentage at the $5 machines than they did at penny machines.

7 "CARD COUNTING IS LEGAL . . ."

Contrary to popular belief, you are perfectly entitled to keep track of how many aces are left in a six-deck blackjack game by using just your brain. If you're good at card counting, you're a casino's worst nightmare. Nonetheless, "There's nothing against using what God gave you to make you a better gambler," says Cory Aronovitz, founder of the Casino Law Group.

Still, while a casino can't have you arrested for counting cards, that doesn't mean it can't make things extremely uncomfortable for you. Casino employees have been known to change the rules in the middle of a blackjack game or even spill drinks on players to deter card counters, according to I. Nelson Rose, a gambling law expert at Whittier Law School in Costa Mesa, Calif. In some states such as Nevada and New Jersey,

casinos can also ask a guest to leave for any—or no—reason. If you refuse, they can have you arrested for loitering.

8 ". . . BUT YOU'RE STILL IN BIG TROUBLE."

At many casinos, employees can legally detain anyone if they have probable cause to suspect a player is cheating or causing a disturbance. If the police get involved, the law often takes the casino's side, say lawyers and civil rights advocates, even if it appears that the casino has overstepped its rights.

In October 2002, Raymond Cagno was having a field day playing blackjack at Las Vegas's El Cortez casino. The dealer was inadvertently showing both her cards (only one of the dealer's cards should be visible), increasing the odds of winning at her table. When casino personnel noticed the error, they asked Cagno to stop playing. It is not illegal to profit from a dealer's mistake, but when Cagno got up to leave, the security guards grabbed him, handcuffed him, and took him to a security holding office. After some heated back and forth between Cagno and the guards, police were called. The officers arrested Cagno for disorderly conduct based, they said, on a complaint from an El Cortez security guard. Cagno was initially convicted, but he appealed, and the conviction was overturned. Later, Cagno's civil suit against the casino was settled for an undisclosed amount. (The El Cortez declined to comment.)

9 "SOME OF US MAY STILL BE 'CONNECTED.'"

Although most casinos today are run by corporations, the business has a lingering reputation for attracting shady characters, and sometimes it's not hard to see why. Consider what happened in Rosemont, Ill. In 2001 state gambling regulators stopped Emerald Casino from opening a riverboat casino in the Chicago suburb, claiming that some of the contractors being used to build the facilities were affiliated with organized crime. Worse, the board alleged that two friends of Rosemont's mayor—who were minority shareholders—also had mob ties. The mayor denies any organized-crime connections, but Emerald's gaming license was revoked, and the firm went into bankruptcy.

In 2004, when the license came up for auction, the political appointees on the gaming board once again awarded it to a company planning to open a casino in Rosemont, despite objections from the board's professional staff. Wary of the mayor's alleged connections, it recommended the license not go to any Rosemont project, and in 2005, the state gaming board revoked the sale of the license to the casino.

10 "POLITICIANS GET RICH OFF US."

Casino executives and groups donated more than $10.8 million to political campaigns in the first half of 2008, according to the Center for Responsive Politics. That's in addition to millions more that get contributed to state and local politicians who have gambling issues in front of them.

In Pennsylvania, the relationship is even cozier. When the state legislature passed a law in 2004 legalizing slot machines in the state, it included a clause allowing Pennsylvania's lawmakers to own up to 1 percent of any company with a casino license—which included everything from a casino to a slot machine manufacturer. The ruling's many critics say it has created a conflict of interest for politicians, who may be tempted to act in their own financial interest instead of their constituents' on gaming issues. But as far as Pennsylvania lawmakers are concerned, such complaints are a day late and a bucket of quarters short.

THINGS TO DO

- **Signing up for loyalty cards** can get you discounts on lodging and food. They also keep track of how much money you're spending—the more you shell out, the more comps you'll receive.

- **The higher the denominations** on a slot or video poker game, the better the payouts. But you can also trick lower-denomination machines by betting the maximum—for instance, 100 nickels in a nickel slot machine will give you better odds than putting the same amount in a $5 slot machine.

- **When playing craps,** the don't pass/don't come line offers better odds than the pass/come line. Also, the numbers 6 and 8 are the most likely numbers to be rolled after a 7, so place your bets accordingly.

10 Things
Theme Parks
Won't Tell You

1 *"NOBODY NEEDS TO PAY FULL PRICE."*

You're waiting in line to get into Sesame Place. Your kids are chomping at the bit to rub shoulders with Elmo, and you've resigned yourself to paying $44.50 per person for admission to the Langhorne, Pa., theme park. Before you flip the big bird to Miss Piggy, go through your wallet and pull out every credit card and organizational membership ID you can find. Chances are that at least one of them will cut the cost of entry.

Discounts flourish at theme parks because admissions account for only part of their revenue. "[A] big thing is having people in the park who are eating pizza, drinking Coke, buying T-shirts and souvenirs," says Tim O'Brien, vice president of publishing and communications for Ripley Entertainment and author of *Ripley's Believe It or Not! Amusement Park Oddities & Trivia*. At Six Flags Great America in Gurnee, Ill., for instance, American Automobile Association membership gets you a few bucks off admission every day except Wednesday—when the discount is three times that amount. In addition, local gas stations often promote park coupons on the back of their receipts. "If you pay full price, you haven't done your homework," says O'Brien.

2 *"YOU'LL SPEND HALF YOUR DAY STANDING IN LINE."*

Show up at your theme park of choice after 11 A.M. and you might not even get into the parking lot, according to Bob Sehlinger, coauthor of *The Unofficial Guide to Walt Disney World 2008*. And if you do get in, chances arc the park will be too crowded for you to enjoy the most popular rides. "If you go during a busy time of year, get your butt out of bed and be one of the first people in the park," says Sehlinger. "Otherwise, you will be pissing away your investment by standing in lines all day."

Want to stay one step ahead of the crowds? You'd better have a plan. That begins with understanding when the place is the least packed—and it's probably not when you think. At Disney World during the summer, for example, weekend crowds tend to be relatively sparse, since most families drive to Florida, using the weekends for travel rather than touring.

As for the rides themselves, Sehlinger suggests "having an itinerary that will allow you to crisscross the park and knock off the five most popular rides before it gets packed."

483

3 "IT DOESN'T PAY TO SLEEP WITH US."

While families who stay at theme-park hotels enjoy special advantages—at Disney World, for example, guests gain early admission to a different park each morning—they often pay a steep premium for on-premise lodging. Although nightly rates at Disney World start at under $100 for a double, those rooms get snapped up quickly; the next-cheapest accommodations start at around $150 and go up to more than $1,000.

Aren't there other hotels nearby? The Disney reservation clerk we spoke with conceded there were, but she painted a picture of hour-long waits to get into the Disney parking lot and hinted that you might find yourself staying in carjack territory. Not necessarily—simply stick with the widely known chains within several miles of the park. For example, AAA gave us the names of a Comfort Inn and a Ramada Inn situated just two and six miles, respectively, from Disney World's main gate. Their discounted rates included a buffet breakfast and were about $20 lower than Disney's cheapest rate. Factor in the money you'll save by eating dinner outside the park, and you'll likely find the benefits of staying off-site outweigh the drawbacks.

4 "IT'S A CLASS-CONSCIOUS WORLD, AFTER ALL."

Theme parks like to present themselves as utopian Valhallas where the CEO waits in line for his ice-cream cone with everyone else. But elitism permeates this seemingly classless society, and you can get "celebrity" treatment—you just have to be willing to buy your way in.

Many parks have VIP packages that give you all sorts of perks, from preferred access to special seats. For example, Steven Weil, a retailer from Fair Lawn, N.J., forked over extra money so that he, his wife, and two of their kids could enjoy the privilege of strolling on Universal's red carpet. "There was a woman leading us around," Weil says. "We were a small group of about 10 people, and she took us through back doors, through side doors, to the head of every line." Weil says that the hostess even babysat their kids while he and his wife went to Planet Hollywood. The only drawback: the reaction of other patrons. "We got a lot of dirty looks," Weil says. "But we didn't care. We didn't have to wait in line; it was well worth the money."

5 "OUR RIDE OPERATORS ARE BARELY OLD ENOUGH TO DRIVE."

Even the most benign ride can turn dangerous when an inexperienced person is operating it. At many parks, especially seasonal ones, ride operators tend to be young summer workers, but there are no federal laws requiring amusement-ride operators to undergo any kind of training program. Some states, including California and Minnesota, have introduced state laws regulating safety and training. Still, "There is no internal consistency from park to park in terms of how they instruct their employees," says Adam Glick, an attorney based in Elizabeth, N.J., who has handled numerous amusement-park injury cases. "The workers tend to be college students on vacation. Most of the ride operators are concerned about flirting with the opposite sex." And even if they're not, disasters can and do occur.

6 "WE'VE GOT A SCREW LOOSE—LITERALLY."

Undertrained operators aren't the only danger amusement parks face. Lurking beneath the glossy, candy-colored ride exteriors may be shoddily maintained gearshifts and missing seat bolts, which can turn a roller coaster ride deadly. And while amusement parks crow about an impressive-sounding .00057 percent industry accident rate, Glick, for one, insists that the number is misleading. "The actual reporting of an accident is made by the park itself," the attorney says. "Every incentive is for the park to underreport accidents—the more you report, the more you get fined and the more trouble you get into."

Surely, a low-accident statistic does nothing to salve the wounds of the customers who've been injured due to poorly maintained rides.

You should give rides a careful once-over, says Ted Moss, an engineering safety consultant who has inspected amusement attractions. "However, as with any mechanical object, you cannot look at the ride and tell when it was last oiled or when the tires were changed," he warns. "If the place in general is poorly maintained, if things aren't painted properly, or if you see the workers sitting around chatting instead of paying attention to their job, those are signs that the park is not stressing safety or care of the rides." For more information on amusement park safety, go to *www.saferparks.org*.

7 "WHEN IT COMES TO REGULATIONS, WE GET A FREE RIDE."

All amusement parks are not inspected equally. Some states—Montana, North Dakota, South Dakota, Alabama, and Kansas—do not regulate rides at all. Some others, like Mississippi and Washington, D.C., regulate traveling carnivals but not permanent ones. Among the safest states are Florida and Pennsylvania, both of which employ full-time inspectors who do nothing but evaluate amusement rides for safety. Elsewhere, you may have a guy checking out the Pressure Drop when he's got time off from inspecting elevators.

In some cases, unfortunately, greater legislative attention comes only on the heels of tragedy. In California, for example, legislation to regulate theme parks was introduced after a 1997 disaster at Waterworld USA in Concord, where a waterslide collapsed, killing one high school student and injuring 32 others after they attempted to climb on together. (California now has permanent theme-park regulations.) "We believe that rides at theme parks are fairly high-risk," says Valerie Brown, former state assembly member who proposed the bill on park regulation. "They're turbulent, doing things against gravity, testing engineering feats."

8 "OUR WATERSLIDE ISN'T EXACTLY A KIDDIE RIDE."

Surely water parks are safer than amusement rides such as roller coasters and other fast-moving machines? Not necessarily. Craig Sklodowski was

22 years old when he followed a line of patrons headfirst down a waterslide at an aqua park in New Jersey. When the six-foot-two, 225-pound Sklodowski hit the end of the slide, he says, he landed in about 3 feet of water. "I either hit the bottom of the pool with my head, or else the force of hitting the water snapped back my neck," says Sklodowski, who is now a quadriplegic. He settled with the park for $4 million. "I think the speed that they design these rides at doesn't take into account that people come in a variety of different shapes and sizes," Sklodowski says. "That mistake has turned my life around 180 degrees." (The park declined to comment.)

Waterslides turn riders into human projectiles hurtling through slicked tubes at speeds as high as 25 miles per hour, requiring levels of physical competence that are simply unnecessary for riding even the scariest roller coaster. While the physical challenge is clearly part of the fun, it also ratchets up the level of risk. These rides "require strength, physical agility, and control," says Anne McHugh, the attorney who represented Sklodowski. "Yet there is the attitude that it's all safe. They sell this as amusement, entertainment, and fun. There's an illusion that it's safe for a five-year-old, a pregnant lady, and an 85-year-old man." How to know when a slide is too much for you or your kids? The majority of water parks have restrictions and recommendations posted at the rides themselves, says a World Waterpark Association spokesperson. You can also look for guidance in a park's brochure or on its website.

9 "WELCOME TO THE TRAGIC KINGDOM."

It's easy to assume that every theme park is a safe haven where your biggest worry is an upset stomach from too much caramel corn. In reality, a park is only as safe as the people who go there. "The largest problem you see in theme parks is unsupervised adolescents," says Captain Joe Vargas, a member of the police department in Anaheim, Calif., Disneyland's hometown. "Parents drop them off, and they run around the park." Vargas says these kids can get into all kinds of trouble—anything from shoplifting to being loud, boisterous, and obscene. In some cases, there's even the threat of violence.

The problem is at its worst during the summer months. In a July 2007 incident, six teenagers were arrested for attacking a 19-year-old boy outside the Six Flags Over Georgia amusement park. The victim suffered from head injuries and was eventually released from intensive care. (A Six Flags spokesperson confirmed the incident but declined to comment.)

How to protect yourself? Forget about the park's image, and do a bit of research before venturing there. Check sites like Theme Park Insider (*www.themeparkinsider.com*) for the lowdown on parks across the country, or speak with friends who've already visited.

10 "DON'T STAND TOO CLOSE TO MICKEY."

It's a hot summer day in Florida, and those cute Disney World characters that your kids are dying to pose with are likewise dying—to get out of those hot costumes. Inside the huge heads of these getups, temperatures can reach as high as 130 degrees in the sun. And while the outside of a costume looks pristine and magical, inside the wearer may well be suffering in his own sweat—or worse. "During summertime it gets busy, it's hot, and a number of people told me they pass out," says Jane Kuenz, coauthor of *Inside the Mouse: Work and Play at Disney World.* "Or else they throw up from the heat. Then they pass out."

That's one of the reasons why costumed employees are supposed to be out and among the patrons for only 20 minutes at a time. But during busy summer days, shifts can sometimes run twice as long. "If they become sick, there's not a whole lot that anybody can do," Kuenz says. "And they won't ever take their heads off, because that is automatic dismissal, so they ham it up and pretend that Minnie Mouse is on her knees for some dramatic reason"—rather than because she is doubled over from cramps and nausea. "I'm not aware of that happening," says a Disney World spokesperson. "We have a very tightly run program designed to look out for the welfare of the employee."

THINGS TO DO

● **Buy your tickets online** before you get to the park. It can save you up to 35 percent, and a theme park's website is the best place to stay up to date on the latest promotions.

● **Credit cards commonly offer** park-related discounts—for instance, American Express's recent $10-off admission special to SeaWorld and Busch Gardens. Check with your card company and the issuing bank to find specials.

● **For sprawling megaparks,** a single-day multipark pass might not be the way to go. You can save 25 percent at Disney World, for example, by getting a single-park pass instead of the park-hopper pass.

● **Planning multiple visits this summer** to your local theme park? A season pass might be your best bet—it typically pays for itself in two visits. Some, like the VIP pass at Kings Dominion in Virginia, offer additional perks like free parking.

10 Things Your
Athletic Coach
Won't Tell You

1 *"YOU WANT A LOWER HANDICAP? YOU CAME TO THE WRONG PERSON."*

Golfers, start your backswing. The snow on your favorite 18-holer has melted away, and your Bertha's ready for some flexing. But before you hit the fairway, you may need to spend 30 minutes or so getting a tune-up from a nearby instructor. Just beware: Finding a reliable golf teacher could drive you bonkers.

Too often "a guy with a good shtick will get your money," says Wayne DeFrancesco, golf instructor at Woodmont Country Club in Rockville, Md., and once named one of *Golf Magazine*'s 100 best teachers in the U.S. Maybe that's why the average male golfer's handicap has stayed around 16 over the past 15 years—even though there are now 28,000 PGA-certified golf pros in the U.S. (that's 6,000 more than in 1997). With golfers spending upwards of $200 an hour on coaching, why isn't the overall game getting better? "Bad teaching," says DeFrancesco. He contends that too many coaches aren't even decent golfers themselves.

You should only hire an instructor who has earned a Class A designation from the PGA. That means he or she has spent around two and a half years training to be a pro and has taken 36 hours of continuing education every three years. (To check, call the PGA at 561-624-8400.) Also, ask for your prospective instructor's scores in recent tournament play. As DeFrancesco puts it, "If you're a good teacher, you should be able to teach yourself to shoot in the 70s."

2 *"I'M NO ROLE MODEL FOR YOUR KIDS . . ."*

Before a high school wrestling match in December 2002, coach Aron Bright of Avon High School in Avon, Ind., bit the head off a live sparrow in front of his wrestlers. As Bright puts it, "Slightly outrageous is what we were going for." Later, though, when word of his stunt got out, he resigned from coaching; Bright, who still teaches at the school, says his motivational technique was branded as "barbaric."

You might say so. And yet, increasingly, coaches are getting reputations for doing more than just mouthing off when looking to inspire their young players or intimidate referees. Attacks by coaches are on the increase and "becoming physical instead of verbal," says Bob

Still, author of *101 Tips for Youth Sports Officials.* For instance, in November 2006, a youth football league coach in Corpus Christi, Tex., tackled a referee and knocked him unconscious after being thrown out of the game by the 18-year-old official. The reason for the coach's ejection in the first place? Repeated warnings about cursing on the sidelines in front of his five- and six-year-old players. "The coach is no longer with the league," says Felix Cornejo, president of the Coastal Bend Corpus Christi Football League.

3 "...AND IT'S NOT SAFE LEAVING THEM WITH ME EITHER."

As you send Junior off to his Little League Baseball games this spring or to swim-team practice this summer, you should be aware that an estimated 15,000 convicted sex offenders currently coach children in out-of-school sports programs, according to Southeastern Security Consultants, a Marietta, Ga., firm specializing in background screening for youth-league coaches. In July 2007, a Massachusetts youth soccer coach was convicted of molesting two teenage girls, and just a couple of months earlier, a Pennsylvania track coach was convicted of videotaping girls undressing.

What can you do to keep your child safe from such predators? Be sure your kid's sports league has done background checks on all coaches and volunteers who come into contact with children. Little League Baseball, for example, the world's largest youth sports organization, requires all local programs to conduct background checks on its coaches. "People forget that many molesters are affable and charming," says Robert Shoop, author of *Sexual Exploitation in Schools: How to Spot It and Stop It.* "They seem like the kinds of people parents want their children to be around."

4 "YOGA ISN'T ALWAYS AS GENTLE AS IT LOOKS."

An estimated 18 million Americans now practice the ancient art of yoga with hopes of increasing their balance and strength. Gina Williams, 48, a Columbia, Md., resident, decided to try yoga because she saw it as a gentler form of exercise than the aerobics that she had been doing. But after one strenuous session, Williams says she wound up with a pulled back muscle and chronic pain that lasted for eight months.

The concern is that injuries among yoga enthusiasts are rising along with the activity's popularity. Gerard Varlotta, director of sports rehabilitation at the New York University/Rusk Institute in New York City, says he has seen about 20 yoga-related ailments per year for the past three years. Tom McCook, a yoga instructor with his own studio in Mountain View, Calif., says the spike in injuries can be traced to "instructors having people do things that are high risk and low return."

How can a yoga novice avoid a painful introduction? Take it easy. "The instructor should start by teaching you breathing and simple postures, such as standing correctly," suggests McCook.

5 "WHEN IT COMES TO SKIING, SAFETY DOESN'T ALWAYS COME FIRST."

Lori McBride, a neurosurgeon at The Children's Hospital in Denver, frequently sees ski accident victims. Fortunately, there have been fewer cases of head trauma in recent years. Why? More people are wearing helmets on the slopes. "Helmets successfully protect the brain," McBride says. "Anybody in ski school should be wearing one." Despite the obvious advantages of enforcing helmet safety, the Professional Ski Instructors of America takes a somewhat laissez-faire attitude toward the gear. "The organization's opinion is that helmets are a matter of choice," says public relations rep Lisa Winston.

Going without a helmet while skiing isn't just dangerous, it can be deadly. In a tragic 2004 incident, 21-year-old Christina Porter wasn't wearing a helmet during a Dartmouth College–sponsored beginner-skiing class in Lyme, N.H., when she crashed into a tree. Porter suffered severe head injuries and was in a coma for six months; she died in January 2005. In April 2007, her parents filed a lawsuit against the college in federal court, seeking more than $20 million in damages. According to the lawsuit, the Dartmouth College ski instructors had sent the skier unaccompanied down a winding slope. The case is pending at press time. "Dartmouth believes its actions in this matter were reasonable and proper and did not lead to the untimely death of Christina Porter, but rather that her death was the result of a tragic accident," a Dartmouth College spokesperson explained in a written statement.

6 "YOU WANT ME TO TEACH YOU PILATES? I CAN BARELY TOUCH MY TOES."

Lucy Beale is one of the 10 million Americans who have found fitness salvation in Pilates, an isometric-style form of exercise. But while attending a class in 2001, she noticed the instructor was starting with a position in which you lie on your stomach and raise your arms, legs, and head. Echoing a belief that is widely held among seasoned Pilates instructors, Beale, who lives in Sandy, Utah, says, "It was the equivalent of starting a weight-training session by lifting 100 pounds without warming up. It's dangerous." Beale says she promptly left in the middle of the session without paying.

With Pilates participation at an all-time high, there are now more people who want to do the regimen than there are qualified instructors to teach it. "A lot of teachers get certified in a weekend—and that's not enough training," says Elyssa Rosenberg, a Pilates instructor in New York. She recommends looking for teachers who are Pilates Guild Certified; they will have spent 600 hours apprenticing and taken three written exams.

> [Look] for teachers who are Pilates Guild Certified; they will have spent 600 hours apprenticing and taken three written exams.

7 "TAKE A DEEP BREATH BEFORE SIGNING OUR SCUBA CONTRACTS."

Each year around 80 recreational divers in North America die while in the water. Christopher Murley became such a victim; he drowned in 1999 while on his third attempt to see the sunken ship *Andrea Doria*, located near Long Island, N.Y. Murley's family attempted to sue his dive instructor and other related parties in federal court, charging negligence and wrongful death. Murley was too inexperienced to take on the *Andrea Doria*, his lawyer Richard Lefkowitz argued, but according to Bill Turbeville, attorney for all but one defendant, Murley had "signed a waiver that releases all parties from any claim of negligence." Murley's lawsuit was eventually dismissed.

"Instructors use releases to insulate themselves from liability," Lefkowitz says. "They need to take responsibility when clients do not meet minimum safety standards." How to protect yourself? Look for a diving instructor who is certified by a reputable organization, such as the Professional Association of Diving Instructors or the National Association of Underwater Instructors. Both groups' sites (*www.padi.com* and *www.naui.org*) provide dive center locators to help you find certified instructors near you.

8 "A PACKAGE OF LESSONS IS A GREAT DEAL—ESPECIALLY FOR ME."

When Mark Pollack signed up for a set of 10 golf lessons at a public course near his home in Hillsdale, N.J., the coach promised to "straighten out" his game. Ten lessons later, says Pollack, "my swing was just as bad as when I started. He offered to give me two free lessons. But I told him that if 10 lessons didn't help, 2 more would not be the answer."

Coaches of every sport from tennis to gymnastics love up-front payments for multiple sessions, expecting that a good number of students will begin to lose interest and eventually miss some of the scheduled lessons or stop coming altogether.

Even worse is when your coach is the one who isn't exactly showing up. "Some instructors come in and go through the motions once a week," says Tom Sadzeck, a 17-year tennis instructor in San Rafael, Calif. "Once he has your money, he can lose incentive to do any better than that."

9 "IF YOU GET HURT, DON'T EXPECT ME TO HELP YOU."

If you're a serious athlete, there's something to the mantra "No pain, no gain." But consider this: A survey by the U.S. Consumer Product Safety Commission found that more than 763,000 children ages 14 and under were severely injured playing sports in 2006. Yet despite such terrible stats, not all states require that an athletic department have a coach on staff trained in CPR and sports first aid— and without that mandate, warns Fred Engh, president of the National Alliance for Youth Sports, "some coaches overlook their responsibility" to protect kids from injury.

That's what a jury said in a district court in Pottawattamie County, Iowa, in 2002. It found the Underwood school district and wrestling coach John Lewis Curtis guilty of negligent supervision for failing to properly care for Nathan Roane, then 16, following a junior varsity wrestling match in 2000. "After Nathan finished wrestling, he got off the mat and could barely stand up," says Laura Pattermann, of Council Bluffs, Iowa, who represented Nathan in the suit. "He was brought into the locker room and left alone on the floor during the varsity matches. He slipped in and out of consciousness and bled internally." But David Woodke, the school district's and Curtis's attorney, contends that "if Mr. Curtis had known the severity of the boy's injury, Mr. Curtis would have stayed with him."

Parents are encouraged to check with their school's athletic director to find out whether coaches are required to train in first aid or CPR, says Don Lauritzen, a health and safety expert at the American Red Cross. And "since many parents attend their children's games," he says, "they, too, should consider taking a course such as Red Cross First Aid, CPR, and AED training." Some states are also stepping up, mandating stricter safety regulations for coaching in schools. New Jersey, for example, ruled that beginning with the 2006–07 school year, all public school athletic coaches must be CPR-certified, with the added recommendation that they complete a Coaching Principles and Sports First Aid course as well.

10 "I CAN BE AN INSENSITIVE JERK."

The parents of Jim Ross, a Mishawaka High School basketball player in Indiana, were fed up with their son's coach when they went to St. Joseph Circuit Court in October 2006 with claims of verbal and psychological abuse. According to the lawsuit, their son's coach made derogatory comments to the six-foot-nine athlete, including, "You are eight feet tall, why can't you make a layup?" and other, more distasteful remarks not fit to print. As a result, the young player, according to allegations, suffered from emotional distress and withdrew psychologically. To add insult to injury, after the parents complained to the school's superintendent, the coach allegedly "intensified his abuse by acting like Jim Ross did not exist," according to the lawsuit—even when Ross fractured his foot during a practice. (The attorneys representing the parents and the superintendent of Mishawaka High School both declined to comment since the case was still pending at press time.)

Tim Flannery, an assistant director of the National Federation of State High School Associations, says that all too often coaches lack the proper training to effectively interact with kids. "Coaches should take a minimum of 40 hours' worth of classes that will teach them to communicate with their players," Flannery suggests. "Tennessee, Washington, and Oregon all have programs which require coaches to continually reeducate themselves on coaching students."

THINGS TO DO

- **Schedule lessons one at a time.** This will help you get a feel for an athletic instructor and see if his or her style suits you.

- **Got the itch to search** for sunken treasure? You can hire a certified scuba diver to take you under, at the Professional Association of Diving Instructors (*www.padi.com*) or the National Association of Underwater Instructors (*www.naui.org*).

- **Pilates used to be popular** primarily with dancers, but now the flexibility- and strength-building program is attracting mainstream athletes, including soccer and baseball players. To find a local Pilates instructor with at least 600 hours of education, visit *www.pilates-studio.com* to search by ZIP code.

- **First-time yoga students** shouldn't get too far ahead of themselves. Experts suggest starting with a style like Iyengar, which emphasizes the slow development of precise alignment, before moving into the more vigorous pace and advanced poses you might find in a style like Ashtanga.

- **Need help with your golf swing?** Hire a coach with a Class A designation from the PGA (you can find one through *www.pga.com*). Also, ask to see some of his recent tournament scores—a good golf instructor should be able to shoot in the low 70s.

10 Things
Major League Baseball
Won't Tell You

1 *"SO MUCH FOR THE NATIONAL PASTIME."*

As of 1985, a quarter of Americans considered baseball their favorite sport. But with NASCAR and soccer on the rise, that figure had dropped to 14 percent by 2006, according to a Harris Poll, or half as much as pro football. Over the same period, according to Nielsen Media Research, postseason TV viewership fell by half; the 10 worst-rated World Series have all been played in the past decade.

Baseball's problems are worsened by inconvenient game times, designed to snare prime-time ad dollars. Afternoon playoff games are a relic, night games on the West Coast don't begin until after 10 in the East, and World Series games routinely end after midnight. "It's not conducive to new fans," says sports writer Buster Olney, who has covered baseball for 18 years. "No kid could stay up that late."

An MLB spokesperson says the game is "quite healthy," pointing to increased attendance, website hits, and fantasy-baseball interest. But Gary Gillette, cochair of the Society for American Baseball Research's Business of Baseball Committee, disagrees. "The diehards will always be there for baseball," says Gillette. "But the casual fans have left in droves."

2 *"SCALPING TICKETS IS ILLEGAL—UNLESS, OF COURSE, WE DO IT."*

In 2002 Richard Kosterman was arrested and convicted under anti-scalping laws after trying to sell an extra ticket to the Mariners' opening day. He challenged the ruling—not because he disputed the charges but because the team was doing the very same thing. Since 2001 teams have partnered with online brokers, allowing ticket holders to sell their seats for whatever the market bears; the team gets the initial sale as well as a 25 percent cut of the profit from the resale. Not only are fans held hostage by this institutionalized price gouging (resale price, and not face value, is printed on the ticket) but any competition is eliminated. In August 2007, MLB tapped StubHub to be its exclusive reseller in the estimated $10 billion market. "Baseball saw ticket resellers as a threat," says lawyer Kim Gordon, who represented Kosterman, "so they decided to get their cut and try to force the other guys out."

Challenges to the policy have generally failed on grounds that online sales fall outside municipal scalping laws. "It's completely legal," says Rebecca Hale, director of public information for the Mariners. "There's nothing left to be said."

3 "WE'RE AS AMERICAN AS APPLE PIE—AND JOB OUTSOURCING."

A study by the Institute for Diversity and Ethics in Sport at the University of Central Florida showed the number of Hispanic players has doubled since 1990, up to 29.1 percent in the 2007 season. Baseball has become "highly dependent" on Latin America, says Adrian Burgos, Jr., author of *Playing America's Game: Baseball, Latinos, and the Color Line.*

Signing bonuses for Latino players are comparable—rarely more than five figures—to those of American players taken in the seventh round of the amateur draft, says Alan Klein, author of *Growing the Game: The Globalization of Major League Baseball.* Compared with the routine seven figures given to top American players, it's no wonder several hundred are signed each year from the Dominican Republic alone. "Teams are looking for a competitive advantage," says Burgos, "sometimes at the expense of exploiting workers." (An MLB spokesperson declined to comment.)

Foreign-born players now account for almost half of minor league rosters—though 98 percent will never make the majors, says José Luis Villegas, coauthor of *Away Games: The Life and Times of a Latin Baseball Player.*

Foreign-born players now account for almost half of minor league rosters— though 98 percent will never make the majors.

---

4 "WE'RE MAKING IT TOUGH FOR YOU TO WATCH YOUR TEAM PLAY."

"Watch every game live!" trumpets MLB.TV, an online video-on-demand service that's designed to let fans keep up with their favorite teams even if they can't see them on TV. Tell that to Steve Buhr. The Cedar Rapids resident, like the rest of Iowa, is unable to watch games for six different teams that claim the state is in their broadcast range. To protect the teams' market share, the league blacks out local games on MLB.TV and Extra Innings, the cable and satellite package, though fans pay around $200 for these services.

The culprit is an arcane map of "broadcast territories," drawn more than 30 years ago. An MLB spokesperson says the league is aware of complaints and is looking into the problem, but that's little consolation for folks like Buhr, who is a four-hour drive from any major league stadium. A fan of the blacked-out Minnesota Twins, Buhr canceled his MLB. TV and has resigned himself to watching highlights the next morning, since his cable company doesn't carry Twins games. "If you picture a wheel with spokes, the hub would be Cedar Rapids," he says. "It's not a good place to be a baseball fan."

5 "WE STILL HAVEN'T CLEANED UP OUR ACT."

According to Major League Baseball, Mark McGwire's 1998 home-run-record chase netted the organization $1.5 billion in ticket, merchandise, and ad sales— though there are now suspicions he was using steroids. Mark Fainaru-Wada and Lance Williams say in *Game of Shadows—*

the book that sparked the infamous "Mitchell Report"—that baseball knew for years steroids were behind the new power-hitting face of the game, but it didn't take action because of the money. "They're seeing these players show up with all this new muscle, and they're not stupid," Williams says. "There's a willful looking the other way."

In the wake of the scandal, MLB has adopted drug testing, but its policy has holes: For example, a maximum of 5 percent of major leaguers are tested off-season. There's also the problem of designer drugs being created for which no tests exist. And where the Olympics has spent almost $10 million trying to develop a reliable test for human growth hormone, baseball gave only one $500,000 grant, to Don Catlin of the Anti-Doping Research Institute. "It can be done," Catlin says, "but I'm not sure it can be done for the budget we have." (A spokesperson for Major League Baseball declined to comment.)

6 "THE PLAYERS AREN'T THE ONLY ONES GETTING INJURED."

A Seattle Mariners game in 2000 would have been only the second one Dee Middleton-Taylor attended, but she never even made it to her seat. "I was thinking, this is a great day, and the next thing I know, I was hit," she recalls. She had been struck in the face by a ball in pregame warm-ups. It shattered bones in her face and lacerated her cornea, requiring multiple surgeries. "You don't expect anything like this to happen," she says.

Maybe you should. Injuries among fans struck by balls are more common

than you might think, says Middleton-Taylor's lawyer, Brad Fulton. The team was compelled to turn over five years' worth of incident reports, and Fulton says the file was five inches thick. "Sometimes there are four or five or six a game," he says. "Way more than they want you to know." A spokeperson speaking for the Mariners says that five injuries in one game does happen but is unusual.) King County's superior court ruled against Middleton-Taylor, holding that fans assume the risk when they enter a ballpark. "There are warnings on the ticket," says an MLB spokesperson, "and announcements made before the game. Fans should be aware."

7 "OUR ACCOUNTING DEFIES THE LAWS OF LOGIC ..."

Baseball Commissioner Bud Selig told Congress in 2001 that the league showed a $232 million loss for the year, but only months later *Forbes* reported the figure as an operating profit of $75 million. Though baseball disputes the methodology, no one denies that the game's finances are as complex as they are secretive. Experts paint them as the antithesis of most accounting scandals: Team owners exaggerate their losses. "When they say they're breaking even, they're making money," Gillette says. "And when they say they're making a small profit, they've got a printing press in the basement."

Owners pay themselves and family members for executive positions (the Yankees' George Steinbrenner has variously employed two sons, two daughters, and three sons-in-law), and the salaries are listed as expenses.

Most significant is the revenue from concessions, parking, and television, which aren't counted as profit even though the money goes straight into the team's coffers. As former MLB President Paul Beeston famously boasted when he was a Toronto Blue Jays executive, "I can turn a $4 million profit into a $2 million loss and get every national accounting firm to agree with me."

8 "... WHILE YOU'RE THE ONE PICKING UP THE SLACK."

Baseball's annual revenue tops $5 billion and has been rising every year. So only by crying poverty can teams like the San Francisco Giants, which raised ticket prices 129 percent from 1995 to 2005, justify quadrupling the national inflation rate. The average cost for a family of four to see a game now tops $175, according to Team Marketing Report, a sports marketing publisher. "If fans think [teams are] making too much money," says Gillette, "they'll be less willing to pay rip-off prices for hot dogs and scorecards."

But where the public gets soaked the most is in the construction of new ballparks. Nineteen new stadiums have been built in the past 15 years, with six more on the way. And with only one exception, those new parks are largely or entirely funded with tax dollars. "They don't have to pay for the stadium, and they don't have to pay property taxes," says Neil deMause, coauthor of *Field of Schemes: How the Great Stadium Swindle Turns Public Money into Private Profit.* "But they get to keep the gate receipts. Does that seem fair?" It's not chump change either; deMause says the new

Yankee Stadium will cost $1.3 billion to build (though the team initially told the city it would run $800 million), with roughly half covered by local, state, and federal tax money.

9 "WE'VE GOT FRIENDS IN HIGH PLACES."

With no equal in American culture, baseball enjoys a lot of special treatment. But perhaps none is more striking than the unique antitrust exemption it has held since it was granted by the Supreme Court in 1922. Calling it a "historical anomaly," Andrew Zimbalist, economist and author of *In the Best Interests of Baseball? The Revolutionary Reign of Bud Selig,* says the ruling came down "partly because at that point in time interstate commerce had a different meaning, and partly because Oliver Wendell Holmes and William Howard Taft were big baseball fans."

A spokesperson for Major League Baseball calls the effects "negligible," but the ruling leaves the league with very few checks on its power. Minor league players are bound to their teams, team owners have major hurdles to jump to sue the league, and the league can decide where a team plays. Montreal Expos fans found this out the hard way, when MLB up and moved their team to Washington, D.C., after the 2004 season.

10 "THE MOST VALUABLE THING IN A PACK OF BASEBALL CARDS IS THE GUM."

Collecting baseball cards sure isn't what it used to be. Over the past quarter-century, many fans have hung on to their childhood collections with the expectation that they'd be worth a lot of money one day. But in today's market, that's highly unlikely. Why? Because everyone else had the same idea. "It used to be, 'My mom threw out my baseball cards,'" says Tracy Hackler, associate publisher for Beckett, the industry's leading price guide. "Well, that's what created the market. Mom throwing out the collection made the ones that weren't thrown out worth something."

Not only have too many cards been saved, but too many are currently being produced. Topps had a virtual monopoly on the baseball card market until 1981, when a court ruling forced MLB to grant licenses to companies including Fleer, Donruss, and Upper Deck, flooding the market. Now it's not the 10-year-old buying a pack for the gum inside who's going to get rich, but the serious collector who already has money to invest in rare cards. As Hackler warns, "Trading cards aren't for you if you look at them and see dollar signs and college educations and second homes."

THINGS TO DO

Ever watch a baseball game and wonder, What the heck are these guys talking about? Here's a quick rundown of some of the terms that get tossed around the horn:

● **On-base percentage.** The OBP is a measure of how often a player gets on base through hits, walks, or hit-by-pitches. Ted Williams is the all-time record holder, having reached base over 48 percent of the time during his 16-year career.

● **WHIP.** A pitcher's WHIP, or walks plus hits per innings pitched, is a better indicator of a pitcher's effectiveness than the classic earned-run average because it takes the ability of the defense out of the equation. Pedro Martinez has the lowest WHIP among all active pitchers; over his career he's allowed an average of 1.04 players on base per inning.

● **Fielding percentage.** The most popular way to measure a player's defensive performance; fielding percentage takes into account the number of assists and putouts, then divides it by the number of chances. In 2007 the National League Champion Colorado Rockies led the Majors with a 98.9 percent fielding percentage.

● **The 999.** The ultimate in fan endurance: Would-be heroes risk gastrointestinal injury in an attempt to consume nine hot dogs and drink nine beers in nine innings. In 2007 the average baseball game lasted around two hours and 55 minutes, according to the Elias Sports Bureau; that means a hot dog and a beer every 19 minutes to make the 999.

Your World

■ The world is definitely a lot noisier than it used to be. With the proliferation of media and technology and an increasingly integrated global economy, more information is coming at us through more and various kinds of channels than ever before. All of which is influencing how we spend our free time, seek to achieve our goals, and participate in civic life.

This chapter is designed to help you sort through the din of all that feedback. Of course, we couldn't possibly fit everything. But here we'll give you informed perspectives on a variety of topics, from what goes on in the halls of Congress to the scruples of reality-television producers. It's your chance to get inside the world of those who seek to enter yours.

10 Things Your
Local News
Won't Tell You

1 *"WE'RE LIVE, LOCAL—AND MORE LURID THAN EVER."*

The audience for local news has steadily declined in recent years. According to the 2005 "State of the News Media" report from research organization the Project for Excellence in Journalism, both early- and late-evening news lost more than 3 percent of their audience a year between 1997 and 2003. An updated 2007 version of the study found that the downward trend has expanded recently to include morning news broadcast, with viewership numbers continuing their decline across the board through 2006.

As a result, local stations have gotten more aggressive in trying to hook viewers. Terry Heaton, a former TV news director now working as a Nashville-based consultant to the industry, recalls being promo-teased one night with "40 DEAD ON I-65," only to discover the casualties were pigs, killed when a livestock truck overturned. "Nothing makes viewers more resentful," he says.

Scott Jones, a former TV reporter, producer, and news director who now runs FTVLive.com, an industry website, says these promos are written by ad copywriters—so what might be a straightforward story about a vice bust gets sold with a lead like "Could your child's teacher be a prostitute at night?" But if the promo entices you to stay tuned after *Law & Order*, as Heaton was, then it has successfully "managed audience flow."

2 *"CRIME WAVE? NO, JUST SWEEPS MONTH."*

In most markets, broadcasters measure their audience four times a year—in February, May, July, and November, during four-week ratings periods known as "sweeps." Although 9 of the top 10 markets get constant monitoring via Nielsen Media Research's "People Meters"—devices installed in sample homes—the rest depend on sweeps weeks to track viewership. This data is used to set ad rates and to stake claims in marketing: "Most watched!" "No. 1!"

That means stations have a lot riding on sweeps periods, which is why they roll out the big guns: flashy projects, like investigative reports—and often stories that tread closest to the line of taste and propriety. "Going into hotel rooms to test for stuff on the sheets was a big one for a while," Heaton says. Cleveland anchor Sharon Reed even got naked for an art piece by photographer Spencer Tunick. The story was shot in June 2004—but didn't run until November sweeps.

Ratings-garnering excesses are an uncomfortable fact of the industry, but one it has learned to live with, says Deborah Potter, president and executive director of NewsLab, an online resource for TV journalists. "This is our bread and butter," she says.

3 "AND NOW A CHECK OF THE FORECAST—WITH OUR WEATHERMAN, CHICKEN LITTLE."

It's no secret that weather coverage is a huge focus for local news. "It's the franchise," says Mark Jurkowitz, associate director of the Project for Excellence in Journalism. "The one thing they do better than anyone else." But it can also confuse viewers, bombarding them with various seals of approval and technological one-upmanship.

According to Dennis Feltgen of the National Weather Service, your local weatherman may or may not be trained in meteorology, and the station probably doesn't rely exclusively on its own forecasts. Many tap the NWS or a private provider such as AccuWeather or Weather Central for a baseline forecast, then augment it with their own, much-hyped Doppler radar system (which tracks precipitation and wind velocity).

Then when skies darken, they go for the kill. "The [weatherman] tries to scare the hell out of you if more than an inch of snow falls," Jurkowitz says. "I've seen schools canceled over what turned out to be less than two inches." The problem, Potter explains, is that station owners are heavily invested in their Doppler equipment and want their money's worth: "The investment justifies the coverage, and vice versa."

4 "OUR CONSULTANTS IN IOWA ARE CALLING THE SHOTS."

Ever wonder why TV news is so similar from city to city? The reason, many in TV say, is a handful of powerful industry consultants who sell station owners on their tried-and-true techniques, right down to stories that get repeated across markets. Perhaps you've seen their work: In 2004, the heyday of the consultant trend, stations in Kansas City, Detroit, Philadelphia, and Milwaukee all did virtually identical stories on chat-room predators, in which men were lured to a rendezvous with a supposedly underage girl they met online who turned out to be a reporter.

Consultants argue they're not the homogenizing behemoth their critics claim them to be. Bill Hague, vice president for corporate development at Frank N. Magid Associates in Marion, Iowa, the largest news-consulting firm, says his company is an advocate for viewers: "Everything we do is based on local research. What works in Dallas may not work in Duluth." Hague admits the

Stations have a lot riding on sweeps periods, which is why they roll out the big guns: flashy projects, like investigative reports—and often stories that tread closest to the line of taste and propriety.

same ideas do tend to spread. "Right now it's MySpace," he says, but claims that isn't Magid's doing. "I don't know how they're all getting the same idea."

5 "SOURCES? WE DON'T NEED NO STINKIN' SOURCES."

Journalism is all about gathering, interpreting, and presenting information, and journalists have evolved a set of principles to help consumers understand it. But TV news doesn't always play by the same rules.

Take VNRs. Video news releases are the TV version of PR, sent in from corporations or other sources but packaged to look like journalism. The controversy over the use of unlabeled VNRs has been building over the past few years. In a well-publicized 2004 case, many stations ran versions of a story on Medicare picked up from the CNN Newsource satellite feed. But it wasn't an independent report; it was a VNR paid for by the Bush administration and "reported" by a PR agent. The Office of National Drug Control Policy drew attention in 2005 for the same thing, which the General Accounting Office called "covert propaganda." And in 2007 the Federal Communications Commission fined Comcast $16,000 for its airing of undisclosed VNRs.

VNRs can be useful, says David Folkenflik, media reporter for NPR. They provide "B-roll," or secondary, footage, which "should always be labeled," he says. But even when VNR footage does get credited, Scott Jones says, it's often under the vague and overused catchall "file footage."

6 "THIS STORY GOES OUT TO ALL THE LADIES IN THE HOUSE."

You may have noticed lately a change in the sports segment of your local newscast. Perhaps it's shorter or seems to focus more and more on the human-interest angle rather than providing scores and highlights. Why? ESPN, for one thing. But it's also part of an attempt to cater to advertisers' most coveted viewers— women ages 25 to 54. Brad Schultz, an assistant professor of journalism at the University of Mississippi, is studying the change. "Support for sports reporting is a mile wide and an inch deep," he says. "It's the least-watched segment, an invitation to tune out."

Less sports isn't the only way women are tweaking TV news. Scott Jones says the quest for female viewers is changing coverage across the board and is a big reason for the increase in health stories. Women not only tend to control a family's spending, they're the family doctor, too, and research shows they're interested in information about health and well-being. Those making the decisions "are convinced that's what the audience wants," Schultz says. And to please their advertisers, TV newscasts are going out of their way to give it to them.

7 "AND NOW A WORD FROM OUR ALL-POWERFUL SPONSOR."

Every news outlet that relies on ad dollars to survive must draw the line at how much influence it will allow advertisers to have on its content. TV news works the same way; its line is just a bit more flexible. "The unwritten rule: If you're doing a 'nice' story on an industry, pick an advertiser [to focus on]," Heaton says. It works the opposite way, too. Jones recalls a case where he was told not to do an item on a local doughnut shop—so popular that it was causing traffic jams—because the shop had refused to advertise with the station. Another story you won't hear, according to Heaton: "People getting ripped off by a local car dealer," since dealerships are big advertisers on local news.

"It's a daily headache in a lot of newsrooms," Potter says. "There's still a fair amount of padding between the sales department and the newsroom in most [local TV] markets, but when radio stations are selling naming rights to their newsrooms"—one in Wisconsin has rechristened itself the "Amcore Bank News Center"—"I think that's crossing a line."

8 "IT'S YOUR FAULT WE STINK."

You might say you want your local TV news to be sober, responsible, and comprehensive, but research shows that the highest ratings go to news that isn't. Research by the Project for Excellence in Journalism bears this out: Its 2006 "State of the Media" report, which analyzed one day's worth of content, found that half of local TV news broadcasts consisted of crime- and accident-related coverage. "That was close to double the percentage on local radio . . . or metro newspapers," the report says.

And it remains true today: If it bleeds, it leads. "Good journalism is often [at odds] with TV news," Heaton says. He explains that TV journalism's finest moments are blockbusters—big, breaking stories such as Hurricane Katrina, when people turn to their television for updates. "Now everyone wants to have blockbusters all the time, and the systems are in place to create artificial ones."

9 "HARD NEWS IS YESTERDAY'S NEWS."

If the local news media have one job to do, it's to cover policy makers and those who spend the public's money—state legislators, city councils, school boards. And yet the accelerated pace of local news broadcasts makes these types of stories tough to cover with any sort of depth. "That's a newspaper story," is how hard news often gets characterized, according to Potter, meaning that it's "complicated, and it doesn't have good pictures."

A report of the Project for Excellence in Journalism found that political and governmental news made up just 11 percent of local TV news stories, while stories on foreign relations comprised a scant 4 percent. Potter thinks the lack of in-depth government news coverage is partly a result of consultants' influence. "[Researchers] tell us people don't want stories about politics, but how are they asking the question? It's one thing to say, 'Do you want more coverage of politics?' and another to ask, 'Do you want to know what your public officials are up to?'"

Jurkowitz agrees. "Consultants have hammered home that no one wants to see politics on TV. That day-in and day-out coverage of state government or city hall has almost vanished from local TV here," he says. "Covering it as process is one thing; covering its relevance to people is another."

10 *"THAT'S INFOTAINMENT, BABY!"*

TV news anchors have been comedy fodder for decades, from *The Mary Tyler Moore Show*'s pompous Ted Baxter to Will Ferrell's smarmy Ron Burgundy in *Anchorman.* "The truth is," Heaton says, "Hollywood has a pretty good handle on some of the characters you run into in this business." Indeed, your local newscast can often be unintentionally comical. Ever snicker at a reporter standing on an abandoned street corner excitedly describing events that took place hours before? What about the weatherman dressed for the Arctic who is braving the elements of the station's parking lot to poke a pocket ruler in a snowbank?

It's all part of the mandate of a visual medium: Show, don't tell. "We're good at sharing experience," Potter says, and visual aids help. Heaton explains that the live-on-location gimmick evolved as part of a consultant-driven "command anchor" strategy, designed to position the main anchor as the show's pilot. The live shot works as a "debriefing" on breaking news, with the anchor serving as the audience's surrogate, like a military commander getting news of troop movements.

"Ask yourself what you're getting," Folkenflik says. "Weather, a crime segment, a tie-in to the network's entertainment programming, a little news, some sports. Are you getting fair value for your time?"

THINGS TO KNOW

Although viewership has dropped in recent years, local broadcast channels continue to enjoy healthy profits from newscasts. A study released in 2008 by the Project for Excellence in Journalism found the following:

- **Local news is a cash cow.** Between 40 and 45 percent of revenue for local stations is generated by news broadcasts.

- **Stations are devoting more time** to news broadcasts. From 2003 to 2006, stations increased news broadcasts by an average of 11 percent.

- **Evening news gets the most viewers.** The highest ratings in local news

broadcasts go to those airing between 5 and 7 P.M. Morning news generally draws the smallest audience.

- **The Web is becoming** a vital platform for local news broadcasts. Around 98 percent of stations include news on their websites, and 40 percent of stations ask their newsroom staff to contribute Web content.

10 Things Your
Congressperson
Won't Tell You

1 *"I CAN'T LOSE."*

When members of the U.S. House of Representatives stand for reelection, for most it's a formality: On average, more than 90 percent of House incumbents win, according to a 2005 report by the Cato Institute. What's behind the incumbency advantage? Campaign financing, for one thing. We taxpayers pick up the tab for incumbents' regular offices, staff, publicity, travel, and mailings, so they needn't raise as much money to run. Challengers, on the other hand, must come up with a fortune—and do so in dribs and drabs, since Congress caps individual contributions at $2,000.

But the biggest factor is partisan gerrymandering. Since the Supreme Court ruled in 1969 that states must ensure that each congressman represents the same number of constituents, the process of redistricting after every census has been aggressively used by state party bosses to protect their incumbents. "Because of gerrymandering, almost 90 percent of Americans live in congressional districts where the outcome is so certain that their votes are irrelevant," concludes the Cato report. And it's bound to get worse: In June 2006 the Court ruled that states can redraw congressional districts as often as they please.

2 *"I'M ABOVE THE LAW."*

Some people were dismayed when Capitol Police didn't give a sobriety test to Rep. Patrick Kennedy (D-R.I.) after he rammed a Capitol Hill security barrier late one night in 2006 and emerged from his Mustang "impaired," with "unsure" balance and "slurred" speech, according to the police report. Georgetown University law professor Paul F. Rothstein wasn't surprised: "They always give [congresspeople] a pass."

Why? *Inside Congress* author Ronald Kessler says that, historically, most officers have operated under the mistaken impression that the Constitution prohibits arresting or even ticketing congresspeople while Congress is in session. The belief was so prevalent at one time that the Justice Department issued a statement in 1976 explaining the "previous policy of releasing members who had been arrested was based on a misunderstanding of the clause in the U.S. Constitution," which forbids only civil arrest, not arrest for a crime. Nonetheless, Capitol Police still coddle and avoid arresting members of Congress. For one thing, protecting congresspeople is part of their mission. For another, Congress controls their budget—including top cops' salaries.

3 "READ THE BILLS I VOTE ON? WHO'S GOT THAT KIND OF TIME?"

In a perfect world, our legislators would vote on each bill based on thorough, firsthand analysis. But that's not how it works in Washington. Most congresspeople don't actually read bills, relying instead on impressions gleaned from staff and lobbyists. And in many cases, they couldn't read them if they wanted to: The 700-plus-page Deficit Reduction Omnibus Reconciliation Act of 2005, for example, surfaced after 1 A.M. and went to vote early the next morning. "That's the way it's done," Rep. Rob Simmons (R-Conn.) told the *Hartford Courant*.

Result: Congresspeople seldom know exactly what they're voting on. Take the 1,600-page Appropriations Bill in 2004 that had already made it through the House before it was discovered that a staffer had slipped in a provision permitting his committee to browse any tax return filed with the IRS.

There have been some attempts to get Congress to change its ways. In 2006, for example, D.C. nonprofit ReadtheBill .org persuaded some reps to introduce a resolution requiring the House to post each bill online for 72 hours before even debating it. But that resolution has been languishing in the House Committee on Rules ever since. A similar bill was introduced in 2007 by Rep. Brian Baird (D-Wash.), but it, too, has since stalled.

4 "CONGRESS IS JUST A STEPPING-STONE TO THE BIG MONEY—IN LOBBYING."

Congress is a pretty good gig, financially speaking. Our senators and representatives currently earn upwards of $165,000 a year—roughly four times the median U.S. household income. But it's not nearly as lucrative as lobbying, a job congresspeople have begun flocking to once they're out of office. "As late as the 1980s, few lawmakers became lobbyists because they considered it beneath their dignity," writes Robert V. Remini in *The House: The History of the House of Representatives*. But today it's the top career choice for former congresspeople.

According to a 2005 report by Public Citizen, since 1998 more than 43 percent of all eligible departing congresspeople went into lobbying. Take William Tauzin. The Louisiana Republican, and former chair of the Energy and Commerce Committee, left the House for a $1-million-plus-a-year job as president of Pharmaceutical Research and Manufacturers of America (PhRMA). According to press reports, PhRMA was wooing Tauzin the same month he pushed through the Medicare bill. Tauzin denies it fueled his zeal for the bill, but you can't help wondering how the prospect of that kind of money might influence one's judgment.

5 "MY HEALTH BENEFITS ARE WAY BETTER THAN YOURS …"

Congresspeople love tinkering with our health care. They virtually created the managed-care industry, for instance, with the Health Maintenance Organization Act of 1973, which tilted the playing field in favor of HMOs, ultimately stripping many Americans of all other choices. Meanwhile, congresspeople enjoy more than a dozen options, including prized indemnity plans, which provide reimbursement without limiting the pool of medical care providers, that few workers in the public sector receive. On top of that, for an annual fee of $480, they can get just about all the medical attention they want at the Capitol Office of the Attending Physician, which has five doctors and a dozen assistants on call for routine checkups, tests, prescriptions, emergency care, and mental health services. Who's making up the difference? Taxpayers, naturally, to the tune of $2.8 million in 2008.

What happens once a congressperson is out of office? She needn't fret: Just five years into the job, she's entitled to keep her regular health coverage until she's ready for Medicare. And she doesn't have to pay extra, as you do for Cobra, under the Health Insurance Portability and Accountability Act, which she voted for in 1996.

6 *"...AND SO IS MY PENSION."*

Congress is forever changing the rules on retirement plans: limiting contributions, punishing pension underfunding, and making it hard for employers to plan ahead. In 2006 Congress passed yet another complex bill that's wreaking more havoc, according to James A. Klein, president of the American Benefits Council. The new Pension Protection Act includes funding rules that, Klein says, "could undermine the retirement security of the very participants the bill's trying to protect." Indeed, less than a month after the PPA took effect, DuPont froze its pension plan and cut back on benefits.

Not that Congress is losing sleep—its members' pensions are exempt. Most qualify for a 401(k)-style plan with a nice match, up to 5 percent of salary. After five years on the job, they're also entitled to a regular pension, bigger than almost all other federal workers' at the same pay and twice what a midlevel executive would expect. If elected before age 30, they can collect in full at age 50; those elected later can retire after 25 years or at age 62. Their pensions rise regularly with the cost of living and can never be taken away—short of a conviction for espionage or treason-related offenses.

7 *"I ENJOY GREAT PERKS AND GIFTS, AND IT'S ALL LEGAL."*

Working on Capitol Hill comes with a lot of fringe benefits. Congresspeople enjoy taxpayer-subsidized gyms, salons and restaurants, free parking, and a nice office. They also get $1-million-plus allowances per year for staff, mail, and travel home, where they can rent another office and lease a car on your dime, according to the National Taxpayers Union.

On top of that, House ethics rules allow them to accept gifts, luxury jet rides, and free overnight trips of up to seven days abroad for meetings, fact-finding missions, and speaking gigs, provided they're related to official duties and not sponsored by lobbyists. Between 2000 and 2005, congresspeople and staff accepted 23,000 of these trips, often to vacation spots and worth nearly $50 million, according to the Center for Public Integrity. Turns out that 90 were sponsored by lobbyists—Mr. and Mrs.

Tom DeLay's infamous $28,000 golfing trip to Scotland among them.

8 *"I SIMPLY CAN'T BE FIRED."*

Once elected, it's almost impossible to kick a congressperson out of office, even if he becomes mentally incompetent or is sent to prison. To oust a member of the House or Senate, it takes a vote of two thirds of his colleagues—which has happened only twice since the Civil War, and five times in all of U.S. history.

House rules do discourage a congressman from participating in committees if convicted of a crime for which he could get two years or more in jail, and his own party may force him from leadership positions even if he's not convicted. For example, Democrats pushed Rep. William Jefferson (D-La.) off the Ways and Means Committee in 2006 because FBI agents swear they caught him accepting a $100,000 bribe and found $90,000 cash in his freezer. (Jefferson denies any wrongdoing.) But even if convicted and sent to prison, Jefferson could seek reelection from his cell, as did former Ohio Democrat James Traficant, Jr., in 2002. Traficant received only 15 percent of the vote and lost his seat—but he was still allowed to collect his full pension.

9 *"LOBBYISTS LOVE ME BECAUSE I DELIVER THE GOODS."*

The reason lobbyists court lawmakers is that they have the power to help friends and hurt foes. For instance, a congressperson can create a specific tax break or other loophole for a lobbyist's clients, giving them an unfair advantage over rivals. Congresspeople also hold the power to steer federal funds to friends by earmarking money for pet projects—a power they often abuse. Case in point: the notorious "Bridge to Nowhere," a Golden Gate–size span between a small town in rural Alaska and a nearly deserted island, for which Rep. Don Young (R-Alaska) persuaded Congress to earmark $223 million in 2005. Similar abuses have increased dramatically in recent years, with the number of earmarks coming out of the House Appropriations Committee nearly tripling, to 15,877 earmarks worth $47.4 billion in 2005, from just 4,126 earmarks worth $23.2 billion in 1994, according to the Congressional Research Service.

Once elected, it's almost impossible to kick a congressperson out of office, even if he becomes mentally incompetent or is sent to prison.

10 *"RULES ARE MEANT TO BE BROKEN."*

Congress is notorious for breaking its own rules: Only a handful of members dock their own pay when absent for reasons other than health, for example. But it's Congress's failure to follow its own legislative procedures that's truly galling. When the joint House-Senate conference committee meets to reconcile different versions of a bill, for instance, House rules forbid adding anything beyond the scope of the version the House has already approved. And once the committee comes up with a compromise bill, the House is supposed to hold at least one public meeting, giving members a written explanation of the changes and three days until the vote. But the conference committee routinely flouts these rules, often making big changes without explanation, then getting the Rules Committee to waive restrictions so they can rush bills through unread. How common is this? In one telling example, the Rules Committee issued so-called blanket waivers for all 18 bills that went through the conference committee from Jan. 4, 2005, through March 2006.

In December 2006, Speaker Hastert took it a step further by letting Sen. William Frist (R-Tenn.) add on to a bill after the conference committee was finished: 40 pages of legislation protecting makers of avian flu vaccine and similar drugs against liability even if they injured or killed patients through gross negligence. Then Hastert got the Rules Committee to make kosher what he'd done. Frist's spokesperson claims there was "bipartisan consensus" for such an incentive, but couldn't explain why it hadn't made it into the text of the bill if it was so popular. Hastert's office failed to return our calls.

THINGS TO DO

Your congressperson works for you—and about 650,000 other constituents. How can you reach him or her and communicate the issues that matter to you? Here are some tips from Norman Ornstein, a congressional expert and resident scholar at the American Enterprise Institute:

- **Catch them at home.** "Most members of congress go back home every weekend—and usually, it's an extended weekend, because they are done by Thursday. It's not difficult for a constituent to get at least a few minutes with the member at home."

- **Send a handwritten letter.** "I know most people these days don't know what a handwritten letter is. But the fact is, most of the mail that members of Congress get otherwise is not much more than form letters. If you write something by hand, it's going to get the notice of the staff member who's processing the mail. And there's a chance that the congressman himself or herself will take it into account."

- **Be realistic.** "If you're writing to change a longtime position of a congressman, you might get a respectful hearing, but you won't be very effective—but if the member is torn, you could have an impact. Also, you can write to whomever you want, but in most cases, you're going to be listened to more if you're a voter in the district of that person."

Bloggers

1 *"HARDLY ANYBODY READS ME."*

If you believe the hype, blogs (short for "Web log")—those online journals where people write about everything from politics and sports to their personal lives—will soon be the only thing most people read. Indeed, the blogging phenomenon, which blossomed from modest beginnings almost a decade ago, seems unstoppable: In 2004 there were roughly 2 million blogs on the Web, according to blog search engine Technorati; by 2007 there were more than 60 million. But the reality behind the stats is that most blogs get few hits.

The most popular do boast huge followings—tech-news site Engadget, for one, has more readers than most print newspapers and magazines. But beyond the elite few, it drops off significantly— the top 25 blogs account for roughly 10 percent of blog readership, according to Web-traffic measurement firm comScore. To be fair, most bloggers aren't seeking a big audience. "The pleasure of blogging is in forming a sense of intimacy readers and fellow bloggers can enjoy," says Rachel Bray, whose Babayaga.ca gets a few hundred hits a day.

So what's the norm? Google CEO Eric Schmidt told a recent gathering of U.K. politicians that the average blog has just one reader: the blogger.

2 *"THE MORE COMPANIES PAY ME, THE MORE I LIKE THEIR STUFF."*

Companies looking for ways to profit from the blogging phenomenon have tried everything from buying ad space on blogs to infiltrating discussion forums with hired PR shills. They've even created fake blogs to hawk their products. In December 2006, Sony went live with AllIWantforXmasIsaPSP.com, a "blog" by two fictitious teenagers clamoring to get a PlayStation Portable for Christmas. The site, which contained videos and strained attempts at youth slang, was quickly exposed as a fraud. "It was designed to be humorous," says a Sony spokesperson. "It didn't come across as intended."

When such tactics aren't enough, companies will even pay bloggers to praise their products. In 2006, Florida outfit PayPerPost sparked controversy by offering to connect advertisers with bloggers willing to drop a company's name into their daily scribbles for a fee (between $4 and $40 per mention). The practice was quickly denounced as online payola, and the Federal Trade Commission weighed in, ruling that word-of-mouth marketers must disclose their sponsorship. Says PayPerPost CEO Ted Murphy, "We're trying to strike a balance that makes everybody happy."

> While more than one third of bloggers consider their work a form of journalism, their news-gathering consists largely of borrowing content and posting links to traditional news sources, along with some added commentary.

3 "DID I MENTION I'M NOT A REAL REPORTER?"

With major newspapers including *The Washington Post* routinely hosting blogs for columnists and reporters, blogging is gaining credibility. But beware: Even those associated with mainstream news outlets aren't subject to the same prepublication safeguards—editing, fact-checking, proofreading—that print publications use. With blogs, "We're shifting to this world where we're publishing first and editing later," says Jeff Jarvis, a journalism professor at the City University of New York and author of the blog BuzzMachine.

While more than one third of bloggers consider their work a form of journalism,

their news-gathering consists largely of borrowing content and posting links to traditional news sources, along with some added commentary. What's more, bloggers don't face the same consequences as journalists for getting it wrong: In a recent libel case against a woman who posted a critical letter about two doctors, the California Supreme Court ruled that those who post content from other sources aren't liable for defamation. In other words, bloggers are off the hook so long as they aren't the original author of the mistake.

4 "I MIGHT INFECT YOUR COMPUTER WITH A VIRUS."

Most Web surfers know better than to click on a link promising free money or a trip to the Bahamas. But blogs can contain malicious code just like any other site. Social-networking hub MySpace, for example, which hosts about 1 in 10 blogs online, has suffered several high-profile attacks. In December 2006 hackers altered hundreds of thousands of MySpace user profiles; the doctored pages directed viewers to a scam site that elicited log-in names and passwords. Another tactic involves targeting innocent blogs and inserting malicious links into the reader comment section—one click and your computer could be infected.

Allysa Myers, a virus-research engineer at security-software maker McAfee, says researchers now see such attacks almost daily. Keeping your operating system, browser, and security software updated may help contain the damage, but the responsibility is partly that of website operators, who need to put proper filters in place so rogue users can't upload bad content. The bottom line for readers: "If you don't know the person doing the linking, don't click on it," Myers says.

5 "I'M REVEALING COMPANY SECRETS."

When Mark Jen started working at Google in 2005, he was so excited about his job that the newly minted associate product manager began writing a blog about it, describing orientation meetings, comparing Google's pay and benefits package with that of his past employer, and recounting a company ski trip. Though Jen revealed nothing earth-shattering, his blog soon drew an audience eager for a peek inside the tight-lipped firm. Two weeks later Jen was fired. He isn't sure just what he wrote that prompted his dismissal, but "was told somebody at the top wanted me gone," Jen says. (Google had no comment on the matter.)

Indeed, companies are only now beginning to realize that employee blogs can be a threat to information security; as of 2007 just 7 percent of firms had policies on personal blogs, according to a survey from the American Management Association and ePolicy Institute. But that doesn't mean you can blog with abandon. "Don't piss off your boss," says Robert Scoble, author of *Naked Conversations: How Blogs Are Changing the Way Businesses Talk with Customers.* Ask about your employer's stance on blogs and what subject matter is out-of-bounds before ever typing a word.

6 "JUST BECAUSE MY NAME'S ON IT DOESN'T MEAN I WROTE IT."

In 2005 New York City mayoral candidate Fernando Ferrer's Web log mentioned he'd attended public schools; in fact, Ferrer had received most of his education in private Catholic schools. When confronted with the error, his campaign admitted the blog was written by a staffer. Ferrer's predicament was hardly unusual: Politicians, business leaders, and other public figures routinely employ ghostwriters to produce books, speeches, and, more recently, blogs. One survey conducted by PR consultant David Davis found that only 17 percent of CEOs who blog do all their own writing.

However common it is, "ghost blogging" remains controversial. "It's a perversion of the real meaning of blogging, which is to put yourself out there," says Debbie Weil, author of *The Corporate Blogging Book.* But not everybody agrees the practice is tantamount to lying. Ed Poll, a law firm management consultant and author of LawBiz Blog, thinks ghost blogging is fine. "I don't think anyone who reads a post should care whether the name on it belongs to the writer," Poll says. "If you believe everything you read, then shame on you."

7 "MY BLOG IS JUST A STEPPING-STONE TO BIGGER AND BETTER THINGS."

In some blogging circles, scorn for the mainstream media, or "MSM," is a virtual religion. Nonetheless, many bloggers have proven eager to join it when the opportunity arises. Melissa Lafsky, author of the popular Opinionistas blog, was stressed and unhappy as a young lawyer in New York City. As a kind of therapy, she began chronicling daily life at her firm, relating tales of tyrannical partners and sleepless, embittered young associates, being careful not to reveal her identity. Her blog soon built a following, gaining mentions in *The New York Times* and Slate.com. Eventually, a literary agent came calling, and Lafsky quit her job to write professionally. "I'd be getting coffee in some newsroom if not for the Internet," she says.

Indeed, bloggers are using their medium to pursue jobs in all sorts of industries. Seeking a spot at Provo Labs, Utah resident Carolynn Duncan created "Why Provo Labs Wants to Hire Carolynn Duncan," a blog detailing her qualifications to work for the startup incubator. "It was kind of a flippant idea," Duncan admits, but it worked—after approaching a company exec at a community dinner and handing him her business card listing her blog's address, Duncan scored an interview and got the job.

8 *"I CAN CONTROL WHAT YOU SEE ON THE INTERNET."*

When search engines like Google calculate their search results—the list you get when you type in specific words—one of the biggest factors in determining order is the number of other sites that link to a given Web page. The reasoning goes that it's a good measure of how useful the content of a website is to readers—and it often works in favor of blogs. "There's no special boost in our algorithm for blogs," according to a Google spokesperson,

"but as part of their nature [for example, routinely providing fresh content], people may link to and from blogs more often."

Knowing how to game the system, some bloggers will use the power of links to get ahead on search-result lists. Kansas lawyer Grant Griffiths started the Kansas Family Law Blog in 2005 to promote his practice. By posting two or three times a day, he says, he soon brought his blog near the top of the list for search terms like "Kansas law" and "divorce lawyers." Within 30 days Griffiths started attracting new business, and now gets two to three new cases per week because of his high-visibility blog.

Bloggers don't just use links to promote themselves; they can also manipulate search results to make their enemies look bad. In a practice known as "Google bombing," a coordinated group of bloggers can boost a site's ranking using negative key words. Such was the case in 2003, when enough bloggers linked to George W. Bush's official White House biography page using the words "miserable failure" to make it No. 1 on the list for a Google search of those words.

9 *"BLOGGING JUST ABOUT RUINED MY LIFE."*

In 2004 Oregon resident Curt Hopkins was getting ready to fly to Minnesota for a job interview at a radio station. But before he got on the plane, the station canceled the meeting. The reason? His blog, Morpheme Tales. Hopkins had made some harsh remarks in it about the Catholic Church a few weeks before the scheduled interview, remarks he suspects sank his chances of getting hired.

Hopkins says he stands by his words, but plenty of people end up regretting a rash posting they didn't expect anyone to read. In an incident that roiled Yale University's campus in January 2008, fraternities at the school faced backlash after members of the Yale Women's Center found pictures on Facebook.com of pledges holding an obscene sign in front of the center.

If you want to blog but still value some measure of privacy, try using one of several blog-hosting services—including Vox, WordPress, or Google's Blogger— that allow you to limit your audience to a select group of your choosing.

10 *"I'M ALREADY OBSOLETE."*

How long can the blog bonanza last? There are already signs of a slowdown:

The growth rate of blogs let up for the first time in 2006, according to Technorati. "There's a certain faddish quality to what's going on," says technology writer Nicholas Carr. "We're probably at or near the peak of popularity of writing blogs."

But that's only a part of the story; indeed, blogs have begun evolving into a multimedia phenomenon. It's now fairly cheap and easy to record video and post it as a video blog, or "vlog." And together with podcasts—audio recordings posted online—the number of video blogs has surged, from 4,000 in 2006 to more than 22,000 in 2007, according to vlog directory Mefeedia. At its core, blogging has always been about showing oneself to the world; with the advent of user-friendly voice and video technology, that idea is becoming more literal every day.

THINGS TO DO

• **With so many blogs out there,** how can you find ones uniquely suited to you and your interests? At *www.technorati.com,* you can search keywords to locate relevant blogs.

• **Need help creating your own** video blog? Check out *www.freeblogs.org*, where you can find a step-by-step tutorial, with tips on everything from setting up a free blog account to uploading your videos.

• **Since blog pages can be doctored** by outside parties to spread viruses, keep up to date on your anti-spy software and try to avoid any links within blogs or their comment pages.

• **Despite the number of dubious** news-source blogs, some mainstream media websites are featuring blogs to provide fresh news content quickly. Major papers like *The New York Times* and *USA Today,* as well as many smaller local newspapers across the country, host blogs online covering everything from politics to travel.

10 Things
Movie Critics
Won't Tell You

1 *"IF YOU SEE ME ON TV, CHANCES ARE I CAN'T BE TRUSTED."*

Ever notice that film critics who ply their trade on the TV infotainment circuit seem to love everything they see? In the past few years the *Today Show*'s Gene Shalit has gushed over such forgettable clunkers as the universally panned *Fantastic Four* ("Fantastic Four . . . everyone!") while over at *Reel Talk*, Alison Bailes raved about big-budget flops like *Beowulf* ("I was gripped and on the edge of my seat!").

Why would these critics be willing to risk their credibility by championing bad movies? To be fair, TV reviewers' tendency to speak in sound bites highly suitable for movie ads is, to some extent, based on the limitations of the medium they work in. Fast-paced entertainment shows spare scant seconds for coverage of anything; you've got to get to the point and make it snappy. *Ebert & Roeper* at least allowed for extended, even passionate, discussion of films up for review.

But TV personalities have to worry about furthering their own brand—themselves. Thus, they tend to play it safe by embracing middling fare or worse. So the next time you hear Larry King praise such low-chuckle-count fodder as

Monster-in-Law as "hysterically funny," you'll know to take his opinion with a barrelful of salt.

2 *"BEWARE OF BLURBS."*

If you really want to know what you're in for when shelling out for the next megahyped blockbuster, it pays to learn the fine art of reading movie ads. The good news for consumers is that most reputable film marketers have cleaned up their act in recent years, no longer cherry-picking words and phrases from reviews so that "a magnificent waste of time" reads on the poster as "Magnificent!" You can thank the overzealous ad execs at Sony—who, it was discovered in 2001, had created a fictional critic, one "David Manning," to churn out enthusiastic blurbs for the films of its subsidiary Columbia Pictures. (In August 2005, Sony agreed to refund $5 to anyone who saw *Hollow Man, The Animal, The Patriot, A Knight's Tale,* or *Vertical Limit* between Aug. 3, 2000, and Oct. 31, 2001.)

But there are still a few useful tricks: When deciphering film ads, use the law of three—that is, every ad should boast full sentences from at least three media sources you've heard of. If you're considering a sci-fi or horror flick and the ad offers up blurbs only from genre-specific publications, pass on it. Finally, if the ad crows something like "America's No. 1 Comedy!" don your skeptic's hat: What, if any, other comedies were released the same week?

3 "IF YOU WANT TO WIN THE OFFICE OSCAR POOL, DON'T LISTEN TO ME."

When asked her take on the Academy Awards, Salon.com film critic Stephanie Zacharek dismisses them as "useless, overrated," while *The Washington Post*'s Ann Hornaday calls them "self-congratulatory, fatuous"—but admits the annual telecast is an "irresistible" guilty pleasure.

The fact is, the job of critics and the interests of the Academy of Motion Picture Arts and Sciences have little to do with each other. But by understanding their antagonism, you can hedge your watercooler Oscar bets. Film critics dote on quality (no matter how exotic their idea of quality may be), whereas the Academy tends to reward monetary success. At the Oscars, stellar filmmaking is routinely eclipsed by sentimental favorites. Which helps explain, for example, how *Rocky* beat out Martin Scorsese's classic *Taxi Driver* in 1976.

Still, critics can help you pick the winners. Veteran reviewers will tell you Oscar tends to tumble for actors laboring under ugly makeup (Charlize Theron in *Monster*) or playing victims (Jodie Foster in *The Accused*). Reviewers are also helpful with Best Picture bets—if only by accident. Scan critic picks and top-10 lists at *www.metacritic.com*; if most really liked something, it's best to bet against it.

4 "HANGING OUT WITH THE STAR OF A FILM COULD NEVER AFFECT MY REVIEW OF IT. I SWEAR!"

An attractive young publicity person leads you to a private room in one of Manhattan's finest hotels, where, along with a handful of other writers, you are met by Russell Crowe, who shakes your hand, asks your name like he really wants to know, then spends a good hour answering questions about most anything within reason. And that was only the beginning of the junket for Twentieth Century Fox's 2003 epic *Master and Commander: The Far Side of the World*. Some of the journalists in attendance had seen the film; others had yet to see it. None left the hotel with their objectivity intact.

Not all junkets lay it on quite so thick as that one did; nonetheless, many responsible critics have begun avoiding them. Says Salon.com's Zacharek, it's a conflict of interest. "Once you talk to these people, you realize that they really are trying to communicate something," she says. But reviewing someone's film after meeting them "is just too weird."

Film critics dote on quality (no matter how exotic their idea of quality may be), whereas the Academy tends to reward monetary success.

Many daily and weekly papers are likewise rebelling against junkets; *Baltimore City Paper*'s arts editor Bret McCabe says, "I won't green-light an interview until I or the writer has seen the movie."

5 "I COULD SAY THIS FILM IS 'ABOUT A LOVABLE MISFIT,' BUT I'D RATHER GO WITH 'IT LIMNS ALTERITY.'"

Even ardent cineastes will sometimes come across a review so steeped in jargon it seems written in another language. Which, in a way, it is. For example, readers may be surprised to discover that 2006's *The Devil Wears Prada* wasn't just a lighthearted comedy, but a *roman à clef* (aka a film using thinly veiled fictional surrogates for real people and events). You may also find yourself tripping over a discussion of *mise-en-scène* (a vague term that can refer to everything from the way actors are placed in a scene to the choice of camera moves).

Aside from these perennial favorites, "schadenfreude" (pleasure derived from the misfortunes of others) is particularly popular right now, while "formalism" doesn't refer to a film about a black-tie event, but rather is an academic term for work that calls attention to its own artificiality (think the opening of *Moulin Rouge*, where the curtains part to reveal a conductor starting up the film's music).

Why do critics sometimes seem to aim to confuse? Zacharek speculates that reviewers go jargon crazy "out of insecurity." She says, "Writers should always write to illuminate, not to obfuscate." That is, they should be more plainspoken.

6 "DON'T BOTHER GOING TO THE MOVIES IN FEBRUARY OR SEPTEMBER."

When Miramax Films' cochairmen, Harvey and Bob Weinstein, officially severed ties with Disney in 2005, Miramax still had a backlog of troubled films it was obligated to release. The company's solution? Dump them in theaters in the postsummer dead zone that lasts from mid-August through September. Which might explain why you've likely never heard of, let alone seen, such fall 2005 "fire sale" releases as *The Great Raid* or *An Unfinished Life*.

But the tail end of summer isn't the only time of year studios like to empty their trash —and when you may want to think twice before heading out to your local multiplex. There's also January and February, once Oscar hopefuls have already hit theaters. That's not to say all films opening during these down periods are dogs. One noteworthy exception: the much lauded *The Assassination of Jesse James by the Coward Robert Ford*, which was released in September 2007. But a look at what it shared marquee space with confirms the trend: the action dud/Clive Owen vehicle *Shoot 'Em Up* was simultaneously limping into theaters.

7 "YOU PROBABLY DON'T WANT TO HEAR THIS, BUT YOU NEED ME."

Want to stir people up? Ask them what they think of movie critics. Jen Davis of Louisville, Ky., is put off by what she sees as a superiority syndrome in the profession. "My opinion is just as valid, dammit!" she says. Tammy Ras of

Pascoag, R.I., is more militant: "If they say, 'Don't see it, it sucks,' that means, 'Go see it, it's great.'" Sounds harsh, but the truth is, filmgoers need reviewers. As Salon.com's Zacharek puts it, "Critics are the only thing standing between consumers and advertising." With hundreds of films released in theaters each year, "Critics are more important now than they ever were," she says. "There are just so many movies, so much aggressive hype."

Skyrocketing ticket and concession prices further underscore the need for prescreening. Keith Phipps, film reviewer for the satire and culture-coverage weekly *The Onion*, gets ticked off at fellow critics for not keeping consumers in mind. "It's that good-enough, three-stars, we'll-give-it-a-pass mentality," he says, that gets people to shell out for unworthy cinematic fare. The catch-22 for critics is that being harder on movies invariably results in more hate mail.

8 "SURE, I'M A BELLWETHER OF TASTE—MY OWN."

Critics have their biases just like the rest of us. For example, don't even mention Johnny Depp to *The Washington Post*'s Stephen Hunter. According to coworker Ann Hornaday, "Stephen isn't a huge fan." Such personal aversions underscore both the catty delights of being a critic—hello, Rex Reed—and the responsibility of not letting one's personal prejudices about particular stars, or even entire genres, interfere with one's critical acumen. That said, you can often tell if a reviewer is of use to you based on what he or she can't stand. Not down with hyperviolent martial arts films? Then Hornaday's your

source. "I really did not get any of the charm," she says. Zacharek, meanwhile, tends to think big, prestige Hollywood movies in general "don't meet anyone's expectations."

How to use critics' predilections to guide you through the thicket of releases? Try making a list of three films you really liked and three you disliked. Then go to *www.rottentomatoes.com* or *www.metacritic.com* to find reviewers whose tastes consistently agree—or disagree—with your own.

9 "IT'S GOTTEN SO BAD, I ACTUALLY PREFER TELEVISION TO MOST MOVIES."

Connie Ogle, who was film critic for *The Miami Herald* before becoming the paper's book editor, always had stacks of to-be-reviewed DVDs atop her television. But what was she more excited about seeing? TV drama *Veronica Mars*.

And it's not just Ogle. With such reliably superior fare as *The Sopranos*, *24*, *The Office*, and *The Wire* in recent years, television has suffered an embarrassment of riches, while the quality of feature films has been sinking steadily. Once frowned upon by Hollywood as middlebrow pap, TV is now drawing talent away from the movies. But why the migration from big screen to small? For one thing, the Hollywood bureaucracy has gotten out of hand. The entire process, according to *The Washington Post*'s Hornaday, "is compromised artistically." As cogs in a vast, slow-churning wheel, many creative minds find their jobs boil down to "stomp[ing] all over other people's work," she says. "They don't do that in TV." And as television production continues to siphon talent from Hollywood, how are the studios filling those slots? By hiring those who make music videos and TV spots to helm feature films—which explains a lot.

10 *"MY TOP-10 LIST IS FULL OF MOVIES NOBODY'S SEEN."*

Is it conceivable for a critic to see everything released in a given year while also finding time to write reviews and take the occasional bathroom break? "Not possible!" Ogle says. And yet a majority of critics are compelled to compile a year-end top-10 list. More troubling is the lack of access most people have to many of the films on these lists: Unless you live in New York or Los Angeles, it's highly unlikely that you've had an opportunity to see such critical darlings as 2005's *The Best of Youth* or 2007's *The Lives of Others.* And yet both films made the year-end lists of critics from *The New York Times* and *Newsweek.*

Granted, the proliferation of top-10s is a flawed system defined by elitism and the trend trade winds, but it doesn't mean they're entirely useless. These lists are an excellent means of sussing out upcoming DVD releases of movies that never made it to your neck of the woods. So if you're ready to load up your Netflix queue with last year's best-loved films that virtually nobody got to see, go to *www.metacritic .com/film* and click on "Film Awards & Top 10s by Year."

THINGS TO KNOW

What separates must-see cinema from a lackluster flick? Lawrence Toppman, movie and theater critic for *The Charlotte Observer,* has some thoughts on the subject:

● **Novelty.** "A good movie must take me some place I have not been. It can be a place, new ideas, creatures I have not seen, but there must be that novel element."

● **Consistency.** "There has to be a universe—whether real or fantasy—where I know how things work, how people live, how things operate. The rules can't change in the middle of the game."

● **Technical competence.** "There should be few continuity mistakes. The photography can't change hue from scene to scene. The editing can't be so choppy that I can't follow the story."

● **Genre integrity.** "If I watch a science fiction film, I have to believe that the science is at least physically possible. In a comedy, it's okay to build a joke over the course of a movie, but it's not funny just to repeat a joke."

10 Things
Celebrity Chefs
Won't Tell You

1 "I'M A CELEBRITY FIRST AND A CHEF SECOND."

Take one part America's obsession with celebrity, stir in a cup of our passion for all things culinary, marinate in a mix of specialty cable channels, and BAM! You've got the perfect recipe for the celebrity chef phenomenon. It's no surprise that more and more chefs are stepping into the media spotlight—"they're the new most likable celebrities," says Susan Ungaro, president of the James Beard Foundation—and they've grown in stature as America has fallen ever deeper in love with food.

At press time the National Restaurant Association was projecting restaurant sales to reach $558 billion for 2008, a 47 percent increase over 2000, and the Food Network, the culinary world's premier stage, has seen its subscribers more than double in that time. As the financial stakes get ever higher, chefs are fleeing their kitchens in search of a bigger piece of the pie. Rachael Ray, the Babe Ruth of celebrity chefs, has ridden her culinary fame to a daytime talk show and her own magazine. The secret? It's not just talent, says Andrea Rademan, VP of the International Food Wine and Travel Writers Association. "Without the marketing, you can't be a celebrity chef."

2 "THERE'S ABSOLUTELY NO REASON TO BUY MY COOKBOOK."

You say you love Bobby Flay's food and want to try to make it at home? Before you spend more than $30 on his *Mesa Grill Cookbook,* check out FoodNetwork .com's recipe database, where among the 36,000-plus recipes you can browse, a quick search will net you 1,914 of the master chef's recipes—or 1,764 more than *Mesa Grill* contains—and it won't cost you a penny. Indeed, free recipe-sharing sites like Recipezaar.com, which offers 271,000 recipes, and Epicurious.com, which holds more than 80,000, also threaten to make your favorite chef's cookbook virtually obsolete. But so far the vast storehouse of free recipes available on the Web hasn't dented cookbook sales; in fact, those authored by celebrity chefs drove overall cookbook sales to $540 million in 2007, a 4 percent increase from 2006.

Do beware, cautions Christopher Kimball, host of *America's Test Kitchen:* Often with free recipes, you get what you pay for. First consider the source; if you don't trust the author, go somewhere else. Also, look for a lot of detail in a recipe. In general, the more specific the descriptions and instructions, the more likely it's going to work, Kimball says.

3 *"JUST BECAUSE I HAVE A COOKING SHOW DOESN'T MEAN I'M A CHEF."*

When the Food Network canceled *Emeril Live* in 2007, it put TV chefs with actual chef experience on the endangered list. The new food faces tend to be cookbook authors and soccer-mom cooks. The problem, says American Culinary Federation President John Kinsella, is that "people call anyone who writes a cookbook a chef. That's not what a chef is."

Foodies, take heart. PBS has been taking in Food Network castoffs, including respected chefs Ming Tsai, Mario Batali, and Sara Moulton.

Rachael Ray will be the first to say she's never run a kitchen—but then neither have a lot of the other big food stars, like Nigella Lawson, Paula Deen, or Dave Lieberman. "It's not necessary that there are professional chefs on the Food Network," says Anthony Bourdain, *Kitchen Confidential* author and a celebrity chef in his own right. "But what they really need are good cooks, and they have precious few of those." A Food Network spokesperson says the idea is "to represent many different perspectives on food."

Foodies, take heart. PBS has been taking in Food Network castoffs, including respected chefs Ming Tsai, Mario Batali, and Sara Moulton. "For us the most important prerequisite is that hosts are experts who are great teachers," says Laurie Donnelly, an executive producer for public TV.

4 *"SEX SELLS, EVEN WITH FOODIES."*

As the celebrity chef phenomenon has exploded, a growing number of chefs are making mouths water for reasons other than their culinary acumen. Actress and model Padma Lakshmi, for one, has gone from guest-starring on *Star Trek: Enterprise* to hosting the popular reality show *Top Chef,* where she muses about plating alongside Tom Colicchio, an accomplished chef and one of *People* magazine's "Sexiest Men Alive" for 2007. Lakshmi's food cred includes two cookbooks, *Easy Exotic* and *Tangy, Tart, Hot & Sweet*—both of which feature glamour shots of the India-born starlet with her own recipes.

Rachael Ray forged new ground for nonmodel chefs when she appeared in the October 2003 issue of *FHM* in a skimpy outfit, seductively licking chocolate off a spoon. How did other women chefs react to the sexy spread? "It didn't hurt her career any," says Cat Cora, an *FHM* veteran herself, who has joined Nigella Lawson and Giada De Laurentiis in ditching traditional cooking togs for tight sweaters with plunging necklines. But not every celebrity chef is making a wardrobe reduction. "My hands do not function if I don't have an apron on or my hair's down," says Sara Moulton, host of *Sara's Weeknight Meals* on PBS.

5 "I'M ADDICTED TO PORN— FOOD PORN, THAT IS."

"Mmmm," moans Nigella Lawson as she "Jackson Pollocks" melted chocolate over chocolate cheesecake on an episode of *Nigella Feasts*. As viewers of the show can attest, there's a little something extra in Lawson's cooking. That something is what's known in the industry as food porn: presenting dishes with an eye toward their sensual appeal. And according to food stylist Wesley Martin, no one does it better than Lawson. "The way she talks about food and describes it is all about the senses," he says.

To that end it's crucial the food look great on-screen. Food stylists like Martin often shop for ingredients, prepare, and even cook the dish, all the while making sure it's ready for its close-up. Lawson, for one, appreciates the help; in particular, she credits director of photography Neville Kidd with making the dishes she creates look so scrumptious. "He's an artist creating beautiful paintings about the food," she gushes. But not all TV chefs are so concerned with presentation. On *Simply Ming*, Chef Ming Tsai likes to plate the food himself and shoot it without too much fuss over how it looks. "You're doing a disservice if you make it look too good," he says.

6 "THE DISHES I MAKE ON TV DON'T ALWAYS WORK SO GREAT AT HOME..."

Sue Gordon, a New Jersey cooking instructor, is a big fan of the Food Network. "I'm always looking for what they'll teach me," she says. Unfortunately, when she tried to duplicate the sweet-potato gnocchi she watched Giada De Laurentiis make on *Everyday Italian*, she learned the age-old lesson that looks aren't everything. "It was so sticky, I had to keep adding flour," Gordon says. "The amounts were completely wrong." Turns out Gordon wasn't the only one who had problems with the recipe—the reviews section of FoodNetwork.com features similar complaints from a number of viewers. (A spokesperson for De Laurentiis declined to comment.)

Often it's a matter of translation. A chef might take a recipe for, say, 24 servings and divide it by four—but then fail to adjust the cooking time properly. These slight variations can make a huge difference, according to Ellen Brown, author of *The Complete Idiot's Guide to Cooking Substitutions*. Also, home cooking and professional cooking are entirely different; even the equipment varies. "It's like getting advice from a race-car driver on how to commute to work," Kimball says. "It's two different skill sets."

7 "...AND SOMETIMES THEY'RE JUST PLAIN GROSS."

Besides having to worry about whether a recipe you got from a cooking show is correct and usable, you also have to be wary of recipes that just don't taste very good. "I've seen chefs on TV create things that make me cringe in horror at the thought that people are going to eat them," says Ellen Brown.

Take the Red Bean Beach Salad that Ingrid Hoffmann made on the beach-picnic episode of *Simply Delicioso*, for example. Users' reviews on the FoodNetwork.com's recipe board slammed the dish for its strange, unappetizing combination of beans and sweet pickles. (We're serious.) "Yuk! It is beyond nasty," posted "Leah" from Philadelphia. (A spokesperson for Hoffmann declined to comment.)

Obviously, it's not fair to condemn a cook for a single dish, especially one she makes on-air. But before attempting a recipe you've seen on television, do your homework. "If it's from a trained chef like Bobby Flay, you're in safe hands," says Gordon.

8 "IT MIGHT BE MY RESTAURANT, BUT THAT DOESN'T MEAN I COOK THERE."

A recent ad campaign for the city of Las Vegas used a commercial featuring Emeril Lagasse, Mario Batali, and Wolfgang Puck, promising that in Vegas you would visit three celebrity chefs in three days. What the ad didn't mention is that you've got a better chance of hitting the jackpot at keno than you do eating food that's actually been cooked by your favorite celebrity chef at one of his many restaurants.

That's not to say the food isn't going to taste good. The menu at these restaurants is prepared from the chef's own recipes, and as Batali's assistant Pamela Lewy says, "Mario is in all of his restaurants all of the time." But while that may be true spiritually, it's simply unrealistic for diners to expect their meal to be prepared by a celebrity chef restaurateur.

But you can improve your odds by checking your favorite chef's tour schedule. If he's going to be traveling to

your city, he's more than likely going to visit his restaurants there. If you're lucky enough to catch Lagasse at one of his places, for example, you could be in for a treat. "If he's at the restaurant, he's behind the line cooking," says a spokesperson for the chef.

9 "MY SHOW IS ONE LONG COMMERCIAL FOR MY COOKBOOKS."

The publishing world sure has changed since cookbook author Mollie Katzen altered the landscape back in 1977 with *The Moosewood Cookbook,* widely credited with introducing vegetarian cooking to the mainstream. Before finding a publisher, Katzen sold the book out of her car, and through word of mouth its popularity exploded, making it one of the 10 bestselling cookbooks of all time, according to *The New York Times.*

With the rise of the Food Network and the birth of celebrity chefdom, it's unlikely that Katzen, who says she was rejected by the Food Network for not being entertaining enough—"I'm too much like Mr. Rogers," she says— could ever have sold as many books if *Moosewood* were released today. (The Food Network had no comment.) That's because celebrity chefs have a stranglehold on the bestseller list, which is proving tough to break. The top five cookbooks of 2006, and four of the top 20 in 2007, belonged to Food Network personalities, according to Simba Information, a Stamford, Conn., market-research firm. "When you're on TV, it's like having a commercial on every week," says Anthony Bourdain.

But things might be changing. Despite Rachael Ray's growing media presence, her books didn't perform as well across the board in 2007 as they did in 2006, according to Michael Norris, a senior analyst at Simba. "Would you be on every box of crackers in the country if you thought your cookbooks were going to pay the freight forever?" he asks.

10 "BOTTOM LINE: MY CELEBRITY STATUS IS GREAT FOR BUSINESS."

Camille Becerra experienced the Midas touch of celebrity chefdom firsthand when she was chosen as a contestant on *Top Chef*. After appearing in four episodes, Becerra estimates that she's seen a 35 to 40 percent increase at her Brooklyn, N.Y., restaurant, Paloma. Not bad for someone who lasted less than half a season.

Little wonder, then, that some chefs, like Melissa Murphy, owner of Sweet Melissa Patisserie in Brooklyn, N.Y., are using brief appearances on food TV to boost their business. Murphy, who won a *Food Network Challenge* making edible ornaments, already has a cookbook out and is currently shopping a show idea of her own. But it's not so easy to climb to the top of the celebrity chef heap. As Tom Colicchio says, he once told a graduating class at the esteemed Culinary Institute of America, "If you got into this business to be the next Emeril, you should apologize to your parents for wasting their money."

THINGS TO KNOW

Celebrity chef Guy Fiere, host of three Food Network shows including *Diners, Drive-Ins and Dives,* offers some quick and easy tips for preparing meat that'll make any home cook seem like a pro:

- **Don't forget to let it sit** for three to five minutes once it's done. "If you cut the meat too soon, juices run out onto the cutting board and that's flavor immediately lost," Fiere says.

- **When marinating, use a resealable** plastic bag—the thicker, the better. Put the meat and marinade inside, then submerge the bottom of the bag in water *before sealing it*. This will push excess air out of the bag, making for much better absorbency.

- **When tailgating or camping,** triple-fold two separate pieces of aluminum foil to create the top and bottom of a flexible cooking pouch that will seal in moisture while heating food on a grill. Same goes for baking fish, potatoes, or vegetables.

10 Things
Reality TV
Won't Tell You

1 *"STEP ASIDE, CRIME DRAMAS. THERE'S A NEW SHERIFF IN TOWN."*

In case you haven't noticed, reality shows are staking out more and more space in network lineups. In 2001, according to Ted Magder, chair of NYU's Department of Media, Culture, and Communications, major networks devoted three hours a week of their prime-time schedule to reality TV and "challenge" game shows. The number increased to eight in 2002 and jumped to more than 20 in 2007. Today, reality TV accounts for 20 percent of prime-time programming on network television.

Fueling the trend is the format's comparatively low production costs: typically less than a third of what it takes to produce hour-long dramas. But the bottom line behind the reality boom is ratings. In a Nielsen report for the 2006-07 season, reality shows accounted for 6 of the top 10 most-watched programs, including all of the top five.

What's behind our fascination with reality TV? Robert Thompson, a Syracuse University communications professor, says that an "evolutionary quirk" compels our curiosity about how others live and function. "It's why we peer into other people's medicine cabinets," he says. "We can't help it; we're naturally voyeuristic."

2 *"THE REALITY IS, IT'S MOSTLY FAKE."*

Seasoned viewers know that what gets called reality on these shows is often fairly contrived. But few fans know the extent to which the producers mold both people and situations to fit their scripts. It's common, for example, to feature actors in the role of supposedly real people, says Jeff Bartsch, a freelance editor who has worked on reality shows: "Producers have to do this sometimes because they're looking for a specific type of person to fit a role."

But it's in filming and editing where the magic truly unfolds. Using endless hours of footage, editors often craft whole sequences using a technique called "Franken-biting" to weave together disparate clips, or they'll dub in contestants' words out of context—something Patrick Vaughn knows all too well. A former contestant on CBS's *The Amazing Race*, Vaughn says he was surprised to hear his own voice encouraging the group to find cabs to finish a leg of the race, and recalls that producers were the ones who instructed them to take taxis. A spokesperson for CBS says the change in transportation was "a safety precaution" and that the dubbing of Vaughn's voice "was done to better describe the scene to the viewer."

Using endless hours of footage, editors often craft whole sequences using a technique called "Frankenbiting" to weave together disparate clips, or they'll dub in contestants' words out of context.

3 *"ONCE YOU SIGN OUR RELEASE, WE OWN YOU."*

It's no joke, according to Jameka Cameron, a former contestant on the CBS reality show *Big Brother:* "When you sign that document, you're basically signing away all of your rights—everything." (Cameron refused to be more specific, due to legal concerns.)

So what exactly does she mean by "everything"? A look at the participant agreement form from CBS's controversial *Kid Nation,* in which unaccompanied minors struggled to create a society in a desert town, sheds some light on the extent of control the makers of these shows wield over contestants. For example, producers had sole discretion in determining what, if any, medical procedures should be sought in cases of injury, even though they didn't guarantee the credentials of their medical staff.

Furthermore, producers were not liable in cases of death or injury of a contestant during the course of filming on location, and they couldn't be held responsible if a child contracted an STD or became pregnant. Says CBS: "The series was filmed responsibly and within all applicable laws in the state of New Mexico at the time of production."

4 *"OUR BACKGROUND CHECK'S A JOKE."*

The way reality shows examine the backgrounds of their participants is an area of concern among legal experts. And for good reason—producers love characters who are great at creating conflict, and they'll overlook important personal information to get them. In 2001's *Big Brother,* contestant Krista Stegall had a knife held to her throat by another cast member who, it turned out, had previously been arrested for theft and assault charges. (Stegall sued; the case was settled out of court.)

Larry Waks, an entertainment lawyer in Texas, says background checks are "still an evolving area" in reality TV and that the big networks are getting stricter. But the problem is far from fixed. In 2007, after one of VH1's *America's Most Smartest Model* contestants was arrested for allegedly groping a woman at a party, it was revealed he'd served time for assault, harassment, criminal contempt, and trespassing. ("We do thorough background checks," says a spokesperson for the show. "We're continuing to investigate the matter.") Los Angeles entertainment lawyer Neville Johnson doesn't like what he sees. "I'm concerned about the characters they recruit for the sake of drama," he says.

5 "EVEN OUR CREW MEMBERS DON'T ALWAYS KNOW WHAT THEY'RE IN FOR."

Participants on reality shows aren't the only ones who don't know what to expect from the experience—crew members are often subjected to highly unpredictable situations as well. Osvaldo Silvera, Jr., a director of photography who's worked on shows including *Top Chef* and *Miami Ink,* says the first rule he learned on a reality set was "always keep your camera rolling no matter what." That included the time he followed a subject into a room only to have the door slammed in his face, hitting his camera and knocking him to the ground. Cinematographer Aaron Schnobrich recalls filming a reality pilot in Red Square during a demonstration. "One of the camera operators was hauled off by officers in front of me, and I barely escaped from being caught," he says.

How do shows prepare crew members for such crazy working conditions? Mostly, they don't. "Not in the sense of confrontation management or anything like that," Schnobrich says. And since the cameras are usually manned by freelancers rather than union labor, producers face little if any resistance. "Especially in reality TV, everyone works freelance," Schnobrich says. "It's the trick of the industry."

6 "AD EXECS ARE THE NEW PRODUCERS."

Product placement is the big thing in TV advertising, and reality shows are the main vehicle. Leading the way is *American Idol,* whose sponsors spend millions to sew their products into the show—which is why, for instance, the Coca-Cola brand on the cups at the judges' table faces the camera. "Reality TV is rife with it," says Mark Andrejevic, author of *Reality TV: The Work of Being Watched.* It's "selling you something without trying, and it works." Indeed, advertisers spent $2.9 billion on product placement in 2007, and double-digit growth is projected over the next five years.

Some advertisers even want to design whole shows around their products. Last fall, for example, MTV premiered *The Gamekillers,* whose concept was developed by Bartle Bogle Hegarty, the agency that pushes Axe deodorant for Unilever PLC. The basis of the show was to see if male contestants could "keep their cool" under pressure—while wearing Axe. Don't be surprised if you start seeing more of these ad-minded concepts, says Andrejevic. "This may be the direction marketing starts going."

7 "GO AHEAD AND SUE US— YOU'LL HAVE A HARD TIME WINNING."

Reality-based shows are famous for subjecting participants to intriguingly dangerous situations. But creators hardly ever have to pay up in the event that someone gets injured or even killed. It's not that people haven't tried to sue—they have—it's just that they virtually never win, according to Eric Robinson, staff attorney for the Media Law Resource Center. Robinson has tracked 14 such cases. Half were dismissed outright, and only one resulted in an arbitration award for the plaintiff.

Just ask Jill Mouser, who in 2003 filed suit in Los Angeles for battery and gross negligence after being held in a harness for 40 minutes for CBS's reality show *Culture Shock*. She claimed that producers failed to warn her just how physically taxing the show would be. The release form she signed said differently; she lost. According to Larry Waks, release forms have gotten increasingly broad to ensure that networks and producers are indemnified from any claims of liability. So if you're intent on participating in a reality show, the most you can do is be aware of the risks and read all the waivers very carefully. Because, says Waks, "They've all stood up. The releases I see have all been found to prevent suits."

8 "REALITY TV? YOU MEAN CELEBRITY TV."

The reality TV landscape has changed rapidly over the past few years. Competition shows and unscripted dramas once dominated the landscape, but it wasn't long before celebrities began infiltrating the reality format. "When reality TV started, its whole appeal was that 'These are not stars—it's unscripted!'" says Robert Thompson. "Then all of a sudden, we have *The Osbournes* and *Surreal Life*." And it wasn't long before network stalwarts like CBS and NBC began catching on to the trend, with celebrity versions of shows like *The Apprentice* and *The Mole*.

Elayne Rapping, professor of American studies at SUNY Buffalo, says that the influx of celebrities into the genre makes sense, because "it became something they could do to keep their careers going." As for viewers, "We want to see [celebrities] being real," Rapping says. "This is a country that's addicted to celebrity." Case in point: ABC's *Dancing With the Stars* drew an impressive 22 million viewers for its first season's finale in 2005, and it was the number-one show in all of television during the fall 2007 season.

9 "WE STEAL A LOT OF OUR BEST IDEAS FROM EUROPE."

If you happen to sally forth across the Pond and catch a show on British TV that's exactly like *Dancing with the Stars*, it means you're watching *Strictly Come Dancing*, the popular U.K. progenitor of the U.S. hit. In fact, of the 9 reality shows listed in the top 50 of Nielsen's ranking report for the 2006–07 season, only three were developed by domestic production companies—and they were among the lowest rated. The reason? Foreign studios have been mining the reality-TV vein for a lot longer than American studios, and they soon started packaging and reselling concepts at a frenzied pace.

Netherlands-based Endemol, the force behind such reality hits as *Extreme Makeover: Home Edition, Deal or No Deal*, and *Big Brother*, farms out formats to other countries, stripping away cultural nuances and tweaking shows so they better suit their new home. The company even throws in a coach with the deal to consult with local producers on how to successfully adapt the show's basic elements. The goal, says David Goldberg, chairman of Endemol in the U.S., is to "exploit our content across as many markets as we can." Indeed, *Big Brother* has variations in almost 40 countries. "It's as if there's nothing original about reality TV," author Andrejevic says.

10 *"GET USED TO IT—WE'RE NOT GOING AWAY ANYTIME SOON."*

Since the 1990s, network television has been strained by the expense of original programming. According to NYU's Magder, producing an hour of original dramatic television averages a cool $3 million and can run much higher (ratings darling *ER,* for example, cost $13 million an episode in its heyday). Compare that with the cost of producing reality shows, which generally run less than $1 million

per hour, and you'll understand why networks won't be abandoning the format anytime soon. "They can't do without them now," says Magder. "The writing overhead is much less. They're easy to produce. It's a good economic model."

Another boon: As the writers' strike aptly demonstrated, reality shows help hedge against union and labor demands related to producing scripted shows. Does that mean reality programming is destined to take over prime time completely? Not necessarily, says Magder. There may be a short-term increase at present, but don't expect the networks to abandon scripted dramas altogether. "The new model of scripted and unscripted shows is too good," he says. For networks to survive, "there must be a mix."

THINGS TO DO

Tired of just watching reality TV? We talked to Lynne Stillman, casting director for CBS's *Survivor,* for some tips on how to get off the couch and onto the show:

- **Know your show.** Before sending in your application, make sure you've seen the show you're applying for. You wouldn't apply for a job if you knew nothing about the company, right?

- **Keep it simple.** When making your audition tape, avoid relying heavily on costumes, props, or other gimmicks. Instead, focus on convincing the casting director not only why you'd be good on the show, but why you would win.

- **Do the paperwork.** Casting directors really do read the application that accompanies an audition tape, so don't rush through it. The two sections that get the most attention: special interests and job history.

- **Communication is key.** A casting director's main concern is that you're a good talker. One sign you may not be ready for prime time is that you have trouble filling two to three minutes for an audition tape.

10 Things
Millionaires
Won't Tell You

1 *"YOU MAY THINK I'M RICH, BUT I DON'T."*

A million dollars may sound like a fortune to most people, and folks with that much cash can't complain—they're richer than 90 percent of U.S. households and earn $366,000 a year, on average, putting them in the top 1 percent of taxpayers. But the club isn't so exclusive anymore. Some 10 million households have a net worth above $1 million, excluding home equity, almost double the number in 2002. Moreover, a recent survey by Fidelity found just 8 percent of millionaires think they're "very" or "extremely" wealthy, while 19 percent don't feel rich at all. "They're worried about health care, retirement, and how they'll sustain their lifestyle," says Gail Graham, a wealth-management executive at Fidelity.

Indeed, many millionaires still don't have enough for exclusive luxuries, like membership at an elite golf club, which can top $300,000 a year. While $1 million was a tidy sum three decades ago, you'd need $3.6 million for the same purchasing power today. And half of all millionaires have a net worth of $2.5 million or less, according to research firm TNS. So what does it take to feel truly rich? The magic number is $23 million, according to Fidelity.

2 *"I SHOP AT WAL-MART ..."*

They may not buy the 99-cent paper towels, but millionaires know what it is to be frugal. About 80 percent say they spend with a middle-class mind-set, according to a 2007 survey of high-net-worth individuals, published by American Express and the Harrison Group. That means buying luxury items on sale, hunting for bargains—even clipping coupons.

In fact, most millionaires come from middle-class households, and roughly 70 percent have been wealthy for less than 15 years, according to the AmEx/Harrison survey. That said, there are plenty of millionaires who never check a price tag. "I've always wanted to live above my means because it inspired me to work harder," says Robert Kiyosaki, author of the 1997 bestseller *Rich Dad, Poor Dad*. An entrepreneur worth millions, Kiyosaki says he doesn't even know what his house would go for today.

3 *"... BUT I DIDN'T GET RICH BY SKIMPING ON LATTES."*

So how do you join the millionaires' club? Your best bet is to run your own business. That's how half of all millionaires made their money, according to the AmEx/

Harrison survey. About a third had a professional practice or worked in the corporate world; only 3 percent inherited their wealth.

Regardless of how they built their nest egg, virtually all millionaires "make judicious use of debt," says Russ Alan Prince, coauthor of *The Middle-Class Millionaire.* They'll take out loans to build their business, avoid high-interest credit card debt, and leverage their home equity to finance purchases if their cash flow doesn't cut it. Nor is their wealth tied up in their homes. Home equity represents just 11 percent of millionaires' total assets, according to TNS. "People who are serious about building wealth always want to have a mortgage," says Jim Bell, president of Bell Investment Advisors. His home is probably worth $1.5 million, he adds, but he owes $900,000 on it. "I'm in no hurry to pay it off," he says. "It's one of the few tax deductions I get."

4 *"I HAVE A CONCIERGE FOR EVERYTHING."*

That hot restaurant may be booked for months—at least when Joe Nobody calls to make reservations. But many top eateries set aside tables for celebrities and A-list clientele, and that's where the personal concierge comes in. Working for retainers that range anywhere from $25 an hour to six figures a year, these modern-day butlers have the inside track on chic restaurants, spa reservations, even an early tee time at the golf club. And good concierges will scour the planet for whatever their clients want—whether it's holy water blessed personally by the Pope, rare Mexican tequila, or artisanal sausages found only in northern Spain. "For some people, the cost doesn't matter," says Yamileth Delgado, who runs Marquise Concierge and who once found those sausages for a client—40 pounds of chorizo that went for $1,000.

Concierge services now extend to medical attention as well. At the high end: For roughly $2,000 to $4,000 a month, clients can get 24-hour access to a primary-care physician who makes house calls and can facilitate admission to a hospital "without long waits in the emergency room," as one New York City service puts it.

5 *"YOU DON'T GET RICH BY BEING NICE."*

Many millionaires privately admit they're "bastards in business," says Prince. "They aren't nice guys." Of course, the wealthy don't exactly look in the mirror and see Gordon Gekko either. Most millionaires share the values of their moderate-income parents, says Lewis Schiff, a private wealth consultant and Prince's coauthor: "Spending time with family really matters to them." Just 12 percent say that what they want most to be remembered for is their legacy in business, according to the AmEx/Harrison study.

Millionaires are also seemingly undaunted by failure. Don Crane, for example, now runs a successful company that screens tenants for landlords. But his first business venture, a real estate partnership, went bankrupt, costing him $20,000—more than his house was worth at the time. "It was the most depressing time in my life, but it was the best lesson I ever learned," he says.

6 "TAXES ARE FOR LITTLE PEOPLE."

Most millionaires do pay taxes. In fact, the top 1 percent of earners paid nearly 40 percent of federal income taxes in 2005—a whopping $368 billion—according to the Internal Revenue Service. That said, the wealthy tend to derive a higher portion of their income from dividends and capital gains, which are taxed at lower rates than wages (15 percent for long-term capital gains versus 25 percent for middle-class wages). Also, high-income earners pay Social Security tax only on their first $97,500 of income.

But the big savings come from owning a business and deducting everything related to it. Landlords can also depreciate their commercial properties and expenses like mortgage interest. And that's without doing any creative accounting. Then there are the tax shelters, trusts, and other mechanisms the super-rich use to shield their wealth.

7 "I WAS A B STUDENT."

According to the book *The Millionaire Mind,* the median college grade point average for millionaires is 2.9, and the average SAT score is 1190—hardly Harvard material. In fact, 59 percent of millionaires attended a state college or university, according to AmEx/Harrison.

When asked to list the keys to their success, millionaires rank hard work first, followed by education, determination, and "treating others with respect." They also say that what they absorbed in class was less important than learning how to study and stay disciplined, says Jim Taylor,

vice chairman of the Harrison Group. Granted, 48 percent of millionaires hold an advanced degree, and elite colleges do open doors to careers on Wall Street and in Silicon Valley (not to mention social connections that grease the wheels). But for every Ph.D. millionaire, there are many more who squeaked through school.

8 "LIKE MY FERRARI? IT'S A RENTAL."

Why spend $3,000 on a Versace bag that'll be out of style as soon as next season when you can rent it for $175 a month? For that matter, why blow $250,000 on a Ferrari when for $25,000 it can be yours for a few weekends a year? Clubs that offer "fractional ownership" of jets have been popular for some time, and now the concept has extended to other high-end luxuries like exotic cars and fine art. How hot is the trend? More than 50 percent of millionaires say they plan to rent luxury goods within the next 12 months, according to a survey by Prince & Associates. Handbags topped the list, followed by cars, jewelry, watches, and art. Online companies like Bag Borrow or Steal, for example, cater to customers who always want new designer accessories and jewelry, for prices starting at $15 a week.

9 "TURNS OUT MONEY CAN BUY HAPPINESS."

It may not be comforting to folks who aren't minting cash, but the rich really are different. "There's no group in America that's happier than the wealthy," says

Taylor, of the Harrison Group. Roughly 70 percent of millionaires say that money "created" more happiness for them, he notes. Higher income also correlates with higher ratings in life satisfaction, according to a new study by economists at the Wharton School of Business. But it's not necessarily the Bentley or Manolo Blahniks that lead to bliss. "It's the freedom that money buys," says Betsey Stevenson, coauthor of the Wharton study.

Concomitantly, rates of depression are lower among the wealthy, according to the Wharton study, and the rich tend to have better health than the rest of the population, says James Smith, senior labor economist at the Rand Corporation. (In fact, health and happiness are as closely correlated as wealth and happiness, Smith says.) The wealthy even seem to smile and laugh more often, according to the Wharton study, to say nothing of getting treated with more respect and eating better food. "People experience their day very differently when they have a lot of money," Stevenson says.

10 "YOU WORRY ABOUT THE JONESES—I WORRY ABOUT KEEPING UP WITH THE TRUMPS."

Wealth may go a long way toward creating happiness, but the middle-class rich still can't afford the life of the billionaire next door—the guy who writes charity checks for $100,000 and retreats to his own private island. "What makes people happy isn't how much they're making," says Glenn Firebaugh, a sociologist at Pennsylvania State University. "It's how much they're making relative to their peers."

Indeed, for all their riches, some 40 percent of millionaires fear that their standard of living will decline in retirement and that their money will run out before they die, according to Fidelity. Of course, it may not help if their lifestyle is so lavish that they're barely squeaking by on $400,000 a year. "You can always be happier with more money," says Stevenson. "There's no satiation point." But that's the trouble with keeping up with the Trumps. "Millionaires are always looking up," says Schiff, "and think it's better up there."

THINGS TO DO

Russ Alan Prince, coauthor of *The Middle-Class Millionaire*, shares five tips on how to become a millionaire:

● **Decide that you want to be rich.** People who get rich want to be rich, Prince says. "You have to put yourself in the line of money."

● **Start your own business.** Working for yourself keeps you motivated. You're also likely to have an opportunity to sell your equity at some point in the future.

● **Be willing to work really hard.** Focus on your strengths, and work really hard to continually improve them and use them in situations that translate into real money.

● **Play hardball.** Forget about win-win negotiations—just make sure *you* win. "Too many people give things away to meet a compromise," Prince says.

● **Always look for opportunity.** Never sit back and wait for things to happen. Being proactive helps you create your own luck.

Credits

Planner Won't Tell You" by Nkiru Asika Oluwasanmi; p. 187: "10 Things Your Estate Planner Won't Tell You" by Michele Marchetti; p. 192: "10 Things Your Charity Won't Tell You" by Sam Jaffee; p. 200: "10 Things Your Cell Phone Service Won' t Tell You" by Ryan Malkin; p. 206: "10 Things Your Cable Company Won't Tell You" by Amy Gunderson; p. 212: "10 Things Your Utility Company Won't Tell You" by Eleanor Laise; p. 217: "10 Things Your Dry Cleaner Won't Tell You" by Daisy Chan; p. 222: "10 Things Your Warehouse Club Won't Tell You" by Noah Rothbaum; p. 227: "10 Things Your Lawyer Won't Tell You" by Brigid McMenamin; p. 233: "Ten Things Your Ticket Broker Won't Tell You" by Jason Kephart; p. 238: "10 Things Your Florist Won't Tell You" by Renée DeFranco; p. 243: "10 Things the Pet Industry Won't Tell You" by Betsy Cummings; p. 249: "10 Things Your Mail Delivery Service Won't Tell You" by Erin Strout; p. 255: "10 Things Your Jeweler Won't Tell You" by Stephanie Williams and Noah Rothbaum; p. 260: "10 Things Your Retailer Won't Tell You" by Michael Kaplan; p. 264: "10 Things Your Antiques Dealer Won't Tell You" by Trevor Delaney; p. 270: "10 Things Your Headhunter Won't Tell You" by Chris Taylor; p. 276: "10 Things Your Bartender Won't Tell You" by Neil Parmar; p. 281: "10 Things Your Restaurant Won't Tell You" by Christine Bockelman; p. 286: "10 Things Your Butcher Won't Tell You" by Jane Black; p. 291: "10 Things Your Farmer's Market Won't Tell You" by Kelly Barron; p. 296: "10 Things Your Caterer Won't Tell You" by Nancy Nall Derringer; p. 301: "10 Things Your Health Food Store Won't Tell You" by Sarah Breckenridge; p. 306: "10 Things Your Supermarket

Won't Tell You" by Anne Kadet; p. 312: "10 Things Your Wine Merchant Won't Tell You" by Michael Kaplan; p. 317: "10 Things Your Gourmet Grocer Won't Tell You" by Michael Kaplan; p. 324: "10 Things Your Fitness Club Won't Tell You" by Reshma Kapadia; p. 329: "10 Things Your Personal Trainer Won't Tell You" by Renée DeFranco; p. 334: "10 Things Your Yoga Instructor Won't Tell You" by Christine Ryan; p. 339: "10 Things the Weight-Loss Industry Won't Tell You" by Trevor Delaney; p. 344: "10 Things Your Therapist Won't Tell You" by Anne Field; p. 349: "10 Things Your Spa Won't Tell You" by Eleanor Laise; p. 354: "10 Things Your Alternative Healer Won't Tell You" by Michael Kaplan; p. 360: "10 Things Your Plastic Surgeon Won't Tell You" by Jim Rendon; p. 366: "10 Things Your Primary-Care Physician Won't Tell You" by Jim Rendon; p. 371: "10 Things Your Hospital Won't Tell You" by Reshma Kapadia; p. 376: "10 Things Hospital CEOs Won't Tell You" by Angie C. Marek; p. 381: "10 Things Your Dentist Won't Tell You" by William Mauldin; p. 386: "10 Things Your Eye Doctor Won't Tell You" by Katrina Brown Hunt; p. 391: "10 Things Your Orthodontist Won't Tell You" by Sarah C. Robertson; p. 396: "10 Things Your Pharmacist Won't Tell You" by Michael Kaplan; p. 401: "10 Things Drug Companies Won't Tell You" by Michael Kaplan; p. 408: "10 Things the DMV Won't Tell You" by Kristen Vala; p. 413: "10 Things Your Gas Station Won't Tell You" by Jim Rendon; p. 418: "10 Things Your Rental Car Company Won't Tell You" by Noah Rothbaum; p. 423: "10 Things Your Auto Insurer Won't Tell You" by Sarah Breckenridge; p. 428:

"10 Things Your Car Dealer Won't Tell You" by Sarah Breckenridge; p. 433: "10 Things Your Car-Leasing Company Won't Tell You" by Demetra Navab; p. 438: "10 Things Your Mechanic Won't Tell You" by Walecia Konrad; p. 444: "10 Things Your iPod Won't Tell You" by Noah Rothbaum; p. 449: "10 Things Your Airline Won't Tell You" by Jim Renden; p. 454: "10 Things Your Cruise Line Won't Tell You" by Chuck Colman; p. 459: "10 Things Your Ski Resort Won't Tell You" by Vera Gibbons; p. 464: "10 Things Your Bed-and-Breakfast Won't Tell You" by Sarah C. Robertson; p. 469: "10 Things Your All-Inclusive Resort Won't Tell You" by Jena McGregor; p. 474: "10 Things Your Country Club Won't Tell You" by Maggie Dunphy and Dawn Wotapka; p. 479:

"10 Things Your Casino Won't Tell You" by Russell Pearlman; p. 483: "10 Things Theme Parks Won't Tell You" by Michael Kaplan; p. 488: "10 Things Your Athletic Coach Won't Tell You" by Michael Kaplan; p. 494: "10 Things Major League Baseball Won't Tell You" by Barry Petchesky; p. 500: "10 Things Your Local News Won't Tell You" by Nancy Nall Derringer; p. 505: "10 Things Your Congressperson Won't Tell You" by Brigid McMenamin; p. 510: "10 Things Bloggers Won't Tell You" by Daniel Cho; p. 515: "10 Things Movie Critics Won't Tell You" by Ian Grey; p. 520: "10 Things Celebrity Chefs Won't Tell You" by Jason Kephart; p. 525: "10 Things Reality TV Won't Tell You" by Kedon Willis; p. 530: "10 Things Millionaires Won't Tell You" by Daren Fonda.